S0-DYU-753

Issues in Race, Ethnicity and Gender

Selections from *The CQ Researcher*

A Division of Congressional Quarterly Inc.
Washington, D.C.

CQ Press
A Division of Congressional Quarterly Inc.
1255 22nd Street, N.W., Suite 400
Washington, D.C. 20037

(202) 822-1475; (800) 638-1710

www.cqpress.com

Copyright © 2002 by Congressional Quarterly Inc.

All rights reserved. No part of this publication may be reproduced or transmitted in any form or by any means, electronic or mechanical, including photocopy, recording, or any information storage and retrieval system, without permission in writing from the publisher.

∞ The paper used in this publication meets the minimum requirements of the American National Standard for Information Sciences—Permanence of Paper for Printed Library Materials, ANSI Z39.48-1992.

Printed and bound in the United States of America

06 05 04 03 02 5 4 3 2 1

A CQ Press College Division Publication

Director	Brenda Carter
Acquisitions editor	Charisse Kiino
Assistant editor	Amy Briggs
Marketing manager	Rita Matyi
Managing editor	Ann Davies
Production editor	Precious Sherry
Cover designer	Dennis Anderson
Composition	Paul Cederborg, Jessica Forman
Print buyer	Liza Sanchez
Sales	James Headley

Photos: American Association of University Women: 272; AP/Wide World: 6, 8, 12, 21, 23, 26, 32, 36, 41, 66, 67, 133, 145, 155, 157, 161, 169, 171, 176, 228, 232, 236, 245; Environmental Justice Resource Center: 97, 98, 99, 102, 104, 107, 108, 109, 110; Reuters: 22, 31, 53, 55, 58, 69, 72, 83, 115, 118, 128, 162, 192, 195, 225, 238, 268, 287, 292; Barbara Sassa-Daniels: 207; ESPN: 230; Lock Haven University: 237; Hales Franciscan H.S.: 271; Nativity Mission School: 276; University of Michigan: 1, 4.

"At Issue" pieces: p. 279: Reprinted with permission of Patricia Dalton; p. 299: Copyright © 1997 by *The New York Times*. Reprinted by permission; p. 299: Copyright © 1996 by *The New York Times*. Reprinted by permission.

Library of Congress Cataloging-in-Publication Data

in process

ISBN: 1-56802-718-4

Contents

ETHNICITY AND IMMIGRATION

GENDER ROLES AND VALUES

Annotated Table of Contents

The 16 *CQ Researcher* articles reprinted in this book have been reproduced essentially as they appeared when first published. In a few cases in which important new developments have occurred since an article was published, these developments are noted in the following overviews, which highlight the principal issues that are examined.

RACE

Affirmative Action

A major battle over the use of race in college admissions may be headed for the U.S. Supreme Court. Unsuccessful white applicants to the University of Michigan's undergraduate college and law school are challenging policies that give an advantage to minority applicants. The university says the policies are needed to ensure racial and ethnic diversity on campus. A federal judge approved the current undergraduate admissions policy, but another judge struck down the law school's system. A federal appeals court will hear the two cases in October 2001. Both sides say the cases may reach the Supreme Court, which has not examined the issue since the famous *Bakke* decision in 1978 barred racial quotas but allowed colleges to consider race as one factor in admissions.

Reparations

After the Civil War, efforts to compensate former slaves were blocked. Now calls are getting louder for payments to the descendants of slaves to help the nation come to terms with a gross historical injustice. But opponents worry that reparations would only widen the divide between the races. Meanwhile, survivors of the Nazi Holocaust have had considerable success in obtaining restitution from governments and corporations linked to Hitler's "final solution." Seeking reparations is not about money, they say, but about winning justice for the victims. But some Jewish Americans argue that the reparations movement has turned a historical tragedy into a quest for money. Other mistreated groups recently have picked up the call for reparations, including World War II "comfort women" and Australian Aborigines.

Redistricting

The release of 2000 Census figures in December 2000 kicked off one of the fiercest political battles the nation has faced: the redrawing of congressional districts based on population changes. The delicate job — whether by state legislators or members of special commissions — invariably is accompanied by intense pressure from partisan political interests whose power may shift along with the boundary lines. In addition to partisan considerations, state legislators may redraw boundaries to suit their own political ambitions. And ethnic and racial minorities may push for districts that will ensure them greater political power. Meanwhile, lawsuits from interest groups are likely to threaten virtually any new districts, especially ones where minority groups comprise the majority.

Policing the Police

Police departments around the country are on the defensive because of accusations of abuse of authority. Los Angeles is being rocked by a corruption scandal involving planted evidence and shooting unarmed suspects. New York City officers have been convicted of torturing a suspect and covering up the crime but acquitted in the shooting death of an unarmed civilian. State and local law enforcement agencies are accused of using "racial profiling" in traffic stops. Critics say stronger controls are needed. Law enforcement groups say most police obey the law and that the abuses are being exaggerated. Meanwhile, the U.S. Supreme Court is set to consider a controversial law aimed at partly overturning the famous *Miranda* decision on police interrogation.

Racism and the Black Middle Class

Despite steady growth in the black middle class over the past thirty years, many African-Americans still believe they face race-based obstacles. As a result, they argue that affirmative action is still necessary to give even highly qualified blacks a fair chance at getting ahead. Others dispute the notion that discrimination is a serious problem and warn that the policy will hurt rather than help blacks by giving them a disincentive to work hard. At the same time, another debate rages over black flight to the suburbs. The American dream of a house in the suburbs only recently has become reality for many African-Americans. But some members of the black community say that successful blacks should move back to the cities in order to help disadvantaged African-Americans left behind.

Environmental Justice

Toxic-waste dumps, sewage-treatment plants and other pollution sources rarely are found near middle-class or affluent communities. Inner-city neighborhoods, rural Hispanic villages and Indian reservations are far more likely to suffer. But a burgeoning new movement is helping poor communities across the country to close the door on unwelcome dumps and factories. Charging that they are victims of environmental racism, activists are winning court battles on the ground that siting polluting facilities among disadvantaged people violates Title VI of the 1964 Civil Rights Act. But business representatives and residents of some affected minority communities say that the movement is stifling their opportunities for economic development and growth.

Income Inequality

The gap between the incomes of poor and wealthy citizens is larger in the United States than in any other industrialized country. Last year, for the first time in almost two decades, low unemployment and increases in the minimum wage helped boost the earnings of Americans at the bottom of the pay scale. But tax policies and the use of stock options as part of corporate executives' compensation packages are helping to divert a growing portion of the nation's wealth to the richest Americans and away from the poor and the middle class. If the current economic boom continues, unskilled workers and those at the low end of the compensation pool will continue to benefit, experts say. But the disparity in Americans' incomes is not likely to disappear.

ETHNICITY AND IMMIGRATION

Diminishing Diversity of Language

More than 6,000 languages are spoken in the world today. But some linguists believe that by the end of the century the influence of globalization and new technologies like the Internet will have most people speaking one language — English. Other experts say that the most widely used tongues, like French, Arabic and Chinese, will remain in everyday use despite the growing popularity of English. While the experts disagree about the prospects for a global language, almost all are concerned that many more obscure tongues are on the verge of being lost forever. Meanwhile, some Americans believe that the United States is in danger of losing its native tongue and argue that English should be the nation's official language.

Debate Over Immigration

More than 1 million immigrants enter the United States, legally and illegally, each year. Many experts credit the new arrivals with helping to create and sustain the nation's current economic prosperity. But others argue that while immigration gives employers access to a cheap and plentiful labor force, American workers suffer because the newcomers take jobs and suppress wage levels. Critics of the current policies call for stricter limits on immigration and a crackdown on U.S. employers who knowingly hire undocumented workers. But supporters of liberal immigration policies warn that severely limiting legal immigration will hurt the economy and that, in any event, employer sanctions are not effective.

Hispanic-Americans' New Clout

Since 1990, the Hispanic-American population has grown from 22.4 million to 35.3 million, increasing by more than 50 percent in just 10 years. As their political clout grows, Latinos are making their presence felt. Democrats have corralled a large share of the Latino vote, but Republicans say Latinos are beginning to embrace GOP positions, such as opposition to bilingual learning, because it is not effectively teaching children to speak English. Others argue that bilingual education does lead to English proficiency and that any opposition to it among Latinos is probably misplaced anger over the poor state of public education in general.

The New Immigrants

The history of the American "melting pot" reflects alternating tensions and accommodations between newcomers and the old guard. No country on Earth, it is said, has absorbed immigrants in greater numbers or variety, or has done more to incorporate immigrants into the national culture. But in today's era of globalizing trade and mass communications, immigrants coming to the U.S. are more diverse in appearance and language than earlier generations of newcomers, more prosperous and more assertive about seeking changes in the cultural and political landscape. Critics charge that the American identity is threatened by the government's overly accommodating immigration policy. Defenders of new immigrants say that putting roadblocks to citizenship in the path of patriotic foreign-born residents is unnecessary and unjust.

Native American's Future

American Indians have the highest unemployment, poverty and disease rates of any ethnic group in the country. Yet Indian leaders say Americans are indifferent to their plight, as reflected in recent funding cuts for Indian programs. Congressional budget-cutters argue that Indians should share the burden of balancing the federal budget, but Indian advocates say aid programs for Indians are cited — and protected — in scores of treaties between tribes and the federal government. Many tribes see the key to their survival in economic development fueled by revenues from gambling. But Indian advocates say that mounting efforts to curtail their casino operations and other moves toward self-determination are only the latest in a long history of violations of Indian sovereignty guaranteed in the Constitution.

GENDER ROLES AND VALUES

Women in Sports

From sandlot T-ball games to professional basketball, athletic opportunities for females continue to expand. Girls' participation is up dramatically in secondary schools, even in such unlikely sports as wrestling. More than 41 percent of varsity college athletes were women last year, and a record 4,400 females competed in the last Olympics, nearly half the total. However, success has come at a cost. Far fewer women are coaching, and men's sports are losing funds or being eliminated as the impact of Title IX is felt. The landmark 1972 gender-equity law requires equal treatment of athletes at universities and secondary schools. Now, a new presidential administration may change its impact. Meanwhile, women's complaints have shifted to parity in scholarship money and playing facilities.

Gay Rights

Vermont has become the first state to grant marriage-like status to gay and lesbian couples. Elsewhere in the country, however, opposition to same-sex marriage remains strong. Meanwhile, other gay-rights measures are gaining support despite continuing opposition from conservatives. Eleven states and some 124 municipalities have anti-discrimination legislation, and many school districts have allowed high school students to form "gay-straight alliance" clubs. On the military front, the Defense Department is promising a crackdown on anti-gay harassment but defending the "don't ask, don't tell" policy. The issues even divided the major presidential candidates during the 2000 campaigns: Democrat Al Gore backed gay-rights measures while Republican George W. Bush was opposed.

Boys' Emotional Needs

The carnage committed in April 1999 by two boys in Littleton, Colorado, forced the nation to reexamine the nature of boyhood in America. Some psychologists contend that societal pressures on boys force them to suppress their most vulnerable emotions in service to a rigid idea of manhood. They say the result is a nation of boys depressed, failing in school and occasionally exploding with murderous rage. The new concern about boys follows a decade in which adolescent girls were thought to be suffering a loss in self-esteem and academic achievement, in part because teachers gave them less attention than boys. But now it is the boys who are falling behind and more likely to be in remedial classes, to be suspended and to drop out of school.

Roe v. Wade

The Supreme Court's decision last year striking down a Nebraska ban on so-called "partial-birth abortion procedures" has taken the steam out of one of the anti-abortion movement's most powerful issues. The Court's decision rendered invalid all of the 31 state bans and stalled the move to pass a similar ban in Congress. The decision was hailed as a victory by the pro-choice movement for upholding the principles of the Supreme Court's landmark 1973 *Roe v. Wade* ruling guaranteeing the right to an abortion. But the surprisingly slim 5–4 majority on the ruling means the judicial climate favoring *Roe* could be reversed if just one justice from the majority retires and is replaced by a justice sharing President George W. Bush's strongly pro-life views.

Preface

The American people are, simply put, a diverse bunch. Whether a man or a woman, of African or European descent, a Daughter of the American Revolution or an immigrant new to this country, external differences separate U.S. citizens and can lead to cultural and policy conflicts. Whether debating the merits of gays in the military or the subtle influences of racism, a multitude of perspectives must be considered when studying these sensitive matters. *Issues in Race, Ethnicity and Gender* does not champion a particular point of view. Instead, through balanced accounts, instructors can thoroughly and fairly explore opposing sides of some of today's most controversial and most personal issues. Students will be challenged to weigh in and form their own opinions on such topics as affirmative action, abortion and immigration.

This reader is a compilation of 16 recent articles from *The CQ Researcher*, a weekly policy brief that brings into focus the often complicated and controversial issues on the public agenda. *The CQ Researcher* makes complex issues less intimidating. Difficult concepts are not oversimplified but are explained in plain English. Offering in-depth, objective and forward-looking reporting on a specific topic, each selection chronicles and analyzes past actions in addition to current and possible future maneuvering. *Issues in Race, Ethnicity and Gender* is designed to encourage discussion, to help readers think critically and actively about these vital issues and to facilitate future research. Real-world examples give a flavor of the substantive detail in a variety of areas while showing how these important issues at all levels of government — federal, state and local — affect all students' lives and futures.

This collection is organized into three sections—"Race," "Ethnicity and Immigration" and "Gender Roles and Values." Each section covers a broad range of policy concerns and will expose students to a wide range of subjects, from the growth of women in sports to the concerns of how redistricting will affect minority representation in Congress. We believe this volume will be an attractive supplement for courses in minority and gender issues in political science and sociology departments.

The CQ Researcher

The CQ Researcher was founded in 1923 under a different moniker: *Editorial Research Reports*. ERR was sold primarily to newspapers, which used it as a research tool. The magazine was given its current name and a design overhaul in 1991. Today, *The CQ Researcher* is still sold to many newspapers, some of which reprint all or part of each issue. But the audience for the magazine has shifted significantly over the years, and today many libraries subscribe. Students, not journalists, are now the primary audience for *The CQ Researcher*.

People who write for the *Researcher* often compare the experience with that of drafting a college term paper. Indeed, there are many similarities. Each article is as long as many term papers—running about 11,000 words—and is written by one person, without any significant outside help.

Like students, staff writers begin the creative process by choosing a topic. Working with the publication's editors, the writer comes up with a subject that has public policy implications and for which there is at least some controversy. After a topic is set, the writer embarks on a week or two of intense research. Articles are clipped, books ordered and information gathered from a variety of sources, including interest groups, universities and the government. Once a writer feels well informed about the subject, he or she begins a series of interviews with experts—academics, officials, lobbyists and people working in the field. Each piece usually requires a minimum of 10 to 15 interviews. Some especially complicated subjects call for more. After much reading and interviewing, the writer begins to put the article together.

Chapter Format

Each issue of the *Researcher*, and therefore each selection in this book, is structured in the same way, beginning with an introductory overview of the topic. This first section touches briefly on the areas that will be explored in greater detail in the rest of the chapter.

Following the introduction is a section that chronicles the important debates currently going on in the field. The section is structured around a number of "Issue

Questions," such as "Should the use of racial profiling be prohibited?" or "Should same-sex relationships be legally recognized?" This section is the core of each selection; the questions raised are often highly controversial and usually the object of argument among those who work and think in the field. Hence, the answers provided by the writer are never conclusive. Instead, each answer details the range of opinion within the field.

Following these questions and answers is the "Background" section, which provides a history of the issue being examined. This look back includes important legislation, executive actions and court decisions from the past. Readers will be able to see how current policy has evolved.

An examination of existing policy (under the heading "Current Situation") follows the background section. Each "Current Situation" provides an overview of important developments that were occurring when the article was published.

Each selection concludes with an "Outlook" section, which gives a sense of what might happen in the near future. This part looks at whether there are any new regulations afoot, anticipates court rulings and considers possible legislative initiatives.

All selections contain other regular features that augment the main text. Each selection includes two or three sidebars that examine issues related to the topic. An "At Issue" page, from two outside experts, provides opposing answers to a relevant question. Also included is a chronology that cites important dates and events and an annotated bibliography that details some of the sources used by the author of each article.

Acknowledgments

We wish to think the many people who were helpful in making this collection a reality. First is Tom Colin, editor of *The CQ Researcher*, who gave us his enthusiastic support and cooperation as we developed this collection. He and his talented staff of editors have amassed a first-class library of *Researcher* articles, and we are privileged to have access to that rich cache. We also acknowledge the advice and feedback from the scholars who commented on our plans for the volume. In particular, we thank Louis DeSipio at the University of Illinois at Urbana–Champaign, Regina Freer at Occidental College, F. Chris Garcia at the University of New Mexico, Daniel Holliman at Syracuse University and Dean Robinson at the University of Massachusetts.

Some readers of this collection may be learning about *The CQ Researcher* for the first time. We expect that many readers will want regular access to this excellent weekly research tool. Anyone interested in subscription information or a no-obligation free trial of the *Researcher* can contact CQ Press at www.cqpress.com or at (800) 638-1710.

We hope that you are as pleased with *Issues in Race, Ethnicity and Gender* as we are. We welcome your feedback and suggestions for future editions. Please direct comments to Charisse Kiino, in care of CQ Press, 1255 22nd Street, NW, Suite 400, Washington, DC 20037, or by email at ckiino@cqpress.com.

— The Editors of CQ Press

Contributors

Thomas J. Colin, managing editor, has been a magazine and newspaper journalist for more than 25 years. Before joining Congressional Quarterly in 1991, he was a reporter and editor at the *Miami Herald* and National Geographic and editor in chief of *Historic Preservation* magazine. He has degrees from the College of William and Mary (English) and the University of Missouri (journalism).

Charles S. Clark, a former *CQ Researcher* staff writer, is currently a senior editor at the Association of Governing Boards of Universities and Colleges. He previously was a writer and editor for the *Washington Post, National Journal* and Time-Life Books. His articles appear in newspapers and magazines nationwide.

Mary H. Cooper specializes in environmental, energy and defense issues. Before joining the *CQ Researcher* as a staff writer in 1983, she was a reporter and Washington correspondent for the Rome daily newspaper *l'Unità*. She is the author of *The Business of Drugs* (CQ Press, 1990). She also is a contract translator-interpreter for the U.S. State Department. Cooper graduated from Hollins College in English.

Jennifer Gavin is a freelance writer and veteran reporter in Rockville, Maryland. She has covered politics and government for the Associated Press, *Orlando Sentinel* and *Denver Post.*

Sarah Glazer is a New York freelancer who specializes in health, education and social policy issues. Her articles have appeared in the *Washington Post, Glamour, Public Interest* and *Gender and Work,* a book of essays. Glazer covered energy legislation for the Environmental and Energy Study Conference and reported for United Press International. She graduated from the University of Chicago with a B.A. in American history.

Kenneth Jost has covered legal affairs as a reporter, editor and columnist since 1970 and has been a *CQ Researcher* staff writer since 1996. He served as chief legislative assistant to Rep. Al Gore from 1977 to 1980. Jost is a graduate of Harvard College and Georgetown University Law Center, a member of the District of Columbia Bar and an adjunct professor in communications law at Georgetown's law school. He is the author of the *Supreme Court Yearbook* series (CQ Press) and contributes to the *American Bar Association Journal* and other publications.

David Masci specializes in social policy, religion and foreign affairs. Before joining the *CQ Researcher* as a staff writer in 1996, he was a reporter at CQ's *Daily Monitor* and the *CQ Weekly.* He holds a B.A. in medieval history from Syracuse University and a law degree from George Washington University.

Jane Tanner is a freelance writer in Charlotte, N.C., who writes for Congressional Quarterly, the *New York Times* and Ballard & Tighe Publishers. Her analysis of Florida's prepaid university-tuition program for *Florida Trend* magazine won a first-place feature award from the National Association of Area Business Publications. Tanner is also the author of *A History of a U.S. Navy Aircraft Carrier* (1994). She holds a B.S. in social policy and an M.S. in journalism from Northwestern University.

1 Affirmative Action

KENNETH JOST

Jennifer Gratz wanted to go to the University of Michigan's flagship Ann Arbor campus as soon as she began thinking about college. "It's the best school in Michigan to go to," she explains.

The white suburban teenager's dream turned to disappointment in April 1995, however, when the university told her that even though she was "well qualified," she had been rejected for one of the nearly 4,000 slots in the incoming freshman class.

Gratz was convinced something was wrong. "I knew that the University of Michigan was giving preference to minorities," she says today. "If you give extra points for being of a particular race, then you're not giving applicants an equal opportunity."

University of Michigan

First-year engineering students at the University of Michigan-Ann Arbor gather during welcome week last year. A federal judge ruled in December 2000 that the school's race-based admissions system in 1995 was illegal but that a revised system adopted later was constitutional. The case is widely expected to reach the Supreme Court.

Gratz, now 24, has a degree from Michigan's less prestigious Dearborn campus and a job in San Diego. She is also the lead plaintiff in a lawsuit that is shaping up as a decisive battle in the long-simmering conflict over racial preferences in college admissions.

On the opposite side of Gratz's federal court lawsuit is Lee Bollinger, Michigan's highly respected president and a staunch advocate of race-conscious admissions policies.

"Racial and ethnic diversity is one part of the core liberal educational goal," Bollinger says. "People have different educational experiences when they grow up as an African-American, Hispanic or white."

Gratz won a partial victory in December 2000 when a federal judge agreed that the university's admissions system in 1995 was illegal. But the ruling came too late to help her, and Judge Patrick Duggan went on to rule that the revised system the university adopted in 1998 passed constitutional muster.

Some three months later, however, another federal judge ruled in a separate case that the admissions system currently used at the university's law school is illegal. Judge Bernard Friedman said the law school's admissions policies were "practically indistinguishable from a quota system."

The two cases — *Gratz v. Bollinger* and *Grutter v. Bollinger* — are now set to be argued together late next month before the federal appeals court in Cincinnati.[1] And opposing lawyers and many legal observers expect the two cases to reach the Supreme Court in a potentially decisive showdown. "One of these cases could well end up in the Supreme Court," says Elizabeth Barry, the university's associate vice president and deputy general counsel, who is coordinating the defense of the two suits.

"We hope the Supreme Court resolves this issue relatively soon," says Michael Rosman, attorney for the Center for Individual Rights in Washington, which represents plaintiffs in both cases. "It is fair to say that there is some uncertainty in the law in this area."

The legal uncertainty stems from the long time span — 23 years — since the Supreme Court's only previous full-scale ruling on race-based admissions policies: the famous *Bakke* decision. In that fractured ruling, *University of California Regents v. Bakke*, the high court in 1978 ruled that fixed racial quotas were illegal but allowed the use of race as one factor in college admissions.[2]

Race-based admissions policies are widespread in U.S. higher education today — "well accepted and entrenched," according to Sheldon Steinbach, general counsel of the pro-affirmative action American Council on Education.

Roger Clegg, general counsel of the Center for Equal Opportunity, which opposes racial preferences, agrees with Steinbach but from a different perspective. "Evidence is overwhelming that racial and ethnic discrimination occurs frequently in public college and university admissions," Clegg says.[3]

Higher-education organizations and traditional civil rights groups say racial admissions policies are essential to ensure racial and ethnic diversity at the nation's elite universities — including the most selective state schools, such as Michigan's Ann Arbor campus. "The overwhelming majority of students who apply to highly selective institutions are still white," says Theodore Shaw, associate director-counsel of the NAACP Legal Defense Fund, which represents minority students who intervened in the two cases. "If we are not con-

From *The CQ Researcher,* September 21, 2001.

Despite Progress, Minorities Still Trail Whites

A larger percentage of young adult African-Americans and Hispanics have completed college today than 20 years ago. But college completion rates for African-Americans and Hispanics continue to be significantly lower than the rate for whites. Today, the national college completion rate — 30 percent — is more than triple the rate in 1950.

Percentages of College Graduates, Ages 25–29

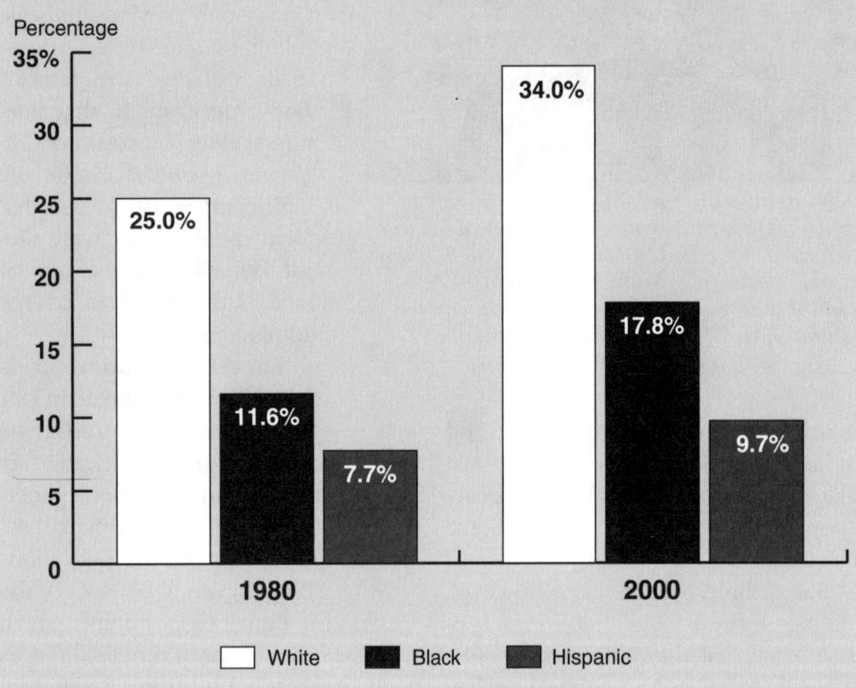

Source: U.S. Department of Education, "Digest of Education Statistics," 2001 edition (forthcoming)

scious of selecting minority students, they're not going to be there."

Opponents, however, say racial preferences are wrong in terms of law and social policy. "It's immoral. It's illegal. It stigmatizes the beneficiary. It encourages hypocrisy. It lowers standards. It encourages the use of stereotypes," Clegg says. "There are all kinds of social costs, and we don't think the benefits outweigh those costs."

The race-based admissions policies now in use around the country evolved gradually since the passage of federal civil rights legislation in the mid-1960s. By 1970, the phrase "affirmative action" had become common usage to describe efforts to increase the number of African-Americans (and, later, Hispanics) in U.S. workplaces and on college campuses.[4] Since then, the proportions of African-Americans and Hispanics on college campuses have increased, though they are still underrepresented in terms of their respective proportions in the U.S. population. (*See chart, p. 3.*)

Michigan's efforts range from uncontroversial minority-outreach programs to an admissions system that explicitly takes an applicant's race or ethnicity into account in deciding whether to accept or reject the applicant. The system formerly used by the undergraduate College of Literature, Science and the Arts had separate grids for white and minority applicants. The current system uses a numerical rating that includes a 20-point bonus (out of a total possible score of 150) for "underrepresented minorities" — African-Americans, Hispanics and Native Americans (but not Asian-Americans). The law school's system — devised in 1992 — is aimed at producing a minority enrollment of about 10 percent to 12 percent of the entering class.

Critics of racial preferences say they are not opposed to affirmative action. "Certainly there are some positive aspects to affirmative action," Rosman says, citing increased recruitment of minorities and reassessment by colleges of criteria for evaluating applicants. But, he adds, "To the extent that it suggests that they have carte blanche to discriminate between people on the basis of race, it's not a good thing."

Higher-education officials respond that they should have discretion to explicitly consider race — along with a host of other factors — to ensure a fully representative student body and provide the best learning environment for an increasingly multicultural nation and world. "Having a diverse student body contributes to the educational process and is necessary in the 21st-century global economy," Steinbach says.

As opposing lawyers prepare for the appellate arguments next month in the University of Michigan cases, here are some of the major questions being debated:

Should colleges use race-based admissions policies to remedy discrimination against minorities?

The University of Michigan relies heavily on high school students' scores on standardized tests in evaluating applications — tests that have been widely criticized as biased against African-Americans and other minorities. It gives preferences to children of Michigan alumni — who are disproportionately white — as well as to applicants from "underrepresented" parts of the state, such as Michigan's predominantly white Upper Peninsula.

Even apart from the university's past record of racial segregation, those factors could be cited as evidence that Michigan's current admissions policies are racially discriminatory because they have a "disparate impact" on minorities. And the Supreme Court, in *Bakke*, said that racial classifications were constitutional if they were used as a remedy for proven discrimination.

But Michigan is not defending its racial admissions policies on that basis. "Every public university has its share of decisions that we're now embarrassed by," President Bollinger concedes. But the university is defending its use of race — along with an array of other factors — only as a method of producing racial diversity, not as a way to remedy current or past discrimination.

Some civil rights advocates, however, insist that colleges and universities are still guilty of racially biased policies that warrant — even require — explicit racial preferences as corrective measures.

"Universities should use race-conscious admissions as a way of countering both past and ongoing ways in which the admission process continues to engage in practices that perpetuate racism or are unconsciously racist," says Charles Lawrence, a professor at Georgetown University Law Center in Washington.

Opponents of racial preferences, however, say colleges should be very wary about justifying such policies on the basis of past or current discrimination against minorities. "The Supreme Court has been pretty clear that you can't use the justification of past societal discrimination as a ground for a race-based admissions policy at an institution that did not itself discriminate," says Stephen Balch, president of the National Association of Scholars, a Princeton, N.J.-based group of academics opposed to racial preferences.

Minority Enrollments Increased

African-Americans and Hispanics make up a larger percentage of the U.S. college population today than they did in 1976, but they are still underrepresented in comparison to their proportion of the total U.S. population. Hispanics comprise 12.5 percent of the population, African-Americans 12.3 percent.

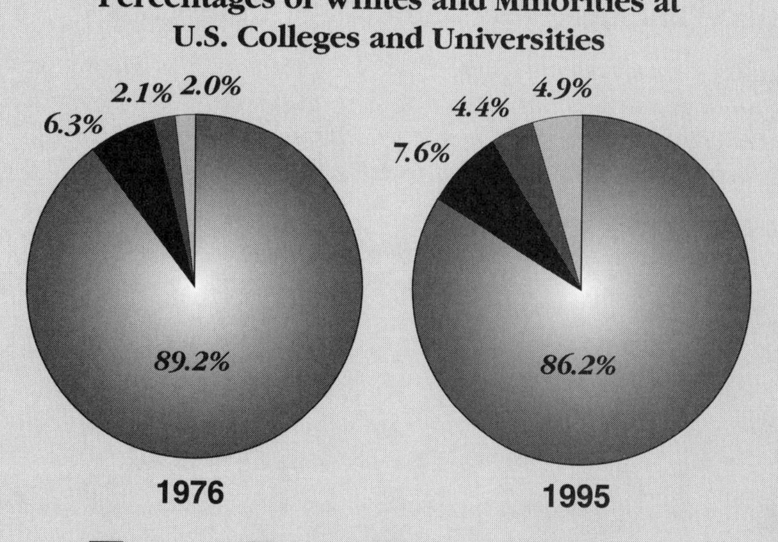

Note: Percentages do not add to 100 due to rounding.

Source: U.S. Dept. of Education, "Digest of Education Statistics," 2001 edition (forthcoming)

Balch defends alumni preferences, the most frequently mentioned example of an admissions policy that disadvantages minority applicants. "It's not at all unreasonable for colleges and universities to cultivate their alumni base," Balch says. In any event, he adds, "As student bodies change, the effect of that policy will change."

For his part, Rosman of the Center for Individual Rights says racial preferences are not justified even if colleges are wrong to grant alumni preferences or to rely so heavily on standardized test scores. "If you have criteria that discriminate and are not educationally justified, then the appropriate response is to get rid of those criteria, not to use 'two wrongs make a right,'" Rosman says.

Minority students intervened in both the undergraduate and law school suits to present evidence of discrimination by the university and to use that evidence to justify the racial admissions policies. In the undergraduate case, evidence showed that the university refused to desegregate fraternities and sororities until the 1960s, allowed white students to refuse to room with black students and did not hire its first black professor until 1967. The evidence also showed that black students reported continuing discrimination and racial hostility through the 1980s and into the '90s.

In a Feb. 26 ruling, Judge Duggan acknowledged the evidence but rejected it as a justification for the admissions policies. The racial segregation occurred too long ago to be a reason for current policies, Duggan said. He also rejected the minority students' argument that the racial impact of alumni preferences, standardized test scores and other admissions criteria justified preferences for minority applicants.

Judge Friedman rejected similar arguments in the final portion of his March 26 ruling in the law school case. "This is a social and political matter, which calls for social and political solutions," Friedman wrote. "The solution is not for the law school, or any other state institution, to prefer some applicants over others because of race."

Should colleges use race-based admissions policies to promote diversity in their student populations?

Michigan's high schools graduated some 100,000 students in 1999. Out of that number, only 327 African- American students had a B-plus average and an SAT score above 1,000 — the kind of record needed to make them strong contenders for admission to the University of Michigan's Ann Arbor campus based on those factors alone.

University officials cite that stark statistic to underline the difficulty they face in admitting a racially diverse student body — and to justify their policy of giving minority applicants special consideration in the admissions process. Without the current bonus for minority applicants, Barry says the number of African-American and Hispanic students "would drop dramatically" from the current level of about 13 percent of undergraduates to "somewhere around 5 percent."

Opponents of racial preferences dismiss the warnings. "It's certainly not inevitable that the number of students from racial and ethnic minorities will decline" under a color-blind system, Rosman says. In any event, he says that diversity is "not a sufficiently powerful goal to discriminate and treat people differently on the basis of race."

The dispute between supporters and opponents of racial admissions policies turns in part on two somewhat rarefied issues. Supporters claim to have social-science evidence to show that racial and ethnic diversity produces quantifiable educational benefits for all students — evidence that opponents deride as dubious at best. (*See story, p. 12.*) The opposing camps also differ on the question of whether the *Bakke* decision allows colleges to use diversity as the kind of "compelling government interest" needed to satisfy the so-called strict-scrutiny standard of constitutional review. (*See story, p. 6.*)

Apart from those specialized disputes, opponents of racial preferences argue simply that they constitute a form of stereotyping and discrimination. "We don't believe that there is a black outlook or an Asian outlook or a white experience or a Hispanic experience," Clegg says. "Students are individuals, and they should be treated as individuals, not as fungible members of racial and ethnic groups."

Some critics — including a few African-Americans — also say racial preferences "stigmatize" the intended beneficiaries by creating the impression that they could not be successful without being given some advantage over whites. "There is no way that a young black at an Ivy League university is going to get credit for

Gratz v. Bollinger: Race and College Admissions

Jennifer Gratz, a white woman, sued the University of Michigan contending she was improperly denied admission because of race. The lawsuit is shaping up as a key battle in the long-simmering conflict over racial preferences in college admissions.

"I see benefits from different opinions, different thoughts on any number of subjects. But I don't think that's necessarily race coming through. I don't think like every other white person. . . . Your race doesn't mean that you're going to think this way or that way."

Jennifer Gratz, B.S., University of Michigan, Dearborn

"You get a better education and a better society in an environment where you are mixing with lots of different people — people from different parts of the country, people from different parts of the socioeconomic system, people from abroad, and people from different races and ethnicities."

Lee Bollinger, President, University of Michigan

[doing well]," says Shelby Steele, a prominent black critic of racial preferences and a research fellow at the Hoover Institution at Stanford University. "There's no way that he's going to feel his achievements are his own."

Supporters of racial admission policies, however, say that race plays an independent and important role in American society that colleges are entitled to take into account. "It is reasonable for educational institutions to believe that race is not a proxy for something else," Bollinger says. "It is a defining experience in American life — and therefore an important one for this goal" of educational diversity.

White supporters of affirmative action generally deny or minimize any supposed stigmatization from race-conscious policies. Some blacks acknowledge some stigmatizing effects, but blame white racism rather than affirmative action. "The stigmatizing beliefs about people of color," Professor Lawrence writes, "have their origin not in affirmative action programs but in the cultural belief system of white supremacy."[5]

The two judges in the Michigan cases reached different conclusions on the diversity issue. In his ruling in the undergraduate case, Duggan agreed with the university's argument that a "racially and ethnically diverse student body produces significant education benefits, such that diversity, in the context of higher education, constitutes a compelling governmental interest under strict scrutiny."

Ruling in the law school case, Judge Friedman acknowledged that racial diversity may provide "educational and societal benefits," though he also called for drawing "a distinction . . . between viewpoint diversity and racial diversity." Based on his interpretation of *Bakke*, however, Friedman said these "important and laudable" benefits did not amount to a compelling interest sufficient to justify the law school's use of race in admissions decisions.

Should colleges adopt other policies to try to increase minority enrollment?

Texas and Florida have a different approach to ensuring a racial mix in their state university systems. Texas' "10 percent plan" — adopted in 1997 under then-Gov. George W. Bush — promises a spot in the state university to anyone who graduates in the top 10 percent of any high schools in the state. Florida's plan — adopted in 1999 under Gov. Jeb Bush, the president's brother — makes the same commitment to anyone in the top 20 percent.

The plans are drawing much attention and some favorable comment as an ostensibly race-neutral alternative to racial preferences. But major participants on both sides of the debate over racial admissions policies view the idea with skepticism.

"It's silly to suggest that all high schools are equal in terms of the quality of their student body," Clegg says. "And therefore it makes no sense to have an across-the-board rule that the top 10 percent of every high school is going to be admitted."

Both Clegg and Rosman also say that a 10 percent-type plan is dubious if it is adopted to circumvent a ban on explicit racial preferences. "Any neutral policy that is just a pretext for discrimination would have to survive strict scrutiny," Rosman says.

Supporters of race-based admissions are also unenthusiastic. "The only reason they work is because we have segregated high schools, segregated communities," Shaw says. "From a philosophical standpoint, I'd rather deal with race in a more honest and upfront way and make a more principled approach to these issues."

In the Michigan lawsuits, the university cited testimony from a prominent supporter of racial admissions policies in opposition to 10 percent-type plans. "Treating all applicants alike if they finished above a given high school class rank provides a spurious form of equality that is likely to damage the academic profile of the overall class of students admitted to selective institutions," said former Princeton University President William G. Bowen, now president of the Andrew W. Mellon Foundation in New York City.

Rosman looks more favorably on another alternative: giving preferences to applicants who come from disadvantaged socioeconomic backgrounds. "It's not a bad idea to take into account a person's ability to overcome obstacles," he says. "That's useful in assessing a person's qualifications."

In his testimony, however, Bowen also criticized that approach. Youngsters from poor black and Hispanic families are "much less likely" to excel in school than those from poor white families, Bowen said. On that basis, he predicted that a "class-based" rather than race-based admissions policy "would substantially reduce the minority enrollments at selective institutions."

For its part, the university stresses that its current system gives up to 20 points to an applicant based on socioeconomic disadvantage — the same number given to minority applicants. "We consider a number of factors in order to enroll a diverse student body," Barry says, "because race is not the only element that's important to diversity in education."

In their rulings, Duggan and Friedman both favorably noted a number of alternatives to race-based admissions policies. Friedman suggested the law school could have increased recruiting efforts or decreased the emphasis on undergraduate grades and scores on the Law School Aptitude Test. He also said the school could have used a lottery for all qualified applicants or admitted some fixed number or percentage of top graduates from various colleges and universities. Friedman said the law school's "apparent failure to investigate alternative means for increasing minority enroll-

What Does *Bakke* Mean? Two Judges Disagree

The Supreme Court's 1978 decision to prohibit fixed racial quotas in colleges and universities but to allow the use of race as one factor in admissions was hailed by some people at the time as a Solomon-like compromise.

But today the meaning of the high court's famous *Bakke* decision is sharply disputed. And the disagreement lies at the heart of conflicting rulings by two federal judges in Michigan on the legality of racial preferences used at the University of Michigan's flagship Ann Arbor campus.

In upholding the flexible race-based admissions system used by the undergraduate College of Literature, Science and the Arts in December, Judge Patrick Duggan said *Bakke* means that colleges can evaluate white and minority applicants differently in order to enroll a racially and ethnically diverse student body.

But Judge Bernard Friedman rejected that widely held interpretation in a March 27 decision striking down the law school's use of race in admissions. Friedman — like Duggan an appointee of President Ronald Reagan — said that racial and ethnic diversity did not qualify as a "compelling governmental interest" needed under the so-called strict scrutiny constitutional standard to justify a race-based government policy.

The differing interpretations stem from the Supreme Court's unusual 4-1-4 vote in the case, *University of California Regents v. Bakke*. Four of the justices found the quota system used by the UC-Davis Medical School — reserving 16 out of 100 seats for minorities — to be a violation of the federal civil rights law prohibiting racial discrimination in federally funded institutions. Four others — led by the liberal Justice William J. Brennan Jr. — voted to reject Alan Bakke's challenge to the system.

In the pivotal opinion, Justice Lewis F. Powell Jr. found the UC-Davis admissions system to be a violation of the constitutional requirement of equal protection but said race could be used as a "plus" factor in admissions decisions. The "attainment of a diverse student body," Powell wrote, "clearly is a constitutionally permissible goal for an institution of higher education."

AP Photo/Walt Zeboski

Reporters follow Allan Bakke on his first day at the University of California-Davis Medical School on Sept. 25, 1978. The Supreme Court ordered him admitted after ruling that the school violated his rights by maintaining a fixed quota for minority applicants.

Under Supreme Court case law, it takes a majority of the justices — five — to produce a "holding" that can serve as a precedent for future cases. In a fractured ruling, the court's holding is said to be the "narrowest" rationale endorsed by five justices. But Brennan's group did not explicitly address the question of diversity. Instead, they said that race-based admissions decisions were justified to remedy past discrimination — a proposition that Powell also endorsed.

Critics of racial preferences in recent years have argued that the Brennan group's silence on diversity means that they did not join Powell's reasoning. On that basis, these critics say, Powell's opinion cannot be viewed as a controlling precedent. They won an important victory when the federal appeals court in New Orleans adopted that reasoning in the so-called *Hopwood* case in 1996 striking down the University of Texas Law School's racial preferences.

In his ruling in the Michigan law school case, Friedman also agreed with this revisionist view of *Bakke*. "The diversity rationale articulated by Justice Powell is neither narrower nor broader than the remedial rationale articulated by the Brennan group," Friedman wrote. "They are completely different rationales, neither one of which is subsumed within the other."

But in the undergraduate case, Duggan followed the previous interpretation of *Bakke*. Brennan's "silence regarding the diversity interest in *Bakke* was not an implicit rejection of such an interest, but rather, an implicit approval of such an interest," Duggan wrote.

The two judges also differed on how to interpret later Supreme Court decisions. Duggan cited Brennan's 1990 majority opinion in a case upholding racial preferences in broadcasting — *Metro Broadcasting, Inc. v. Federal Communications Commission* — as supporting the use of diversity to justify racial policies. But Friedman said other recent rulings showed that the Supreme Court had become much more skeptical of racial policies than it had been in 1978. Among the decisions he cited was the 1995 ruling, *Adarand Constructors v. Peña* that overruled the *Metro Broadcasting* holding.

ment" was one factor in rejecting the school's admissions policies.

For his part, Duggan noted the possibility of using race-neutral policies to increase minority enrollment when he rejected the minority students' critique of such policies as alumni preferences. "If the current selection criteria have a discriminatory impact on minority applicants," Duggan wrote, "it seems to this court that the narrowly tailored remedy would be to remove or redistribute such criteria to accommodate for socially and economically disadvantaged applicants of all races and ethnicities, not to add another suspect criteria [sic] to the list." ■

BACKGROUND

Unequal Opportunity

African-Americans and other racial and ethnic minority groups have been underrepresented on college campuses throughout U.S. history. The civil rights revolution has effectively dismantled most legal barriers to higher education for minorities. But the social and economic inequalities that persist between white Americans and racial and ethnic minority groups continue to make the goal of equal opportunity less than reality for many African-Americans and Hispanics.

The legal battles that ended mandatory racial segregation in the United States began with higher education nearly two decades before the Supreme Court's historic ruling in *Brown v. Board of Education*.[6] In the first of the rulings that ended the doctrine of "separate but equal," the court in 1938 ruled that Missouri violated a black law school applicant's equal protection rights by offering to pay his tuition to an out-of-state school rather than admit him to the state's all-white law school.

The court followed with a pair of rulings in 1950 that similarly found states guilty of violating black students' rights to equal higher education. Texas was ordered to admit a black student to the state's all-white law school rather than force him to attend an inferior all-black school. And Oklahoma was found to have discriminated against a black student by admitting him to a previously all-white state university but denying him the opportunity to use all its facilities.

At the time of these decisions, whites had substantially greater educational opportunities than African-Americans. As of 1950, a majority of white Americans ages 25–29 — 56 percent — had completed high school, compared with only 24 percent of African-Americans. Eight percent of whites in that age group had completed college compared with fewer than 3 percent of blacks. Most of the African-American college graduates had attended all-black institutions: either private colleges established for blacks or racially segregated state universities.

The Supreme Court's 1954 decision in *Brown* to begin dismantling racial segregation in elementary and secondary education started to reduce the inequality in educational opportunities for whites and blacks, but changes were slow. It was not until 1970 that a majority of African-Americans ages 25–29 had attained high school degrees.

Changes at the nation's elite colleges and universities were even slower. In their book *The Shape of the River*, two former Ivy League presidents — Bowen and Derek Bok — say that as of 1960 "no selective college or university was making determined efforts to seek out and admit substantial numbers of African-American students." As of 1965, they report, African-Americans comprised only 4.8 percent of students on the nation's college campuses and fewer than 1 percent of students at select New England colleges.[7]

As part of the Civil Rights Act of 1964, Congress included provisions in Title IV to authorize the Justice Department to initiate racial-desegregation lawsuits against public schools and colleges and to require the U.S. Office of Education (now the Department of Education) to give technical assistance to school systems undergoing desegregation. A year later, President Lyndon B. Johnson delivered his famous commencement speech at historically black Howard University that laid the foundation for a more proactive approach to equalizing opportunities for African-Americans. "You do not take a person," Johnson said, "who, for years, has been hobbled by chains and liberate him, bring him up to the starting line of a race and then say, 'You are free to compete with all the others,' and still justly believe that you have been completely fair."[8]

Affirmative Action

Colleges began in the mid-1960s to make deliberate efforts to increase the number of minority students. Many universities instituted "affirmative action" programs that included targeted recruitment of minority applicants as well as explicit use of race as a factor in admissions policies. White students challenged the use of racial preferences, but the Supreme Court — in the *Bakke* decision in 1978 — gave colleges and universities a flashing green light to consider race as one factor in admissions policies aimed at ensuring a racially diverse student body.

The federal government encouraged universities to look to enrollment figures as the criterion for judging the success of their affirmative action policies. By requiring universities to report minority enrollment figures, the Nixon administration appeared to suggest that race-conscious admissions were "not only permissible but mandatory," according to Bowen and Bok. But universities were also motivated, they say, to remedy past racial discrimination, to educate minority leaders and to create diversity on campuses.

As early as 1966, Bowen and Bok report, Harvard Law School moved to increase the number of minority students by "admitting black applicants with test scores far below those of white classmates." As other law schools adopted the strategy, enrollment of African-Americans increased — from 1 percent of all law students in 1965 to 4.5 percent in 1975. Similar efforts produced a significant increase in black students in Ivy League colleges. The proportion of African-American students at Ivy League schools increased from 2.3 percent in 1967 to 6.7 percent in 1976, Bowen and Bok report.[9]

AP Photo

President Lyndon B. Johnson signs the Civil Rights Act on July 2, 1964. Race-based admissions policies now in use around the country evolved gradually from the landmark law.

Critics, predominantly but not exclusively political conservatives, charged that the racial preferences amounted to "reverse discrimination" against white students and applicants. Some white students challenged the policies in court. The Supreme Court sought to resolve the issue in 1978 in a case brought by a California man, Alan Bakke, who had been denied admission to the University of California Medical School at Davis under a system that explicitly reserved 16 of 100 seats for minority applicants. The 4–1–4 decision fell short of a definitive resolution, though.

Justice Lewis F. Powell Jr. cast the decisive vote in the case. He joined four justices to reject Davis' fixed-quota approach and four others to allow use of race as one factor in admissions decisions. In summarizing his opinion from the bench, Powell explained that it meant Bakke would be admitted to the medical school but that Davis was free to adopt a more "flexible program designed to achieve diversity" just like those "proved to be successful at many of our great universities."[10]

Civil rights advocates initially reacted with "consternation," according to Steinbach of the American Council on Education. Quickly, though, college officials and higher-education groups took up the invitation to devise programs that used race — in Powell's terms — as a "plus factor" without setting aside any seats specifically for minority applicants. The ruling, Steinbach says, "enabled institutions in a creative manner to legally provide for a diverse student body."

The Supreme Court has avoided re-examining *Bakke* since 1978, but has narrowed the scope of affirmative action in other areas. The court in 1986 ruled that government employers could not lay off senior white workers to make room for new minority hires, though it upheld affirmative action in hiring and promotions in two other decisions that year and another ruling in a sex-discrimination case a year later. As for government contracting, the court ruled in 1989 that state and local governments could not use racial preferences except to remedy past discrimination and extended that limitation to federal programs in 1995.[11]

All of the court's decisions were closely divided, but the conservative majority made clear their discomfort with race-specific policies. Indeed, as legal-affairs writer Lincoln Caplan notes, none of the five current conservatives — Chief Justice William H. Rehnquist and Associate Justices Sandra Day O'Connor, Antonin Scalia, Anthony M. Kennedy and Clarence Thomas — has ever voted to approve a race-based affirmative action program.[12]

Negative Reaction

A political and legal backlash against affirmative action emerged with full force in the 1990s — highlighted by moves in California to scrap race-conscious policies in the state's uni-

Chronology

Before 1960

Limited opportunities for minorities in private and public colleges and universities.

1938
Supreme Court says Missouri violated Constitution by operating all-white law school but no school for blacks.

1950
Supreme Court says Texas violated Constitution by operating "inferior" law school for blacks.

1954
Supreme Court rules racial segregation in public elementary and secondary schools unconstitutional; ruling is extended to dismantle racially segregated colleges.

1960s-1970s

Civil rights era: higher education desegregated; affirmative action widely adopted, approved by Supreme Court if racial quotas not used.

1964
Civil Rights Act bars discrimination by federally funded colleges.

1978
Supreme Court rules in *Bakke* that colleges and universities can consider race as one factor in admissions policies.

1980s **_Supreme Court leaves_ Bakke _unchanged._**

1986
Supreme Court limits use of affirmative action by employers if plan leads to layoffs of senior workers, but upholds racial preferences for union admission and promotions.

1987
Supreme Court rules, 6–3, that voluntary affirmative action plans by government employers do not violate civil rights law or Constitution.

1989
Supreme Court says state and local governments can adopt preferences for minority contractors only to remedy past discrimination.

1990s **_Opposition to race-based admissions policies grows._**

1995
Supreme Court, in *Adarand* case, limits federal minority-preference programs for contractors; President Clinton defends affirmative action; University of California ends use of race and sex in admissions.

1996
University of Texas law school's use of racial preferences in admissions ruled unconstitutional in *Hopwood* case; California voters approve Proposition 209 banning state-sponsored affirmative action in employment, contracting and admissions.

1997
Texas Gov. George W. Bush signs law guaranteeing admission to University of Texas to top 10 percent of graduates in state high schools.

1998
Washington state voters approve initiative barring racial preferences in state colleges and universities.

1999
Gov. Jeb Bush of Florida issues executive order banning racial preferences but granting admission to state colleges to top 20 percent of graduates in all state high schools.

2000s **_Legal challenges to affirmative action continue._**

Dec. 4, 2000
University of Washington Law School's former admissions system — discontinued after Proposition 200 — is upheld by federal court.

Dec. 13, 2000
University of Michigan undergraduate admissions policies upheld by federal judge, though former system ruled illegal.

March 26, 2001
Supreme Court agrees to hear new appeal in *Adarand* case.

March 27, 2001
University of Michigan Law School admissions policies ruled unconstitutional by federal judge.

June 2001
Supreme Court declines to review conflicting rulings in *University of Washington, University of Texas* cases.

Aug. 27, 2001
Federal appeals court in Atlanta rules University of Georgia admissions system giving bonuses to all non-white applicants is unconstitutional.

October 2001
Federal appeals court in Cincinnati to hear appeals in *University of Michigan* cases on Oct. 23; Supreme Court to hear *Adarand* case Oct. 31.

Should Minority Contractors Get Preferences?

Six years ago, the Supreme Court cast doubt on the constitutionality of federal preferences for minority-owned road contractors. Now a white Colorado contractor, Randy Pech, is asking the court to rule that a revised program approved by Congress during the Clinton administration also doesn't pass constitutional muster.

The justices will hear arguments on Oct. 31 in a renewed challenge by Pech, whose company, Adarand Constructors, Inc., waged an earlier battle against a Department of Transportation (DOT) program giving contractors a 10 percent bonus for awarding subcontracts to minority-owned firms.

In a 5–4 decision in *Adarand Constructors, Inc. v. Peña*, the court in 1995 held that minority set-asides, or preferences, are constitutional only if they serve a compelling government interest and are narrowly tailored to meet that goal.[1] Applying that standard, lower courts later ruled the subcontractor-compensation clause unconstitutional.

The federal government then revised the overall program somewhat. Among other things, the revision allows white-owned businesses to apply for status as a disadvantaged company. The government dropped the subcontractor-compensation clause, but retained a provision setting aside 10 percent of federal highway contractors for "disadvantaged business enterprises." The Denver-based 10th U.S. Circuit Court of Appeals ruled last year that the revised program satisfied the "strict scrutiny" standard of constitutional review.

The new case, *Adarand Constructors, Inc. v. Mineta*, finds the Bush administration in the unanticipated position of defending an affirmative action program. President Bush was critical of racial preferences during his presidential campaign. But his newly appointed solicitor general, Theodore Olson, filed a brief in late August defending the DOT program as constitutional. Court observers note that it would have been unusual for the government to change positions after the justices agreed to review the case.[2]

In its brief, *Adarand* asks the court to rule that racial preferences are "intolerable, always." As an alternative, the company urges the justices to rule that the government did not have adequate evidence of racial discrimination against minority contractors to justify the program and that the mandatory presumption of disadvantage in favor of minority-owned firms was not narrowly tailored to remedy past discrimination.

In its brief, however, the government contends that Congress had "extensive evidence of public and private discrimination in highway contracting" and created the preferences system "only after race-neutral efforts . . . had proved inadequate."

---

[1] The legal citation is 515 U.S. 200 (1995). For background, see Kenneth Jost, *The Supreme Court Yearbook*, 1994–1995, pp. 27–32.

[2] The Mountain States Legal Foundation, the public interest law firm representing Adarand, has a summary of the case on its Web site: www.mountainstateslegal.org. The government's brief can be found at www.usdoj.gov/osg.

---

versity system and a federal appeals court decision barring racial preferences in admissions in Texas and two neighboring states. But President Bill Clinton rebuffed calls to scrap federal affirmative action programs. And colleges continued to follow race-conscious admissions policies in the absence of a new Supreme Court pronouncement on the issue.

In the first of the moves against race-conscious admissions, the 5th U.S. Circuit Court of Appeals in New Orleans in March 1996 struck down the University of Texas Law School's system that used separate procedures for white and minority applicants with the goal of admitting a class with 5 percent African-American and 10 percent Mexican-American students.[13] The ruling in the *Hopwood* case unanimously rejected the university's attempt to justify the racial preferences on grounds of past discrimination. Two judges also rejected the university's diversity defense and directly contradicted the prevailing interpretation of Bakke that diversity amounted to a "compelling governmental interest" justifying race-based policies.[14]

The ruling specifically applied only to the three states in the 5th Circuit — Louisiana, Mississippi and Texas — but observers saw the decision as significant. "This is incredibly big," said John C. Jeffries Jr., a University of Virginia law professor and Justice Powell's biographer. "This could affect every public institution in America because all of them take racial diversity in admissions."[15]

Four months later, the University of California Board of Regents — policymaking body for the prestigious, 162,000-student state university system — narrowly voted to abolish racial and sexual preferences in admissions by fall 1997. The 14–10 vote approved a resolution submitted by a black businessman, Ward Connerly, and supported by the state's Republican governor, Pete Wilson. Connerly was also the driving force behind a voter initiative — Proposition 209 — to abolish racial preferences in state government employment and contracting as well as college and university admissions. Voters approved the measure, 54 percent to 46 percent, in November 1996.

In the face of opposition from UC President Richard Atkinson, the move to scrap racial preferences was delayed to admissions for the 1998–1999 academic year. In May 1998, the university released figures showing a modest overall decline in acceptances by non-Asian minorities to 15.2 percent for the coming year from 17.6 percent for the 1997–1998 school year. But the figures also showed a steep drop in the number of black and Hispanic students in the entering classes at the two most prestigious campuses — Berkeley and UCLA. At Berkeley, African-American and Hispanic acceptances fell to 10.5 percent from 21.9 percent for the previous year; at UCLA, the drop was to 14.1 percent from 21.8 percent.

The Supreme Court did nothing to counteract the legal shift away from racial preferences in education. It declined in 1995 to review a decision by the federal appeals court in Richmond, Va., that struck down a University of Maryland scholarship program reserved for African-American students. A year later, the justices refused to hear Texas' appeal of the *Hopwood* decision; and a year after that they also turned aside a challenge by labor and civil rights groups to Proposition 209. Instead, the high court concentrated on a series of rulings beginning in June 1993 that limited the use of race in congressional and legislative redistricting.[16] And in June 1995 the court issued a decision, *Adarand Constructors, Inc. v. Peña,* that limited the federal government's discretion to give minority-owned firms preferences in government contracting.[17]

With affirmative action under sharp attack, Bowen and Bok came out in 1998 with their book-length study of graduates of selective colleges that they said refuted many of the criticisms of race-based admissions. Using a database of some 80,000 students who entered 28 elite colleges and universities in 1951, 1976 and 1989, the two former Ivy League presidents confirmed the increase in minority enrollment at the schools and the impact of racial preferences: More than half the black students admitted in 1976 and 1989 would not have been admitted under race-neutral policies, they said. But they said dropout rates among black students were low, satisfaction with their college experiences high and post-graduation accomplishments comparable with — or better than — white graduates.[18]

The Bowen-Bok book buttressed college and university officials in resisting calls to scrap racial preferences. While voters in Washington state moved to eliminate race-based admissions with an anti-affirmative action initiative in 1998, no other state university system followed the UC lead in voluntarily abolishing the use of race in weighing applications.

In Texas, then-Gov. George W. Bush sought to bolster minority enrollment in the UT system after *Hopwood* by proposing the 10 percent plan — guaranteeing admission to any graduating senior in the top 10 percent of his class. (Florida Gov. Jeb Bush followed suit with his 20 percent plan two years later.) Many schools — both public and private — re-examined their admissions policies after *Hopwood.* But, according to Steinbach, most of them "found that what they had was satisfactory."

Legal Battles

Critics of race-based admissions kept up their pressure on the issue by waging expensive, protracted legal battles in four states: Georgia, Michigan, Texas and Washington. The cases produced conflicting decisions. The conflict was starkest in the two University of Michigan cases, where two judges both appointed in the 1980s by President Ronald Reagan reached different results in evaluating the use of race at the undergraduate college and at the law school.

The controversy in Michigan began in a sense with the discontent of a longtime Ann Arbor faculty member, Carl Cohen.[19] A professor of philosophy and a "proud" member of the American Civil Liberties Union (ACLU), Cohen had been troubled by racial preferences since the 1970s. In 1995 he read a journal article that described admissions rates for black college applicants as higher nationally than those for white applicants. The article prompted Cohen to begin poking around to learn about Michigan's system.[20]

As Cohen tells the story, administrators stonewalled him until he used the state's freedom of information law to obtain the pertinent documents. He found that the admissions offices used a grid system that charted applicants based on high school grade point average on a horizontal axis and standardized test scores on a vertical axis — and that there were separate grids or different "action codes" (reject or admit) for white applicants and for minority applicants. "The racially discriminatory policies of the university are blatant," Cohen says today. "They are written in black and white by the university. It's just incredible."

Cohen wrote up his findings in a report that he presented later in the year at a meeting of the state chapter of the American Association of University Professors. The report also found its way to a Republican state legislator, Rep. Deborah Whyman, who conducted a hearing on the issue and later held a news conference to solicit unsuccessful applicants to challenge the university's admission system. They forwarded about 100 of the replies to the Center for Individual Rights, a conservative public-interest law firm already active in challenging racial preferences.

Gratz and a second unsuccessful white applicant — Patrick Hamacher — were chosen to be the named plaintiffs in a class-action suit filed in federal court in Detroit in October 1997. The center filed a second suit against the law school's admission system in December 1997. The lead plaintiff was Barbara Grutter, who applied to the law school in December 1996 while in her 40s after raising a family and working as a health-care consultant. Grutter, who is white, thought she deserved admission based on her 3.8 undergraduate grade-point average 18 years earlier and a respectable score on the law school admission test (161, or 86th percentile nationally). Since the rejection, she has not enrolled elsewhere.

Evidence of Diversity Benefits Disputed

The University of Michigan is defending its race-based admissions policies not only with law but also evidence of the educational benefits of having a racially mixed student body. But opponents of racial preferences dismiss the evidence as distorted and biased.

The largest of the studies introduced as evidence in the two federal court lawsuits over the university's undergraduate and law school admissions policies runs 850 pages. Written by Patricia Gurin, chairman of the Psychology Department, it contains detailed statistics derived from a national student database and surveys of Michigan students. Gurin contends that students "learn more and think in deeper, more complex ways in a diverse educational environment."[1]

In addition, Gurin says students "are more motivated and better able to participate in an increasingly heterogeneous and complex democracy." And students who had "diversity experiences" during college — such as taking courses in Afro-American studies — also had "the most cross-racial interactions" five years after leaving college.

AP Photo/Paul Sancya

University of Michigan student Agnes Aleobua speaks out against a court ruling last March that the law school's race-based admission policy is illegal.

The National Association of Scholars, which opposes racial preferences, released two lengthy critiques of Gurin's study after the trials of the two suits. The studies were included in a friend-of-the-court brief filed in the appeals of the rulings.[2]

In the major critique, Thomas E. Wood and Malcolm J. Sherman contend that the national student database actually shows "no relationship" between the proportion of minorities on campus and educational benefits. They also say that "diversity activities" had only a "trivial impact" on educational outcomes.

The university also included "expert reports" from William G. Bowen and Derek Bok, the two former Ivy League university presidents who co-authored the pro-affirmative action book *The Shape of the River*. Bowen and Bok repeat their conclusions from the 1998 book that black students admitted to the "highly selective" colleges and universities studied did "exceedingly well" after college in terms of graduate degrees, income and civic life.[3] About half of the blacks admitted to the schools would not have been admitted under race-neutral policies, Bowen and Bok say.

In their reports for the Michigan suits, Bowen and Bok briefly acknowledge that black students at the schools had lower grades and lower graduation rates than whites. In an early critique of the book, two well-known critics of racial preferences — Abigail and Stephan Thernstrom — call Bowen and Bok to task for glossing over the evidence of poor performance by black students. They note that the dropout rate for black students — about 20 percent — was three times higher than for whites and that black students' grades overall were at the 23rd percentile — that is, in the bottom quarter.[4]

The studies are the tip of a large iceberg of academic literature that has sought to examine the effects of diversity in colleges and universities. In the most recent of the studies to be published, a team of authors from Pennsylvania State University concludes that the evidence is "almost uniformly consistent" that students in a racially or ethnically diverse community or engaged in "diversity-related" activities "reap a wide array of positive educational benefits."[5] In their own study of students at seven engineering schools, the scholars found what they called "a small, if statistically significant, link between the level of racial/ethnic diversity in a classroom and students' reports of increases in their problem-solving and group skills."

---

[1] Gurin's report can be found on the university's Web site: www.umich.edu.

[2] Thomas E. Wood and Malcolm J. Sherman, "Is Campus Racial Diversity Correlated With Educational Benefits?", National Association of Scholars, April 4, 2001 (www.nas.org). Wood is executive director of the California Association of Scholars; Sherman is an associate professor of mathematics and statistics at the State University of New York in Albany.

[3] William G. Bowen and Derek Bok, *The Shape of the River: Long-Term Consequences of Considering Race in College and University Admissions*, 1998. Bowen is a former president of Princeton University, Bok a former president of Harvard University.

[4] Stephan Thernstrom and Abigail Thernstrom, "Reflections on The Shape of the River," *UCLA Law Review*, Vol. 45, No. 5 (June 1999), pp. 1583–1631. Stephan Thernstrom is a history professor at Harvard; his wife is a senior fellow at the Manhattan Institute and a member of the Massachusetts Board of Education.

[5] Patrick T. Terenzini *et al.*, "Racial and Ethnic Diversity in the Classroom: Does It Promote Student Learning?", *Journal of Higher Education* (September/October 2001), pp. 509–531. Terenzini is a professor and senior scientist with the Center for the Study of Higher Education at Pennsylvania State University.

The cases proved to be long and expensive. By last fall, the university said it had spent $4.3 million defending the two suits, not counting personnel costs; the center had spent $400,000, including salaries, and also received the equivalent of $1 million in pro bono legal services from a Minneapolis firm helping to litigate the suits. Among the key pieces of evidence was a long report by an Ann Arbor faculty member — psychology Professor Patricia Gurin — concluding that diversity in enrollment has "far-reaching and significant benefits for all students, non-minorities and minorities alike." The center countered with a lengthy study issued under the auspices of the National Association of Scholars that analyzed the same data and found "no connection . . . between campus racial diversity and the supposed educational benefits."

In the meantime, the university revised its undergraduate admissions system, beginning with the entering class of 1999. The race-based grids and codes were replaced by a numerical system that assigned points to each applicant based on any of a number of characteristics. An applicant from an "underrepresented minority group" — African-Americans, Hispanics and Native Americans — is given 20 points. (One hundred points is typically required for admission, according to Cohen.) The same number is given to an applicant from a disadvantaged socioeconomic status, to a white student from a predominantly minority high school or to a scholarship athlete, according to university counsel Barry. The most important single factor, she adds, is an applicant's high school grades.

Judge Duggan's Dec. 13 ruling in the undergraduate case sustained the plaintiffs' complaint against the system used when Gratz and Hamacher had been rejected. Duggan said that the "facially different grids and action codes based solely upon an applicant's race" amounted to an "impermissible use of race." But Duggan said the revised system was on the right side of what he called "the thin line that divides the permissible and the impermissible."

Ethnicity at the University of Michigan

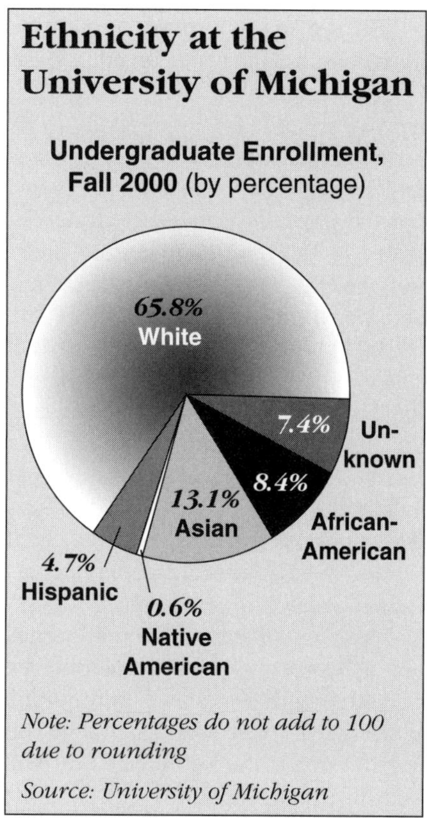

Note: Percentages do not add to 100 due to rounding

Source: University of Michigan

Three months later, however, Judge Friedman on March 27 struck down the law school's admission system. Evidence showed that the school had used a "special admissions" program since 1992 aimed at a minority enrollment of 10 percent to 12 percent.

Friedman relied on a statistical analysis that showed an African-American applicant's relative odds of acceptance were up to 400 times as great as a white applicant's. Friedman rejected the use of diversity to justify the racial preferences, but in any event said the law school's system was not "narrowly tailored" because there was no time limit and there had been no consideration of alternative means of increasing minority enrollment.

The two Michigan cases took on added significance in June when the Supreme Court declined for a second time to hear Texas' appeal in the *Hopwood* case or to hear the plaintiffs' appeal of a ruling by the 9th U.S. Circuit Court of Appeals upholding a discontinued system of racial preferences at the University of Washington Law School. As the lawyers in the Michigan cases prepared for their scheduled appellate arguments, the 11th U.S. Circuit Court of Appeals issued a ruling on Aug. 27 striking down the University of Georgia's admissions system. With less extensive evidence in the Georgia case, however, legal observers viewed the two Michigan cases as the most likely to be accepted by the Supreme Court for its first full look at race-based admissions since *Bakke*.[21] ■

CURRENT SITUATION

Legal Confusion

A half-decade of legal and political challenges to race-based admissions policies has forced changes at some of the country's biggest state universities and produced widespread uncertainty throughout higher education.

"Colleges and universities are mystified with the confusing landscape as to what is and what is not permissible when it comes to admission practices," says Barmak Nassirian, associate executive director of the American Association of Collegiate Registrars and Admissions Officers. With the law unclear, Nassirian says, "institutions are essentially left to fend for themselves when it comes to compliance."

State universities in Texas and Florida are implementing new policies that eliminate explicit preferences for minority applicants but substitute guaranteed admission to high-ranking graduates of all high schools in the state — the top

10 percent of graduates in Texas, top 20 percent in Florida. The University of California in June approved a similar plan — guaranteeing admission to the top 12.5 percent of any high school class — that is to go into effect in fall 2003.

Both California and Texas reported significant declines in minority enrollment immediately after Proposition 209 and the *Hopwood* decision forced the state universities to eliminate racial preferences. Officials in Texas and Florida say the new policies are proving effective in minimizing the impact on minority enrollment.

Black and Hispanic enrollment dropped at the University of Texas and Texas A&M University immediately after *Hopwood*, but is now said to be back to levels immediately before the ruling. "It's maintained our course," state Rep. Irma Rangel, a Democrat and one of the authors of the 10 percent law, told the *Fort Worth Star-Telegram* earlier this year.[22]

University of Florida officials braced for reduced minority enrollment under the top 20 percent plan that first went into effect for the freshman class entering this fall. In June, university officials were projecting a drop in the number of African-American students — from 12 percent the previous year to 9 percent for the incoming class — but a modest increase in Hispanic students. "We expected we would have reductions here, but we've done everything we know how to keep it from happening," Charles E. Frazier, the university's vice provost, told The Associated Press.[23]

Public universities have the biggest problem in devising acceptable admissions policies, Nassirian says, because of the large number of applications they receive. Elite private universities have the resources to make a "very comprehensive assessment of an applicant's full portfolio," Nassirian explains. With more applications and fewer resources, he concludes, big state universities have to use less individualized ways "to make a first cut as to whose application moves up and gets reviewed."

The University of Georgia — which receives about 14,000 applications a year — defended its racial system by noting the difficulty of individual review, but the appeals court rejected the defense. "If UGA wants to ensure diversity through its admissions decisions, and wants race to be part of that calculus," Judge Stanley Marcus wrote, "then it must be prepared to shoulder the burden of fully and fairly analyzing applicants as individuals and not merely as members of groups." [24] For its part, the University of Michigan says every application is individually reviewed by one of 21 admissions counselors assigned to specific geographic areas.

Nassirian contends racial preferences are an issue only for a minority of colleges with selective admissions policies. For those schools, though, he says he hopes the Supreme Court will take up the issue soon.

"It is regrettable that the law of the land has to get so overly complicated that you need a whole team of attorneys to guess what is allowable and what is not," Nassirian says. "That is not generally a sign of health — when people cannot get definitive answers as to what the law is."

Legal Appeals

Opposing lawyers for the two major sides in the University of Michigan cases are projecting confidence as they prepare for Oct. 23 arguments in the most closely watched case on racial preferences in college admissions since *Bakke*.

The federal appeals court in Cincinnati has scheduled a total of 90 minutes to hear from lawyers representing the university, the plaintiffs and the minority intervenors in the undergraduate and law school cases — 15 minutes for each lawyer in each case. The three judges who will hear the case are to be picked at random shortly before the arguments: The court's 11 judges include five appointed by Republican presidents and six named by Democrats.

Representing the unsuccessful applicants, Rosman of the Center for Individual Rights says he is "cautiously optimistic" about the outcome. "We think we have a strong case, but you can never predict what a court will do," Rosman says. The university's attorney — John Payton, a lawyer with a prominent Washington law firm — says, "I feel very good about where we are."

Payton says *Bakke* is the key to the case, and he discounts the significance of the court rulings that have questioned its status as a precedent for using diversity to justify race-conscious admissions policies. "I don't think you can find a trend in that small group of cases," he says, "and I don't think there is a trend."

For his part, Rosman warns that justifying racial admissions policies on the basis of diversity could invite similar policies elsewhere in government. "If you think that racial diversity leads to intellectual foment that leads to new and better ideas, it's not clear why you wouldn't want to have different perspectives from different races in a lot of different areas of government," he says.

Payton thinks the evidence introduced by the university to defend its policies may influence the judges. "The social-science evidence confirms the consensus among educators that there is a very significant educational impact [from having] a diverse student body," he says. Rosman is dubious. "I don't think they're going to be too overwhelmingly fascinated by the social-science evidence," he says.

Both sides have drawn support from outside groups in the form of friend-of-the-court briefs, but the university rallied a more impressive list of allies. More than a dozen briefs supporting the university's position were filed by, among others, the American Bar As-

At Issue:

Should colleges eliminate the use of race in admissions?

THOMAS E. WOOD
EXECUTIVE DIRECTOR, CALIFORNIA ASSOCIATION OF SCHOLARS, CO-AUTHOR OF CALIFORNIA PROP. 209

WRITTEN FOR THE CQ RESEARCHER, SEPTEMBER 2001

Colleges should eliminate the use of race in admissions. One cannot prefer on the basis of race without discriminating against others on the basis of race. Treating people differently on the basis of their race violates the Constitution's guarantee of equal protection under the laws.

There is only one national database for higher education that is in a position to adequately address this question whether, or to what extent, campus racial diversity is a necessary component of educational excellence. So far, the American Council on Education/Higher Education Research Institute database has failed to find any connection between campus racial diversity and any of the 82 cognitive and non-cognitive outcome variables incorporated in the study.

Proponents claim that the abandonment of racial classifications will result in the resegregation of higher education. Since preferences have been used to increase the number of minorities in the past, their abandonment will lead in the near term to lower numbers for minorities (though only in the most elite institutions of higher education).

But the claim that abandoning the use of race in college admissions will lead to resegregation implies that all or virtually all minorities who are presently enrolled in the most elite institutions are there only because they have been given preferences, which is both untrue and demeaning. The claim also ignores the fact that the country was making significant progress toward diversity *before* the advent of racial preferences in university admissions in the mid-to-late 1970s.

This analysis is confirmed by the experience of Texas, California and Washington, which already have bans on racial classifications in university admissions. The experience in these states has been that while there is an initial decline when racial classifications are abandoned (though only in the most elite institutions), the underlying trend toward greater diversity resumes after the initial correction.

For some, of course, any regression from the numbers that are obtainable through the use of preferences is unacceptable. At its heart, this is the view that racial diversity is a value that trumps all others. But that is a view that has clearly been rejected by the courts, and for good reason. Diversity is an important public policy goal, but there is a right way and a wrong way to pursue it. Racial classifications are the wrong way.

ANGELO ANCHETA
DIRECTOR, LEGAL AND ADVOCACY PROGRAMS, CIVIL RIGHTS PROJECT, HARVARD LAW SCHOOL

WRITTEN FOR THE CQ RESEARCHER, SEPTEMBER 2001

Affirmative action policies advance the tenet that colleges, like the workplace and our public institutions, should reflect the full character of American society. Race-conscious admissions policies not only promote the integration ideal first realized in *Brown v. Board of Education* but also help create educational environments that improve basic learning and better equip students for an increasingly diverse society.

The U.S. Supreme Court upheld race-conscious admissions over 20 years ago in *Regents of the University of California v. Bakke*. Yet, affirmative action opponents, armed with the rhetoric of quotas and tokenism for the unqualified, persist in trying to undermine *Bakke*. Educators know that quotas are illegal under *Bakke* and that granting admission to the unqualified serves no one's interest. Colleges have been highly circumspect, employing carefully crafted policies that consider all applicants competitively and that use race as only one of many factors in admissions decisions.

Nevertheless, recent litigation challenging affirmative action in Texas, Washington, Georgia and Michigan portends that the Supreme Court will soon revisit *Bakke*. But the case that promoting educational diversity is, in the language of the law, "a compelling governmental interest" and that race-conscious admissions policies can best serve that interest has only strengthened in recent years.

The latest findings show that student-body diversity significantly improves the quality of higher education. Studies at the University of Michigan have found that diverse learning environments can enhance students' critical-thinking skills, augment their understanding and tolerance of different opinions and groups, increase their motivation and participation in civic activities and better prepare them for living in a diverse society. Several studies support these findings and further show that interaction across races has positive effects on retention rates, satisfaction with college, self-confidence and leadership ability.

Without race-conscious admissions, the student-body diversity necessary to advance these educational outcomes would be lost. The declining enrollment of minority students at public universities that have abandoned affirmative action strongly suggests that the "color-blind" path is not the path to equal opportunity; nor is it the path to the highest-quality education.

Affirmative action policies reflect the reality that race has always shaped our educational institutions. Justice Blackmun's admonition in *Bakke* thus remains as vital as ever: "In order to get beyond racism, we must first take account of race. There is no other way."

sociation, General Motors, a group of 33 other *Fortune* 500 companies, and a long roster of higher education and civil rights groups. The eight briefs in support of the plaintiffs came from such conservative groups as the National Association of Scholars, the Center for Equal Opportunity and the Independent Women's Forum.

The minority intervenors will also repeat their arguments that the race-conscious admissions policies are justified as a remedy for the university's overt discrimination in the past and the disparate impact of other admissions policies on minorities. They face an uphill fight since both judges rejected their arguments. But Miranda Massie, the Detroit lawyer representing minority students in the law school case, says pro-affirmative action groups will mount a march and rally in Cincinnati on the day of the appeals court hearing.

Whatever the three-judge panel decides, the losing parties are certain to appeal to the Supreme Court. "Eventually, the Supreme Court will decide in all probability," Univeristy of Michigan President Bollinger says. Rosman agrees: "To the extent that the Supreme Court can resolve the uncertainty, it would be appropriate." ■

OUTLOOK

Ideals and Reality

Michigan graduate Jennifer Gratz and President Bollinger agree that someday colleges should stop using race as a factor in admissions decisions. "They can make up whatever policy they want as long as they as don't discriminate," Gratz says.

Bollinger, too, says he views color-blind admissions as an ultimate goal. "If it eventually came about that we got racial and ethnic diversity without taking race or ethnicity into account, we would no longer do so," Bollinger says.

Critics think the time for abolishing racial preferences has come. "We don't think institutionalized discrimination against African-Americans any longer exists," says Clegg of the Center for Equal Opportunity. "So institutionalized discrimination in their favor shouldn't exist."

Supporters say the critics overestimate the racial progress made since the peak of the civil rights era in the mid-1960s. "Thirty-five years — when you stack it up against 300 years — is peanuts," says Shaw of the NAACP Legal Defense Fund. "To think that we have solved all of these problems in 35 years is shortsighted and just wrong."

Public opinion and political sentiment on the issue appear to be somewhat malleable. Polls generally register support for "affirmative action" and opposition to "racial preferences." At Michigan, Cohen says he has few faculty allies in opposing race-conscious admissions. As for students, "it seems to me plain that a majority supports the university's position," he says.

Democrats in Congress have generally defended affirmative action even when the issue was hot in the mid-1990s. Republican leaders initially staked out positions against preferences after taking control of Congress following the 1994 elections, but then put the issue on a back burner.

The Supreme Court has also charted an uncertain course on the issue. The justices are divided along ideological lines on the issue, with the five conservatives generally opposed to racial policies and aligned against the four more liberal justices: John Paul Stevens, David H. Souter, Ruth Bader Ginsburg and Stephen G. Breyer.

Two of the conservatives — Scalia and Thomas — have staked out the strongest position against considering race in government policies. But O'Connor has a pivotal vote on the subject and has consistently stopped short of flatly prohibiting the government from taking race into account in employment, contracting or redistricting.

Bollinger — a legal scholar as well as university administrator — says *Bakke* remains "a firm constitutional precedent" for the university's policy. He says he is optimistic about the outcome of the two lawsuits — and about the future course of race relations in academia and beyond.

"I really do believe people of good sense will see the importance of maintaining the course that *Brown v. Board of Education* put us on — to work very hard on issues of race and ethnicity in this society," Bollinger says. "We have much to learn, much to overcome, and our great educational institutions are one of the most meaningful ways of addressing the experience of race."

For her part, Gratz says she had a "diverse group" of friends in high school and college, but acknowledges they were predominantly other whites. Still, she believes race relations in the United States today are "pretty good."

"I think that the more emphasis that we put on race, the more people are going to look at race," she concludes. "And I would like to see that in the future we really do have equal opportunity for all, regardless of race."

Does she think that will happen? "Yes," Gratz says, "it can happen." ■

Notes

[1] For extensive information on both cases, including the texts of the two rulings and other legal documents, see the University of Michigan's Web site (www.umich.edu) or the Web site of the public-interest law firm representing the plaintiffs, the Center for Individual Rights (www.cir-usa.org).

[2] The legal citation is 438 U.S. 265; Supreme Court decisions can be found on a number of Web sites, including the court's official site: www.supremecourtus.gov. For background, see Kenneth Jost, "Rethinking Affirmative Action," *The CQ Researcher*, April 28, 1995, pp. 369-392.

FOR MORE INFORMATION

American Council on Education, 1 Dupont Circle, N.W., Suite 800, Washington, D.C. 20036; (202) 939-9300; www.acenet.edu. The council was the lead organization in a friend-of-the-court brief filed by 30 higher-education groups in support of the University of Michigan's race-conscious admissions policies.

Center for Equal Opportunity, 815 15th St., N.W., Suite 928, Washington, D.C. 20005; (202) 639-0803; www.ceousa.org. The center filed a friend-of-the-court brief in support of the plaintiffs challenging University of Michigan admissions policies.

Center for Individual Rights, 1233 20th St., N.W., Washington, D.C. 20036; (202) 833-8400; www.cir-usa.org. The public-interest law firm represents plaintiffs in the University of Michigan cases and others challenging race-conscious admission policies.

NAACP Legal Defense Fund, 99 Hudson St., Suite 1600, New York, N.Y. 10013; (212) 965-2200; www.naacpldf.org (under construction, September 2001). The Legal Defense Fund represents the minority student intervenors in the two suits contesting admission policies at the University of Michigan.

National Association of Scholars, 221 Witherspoon St., Second Floor, Princeton, N.J. 08542-3215; (609) 683-7878; www.nas.org. The organization studies and advocates on academic issues including race-based admissions policies.

[3] See Robert Lerner and Althea K. Nagai, "Pervasive Preferences: Racial and Ethnic Discrimination in Undergraduate Admissions Across the Nation," Center for Equal Opportunity, Feb. 22, 2001 (www.ceo-usa.org).

[4] For background, see David Masci, "Hispanic Americans' New Clout," *The CQ Researcher*, Sept. 18, 1998, pp. 809-832; David Masci, "The Black Middle Class," *The CQ Researcher*, Jan. 23, 1998, pp. 49-72; and Kenneth Jost, "Diversity in the Workplace," *The CQ Researcher*, Oct. 10, 1997, pp. 889-912.

[5] Charles R. Lawrence III and Mari J. Matsuda, *We Won't Go Back: Making the Case for Affirmative Action* (1997), p. 127. Matsuda, Lawrence's wife, is also a professor at Georgetown law school.

[6] For background, see Joan Biskupic and Elder Witt, *Guide to the U.S. Supreme Court* (3d ed.), 1997, pp. 362-363. The cases discussed are *Missouri ex rel. Gaines v. Canada*, 305 U.S. 337 (1938); *Sweatt v. Painter*, 339 U.S. 629 (1950); and *McLaurin v. Oklahoma State Regents for Higher Education*, 339 U.S. 637 (1950).

[7] William G. Bowen and Derek Bok, *The Shape of the River: Long-Term Consequences of Considering Race in College and University Admissions* (1998), pp. 4-5. Bowen, a former president of Princeton University, is now president of the Andrew W. Mellon Foundation in New York City; Bok is a former president of Harvard University and now University Professor at the John. F. Kennedy School of Government at Harvard.

[8] Reprinted in Gabriel J. Chin (ed.), *Affirmative Action and the Constitution: Affirmative Action Before Constitutional Law, 1964-1977*, Vol. 1 (1998), pp. 21-26.

[9] Bowen and Bok, *op. cit.*, pp. 6-7.

[10] Description of the announcement of the decision taken from Bernard Schwartz, *Behind* Bakke: *Affirmative Action and the Supreme Court* (1988), pp. 142-150.

[11] The cases are *Wygant v. Jackson Bd. of Education*, 476 U.S. 267 (1986); *Johnson v. Transportation Agency of Santa Clara County* 480 U.S. 646 (1987); *City of Richmond v. J.A. Croson Co.* 488 U.S. 469 (1989); and *Adarand Constructors, Inc. v. Peña* 575 U.S. 200 (1995).

[12] Lincoln Caplan, *Up Against the Law: Affirmative Action and the Supreme Court* (1997), p. 16.

[13] The case is *Hopwood v. Texas*. Some background on this and other cases in this section drawn from Girardeau A. Spann, *The Law of Affirmative Action: Twenty-Five Years of Supreme Court Decisions on Race and Remedies* (2000).

[14] The legal citation is *Hopwood v. Texas*, 78 F.2d 932 (5th Cir. 1996). In a subsequent decision, the appeals court on Dec. 21, 2000, reaffirmed its legal holding, but upheld the lower court judge's finding that none of the four plaintiffs would have been admitted to the law school under a race-blind system. See *Hopwood v. Texas*, 236 F.2d 256 (5th Cir. 2000).

[15] Quoted in Facts on File, March 28, 1996.

[16] For background, see Jennifer Gavin, "Redistricting," *The CQ Researcher*, Feb. 16, 2001, pp. 113-128; Nadine Cahodas, "Electing Minorities," *The CQ Researcher*, Aug. 12, 1994, pp. 697-720.

[17] The legal citation is 515 U.S. 200.

[18] For a critique, see Stephan and Abigail Thernstrom, "Reflections on the Shape of the River," *UCLA Law Review*, Vol. 46, No. 5 (June 1999), pp. 1583-1631.

[19] For a good overview, see Nicholas Lemann, "The Empathy Defense," *The New Yorker*, Dec. 18, 2000, pp. 46-51. See also Carl Cohen, "Race Preference and the Universities — A Final Reckoning," *Commentary*, September 2001, pp. 31-39.

[20] "Vital Signs: The Statistics that Describe the Present and Suggest the Future of African Americans in Higher Education," *The Journal of Blacks in Higher Education*, No. 9 (autumn 1995), pp. 43-49.

[21] The Washington case is *Smith v. University of Washington Law School*, 9th Circuit, Dec. 4, 2000; the Georgia case is *Johnson v. Board of Regents of the University of Georgia*, 11th Circuit, Aug. 27.

[22] See Crystal Yednak, "Laws Meant to Boost Diversity Paying Off," *Fort Worth Star-Telegram*, Jan. 13, 2001, p. 1.

[23] Ron Word, "State Universities Have Differing Results Recruiting Minorities," The Associated Press, June 19, 2001.

[24] See Edward Walsh, "Affirmative Action's Confusing Curriculum," *The Washington Post*, Sept. 4, 2001, p. A2.

Bibliography

Selected Sources Used

Books

Bowen, William G., and Derek Bok, *The Shape of the River: Long-Term Consequences of Considering Race in College and University Admissions*, Princeton University Press, 1998.

The book analyzes data on 80,000 students admitted to 28 selective private or public colleges and universities in 1951, 1976 and 1989 to examine the impact of race-based admissions on enrollment and to compare the educational and post-graduation experiences of white and minority students. Includes statistical tables as well as a nine-page list of references. Bowen, a former president of Princeton University, heads the Andrew W. Mellon Foundation; Bok is a former president of Harvard University and now a professor at Harvard's John F. Kennedy School of Government.

Caplan, Lincoln, *Up Against the Law: Affirmative Action and the Supreme Court*, Twentieth Century Fund Press, 1997.

The 60-page monograph provides an overview of the Supreme Court's affirmative action rulings with analysis written from a pro race-conscious policies perspective. Caplan, a longtime legal-affairs writer, is a senior writer in residence at Yale Law School.

Chin, Gabriel J. (ed.), *Affirmative Action and the Constitution: Affirmative Action Before Constitutional Law, 1964–1977* (Vol. 1); *The Supreme Court "Solves" the Affirmative Action Issue, 1978–1988* (Vol. 2); *Judicial Reaction to Affirmative Action, 1988–1997* (Vol. 3), Garland Publishing, 1998.

The three-volume compendium includes a variety of materials on affirmative action from President Lyndon B. Johnson's famous speech at Howard University in 1965 to President Bill Clinton's defense of affirmative action in 1995 as well as the full text of the federal appeals court decision in the 1995 *Hopwood* decision barring racial preferences at the University of Texas Law School. Chin, who wrote an introduction for each volume, is a professor at the University of Cincinnati College of Law.

Edley, Christopher Jr., *Not All Black and White: Affirmative Action, Race, and American Values*, Hill & Wang, 1996.

Edley, a Harvard Law School professor, recounts his role in overseeing the Clinton administration's review of affirmative action in 1995 as part of a broad look at the issue that ends with measured support for affirmative action "until the justification for it no longer exists."

Schwartz, Bernard, *Behind Bakke: Affirmative Action and the Supreme Court*, New York University Press.

Schwartz, a leading Supreme Court scholar until his death in 1997, was granted unusual access to the private papers of the justices for this detailed, behind-the-scenes account of the *Bakke* case from its origins through the justices' deliberations and final decision.

Spann, Girardeau A., *The Law of Affirmative Action: Twenty-Five Years of Supreme Court Decisions on Races and Remedies*, New York University Press, 2000.

The book includes summaries — concise and precise — of major Supreme Court decisions from *Bakke* in 1978 to *Adarand* in 1995 Spann is a professor at Georgetown University Law Center.

Steele, Shelby, *A Dream Deferred: The Second Betrayal of Black Freedom in America*, HarperCollins, 1998.

Steele, a prominent black critic of affirmative action and a research fellow at the Hoover Institution at Stanford University, argues in four essays that affirmative action represents an "extravagant" liberalism that "often betrayed America's best principles" in order to atone for white guilt over racial injustice.

Articles

Lawrence, Charles R. III, "Two Views of the River: A Critique of the Liberal Defense of Affirmative Action," *Columbia Law Review*, Vol. 101, No. 4 (May 2001), pp. 928–975.

Lawrence argues that liberals' "diversity" defense of affirmative action overlooks "more radical substantive" arguments based on "the need to remedy past discrimination, address present discriminatory practices, and reexamine traditional notions of merit and the role of universities in the reproduction of elites." Lawrence is a professor at Georgetown University Law Center.

PBS NewsHour, "Admitting for Diversity," Aug. 21, 2001 (www.pbs.org/newshour).

The report by correspondent Elizabeth Brackett features interviews with, among others, Barbara Grutter, the plaintiff in the lawsuit challenging the University of Michigan Law School's race-based admissions policies, and the law school's dean, Jeffrey Lehman.

Thernstrom, Stephan, and Abigail Thernstrom, "Reflections on The Shape of the River," ***UCLA Law Review*****, Vol. 46, No. 5 (June 1999), pp. 1583–1631.**

The Thernstroms contend that racial preferences constitute a "pernicious palliative" that deflect attention from real educational problems and conflict with the country's unrealized egalitarian dream. Stephan Thernstrom is a professor of history at Harvard University; his wife Abigail is a senior fel-

2 Reparations

DAVID MASCI

A memorial at the Nazi concentration camp at Buchenwald honors the hundreds of thousands of Jews who were murdered there. Billions of dollars have been paid to Holocaust survivors.

Rep. John Conyers Jr. is not a man who gives up easily. Six times since 1989, the feisty 19-term Michigan Democrat has introduced a measure in the House of Representatives to create a commission to study paying reparations to African-American descendants of slaves. Each time, the bill has died.

But Conyers is optimistic. He claims that beating the same legislative drum so long has helped bring the reparations issue to the attention of the American people.

"Twelve years ago, most people didn't even know what reparations were, and now it's a front-burner issue," he says. "It's like those first [unsuccessful] bills making Martin Luther King's birthday a holiday: You have to build up a critical mass of support, or you don't get anyplace."

Indeed, several local governments have passed resolutions favoring reparations, and the issue has caught the attention of a growing cadre of prominent black advocates and scholars, who have begun holding conferences and symposia on the subject. "It's time to address this issue we've so long denied — the lingering effects of slavery," said Johnnie Cochran, former counsel for O.J. Simpson and a member of a "dream team" of attorneys preparing to sue the federal government and others for slavery reparations. [1]

In addition, several African nations are trying to put the issue on the agenda of the upcoming United Nations World Conference Against Racism, in Durban, South Africa. They hope the United States and former colonial powers like Britain and France will increase aid to African countries to compensate for centuries of slave trading.

Until 50 years ago, debates over reparations for victims of persecution were largely theoretical. But in the wake of World War II, reparations increasingly have been seen as a viable means of addressing past injustices — not just to Jews slaughtered in the Holocaust but to Japanese-Americans, Native Americans and even Australian Aborigines. In fact, the debate over slavery reparations comes on the heels of a string of victories for groups seeking restitution.

In 1988, for instance, Congress passed a law authorizing the U.S. government to apologize for interning Japanese-Americans during the war and award $20,000 to each surviving victim. More recently, European countries and companies from Bayer AG to Volkswagen have paid billions of dollars to victims of Nazi Germany's effort to exterminate Europe's Jews and other "undesirables."

Now it is time for slavery reparations, proponents say. Randall Robinson, author of the bestseller *The Debt: What America Owes to Blacks*, argues that acknowledging the nation's debt to African-Americans for slavery and a subsequent century of discrimination will help heal the country's existing racial divide. "We cannot have racial reconciliation until we make the victims of this injustice whole," says Robinson, president of TransAfrica, a Washington, D.C.-based black advocacy group.

Besides raising a moral question, reparations for slavery is also an economic issue, Robinson says. Many of the problems facing black America are directly linked to slavery and the 100 years of forced segregation that followed emancipation in 1865, he says. "It's foolish to argue that the past has nothing to do with the present," Robinson says. "There's a reason why so many African-Americans are poor: It's because a terrible wrong occurred in our history that produced a lasting inequality." Reparations will help right that wrong, advocates say, by helping black Americans reach social and economic parity.

But other black Americans warn that paying reparations for slavery will drive a new wedge between blacks and whites, leading to greater racial polarization. "Doing something like this would create a tremendous amount of resentment among whites," says Walter Williams, chairman of the Economics Department at George Mason University in Fairfax, Va.

Williams says whites and other Americans would understandably be opposed to paying restitution for a crime that ended more than 135 years ago and to a community now making great social and economic strides.

From *The CQ Researcher*, June 22, 2001.

Seeking Justice for Australia's Aborigines

Australian Olympic gold medal winner Cathy Freeman knew all about the "stolen generation" of Aborigines. Her grandmother was one of the thousands of youngsters taken from their parents by white authorities.

Winning the 400-meter dash at last year's Summer Games gave Freeman a chance to speak out on the centuries of mistreatment of Australia's indigenous people.

Aborigines have lived in Australia for at least 40,000 years, most likely migrating from Southeast Asia. Their downfall as a people began in 1788, when British ships brought 1,000 settlers, including more than 500 convicts from overcrowded jails. Clashes began almost immediately, but the Aborigines' primitive weapons were no match for British guns and mounted soldiers.

Because the convicts provided free labor, the white settlers treated the Aborigines as little more than useless pests. Those who were not killed were driven away to fenced reser-vations in the most inhospitable parts of the "outback" territory. Crimes against Aborigines often went unpunished.

Aborigines, who make up 2 percent of Australia's largely white population of 19 million, were not allowed to vote until 1962; they were not counted in the census until 1967. Moreover, Aborigines' life expectancy is 20 years less than the national average and they occupy the lowest rung of the nation's economic ladder.

But in 1992, they won a significant victory when courts recognized that the Aborigines had "owned' Australia before whites arrived. Today, they own more than 15 percent of the continent, mostly in the remote northern territory.

Nevertheless, some Aboriginal leaders are seeking reparations for perhaps the worst injustice perpetrated against their group — the state-sponsored abduction of Aboriginal children from their parents.

From the early 1900s until the 1970s, as many as 100,000 Aboriginal children were taken from their parents to be raised among whites in orphanages or foster families. State and federal laws that permitted the practice were based on the belief that full-blooded Aborigines would eventually die out and that assimilating the children into white society was the best way to save them.

Reuters Photo/Jerry Lampen

Olympic gold medalist Cathy Freeman has used her celebrity to call attention to her fellow Aborigines.

In 1997, the Australian Human Rights and Equal Opportunity Commission reported that many of the children had been physically and sexually abused and suffered long-term psychological damage from the loss of family and cultural ties.

But Australian Sen. John Herron called the 1997 report "one-sided" and said the stories about removing Aboriginal children from their families was greatly exaggerated." [1]

His comments stung Aden Ridgeway, the only Aborigine senator in Parliament, who angrily compared Herron's statements to "denying the Holocaust." [2]

"They were denying they had done anything wrong, denying that a whole generation was stolen," Freeman said. "The fact is, parts of people's lives were taken away." [3]

Herron recognizes the removal of Aboriginal children as a blemish on Australia's history, but he claims many were taken with their parents' consent and for their own welfare. He believes amends are the responsibility of states and churches and has suggested that reparations claims be filed individually via the courts.

"Blacks have come so far; this is nothing but counterproductive," he says.

Opponents also argue that, rather than correcting economic disparity, reparations would take money and attention away from more pressing social and economic issues facing black Americans, such as a substandard education system and high incarceration rates for young African-American men. "This would be such a huge waste of resources, at a time when so much needs to be done in education and other areas," Williams says.

To counter such arguments, slavery reparations advocates have begun modeling their efforts on successful techniques used by Holocaust victims. Recent battles for Holocaust-related reparations have netted survivors and their families more than $10 billion in compensation for slave labor, recovered bank accounts and unclaimed life insurance policies.

But reparations proponents say it is difficult to prove abuse in the absence of documents and witnesses. They cite the first stolen-generations case, brought last year, which was dismissed for lack of evidence.

Many advocates for the Aborigines favor creation of a national compensation board to adjudicate all "stolen generation" claims.

But Prime Minister John Howard dismisses the idea. He refuses to issue an apology, stating today's Australians should not be held responsible for the mistakes of past generations. He also points to a $63 million government program designed to reunite families of the stolen generation.

However, former Prime Minister Malcolm Fraser says an apology is essential. "We can't undo the past, but we can, in an apology, recognize the fact that many actions in the past did a grave injustice to the Aboriginal population of Australia. We have a commitment to recognize that and other past injustices in walking together into a new future." [4]

Last year, the government spent $1.5 billion on health, education, housing and job-training programs for Aborigines.

But monetary payments and programs are not enough, say some reparations supporters. Geoff Clark, chairman of the Aboriginal and Torres Strait Islander Commission, which oversees indigenous affairs, wants the government not only to apologize but also to sign a treaty with the indigenous population that would provide limited autonomy for Aboriginal communities. His group cites similar treaties in the United States and Canada.

Howard says a treaty would be too divisive. "One part of Australia making a treaty with another part is to accept that we are in effect two nations," he said in a radio interview last year." [5]

Ridgeway supports the treaty. "I think the prime minister's kidding himself if he thinks that a treaty's going to be divisive. The goal is about a formal document that better defines black and white relations and the unfinished business of reconciliation." [6]

A national election later this year is widely expected to usher in a new prime minister. Howard's rival has supported the idea of a government apology to the Aborigines.

— ***Scott Kuzner***

AP Photo/David Guttenfelder

Australians protesting outside the federal court in Darwin in August 2000 call for government compensation for indigenous Australians of the "stolen generations."

[1] "Separated, But Not a Generation," *Illawarra Mercury*, Aug. 19, 2000, p. 9.

[2] Mitchell Zuckoff, "Golden Opportunity, Australian Aboriginal Activists Hope to Exploit the Olympics to Publicize Their De-mands for an Apology, Cash Reparations and Limited Sov-ereignty," *The Boston Globe*, Sept. 18, 2000, p. 1E.

[3] Michael Gordon, "Beginning Of The Legend," *Sydney Morning Herald*, Sept. 25, 2000, p. 10.

[4] Malcolm Fraser, "Apology Must Be First Step," *Sydney Morning Herald*, April 8, 1999, p. 15.

[5] Tony Wright and Kerry Taylor, "PM Rules Out 'Divisive' Treaty," *The Age*, May 30, 2000, p. 2.

[6] *Ibid.*

But some argue that compensating victims of injustice cheapens their suffering. Indeed, a group of mostly Jewish-American scholars and journalists has criticized some of the efforts to obtain relief for Holocaust survivors. They say the lawyers and Jewish groups involved have turned the legitimate quest for restitution into a shameless money grab that degrades the memory of the millions who perished.

"Fighting for money makes it much harder to see a tragedy in the right light," says Melissa Nobles, a professor of political science at the Massachusetts Institute of Technology (MIT) in Boston.

"They have hijacked the Holocaust and appointed themselves saviors of the victims — all in the name of money," says Norman Finkelstein, a history professor at Hunter College in New York City and author of *The Holocaust Industry: Reflections on the Exploitation of Jewish Suffering*.

Finkelstein points out that those representing the victims have used hardball tactics to "blackmail" Germany, Switzerland and other countries into paying huge sums to satisfy what are often dubious claims. Besides cheapening the historical legacy of the Holocaust, he argues, such actions could potentially trigger an anti-Semitic backlash in Europe.

Supporters say they are only working aggressively to obtain some small measure of justice for the victims. "We are trying to compensate slave laborers and return the assets of survivors," says Elan Steinberg, executive director of the World Jewish Congress, one of the groups leading the Holocaust reparations efforts. "In doing this, we must uncover the truth, which is often hard for these countries to confront."

He says Holocaust victims should not be denied their assets or rightful compensation just because confronting European countries with their past might lead to an anti-Jewish backlash. "Survivors have a right to pursue legitimate claims," he insists. "This is about justice."

"It is good that we try to make some effort to acknowledge someone's suffering, even if it is inadequate," says Tim Cole, a professor of 20th century European history at the University of Bristol in England. At the very least, reparations are important symbolic gestures to the victims from the victimizers, he adds.

As the debate over reparations continues, here are some of the questions experts are asking:

Should the United States pay reparations to African-American descendants of slaves?

For much of its 250-year history on these shores, slavery was America's most divisive and controversial issue. The Founding Fathers fought over the status of African slaves when drafting both the Declaration of Independence and the Constitution. And of course, in 1861 slavery helped trigger the nation's most costly conflict, a four-year Civil War that tore the country apart.

Today, few Americans of any race would disagree that slavery was the most shameful and tragic episode in American history. Many would also agree that African-Americans as a whole, including the descendants of slaves, are still suffering from its effects.

> **"Whites need to realize that we'll have no chance of cohering as a nation in the future unless we deal with this issue now."**
>
> ***— Randall Robinson, President, TransAfrica***

Proponents say compensation is justified on a variety of levels, beginning with the fact that African-Americans remain severely handicapped by the legacy of slavery, lagging behind the nation as a whole in virtually every measure. As a result, supporters say, they need and deserve extra help to overcome the economic and social disadvantages they face.

"Our entire economic sector has been and remains truncated because of slavery," says Ronald Walters, a political science professor at the University of Maryland. "We need something to help reverse this terrible harm done to blacks in this country."

"You have an enormous, static and fixed inequality in America due to a 350-year human-rights crime," Robinson says. "We have an obligation to compensate the people still suffering for the wrong that occurred."

Robinson, Walters and others argue that reparations are justified by the fact that the United States grew prosperous largely through the toil of unpaid African-Americans. "Exports of cotton, rice and tobacco swelled the coffers of the U.S. Treasury, yet the people who produced it were never paid," Robinson says.

However, an overwhelming majority of Americans do not believe the nation owes black Americans reparations. A March poll found that 81 percent of registered voters oppose reparations, while only 11 percent support them. [2]

Some Americans feel that the nation has already paid reparations for slavery by passing civil rights and affirmative action laws and by funding myriad social programs designed to help African-Americans and other disadvantaged peoples. "Since the War on Poverty in the 1960s, the nation has spent $6 trillion on fighting poverty," Williams says.

Others dismiss the whole idea of reparations for slavery out of hand, citing the potentially astronomical cost. Compensating for slavery's injustices could cost as much as $10 trillion, according to some estimates, dwarfing the estimated $10 billion paid to Holocaust victims so far.

Nevertheless, supporters say, reparations would ease African-Americans' feeling that the nation cares little about their plight. "The socioeconomic inequality that exists today because of slavery means that the American promise of egalitarianism remains unfulfilled for blacks," Walters says. "It would make the idea of America and American democracy meaningful to blacks."

Paying reparations would benefit the entire nation by creating a more conducive environment for racial reconciliation, supporters say. "We'll never have any harmony or stability between the races until there is commitment to make the victim whole," Robinson says. "Whites need to realize that we'll have no chance of cohering as a nation in the future unless we deal with this issue now."

Conyers agrees that paying reparations would encourage racial healing — for both blacks and whites. "This could create a bridge that unlocks understanding and compassion between people," he says.

But opponents say compensating slavery victims will have exactly the opposite effect — creating new grounds for racial polarization. "I can't think of a better fortification for racism than reparations to blacks," says George Mason University's Williams. "To force whites today, who were not in any way responsible for slavery, to make payments to black people — many of whom may be better off [than the whites] — will create nothing but great resentment."

"It would create a huge backlash against black people, which is something they don't really need," says Glen Loury, director of the Institute of Race and Social Division at Boston University. "It would also be seen as just another example of black people's inability 'to get over it and move on.' "

Indeed, opponents say, reparations might even have the reverse effect: They could significantly weaken the nation's commitment to lifting poor black Americans out of poverty. "This would be a Pyrrhic victory for African-Americans," says Loury, who is black. "It would undermine the claim for further help down the road, because the rest of America will say: 'Shut up: You've been paid.' "

In addition, Loury says, pushing for restitution detracts from the real issues facing the black community. "This whole thing takes the public's attention away from important issues, like failing schools and the fact that so many African-Americans are in jail."

"I can't think of a better fortification for racism than reparations to blacks."

— Walter Williams, Chairman, Economics Department, George Mason University

Have efforts to collect reparations for Holocaust victims gone too far?

In the last five years, efforts to compensate and recover stolen property for Holocaust victims and their heirs have increased dramatically. What started in the mid-1990s as an action to recover money in long-dormant Swiss bank accounts has snowballed into a host of lawsuits and settlements against European insurance companies, German and American manufacturers and art galleries around the world. [3]

By and large, these actions have been hailed as a great victory for victims of oppression. Yet a small but growing circle of critics questions the efforts. They charge the lawyers working on behalf of Holocaust victims — as well as the World Jewish Congress, the International Commission on Holocaust Era Insurance Claims (known as the Claims Conference) and other groups — with exploiting a historical tragedy for monetary gain.

"This whole thing has gone way too far," says Gabriel Shoenfeld, senior editor of *Commentary*, a conservative opinion magazine that examines issues from a Jewish perspective. "This is a case of a just cause that has been traduced by overzealous organizations and some rather unscrupulous lawyers." Hunter College's Finkelstein goes further, branding those who work on behalf of survivors as "the Holocaust industry" and their actions "nothing short of a shakedown racket."

Shoenfeld and Finkelstein are troubled by the fact that Jewish groups and attorneys working on the cases have taken it upon themselves to represent Holocaust survivors. "Groups like the World Jewish Congress don't really represent anyone," Finkelstein says. "They weren't elected by anyone to do this, and most Jews don't even know who they are."

He argues that such groups are using the survivors' high moral status as a cudgel to beat countries and corporations into submission. "They've wrapped themselves in the mantle of the needy Holocaust victims against the greedy, fat Swiss bankers and Nazi industrialists," Finkelstein says. "They are out of control and reckless."

Shoenfeld says the claims often are either overblown, dubious or

For Native Americans, a Different Struggle

Unlike African-Americans, Native Americans are not seeking a huge settlement to right the wrongs of the past. Instead, they're working on the present.

"We don't want reparations," says John Echohawk, executive director of the Native American Rights Fund, an Indian advocacy group in Boulder, Colo. "What we do want is the government to honor its duty to us — and we want our land and our water back." They also want up to $40 billion they say the government owes them.

Tribes have been making land claims against the government for more than a century. Today, dozens of claims are being dealt with (*see p. 30*).

But the biggest fight for restitution has come over allegations of government mishandling of a huge trust fund for Native Americans. Indian advocates say the federal government will end up owing between $10 billion and $40 billion to Native Americans when the matter is cleared up.

AP Photo/Jeff Robbins

Penny Manybeads stands beside her hogan at the Navajo Indian reservation in Tuba City. Ariz., in 1993. Native Americans want the government to pay for the mismanagement of their natural resources trust fund.

Since 1887, the federal government's Bureau of Indian Affairs (BIA) has managed many of the natural resources on Indian lands, such as oil and mineral deposits and grazing and water rights. Proceeds from the sale or use of these resources are, in theory at least, put into a trust fund administered by the government on behalf of members of the tribes who own the assets — some 500,000 Native Americans throughout the country.

In the 1970s, Elouise Cobell, a member of the Blackfoot tribe, began to question the government's management of these accounts. Other Indians had long suspected mismanagement, but no one had challenged the BIA officials who controlled the fund.

Over the next two decades, Cobell, who has an accounting background, concluded that billions of dollars had been lost, and that many Indians were being cheated out of money that was rightfully theirs. Her efforts to get BIA officials to pay attention to the problem came to naught. "They tried to belittle me and intimated that I was a dumb Indian," she says.

In 1996, after years of what Cobell calls stonewalling by federal officials, she and four other Native Americans filed a class action suit in federal court against the Department of the Interior, which controls BIA. "The suit was a last resort, because no one would listen to us," Echohawk says. "No one did anything."

The plaintiffs charged that many records had been destroyed; that officials had improperly invested much of the money coming into the trust; and that no effort was made to keep individual Indians informed about the individual accounts the government kept for them. [1] These claims were later buttressed by a government official, who acknowledged that trust managers could not locate some 50,000 account holders because of poor recordkeeping.

Even before the suit was filed, the federal government had made some attempts to address the problem. In 1994, Congress passed the Native American Trust Fund Accounting and Management Reform Act, authorizing the appointment of a special trustee to manage and reform the fund. But the first such trustee, former Riggs Bank President Paul Homan, resigned in protest in 1999, complaining that the Interior Department was not adequately committed to reform.

Meanwhile, Cobell's suit against the government succeeded. In December 2000, a federal court ruled against the Interior Department and took control of the trust fund. "The government kept arguing that they were doing the best they could, but that just wasn't true," Echohawk says. "Fortunately, the court didn't believe them."

The government lost a subsequent appeal. Most recently, the new Bush administration decided not to continue to appeal the ruling, ending resistance to a court-administered solution.

The parties now must decide how much the government owes the trust fund. "We hope we can avoid a protracted legal battle over damages and settle out of court," Echohawk says, adding that Bush's decision not to continue appealing the ruling is a good sign the administration is committed to solving the problem.

Still, Echohawk is wary. "I'm cautious because until now, the government has fought us every inch of the way," he says. "Federal stonewalling and neglect are part of the story of the American Indian."

---

[1] Colman McCarthy, "Broken Promises Break Trust," *The Baltimore Sun*, March 7, 1999.

simply not valid. "It's clear that they're trying to humiliate these countries into giving in," he says.

Shoenfeld cites a recent case against Dutch insurers, who had already settled with the Netherlands' Jewish community for unpaid wartime insurance policies. "These guys then came in and tried to unfairly blacken Holland's reputation by painting their behavior during the war in an unfavorable light, without acknowledging all of the good things Dutch people did for Jews during that time," he says. "It was all an effort to blackmail them, to extract more money from them."

Even the much-publicized victory against the Swiss banks was marred by unscrupulous tactics, Finkelstein contends. After forcing the banks to set up a commission headed by former U.S. Federal Reserve Chairman Paul A. Volcker to investigate claims, they demanded a settlement before the commission finished its work, he says.

The Swiss caved in and paid $1.25 billion, Finkelstein says, because the groups were creating public hysteria and had American politicians threatening an economic boycott. "They honed this strategy against the Swiss and then turned to the French, Germans and others and used it successfully against them."

Such heavy-handed tactics create unnecessary ill will against European Jews, critics say. "By bludgeoning the Europeans into submission, the Holocaust industry is fomenting anti-Semitism," Finkelstein says.

Shoenfeld says the tactics have already spurred an anti-Semitic backlash in Germany and Switzerland. "Don't Jews have enough problems in the world without bringing upon themselves the wrath of major European powers?" he asks.

But groups pursuing Holocaust reparations say their opponents are misguided. "How can anyone ask [if] we are going too far in attempting to get restitution for people who were driven from their homes, forced into hiding, persecuted and forced to work?" asks Hillary Kessler-Godin, director of communications for the Claims Conference in New York City.

Supporters also argue that their tactics are not "heavy-handed" or designed to blackmail European countries. "We're not out to humiliate anyone," says the World Jewish Congress' Steinberg. "But sometimes the truth is hard and difficult for everyone to accept."

For instance, it would not serve the truth or the victims to sugarcoat Holland's dismal record of protecting Jews during the Holocaust, Steinberg says. "Holland had the worst record of any Western European country," he argues. "Eighty percent of its Jews were wiped out."

He also points out that his group rushed to settle the Swiss case before the Volcker commission finished its work in order to begin repaying survivors before they died. "Many survivors are very old and dying at such a rapid rate — some 10,000 to 15,000 a year. We had to move on this," he says. The commission will continue its work, so that all 55,000 Holocaust-era accounts can be investigated and paid out, he adds.

Proponents also counter the criticism that their actions foment anti-Semitism. "Anti-Semitism is not caused by Jewish actions, but by people who don't like Jews," Kessler-Godin says. "To temper our actions on behalf of people who have suffered the worst form of anti-Semitism possible in the name of not causing anti-Semitism defies logic."

"Holocaust survivors should not have to abrogate their rights simply for political expediency," Steinberg adds, pointing out that most people, regardless of their religious background, understand and support his group's efforts. "At the end of the day, most non-Jews — except those who represent the banks or insurance companies — see this as an act of justice."

Does putting a price tag on suffering diminish that suffering?

On Dec. 7, 1998, the leader of one of the pre-eminent Jewish organizations in the United States shocked many American Jews by publicly questioning efforts to obtain reparations for Holocaust survivors. In a *Wall Street Journal* editorial, Abraham Foxman, national director of the Anti-Defamation League, argued that when "claims become the main focus of activity regarding the Holocaust, rather than the unique horror of 6 million Jews, including 1.5 million children, being murdered simply because they were Jewish, then something has gone wrong." [4]

Foxman worried that the drive to obtain restitution would shift modern attitudes about the Holocaust from one of reverence for the victims and their suffering to an accounting of their material losses.

"I fear that all the talk about Holocaust-era assets is skewing the Holocaust, making the century's last word on the Holocaust that the Jews died, not because they were Jews, but because they had bank accounts, gold, art and property," he wrote. "To me that is a desecration of the victims, a perversion of why the Nazis had a Final Solution, and too high a price to pay for a justice we can never achieve." [5]

Foxman's editorial provoked an immediate response from many prominent Jews. Nobel Peace Prize winner Elie Wiesel argued that compensating Holocaust survivors does not sully their memory but is the right thing to do.

"It is wrong to think of this as about money," said Wiesel, a Holocaust survivor himself. "It is about justice, conscience and morality." [6]

But critics point out that reparations, almost by their nature, are tainted, because they mix the sacredness of a people's suffering and pain with the world's greatest source of corruption: money. "Although there might be a way to handle this whole thing with dignity, it inexorably becomes a sordid business," Finkelstein says. "I believe money always corrupts things."

"There is a real danger here that most people will say: Hey wait a minute. This is all really about money," says MIT's Nobles. "Money can profoundly obscure the nature of a tragedy."

Some critics also contend that monetary reparations can do victims more harm than good. "People who have been victimized need to become free internally in order to move beyond the tragedy that has occurred," says Ruth Wisse, a professor of Yiddish and comparative literature at Harvard University. "In this sense, reparations can be harmful because they make victims less dependent on themselves."

Instead of monetary payments, she says, nations should take steps to resolve the political problems that led to the suffering in the first place. "Reparations should be made on political terms, not economic terms," she says. For example, she said a country like Turkey, which many historians say exterminated more than a million Armenians at the beginning of the 20th century, might want to help protect Armenia from outside threats.

But advocates for reparations argue that the money is more a powerful symbol than a primary motive. "We're really talking about justice," says the University of Bristol's Cole. "It's a symbolic act, a gesture."

Although, Cole says, "no amount of money can ever compensate for the suffering of history's victims," restitution can aid them in some small way. "There are things we can do to ease people's suffering or bring them some sense that justice is being done."

"Of course you can't put a price tag on suffering," says the University of Maryland's Walters. "But what you can do is ask: What will bring the victims a measure of dignity? Isn't that the most important thing?"

Proponents also contend that, in the real world where victims of past oppression may still be suffering, monetary compensation can make a huge difference in their lives. For instance, says Kessler-Godin, many Eastern European Holocaust survivors live in poverty and need assistance. "It's OK for Abraham Foxman, living his comfortable American life, to say that it cheapens the memory of victims, but there are people who are living hand to mouth who don't have that luxury."

Finally, supporters say, forgoing reparations allows the victimizers to retain their financial wealth. "When you argue that a victim shouldn't pursue restitution, you are essentially rewarding the oppressors," Steinberg says. ■

BACKGROUND

Ancient Notion

The payment of reparations for genocide or other injustices is a relatively new phenomenon, which began with Germany's 1951 pledge to aid Israel and to compensate individual victims of the Holocaust. "Before World War II, nations saw what they did to other people during wartime as a natural byproduct of war," MIT's Nobles says. "The vanquished simply had to accept what had happened to them."

But while the use of reparations may be a relatively new remedy, the ideas behind them have a long, if circuitous, intellectual pedigree stretching back for millennia. For instance, the ancient Greeks and Romans explored the notion that the weak and oppressed deserve sympathy and possibly assistance. The 4th century B.C. Athenian philosopher Plato addressed this issue in his most famous dialogue, *The Republic*. A generation later Aristotle, another Athenian philosopher, wrote that the best kind of government was one that helped those who had been deprived of happiness. [7]

Judeo-Christian doctrine also grappled with what individuals and society owe to the downtrodden and oppressed. For instance, in the *New Testament*, Jesus Christ singled out the persecuted as being particularly deserving of compassion and assistance. [8]

The first modern articulation of these principles came in the 18th century during the Enlightenment. Ironically, it was the intellectual father of free market economics — Scottish philosopher Adam Smith — who wrote most forcefully and eloquently about guilt and the resulting sympathy it causes.

In his 1759 treatise, *The Theory of Moral Sentiments*, he wrote: "How selfish soever man may be supposed, there are evidently some principles in his nature, which interest him in the fortunes of others, and render their happiness necessary to him, though he derives nothing from it, except the pleasure of seeing it. Of this kind is pity or compassion, the emotion we

Chronology

1945-1980 *After World War II, West Germany moves to pay restitution to Jewish survivors of the Holocaust.*

1948
Congress passes the Japanese-American Evacuations Claims Act to compensate Japanese-Americans who lost property as a result of being interned during World War II.

1951
West German Chancellor Konrad Adenauer proposes paying assistance to Israel and reparations to Jewish survivors of the Nazi Holocaust.

1953
Israel and West Germany agree on payment of reparations and aid. Over the next nearly 50 years, Germans will pay more than $60 billion in Holocaust-related restitution.

1956
Swiss government asks banks and insurers to reveal their Holocaust-related assets. The companies say such "dormant accounts" hold less than 1 million Swiss francs.

1962
A second request for an accounting of Holocaust-related assets leads to the discovery of about 10 million Swiss francs in dormant accounts.

1965
West Germany ends state-to-state payments to Israel. Holocaust survivors continue to receive payments from German government through the present.

1980s-Present *Oppressed groups begin seeking reparations.*

1980
Congress creates the Commission on Wartime Relocations and Internment of Civilians to study possible reparations for Japanese-Americans interned during World War II.

1987
National Coalition of Blacks for Reparations in America (N'COBRA) is founded.

1988
Congress passes the Civil Liberties Act, which apologizes for the wartime internment of Japanese-Americans and authorizes the payment of $20,000 to surviving internees. Eventually, 80,000 Japanese-Americans receive an apology and a check.

1989
Rep. John Conyers Jr., D-Mich., introduces legislation to create a commission to study the African-American reparation issue. He will reintroduce the bill five more times in the coming years.

1990
The first Japanese-American internees begin receiving reparations checks.

1995
European and American media exposés document the role of Swiss banks in financing the Nazi war effort and in failing to make restitution to Holocaust survivors.

October 1996
Class action suit is filed in New York federal court against Swiss banks, seeking funds from "dormant accounts" of Holocaust victims.

1998
Though not an apology, President Clinton says in a speech at a Ugandan village school that it was wrong for European Americans to have received "the fruits of the slave trade."

August 1998
Swiss government agrees to pay $1.25 billion to settle claims against Swiss banks.

December 1998
In a *Wall Street Journal* op-ed piece, Anti-Defamation League national director and Holocaust survivor Abraham Foxman questions the tactics employed by those seeking reparations for Holocaust survivors.

December 1999
The German government and corporations that used slave labor during the war establish a $4.3 billion fund to compensate surviving slave laborers.

2000
TransAfrica founder Randall Robinson publishes *The Debt: What America Owes to Blacks*, a bestselling book arguing for reparations for slavery.

2001
Conservative commentator David Horowitz creates a controversy on many American campuses when he tries to publish an ad in college newspapers entitled "Ten Reasons Why Reparations for Slavery is a Bad Idea — and Racist, Too."

2002
Prominent African-American attorneys promise to sue the federal government and private companies for slavery reparations.

THE WHITE HOUSE
WASHINGTON

A monetary sum and words alone cannot restore lost years or erase painful memories; neither can they fully convey our Nation's resolve to rectify injustice and to uphold the rights of individuals. We can never fully right the wrongs of the past. But we can take a clear stand for justice and recognize that serious injustices were done to Japanese Americans during World War II.

In enacting a law calling for restitution and offering a sincere apology, your fellow Americans have, in a very real sense, renewed their traditional commitment to the ideals of freedom, equality, and justice. You and your family have our best wishes for the future.

Sincerely,

GEORGE BUSH
PRESIDENT OF THE UNITED STATES

OCTOBER 1990

In October 1990, Japanese-Americans interned during World War II received this letter of apology from President George Bush, in addition to a check for $20,000.

feel for the misery of others, when we either see it, or are made to conceive it in a very lively manner." [9]

Smith argued further that this sympathy is a cornerstone of justice. It is necessary for creating and maintaining general social order, he believed.

Native Americans

In the 18th and 19th centuries, compassion for the plight of others — whether out of Christian duty or to promote the greater good — fueled movements to abolish slavery and the slave trade in Europe and the United States. Later, these impulses led the United States, albeit very slowly, to consider compensating Native Americans for the government's taking of their land and the resulting destruction of much of their population and culture.

The expansion of the American frontier during the 19th century resulted in American Indians being forcibly moved to reservations, where many remain today. Millions of acres, primarily in the Great Plains, were taken from tribes with little or minimal compensation.

But the U.S. government did not consider compensating Native Americans for the loss of this property until 1946, when Congress established a Claims Commission to handle Indian land claims. The body soon became bogged down in the flood of claims, many of which were substantial. When the commission was eliminated in 1978, it had adjudicated only a fraction of the disputes between tribes and the government and had paid Native Americans only token compensation for the lost land. [10]

Meanwhile, the courts became much more sympathetic to Indian claims. In 1980, for instance, the Supreme Court awarded the Sioux $122 million for the theft of lands in South Dakota's Black Hills. It remains the largest award for a Native American land claim in U.S. history. *(See story, p. 26.)*

Today, Native Americans are still pressing land claims, particularily in the Eastern United States. "Many of these claims revolve around treaties made between states and Indian nations early in the country's history," says John Echohawk, executive director of the Native American Rights Fund, an Indian advocacy group in Boulder, Colo. Since the U.S. Constitution leaves the power to negotiate Indian treaties with the federal government, many of these agreements with the states are now being challenged, he adds.

One of the biggest such disputes involves three bands of Oneida Indians, who are trying to recover 300,000 acres of land in central New York state. The case hinges on a treaty negotiated in 1838.

Restitution to "Comfort Women"

On the other side of the globe, victims of a more recent tragedy — Japan's sexual enslavement of thousands of Asian women during World War II — are also seeking restitution. An estimated 200,000 "comfort women" were forced to serve the Japanese military at its far-flung outposts. They claim they were kidnapped or tricked into working as sexual slaves for the Japanese soldiers, who beat and raped them.

Reuters Photo/Yun Suk-bong

South Korean "comfort women" who were forced to provide sex for Japanese soldiers in World War II demand compensation during a protest at the Japanese Embassy in Seoul last March.

In 1995, then Japanese Prime Minister Tomiici Murayama officially apologized for the practice, but the government has yet to pay any reparations to the surviving women.

Other groups that have been victimized, like Armenians, also want restitution. And still others — like Latinos, Chinese-Americans and women in the United States — who suffered varying degrees of discrimination over the years, have not organized significant reparations movements, in part because their suffering is perceived as being different from the official policies that led to genocide or slavery.

Japanese-Americans

On Feb. 19, 1942, less than three months after the Japanese bombing of Pearl Harbor, President Franklin Delano Roosevelt signed Executive Order 9066, authorizing the removal of Japanese immigrants and their children from the western half of the Pacific coastal states and part of Arizona.

Within days, the government began removing 120,000 Japanese-Americans — two-thirds of them U.S. citizens — from their homes and businesses. Many were forced to sell their property at far below market value in the rush to leave. All were eventually taken to hastily built camps in Western states like California, Idaho and Utah, where most remained until the war was almost over. Some young Japanese-American men were allowed to leave the camps to serve in the armed forces — and many did so with valor — and a handful of mostly young internees were also permitted to relocate to Midwestern or Eastern states.

The camps were Spartan, but in no way resembled Nazi concentration camps or Stalinist Russia's gulags. Still, the internees were denied their freedom and, in many cases, their property.

During this time, internee Fred Korematsu and several other Japanese-Americans challenged the constitutionality of the internment. Korematsu's case ultimately found its way to the Supreme Court, which ruled that during national emergencies like war Congress and the president had the authority to imprison persons of certain racial groups.

After the war, Congress passed the Japanese-American Evacuations Claims Act of 1948 to compensate those who had lost property because of their internment. Over the next 17 years, the government paid $38 million to former internees. [11]

But efforts to make the government apologize for its wartime actions and pay reparations to internees over and above the property claims remained on a back burner until the 1970s. During that decade, Japanese-American activists — led by the community's main civic organization, the Japanese-American Citizens League (JACL) — began building support for redress.

Initially, only about a third of Japanese-Americans favored reparations. Many felt the painful war years should be forgotten. Others worried that vocal demands, coupled with growing fears among the U.S. public over the rising economic power of Japan, would provoke another backlash against Japanese-Americans. [12]

But by the end of the decade, a

majority of Japanese-Americans supported the effort, and the JACL began effectively lobbying Congress for redress. In 1980, Congress created the Commission on Wartime Relocations and Internment of Civilians to study the issue.

During public hearings over the next two years, the commission heard emotional testimony as former internees shared their personal sagas. Publicity generated by the hearings helped awaken the American public to the injustice done to the internees.

AP Photo/National Archives

Japanese-Americans were housed in hastily erected internment camps, like this one near Phoenix, Arizona, after the Japanese attack on Pearl Harbor. The U.S. later paid $20,000 to each person confined.

One former internee, Kima Konatsu, told about her family's experience while incarcerated near Gila River, Ariz. "During that four years we were separated [from my husband] and allowed to see him only once," Konatsu told the commission. Eventually he became ill and was hospitalized, she said. "He was left alone, naked, by a nurse after having given him a sponge bath. It was a cold winter and he caught pneumonia. After two days and two nights, he passed away. Later on, the head nurse told us that this nurse had lost her two children in the war and that she hated Japanese." [13]

In 1983, the commission concluded that there had been no real national security reason to justify relocating or incarcerating the Japanese-Americans, and that the action had caused the community undue hardship. A second report four months later recommended that the government apologize for the internment and appropriate $1.5 billion to pay each surviving internee $20,000 in reparations. [14]

That same year, a new National Council for Japanese-American Redress (NCJAR) emerged, which opposed what it saw as the JACL's accommodationist approach to reparations. NCJAR filed a class action suit against the government on behalf of the internees, demanding $27 billion in damages. But the suit was dismissed in 1987 on procedural grounds. [15]

Nevertheless, the lawsuit created restitution momentum in Congress, where support had been building since issuance of the commission's 1983 reports. Because many former internees were elderly, proponents argued that something should be done quickly, before most of the intended beneficiaries died. [16]

In 1988, Congress passed the Civil Liberties Act, which authorized $1.25 billion over the next 10 years to pay each internee $20,000. The law also contained an apology to Japanese-Americans who had been incarcerated [17] *(see p. 30)*.

On Oct. 9, 1990, the government issued its first formal apologies and checks to Japanese-Americans in a moving ceremony in Washington, D.C. A tearful Sen. Daniel K. Inouye, D-Hawaii — a Japanese-American who lost an arm fighting for the United States during World War II — told the internees and assembled guests that day: "We honor ourselves and honor America. We demonstrated to the world that we are a strong people — strong enough to admit our wrongs." [18]

Since then, some 80,000 former internees have received compensation. [19]

The Holocaust

In many ways, the modern debate over reparations began on Sept. 27, 1951. On that day West German Chancellor Konrad Adenauer appeared before the country's legislature, or Bundestag, and urged his fellow Germans to make some restitution for the "unspeakable crimes" Germany had committed against the Jewish people before and during World War II. His proposal — to provide assistance to the newly founded state of Israel as well as restitution to individual Holocaust survivors — was supported by both his own Christian Democratic party and the opposition Social Democrats.

Ironically, West Germany's offer of reparations was much more controversial in Israel, where a sizable minority, led by then opposition politician Menachem Begin, opposed taking "blood money" from Holocaust perpetrators. Begin and others argued that by receiving compensation from the Germans, Israel would literally be selling the moral high ground. [20]

But Israeli Prime Minister David Ben Gurion argued forcefully that

Italian-Americans Were Also Mistreated

Japanese-Americans were not the only ethnic group to suffer from discrimination during World War II. Many Italian-Americans also were victimized in the name of national security.

The United States was at war with Italy from the end of 1941 until it surrendered to the Allies in 1943. During that time, some 600,000 Italian immigrants were classified as "enemy aliens," even though many had sons fighting for the United States against Italy, Germany and Japan.

Tens of thousands were subjected to search and arrest, and 250 were interned in camps. In California, an evening curfew was imposed on more than 50,000 Italian-Americans. Some 10,000 were forced to move away from areas near military installations. Authorities even impounded the boats of Italian-American fishermen.

While generally recognized as a gross violation of civil liberties, the federal government's mistreatment of Italians was much less far-reaching than the internment suffered by 120,000 Japanese. Indeed, more German-Americans were interned — about 11,000 in Texas, North Dakota and elsewhere. Perhaps that's why Italian-American groups have not demanded reparations. Instead, they have asked the government to "acknowledge" what happened.

In 2000, Congress agreed, passing legislation authorizing the Justice Department to conduct an investigation into the episode. The department's work is expected to be finished by the end of the year.

Israel had a duty to see that Germany did not profit from its heinous crimes. "He understood that we are obligated to ensure that murderers are not inheritors," says the World Jewish Congress' Steinberg.

Ben Gurion prevailed, in part because Israel desperately needed funds to resettle European Jews who had survived the Holocaust. The German government began paying restitution to Holocaust survivors around the world in 1953 and has since paid out about $60 billion for both individual claims and aid to Israel. The state-to-state payments ended in 1965, but the German government still sends monthly pension checks to about 100,000 Holocaust survivors.

After West Germany's agreement with Israel, little was done to obtain further restitution for Holocaust victims. Many who had survived the camps were more concerned with getting on with their new lives and wanted to forget about the past. In addition, the Soviet Union and its Eastern bloc allies — where most Holocaust victims had come from — made no effort to aid the quest for restitution. Even the United States was content to let the issue lie, partly in order to focus on integrating West Germany and other Western allies into a Cold War alliance. [21]

Still, the issue did not disappear entirely. In Switzerland — a banking and finance mecca and a neutral country during the war — the government was taking small, inadequate steps to discover the extent of Holocaust-related wealth. Many Jews killed by the Germans had opened accounts in Swiss banks and taken out insurance policies from Swiss companies before the war as a hedge against the uncertainty created by the Nazi persecution.

In 1956, the Swiss government surveyed its banks and insurance companies to determine the value of accounts held by those who had died or become refugees as a result of the Holocaust. The companies replied that there were less than a million Swiss francs in those accounts.

In 1962, the government once again requested an accounting of Holocaust-related assets. This time, the companies came up with about 10 million francs, some of which was paid to account holders or their heirs. In the 1960s, '70s and '80s, other efforts by individuals seeking to recover Swiss-held assets were largely unsuccessful because the banks and insurers required claimants to have extensive proof of account ownership, proof that often had been lost or destroyed during the war.

But in the 1990s the situation changed dramatically. First, the collapse of communist regimes throughout Eastern Europe opened up previously closed archives containing Holocaust-related records. In addition, many Holocaust survivors lost their reticence about pursuing claims, in part because films like "Schindler's List" brought greater attention to their plight and made it easier to go public.

In the mid-1990s, journalists and scholars began uncovering evidence that Switzerland had been a financial haven for Nazi officials, who had deposited gold looted from Holocaust victims in Swiss banks. The investigation stimulated new interest in dormant bank accounts and insurance policies.

In 1996 a class action suit on behalf of victims and their heirs was filed in New York against Swiss banks and insurance companies. Swiss efforts to get the suit dismissed failed. Meanwhile, pressure from the U.S. Congress and local officials threatening economic sanctions against the companies forced the banks and insurers to acknowledge the existence of a large number of dormant accounts. By 1999, the Swiss had negotiated a settlement to set aside $1.25 billion to pay out dormant accounts and fund other Holocaust-related philanthropies.

The Swiss case prompted other Holocaust claims. For instance, in 1998 U.S. and European insurance regulators, Jewish groups and others formed a commission — headed by former Secretary of State Lawrence Eagleburger — to investigate claims against European insurance companies outside Switzerland.

The commission was an attempt to bypass lawsuits and to get the insurers — which include some of Europe's largest, like Italy's Generali and Germany's Allianz — to pay elderly claimants before they died. So far, the companies have paid out very little in compensation, because of bureaucratic wrangling at the commission and unwillingness on the part of survivors to accept what have in many cases been only small offers of restitution from the companies. [22]

Meanwhile, former prisoners who had been forced to work without pay for German manufacturers during the war began seeking restitution for their labor. The Nazis had drafted an estimated 12 million people — including 6 million mostly Jewish concentration camp inmates — to provide unpaid labor for some of the biggest names in German industry, including giant automaker Volkswagen. Many were worked to death. [23]

Initially Germany and then-Chancellor Helmut Kohl resisted efforts to pay reparations to slave laborers, citing the 1953 settlement with Israel. But in 1998 the country elected a new leader, Gerhard Schröeder, who authorized negotiations to settle the issue.

Last July, the German government and companies that had used slave labor established a $4.3 billion fund to compensate an estimated 1.5 million survivors. The deal, negotiated with German and American lawyers for the slave laborers and ratified in the Bundestag on May 30, indemnifies German industry from further lawsuits on behalf of slave laborers. ■

CQ/Scott Ferrell

Rep. John Conyers Jr., D-Mich., wants Congress to create a commission on reparations for descendants of slaves. "Twelve years ago, most people didn't even know what reparations were, and now it's become a front-burner issue," he says.

CURRENT SITUATION

Reparations for Slavery

Efforts to compensate African-Americans for slavery began formally on Jan. 16, 1865, months before the Civil War ended. On that day, Union General William Tecumseh Sherman issued Special Field Order 15, directing his soldiers — who were then marching through the South — to divide up confiscated Confederate farms into 40-acre plots and redistribute the land to slaves. Farm animals were also to be redistributed.

But Sherman's promise of "40 acres and a mule" was never realized. Four months after the order was signed, President Abraham Lincoln was assassinated. His successor, Southerner Andrew Johnson, largely opposed reconstruction and quickly rescinded Sherman's order. More than 40,000 slaves were removed from farms they had recently occupied.

In the years since Special Field Order 15, the idea of compensating African-Americans arose only occasionally in the public arena and at-

At Issue:

Should the U.S. government apologize to African-Americans for slavery?

REP. TONY P. HALL
D-OHIO

WRITTEN FOR THE CQ RESEARCHER, JUNE 2001

yes

America's history has changed the course of humanity. As an enemy of tyrants, an advocate of liberty and a defender of freedoms, America has proven herself again and again. Our achievements stir other peoples' pride, and our history bestows upon us the courage to conquer new challenges.

But our achievements and our history are blemished by the shameful decades when U.S. laws permitted the enslavement of African-Americans. This long chapter ensured that many of the hands that built our young nation were not those of full participants in an emerging American dream, but of men, women and children forced to obey the tyranny of "masters."

In recent years, we have apologized for racist medical experiments that inflicted pain and eventually death on many young, innocent men in Tuskegee, Ala. We have paid reparations for forcibly interning thousands of Japanese-Americans during World War II. And we helped to broker an apology and reparations for victims of the Holocaust.

Of course, the fact we have acknowledged these wrongs doesn't make up for the pain of the past. But if what we've done in these cases wasn't sufficient to fulfill that impossible goal, it was necessary to restore the goodwill needed to change our future. In giving these and other Americans the dignity of an honest admission that our nation was wrong, these apologies have given us all a measure of healing.

Nearly 14 decades after slavery was abolished, its legacy still reverberates through Americans' daily lives. Neither former slaves nor slave owners are alive today, and few Americans trace their own roots to slavery. But all Americans bear slavery's bitter burdens — the lingering racial tensions, the stubborn poverty and dysfunction that is disproportionately high among African-Americans, the persistence that justice has not yet been done.

"I am sorry" are the first words uttered by anyone sincere about righting a wrong. And yet in the case of our nation's greatest moral failing, we have yet to say these words. We have pursued countless policies toward the goal of racial healing. We have been enriched by the determination of African-Americans to overcome the problems rooted in their ancestors' enslavement. But neither their success, nor the blood spilled in our Civil War, excuses our country's continuing silence.

Some critics say an apology may open old wounds. Some say that paying reparations is essential to atonement. But no one can say those three words don't ring true.

ROBERT W. TRACINSKI
FELLOW, AYN RAND INSTITUTE, MARINA DEL REY, CALIF.

JUNE 2001

no

An apology for slavery on behalf of the nation presumes that whites today, who mostly oppose racism and never owned slaves, still bear a collective responsibility — simply by belonging to the same race as the slaveholders of the Old South. Such an apology promotes the very idea at the root of slavery: racial collectivism.

Slave owners were certainly guilty of a grave injustice. But by what standard can other whites be held responsible for their ideas and actions? By what standards can today's Americans be obliged to apologize on the slaveholders' behalf? The only justification for such an approach is the idea that each member of the race can be blamed for the actions of every other member, that we are all just interchangeable cells of the racial collective.

Critics of the proposed apology oppose it, not because it embraces this racist premise but because it does not go far enough. They want to apply the notion of racial collectivism in a more "substantial" form, by increasing welfare and affirmative-action programs designed to compensate for the wrongs of slavery. Such compensation consists of punishing random whites, by taxing them and denying them jobs and promotions in order to reward random blacks.

The ultimate result of this approach is not racial harmony or a color-blind society but racial warfare. It is precisely this kind of mentality that has devastated the Balkans, with each ethnic tribe continually exacting revenge on the other in retaliation for centuries-old grievances.

The idea of a national apology for slavery merely reinforces this same kind of racial enmity in America. By treating all whites as the stand-ins or representatives for slaveholders, it encourages the view of blacks and whites as a collective of victims pitted against an opposing and hostile collective of oppressors, with no possibility for integration or peaceful coexistence.

The only alternative to this kind of racial Balkanization is to embrace the opposite principle: individualism. People should be judged based on their choices, ideas and actions as individuals, not as "representatives" of a racial group. They should be rewarded based on their own merits — and they must not be forced to pay, or to apologize, for crimes committed by others, merely because those others have the same skin color.

Americans both black and white should reject the notion of a collective guilt for slavery. They should uphold the ideal of a color-blind society, based on individualism, as the real answer to racism.

tracted little attention. But lately the idea has gained considerable steam, propelled by several high-profile events, such as academic conferences on the subject and the threat of reparations lawsuits by prominent black attorneys.

In addition, Chicago, Detroit and Washington, D.C., have passed resolutions supporting federal reparations legislation. And slavery reparations has become a hot topic on college campuses, as more and more scholars study the idea. "This is the fourth paper I've delivered on reparations this year alone," University of San Diego Law Professor Roy Brooks said at a May conference on the issue. "That suggests there's much to say about the subject and that reparations is a hot issue internationally." [24]

AP Photo/Lou Krasky

South Carolina Gov. Jim Hodges helps to break ground for an African-American monument last year in Columbia. In spite of efforts by several states to come to terms with the history and contributions of black Americans, many advocates for slavey reparations say that only restitution will close the racial divide.

The lawsuits being prepared by several prominent black attorneys and advocates are expected to be filed early next year. They are the brainchild of a legal team that includes TransAfrica's Robinson, O.J. Simpson attorney Cochran, Harvard University Law School Professor Charles Ogletree and Alexander Pires, who recently won a $1 billion settlement from the Department of Agriculture on behalf of black farmers who were denied government loans.

"The history of slavery in America has never been fully addressed in a public forum," Ogletree said. "Litigation will show what slavery meant, how it was profitable and how the issue of white privilege is still with us. Litigation is a place to start, because it focuses attention on the issue." [25]

The team wants the federal government to officially apologize for slavery and for the century of state-supported discrimination — such as the South's segregationist "Jim Crow" laws — that followed emancipation. Moreover, the lawyers are likely to ask for some kind of monetary remedy, although no agreement has been reached either on how much is owed or how reparations would be dispersed.

Estimates vary wildly over how much black Americans are owed for slavery. Larry Neal, an economics professor at the University of Illinois at Urbana-Champaign, has calculated that the United States owes African-Americans $1.4 trillion in back wages for work completed before emancipation. Georgetown University Business School Professor Richard America, however, estimates the debt is closer to $10 trillion. [26]

Robinson doesn't want direct cash payments to African-Americans, especially people like himself, who are in the middle- or upper-income brackets. He favors establishment of a trust fund to assist underprivileged blacks. "The question we need to be asking is: How do we repair the damage?" Robinson asks. "We need a massive diffusion of capital to provide poor African-American youth with education — from kindergarten through college — and some sort of fund to promote economic development."

Most legal experts do not expect Cochran, Ogletree and the others to succeed, noting that the claim is almost 150 years old and thus the statute of limitations expired long ago.

"Even in a friendly court, there are going to be statute of limitations problems," Tulane University Law School Professor Robert Wesley says. [27] Moreover, experts point out, under the doctrine of sovereign immunity governments are protected from most legal actions.

Still, some legal scholars say the suit is not wholly a pipe dream, noting that civil rights attorneys in the 1950s and '60s also faced long odds in their battle to end race discrimination. "This will be a daunting task, but it is certainly not impossible," says Robert Belton, a Vanderbilt University law professor.

Even if the suit does not ultimately lead to redress or an apology, it may succeed on another level, says David Bositis, senior political analyst at the Joint Center for Political and Economic Studies, a think tank focusing on African-American issues. "Even if they just got some federal district judge to hear the case, it would become a much larger news item and so would stimulate discussion and debate," he says. "They would consider that a victory."

The black legal team is also planning to sue private companies that benefited from slavery, including banks, insurance companies, shipping firms and other businesses that may have profited from the slave trade.

Research by New York City lawyer and activist Deadria Farmer-Paellmann revealed that several insurance companies — including Aetna and New York Life — insured slave owners against the loss of their "property."

"If you can show a company made immoral gains by profiting from slavery, you can file an action for unjust enrichment," she said. [28] Her work coincides with a new California law requiring all insurance companies in the state to research past business records and disclose any connections to slavery.

In addition, a growing chorus of civil rights leaders, including the Rev. Jesse L. Jackson, has called on insurers to pay some form of restitution. "We call on the insurance companies to search their national files and disclose any and all policies issued to insure slave owners during the period of slavery," Jackson said. [29]

Some black leaders have suggested that culpable corporations establish scholarship funds for underprivileged black students.

But, while Aetna has publicly apologized for insuring owners against the loss of slaves, it has refused to provide compensation, arguing that slavery was legal when the policies were issued. New York Life is withholding comment until it finishes reviewing its historical records. ■

OUTLOOK

Starting a Dialogue

Those working to obtain reparations for slavery often compare the fight with the long, uphill struggle faced by civil rights activists in the 1950s and '60s. "The relative powerlessness of our community is not a new thing for African-Americans," the University of Maryland's Walters says. "We've been here before and have won, and I think we're going to win this time, too."

"The uneasiness that some express about reparations is the same uneasiness that we had about integration and about a woman's right to choose," Harvard's Ogletree said. "We've gained some important mainstream viability, but these things take time." [30]

For now, reparations proponents say that they hope to get the government to consider the issue, just as it did for Japanese-American internees and Holocaust survivors. "Right now this is about process," Walters says. "With Japanese-Americans, nothing really happened until after the government took some time to study the issue."

But opponents and others are confident the effort will fail. "This is going to die out because it makes no sense," George Mason's Williams says. "Conyers' bill is languishing in Congress and will continue to languish in Congress, because white politicians cannot sell this to white America."

MIT's Nobles agrees. "The best they can hope for from Congress is some sort of formal apology," she says. A claim based on an injustice that occurred so long ago is simply too nebulous to warrant serious consideration by lawmakers or judges, she says. "This isn't like the case of Japanese-Americans, where you had direct survivors of the act in question. [The former internees'] suffering was identifiable and for a specific period of time — four years — making it much less complicated."

Efforts against private firms — like insurance companies — have a better chance of producing some monetary reward, she predicts. "Eventually, some company will feel the heat, cave in and set up some sort of trust fund or something," she says, adding that Cochran, Ogletree and the other attorneys are unlikely to quit without something to show for their efforts. "To prove that all of this [effort] was worthwhile, they're going to work for a real win."

Others agree the movement will probably achieve at least some of its goals. "The less sophisticated supporters may think that they're going to win reparations, but the more sophisticated ones know that, in the near term, the chance of this happening is very unlikely," says Bositis, of the Joint Center for Political and Economic Studies.

"For these more realistic people, the principal thing they are trying to do is to start a dialogue on the issue, to get people talking about it," he concludes. ■

Notes

[1] Quoted in Jane Clayson, "Some Civil Rights Leaders Say Descendants of Slaves Should

Be Compensated," CBS News: "The Early Show," Jan. 11, 2001.
[2] Larry Bivins, "Debate on Reparations for Slavery Gaining Higher Profile," Gannett News Service, April 21, 2001.
[3] For background, see Kenneth Jost, "Holocaust Reparations," *The CQ Researcher*, March 26, 1999, pp. 257-280.
[4] Quoted in Abraham H. Foxman, "The Dangers of Holocaust Restitution," *The Wall Street Journal*, Dec. 7, 1998.
[5] Quoted in *Ibid.*
[6] Mortimer Adler, *Aristotle for Everybody* (1978), p. 126.
[7] Quoted in Arthur Spiegelman, "Leaders of Fight for Holocaust Reparations Under Attack," *The Houston Chronicle*, Dec. 27, 1998
[8] Matthew 5:10.
[9] Adam Smith, *The Theory of Moral Sentiments* (1759), pp. 47-48.
[10] Elazar Barkan, *The Guilt of Nations: Restitution and Negotiating Historical Injustices* (2000), p. 183.
[11] Mitchell T. Maki, *et al.*, *Achieving the Impossible Dream: How Japanese-Americans Obtained Redress* (1999), p. 54.
[12] Barkan, *op. cit.*, p. 34.
[13] Maki, *op. cit.*, p. 107.
[14] *Ibid.*
[15] *Ibid.*, pp. 121-128.
[16] Christine C. Lawrence, ed., *1988 CQ Almanac* (1988), p. 80.
[17] *Ibid.*
[18] Maki, *op. cit.*, p. 213.
[19] *Ibid.*, p. 214.
[20] Barkan, *op. cit.*
[21] Jost, *op. cit.*
[22] Henry Weinstein, "Spending by Holocaust Claims Panel Criticized," *Los Angeles Times*, May 17, 2001.
[23] "Key Dates in Nazi Slave Labor Talks," *The Jerusalem Post*, May 21, 2001.
[24] Quoted in Erin Texeira, "Black Reparations Idea Builds at UCLA Meeting," *Los Angeles Times*, May 12, 2001.
[25] Quoted in Tamar Lewin, "Calls for Slavery Restitution Getting Louder," *The New York Times*, June 4, 2001.
[26] Kevin Merida, "Did Freedom Alone Pay a Nation's Debt?" *The Washington Post*, Nov. 28, 1999.
[27] Quoted in Tovia Smith, "Legal Scholars Considering Class Action Lawsuit to Seek Restitution for Descendants of African Slaves," Weekend Edition Saturday, National Public Radio, April 1, 2001.
[28] Quoted in Lewin, *op. cit.*
[29] Quoted in Tim Novak, "Jackson: Companies Owe Blacks," *The Chicago Sun Times*, July 29, 2000.
[30] Quoted in Lewin, *op. cit.*

FOR MORE INFORMATION

Anti-Defamation League, 823 United Nations Plaza, New York, N.Y. 20017; (212) 490-2525; www.adl.org. Fights anti-Semitism and represents Jewish interests worldwide.

Conference on Jewish Material Claims Against Germany, 15 East 26th St., Room 906, New York, N.Y. 10010; (212) 696-4944; www.claimscon.org. Pursues reparations claims on behalf of Jewish victims of the Nazi Holocaust.

Japanese American Citizens League (JACL), 1765 Sutter St., San Francisco, Calif. 94115; (415) 921-5225. www.jacl.org. The nation's oldest Asian-American civil rights group fights discrimination against Japanese-Americans.

Joint Center for Political and Economic Studies, 1090 Vermont Ave., N.W., Suite 1100, Washington, D.C. 20005; (202) 789-3500; www.jointctr.org. Researches and analyzes issues of importance to African-Americans.

National Coalition of Blacks for Reparations in America, P.O. Box 62622, Washington, D.C. 20029; (202) 635-6272; www.ncobra.com. Lobbies for reparations for African-Americans.

Native American Rights Fund, 1712 N St., N.W., Washington, D.C. 20036; (202) 785-4166; www.narf.org. Provides Native Americans with legal assistance for land claims.

TransAfrica, 1744 R. St., N.W., Washington D.C. 20009; (202) 797-2301; www.transafricaforum.org. Lobbies on behalf of Africans and people of African descent around the world.

U.S. Holocaust Memorial Museum, 100 Raoul Wallenberg Place, S.W., Washington, D.C. 20024; (202) 488-0400; www.ushmm.org. Preserves documentation and encourages research about the Holocaust.

World Jewish Congress, 501 Madison Ave., 17th Floor, New York, N.Y., 10022; (212) 755-5770; www.wjc.org.il. An international federation of Jewish communities and organizations that has been at the forefront of negotiations over Holocaust reparations.

Bibliography

Selected Sources Used

Books

Elazar Barkan, *The Guilt of Nations: Restitution and Negotiating Historical Injustices*, W.W. Norton (2000).
A professor of history at Claremont Graduate University has written an excellent and thorough history of restitution efforts in the 20th century, from attempts by Holocaust survivors to recover stolen property to the campaign to compensate "comfort women" forced to provide sex to Japanese soldiers. Barkan also examines the intellectual origins of the reparations movement.

Finkelstein, Norman G., *The Holocaust Industry: Reflections on the Exploitation of Jewish Suffering*, Verso, 2000.
Finkelstein, a professor of political theory at Hunter College, charges lawyers and Jewish groups with exploiting the Holocaust for financial and political gain, using unethical and immoral tactics. He contends that much of the money "extorted" from European companies and countries is not going to survivors, and that the entire process is degrading the historical legacy of the Holocaust.

Maki, Mitchell T., Harry H. L. Kitano and S. Megan Berthold, *Achieving the Impossible Dream: How Japanese Americans Obtained Redress*, University of Illinois Press (1999).
The authors trace the history of efforts to get the U.S. government to pay reparations to Japanese-Americans interned during World War II.

Robinson, Randall, *The Debt: What America Owes to Blacks*, Plume, 2000.
The president of TransAfrica argues for reparations for African-Americans, writing: "If . . . African Americans will not be compensated for the massive wrongs and social injuries inflicted upon them by their government, during and after slavery, then there is no chance that America can solve its racial problems — if solving these problems means, as I believe it must, closing the yawning economic gap between blacks and whites in this country."

Articles

Bivis, Larry, "Debate on Reparations for Slavery Gaining Higher Profile," Gannett News Service, April 21, 2001.
The article examines African-Americans' growing call for reparations.

Dyckman, Martin, "Our Country has Paid the Bill for Slavery," *St. Petersburg Times*, June 25, 2000.
Dyckman makes a strong case against reparations to black Americans, arguing that the Union soldiers who died in the Civil War to free the slaves paid the country's debt to African-Americans.

Jost, Kenneth, "Holocaust Reparations," *The CQ Researcher*, March 26, 1999.
Jost gives an excellent overview of the debate over reparations for the survivors of the Nazi Holocaust. His description of the fight over dormant bank accounts and insurance policies in Switzerland is particularly illuminating.

McTague, Jim, "Broken Trusts: Native Americans Seek Billions They Say Uncle Sam Owes Them," *Barron's*, April 9, 2001.
McTague examines the Native American lawsuit against the federal government for decades of mishandling of the trust fund derived from the lease and sale of natural resources on Indian lands. The tribe recently won a judgment against the federal government, and the suit may result in native tribes receiving up to $10 billion.

Merida, Kevin, "Did Freedom Alone Pay a Nation's Debt?" *The Washington Post*, Nov. 28, 1999.
Merida examines the movement to obtain reparations for the African-American descendants of slaves, providing a good historical overview of efforts to compensate newly freed slaves after the Civil War.

Schoenfeld, Gabriel, "Holocaust Reparations — A Growing Scandal," *Commentary Magazine*, Sept. 2000.
The magazine's senior editor takes Jewish groups to task for their hardball tactics against Germany and other European countries in their Holocaust reparations efforts. He worries they will foment bad feeling in Europe against Jews and Israel.

Trounson, Rebecca, "Campus Agitator," *Los Angeles Times*, April 10, 2001.
The article chronicles the controversy surrounding recent attempts by conservative commentator David Horowitz to place ads in college newspapers that argue against reparations for African-Americans.

Zipperstein, Steven J., "Profit and Loss," *The Washington Post*, Sept. 24, 2000.
A professor of Jewish studies at Stanford University accuses author Norman G. Finkelstein of making wild and unsubstantiated charges in *The Holocaust Industry* (see above). "Imagine an old-style rant, with its finely honed ear for conspiracy, with all the nuance of one's raging, aging, politicized uncle," he writes.

3 Redistricting

Jennifer Gavin

Special elections for the Missouri Senate may not seem important enough to make national Republican leaders pull out their checkbooks.

AP Photo/Martin Lueders

The announcement of new census figures last Dec. 28 set the stage for the reapportionment of House seats and then redistricting. The new U.S. population is 281.4 million.

But that's just what happened in January, when the National Republican Congressional Committee (NRCC) poured $125,000 into Missouri to help local candidates vying for three vacant seats. Republicans won two of the three races, giving the GOP control of the state Senate for the first time since 1948.

The payoff for national party officials will come later this year, when the legislature redraws Missouri's nine congressional districts.

"Republicans will now have a seat at the table in Missouri's redistricting process," said Rep. Thomas M. Davis III, R-Va., a top NRCC official. "It will now be difficult for the Democrats [who control the Missouri House] to go through the redistricting process unchecked."

Every 10 years, as soon as the Census Bureau finishes its count, the 435 seats in Congress are reapportioned, or reassigned to the states based on their new populations. Then the once-a-decade political housekeeping task of redistricting begins.

Often bitterly partisan, redistricting has been dubbed political "housekeeping" for good reason: It often determines which political party will "keep" control of the House for the next decade. District maps are redrawn either by specially appointed commissions or by state legislatures — hence the NRCC's interest in the Missouri Senate race.

Depending on how the districts are redrawn within each state, various groups of voters can be included or excluded from a particular district. The results can skew future election outcomes to favor one party or affect whether minorities can elect members of their own groups. In fact, the past four redistricting cycles were fraught with legislative and legal actions resulting from allegations that minority groups were harmed, or unfairly helped, by how district lines were drawn.*

With a presidential election so close it took weeks to finalize, an evenly divided Senate and a slim 10-seat Republican margin in the House, the upcoming redistricting process could become even more contentious than usual.

"You're talking about self-survival politics," says University of South Florida political science Professor Susan A. MacManus, a specialist in redistricting.

Nearly all of the 435 House districts could be affected. Although only 18 states gained or lost congressional seats as a result of interstate population shifts revealed by the 2000 census, 43 states will redraw their district lines to reflect intrastate population changes.

At the outset, the Republicans appear to have more control over the process than they did in 1990, when Democrats controlled redistricting in 172 districts and the GOP controlled only five. The rest of the districts were drawn up by either split party control or by independent commissions. [1] (*See map, p. 42.*)

In the past decade, however, Republicans have gained control over more state legislatures, which typically draw the district lines, and more governorships, which can veto the proposed maps. Even though Democrats still control the process in 144 districts, Republicans will now control 98 districts, according to the Republican National Committee (RNC). "The GOP's redistricting position is almost 20 times better than it was in 1991," said Tom Hofeller, RNC redistricting director. "But remember, Democrats are still ahead." [2]

Further, the reapportionment of congressional seats based on population shifts has awarded new seats to states that typically trend Republican. Eight Republican-dominated, mostly Western and Sun Belt states gained seats while Democratic stronghold states in the Northeast and Midwest lost 10 seats. Nonetheless, Democrats still control legislatures and governorships in several of the largest states, including California. [3]

Democrats, however, challenge the belief that demographic shifts away from traditionally Democratic-leaning states will largely benefit Republicans. For one thing, they cite the close presidential vote in Florida, where the Republicans control the governorship and legislature. In addition, Democratic officials believe underlying trends favor their party in Arizona, Nevada, Colorado and other Western states.

"If you look at the electoral map and project ahead to 2004, I don't think George Bush gets any gains [from the census] except for being

* Redistricting does not affect the U.S. Senate, where each state has two senators regardless of population.

From *The CQ Researcher,* February 16, 2001.

Many Factors Affect Redistricting

Every 10 years, states must redraw their congressional districts to compensate for population shifts. In most states, partisan control of redistricting appears to depend largely on which party controls the state House, Senate and governorship. But incumbent clout, alliances and race also affect district lines. Redistricting usually is handled by the legislature and must be completed in time for the next congressional elections.

able to pick up a vote or two more out of Texas," said Jenny Backus, spokeswoman for the Democratic National Committee (DNC). [4]

The Constitution does not require congressional districts to be equal in population, or even that districts be created. It simply says states should be assigned congressional representation "according to their respective numbers."

But over time — first pressed by fairness arguments and later by court rulings — districts have become roughly equal in population. Currently, each House seat represents about 572,000 persons. Based on the new census totals, each seat will represent 647,000 people after redistricting.

As politicians and political parties seek to gain or hold onto power, they draw district lines to include enclaves of supporters and exclude opponents. In extreme cases, the practice is known as gerrymandering, after a distorted district — said to resemble a salamander — drawn in 1812 by the Massachusetts Legislature to benefit the party of Democratic Gov. Elbridge Gerry.

Lawsuits will probably be inescapable during the coming redistricting cycle, most of which must be completed before the 2002 congressional elections. Redistricters must walk a legal tightrope to avoid charges that disproportionately rural districts violate the constitutional equal-protection rights of urbanites and minorities. Such fears during the 1980s and early '90s led map drawers to create districts in which a majority of voters were members of minority groups.

But such "majority-minority" districts have themselves been challenged, and the U.S. Supreme Court — in a series of 5-4 rulings — has generally upheld the challenges.

"We have to mobilize the community so we do not go back" and lose minority voting power, says Melanie Campbell, executive director of the National Commission on Black Civic Participation.

Controversy and litigation may also erupt over whether redistricters should use actual head-count numbers or figures based on statistical sampling. After it was found that certain population subgroups are not being accurately counted by the census, the National Science Foundation recommended in 1995 that statistical sampling be combined with actual census numbers to produce a more accurate population picture. [5]

The GOP has long opposed sampling, fearing it would turn up more minorities and thus skew districts toward the Democrats. In 1999, the Supreme Court ruled that reapportionment must be based on direct census counting rather than sampling. But the ruling does not affect redistricting or the use of such data for distributing federal funds.

Under the Clinton administration, the Census Bureau generated the statistical sample numbers and will make them available to states and other political entities if President Bush allows it. A decision is expected by early spring. [6]

"Obviously, it's a very sensitive issue," said Commerce Secretary Donald L. Evans, whose agency oversees the census. And while he said he had not yet had time to review the issue, "It's at the top of the list." [7]

As redistricting begins across the nation, these are some key questions being asked:

Do recent Supreme Court rulings undermine minority representation in Congress?

Minority groups are deeply concerned that their representation in Congress will be reduced by recent Supreme Court decisions, particularly two precedent-setting rulings handed down in the last decade.

The two cases — *Shaw v. Reno* in 1993 and *Miller v. Johnson* in 1995 — addressed the use of race as the predominant factor in drafting districts. *Shaw* found that while a district's "gerrymandered" shape may not be unconstitutional, the odd shape might indicate that race played an inordinate part in a district's creation. The court created a "strict scrutiny" standard, whereby if race was found to have outweighed other significant factors when the district was drafted, redistricters would need to show that making race the predominant consideration was necessary due to a compelling governmental interest.

Miller took that argument a step farther, disallowing race as the predominant factor in drafting district lines. Supreme Court Justice Anthony Kennedy, writing for the majority in the 5-4 ruling, stated, "Just as the state may not, absent extraordinary justification, segregate citizens on the basis of race in its public parks, buses, golf courses, beaches, and schools," the government also "may not separate its citizens into different voting districts on the basis of race." [8]

When the *Miller* decision was handed down June 29, 1995, a *New York Times* editorial said it "eviscerated" the Voting Rights Act. [9] Rep. Cynthia A. McKinney, a Democrat whose suburban Atlanta, Ga., district was the subject of the ruling, warned it could lead to "the ultimate bleaching of the U.S. Congress." [10]

"These decisions raise the most serious questions concerning the future of minority political participation," civil rights lawyer Frank R. Parker wrote in the *American University Law Review*. "If, because of white bloc voting, minorities are unable to elect representatives of their choice except in majority-minority districts, then the elimination of these majority-minority districts is sure to negate the voting strength of minority voters, reduce minority representation in Congress and increase white political power in Congress." [11]

However, political scientists Stephan and Abigail Thernstrom note, in their book *America in Black and White: One Nation, Indivisible*, that McKinney and other black lawmakers were re-elected after the ruling. [12] In fact, since 1992 McKinney has won re-elections with up to 73 percent of the vote. And Rep. Melvin Watt, a black Democrat, has been regularly re-elected even though his North Carolina district no longer has a black majority and has been redrawn repeatedly, most recently in 1997. [13]

Watt's district was the legal battleground for *Shaw v. Reno* and another court challenge pending before the U.S. Supreme Court. [14]

Some minority-group organizations say the Supreme Court rulings don't wipe out the potential for majority-minority districting — they just raise the bar. "While it makes it more difficult, because of the higher level of scrutiny, we believe it is still legal to draw such districts," says Marisa J. Demeo, a lawyer for the Mexican-American Legal Defense and Education Fund (MALDEF). "The record has to be established better, when districts are being drawn, as to all the other factors being taken into account."

The courts made it clear, she continues, that drafters could consider the need to keep "communities of interest" together. "We don't think that's a direct parallel to race, but it is true, certain communities of color also share many interests," Demeo says.

Margaret Fung, executive director of the Asian American Legal Defense and Education Fund, points out that the Supreme Court still allows race to be considered in the redistricting process. "The reality is, there are a number of factors," she says. "It's important to understand that race may still be considered."

Vanderbilt University political scientist Carol M. Swain views the changed legal scene as a boon, not a blow, to minority representation in Congress. She argues in her book, *The Future of Black Representation*, that majority-minority districts focus too much on the color of their residents, rather than on which representatives — regardless of color — will be likely to support minority-friendly policies. She notes that *Miller* did not strike down the precedent set in *Beer v. United States*, a 1976 case that prompted courts to bar redistricting plans that leave minority voters worse off than they were before.

Swain says there is evidence that the majority-minority districts drawn in the early 1990s undercut the ability of white Democrats in adjacent districts to be re-elected — leading to their being replaced by Republicans, whose policy views are not always in step with minority agendas. When the GOP seized control of the House in 1994, three black Democratic members eventually lost committee chairmanships, 17 lost subcommittee chairmanships and many others lost important leadership posts, she notes.

In addition, Swain says, congressional voting patterns show that when white Democratic members lost black voters to black supermajorities in neighboring districts, they began voting more conservatively than before — diluting their support for black policy agendas.

"The upshot was that black voters lost power and influence," Swain writes. "The *Miller* ruling is good for the Democratic Party, good for the Congressional Black Caucus and good for the vast majority of African-Americans who need more representation of their liberal views of policy than they need people who look like them." [15]

When Minority Groups Collide

In recent years, redistricting efforts have paid special attention to creating congressional districts where ethnic and racial minority groups are in the majority — or at least have greater voting clout. These so-called majority-minority districts seek to give minority groups a stronger shot at electing one of their own to Congress.

But efforts to create majority-minority districts face two problems. The U.S. Supreme Court's 1995 *Miller v. Johnson* ruling essentially disallowed using race as the predominant factor in drafting district lines.

Justice Anthony M. Kennedy, writing for the majority, stated, "Just as the state may not, absent extraordinary justification, segregate citizens on the basis of race in its public parks, buses, golf courses, beaches, and schools," the government also "may not separate its citizens into different voting districts on the basis of race."

The second problem for majority-minority districts stems from the nation's increasing ethnic diversity: What if an area is home to two or more minority groups in significant numbers? Since congressional districts can have only one representative at a time, the question for those drawing the boundary lines is which minority group should have the most voting power?

"That's a huge problem in some of our metropolitan areas," says Susan MacManus, a professor of political science at the University of South Florida in Tampa and an expert on redistricting. "More and more in these kind of situations, it's going to be very difficult to appease both minority groups."

MacManus says the problem is particularly acute in the Miami-Dade County area, which has large numbers of African-Americans and Cuban-Americans. During the post-1992 redistricting in Florida, the proposed state Senate districts drawn in Miami-Dade came under attack by Cuban-Americans. But the courts ruled that an increase in the number of Hispanic-majority districts would have unfairly impacted African-American representation. MacManus says the Florida Supreme Court determined that the redistricters "did the best they could — if they had drawn the district any differently, it would have disadvantaged one group more than another."

Ultimately, MacManus says, multiethnic districts will be increasingly challenged in the courts as African-Americans, Hispanics and other minorities compete for political clout.

"It's not going to suffice in certain instances to lump them together and say, 'This is a minority district,' because their priorities don't always coincide," she says.

Margaret Fung, executive director of Asian American Legal Defense and Education Fund, says even with a population of more than 800,000, Asian-Americans in New York City have yet to elect a member of Congress, state legislator or City Council member.

From her group's perspective, the next cycle of redistricting will be about raising Asians' awareness of the need to be more politically involved in the process. It also will be about finding ways to amass Asian voting power in a district without the courts throwing out the district as excessively race-focused, Fung says. The key, Fung says, will be finding ways to show redistricting officials that Asians constitute a community of interests that does not depend on race alone.

Will redistricting shift the partisan balance of power in Congress?

Redistricting, it has been said, is a mirror into which every state legislator gazes and sees himself, or herself, as a member of Congress. Protecting incumbents of one's own party, carving the political base out from under the opposition and crafting customized districts from which state lawmakers launch federal careers — these are the time-honored, and not even very hidden, agendas of the districting process.

But given the results of the 2000 election and the tenuousness of the current 10-vote Republican control of the House, the coming redistricting battle is expected to be particularly intense.

Legislatures with decisive majorities in either party are expected to try to ensure that any seats their state lost in reapportionment will not be lost by one of their own, and that any seats gained will be won by the party in power.

The potential fallout could touch House Minority Whip David Bonior, D-Mich., the second-ranking lawmaker in the House Democratic Caucus. He may retire after 24 years in Congress and run for governor. His decision will no doubt be strongly influenced by the likelihood that his home district may be significantly altered, if not eliminated, in the coming redistricting. Michigan is losing a seat due to a population decrease. [16]

Reapportionment triggers political turmoil not only in states losing seats but also in states gaining them. That's because all the districts in a state are redrawn when a state's total changes. "People think you get two new seats," said Mark Fleisher, chairman of the Democratic Party in Arizona, which is about to go from six to eight seats. "You don't. You get eight new seats. It's going to be a whole new ballgame." [17]

Republicans and Democrats offer different predictions as to which party "controls" various congressional seats in redistricting. Typically, a state with a governor and legislature of the same party is assumed to control the redistricting process in that state. But in many states, the GOP controls one chamber while the Democrats hold sway in the other; or one party controls the legisla-

Chronology

ture but a governor of another party has veto power over its actions.

The crystal ball is further clouded by the fact that in five states independent special commissions will tackle redistricting. But because politicians select commission members, their activity often is not completely nonpartisan.

Others warn that even when one party controls redistricting, there is no guarantee that the party will win in the next election. For instance, the Democrats held a commanding advantage in redistricting after the 1990 census and state legislative elections, but Republicans won control of the House in 1994.

In addition, Republicans and Democrats disagree over which party will gain the most from population shifts and other trends.

"Clearly, the electoral shift based on the census will help Republicans in 2004," said GOP strategist Scott Reed, who managed Bob Dole's 1996 presidential campaign. "The movement is from the liberal Northeast, Democrat country, to the South and West, which are trending Republican." [18]

But the DNC's Backus said influxes of moderate and immigrant voters mean the South and West may be more in contention than the GOP believes. "The growth states are states with a diverse population, and we are the party of inclusion. . . . Those states are becoming more and more up for grabs." [19]

For instance, in Georgia — which will gain two new seats — it may not matter that Democrats control both legislative chambers and the governorship, because the areas of greatest population growth are trending Republican. Those voters may defy any partisan efforts to water down their voting strength.

In addition, experts on redistricting say, outcomes don't hinge solely on the political leanings of the governor and legislature. Personal relationships, alliances and animosities can sometimes trump party politics in redistricting.

1900s-Present

Current size of the House is set. Voting-rights legislation takes up dilution of black voting strength.

1911

Membership of the House is fixed at 433, plus one representative each for future states New Mexico and Arizona.

1920

Reapportionment controversy breaks out after the census shows that, for the first time in history, the majority of Americans are urban residents. Rural representatives insist that the farm population is undercounted.

1965

Voting Rights Act bans redistricting plans that dilute the voting strength of black communities. Other minority groups, including Hispanics, Asian-Americans and Native Americans, subsequently are covered by the law.

1992

National Science Foundation and Census Bureau conclude that statistical sampling should be combined with actual census counts to help generate a more accurate snapshot of the population.

1993-1997

U.S. Supreme Court rulings raise the standard for using race as a predominant factor in redrawing congressional districts. The high court establishes a "strict scrutiny" test but allows minority districts if they are due to a compelling governmental interest.

Dec. 28, 2000

New census figures show a population shift from the Northeast to the South and West.

2001

States begin redistricting for November 2002 elections.

"It's very unpredictable — it's survival politics, not always along straight party lines. Sometimes it's along personal lines," says the University of South Florida's MacManus. In some cases, family dynasties are created and nurtured, she says. In other cases, incumbents are harried by redistricters of their own party who want to run for Congress themselves.

No matter what forces tilt the balance, redistricting is expected to help defeat incumbents in 2002. In the past four elections immediately following redistricting — in 1962, '72, '82 and '92 — an average of 13 House incumbents were defeated in primaries, many of them because redistricting had thrown them into new political territory or forced them to run against other incumbents. [20]

Now, a major new wrinkle in the process could change the outcome. Thanks to the Internet, the public will have more access to what's going on, and thus will be able to participate in the process more than ever before.

During the 1991 redistricting, special computer programs, accessible only to legislative staffers or similar insiders, were used to generate proposals. Today, computing has become so ubiquitous many more people will be able to offer viable proposals to the lawmakers or commissioners who draw the lines.

"This time around, you're going to have a lot more players in the game," MacManus says. ■

BACKGROUND

Early Controversies

The Constitution specified that seats in the House of Representatives be apportioned among the states by population at least every 10 years and provided an initial apportionment of 65 seats among the original 13 states. But the charter did not specify that states had to create districts, how districts were to be drawn or whether districts had to be roughly equal in population. Congress did establish requirements for contiguous, single-member districts in 1842 and for equal-population districts in 1872. But sporadic efforts to enforce the law in states with districts of unequal population were unsuccessful. [21]

In the early years, some states elected representatives from districts but others did not. Beginning in 1800, several attempts were made to mandate the use of districts. By 1840, single-member districts had been adopted by 22 of the 31 states. And in 1842 an apportionment law required representatives to be "elected by districts composed of contiguous territory."

The 1872 apportionment act added for the first time a requirement that congressional districts contain "as nearly as practicable an equal number of inhabitants." Similar provisions were included in apportionment acts passed in 1881, 1891, 1901 and 1911.

But twice at the beginning of the 20th century, the House failed to enforce the requirements it had laid down for districting. In 1901, when a Kentucky redistricting law was challenged, a House committee failed to act, arguing that the Constitution did not give Congress power to revise the boundaries of districts set by state legislatures. In 1908, the election of a Virginia representative was challenged on the grounds of unequal population between districts. A House committee upheld the challenge, saying the state's districting law did not conform to the congressional act. But the House never took action on the committee's report, and the challenged representative was seated.

Legal Challenges

Reapportionment and redistricting became major political issues in the 20th century because of growing urbanization. As the populations of urban districts mushroomed and rural-dominated legislatures refused to redistrict to account for those population shifts, city-dwellers complained that they were grossly under-represented.

But rural legislators sought to preserve political power by blocking redistricting of state legislatures to take account of the population shift to the cities.

Following the 1920 census, rural interests held sufficient power to block the constitutionally mandated reapportionment of House seats for most of the 1920s. Congress in 1929 dropped previous anti-gerrymandering requirements that congressional districts be equal in population, contiguous and compact, and in 1932 the Supreme Court upheld the law.

A decade later, the high court agreed to hear a constitutional challenge brought by urban Illinois voters challenging population inequalities among the state's congressional districts. Plaintiffs said the population disparities violated their rights under the Equal Protection Clause, but the court in 1946 voted 4-3 to dismiss the suit. "Courts ought not enter this political thicket," Justice Felix Frankfurter wrote in the main opinion.

However, the court reversed directions in the 1960s, by establishing the now-famous "one-person, one-vote" rule, requiring as a matter of federal constitutional law that both legislative and congressional districts be very nearly equal in population. Beginning with its landmark decision in a Tennessee case, *Baker v. Carr* (1962), the court said it did have the power to rule on state redistricting challenges. In a trio of cases over the next two years, the court established the rule that state legislative districts and congressional districts be equal in population. "[A]s nearly as practicable, one man's vote in a congressional election is to be worth as much as another's," Justice Hugo L. Black wrote in *Wesberry v. Sanders* (1964).

A year later, Congress passed the Voting Rights Act, which culminated a decades-long effort by civil rights groups to break down barriers to voting by African-Americans. The law included a provision — section 5 — empowering the Justice Department to review any state or local law or policy affecting voting rights in jurisdictions with histories of discrimination against minorities.

Civil rights groups used the section to challenge state plans to shift from district to at-large elections. The Supreme Court in 1973 ruled that multimember districts could amount to illegal "vote dilution" against minorities under the 1965 law. But two years later the court disappointed civil rights groups by holding that districting plans did not have to maximize the number of majority-minority districts as long as there was "no retrogression" in racial minorities' voting power.

The court again disappointed civil rights groups in 1980 by ruling that in order to prove a violation of the Voting Rights Act, one must prove an intent to discriminate. Two years later, Congress partly reversed the decision, by providing that an election procedure that "results in the denial or abridgment" of the right to vote could be ruled illegal even if no intent to discriminate was found.

"Racial Gerrymanders"

After the 1990 census, civil rights groups sought to use the Voting Rights Act to require states to create more congressional districts with majority African-American or Hispanic populations. Beginning in 1993, however, Supreme Court rulings allowed white voters to challenge majority-minority districts and eventually established a rule against using race as the predominant factor in redistricting.

The Justice Department — under former President George Bush — had sided with civil rights groups after the 1990 census in pressuring states to create more majority-minority districts. New districting plans created for the 1992 congressional elections contributed to the election of a record number of African-Americans and Hispanics. Some of the districts, however, were criticized for their irregular shapes.

One of those districts, in North Carolina, combined predominantly African-American sections of three metropolitan areas by stretching some 160 miles across the center of the state. A group of white voters sued, claiming that the bizarrely shaped district amounted to an unconstitutional racial gerrymander. A lower federal court rejected the challenge, but the Supreme Court, in *Shaw v. Reno*, voted 5-4 to reinstate the suit.

Writing for the majority, Justice Sandra Day O'Connor said that white voters could use the Constitution's Equal Protection Clause to challenge a district that is "highly irregular" in shape and drawn to "segregate voters by race." And the districting plan could be upheld only if it satisfied the strict scrutiny test of meeting a compelling government interest.

Two years later, the court in *Miller v. Johnson* struck down a Georgia plan that had created three majority-black districts, including one stretching from the Atlanta suburbs to the Atlantic coast. Writing for the same five-member majority, Justice Kennedy said that redistricting plans were subject to constitutional challenge whenever race was "the predominant factor motivating the legislature's decision to place a significant number of voters within or without a particular district."

The court continued to make it harder to draw majority-minority districts with decisions in 1996 that threw out districts in Texas and the challenged district in North Carolina — which the lower federal court had upheld on remand. In both cases, the court ruled that a state's effort to comply with the Voting Rights Act or to remedy past discrimination did not justify a racially motivated districting scheme.

Civil rights groups complained that the rulings would make it harder for African-Americans or Hispanics to be elected to Congress or to state legislatures. Dissenting justices also forcefully argued that the rulings improperly injected the federal courts into an inherently political process.

But the Supreme Court's conservative majority showed no sign of retreating. Indeed, the North Carolina case returned to the court for a third and fourth time as white voters continued to challenge a redistricting plan that the state argued complied with the court's guidelines. ■

CURRENT SITUATION

The Fighting Begins

Now that population figures have been announced, jockeying for position on redistricting is already under way in several states.

As a result of the 2000 Census, Connecticut, Illinois, Indiana, Michigan, Mississippi, Ohio, Oklahoma and Wisconsin will each lose one seat; New York and Pennsylvania each will lose two seats. Meanwhile, California, Colorado, Nevada and North Carolina gain a seat each, while Arizona, Florida, Georgia and Texas will pick up two new seats. [22]

In Texas, a 27 percent increase made the likelihood of new districts so obvious that political maneuvering has been under way there for some time. Knowing that the makeup of the legislature would affect redistricting, the GOP has been trying hard — albeit it unsuccessfully — to win a majority in the Texas House.

Meanwhile, the Texas redistricting plan is expected to end up before a three-judge panel that could redraw the lines if it believes the original plan violates the Voting Rights Act. In 1996, such a panel declared three districts racially gerrymandered and redrafted them, which affected not just three but 13 districts and forced congressional candidates in all those districts into special elections. [23]

In Connecticut, which is set to lose a congressional district for the first time since 1840, state lawmakers already are deliberating how to reduce the number of districts from six to five and keep the process even-handed. "Those who love Connecticut should think long and hard before screwing up the social, economic and political community that is eastern Connecticut in the name of giving a hard time to a freshman congressman," said first-term Republican Rep. Rob Simmons, who may see a chunk of his district parceled out. [24]

Meanwhile, redistricting is expected to be more contentious in several key states. For instance, all eyes will be on California, where Democrats control both chambers of the legislature and the governorship, and where 53 congressional seats are at stake. In New York, each party is expected to lose one seat, since the state has a GOP governor and two legislative chambers controlled by different parties.

In Pennsylvania, which also will lose two seats, Republicans are in firm control of both chambers and the governor's office, so it is assumed that the state's two Democratic congressmen may be threatened by new boundaries or even shoved into each other's districts. In Michigan, which is losing one seat, the GOP controls the legislature and the governor's office, making it likely the 9-5 Democratic advantage in the House delegation will be narrowed.

Sometimes term limits give the process a new twist. Before such policies were adopted — largely during the past decade — some state legislators were happy to hang onto their state House or Senate seats indefinitely. Now, "they're thinking about drawing themselves something else" in order to perhaps still have a political future by moving up into Congress, MacManus says.

Statistical Sampling

By this spring, the Bush administration is expected to determine whether to release sampling-based census data. Commerce Secretary Evans has said the decision will be based on the best available information, including a Census Bureau survey of 300,000 households to gauge the accuracy of the 2000 Census.

President Bush strongly supports traditional counting. "The head count is the best way to conduct the census rather than risking the uncertainty and manipulation inherent in statistical sampling methods," said his campaign spokesman, Scott McClellan. "We need an administration committed to counting every person in America." [25]

Lawsuits are likely either way, MacManus says. "If somebody loses and you've got sampling data in place, they'll sue to get the actuals — and vice versa," she says.

Some groups representing minorities — joined by local government agencies facing loss of money that is distributed based on population — are pressing the new administration to allow the adjusted data to be used.

The Clinton administration made a commitment to release the most accurate data in 2001, says MALDEF's Demeo. "We expect the Bush administration to adhere to that commitment if it is going to fulfill its promise of representing the Latino community," she says.

MALDEF contends that Hispanics were seven times more likely to be uncounted by the 1990 census than non-Hispanic whites. Although the most recent census may have improved on that situation, undercounting is still probable, the group says.

Likewise, the Asian American Legal Defense Fund supports sampling. "Most experts have said it leads to the most accurate count," says Executive Director Fung. "Many people were missed by the census, never got forms in the mail or were not approached by enumerators."

"If the new administration is serious in its call for inclusiveness and cooperation, it must allow the professionals at the Census Bureau to do their job and use modern scientific methods, so that we do not repeat the undercounts that have occurred in the past, which have disproportionately affected African-American and other minorities," said Barbara R. Arnwine, executive director of the Lawyers' Committee for Civil Rights Under Law.

Republican lawmakers are bitterly opposed to statistical sampling, which many view as a threat to their control of the House. Sampling amounts to nothing more than guesswork and invites manipulation of numbers for partisan gain, they argue.

"This is simply a bad idea," wrote Rep. Dan Miller, R-Fla., former chairman of the House Government Reform and Oversight Subcommittee on the Census. "Its constitutionality and legality are suspect." [26]

And it would not meet the constitutional requirement that the government conduct "an actual enumeration" of the population every 10 years, opponents add. [27]

"The Republicans are convinced that this is just a big Democratic plot," says Margo Anderson, a history professor at the University of Wisconsin. "And the Democrats are convinced the Republicans are out to lower the population counts in areas that vote Democratic."

In fact, a Republican political consultant on redistricting issues, Clark Bensen, calculated that if sampling had been used before the 1990 races, it could have shifted the results in 24 House races — enough to nearly eliminate the 22-vote edge enjoyed by the GOP in the House before last year's election. ■

OUTLOOK

Minority Concerns

Some Democrats believe African-Americans are willing to trade majority-minority districting for more party-based support of black issues. They plan to remind their minority compatriots that the Voting Rights Act itself is up for congressional renewal in 2007, when the partisan makeup of Congress will reflect this year's redistricting.

But other observers expect the push for majority-minority districts to continue, even if it results in more Republican seats in Congress.

Because the case-law path leading to 2001 is complex — with redistricters having to be careful about addressing minority concerns — litigation is virtually certain, and some states are beefing up their budgets accordingly.

At Issue:

Should race be a focal consideration in redistricting decisions?

KEITH W. REEVES
Associate Professor, Swarthmore College

WRITTEN FOR THE CQ RESEARCHER, FEBRUARY 2001

yes

On Aug. 6, 1965, President Lyndon B. Johnson signed into law the most stringent and comprehensive federal voting rights legislation in the nation's history. Only five months before, the nation watched in horror and disbelief as blacks — peacefully participating in a voting rights protest march from Selma to Montgomery — were brutally attacked by Alabama troopers and deputy sheriffs. "Bloody Sunday" would become the catalyst for an invigorated commitment by the Johnson administration to secure comprehensive legislation guaranteeing the right to vote without regard to "race, color or previous condition of servitude."

Passage of the Voting Rights Act represented the pinnacle of black Americans' prolonged struggle to participate fully and freely in American life and society, Johnson said. Yet more than 30 years later, minority political representation continues to be the focal point of an immensely complex political and public policy debate.

The debate has been made all the more contentious by Supreme Court rulings. The fundamental question is: Should states with sizable black and Latino populations create electoral districts that give minorities a reasonable chance to elect candidates of their choice — by inference, minorities? Or are these districts simply "affirmative action tools in the electoral realm" that pull the nation back from its cherished ideal of a color-blind society?

On the contrary, say voting and civil rights advocates. That minorities remain significantly underrepresented in elective office (especially at the federal level) is a troubling, if not shameful, imperfection in the democratic functioning of this country. And, racial discrimination by whites, voting rights advocates argue, still remains a prodigious barrier for minority candidates in majority-white settings.

Given the limitations of remedial alternatives, race-conscious districting — albeit imperfect — is a demonstrably effective corrective action that brings about a level playing field for minority office-seekers. Racial bloc voting among whites coupled with continued racial prejudice and discrimination perniciously stacks the electoral deck against them. And until it diminishes, race-based districting is perhaps the only means of ensuring that minorities are afforded an equal opportunity to compete for — not necessarily win — elected office. This is neither a special privilege nor a means of insulating blacks and Latinos from white electoral competition, as has been suggested. Rather, it is a remedy to offset the voting discrimination against minority candidates on account of race.

ROGER CLEGG
General Counsel, Center for Equal Opportunity

WRITTEN FOR THE CQ RESEARCHER, FEBRUARY 2001

no

For years, racial gerrymandering was used to ensure that some kinds of candidates won and that others lost. Civil rights organizations and their allies rightly decried this, and eventually the Supreme Court and the Voting Rights Act called it to a halt. Now, however, we are told that sometimes racial gerrymandering can be good.

While the two situations are not morally identical, the basic problem remains the same. It is deeply troubling when the government uses race to determine the winners and losers in an election.

Rather than being colorblind, the government is color-coding its districts. What's more, and worse, is that parties and voters are encouraged to play identity politics, too.

Voters and parties are told: Here are black districts, where the people have certain interests, and vote a certain way. And here are white districts, where the interests are necessarily different, and people vote another way. So voters and parties are encouraged to view politics and policy through the prism of race. And while black voters may be guaranteed a few representatives, their influence in all other districts is minimized.

The premise of gerrymandering — that race is political destiny — is wrong. In a recent *New York Times* poll, for instance, as many blacks as whites classified themselves as "conservative." Alan Keyes is the darling of black and white conservatives alike, as Ted Kennedy is lionized by black and white liberals. A conservative state like Virginia elected a black governor not long ago, and a Southern white like Bill Clinton was beloved of blacks. As Jim Sleeper points out in his book *Liberal Racism*, two of the black congressmen to represent majority-white districts in recent years were Republicans: J.C. Watts of Oklahoma and Gary Franks of Connecticut. And when majority-black districts have been un-gerrymandered after court intervention, no black incumbent was defeated.

But interracial coalition building is not only discouraged by racial gerrymandering but also made impossible. What incentive is there — what possibility is there — for white and black voters to find common ground when they are told by the government that they must vote in separate districts?

Instead of relying on race and racial stereotypes, redistricting should rely on existing and natural boundaries — like school-attendance zones, waterways and so forth — leaving communities intact. Common issues such as schools and crime will, as the Supreme Court has said, "do more to unite people who live close to one another than their race can do to separate them."

Officials complain that the Supreme Court's redistricting decisions have made it more difficult than ever for states and independent commissions to redraw congressional districts. The decisions made it clear that race cannot be the predominant factor in shaping a district, but still can influence the process. States, as a result, will pay increased attention to non-race factors, such as the compactness of a district or protecting incumbents. [28]

Even before the Supreme Court decisions beginning with *Shaw v. Reno*, redistricting was a legally contentious process. Following the 1990 decennial census, more than 130 suits were filed in 40 states challenging either individual districts or a state's overall redistricting plan.

Some lawsuits have already been filed, well before redistricting plans can even be drawn. "States are setting aside money to defend their plans in court, because they know everything they do is going to be examined under a microscope," said Tim Storey, a redistricting specialist with the National Council of State Legislatures.

As for those states where suits precede even the release of districting data, "Part of it is, some of the plaintiffs just want to get a lawsuit in to have standing" when the issues are finally adjudicated, Storey says.

Considering that the cases of the 1990s all came down in 5-4 votes, what is the likelihood the vote pattern will continue? Legal observers note that Justice O'Connor, the swing vote in most of the rulings, appeared to be moving away from the majority line with each case.

Last November, another race-related redistricting case was argued before the U.S. Supreme Court. *Hunt v. Cromartie* focuses on the redrawing of North Carolina's 12th District in 1997 to meet earlier court challenges to the 1992 version. A North Carolina federal district court ruled that the 1997 redraw had race as its chief consideration; that was rejected by the Supreme Court. A ruling on *Hunt v. Cromartie* may be imminent.

The Census Bureau is scheduled to deliver final Census 2000 numbers to the states by April 1 so they can begin their redistricting. The Bush administration must decide before then whether the head count numbers should be revised by the results obtained by sampling. President Bush's decision will determine more than whether minorities — and thus Democrats — will receive greater representation in Congress. It will also help decide whether minority communities will receive billions of dollars in federal funds each year.

New York Rep. Carolyn B. Maloney, the ranking Democrat on the House Census Subcommittee, calls the dispute the "bloodiest political war" she has ever seen. If Democrats lose, Bush's decision "will clearly make Florida look like a case of petty theft," she said. [29]

Using raw census numbers is expected to boost Republican prospects in at least 12 House races in 2002. "The president supports an actual head count, because he believes it's the best and the most-accurate way to conduct the census," said White House spokesman Ari Fleischer. But he said no final decision has been made. ■

Notes

[1] See Gregory L. Giroux, "GOP in Position to Have Its Say When States Redraw Congressional Districts," *CQ Weekly*, Jan. 6, 2001, pp. 39-40.

[2] *Ibid.*

[3] New seats went to Arizona, California, Colorado, Florida, Georgia, Nevada, North Carolina and Texas. Meanwhile, Connecticut, Illinois, Indiana, Michigan, Mississippi, New York, Ohio, Oklahoma, Pennsylvania and Wisconsin lost seats.

[4] See Nick Anderson, "Census Data Likely to Benefit GOP Statistics," *Los Angeles Times*, Dec. 28, 2000 p. A6.

[5] For background, see Kenneth Jost, "Census 2000," *The CQ Researcher*, May 1, 1998, pp. 385-408.

[6] Giroux, *op cit.*

[7] *Ibid.*

[8] Linda Greenhouse, "Justices, in 5-4 vote, Reject Districts Drawn with Race the 'Predominant Factor,'" *The New York Times*, June 30, 1995 p. A1.

[9] "The Supreme Court's Final Day — Gutting the Voting Rights Act," *The New York Times*, June 30, 1995 p. A26.

[10] Quoted in Ronald Smothers, "GOP Anxiously Awaits Redistricting," *The New York Times*, June 30, 1995 p. A23.

[11] *Ibid.*

[12] Stephan Thernstrom and Abigail Thernstrom, *America in Black and White: One Nation, Indivisible* (1997), p. 484.

[13] See Congressional Quarterly, *2000 Politics in America* (1999).

[14] Linda Greenhouse, "Justices Reconsider Race and Redistricting," *The New York Times*, Nov. 28, 2000, p. A18.

[15] Carol M. Swain, "The Future of Black Representation," *The American Prospect*, No. 23, fall 1995.

[16] See Karen Foerstal, "Bonior Ponders Governor Bid," *CQ Weekly*, Jan. 13, 2001.

[17] Scott Thomsen, "Arizona Politics May Change," The Associated Press, Dec. 29, 2000.

[18] Nick Anderson, "Census Data Likely to Benefit GOP Statistics," *Los Angeles Times*, Dec. 28, 2000, p. A6.

[19] Maurice Tammen, "Parties spin census data differently," *Atlanta Journal-Constitution*, Dec. 31, 2000, p. C1.

[20] *Ibid.*

[21] Unless otherwise noted, material in this section is from Congressional Quarterly's *Guide to Congress, 5th Edition* (2000).

[22] Giroux, *op. cit.*

[23] Suzanne Gamboa, "Texas Displaces New York with two new seats in Congress," The Associated Press, Dec. 28, 2000.

[24] See Maura Casey, "For Lawmakers, Push May Come to Shove When Six Congressional Districts Become Five," *The New York Times*, Jan. 28, 2001, p. A1.

[25] Quoted in Leslie Casimir, "Bush Stance on Sampling Makes No Census — Latinos, *New York Daily News*, July 6, 2000.

[26] See Jost, *op. cit.*

[27] Jost, *op. cit.*

[28] See Robert Pear, "Race Takes Back Seat as States Prepare to Redistrict," *The New York Times*, Feb. 4, 2001, p. A17.

[29] Quoted in Jim VandeHei, "Bush's Next Recount Battle: Should Census Tallies Be Adjusted?" *The Wall Street Journal*, Feb. 8, 2001.

Bibliography

Selected Sources Used

Books

Thernstrom, Abigail, *Whose Votes Count? Affirmative Action and Minority Voting Rights*, Harvard University Press, 1987.
A history and analysis of minority voting rights. Includes forward look at possible action by the Supreme Court.

Thernstrom, Stephan, and Abigail Thernstrom, *America in Black and White: One Nation, Indivisible*, Simon & Schuster, 1997.
A study of African-American political involvement, with focus on recent political and legal trends in redistricting.

***Politics in America 2000*, CQ Press, 1999.**
Detailed profiles of all 535 members of Congress and characteristics of their districts.

Articles

Anderson, Nick, "Census Data Likely to Benefit GOP Statistics," *Los Angeles Times*, Dec. 28, 2000.
Analysis of census data against backdrop of November 2000 election results.

Casey, Maura, "For Lawmakers, Push May Come to Shove When Six Congressional Districts Become Five," *The New York Times*, Jan. 28, 2001, p. A1.
Connecticut reaction to redistricting caused by population loss.

Foerstal, Karen, "Bonior Ponders Governor Bid," *CQ Weekly*, Jan.13, 2001.
Minority Whip David Bonior, D-Mich., begins talking publicly about ending his 24-year House career and running for governor, amid speculation his district is likely to change substantially during redistricting.

Giroux, Gregory L., "Myriad Forces Will Influence Redistricting Process," *CQ Weekly*, Jan. 13, 2001, pp. 114-119.
An overview of political and non-political factors influencing redistricting in the wake of the 2000 census.

Greenhouse, Linda, "Justices Reconsider Race and Redistricting," *The New York Times*, Nov. 28, 2000, p. A18.
A look at the issues behind an upcoming U.S. Supreme Court redistricting case.

Parker, Frank R., "The Damaging Consequences of the Rehnquist Court's Commitment to Color-Blindness Versus Racial Justice," *American University Law Review*, Vol. 45 No. 3, February 1996.
Academic analysis of court decisions of the 1990s and the possible effects on African-American representation.

"The Supreme Court's Final Day — Gutting the Voting Rights Act," *The New York Times*, June 30, 1995, p. A26.
Editorial following the court's decision in *Miller v. Johnson*.

Swain, Carol M., "The Future of Black Representation," *The American Prospect*, No. 23, fall 1995.
Academic analysis of the *Miller* decision, suggesting it could strengthen black Americans' political clout by continuing ties with white, Democratic politicians.

Reports

U.S. Bureau of the Census, "Strength in Numbers — Your Guide to Census 2000 Redistricting Data," online: www.census.gov/clo/www/strength2.pdf.

FOR MORE INFORMATION

Democratic National Committee, 430 S. Capitol St. S.E., Washington, D.C. 20003; (202) 863-8000; www.democrats.org. The DNC monitors redistricting efforts, coordinates recruitment of candidates and conducts party constituency outreach and voter registration in individual districts.

Republican National Committee, 310 First St. S.E., Washington, D.C. 20003; (202) 863-8600; www.rnc.org. The Republican counterpart to the Democratic National Committee.

Lawyers' Committee for Civil Rights Under Law, 1401 New York Ave. N.E., Suite 400, Washington, D.C. 20005; (202) 662-8600; www.lawyerscomm.org. A nonprofit group that addresses racial discrimination issues.

Asian American Legal Defense and Education Fund (AALDEF), 99 Hudson St., 12th Floor, New York, N.Y. 10013; (212) 966-5932; www.aaldef.org. Dedicated to achieving social and economic justice for Asian-Americans.

Mexican American Legal Defense and Educational Fund (MALDEF), 1518 K St. N.W., Suite 410, Washington, DC 20005; (202) 628-4074; www.maldef.org. Protects the civil rights of Latinos in the United States.

4 Policing the Police

KENNETH JOST

Rafael Perez had wanted to be a policeman since childhood After four years in the Marines, he joined the Los Angeles Police Department in 1989. He did well and was assigned to a special anti-gang squad in the Rampart Division, just west of downtown.

The densely populated Rampart area is home to many Asian and Hispanic immigrants and to some of the city's most feared street gangs. When Perez started in the elite squad, Rampart had one of the highest murder rates among the city's 18 police divisions. Today, violent crime has declined there — perhaps a credit to the LAPD's aggressive anti-gang and anti-drug efforts.

The Rampart Division, however, is taking no bows for its work these days. Instead, Rampart has become the name of a stunning scandal of police misconduct ranging from manufacturing evidence and committing perjury to stealing drugs and shooting unarmed suspects. The spreading scandal threatens hundreds, perhaps thousands, of criminal convictions and deals a body blow to the LAPD's efforts to regain public confidence after a troubled decade marked by the Rodney King beating and the O. J. Simpson murder trial. (*See story, p. 56.*)

Perez was once in the middle of the corruption but is now the source of the scandal's most damning disclosures. Facing trial in September on charges of stealing 6 pounds of cocaine from a police evidence room, Perez negotiated a plea bargain by promising to tell all he knew about misconduct in the Rampart Division.

"There's a lot of crooked stuff going on in the LAPD," Perez told authorities, according to transcripts of the interviews obtained by the *Los Angeles Times*. [1]

From *The CQ Researcher*, March 17, 2000.

Reuters

Former LAPD officer Rafael Perez revealed corruption in the Rampart Division as part of a plea bargain on cocaine charges. He was sentenced to five years in prison.

The Rampart scandal emerged as law enforcement agencies around the country were coming under renewed scrutiny on a variety of issues. The New York City Police Department was still reeling from the brutal sodomizing of a Haitian immigrant in 1997 when four white officers last year shot and killed an unarmed West African immigrant, Amadou Diallo, in the vestibule of his Bronx apartment building. Their trial, moved to Albany because of massive local publicity about the case, ended last month with the officers' acquittal on all counts — a verdict that served only to renew the debate over police tactics and racial attitudes (*see p. 72*).

Meanwhile, civil-rights and civil-liberties organizations were mounting attacks on "racial profiling," the practice of making traffic or other investigative stops on the basis of an individual's race or ethnicity. Two states, Maryland and New Jersey, have signed federal court consent decrees agreeing to end the practice after lawyers from the American Civil Liberties Union (ACLU) gathered evidence showing racial patterns in highway stops by state police. Other suits are pending. Critics also want to require police to collect racial data on traffic stops in other states to determine the extent of the practice — which law enforcement officials insist is not widespread (*see p. 69*).

The public focus on police practices comes at a time of declining crime rates and generally increasing police professionalism. A recent survey of both rank-and-file police personnel and officers suggests that the vast majority of police recognize legal constraints on their conduct, try to stay within the law and disapprove of colleagues who do not. (*See poll, p. 66.*)

Still, policing the police — either through internal management or external review — remains a difficult job. "Cops and teachers exercise the most unsupervised discretion of any government employees in living up to the public trust or not," says Edwin Delattre, dean of Boston University's School of Education and author of a book on police ethics. "If you look at a cop on the street, there's nobody immediately looking over the cop's shoulder."

"The gap between the best and worst police departments is bigger than ever," says Samuel Walker, a professor of criminal justice at the University of Nebraska in Omaha and author of a history of U.S. law enforcement. "In places like San Diego

Black Motorists on I-95 Still Targeted

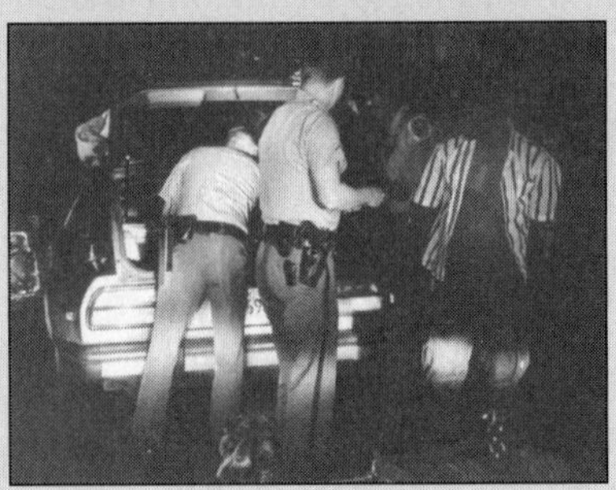

The state of Maryland settled a racial-profiling suit in January 1995 by agreeing to halt the practice and to furnish racial data on traffic stops to the American Civil Liberties Union of Maryland to monitor the agreement. Despite the settlement, the data showed that a disproportionate number of motorists stopped since then along the I-95 corridor in Maryland — more than two-thirds — were people of color.

Detentions and Searches
January 1995 – June 1999

	Number of Stops	Percent
African-Americans	1,205	60.7%
Hispanics	117	5.9
Whites	641	32.3
Other	23	1.2
Total non-white	1,322	67.8
Total searches	**1,986**	

Note: Total does not add to 100 percent due to rounding.

Source: American Civil Liberties Union of Maryland

and Charlotte, there is good discipline. They care about their citizens. That's simply not true in New York and Los Angeles."

Police officials tend to simultaneously minimize the extent of abusive practices while insisting they are taking steps to prevent them. Abuse-of-force cases are "insignificant arithmetically," says James Powers, chief of the Fredericksburg, Va., police department and an adviser to an International Association of Chiefs of Police (IACP) study on the use of force. "But perception-wise, it's very significant. One misuse of force to us is catastrophic. And for a long, long time, we've been taking every step we know to restrict or prohibit the improper use of force."

"There is no excuse for stopping someone because they're black or Hispanic or because they're a black person in a white neighborhood," says Earl Sweeney, director of the New Hampshire Police Standards and Training Council and chair of the IACP's highway safety committee. But Sweeney says racial-profiling abuses "have been perpetrated by a minority of individuals, in some cases well-motivated but poorly trained. We really think the answer is in policy, training and supervision."

Many of the most volatile police controversies — such as the two recent New York City cases — are racially charged. Public mistrust of police remains high in many minority communities.

"Given the large numbers of African-Americans today in prison or under the jurisdiction of the criminal justice system, there are questions in the black community whether this has resulted from discriminatory practices on the part of the police," says Hubert Williams, president of the Police Foundation, a Washington-based research organization.

In Los Angeles, however, many of the officers implicated so far, including Perez, are Hispanics who were targeting Hispanic offenders and suspects.

"This is not a black-white or white-brown incident," says Elizabeth Schroeder, associate director of the ACLU of Southern California. "You've got minority cops who are beating up minorities."

The efforts to control police conduct from the outside began in earnest in the 1960s, when the U.S. Supreme Court, under Chief Justice Earl Warren, handed down a series of decisions aimed at protecting the rights of suspects and criminal defendants. The best known of those rulings — the so-called *Miranda* decision in 1966 — required police to advise suspects after their arrest of their right to remain silent and to have a lawyer present during any questioning.

At around the same time, efforts were being made to increase the number of minority officers on urban police forces. In addition, police critics sought to establish civilian review boards to receive and in some cases adjudicate complaints regarding police conduct.

Today, those changes are widely, but not universally, accepted. In particular, the *Miranda* rule has become an ingrained police practice — and universally known through three decades of police stories on television and film. But law enforcement groups are lining up behind an effort to relax the *Miranda* decision by breathing life into a 1968 law that sought to partly lift its enforcement in federal courts.

The Justice Department has generally refused to invoke the law — known as Section 3501 — because of doubts about its constitutionality. But the Supreme Court will consider a case next month in which a federal appeals court invoked the law to turn back a defendant's challenge to a confession that he claimed police obtained before giving him his *Miranda* warnings.

"We do not want to be in a situation where officers know that they can torture a suspect to get a confession" says Gene Voegtlin, legislative counsel for the IACP, which filed a brief urging the court to uphold Section 3501. "But we believe you need to have some flexibility so that society is not punished for small oversights by having confessions thrown out and convictions lost."

But Williams says there is no need to relax or overturn *Miranda*. "Why would we — at a time when the crime rate is spiraling down, when we're trying to focus on community policing — why open up the door for inappropriate practices by some officers that in the past have vastly colored the reputation of the whole force?" Williams asks.

As the justices prepare to hear the *Miranda* case, here are some of the questions being debated by police and their critics:

Should the Miranda *rule regarding police interrogation be relaxed?*

Charles Dickerson was not physically mishandled or psychologically coerced when an FBI agent and an Alexandria, Va., police detective questioned him about a 1997 bank robbery. But a federal judge found that Dickerson — contrary to the FBI agent's testimony — had not been "Mirandized" before he gave a statement linking himself to the getaway vehicle used in the holdup. On that basis, the judge blocked the government from using Dickerson's statement in his scheduled trial.

Three years later, Dickerson has yet to be tried. Instead, his case goes before the U.S. Supreme Court next month in a crucial test of the federal law aimed at partially overturning *Miranda* — Section 3501. Critics of *Miranda* hope the court will use the case to relax the application of a decision that they say has hurt law enforcement by making confessions harder to get and allowing some defendants to avoid conviction because of technical mistakes unrelated to any improper conduct by police.

"When you have technical errors or inadvertent oversights — good-faith mistakes — you end up punishing society by excluding evidence that could be used to keep dangerous people off the streets," says Voegtlin of the police chiefs' association.

Supporters of the *Miranda* decision deny that the ruling has greatly hampered law enforcement, but also insist that the mandatory warnings are essential to protect suspects' rights in police interrogation.

"It's ridiculous to think that a lay person understands their rights under the Fifth Amendment," says Lisa Kemler, co-author of a brief in the case on behalf of the National Association of Criminal Defense Lawyers. "The police setting is inherently coercive. All of the things that the [Supreme Court] talked about in the *Miranda* decision are still true today."

Reuters / Brad Rickerby

Demonstrators in New York City protest the Feb. 25 acquittal of four NYPD officers in the shooting death of Amadou Diallo, an unarmed street vendor from West Africa. He was shot in the vestibule of his apartment building while reaching for his wallet.

The effects of the *Miranda* decision have been debated ever since the Supreme Court handed down its decision on June 13, 1966. In recent years, an academic critic of the decision, University of Utah law Professor Paul G. Cassell, has sought to prove the ruling's adverse effects on law enforcement in voluminous scholarly articles as well as in court briefs (*see p. 72*).

The Supreme Court case, however, does not directly concern the pros and cons of the *Miranda* ruling. Instead, the case tests Congress' power to pass a law to change a decision that the Supreme Court itself indicated might be subject to legislative revision.

Despite LAPD's Investigation of Rogue Unit . . .

Six months after the Rampart Division scandal broke in Los Angeles, Police Chief Bernard Parks laid out the department's explanation of how a supposedly elite anti-gang unit had turned into a rogue outfit. In a damning 362-page report, investigators blamed the department itself for tolerating sloppy recruiting, inadequate discipline, lax supervision and a general culture of mediocrity.

"We as an organization provided the opportunity," Parks wrote in a preface to the report, which was released on March 1. [1]

Parks, a career cop in his third year as chief of the nation's second-largest police department, hoped the report would convince a skeptical press and public that the department could be trusted to investigate the scandal and institute reforms. But the report did little to quiet criticism of the department or to derail calls for an independent investigation.

"The city and its police department need an independent commission, and we need it now," said Ramona Ripston, executive director of the American Civil Liberties Union (ACLU) of Southern California. "Relying on the police department to ferret out all of the underlying problems is like having a cancer patient operate on himself."

Police experts outside Los Angeles also voiced skepticism and distrust. "The LAPD is incapable of ensuring accountability of itself," Samuel Walker, a professor of criminal justice at the University of Nebraska at Omaha and an expert on police reform, told *The New York Times.*

"Unlike every other major city police department in the country, the Los Angeles Police Department has been able to resist self-scrutiny and reform," says Joseph McNamara, a former Kansas City and San Jose police chief and now a scholar at the Hoover Institution at Stanford University. "The Watts riot in 1965 showed clearly that the department was insensitive and not geared to providing the kind of service that minority communities needed. They've had one bad case after another, but they continued to embrace a very confrontational style of policing."

The scandal does not lack for other investigations. The Los Angeles District Attorney's office has been reviewing police misconduct in individual cases since the scandal broke. Already, about 40 convictions have been overturned as a result. District Attorney Gil Garcetti said in December that as many as 3,000 cases will have to be reviewed because of the scandal.

In addition, two federal law enforcement agencies recently announced plans to look into the scandal. U.S. Attorney Alejandro Mayorkas said on Feb. 23 that federal prosecutors and at least a dozen FBI agents would begin investigating alleged civil rights abuses by LAPD officers. The next day, the Immigration and Naturalization Service (INS) said it would look into accusations that INS agents helped Rampart Division officers arrange for the deportation of at least 160 Latino immigrants and the prosecution of 40 others for illegal re-entry into the United States.

Prospects for a specially created commission to investigate the scandal, however, are uncertain. Mayor Richard Riordan had high praise for the department's internal report — while acknowledging that he had not read all of it. "I have never been so proud of the Police Department," Riordan told a radio interviewer the day the report was released. Parks himself answered brusquely when a reporter at the news conference asked whether an independent commission was needed. "No," Parks said. "Next question."

Following the beating of black motorist Rodney King by four white police officers a decade ago, an independent commission was created to improve police accountability

Section 3501 of the federal Criminal Code provides that any "voluntary" confession can be introduced in federal courts. The law lists the giving of warnings as two out of five factors for a court to consider in determining whether a statement was voluntary. (*See box, p. 65.*)

The defenders of Section 3501 note that the court itself said that the procedures laid out in the *Miranda* decision might not be the only way to protect suspects' rights.

"*Miranda* itself is not a constitutional mandate," says Kent Scheidegger, legal director of the California-based Criminal Justice Legal Foundation. "The court created some rules for the implementation of constitutional rights that are not themselves constitutionally required, and those rules are subject to revision by Congress."

Critics of the law, however, insist that Congress had no power to overturn a decision defining constitutional rights. "If Congress can overrule *Miranda* by legislation, then it can overrule anything," says Yale Kamisar, a University of Michigan law professor and longtime defender of the ruling.

"The *Miranda* opinion says that these warnings aren't the only solution as long as you come up with an alternative that is equally effective," Kamisar adds. "The proponents of the statute never mention the [court's] statement that you'd have to come up with an alternative that is equally effective."

Cassell, who will present the arguments in defense of the law before

. . . Critics Call for Outside Probe

and oversight. Headed by former Secretary of State Warren Christopher, it called for the establishment of an inspector general's office and the creation of a tracking system for problem officers. Both recommendations were put into effect, but only after several years' delay.

In August 1998, Parks told the Los Angeles Police Commission — the five-member civilian board that exercises nominal authority over the department — that virtually all of the Christopher Commission's recommendations had been implemented. But the new report acknowledges that the computerized system for tracking complaints against officers has fallen short of expectations in part because some personnel investigations never got into the system.

ACLU officials say the problems with implementing the Christopher Commission recommendations demonstrate the need for an independent commission this time, too. "We want to make sure that there is a procedure in place that will do periodic reports on where we stand with regard to the recommendations, so that the public doesn't forget and public officials don't forget that these things are outstanding," says Elizabeth Schroeder, ACLU associate director in Southern California.

So far, 20 Rampart Division police officers have been either fired or suspended or have resigned. The report attributed wrongdoing to "a few individuals" whose behavior "had a contagion effect" on others around them. Schroeder said she was worried that the department had not looked at "the larger problems in the department, other areas outside Rampart."

The report makes 108 recommendations for consideration by the Police Commission, mostly aimed at strengthening management and oversight within the department. (*See box, p. 59.*) The commission itself is apparently divided over how to proceed. Two members — including Chairman Gerald Chaleff, a noted criminal defense attorney — are said to want the commission itself to institute a broad inquiry, while the others are thought either to favor a more limited review or are uncertain.

Meanwhile, Rafael Perez, the officer who blew the whistle on the Rampart scandal, was sentenced last month to five years in prison as part of a plea bargain to charges of stealing 6 pounds of cocaine from the police department's evidence room. Appearing in court in a jail-issued orange jump suit, Perez tearfully apologized for what he called his "atrocities."

The ex-Marine has implicated himself and others in covering up at least three potentially unjustified police shootings, including one fatal incident. In one of the cases, Perez said he and a partner shot an unarmed gang member, Javier Francisco Ovando, and then planted a gun on him to try to justify the shooting. Ovando, whose injuries left him in a wheelchair, was convicted of assault on an officer and given a 23-year prison sentence; he was freed from prison in September.

In court, Perez said that he had allowed himself to be consumed by "the us-against-them ethos of the overzealous cop" while working with the anti-gang unit — which was known by the acronym CRASH (Community Resources Against Street Hoodlums). "We vaguely sensed that we were doing wrong things for the right reasons," Perez said. He concluded, "Whoever chases monsters should see to it that in the process he does not become a monster himself."

[1] Coverage drawn from *Los Angeles Times*, March 1, 2000, p. A1; March 2, 2000, p. A1; *The New York Times*, March 2, 2000; *The Washington Post*, March 2, 2000, p. A3. For extensive previous coverage, see the *Los Angeles Times*' Web site: www.latimes.com/rampart. The police department report can be found at www.lapdonline.com.

the Supreme Court next month, says that police will "absolutely" continue to give the warnings even if the statute is upheld. "The warnings aren't the problems," Cassell says. "The problems are the vast procedural apparatus that's been erected around the warnings."

In fact, some pro-law enforcement observers say *Miranda* has actually benefited police. "*Miranda* is probably the best thing that's ever happened to police, even though they may not know it," says Craig Bradley, a law professor at Indiana University in Bloomington and former federal prosecutor and Justice Department official.

The ruling "gives police something very easy to comply with," Bradley continues. And compliance with the warnings typically limits further inquiry into police conduct.

"In *Miranda*, the court condemned a number of techniques" such as psychological pressure and deceptive tactics, Bradley says. "After *Miranda*, no one looks into that any more. There's very little examination of police tactics short of outright brutality."

Voegtlin agrees on some of the benefits of the ruling. "The *Miranda* decision gave law enforcement some valuable guidelines," he says. "It put policies and procedures into place to protect officers as well as suspects. Once it was certified that the warnings were given, there wasn't a question of the voluntariness of the confession."

Still, the police chiefs' group is joining other law enforcement organizations in urging the court to uphold the law limiting *Miranda*'s impact. "For someone to go free because of a technical oversight is wrong," Voegtlin says, "and that's what we're trying to remedy."

Are stronger measures needed to prevent use of excessive force by police officers?

Public confidence in New York City's finest was still recovering from the brutal sodomizing of Haitian immigrant Abner Louima in 1997 when it was shaken again a year ago by the Amadou Diallo shooting. But NYPD officials say that the controversy over Diallo's death and the prosecution of four white police officers for the shooting obscures an encouraging trend: a decline in police shootings and civilians killed or wounded by police fire.

In all, New York City police shot and killed 11 civilians in 1999. That figure is sharply down from the previous year's total of 19. Moreover, the number has been declining steadily since 1990, when 41 civilians were killed. The number of wounded also fell to 31 last year from 43 in 1998, and the number of incidents dropped to 155 from 249 in the same period.

"Generally, when it comes to the use of firearms, we are the most restrained large city police department in the United States," New York City Police Commissioner Howard Safir told a *New York Times* columnist last month. [2]

Police organizations nationwide are also trying to reassure the public about improper use of force by officers. A study released by the IACP in January showed that police used force fewer than 3.5 times per 10,000 calls for service, and suspects were injured in fewer than 3 percent of the instances when force was used.

"The incidence of use of force is minuscule compared to the number of citizen contacts, and the incidence of use of improper force is also minuscule in relation to that number," Fredericksburg Police Chief Powers said. [3]

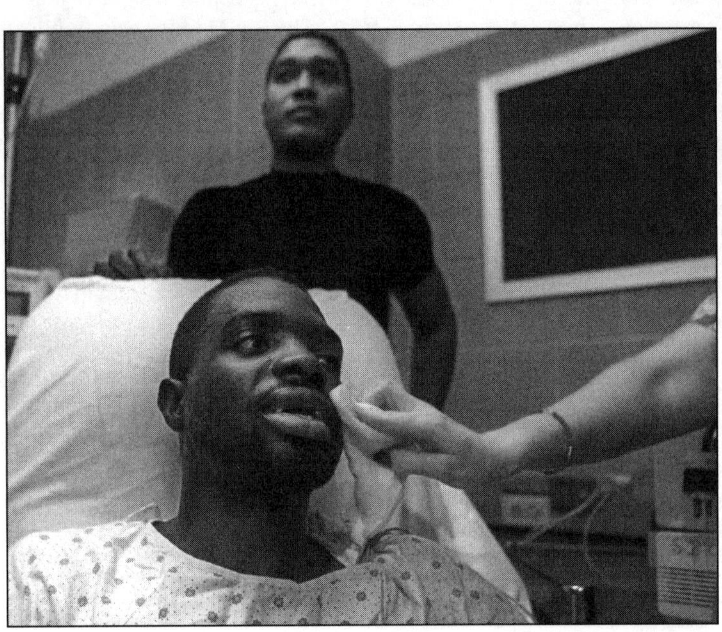

Reuters

Abner Louima, a Haitian immigrant, was beaten and sodomized with a broken broomstick handle by New York City police officers after a nightclub altercation in 1997.

Outside critics and observers, however, see no cause for complacency. "Excessive force has long been and continues to be a serious problem with enormous racial overtones in New York City," says Norman Siegel, executive director of the New York Civil Liberties Union. "And it will probably continue as long as mayors and police commissioners continue to deny the painful problem of police brutality, until civilian review boards become more effective, until police departments such as New York City's become more racially representative of the people they police and until they get better training."

"Whenever police abuse their authority, it's a social problem that needs to be controlled," says Geoffrey Alpert, a professor at the University of South Carolina's College of Criminal Justice in Columbia and an adviser to police departments on use of force. "It's a very powerful tool that they're given, and to abuse it flies in the face of why we give it to them."

Civil-rights and civil-liberties organizations often emphasize external mechanisms to try to control use of excessive force by police, such as civilian review boards, civil damage suits and criminal prosecutions. The effectiveness of civilian-review mechanisms is a subject of sharp dispute between civil-rights advocates and police unions and public officials in many cities. In New York, for example, Mayor Rudolph Giuliani is strongly opposed to the city's civilian review board, although the City Council voted overwhelmingly several years ago to keep it in existence.

"A number of them are very successful and have documented records of achievements," says the University of Nebraska's Walker, author of a forthcoming book on police accountability. "A number of them are abject failures. It's a question of determining which ones work, and why."

"Civilian review can be useful if it's a cooperative venture that doesn't just have to do with problems," Delattre says. "If the only time they're engaged is over some type of crisis,

The "Rampart Corruption Incident"

The Los Angeles Police Department's Board of Inquiry Report into the "Rampart Corruption Incident" detailed 108 recommendations for improvements in the department. The complete report, with an executive summary tracing the history of the scandals, can be found on the LAPD's Web site: www.lapdonline.com.

Here are some of the board's major recommendations:

■ **Testing and screening of police officer candidates** — Obtain all publicly available information, including criminal records, on candidates; give polygraph examinations to all candidates prior to background investigations.

■ **Personnel practices** — Improve tracking of personnel investigations; "restore integrity" to evaluation system; standardize selection for specialized units; limit tour of duty in specialized units.

■ **Personnel investigations and management of risk** — Expand internal-affairs investigations to cover all but most minor complaints; expand sting operations and checks of officers' financial records; eliminate city charter provisions setting time limits for administrative investigations.

■ **Corruption investigations** — Expand anti-corruption unit within Internal Affairs section; improve consultation with city attorney and district attorney; allow anti-corruption investigations to be conducted from non-city facilities to ensure confidentiality.

■ **Operational controls** — Increase number of field sergeants to improve supervision; improve oversight of specialized units; establish uniform rules on use of informants; strengthen security of Property Division and disposition of evidence; improve review of use of force to detect patterns involving individual officers.

■ **Anti-corruption inspections and audits** — Improve audits of investigations.

■ **Ethics and integrity training** — "Greatly increase" ethics and integrity training for all employees.

■ **Job-specific training** — Improve training in particular for supervisors and watch commanders; develop comprehensive training on cultivating and managing informants.

or if it has inordinate power, you're not going to have anything except a higher wall of resistance and silence [from police]."

Legal actions also have mixed results on officer conduct, experts say. Alpert says civil damage suits don't radically affect police behavior. "A lot of that information stays in the legal offices and never filters back to the police department," he says.

As for criminal prosecutions of questionable police behavior — which are relatively few in number in any event — Alpert says officers on patrol often respond by becoming more reluctant to initiate investigations of suspicious circumstances. "For a lot of these shootings that are relatively close calls, they're likely to say 'the system is just punishing us for doing our jobs' and become more careful in not going out on a limb," he says.

Police officials are more likely to emphasize improved recruitment and training as ways to prevent excessive use of force. "We now give psychological tests and do extensive interviews before hiring," says Fredericksburg Police Chief Powers. "We take every step we can to make sure that officers are not predisposed to that. And we do extensive training and talk about what is the proper use of force."

Categorical rules on use of force also may reduce civilian injuries, according to Carl Klockars, a professor of criminal justice at the University of Delaware in Newark. Departments that specifically prohibit high-speed chases or the use of warning shots, for example, appear to have few civilians killed or injured by police conduct, Klockars says.

"Excessive force has been with us forever, and it's still with us," says the Police Foundation's Williams. "It has not abated significantly at all. But you've got to understand the environment police are working in. It's a very tough job, and in many instances they're just trying to do the best they can do."

Critic Says *Miranda* Hurt Law Enforcement . . .

When he dissented from the Supreme Court's *Miranda* decision in 1966, Justice Byron White bitterly warned that the new rules on police interrogation would result "in some unknown number of cases" in which "a killer, a rapist, or other criminal" was returned to the streets to commit more crimes. After a period of initial opposition, however, police adapted to the new rules, and concern about its impact abated.

Three decades later, *Miranda* is second nature to virtually all police officers and is widely regarded — by police, prosecutors, and criminal-justice experts — as having had little, if any, adverse impact on law enforcement.

For the past five years, however, Paul G. Cassell, a law professor at the University of Utah and former federal prosecutor and Justice Department official, has waged a relentless campaign to reverse the conventional wisdom about the effects of the *Miranda* decision. In a series of eight strongly argued, densely statistical law-review articles, Cassell contends that *Miranda* has resulted in thousands of "lost confessions" over the years and caused a lasting drop in the percentage of crimes "cleared" by police.

"My statistics suggest that *Miranda* is the most devastating blow inflicted on law enforcement in the last half-century," Cassell says.

Other scholars sharply disagree. In one detailed critique, University of Chicago law Professor Stephen J. Schulhofer says *Miranda* has produced "substantial benefits" and "vanishingly small social costs." Another critic, Richard A. Leo, a criminologist at the University of California at Irvine, says *Miranda* "has not had any dramatic rate on how successfully police interrogate and obtain confessions." Cassell "is a one-man panic," Leo says. "He is a brilliant ideologue and an extraordinarily skillful legal advocate. He also manipulates and sometimes misrepresents the data."

Cassell, a former law clerk to Chief Justice Warren E. Burger and to Justice Antonin Scalia when he was on the federal appeals court in Washington, will take his thesis to the Supreme Court itself in a pivotal case involving the *Miranda* ruling next month. He will be asking the high court to uphold a 1968 law — so-called Section 3501 of the federal Criminal Code — that purported to override the use of *Miranda* in federal courts. The high court appointed Cassell to argue the case after the Justice Department decided not to defend the constitutionality of the law.

As one of his major points, Cassell will argue that the court has to defer to Congress' judgment at that time about the effects of the *Miranda* ruling. "Congress' judgment was that *Miranda* did indeed have a harmful effect on law enforcement," Cassell says. "That's the posture that this case will go before the court in, and the court is in no position to second-guess that judgment."

Cassell came to the *Miranda* issue while serving as an associate deputy attorney general in the Justice Department in the late 1980s. One of his assignments was to look for test cases to use Section 3501. After three years as a federal prosecutor in Alexandria, Va., outside Washington, he joined the Utah law faculty and threw himself into a variety of pro-law enforcement issues, including a proposed constitutional amendment on victims' rights.

In his first article on the effects of *Miranda*, Cassell acknowledged that court decisions suppressing confessions or overturning convictions because of *Miranda* violations are "quite rare." But he contended that the true measure of *Miranda*'s effects was the number of confessions "lost" to police because suspects invoked their right to remain silent. Reanalyzing data from a dozen studies done shortly after *Miranda*, Cassell estimated that confessions were

Should the use of "racial profiling" be prohibited?

Christopher Darden and Johnnie Cochran squared off against each other in a Los Angeles courtroom as prosecutor and defense lawyer in the O. J. Simpson murder case. But the two African-American attorneys had something in common before the trial. Both had been victims of what they regarded as racially motivated traffic stops by police while working for the Los Angeles district attorney's office.[4]

Darden and Cochran are just two of the many African-Americans from all walks of life who have stepped forward during recent years to complain about being stopped for the not-so-fictitious offense of DWB — "driving while black." Minority groups representing blacks as well as Hispanics complain that police use racial or ethnic stereotypes in traffic enforcement or other investigative stops.

"This is not a new thing, by any means," says David Harris, a law professor at the University of Toledo who has studied the issue for the ACLU. "What is new is that we have begun over the last few years to see the collection of some of the data to substantiate what blacks and other minorities have been saying for a long time."

Some police officials acknowledge the practice while also expressing strong disapproval. "Whether racial profiling is existent in the United States — I'm sure that it probably is," says Jack Grant, manager of the Division of State and Provincial Police at the police chiefs' association. "We discourage it. Responsible police administrators do everything they

. . . But Most Experts Disagree, Support Ruling

lost in 16 percent of criminal cases.

Cassell further calculated that confessions were "necessary" to obtain a conviction in 24 percent of criminal cases. On that basis, he calculated that *Miranda* costs law enforcement convictions in about 3.8 percent of cases. Using 1993 figures, Cassell concluded that 28,000 arrests for violent crimes and 79,000 arrests for property offenses that year "slipped through the criminal-justice system due to *Miranda*." [1]

In a response published in the same issue, Schulhofer described Cassell's conclusions as far short of the catastrophic effect that *Miranda*'s critics had predicted. But he proceeded to challenge Cassell's reading of the previous studies and a number of the assumptions he used in making his calculations. On that basis, Schulhofer estimated that *Miranda* caused at most a 4 percent decline in the confession rate and lost convictions in fewer than 1 percent of all arrests. [2]

In a subsequent article, Cassell also blamed *Miranda* for a drop in the crime-clearance rate from about 60 percent before the ruling to about 45 percent after — a level that continues today. Schulhofer responded by contending that the apparent drop was more likely due to the overall increase in crime and the overtaxing of police resources. [3] Others, including Professor Yale Kamisar of the University of Michigan Law School, also have contended that pre-*Miranda* clearance rates were probably inflated and that current figures represent a more accurate picture of police success in identifying and arresting suspects.

Leo weighed in on the academic debate by conducting firsthand observation of more than 180 police interrogations in three unidentified cities. [4] He concluded that police had avoided any dramatic impact from *Miranda* by adapting to the ruling — though sometimes with strategies that "straddle the ambiguous margins of legality." At the same time, Leo credits *Miranda* with improving police professionalism and civility. "Most police like *Miranda*," Leo says. "They've embraced it as a symbol of professionalism."

For his part, Cassell expects most law enforcement officers will continue to give *Miranda* warnings even if the federal statute easing the requirement is upheld. As for the academic debate, "I'm the first to concede that there's conflicting evidence," he says. But he insists that he has punctured a myth that the ruling has had no impact and that law enforcement groups all support the ruling.

"All the leading law enforcement organizations in the country are filing [briefs] in support of [Section 3501]," Cassell says. "All of those groups are coming in and explaining that they're concerned about the harmful effects of *Miranda*."

[1] Paul G. Cassell, "Miranda's Social Costs: An Empirical Reassessment," *Northwestern University Law Review*, Vol. 90, No. 2 (winter 1996), pp. 387-499. Cassell has posted his law review articles on a Web site: www.law.utah.c/faculty/bios/cassell.

[2] Stephen J. Schulhofer, "Miranda's Practical Effect: Substantial Benefits and Vanishingly Small Social Costs," *ibid.*, pp. 500-563. Some of Schulhofer's points can be found in the American Civil Liberties Union's brief in the *Dickerson* case: www.aclu.org.

[3] Paul G. Cassell, "All Benefits, No Costs: The Grand Illusion of Miranda's Defenders," *Northwestern University Law Review*, Vol. 90, No. 3 (spring 1996), pp. 1084-1124; Stephen J. Schulhofer, "Miranda and Clearance Rates," *Northwestern University Law Review*, Vol. 91, No. 1 (fall 1996), pp. 278-294. For a rebuttal, see Paul G. Cassell and Richard Fowles, "Handcuffing the Cops? A Thirty-Year Perspective on Miranda's Harmful Effects on Law Enforcement," *Stanford Law Review*, Vol. 50, No. 4 (April 1998), pp. 1055-1145.

[4] Richard A. Leo, "The Impact of Miranda Revisited," *Journal of Criminal Law and Criminology*, Vol. 86, No. 3 (Spring 1996), pp. 621-692.

can to prevent it. It cannot be tolerated as a practice in police work."

Many police officials and law enforcement supporters, however, also insist that race can sometimes be a legitimate factor for officers to consider in police investigations. "Racial profiling is wrong," says Cornelius Behan, retired police chief in Baltimore County, Md., "but it gets confused with sensible police procedures. It's wise to try to develop a profile of who the offenders are, and sometimes a legitimate profile would have race in it."

"The distinction is between profiling and discriminatory profiling," Delattre says. "Anybody who says you can enforce the law and protect public safety without profiling is trying to sell you a pipe dream. What you need are clear statements of policy about how to justify responsible profiling from profiling that's based on bigotry and that has the effect that bigotry has."

Racial and ethnic minorities have long been accustomed to being regarded with suspicion when they frequent "white" neighborhoods, whether on foot or in vehicles. The "driving while black" issue has become more visible in recent years because of stepped-up traffic enforcement aimed in large part at detecting drug offenses. "These pretext stops are about drugs," Harris says. "That's what the federal government has trained local law enforcement to use them for."

Harris and other critics of racial profiling say police who target blacks or other minorities in drug-interdiction efforts are operating on a false assumption that use of drugs is highest among African-Americans. "Police are focused on the drug market in the inner city, and that's in African-American communities and other minority communities," the Police Foundation's Williams explains. "They look at the people they're arresting, and that's where they get their profile. So it always winds up with a heavy representation of African-Americans and Hispanics."

Critics also question the value of using traffic stops for drug enforcement, noting that the vast majority of people stopped in drug-related patrolling end up not being charged with any drug offenses. John Crew, director of the ACLU of Northern California's Police Practices Project, says data gathered for a class-action suit against the California Highway Patrol indicate that the CHP stopped about 33,000 motorists in 1997 in drug-related investigations but had a "hit rate" of less than 2 percent. "If you use a tactic that fails 98 percent of the time," Crew says, "normally that's not something that you would view as successful."

But Sweeney, who oversees training for all of New Hampshire's state and local police, defends the use of traffic enforcement for other anti-crime purposes. "Aggressive enforcement of the traffic laws keeps crime down," Sweeney says. "You have a tendency to detect people who are violating the laws."

"People who have been arrested tell you that they stay away from communities and areas where there is intensive enforcement of traffic laws," Sweeney continues. "If they're carrying drugs, carrying burglary tools, they're likely to be stopped while driving along that stretch of the highway."

While condemning racial profiling, police officials generally contend the problem is relatively isolated. Critics insist the practice is more widespread. To try to substantiate their beliefs, the ACLU and other critics favor legislation — passed in two states and pending in Congress and at least 18 other states — to require state and local law enforcement agencies to gather data on the race of persons stopped for traffic violations. Police groups generally oppose such proposals as unnecessary and expensive.

But Crew also notes that many police leaders have become more attuned to the problem, in part because of the effect that the perception of racial profiling has on public confidence in law enforcement.

"It's interesting to hear law enforcement groups talk about this not just as a civil-rights issue, not just a justice issue, but as an effective-policing issue," Crew says. "If they're going to be effective, they can't afford to have a large segment of the American population, people of color, disaffected from police." ■

BACKGROUND

A Checkered Past

The creation of the first full-time police departments in the United States in Philadelphia and Boston in the 1830s came not long after Sir Robert Peel established what is regarded as the first modern force, the London Metropolitan Police, in 1829. The London police quickly gained a reputation for professionalism, but urban police departments in the United States were beset by continuing scandals through the 19th century. Police departments were guilty of "pervasive brutality and corruption," according to historian Walker, and "did little to prevent crime or provide public services." [5]

A police-reform movement developed in the early 20th century. The reformers sought to rid police departments of political influence and cronyism and turn them into efficient, nonpartisan agencies committed to public service. They wanted police departments to be run by trained experts with job tenure to insulate them from political interference. They also wanted to improve the recruitment and training of officers and to centralize a command structure for better accountability. Some progress was made on all of those goals. Still, a federal crime commission — the famous Wickersham Commission — reported in 1931 that physical brutality was "extensively practiced" by police departments around the country. [6]

The Supreme Court first stepped in to police the interrogation process in 1936 in a flagrant case in which three black tenant farmers "confessed" to the murder of a white farmer after being brutally tortured by local sheriff's deputies in Mississippi. An involuntary confession was unreliable, the court reasoned, and its use in court would violate the 14th Amendment's prohibition against depriving anyone of life or liberty without due process of law. In a second confession case six years later, the court shifted its focus by declaring that the Due Process Clause prohibited the use of any evidence — whether true or false — that police obtained through techniques that "shocked the conscience" of the community or violated fundamental standards of fairness. [7]

The high court ruled on more than 30 confession cases between 1936 and 1964, deciding whether a confession was voluntary by looking at the totality of the circumstances in each case. [8] In some cases, the court established that certain interrogation methods — including physical force, threats of harm or punishment, lengthy or incommunicado question-

Chronology

Before 1900 ***Corruption and brutality are pervasive in U.S. police forces.***

1900-1960 ***Police reform movements advance; Supreme Court begins to review confession cases.***

1936
First Supreme Court decision to bar confession as involuntary.

1960s ***Warren Court seeks to control police conduct.***

1961
Supreme Court rules illegally seized evidence cannot be used in state court trials.

1966
Supreme Court in *Miranda v. Arizona* requires police to advise suspects of rights.

1968
Kerner Commission warns of deep mistrust of police by African-Americans; Congress passes law aimed at overturning *Miranda* in federal courts.

1970s ***Burger Court restricts* Miranda*, but does not overturn it.***

1971
Confession obtained in violation of *Miranda* can be used to impeach defendant's testimony at trial, Supreme Court rules.

1980s ***Conservative era in law enforcement.***

1986
Justice Department unit proposes effort to overturn *Miranda*, but plan is not pursued.

1990s ***Police brutality and racial profiling emerge as major issues.***

1991
Black motorist Rodney King is kicked and beaten by white Los Angeles police officers; they are acquitted in state trial in 1992, but two are convicted a year later of civil-rights violations.

1993
Black lawyer Robert Wilkins files anti-racial profiling suit after being stopped by Maryland state troopers; state settles suit in 1995 by agreeing to end racial profiling and provide racial data on traffic stops to ACLU.

1996
Supreme Court upholds pretextual traffic stops for drug enforcement.

1997
Black immigrant Abner Louima is sodomized by white New York police officers; Justin Volpe pleads guilty in 1999 and draws 30-year prison term.

February 1999
Black immigrant Amadou Diallo is fatally shot by four white NYPD officers; murder trial moved to Albany because of publicity in New York City.

April 1999
New Jersey attorney general issues report acknowledging racial profiling by state police; state settles Justice Department suit in December by agreeing to end practice.

September 1999
Rafael Perez implicates himself and other LAPD anti-gang officers in city's Rampart Division in widespread abuse, including planting evidence and shooting suspects.

December 1999
Supreme Court agrees to review appeals court ruling upholding 1968 law aimed at overturning *Miranda* in federal courts.

2000s ***Racial profiling, police brutality continue as high-profile issues.***

January 2000
Democratic presidential candidates Al Gore and Bill Bradley oppose racial profiling; GOP front-runner George W. Bush is ambiguous.

Feb. 25, 2000
NYPD officers are acquitted in Diallo shooting; former LAPD officer Perez gets five years in prison for stealing cocaine from police evidence room.

March 1, 2000
LAPD report blames Rampart scandal on lax supervision and "culture of mediocrity."

April 19, 2000
Supreme Court set to hear arguments on anti-*Miranda* law.

Controversial *Miranda* Ruling Still Stands

The U.S. Supreme Court's 1966 *Miranda* decision requiring police to advise suspects of their constitutional rights against self-incrimination before interrogation has been narrowed over the years by subsequent high court decisions, but not overturned.

CASE	VOTE	RULING
Miranda v. Arizona (1966)	5-4	Police must advise suspect before interrogation of right to remain silent, right to a lawyer, right to have lawyer appointed, and give warning that any statement can be used against him; police cannot use any statement obtained without such warnings.
Orozco v. Texas (1969)	6-2	Police must give *Miranda* warnings whenever a suspect is effectively in custody — in this case, in his home.
Harris v. New York (1971)	6-3	Statement obtained in violation of *Miranda* can be used to cross-examine defendant or impeach testimony at trial.
Michigan v. Tucker (1974)	8-1	Police can use statement in violation of *Miranda* as a lead for obtaining other evidence; Rehnquist opinion emphasizes *Miranda* not constitutionally required.
Michigan v. Mosley (1975)	7-2	Police did not violate *Miranda* by questioning suspect who invoked his right to silence about a second offense after they gave a second warning.
United States v. Mandujano (1976)	8-0	No *Miranda* warning needed for grand jury witness.
Brewer v. Williams (1977)	5-4	Police officer's speech pleading for "Christian burial" of child murder victim was "tantamount to interrogation" and violated suspect's *Miranda* rights.
Fare v. Michael C. (1979)	5-4	Probation officer need not give *Miranda* warnings before questioning juvenile suspect.
Rhode Island v. Innis (1980)	6-3	Police appeal to suspect's conscience did not amount to interrogation in violation of *Miranda*.
Edwards v. Arizona (1981)	9-0	Police must stop interrogation after suspect asks for lawyer.
Minnesota v. Murphy (1984)	5-4	No *Miranda* warning needed before interview with probation officer.
New York v. Quarles (1984)	5-4	Police did not violate *Miranda* by asking suspect, "Where's the gun?" before giving warnings; suspect's answer could be used as evidence at trial ("public safety exception").
Withrow v. Williams (1993)	5-4	*Miranda* violation can be basis for challenging state court conviction in federal habeas corpus proceeding.

Law OKs "Voluntary" Confessions

Section 3501 of the federal Criminal Code (Title 18) attempts to partly overturn the *Miranda* decision as used in federal courts. The law provides that a confession "shall be admissible in evidence" in any federal prosecution "if it is voluntarily given." The law lists five situations — some of which track the four warnings required under *Miranda* — that a judge should consider in determining whether a confession was voluntary:

- The time between the defendant's arrest and arraignment in court.*
- Whether the defendant knew the nature of the offense with which he was being charged when he confessed.**
- Whether the defendant "was advised or knew that he was not required to make any statement and that any such statement could be used against him.
- Whether the defendant "had been advised prior to questioning of his right to the assistance of counsel."
- Whether the defendant "was without the assistance of counsel when questioned."

** This recognizes that the longer a suspect is held without charges the greater the possibility that mistreatment prompted the confession.*

*** This recognizes the possibility that police sometimes threaten to hold suspects incommunicado until they confess.*

ing, solitary confinement, denial of food or sleep and promises of leniency — were presumptively coercive and therefore constitutionally impermissible. But the court did not attempt to set out a specific checklist of procedures for police to assure that a suspect's statement would be deemed voluntary and therefore admissible in court.

Police professionalism "continued to make steady advances" during this period, according to historian Walker. [9] A "new generation" of police chiefs provided better leadership, while officers became more productive because of technological advances, such as patrol cars with sophisticated communications systems.

At the same time, racial flareups foreshadowed the crisis in police-community relations that fully developed in the 1960s. Racial disturbances in Detroit and New York City's Harlem in 1943 produced accusations of discriminatory enforcement against the cities' African-American populations, while the "Zoot Suit" riots in Los Angeles exposed tensions between blacks, Hispanics and the city's overwhelmingly white police force.

Some police chiefs and national organizations responded with programs to improve race relations. But, as Walker notes, recruitment of black police officers lagged, and the "pioneering efforts" in improving police-community relations did not keep pace with the rapidly changing context of race relations in the decades after World War II.

By the mid-1960s, the Supreme Court had a liberal majority that was determined to continue the civil-rights revolution it had launched with the landmark school-desegregation rulings of the 1950s. The court also was determined to bring about a due-process revolution in the administration of criminal justice across the country. In 1961 the court ruled that illegally obtained evidence could not be used in state trials; two years later it ruled that the states had to provide lawyers for indigent criminal defendants in felony trials if they could not afford to pay for one themselves. [10]

Then in 1964 the court held in *Escobedo v. Illinois* that a suspect has a right under the Sixth Amendment to consult with his lawyer during police interrogation once an investigation had moved from a general inquiry to focus specifically on him. The implications of the decision were unclear; one reading suggested that it applied only to suspects like Escobedo who already had an attorney.

But two years later the court made clear it had a broader interest in police interrogations by scheduling arguments in four consolidated cases in which defendants challenged their convictions by claiming that police had obtained confessions from them in violation of their constitutional rights.

Miranda's Rights

Ernest Miranda confessed to the kidnap-rape of a Phoenix, Ariz., teenager in 1963 after an interrogation session with no overt indications of coercion. Police found Miranda, a 23-year-old laborer, after tracking the license plate of a truck driven by the

What Cops Say About Police Abuse

Most police officers recognize legal constraints on police and say they reject the so-called code of silence on abuses by colleagues, according to a federally financed survey. The survey found, however, that many officers disagree with strict limits on police behavior. Nearly one-fourth, for example, said it was sometimes justifiable to use more force than legally permitted. "Most officers have the kind of values about police abuse that we want, but there's still a substantial group out there that's saying things that are disturbing," says study director David Weisburd, director of the Institute of Criminology at the Hebrew University Law School in Jerusalem.

Some questions and answers from the survey

- It is sometimes acceptable to use more force than is legally allowable to control someone who physically assaults an officer.
  24.5% agree 75.5% disagree
- Do you think ethics in law enforcement training is effective in preventing abuse of authority?
  82.2% yes 17.8% no
- Do you think human-diversity or cultural-awareness training is effective in preventing abuse of authority?
  74.9% yes 25.1% no
- The code of silence is an essential part of the mutual trust necessary to good policing.
  16.9% agree 83.1% disagree

AP Photo/Tina Fineberg

New Yorkers protest the acquittal of four NYPD officers in the death of Amadou Diallo, who died in a hail of 41 bullets.

Source: Police Foundation. The survey consisted of anonymous telephone interviews with 925 officers and rank-and-file street cops conducted in late 1997 and early 1998. The Justice Department's Office of Community Policing Services financed the survey.

assailant. Detectives went to his home, asked him to accompany them to the police station and there began questioning him about the crime. A line-up was inconclusive, but police told Miranda he had been identified. At that point, he admitted that he had raped the girl. [11]

The Supreme Court heard arguments in Miranda's effort to reverse his state court conviction and in three other confession cases on March 2 and 3, 1966. When he announced the decision in the cases on June 13, Chief Justice Warren acknowledged that Miranda's statement might not be deemed involuntary "in traditional terms." But Warren, a former district attorney in California, said that "incommunicado interrogation" and such recognized police techniques of undermining a suspect's will through flattery, isolation or trickery were inherently compulsive and violated the Fifth Amendment's "cherished" principle against self-incrimination.

To protect that right, Warren continued, police must advise a suspect of the right to remain silent, the right to an attorney and the right to have an attorney appointed if he cannot afford one, and must warn that any statement given after waiving those rights could be used in court against him. Warren acknowledged that the Constitution might not require this particular set of safeguards. But unless equally effective safeguards were established, police had to give those warnings for a suspect's statement to be admissible later in court.

The 5-4 decision stopped short of the most restrictive position urged in arguments: an absolute requirement to have an attorney present during any police interrogation. The dissenting justices nonetheless forcefully criticized the ruling. They argued for retaining what Justice Byron White called the "more pliable" method of testing confessions on the totality of the circumstances. And each of the four dissenters warned of a likely adverse effect on law enforcement. "We do know that some crimes cannot be solved without confessions," Justice John Marshall Harlan wrote, "and that the Court is taking a real risk with society's welfare in imposing its new regime on the country."

Those warnings were quickly picked up and amplified by police, prosecutors and politicians. The court, critics said, had "handcuffed" the police. Congress responded in 1968 with a provision in the Omnibus Crime Control and Safe Streets Act seeking to overturn *Miranda* in federal courts and return to a voluntariness test. The main sponsor, Sen. John McClellan, D-Ark., had proposed a constitutional amendment shortly after the decision was announced, but turned to the easier legislative route instead.

Also in 1968, Republican presidential nominee Richard M. Nixon made the Supreme Court's criminal-procedure decisions a major focus of his campaign and promised to appoint law-and-order justices to the court if elected. The next year, as president, Nixon chose Warren E. Burger, a conservative judge from the federal appeals court in Washington, D.C., to succeed Warren as chief justice.

During Burger's 17 years as chief justice, both supporters and critics of *Miranda* found cause for disappointment. Initially, the court somewhat expanded the ruling — for example, to cover custodial interrogation outside a police station. In 1971, however, Burger and the four *Miranda* dissenters joined in a 6-3 decision carving out a major exception that allowed prosecutors to use a statement obtained in violation of the decision to cross-examine a defendant at trial. Other exceptions and restrictions followed.

AP Photo/John Gaps III

Looting suspects are arrested during the riots in Los Angeles in May 1992 following the acquittal of four LAPD officers in the videotaped beating of motorist Rodney King.

Still, the Burger Court stopped short of overturning *Miranda*. And police attitudes toward *Miranda* changed from hostility to acceptance. By the late 1980s, an American Bar Association survey found that "a very strong majority" of police, prosecutors and judges believed *Miranda* "does not present serious problems for law enforcement." [12]

Critics of the Warren Court's criminal-procedure rulings saw a better chance for undoing some of the decisions after President Ronald Reagan chose William H. Rehnquist to succeed Burger as chief justice in 1986. Within the Justice Department, the Office of Legal Policy proposed a direct challenge to *Miranda*, but Solicitor General Charles Fried largely rebuffed the idea.

"Most experienced federal prosecutors in and out of my office were opposed to the project, as was I," Fried wrote in his memoir. [13] Cassell points to cases in which federal prosecutors did try to use Section 3501, and their efforts were supported by the department on appeal.

Still, Justice Antonin Scalia, writing in a 1994 case, complained about the government's "repeated refusal" to invoke the provision in confession cases. [14] And a year earlier, the Rehnquist Court signaled a sort of acceptance of by reaffirming — on a 5-4 vote with Rehnquist in dissent — that federal courts can set aside state court convictions if police violated a suspect's *Miranda* rights during questioning. [15]

Use of Force

Police came under intense, renewed criticism in the 1990s despite the easing of the controversy

Race Colors Attitudes About Police Conduct

Most Americans — including a majority of blacks and a substantial majority of whites — have a favorable opinion of their local police. Aftican-Americans are nearly four times as likely as whites to feel they are treated unfairly by local police, according to a recent Gallup Poll. Among blacks, younger men were nearly twice as likely as younger women to feel unfairly treated. Here are some questi ons from the poll:

1. Do you have a favorable or unfavorable opinion of your local police?

	Favorable	Unfavorable	Don't know
Blacks	58%	36%	6%
Whites	85%	13%	2%

2. Do you feel you're treated fairly by the local police in your area?

	Fairly	Not Fairly	Not Applicable/ Did not answer
Blacks	66%	27%	7%
Whites	91%	7%	2%

3. Do you feel you're treated fairly by the local police in your area?

Black men	**Treated Fairly**	**Not Treated Fairly**
Ages:		
18-34	43%	53%
35-49	71%	23%
50+	68%	22%
Black women	**Treated Fairly**	**Not Treated Fairly**
Ages:		
18-34	67%	26%
35-49	75%	19%
50+	71%	18%

Source: The Gallup Organization. The survey is based on 2,006 phone interviews with a random sample of adults in the continental U.S. from Sept. 24, 1999, to Nov. 16, 1999.

over interrogation practices. The issue was police use of force — a problem that flared up most dramatically in the beating of black motorist King in Los Angeles in 1991 and the sodomizng of Haitian immigrant Louima in New York City in 1997. [16] The incidents provoked new accusations of racism against both police departments from minority and civil rights groups and new concerns among police executives and governments officials about how to control use of excessive force by police.

Police shootings of black civilians had touched off several of the racial disturbances that had erupted in the nation's big cities three decades earlier. The 1968 report by a presidential panel appointed to study the cause of the riots — the so-called Kerner Commission — found "deep hostility between police and ghetto communities" to have been a "primary cause" of the disorders.

Historian Walker also blames the lack of controls on the use of force by police. "Even the best departments had no meaningful rules on deadly force," Walker writes, "offering their officers many hours of training on how to shoot but not on when to use their weapons." [17]

Much progress was made over the next 25 years, according to Walker. Civilian review boards — favored by groups seeking to hold police accountable — gradually achieved a measure of acceptance after having been stoutly resisted by police unions, local politicians and some segments of the public. By the 1990s, Walker reports, more than three-fourths of the police departments in the nation's biggest cities had some form of external or civilian review of complaints.

In addition, local police departments began adopting rules to guide officers in the use of force. The rules appeared to bring results. New York City Police Commissioner Patrick Murphy instituted a rule in 1972 allowing officers to shoot only in "the defense of life" and requiring reports and reviews of any weapons discharge. Officer-involved shootings declined 30 percent over the next three years, according to research by James Fyfe, a professor of criminal justice at Temple University in Philadelphia and an expert on use-of-force issues. [18]

The beating of King by four white Los Angeles police officers after a high-speed car chase on March 3, 1991, put the issue of police brutality back on the national agenda. An 81-second videotape shot by a resident of a nearby apartment — broadcast countless times around the world over the next two years — showed the officers repeatedly kicking King and hitting him 56 times with their batons as he lay on the ground.

The episode produced a national outcry, but criminal prosecutions of the officers ended with mixed results. A predominantly white jury in a neighboring county acquitted the officers of state charges in April 1992; two officers were convicted of violating King's civil rights in a federal court trial in April 1993, but they were given relatively light sentences of 30 months each.

Meanwhile, though, a special commission appointed by Los Angeles Mayor Tom Bradley concluded that the incident was merely one example of what it described as "a tolerance within the LAPD of attitudes condoning violence against the public." [19]

Six years after the King beating, police brutality again became a national issue with an episode in New York that had none of the ambiguity or arguable justifications of the Los Angeles incident. New York police officers arrested Louima on Aug. 9, 1997, following an altercation outside a Brooklyn nightclub. Officer Justin Volpe later acknowledged that he struck Louima while taking him to the patrol car. Once at the station house, Volpe took Louima into a restroom and plunged a broken broomstick handle into the Haitian's rectum. Volpe pleaded guilty to six federal charges in May 1999 and was later sentenced to 30 years in prison; a second officer, Charles Schwarz, was convicted of beating Louima and holding him down during the sodomizing.*

The incident produced universal revulsion, even among sympathetic police observers. "This was clearly a case of sadism and racism," says Boston University's Delattre. Nonetheless, New York Mayor Giuliani, a strong police supporter, saw a positive sign in the willingness of Volpe's fellow officers to aid investigators in uncovering the incident and to testify against him. The trial, Giuliani said, "destroys the myth of the blue wall of silence" among police officers.

Reuters/Lee Celano

Los Angeles motorist Rodney King was severely beaten by LAPD officers in 1991 after a high-speed chase. The shocking incident was captured on videotape and shown around the world.

For his part, though, Walker says the King and Louima cases represented a setback for public perceptions of police accountability.

"All of the positive developments have been obscured by these horrific examples in New York and Los Angeles, which make it appear to the average citizen that nothing has changed, and maybe things have gotten worse," Walker says.

"Driving While Black"

Racial profiling became the new flashpoint of police-community relations during the 1990s. African-Americans from many walks of life testified to their experiences of having been stopped and questioned by police seemingly for no reason other than their race.

By the end of the decade, the leading law enforcement groups were joining civil-rights and civil-liberties groups in saying that race alone should never be the basis for a traffic stop or other police investigation. But police were also continuing to defend the use of race as one factor in criminal profiling, particularly in anti-drug enforcement.

Police explained their use of race in deciding what drivers or pedestrians to stop for investigation by pointing to the statistics showing that African-Americans are more likely than whites to be arrested or convicted of many of the most common crimes, especially drug offenses and so-called street crimes. Courts up to and including the U.S. Supreme Court sanctioned the practice.

In one representative case, the Ari-

* Schwarz was fired from the force; he and two other current officers — Thomas Bruder and Thomas Wiese — were convicted in federal court in Brooklyn on March 6, 2000, of conspiracy to obstruct justice for attempting to cover up the incident; attorneys for the three defendants said they would appeal. Schwarz faces up to a life sentence in the first case; the three face up to five years in the second case.

Community Policing Widely Accepted . . .

In Boston, police enlisted the help of black ministers to warn drug dealers and young gang members that they risked tough federal prosecutions unless gun violence was curbed.

In San Diego, police gave 1,200 citizen volunteers training and police-like uniforms as part of a neighborhood-based crime-prevention effort.

In Chicago, police work with social-service agencies and organizations to try to improve community life and reduce crime.

The crime-fighting strategies adopted by the three cities reflect different aspects of "community policing," an approach that has advanced over the past decade from experimental innovation to nearly universal acceptance. The philosophy calls for tying police work more closely to citizen concerns, decentralizing police decision-making, and adopting a proactive approach to crime prevention in place of a reactive approach tied to solving crimes after they have occurred. [1]

CQ Photo/R. Michael Jenkins

In Washington, D.C., community policing includes a visit to Young's Supermarket.

Proponents say the no-longer-new approach has improved police-community relations and contributed to reducing crimes in cities from coast to coast. "Community policing is what most people would argue is playing a big role in the reductions of crime," says Hubert Williams, a former Newark, N.J., police chief and now president of the Police Foundation. "Large numbers of police officers working in concert with the public can make a difference."

Critics and skeptics, however, say the results are either disappointing or unproven. "Many people in the field say that it has not really taken root," says Samuel Walker, a professor of criminal justice at the University of Nebraska in Omaha. "It's not clear that this has really changed the fundamental ways that police departments operate."

Some traditionalists also view community policing as soft on serious crime. Some go so far as to dismiss it as more like social work than policing. Proponents scoff at the criticism." It's not soft on crime," says Williams. "It's the key thing to crime control."

"The police are small in numbers, and they cover large areas," Williams continues. "Usually when a crime is occurring, they are not there. It's the public that sees it. They have the information. And that information base is absolutely vital to police solving crimes."

Community policing stems in part from a reaction against an overly technological approach to policing almost universally adopted in the last half-century. "We kind of enclosed ourselves in these metal vehicles and separated ourselves through technology and other means from the people we were serving," Williams says.

Williams, an African-American, says the philosophy also reflects the need for police to gain the confidence of racial and ethnic minority groups. "The problem we have

zona Supreme Court in 1975 upheld a police officer's decision to question a Mexican male because he was sitting in a parked car in a predominantly white neighborhood. The use of race, the court said, was "a practical aspect of good law enforcement." [20]

Two decades later, the Supreme Court in 1996 gave police a blank check to use traffic violations as a pretext for stopping motorists for suspected drug violations. The ruling in *Whren v. United States* turned aside the plea by two black defendants that they had been stopped because of their race.

By the 1990s, though, racial profiling was being challenged not only by convicted defendants but also by the innocent victims of the practice — people who were stopped, questioned, perhaps searched and then allowed to go on their way when police found no evidence of crime. The first major victory for critics of the practice came in a case brought by Robert Wilkins, a public defender in Washington, D.C., who was stopped by Maryland state police in May 1992 while driving with his family back to Washington. When Wilkins refused to consent to a search of his car, troopers called for a trained narcotics dog to try to detect drugs, but no drugs were found.

Wilkins, represented by the ACLU of Maryland and two private Washington lawyers, filed a federal civil rights damage suit in May 1993 contending that the use of a racial profile violated his constitutional rights. The state agreed to settle the suit in Janu-

. . . But Critics Question the Benefits

is that we are not fully prepared to engage these multicultural communities," he says. "We don't know how to overcome the racial and cultural barriers that exist there."

Walker says the philosophy is akin to an approach called "team policing" that gained popularity in the 1970s but then disappeared in the more conservative '80s. By the early '90s, however, community policing was being widely discussed in law enforcement circles and drawing support from academic circles.

In 1992, Democratic presidential candidate Bill Clinton endorsed the idea. Once in office, his administration has supported community policing with money and other institutional support.

Community policing got another boost — but with a different emphasis — from two conservative-leaning researchers who called for police to give greater emphasis to seemingly minor crimes such as vandalism or public urination and less attention to so-called "index" crimes such as robbery, burglary and the like. In their book *Fixing Broken Windows*, George Kelling and Catherine Coles argued that police could simultaneously improve community life and reduce crime by focusing on these "public order" offenses.

"Crime is prevented by order maintenance," says Kelling, now a professor at Rutgers University's School of Criminal Justice in Newark. [2]

New York City Mayor Rudolph Giuliani and two of his police commissioners — William Bratton and the current commissioner, Howard Safir — put Kelling's philosophy into practice by, for example, cleaning up graffiti in the city's subways. Giuliani and police officials attribute the city's sharp reduction in crime in part to the public-order maintenance approach.

Critics, however, say New York's predominantly white police force has also been guilty of overly aggressive enforcement, especially in minority neighborhoods. They also say that the declining crime rate in the city mirrors trends nationwide that may be due in large part to economic factors, such as the decline in unemployment.

Kelling acknowledges the criticism of New York police in the torture of Haitian immigrant Abner Louima in 1997 and the killing of West African immigrant Amadou Diallo last year. But he calls the Louima case an isolated incident and the Diallo killing a "terrible tragedy" that reflected the risks of police enforcement in high-crime neighborhoods. "The rap that the police of New York City are out there ravaging the African-American community is just a sound bite," Kelling says.

The criticism of New York police, Kelling says, reflects a politicization that obscures a broad consensus in favor of making police departments more accountable on a neighborhood level. "The middle left and the middle right should be rejoicing together," he says.

For his part, Williams says that police themselves have come to view community policing more favorably.

"When I became a police officer 30 years ago, the police didn't want community involvement," Williams says. "We saw that as interference. Now we see the community as a valuable partner in crime control. One of the big changes is this idea that working with the community is positive."

---

[1] For background, see Richard L. Worsnop, "Community Policing," *The CQ Researcher*, Feb. 5, 1993, pp. 97-120; Samuel Walker, *Popular Justice: A History of American Criminal Justice* (2d ed., 1998), pp. 238-239.

[2] George L. Kelling and Catherine M. Coles, *Fixing Broken Windows: Restoring Order and Reducing Crime in Our Communities* (1996). Coles is a research associate at the Rutgers University School of Criminal Justice, and is Kelling's wife.

ary 1995. The state said it would adopt an official policy prohibiting racial profiling and, significantly, maintain detailed records of motorist stops to be provided to the ACLU to monitor any patterns of discrimination. Wilkins and his family were also awarded $50,000 plus attorney fees.

Critics of racial profiling won another settlement late last year after New Jersey officials acknowledged that some state troopers had singled out black and Hispanic motorists for anti-drug enforcement. The long-simmering issue recently erupted in the state when the head of the state police, Carl Williams, was quoted as saying it was "most likely a minority group" that was involved with marijuana or cocaine. The state's Republican governor, Christine Todd Whitman, fired Williams on Feb. 28.

Less than two months later, Whitman appeared with the state's attorney general at a news conference on April 20 to release a two-month study that confirmed a stark racial pattern in traffic stops by troopers at some stations. At year's end, the state signed an agreement with the U.S. Justice Department mandating an overhaul of the state police to end racial profiling and agreeing to the appointment of a federal monitor to oversee implementation of the accord.

The shift of opinion on the issue could be seen in comments by candidates in the 2000 presidential campaign. The two leading Democrats — Vice President Al Gore and former New Jersey Sen. Bill Bradley — both spoke out against racial profiling in a Jan. 17 debate in Iowa. Bradley drew blood on the issue by challenging Gore to "walk down that hallway" in the White House and get President Clinton to sign an executive order barring racial profiling by federal law enforcement agents. Gore aides later noted that Clinton has ordered federal agencies to collect data on the practice.

For his part, the Republican front-runner, Texas Gov. George W. Bush, also criticized racial profiling in a Jan. 10 campaign debate in Michigan. "No one wants racial profiling to take place in any state," Bush said. But Bush also said, "It's not the federal government's role to run state police departments." The ACLU criticized what it called Bush's "vague" statements and challenged him to issue an executive order in Texas barring the practice. ■

CURRENT SITUATION

Debating *Miranda*

The University of Utah's Cassell began his efforts to undercut the Supreme Court's *Miranda* decision when he worked for the Justice Department in the 1980s. Next month, he finds himself in the unusual position of arguing against an accused bank robber, Charles Dickerson, and the government itself in urging the high court to uphold a statute Congress passed to try to partly overturn *Miranda*.

Cassell has worked with the conservative Washington Legal Foundation (WLF) in several cases in an attempt to validate the law, Section 3501 of the federal Criminal Code, which seeks to replace the *Miranda* rule with a provision allowing the use of any "voluntary" confession. WLF intervened in Dickerson's case as the federal appeals court in Richmond, Va., took up the government's appeal of a trial judge's decision to bar his statements to police on grounds of a *Miranda* violation.

In its appeal, the government ignored Section 3501 and instead challenged the judge's finding that Dickerson had not been Mirandized before making a crucial admission that he had driven the pickup truck used by the suspect accused of actually carrying out the robberies. But Cassell argued that the trial judge had been wrong to disregard Section 3501 in determining whether the government could introduce Dickerson's statements as evidence at trial.

Reuters/Sam Mircovich

The four LAPD officers accused in the beating of Rodney King in March 1991 were, clockwise from top left, Laurence Powell, Stacey Koon, Theodore Briseno, and Timothy Wind. The four were acquitted in state court, but Koon and Powell were convicted in federal court of violating King's civil rights.

The appeals court panel agreed and went on to declare that Congress had acted within its power in passing the law. "Congress has the power to overrule judicially created rules of evidence and procedure that are not required by the Constitution," Judge Michael Williams wrote in the 2-1 decision. "As a consequence, we hold that the admissibility of confessions in federal court is governed by Section 3501, rather than the judicially created rule of *Miranda*." [21]

In urging the Supreme Court to overturn the ruling, Dickerson's attorney, James W. Hundley, argued that the law was unconstitutional. "Only the Supreme Court may alter *Miranda*'s requirements," the Fairfax, Va., lawyer wrote. Hundley acknowledged that the *Miranda* court suggested that Congress and state legislatures might craft their own procedural protections for police interrogation. But Section 3501, he said, "makes no provision whatsoever for procedures at least as effective in apprising individuals of their right to remain silent and assuring that exercise of that right will be honored."

The Justice Department joined Dickerson in urging the high court to invalidate the law. *Miranda* and subsequent cases refining the decision "represent an exercise of this Court's authority to implement and effectuate constitutional rights, and, accordingly, those decisions are binding on Congress," the government lawyers argued. Nor is there any reason to overrule *Miranda*, the government said. The ruling has proved to be easy for both police and courts to administer, the government lawyers argued, and overruling the decision would weaken public confidence in the criminal-justice system as well as in the Supreme Court itself.

With both of the parties urging reversal of the appeals court opinion, the high court appointed Cassell as a "friend of the court" to urge an affirmance. In his brief — filed on March 9 — he insisted that Congress had the power to "modify" what he called *Miranda*'s "overprotective and extraconstitutional features." He also contended that the list of factors cited in the law for evaluating the voluntariness of a confession — including the giving of *Miranda*-type warnings — "amply provides" needed protections for criminal suspects. In fact, Cassell said, police would probably continue to give *Miranda* warnings if the law was upheld. "The statute, as well as numerous other legal rules, makes it very much in every officer's interest to continue to give them," he said.

Civil-liberties groups and law enforcement organizations weighed in with friend-of-the-court briefs on both sides of the case. The ACLU maintained that even with *Miranda*, police go to "sometimes illegal lengths" to get a confession from a suspect. Those incidents, the ACLU warned, "provide a disturbing glimpse of what police practices could become in a world without *Miranda* — where police need not tell citizens of their right to remain silent, and need not respect that right once invoked."

In an opposing brief, however, lawyers representing the IACP, the National Sheriffs Association and Americans for Effective Law Enforcement echoed Cassell's prediction that police would continue to warn suspects of their rights even if the law was upheld. A court ruling upholding the law, the law enforcement brief concluded, would "take *Miranda*'s salutary purpose of ensuring voluntary confessions to a higher level of refinement and development."

Cassell says he is "optimistic that I'm going to prevail." But Scheidegger of the Criminal Justice Legal Foundation concedes that upholding the law is "an uphill battle. It requires the court to embrace the idea that it imposed rules on the states that aren't required by the Constitution."

On the opposite side, defenders of *Miranda* also expect a close fight, though they expect the court to nullify the law. "It's going to be a really close decision, 5-4, upholding *Miranda*," defense lawyer Kemler predicts.

For his part, though, Indiana law Professor Bradley feels certain that the court will not uphold the law. "There's no reason to think that the Supreme Court's going to do it," Bradley says. "If *Miranda* were gone, the whole voluntariness can of worms would be reopened in every confession. You'd see courts climbing into the whole interrogation thing again."

Judging Police

Four New York City police officers, in plainclothes and an unmarked car, are patrolling a high-crime neighborhood around midnight in the Bronx. They spot a figure that appears to be lurking at the entrance to an apartment building. Their suspicions aroused, they stop, get out of the car, and call out, "Sir, please. New York police. We need a word with you."

The man turns and goes into the vestibule of the building. He does not respond to the officers' request to show his hands. Instead, he reaches in his pocket and pulls out a black object. "Gun! He's got a gun!" Officer Sean Carroll yells. Carroll and Edward McMellon begin firing. By the end of the incident, they have emptied their pistols — 16 rounds each; officers Kenneth Boss and Richard Murphy fire five and four rounds, respectively.

That is how the four white officers say Amadou Diallo, a 22-year-old immigrant from Guinea, died on the night of Feb. 4, 1999. Only as the West African street vendor lay dying — inside the building where he lived — did the officers realize that the black object in his hand was a wallet, not a gun.

In emotional testimony to a biracial jury in Albany, N.Y., last month, the officers described the incident as a tragic mistake. [22] The jurors — including four black women — apparently agreed. After deliberating for 21 hours over 2½ days, the state court jury on Feb. 25 acquitted the officers of all charges — including murder, manslaughter and reckless homicide.

New Yorkers — politicians and public alike — were divided in their reactions to the verdict. [23] "I think this jury reaffirms our belief in the American system of justice," Giuliani declared. But former Mayor David Dinkins, who is black, was outraged by the verdict. "This will send the wrong message to those members of the Street Crime Unit who walk around saying, 'We own the night,' " Dinkins said.

Lawyers in the case aired similarly divergent views. Defense attorney Stephen Worth, who represented McMellon, said the verdict showed the jurors understood the difficulties faced by police. "The point is the police officers have to be able to do their job and do it the right way." But Bronx District Attorney Robert Johnson said, "This case raises a lot of issues about police tactics."

The acquittals did not end the legal proceedings stemming from the shooting. U.S. Attorney Mary Jo White said her office and the Justice Department's Civil Rights Division will review the case to determine whether any federal civil rights laws were violated. Diallo's parents plan to file a civil lawsuit against the city. And the officers could still face administrative charges within the department.

One expert said the case illustrates the risks of New York's aggressive "zero-tolerance" enforcement — a policing strategy that its supporters say has helped bring down the city's crime rate.

"The strategy is difficult to manage in a way that achieves the crime-control benefits that it is intended to achieve and at the same time respects civil liberties and also doesn't generate ill will in the community," says Robert Worden, a professor of criminal justice and public policy at the State University of New York in Albany.

"It's possible, in principle, to do that, but it's difficult in practice," Worden says. "It's difficult to retain a commitment to that kind of proactive policing while ensuring that the officers do so with respect for the individuals."

Watching for Profiling

Alberto Lovato, a professional musician and preschool teacher, was stopped by Los Angeles police officers last year, ordered out of his truck at gunpoint, forced to lie face down on the ground, handcuffed and accused of being a gang member — all before the officers looked at his driver's license or registration. "I was afraid for my life," Lovato recalled last month at a news conference announcing a federal civil rights suit brought by three African-Americans and Lovato and a second Latino seeking to block the Los Angeles Police Department from using race as a factor in investigative stops.

All five of the plaintiffs committed no offense other than "driving while black or brown," Ramona Ripston, executive director of the ACLU of Southern California, remarked at the Feb. 10 news conference. "There is no way in the world what happened to them would have occurred if they were white."

> **"There was a grossly disproportionate number of minority motorists who were being stopped and searched on I-95."**
>
> ***— Deborah Jeon, Attorney, ACLU of Maryland***

The suit asks for a court order barring racial profiling and requiring the police department to collect and maintain racial data on traffic stops. ACLU officials noted that 70 municipalities in California have already agreed to gather such information on a voluntary basis. LAPD officials declined to comment on the suit or on the general issue of profiling. In the past, however, Chief Bernard Parks, who is black, has said that race can be used "in conjunction with other circumstances" to justify a detention. [24]

The Los Angeles suit now joins with other ACLU legal attacks on racial profiling on both coasts. The ACLU of Northern California filed suit against the California Highway Patrol and the state's Bureau of Narcotics Enforcement (BNE) last June on behalf of a Latino attorney, Curtis Rodriguez. Rodriguez became suspicious while he was driving on a state highway in June 1998 after he observed five Latino drivers stopped by CHP or BNE officers within a 10-mile stretch. Rodriguez himself was stopped a while later and his car searched without his permission. The officer let him go after 20 minutes without issuing a ticket.

The ACLU's suits in Maryland and New Jersey are both continuing despite agreements by both states to end racial profiling. In Maryland, ACLU lawyers went back into court in late 1996 claiming that the state was not complying with the January 1995 settlement. As evidence, the lawyers cited racial data that the state had agreed to collect and turn over to the ACLU to check implementation of the agreement.

"The numbers began to come in and immediately it jumped out at you that when you looked at the Interstate-95 corridor, there was a grossly disproportionate number of minority motorists who were being stopped and searched," says Deborah Jeon, a managing attorney with the ACLU of Maryland. Jeon says initially about 85 percent of motorists stopped were minorities; the number fell to 70 percent but has remained near that level since.

In New Jersey, the ACLU is proceeding with its class-action suit filed in state court in New Brunswick even though the Justice Department nego-

At Issue:

Is the federal law limiting enforcement of the Miranda *decision constitutional?*

yes

Paul G. Cassell
Professor, University of Utah College of Law

BRIEF OF COURT-APPOINTED AMICUS CURIAE, *CHARLES THOMAS DICKERSON v. UNITED STATES*, MARCH 9, 2000

The ultimate question in this case is whether the federal criminal-justice system must exclude from evidence a criminal suspect's voluntary statement, despite an Act of Congress to the contrary. *Miranda v. Arizona* automatically excludes such a statement if it was given in response to custodial questioning without the required warnings. It enforces that exclusion on the basis of an irrebuttable presumption that such questioning by police must in every case have coerced the confession. . . . Nothing in the Constitution requires this uncompromising rule or strips the elected branches of their authority to modify it.

Congress' decision to enact Section 3501 was consistent with the Constitution. *Miranda* did not, and of course could not, simply redraft the Fifth Amendment to include a new constitutional right . . . Later pronouncements by the Court have confirmed that *Miranda*'s exclusionary rule was instead a preventive measure. . . . Because *Miranda*'s exclusionary rule was in this sense judicially improvised, rather than constitutionally required, *Miranda* necessarily accommodates legislative modification. Accordingly, there is neither need nor reason to overrule *Miranda* in order to uphold Section 3501.

The benefits of *Miranda* are preserved virtually intact by Section 3501. There is ample reason to believe that *Miranda* warnings will remain a standard [police] practice, because the statute, as well as numerous other legal rules, makes it very much in every officer's interest to continue to give them.

What Section 3501 changes is not so much the officer's incentive to give warnings but rather *Miranda*'s draconian remedy for any defect in giving them . . . As Congress understood, the automatic character of *Miranda*'s exclusionary rule is excessive because, heedless of the costs, it excludes confessions that manifestly were not produced by the police coercion that was *Miranda*'s principal target.

So long as involuntary confessions remain banned, as they are under Section 3501, and so long as trial courts are empowered [to] thwart any police behavior that produces involuntary confessions — again as they are under the statute — *Miranda*'s automatic exclusionary rule is unnecessary to preserve the full breadth of a suspect's Fifth Amendment right. . . . Because *Miranda*'s automatic rule excluding unwarned statements extends beyond the Fifth Amendment's bar on actually compelled statements, Congress was free to balance for itself the costs and benefits of that automatic rule and to supersede it with a rule more in keeping with the facts of each case and more faithful to the . . . Fifth Amendment.

no

Seth P. Waxman
Solicitor general of the United States

BRIEF FOR THE UNITED STATES, *CHARLES THOMAS DICKERSON v. UNITED STATES, JAN. 28, 2000*

Because the *Miranda* decision is of constitutional dimension, Congress may not legislate a contrary rule unless this Court were to overrule *Miranda*. We submit that principles of stare decisis do not favor the overruling of *Miranda* . . . In the 34 years since that decision was handed down, it has become embedded in the law. . . . If *Miranda* were to be overruled, this Court would have to disavow a long line of its cases that have interpreted *Miranda*, and it would have to overrule directly at least 11 cases that have reaffirmed that a confession obtained in violation of *Miranda* must be suppressed in the government's [main case]. At this date, there is no sufficient justification to overrule the balance struck in *Miranda* between the need for police questioning and the privilege against compelled self-incrimination, and there are substantial benefits to retaining that balance.

We acknowledge that there is a profound cost to the truth-finding function of a criminal trial when probative evidence is suppressed. . . . In many respects, however, *Miranda* is beneficial to law enforcement. Its core procedures provide clear guidance to law enforcement officers, and thus are not difficult to administer. If those procedures are followed, a defendant will frequently forgo any challenge to the voluntariness of an ensuing confession. . . . By contrast, the totality-of-the-circumstances test that was the sole measure of a confession's admissibility before *Miranda*, and that would govern in its absence, would be much more difficult for the police and the courts to apply and much more uncertain in application.

There is no sufficient change in the factual premises on which this Court based its decision in *Miranda* that would justify revisiting its holding. Although technological changes such as the availability of videotaping — might be of relevance as a part of a package of safeguards intended to provide alternative protection for the Fifth Amendment privilege, Section 3501 does not adopt those safeguards or any others to ensure that a suspect is aware of his rights and has an opportunity to exercise them.

Finally, both the confidence of the public in the fairness of the criminal-justice system and the stability of this Court's constitutional jurisprudence . . . may be expected to suffer if *Miranda* were overruled. Those values weigh heavily against discarding the essence of the balance that the Court struck in *Miranda*. Accordingly, *Miranda* should not be overruled. . . .

tiated an agreement with the state to end racial profiling in December.

"What's in the consent decree hasn't happened yet," says Lenore Lapidus, legal director of the ACLU of New Jersey. "Until we see what changes are actually made, we're not willing to forgo our claims." The ACLU's suit, filed under the state's anti-discrimination law, seeks damages as well as court-ordered changes to bar profiling.

Meanwhile, two states — Connecticut and North Carolina — have begun collecting racial data on traffic stops under laws that went into effect at the start of the year. In California, however, the state's Democratic governor, Gray Davis, vetoed a bill in September that would have required state and local law enforcement agencies to gather such information. ■

FOR MORE INFORMATION

American Civil Liberties Union, 125 Broad St., New York, N.Y. 10004; (212) 549-2500; www.aclu.org. The ACLU has been active on racial profiling, use of force and other police practices issues.

Community Policing Consortium, 1726 M St. N.W., Suite 801, Washington, D.C. 20036; (800) 833-3085; www.communitypolicing.org. The federally funded project is a consortium of five law enforcement groups aimed at promoting community-policing projects throughout the country.

Fraternal Order of Police, Grand Lodge, 1410 Donelson Pike, A-17, Nashville, Tenn. 37217; (615) 399-0900; www.grandlodgefop.org. The FOP is the largest membership organization representing rank-and-file law enforcement officers.

International Association of Chiefs of Police, 515 N. Washington St., Alexandria, Va. 22314-2357; (703) 836-6767; www.theiacp.org. The IACP is the world's largest organization of police executives.

National Association of Criminal Defense Lawyers, 1025 Connecticut Ave. N.W., Suite 901, Washington, D.C. 20036; (202) 872-8600; www.criminaljustice.org. NACDL is the largest organization exclusively representing criminal defense lawyers.

Police Foundation, 1201 Connecticut Ave. N.W., Suite 200; Washington, D.C. 20036; (202) 833-1460; www.policefoundation.org. The foundation sponsors research evaluating and promoting innovation in policing.

OUTLOOK

The Public's Trust

In its report on corruption in the Rampart Division, the LAPD Board of Inquiry acknowledged that the scandal had "devastated our relationship with the public we serve." In New York City, there was also evidence that the Louima and Diallo cases had weakened public confidence in the police.

Some New York prosecutors reported that grand jurors are more skeptical of police officers' testimony than in the past. And a *New York Times* survey of about 100 city residents after the acquittal in the Diallo shooting found that many people believe police show too little respect for citizens — although many also recognized the difficulties police face in doing their jobs. [25]

Americans also have become concerned about police conduct on the issue of racial profiling. A Gallup Poll conducted last fall found that 59 percent of those surveyed believed that racial profiling is "widespread" — including 56 percent of whites and 77 percent of blacks. And 81 percent of respondents said they disapprove of the practice.

Still, the Gallup Poll found that most Americans — including a majority of blacks and a substantial majority of whites — have a favorable opinion of their local and their state police. (*See box, p. 68.*) Some local police departments have their own evidence of public confidence. San Diego's police department — often cited as a model of "community policing" — said that a recent survey by an outside consultant found that 89 percent of those surveyed expressed approval of the police. [26]

Public confidence in police will continue to be tested as the current controversies are played out. In Los Angeles, the police department is continuing with disciplinary investigations against officers implicated in the Rampart scandal. Criminal investigations by the district attorney's office are proceeding slowly, and probes by federal agencies are only now getting under way. The city is also bracing for a flurry of civil lawsuits: The City Council has been told that the city's liability in wrongful-injury and imprisonment cases could reach $120 million.

In New York, meanwhile, the four officers acquitted of criminal charges in the Diallo shooting still face administrative proceedings that could result in anything from a reprimand to dismissal. The Justice Department is promising to complete its review of the incident within a few weeks.

A federal civil-rights prosecution appears unlikely, however, given the lack of evidence of any intent by the officers to violate Diallo's rights.

The Supreme Court's airing of the *Miranda* case next month also will revive public interest in the question of police interrogation and use of confessions. Most legal experts expect the court to reaffirm *Miranda* and strike down the federal law (Section 3501) aimed at limiting the ruling. And some police executives say that a decision to relax *Miranda* would actually unsettle public confidence in police.

"Once you say that a confession is valid without informing people of their rights, you've got problems," says the Police Foundation's Williams.

Police work has clearly changed dramatically in the three decades since the *Miranda* ruling. Today, police chiefs and officers appear to be more careful about staying within legal limits and more willing to discipline individual officers who step over the line. "I've never met a chief who didn't want to prosecute someone" who was found to have used improper force, says Fredericksburg Police Chief Powers.

"It's now more true than it was in the past that officers will report misconduct by other officers," Walker says. "In some of the better departments, they've taken some important steps toward self-policing."

For his part, Boston University's Delattre says the news media's focus on misconduct cases may give the public a misleading image of police.

"I've met a fair number of people who don't belong in policing, who should have been weeded out, and I've met many, many more cops who are basically decent people," Delattre says. "There are a lot of police who belong there, and they don't get much acknowledgment." ■

Notes

[1] Scott Glover and Matt Lait, "L.A. Police Group Often Broke Law, Transcripts Say," *Los Angeles Times*, Feb. 10, 2000, p. A1. For other articles, see the *Times'* Web site: www.latimes.com/rampart.

[2] Clyde Haberman, "Despite Diallo, Data Show Gun Restraint," *The New York Times*, Feb. 4, 2000, p. B1.

[3] International Association of Chiefs of Police, "Police Use of Force in America," October 1999.

[4] See Christopher A. Darden, *In Contempt* (1996), p. 110; "Cochran & Grace," "Johnnie Cochran: Driving While Black," Court TV, March 23, 1997, cited in David A. Harris, "The Stories, the Statistics, and the Law: Why 'Driving While Black' Matters," *Minnesota Law Review*, Vol. 84 (1999), pp. 265-266.

[5] Samuel Walker, *Popular Justice: A History of American Criminal Justice* (1980), p. 61. Other historical background is also drawn from this first edition and from a revised and updated edition published in 1998.

[6] National Commission on Law Observance and Enforcement, *Lawless in Law Enforcement* (1931), p. 103, cited in Walker, *op. cit.*, p. 174.

[7] The cases are *Brown v. Mississippi* (1936) and *Lisenba v. California* (1941).

[8] Background drawn from Yale Kamisar *et al.*, *Modern Criminal Procedure: Cases, Comments, and Questions* (8th ed. 1994), as summarized in Richard A. Leo, "The Impact of Miranda Revisited," *Journal of Criminal Law and Criminology*, Vol. 86, No. 3 (1996), pp. 624-625.

[9] Walker, *op. cit.*, pp. 194-199.

[10] The cases are *Mapp v. Ohio* (1961) and *Gideon v. Wainwright* (1963).

[11] Account of interrogation taken from Paul G. Cassell, "The Statute That Time Forgot: 18 U.S.C. Section 3501 and the Overhauling of Miranda," *Iowa Law Review*, Vol. 85 (1999), pp. 183-191. The teenaged victim said she thought Miranda could be the assailant, but could not be positive. After the line-up, Miranda asked if the teenager and a second assault victim had identified him. "Yes, Ernie, they did," a detective replied.

[12] ABA Special Commission on Criminal Justice in a Free Society, Criminal Justice in Crisis (1988), p. 28.

[13] Charles Fried, *Order and Law* (1990), p. 46.

[14] The case is *Davis v. United States* (1994).

[15] The case is *Withrow v. Williams* (1993).

[16] For background, see Richard L. Worsnop, "Police Brutality," *The CQ Researcher*, Sept. 6, 1991, pp. 633-656.

[17] Walker, *op. cit.* (2d ed.), p. 197.

[18] See *Ibid.*, pp. 232-234.

[19] Cited in Worsnop, *op. cit.*, p. 644.

[20] Cases cited in Randall Kennedy, *Race, Crime, and the Law* (1997), p. 152.

[21] The appeals court ruling in *Dickerson v. United States* can be found on the Web site www.findlaw.com; the decision is also posted on Professor Cassell's Web site: www.law.utah.edu/faculty/bios/cassell, along with many other materials relating to the case.

[22] See *The New York Times*, Feb. 15, 2000, p. A1; Feb. 16, 2000, p. A25.

[23] Reaction drawn from *The New York Times*, Feb. 26, 2000, p. A1; *The Washington Post*, Feb. 26, 2000, p. A1.

[24] See *Los Angeles Times*, Feb. 11, 2000, p. B8.

[25] See *The New York Times*, March 9, 2000 (prosecutors' comments), p. A27; March 5, 2000, p. A1 (public attitudes).

[26] Cited in *The New York Times*, March 4, 2000, p. A1.

Bibliography

Selected Sources Used

Books

Baker, Liva, *Miranda: Crime, Law and Politics*, Atheneum, 1983.
Baker, author of several books on legal topics, traces the history of the *Miranda* case from his initial arrest through the Supreme Court's decision and its political and legal impact over the next decade and a half. The book includes a 15-page bibliography and source notes.

Delattre, Edwin J., *Character and Cops: Ethics in Policing (3d ed.)*, AEI Press, 1996.
Delattre, a philosopher and dean of Boston University's School of Education, examines questions of ethics relating to a variety of police issues, including corruption, discretion, management, recruitment and training.

Fogelson, Robert M., *Big-City Police*, Harvard University Press, 1977.
The book provides a survey history of police in major U.S. cities from the machine-politics days of the late 19th century through the reform efforts of the 20th century, which Fogelson says had stalled as he was writing the book in the mid-1970s. The book includes detailed notes.

Geller, William A., and Hans Toch (eds.), *Police Violence: Understanding and Controlling Police Abuse of Force*, Yale University Press, 1996.
The book includes essays by 20 contributors on issues relating to use of force, including the role of officer selection and training and the role of administrative or outside review. Geller is a former associate director of the Police Executive Research Forum; Toch is a professor at the School of Criminal Justice, State University of New York at Albany. Each chapter has detailed notes; the book also has a 40-page bibliography

Kelling, George F., and Catherine M. Coles, *Fixing Broken Windows: Restoring Order and Reducing Crime in Our Communities*, Free Press, 1996.
This influential book outlines a crime-control strategy for big cities based on maintaining order and devoting attention to disorderly behavior — so-called quality-of-life crimes. Kelling is a professor at Rutgers University's School of Criminal Justice; Coles, his wife, is a research associate at the school.

Kennedy, Randall, Race, *Crime, and the Law*, Pantheon, 1997.
Kennedy, a professor at Harvard Law School, includes a chapter on racial profiling in this strongly argued critique of racial disparities in the criminal-justice system. The book includes detailed notes and a 49-page bibliography.

Rosenbaum, Dennis P. (ed.), *The Challenge of Community Policing: Testing the Promises*, Sage Publications, 1994.
The book includes 19 essays evaluating the impact of community policing within police departments and on communities. Rosenbaum is a professor of criminal justice at the State University of New York in Albany.

Walker, Samuel, *Popular Justice: A History of American Criminal Justice*, Oxford University Press, 1980.
Walker, a professor of criminal justice at the University of Nebraska at Omaha, traces the history of policing in the United States from Colonial times and the creation of the first urban police forces in the 1830s through the professionalization of the police in the 20th century and the changes in policing during the due-process revolution of the 1960s. In a second edition, published in 1998, Walker carries the history through the more conservative law-and-order era of the 1980s and '90s. Walker is also author of the forthcoming *Police Accountability: The Role of Citizen Oversight* (Wadsworth, 2000).

Articles

Harris, David A., "The Stories, the Statistics, and the Law: Why 'Driving While Black' Matters," *Minnesota Law Review*, Vol. 84 (1999), pp. 265-326.
Harris, a law professor at the University of Toledo, provides background about and a strongly argued critique of racial profiling. Harris also authored an earlier report on the issue for the American Civil Liberties Union, "Driving While Black: Racial Profiling on Our Nation's Highways" (June 1999). The report can be found on the ACLU's Web site: www.aclu.org/profiling/report.

Reports and Studies

International Association of Chiefs of Police, "Police Use of Force in America," October 1999.
The 47-page report found that police use force infrequently — about 3.5 times per 10,000 calls for service in 1999 — and that excessive force was used in fewer than one-half of 1 percent of those instances. The report is based on data voluntarily submitted by police forces around the country to a federally funded database.

National Institute of Justice, "Use of Force by Police: Overview of National and Local Data," October 1999.
The 76-page report consists of six chapters written by academic experts on the use of force by police. The report's major conclusion is that the incidence of wrongful use of force by police is "unknown."

5 Racism and the Black Middle Class

DAVID MASCI

By any measure, Wanda Alexander is a success. Just 39, she has built her own real estate consulting business and lives in Upper Marlboro, Md., a comfortable suburb south of Washington.

But Alexander's journey to reach the American dream wasn't easy. As a black woman, she faced obstacles that she believes were placed in her way because of her race. Before striking out on her own, for example, she watched her less experienced white colleagues receive training and promotions ahead of her. "I got tired of people telling me in subtle and sometimes overt ways that I would never do better than I had because of my race and gender," she says.

Stories like Alexander's are common among black professionals. Many feel anger and frustration even as they achieve personal and professional success. Indeed, polls show that a solid majority of well-off African-Americans still feel that racism is an obstacle to their advancement. A 1995 poll commissioned by *The Washington Post*, the Kaiser Family Foundation and Harvard University found that 84 percent of all black Americans with an annual household income of between $30,000 and $75,000, believed that "past and present discrimination is the major reason for the economic and social ills blacks face." Perhaps surprisingly, only 66 percent of poor and working-class blacks felt the same way. [1]

The sense that discrimination is still a problem for middle-class blacks is hard for many Americans to understand. By all accounts, the post-civil rights era has been a time of great growth for the black middle class. Today, more than one-third of all African-Americans meet the fiscal definition of middle class: They reside in households that earn the median national income of $35,000 per year or more. In the 1960s, fewer than 10 percent of black Americans fit this description. Moreover, the number of black doctors, lawyers and engineers has grown exponentially since World War II. Indeed, the percentage of African-Americans in white-collar jobs has jumped from under 6 percent in 1940 to roughly half today. [2]

Douglas Graham/Congressional Quarterly

Blacks also have made great strides in the business world. The number of successful black entrepreneurs is increasing every year in fields as diverse as finance, software and manufacturing. Blacks serve as the presidents of several big U.S. corporations, including American Express and Maytag, putting them just one rung below CEO.

And yet, in the minds of many well-to-do African-Americans, all is not well. "Despite its evident prosperity, much of America's black middle class is in pain," writes *Newsweek* reporter Ellis Cose in his 1993 book, *The Rage of a Privileged Class*. The reason, according to Cose, is that white America has broken its "covenant" with blacks. The idea, he writes, "that if you work hard, get a good education and play by the rules you will be allowed to advance and achieve to the limits of your ability" has never been fully realized. [3]

For many middle-class African-Americans, the "pain" is felt most keenly in the workplace, where they say their race is still a factor in hiring and promotion. "Discrimination still exists, even if it's masked well," says Joanne Dowdell, an African- who is vice president for new product development at Washington Business Information Inc.

Many scholars of race relations echo such sentiments, arguing that while some businesses — especially large corporations — have become more open to blacks and other minorities, racism is still a big problem. "It's still an obstacle. It just takes a more subtle form," says Bart Landry, an associate professor of sociology at the University of Maryland at College Park.

Some white managers mean well and don't know that they are discriminating, Landry and others say. But they feel that many managers still view African-Americans as lazy or less capable than whites, or both. And so, they say, even at companies that pride themselves on hiring and promoting minorities, few African-Americans ever rise to the top or even to positions of real responsibility. "People in control want to work with people who look like them," says Ronald Walters, a professor of government at Maryland. As a result, Walters and others point out, there are no black CEOs at America's largest, most powerful corporations.

But other observers argue that discrimination is no longer a great stumbling block for African-Americans. In fact, says Shelby Steele, a research fellow at the Hoover Institution, universities, companies and

From *The CQ Researcher*, January 23, 1998.

How Are Blacks Doing?

African-Americans don't think they are faring as well as whites think they are, according to a comprehensive Gallup Poll in early 1997. But the poll also showed substantial improvement over time in blacks' satisfaction with their lives.

How are blacks treated in your community?

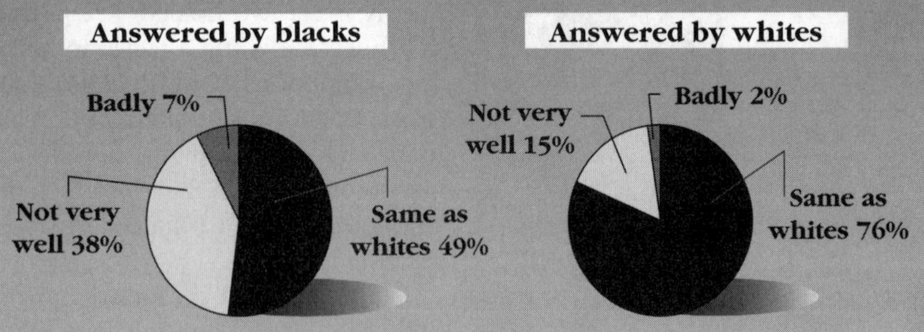

How do you feel about affirmative action?

	Answered by Blacks	Answered by Whites
Increase affirmative action	53%	22%
Keep affirmative action the same	29%	29%
Decrease affirmative action	12%	37%

Blacks in your community have as good a chance as whites to:

	Answered by Blacks	Answered by Whites
Get a job	46%	79%
Get housing	58%	86%
Get an education	63%	79%

Percent who think blacks are treated the same as whites in your community:

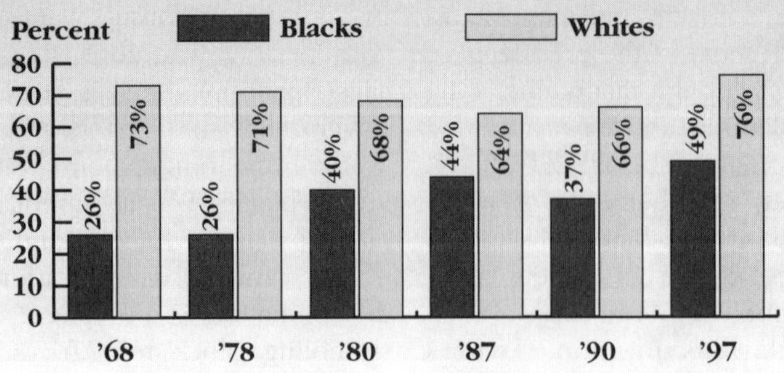

Source: The Gallup Organization conducted a telephone poll of 3,076 black and white Americans between Jan. 4 and Feb. 28, 1997.

the government are working hard to find, hire and promote blacks. "This is the new spirit of corporate America," says Steele, who is black.

Steele and others argue that the problem for African-Americans on the job isn't racism, but lack of progress in education and training. For instance, they point out, blacks — even from middle-class backgrounds — don't score as well on standardized tests and are more likely to drop out of college than whites, even poor whites. [4] "The fact is that in many [occupational] areas there is a very small pool of qualified black applicants, and that's the problem," says Gerald Reynalds, president of the Center for New Black Leadership.

According to Steele, Reynalds and others, the view that racism is still the primary obstacle to black advancement on the job and elsewhere has hurt African-Americans by shifting the emphasis from self-improvement to fighting discrimination. "People put too much stock in discrimination today," says Walter Williams, chairman of the Economics Department at George Mason University in Fairfax, Va. Blaming discrimination, says Williams, has undercut blacks' advancement by leading them to rely on racial preferences instead of their own efforts.

To begin with, Williams and other black conservatives say, preferences created by the policy known as "affirmative action" are damaging to society as a whole because it is fundamentally unfair to judge someone based on race, regardless of the reason. Such efforts lead to resentment among whites and bolster stereotypes of black inferiority.

But, Williams argues, the policy does the greatest harm to those it is intended to help because it lowers the standards by which African-Americans are judged. Giving someone a preference "doesn't do them any favor," he says, because people who don't have to work as hard to get ahead, won't. In other words, by lowering standards for African-Americans, companies, universities and others are giving them a disincentive to achieve on their own.

The net result of such assistance, Williams says, is that it produces problems when the beneficiaries of affirmative action are eventually forced to compete head to head with everyone else. It also makes blacks "passive," in Steele's view. "It makes me into someone who cannot move forward unless white people are benevolent and help me move forward," he says.

But supporters of affirmative action counter that it is necessary simply to give African-Americans a chance to succeed in the face of past and present racism. The bottom line, they say, is that there is no level playing field when it comes to competition between blacks and whites. White men have controlled all the levers of power in American society from the beginning, they say, conferring upon them an advantage that did not go away when the Civil Rights Act of 1964 was passed.

"The effects of discrimination linger," says Cecilia Conrad, a research associate at the Joint Center for Political and Economic Studies, which focuses on issues of interest to blacks. "Whites are still benefiting from Jim Crow," she adds.

But vestiges of traditional discrimination have been felt far beyond the workplace. For instance, until recently, many suburban areas were virtually off-limits to African-Americans. And while housing discrimination has not been entirely eliminated, most neighborhoods that were, in effect, reserved for whites are now open to black homeowners. Not surprisingly, the number of African-Americans living in the suburbs has risen dramatically in the last three decades. [5]

But some black thinkers argue that "black flight" from the inner cities has hurt African-Americans. As the best and the brightest have left for the suburbs, many formerly segregated communities, usually in cities, have degenerated into neighborhoods characterized by high crime, little economic opportunity and hopelessness. "Talented individuals and stable families have left, and left a vacuum," says Roy Brooks, a law professor at San Diego State University.

Brooks is among the blacks who urge middle-class African-Americans to move into black urban areas in order to revitalize them. They argue that black professionals can serve as role models for members of the underclass. In addition, they say, by living and shopping in these areas, professionals and other residents will increase economic opportunities in the neighborhood as businesses are established to serve them.

But many black professionals reject the notion that they should feel obliged to live in a poor, crime-ridden area in order to serve the less fortunate. "I want to live where I'm most comfortable," Alexander says. Elijah Anderson, a professor of ethnography at the University of Pennsylvania, agrees. "The bottom line is that people should be able to do what they want."

Anderson and others argue that there is no sense in working hard and succeeding if you can't live where you want to. In addition, he doubts that an influx of the black middle class back to the cities would make a big difference in the lives of poor African-Americans. Instead, he argues, the underclass needs training and jobs, not role models.

Besides, they contend, one does not have to live next door to someone in order to help them. "There are other ways that you can give back to the community," Dowdell says. Alexander and Dowdell, who lives in a predominantly white part of Washington, both work to help other African-Americans get ahead. Alexander, for instance, helps to finance scholarships for young, black women.

But others are torn over the issue. "You need good role models so that kids can see that there are legitimate alternatives to poverty," says Gavin Jackson, a human resources specialist at the Department of the Treasury, who lives in suburban Burtonsville, Md., with his wife and two children. At the same time, Jackson admits that he is not ready to move out of suburbia. "I can't sacrifice my children. I mean, we moved [to the suburbs] because the schools were better." [6]

Like many black professionals, Jackson feels the tug of group identity even as he strives to build a life for himself and his family. As Jackson and other African-Americans look toward the future, these are some of the questions they are asking:

Is racism still a big obstacle to advancement for many black professionals?

In November 1996, oil giant Texaco agreed to pay $176.1 million to settle a discrimination suit filed by 1,400 current and former black employees. Many of the workers who sued alleged that they had repeatedly lost out on promotions and raises because of their race. They also claimed that they were subjected to racial slurs and other indignities. [7]

For many black Americans, the Texaco case is simply the tip of a very large iceberg. According to recent polls, fully two-thirds of middle-class blacks think that discrimination is still a real problem in their lives. Racism, most of these professionals say, is a fact of life in corporate America, a fact that puts African-Americans at a serious disadvantage as they try to compete with whites in the workplace.

Many whites and others wonder how their black colleagues can still feel discriminated against. After all, they say, the days of Jim Crow, of overt, institutionalized racism, are over.

"It's not a nationwide problem," said Michael Losey, president and CEO of the Society for Human Resource Management. According to

Blacks in White-Collar Occupations

In stark contrast to 1940, when most blacks did manual labor, more than half the black women and a third of the men had white-collar jobs in 1990.

	1940	1970 (Percentage)	1990
Men			
Professionals	*1.8*	*7.8*	*9.4*
Proprietors, managers and officials	*1.3*	*4.7*	*6.7*
Clerical and sales	*2.1*	*9.2*	*15.9*
Total white-collar	*5.2*	*21.7*	*32.0*
Women			
Professionals	*4.3*	*10.8*	*15.9*
Proprietors, managers and officials	*0.7*	*1.9*	*7.6*
Clerical and sales	*1.4*	*23.4*	*35.4*
Total white-collar	*6.4*	*36.1*	*58.9*

Sources: Stephan and Abigail Thernstrom, America in Black and White: One Nation, Indivisible, *1997, based on U.S. Census Bureau,* 'Money Income in the U.S.: *1995."*

Losey, who is white, when a case like Texaco does occur, there is a reason people are shocked. He says that "many people recognize this as inconsistent with what they see in their community, what they see as their company policy where they work, what they see as a practice." [8]

But many black thinkers argue that discrimination encountered by minorities today is harder to recognize because it is much different from the obvious examples of past prejudice. "We are dealing not with overt racism, but a subtler form," says Professor Robert Hill, director of the Institute for Urban Research at Morgan State University in Baltimore.

Hill argues that many white managers don't know that they are discriminating against their black colleagues. "They are doing their best," he says, "but they don't realize that their best is not adequate." For instance, Hill says, whites exclude blacks from their network of close co-workers ("the buddy system"), which in effect excludes African-Americans from important decisions and promotions.

Others argue that many whites still view blacks as their intellectual inferiors. "A lot of white people have not really viewed black people close-up," says the University of Pennsylvania's Anderson, "operating instead on stereotypes."

And so, even at companies that try to hire and promote a lot of minorities, there are few black professionals in any important slots, says Sharon Collins, an associate professor of sociology at the University of Illinois in Chicago. "Black managers tend to go in the personnel or public relations departments," she add. "These don't tend to be the most career-enhancing jobs."

Moreover, says Conrad of the Joint Center for Economics and Politics, African-Americans are excluded from key posts because whites don't trust blacks to do the most important work in the corporation. "They tend not to be in the company's profit centers, like sales or product development," she says.

As a result, Collins and Conrad say, the very top of the corporate hierarchy includes very few black executives. In addition, they say, there are no black CEOs at *Fortune* 500 companies, with the exception of Beatrice Foods Inc., which is black-owned.

But other African-American thinkers reject the idea that black professionals are being held back in large numbers by discrimination. In fact, many say, large companies and government agencies are working overtime to hire and promote minorities. "Every major company is busting its ass looking for brown faces," says Reynalds of the Center for New Black Leadership.

The Hoover Institution's Steele, author of the best-selling treatise on race *The Content of Our Character*, agrees with Reynalds, pointing out that "in corporations, universities and the government, people are looking for ways to encourage and mentor blacks."

Steele, Reynalds and other thinkers are not saying that America is a color-blind society. "People have lost their minds if they think they can do away with prejudice," Reynalds says. But he believes that racism today is not a powerful enough force in our society to hold back minorities who want to succeed.

The problem, Reynalds, Steele and others say, isn't discrimination, but a lack of education and training. For instance, they point out, blacks do score significantly lower on standardized tests and are much more likely to have been involved in the criminal-justice system than whites. "If you've been convicted of a felony or don't have a proper education, that will be a much greater obstacle to job advancement than your race," Reynalds says.

Steele agrees, arguing that poverty and other social factors have "brought us to a point where we're not as competitive as other groups are."

But what about polls showing middle-class blacks' concern over discrimination and anger over the way society is treating them? Some, like Ward Connerly, the

California businessman behind Proposition 209, the ballot initiative ending affirmative action programs in California, say that African-American anger is due to outmoded attitudes about race. "I think part of our racial problem is that my fellow black Americans are so sensitive to the issue of racism that it almost becomes a self-fulfilling prophecy," he says. "You look for it, and by golly, it's there — whether it's real or not." [9]

Others are less forgiving. Steele, for instance, believes that African-Americans, either consciously or unconsciously, often cry racism because it produces results. "If I'm black and I'm angry, I'm more likely to get attention and get preferential treatment than if I'm black and not angry," he says. In short, the accusations of racism and the anger are tools that give black employees leverage over their white managers, who do not want to be accused of racism.

"This [behavior] trips white guilt and obligation and gets [blacks] preferential treatment, like a promotion or an all-black lounge at the office," Steele says. In many cases these African-American professionals convince themselves that they are victims. "We all tend to believe in what serves us, even if it's wrong," he says.

Lou Denatteis/Reuters

Marchers protesting Proposition 209 cross the Golden Gate Bridge led by Jesse Jackson, San Francisco Supervisor Mabel Teng and Mayor Willie Brown.

Do members of the black middle class have an obligation to other blacks to live in predominantly African-American neighborhoods, especially in poorer areas in the inner city?

Buying a home in the suburbs is the quintessential right of passage for middle-class Americans. But before the civil rights movement of the 1950s and '60s, African-Americans were not welcome in most suburban areas.

Today, the situation is different, although housing discrimination is far from eradicated. A recent study in the Washington, D.C., area, for instance, showed that many real estate agencies still "steer" minorities away from certain areas. But by and large, suburban enclaves that were once segregated are now open to African-Americans.

Statistics bear out this new interracial reality. Polls show that since 1960 the number of African-Americans living in suburban areas has more than doubled. Today roughly 32 percent of all black Americans live in the suburbs. [10] And in some areas, blacks comprise the majority of suburbanites. For instance, Prince George's County, Md., outside Washington, is now 62 percent African-American. [11]

For a member of the black middle class, the suburbs have the same allure that they do for their white counterparts: better schools, lower crime rates and bucolic settings usually not found in cities.

But some African-Americans view the middle-class exodus with dread and call for black professionals to move back to the urban areas where they grew up.

"Integration has resulted in a depletion of human and economic resources from the black community," says San Diego State's Brooks. "We need to find a way to reintegrate the black middle class into inner-city areas," Walters adds.

The problem, Brooks, Walters and others say, is that middle-class migration to the suburbs has drained traditionally black areas of some of their most productive and valuable citizens. In the past, when segregation forced all blacks to live together regardless of class, professionals and other accomplished African-Americans served as leaders and role models in the community. Today, they say, there is a void in many areas created by the absence of successful people. "They need to reconnect with their roots and serve as role models to the rest of the community," Walters says.

Walters also argues that "the middle class leaves behind a much weaker institutional base and a citizenry denuded of resources." For example, he says, the presence of middle-class residents gives the areas greater political clout, which in turn could lead to better city services, like police and sanitation. In addition, he says, middle-class children and par-

Blacks Flocked to the Suburbs

Many black Americans moved to the suburbs following the civil rights movement of the 1950s and '60s. From 1960 to 1995, the number of suburban blacks tripled, and the percentage of blacks who were suburbanites doubled.

Blacks in the Suburbs

	Number (in millions)	Percent of total black population	Percent of total suburban population
1950	2.2	15	5.5
1960	2.9	15.2	4.8
1970	3.6	16.1	4.8
1980	5.9	22.3	5.9
1995	10.6	31.9	8.1

Sources: Stephan and Abigail Thernstrom, America in Black and White: One Nation, Indivisible, *1997, based on data from* Statistical Abstract of the U.S.: 1974 *and U.S. Bureau of the Census.*

ents "raise the standards at schools, which benefits everyone."

Finally, Walters and Brooks argue, the presence of a large group of people with disposable income will give blighted areas an economic shot in the arm, which in turn will create needed jobs. "Businesses will be created to serve them, and they will start businesses of their own in the community," Brooks says.

The idea that the presence of a middle class is necessary for healthy community development has prompted a number of cities, including Philadelphia and Cleveland, to offer tax and other incentives to lure professionals back to inner-city neighborhoods long abandoned by all but the poor. Cleveland, for instance, is offering lots in rundown areas for as little as $100 to anyone willing to build a house and live there. The city also offers mortgage assistance and will waive property taxes for up to 15 years. "Cities cannot survive if they are full of old and poor people," says Cleveland Mayor Michael White, an African-American. [12]

The city's plan seems to be working. Since 1990, 2,400 new homes have been built in the special areas, almost all by African-Americans. More broadly, the percentage of black households nationwide with an income of $75,000 or more that have stayed in cities has remained at 48 percent throughout the 1990s. [13]

But while many thinkers on race applaud the back-to-the-city trend, others argue that middle-class African-Americans should not feel obligated to stay in or move back to inner cities. "I like the idea that people have choices . . . and if I want to move to a certain area because it's, say, close to work, I should be able to do that," says Conrad, who grew up in a segregated neighborhood. "If you have the money and wherewithal, you should live where you want to, period," agrees George Mason's Williams.

Others say that trying to push middle-class blacks back into their old, largely African-American neighborhoods is bad for both them and the country. To begin with, they argue, more blacks and whites should be living together, not trying to stay with their own kind. "What we're talking about here is resegregation, plain and simple," Anderson says. "We will lose the idea of making America into a universalist, egalitarian society," he says.

Anderson and others also argue that the middle-class African-Americans who move into inner-city neighborhoods are making a sacrifice in the name of racial unity. For one thing, he says, blacks are financially penalized when they go to sell their city houses because the only people who will want to purchase a home in these areas are other African-Americans. "This is a limited housing market because whites, Asians and other folks aren't interested in these neighborhoods," he says. "That's a bad way to play the capitalist game."

Finally, opponents of efforts to lure professionals back to cities argue that the presence of some middle-class African-Americans in the neighborhood isn't a solution to the real problems of the black underclass. "What inner-city blacks need is not the middle class but a real job base," Landry says. According to Landry and others, the presence of middle-class residents might improve local government and create a few new service jobs, but it won't generate the kind of employment, such as a factory work, that allows poorer residents the opportunity to make a decent living.

Landry also rejects the notion that black professionals will make a difference by serving as role models for their less fortunate brethren. "Black kids don't need these role models in that sense," he says, "because in our media age the role models and avenues to success are well-known."

Do middle-class African-Americans need affirmative action to have equal opportunities at school and work?

On Nov. 5, 1996, proponents of

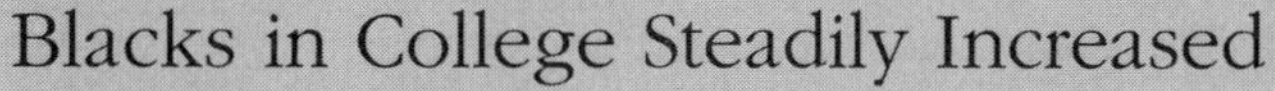

Blacks in College Steadily Increased

Four times as many blacks had attended college for at least four years in 1995 as in 1960.

Percent with Four Years or More of College

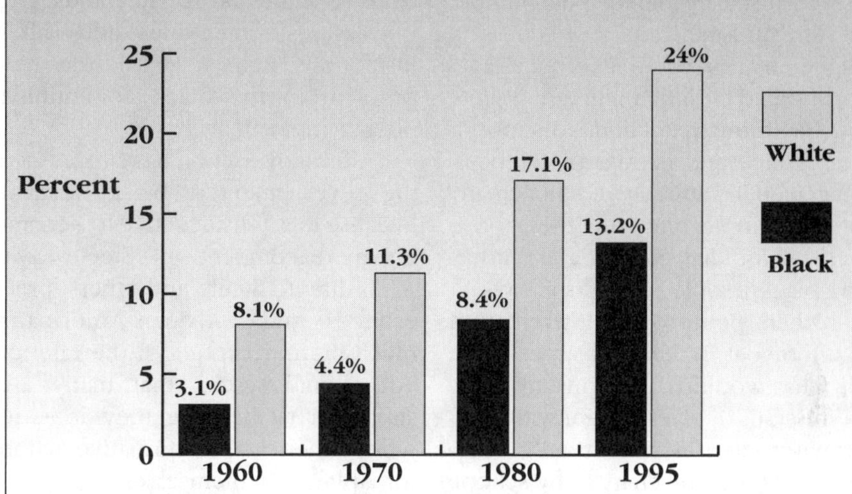

Sources: Stephan and Abigail Thernstrom, America in Black and White: One Nation, Indivisible, *1997, based on U.S. Census Bureau,* "Money Income in the U.S.: *1995."*

affirmative action suffered a stunning blow when voters in California passed Proposition 209, a ballot measure that outlawed the use of racial or gender preferences at all state government institutions. A year later, on Nov. 3, Prop. 209 went into effect when the Supreme Court refused to review an earlier Court of Appeals decision upholding the referendum's constitutionality. [14]

The success of Proposition 209 has inspired similar efforts in other parts of the country. Voters in Colorado and Ohio, among others, will have a chance to eliminate gender and racial preferences in the upcoming 1998 elections.

Meanwhile, recent court challenges to affirmative action programs also have proven successful. For instance, in 1996 the Supreme Court refused to review (and hence effectively upheld) a 5th Circuit Court of Appeals decision prohibiting the University of Texas from using race or gender in admissions. In New Jersey, a discrimination suit brought by a white teacher was settled before it went to the Supreme Court. Settlement was prompted by the likelihood that the court would rule that the affirmative action policy that led to the teacher's dismissal was unconstitutional. She had been laid off and a black teacher retained, although both had equal tenure and qualifications, because the school system wanted to maintain racial diversity.

To many black professionals, the success of efforts to eliminate or scale back affirmative action is both disheartening and misguided. "A lot of white people say: 'We've solved racism, so just get on with [life] already,' " says the University of Pennsylvania's Anderson.

But the reality, according to Anderson and others, is that affirmative action is still needed to give African-Americans simply a fighting chance of competing in a world where the odds are still stacked against them, even three decades after the successes of the civil rights movement.

"You cannot do in 30 years what [America has] done with great success for 300 years — that is, give affirmative action to white people," says historian John Hope Franklin, who heads the advisory panel on race relations established in June by President Clinton. [15]

Wade Henderson, executive director of the Leadership Conference on Civil Rights, agrees that whites have enjoyed such great advantages historically that attempts to rectify past injustices require more than a level playing field. He points out, for example, that African-Americans graduating from college and looking for work might not have either the financial resources or "connections" that their white counterparts may enjoy thanks to their families. "The roots of racism run deep," he says.

In fact, Henderson and others argue, it's not possible to have a level playing field, and so it's counterproductive to pretend otherwise. "Nepotism and favoritism, that's white affirmative action, and it determines a lot of hiring and promotion decisions," says the University of Maryland's Landry. "Blacks don't have those kind of connections, and so they shouldn't feel apologetic if they substitute affirmative action instead," he adds.

Finally, supporters of affirmative action say, the evidence to support the policy is in the numbers. To begin with, they point out, blacks are still woefully underrepresented, both as students in universities and as white-collar workers. For example, according to 1995 Department of Education statistics, only 44.9 percent of African-Americans had attended at least some college, compared with 55.4 percent of whites. [16] In addition, as of 1994, only 14.7 percent of black men and

20.1 percent of black women held what would be considered managerial or professional jobs. By contrast, 27.5 percent of white men and 29.9 percent of white women worked in such jobs.[17] (*See graph, p. 82.*)

The disparity between the number of African-Americans and whites in higher learning and executive-level jobs would be much higher if it were not for affirmative action, say supporters of race and gender preferences. "If you ended affirmative action, many of the people who run these businesses wouldn't give a fig about hiring black people," Anderson says.

Others point to the University of California at Berkeley as an example of what would happen in university admissions of blacks nationwide if affirmative action were totally abolished. At the university's law school, for instance, admission of African-American students dropped 81 percent the year after racial preferences were eliminated. "Imagine if we had Proposition 209 nationwide," Anderson says. "We'd have institutionalized segregation again."

But opponents of affirmative action argue that the policy — far from helping African-Americans — actually has had a detrimental impact on the black middle class. To begin with, they say, affirmative action lowers standards by which black Americans are judged, at school or on the job. This in turn creates what Reynalds calls "perverse incentives" for African-Americans to expect more for less. "If you don't have to work as hard, you won't," he says. "That's just human nature."

The problem, Reynalds argues, comes when black students or workers have to compete head to head with their white counterparts. "Once they get into the real world, they're in for a rude awakening because most folks run into the higher standard sooner or later and often don't know how to handle it." This leads to higher rates of black failure, Reynalds contends. For instance, he says, many more black than white students who get into good colleges and universities drop out before they graduate.

By accepting unqualified candidates, opponents like Reynalds say, universities, companies and other institutions help to mask the real problem in the black community: poor achievement.

"Affirmative action has suppressed the development of black America because it is a disincentive to becoming more competitive," Steele says. According to Steele and others, preferences make African-Americans much more accepting of the inferior educational system that many are subjected to because they look to white America and affirmative action for uplift, not themselves.

Lower standards also fuel false stereotypes of black inferiority, opponents say, because people will always wonder whether African-Americans owe their success to hard work and intelligence or affirmative action. "If you have a white who has graduated from an Ivy League school, you know something about that kid and the work he's had to do to get there," Steele says. But "if someone has been getting a preference since high school, you don't know much about his true worth, regardless of his credentials on paper." In the end, Steele argues, "the big tragedy is that many blacks have high SAT scores, but they're tarred with the same brush." In other words, affirmative action distorts the connection between your credentials and your ability, regardless of the reality of the situation.

Others say that preferences also create white resentment, which in turn leads to race-based anger. "In many places, they'll kick the white guy's butt if he does shoddy work, but not the black guy's," Williams says. "This, of course, creates ill will among the races."

Most important, opponents say, affirmative action is simply immoral in a society that claims to be working toward true equality. "If you believe in equality before the law, you have to be offended by an institution that uses racial preferences," Williams says. ■

BACKGROUND

The Migration North

Until the turn of the century, most black Americans lived in rural areas of the South. Even in 1940, a majority of African-Americans were still working in agriculture below the Mason-Dixon line.

The concentration of blacks in the South retarded African-American progress. On purely economic grounds, few blacks, even after Emancipation, benefited from the industrialization and urbanization taking place in the North and other parts of the country. In the decades following the Civil War, most blacks stayed in the areas where they had been slaves, many working as sharecroppers on land owned by whites.

Meanwhile, throughout the country, but especially in the South, government institutions and businesses treated African-Americans like pariahs. From restaurants to universities to the local Woolworth's, the list of indignities was endless. In many parts of the country, African-Americans were effectively barred from voting or sitting on juries. Public facilities were often segregated, and many businesses refused to serve blacks. Well-funded state universities attended by whites didn't admit blacks.

Still, even in this harsh economic

Chronology

1940s-1950s

World War II and its aftermath presage big changes for African-Americans as the migration north intensifies and the civil rights movement takes off.

1941
U.S. entry into World War II causes an immediate shortage of industrial labor at home, increasing the migration of African-Americans from the South to Northern urban areas.

1946
President Harry S Truman orders an end to racial segregation in the armed forces.

1947
Jackie Robinson joins the Brooklyn Dodgers, becoming the first African-American to play Major League baseball.

1954
The Supreme Court's landmark *Brown v. Board of Education* ruling overturns the previous "separate but equal" policy in public education.

1955
Rosa Parks refuses to give up her seat on a city bus to a white man, sparking the Montgomery, Ala., bus boycott. The Rev. Martin Luther King Jr. emerges as a civil rights leader.

1960s

The civil rights movement becomes a national crusade. Congress enacts a raft of legislation aimed at ending discrimination.

1961
President John F. Kennedy uses the term "affirmative action" for the first time, ordering federal contractors to take affirmative action not to discriminate in hiring, but does not set numerical quotas.

1963
Martin Luther King Jr. gives his stirring "I Have a Dream" speech at the Lincoln Memorial in Washington.

1964
Congress passes the sweeping Civil Rights Act, which prohibits discrimination by employers on the basis of race, sex or national origin.

1965
In August President Lyndon B. Johnson signs the Voting Rights Act, which outlaws unreasonable barriers to voting. In September he issues Executive Order 11246 requiring federal contractors to actively recruit minorities.

1966
The Black Panthers, a group advocating "black power," is founded.

1968
Civil Rights leader Martin Luther King Jr. is assassinated, touching off race riots in many American cities.

1970s-present

In the post-civil rights era, new policies like affirmative action are adopted, sparking a backlash among whites.

1970
President Richard M. Nixon expands upon Executive Order 11246 to require contractors to set goals for minority employment.

1978
In *University of California Regents v. Bakke*, the Supreme Court rules that universities can use race as a factor in admissions, but may not impose quotas.

1980
Affirmative action foe Ronald Reagan is elected to the presidency. The Justice Department begins attacking racial quotas.

1995
Middle-class blacks are widely represented among the hundreds of thousands of people at the Million Man March in Washington, D.C.

1996
Voters in California approve Proposition 209 outlawing the use of race or gender preferences at all state government institutions.

1997
President Clinton names an advisory panel on race relations as part of a "national dialogue on race."

1998
Referendums in Colorado, Ohio, Washington and Florida will give voters a chance to strike down racial preferences in hiring and college admissions.

and social environment, a small black middle class slowly grew. The process was aided in the early part of the century by a migration of African-Americans to Northern industrial areas. The first great wave of this movement occurred during World War I. The conflict cut off the flow of immigrants from Europe, forcing American factories to look for cheap labor elsewhere. By 1920, most Northern cities had sizable black communities.

World War II also played a key role in black population shifts. While heavy industry was expanding almost exponentially to produce weapons and other war materiel to fight the Axis powers, many of the nation's white factory workers were in uniform. Blacks, on the other hand, were not inducted into the armed forces at as great a rate as whites, making them prime candidates to fill the void. As a result, African-Americans moved in large numbers to the industrial North and would continue to do so for the next three decades.

This second great migration ballooned black populations in cities from Los Angeles to New York. By the end of the war, more than one-quarter of all African-Americans lived outside the South. By 1960, the number had risen to 40 percent. [18]

As more and more black Americans shifted from agricultural to factory work, income levels began improving. More money meant more power for blacks, as consumers and voters. It also — along with the GI Bill and other factors — led to a significant increase in black educational attainment. As a result, the number of African-Americans with at least a high school diploma jumped from 12.3 percent in 1940 to 38.6 percent in 1960. During the same period, the percentage of black men doing white-collar work jumped from 10 percent to nearly one-quarter. [19]

But the Second World War altered more than income and education levels. Many blacks, and a few whites, saw the irony of more than 300,000 young, black men fighting — in segregated units — for freedom around the world. By the end of the war, black Americans felt that they had done their part and deserved to be treated accordingly by the broader society. More important, black leaders and liberal, white politicians began to forcefully and openly campaign against the nation's overtly racist policies.

"The Second World War altered more than income and education levels. Many blacks, and a few whites, saw the irony of more than 300,000 young, black men fighting — in segregated units — for freedom around the world."

Their efforts produced some startling results. The armed forces, and, more slowly, professional sports, were integrated. Some colleges and universities began accepting African-Americans, albeit in small numbers. Ten years after the war ended in 1945, however, many barriers to full integration remained.

Civil Rights Era

Still, the winds of change were blowing. In 1954, the Supreme Court's historic *Brown v. Board of Education* decision declared state-sponsored segregation in schools to be unconstitutional. At the same time, the civil rights movement was beginning to attract the attention of white America. Just a year after the *Brown* ruling, Rosa Parks was arrested on a city bus in Montgomery, Ala., for refusing to give up her seat to a white passenger.

The arrest united Montgomery's black community and led to the Montgomery bus boycott. The Parks incident also catapulted a young Atlanta clergyman into the leadership of the boycott and, eventually, the national spotlight. His name: the Rev. Martin Luther King Jr.

After almost a year, the boycott ended when a federal court ruled that segregation on the city's buses was unconstitutional. But the incident had an impact far beyond the city's boundaries. King built on the victory in Montgomery to found a national civil rights organization, the Southern Christian Leadership Conference (SCLC). Run largely by black clergymen, it was dedicated to non-violence as an agent of change. Throughout the late 1950s and early '60s, the SCLC and other civil rights groups scored a number of stunning victories in the fight against racial segregation. From the sit-in at Woolworth's in Greensboro, N.C., to the business boycott in Birmingham, Ala., blacks, sympathetic whites and civil rights groups made slow but steady gains in the struggle for equality.

Outside the South, white America had awakened to the realities of Jim Crow. Television networks regularly broadcast the indignities suffered by

At the NAACP, a Challenge to Integration

The unthinkable occurred at the NAACP's annual meeting in Pittsburgh last July. As the nation's oldest and most respected civil rights organization gathered to chart a course for the coming year, a sizable and vocal minority of members were calling for reconsideration of the group's longstanding support for integration.

The proposal caused a fire storm both within the organization and around the country. After all, the NAACP had been founded on the principle that "separate but equal" was an unworkable fallacy and had to be ended.

Indeed, integration has been the bedrock of mainstream civil rights philosophy for decades. Black leaders ranging from Supreme Court Justice Thurgood Marshall to the Rev. Martin Luther King Jr. to Jesse Jackson have all supported the idea that blacks and whites should strive toward a society where all peoples work, learn and live together. In addition, most of the great grass-roots victories of the civil rights movement involved integrating institutions from universities to lunch counters.

The NAACP's new chairperson, Myrlie Evers-Williams, the widow of slain civil rights leader Medger Evers, led the fight to beat back the anti-integration effort. "We're doing what we have always done, and our position remains the same," she said at the time.[1]

NAACP President Kweisi Mfume

It was not the first time that integration has come under black attack. Scientist Booker T. Washington believed that the races could work better together by working separately. Others, from black nationalist Marcus Garvey to the Nation of Islam's Louis Farrakan have called for black separatism as the only way to encourage African-American advancement.

But the fact that so strong and public a challenge occurred on such a fundamental issue was seen as telling. For a growing number of African-Americans, the question isn't whether to integrate, but how to build prosperous, stable black communities. Many of these critics are not opposed to blacks and whites living and working together. Instead, they argue, civil rights groups should end their quest for integration above and beyond all other concerns. "Integration hasn't served African-Americans well, especially poorer ones," says Roy Brooks, a law professor at San Diego State University.

Brooks and others argue that instead of trying to push people into a broader society that may not fully accept them, groups like the NAACP should work to foster black self-help. "African-Americans, like Italians, Jews and Cubans, must pull together," Brooks says. "These groups were able to succeed within their own segregated communities and used that as a springboard to the wider community."

Such sentiments are especially strong with regard to schools. Critics of integration argue that the civil rights community has focused on busing at the expense of quality education. For one thing, they argue, busing black students to white schools leads to white flight, which in turn leads to resegregated schools. In fact, two-thirds of all black students already attend schools where a majority of the pupils are from minority groups. And if integration as an ideal is sacrificed on the altar of good education, so be it, say these critics. "Our biggest concern now is whether our schools will be equal. Separate but equal would not be too bad," says Amos Quick, an African-American who is a member of a citizens' committee redrawing school boundaries in Greensboro, N.C.[2]

But civil rights leaders, including NAACP President Kweisi Mfume, argue that separating the races will not improve the quality of schools. In addition, Mfume says, "most parents want their children to have the most diverse, comprehensive educational experience they can have. And they want them to have it with different races."[3]

Mfume and other civil rights advocates say that recent talk of ending the fight for integration is a result of African-American frustration after years of trying to gain acceptance by whites. According to Theodore Shaw, associate director-counsel of the NAACP Legal Defense and Education Fund, this frustration is natural in the current environment in which most blacks live. "You're beating your head up against the wall until it's bloody. At some point you have to ask, 'Should I continue to beat up against this wall?' "[4]

But others argue that the civil rights groups are reaping what they have sown by pushing for racial preferences in hiring and education at the expense of the colorblind society. According to Shelby Steele, a research fellow at the Hoover Institution, the growing rejection of integration is "an outgrowth of the same incentive system that created affirmative action."

Black people, he says, have been encouraged to think of themselves in largely racial terms, making integration harder. "They have been rewarded for saying their black identity is their first identity, " he says, "so it's not surprising" that their group identity overrides all other concerns.

---

[1] Quoted on National Public Radio, "Weekend All Things Considered," July 12, 1997.

[2] Quoted in Nat Hentoff, "The Undercutting of Thurgood Marshall — by the NAACP," *The Washington Post,* July 12, 1997.

[3] Quoted on National Public Radio, *op. cit.*

[4] Quoted in James S. Kunen, "Integration Forever?" *Time,* July 21, 1997.

African-Americans who were jailed, beaten and abused for protesting segregation. The dramatic media coverage helped effect a tremendous shift in public opinion in favor of civil rights. By 1963, 83 percent of all whites said they favored equality in the workplace, almost double the number who responded to the same question 19 years earlier.

The campaign for equality culminated in the Civil Rights Act of 1964, which prohibited discrimination based on race. The following year, Congress passed the Voting Rights Act, which put an end to literacy tests and other tactics used by Southern states to prohibit blacks from registering to vote. These two laws, and others that followed, did not end institutional discrimination overnight. But they did reflect the federal government's commitment to rooting out the race-based policies that had long been a part of American life.

Affirmative Action

By the 1970s, most historians agree, the worst excesses of the past had been eliminated. Meanwhile, black Americans were making great strides in catching up to white America. By 1969, median income for a black family was $22,000, a far cry from the white average of almost $36,000 but a significant improvement over the previous decades. Other factors also showed that the gap was closing. For instance, by 1970, 36.1 percent of African-Americans were in white-collar jobs, up from 6.4 percent in 1940. And the percentage of blacks attending college rose by a factor of five, from 7.2 percent in 1960 to 37.5 percent in 1995. [20]

During the civil rights battles of the 1950s and '60s, the vast majority of white Americans came to believe in the justness of the struggle against discrimination. But in the post-civil rights era, this relative consensus broke down. Part of this schism grew out of the "Black Power" movement in the late 1960s and early '70s. Black power represented the repudiation of the civil rights movement. First, it explicitly rejected cooperation between races, which had been a hallmark of the struggle. It also advocated acquiring power "by any means necessary," including violence. Hence, it rejected King's strategy of non-violent action.

At the same time, America's cities experienced a sharp increase in crime and an explosion of race-related riots. All of this made white America, as well as many blacks, highly uncomfortable.

In addition, new initiatives aimed at fighting poverty and fostering black advancement in general have proven much more controversial than the original anti-discrimination laws of the early 1960s. The new initiatives, part of President Lyndon B. Johnson's "Great Society" program, did not entirely achieve their goals. Many of these programs have since been altered or eliminated.

One policy from this era that has become increasingly controversial is affirmative action. President John F. Kennedy first used the term in 1961, when he issued an executive order requiring federal contractors to take "affirmative action" to ensure that they did not discriminate. In 1965, President Johnson put teeth into the policy, issuing an executive order that required federal contractors not merely not to discriminate, but to actively recruit minorities. During the Nixon administration, the mandate was strengthened to require contractors to establish and meet specific minority-hiring goals.

By the end of the 1970s, affirmative action had spread to most sectors of society. Colleges and universities were using it in admissions. The federal government had expanded it to "set aside" a certain percentage of contracts for minority-owned businesses. [21] And corporations were voluntarily setting up minority-recruitment and other affirmative action programs.

But even as affirmative action was becoming more commonplace, it was coming under attack. During the 1970s, the Supreme Court heard a number of challenges to the policy, including the landmark 1978 case, *University of California Regents v. Bakke*. The case involved a white law school applicant, who claimed that he had been rejected in favor of less-qualified blacks under the university's affirmative action program. The justices agreed, outlawing the use of numerical racial quotas in university admissions. The court also ruled, however, that while quotas were unconstitutional, race could still be a *factor* in making admission decisions.

Attacks against affirmative action intensified in the 1980s. President Ronald Reagan and his successor, George Bush, were opposed to race-based preferences, and the Justice Department in their administrations worked to eliminate quotas and other race-based hiring programs. In addition, the six new justices chosen for the Supreme Court during this period either opposed or had serious reservations about the policy. In the 1990s, as a result, the high court has handed down several decisions striking down affirmative action programs. [22]

At the same time, the policy has been attacked at the grass-roots level. In 1996, Californians voted to approve Proposition 209, the first statewide repeal of affirmative action programs. Similar referenda are slated for votes this year in Washington, Ohio, Florida and Colorado.

Today, according to recent polls, roughly 60 percent of whites and 40 percent of blacks oppose affirmative action.[23] It has become a litmus test in most debates over race. For instance, the recent GOP opposition to Bill Lann Lee, President Clinton's nominee to head the Civil Rights Division at the Justice Department, revolved around Lee's support for preferences. And at the president's recent "town hall" meeting in Akron, Ohio, part of his national dialogue on race, affirmative action sparked the fiercest debate.[24]

For members of the black middle class, affirmative action is often a difficult issue. But, regardless of their position, many blacks worry that it will lead whites to devalue all achievement by African-Americans, be it in the workplace or the classroom.

"You know, I just want the opportunity to succeed, nothing more," says Alexander, who supports the policy. ■

Blacks' Income and Assets Lag

The median income of white families was 65 percent more than that of blacks in 1995. White households had 10 times the material assets of black households in 1993.

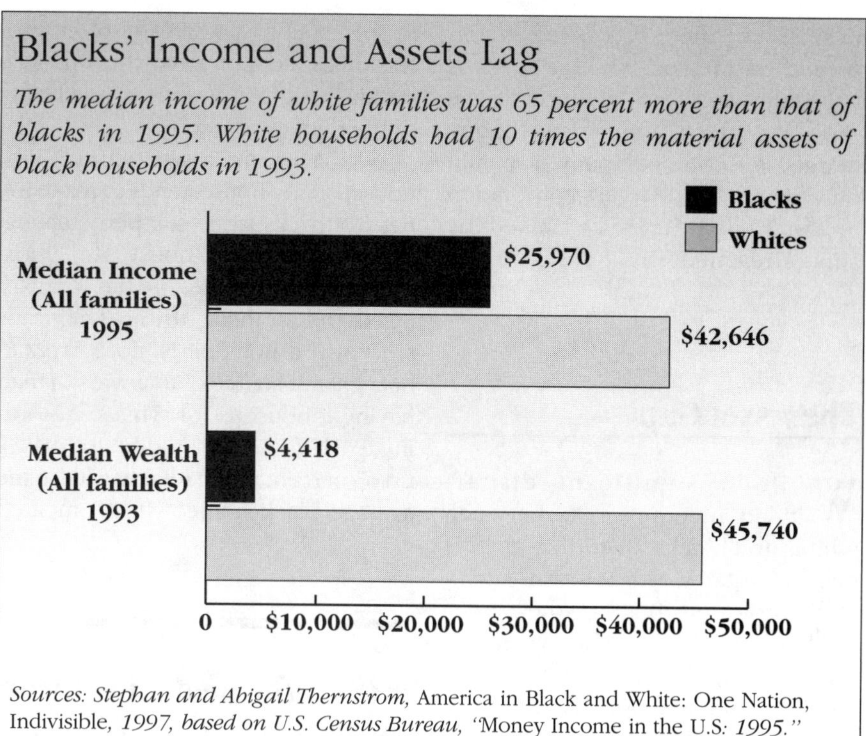

Sources: Stephan and Abigail Thernstrom, America in Black and White: One Nation, Indivisible, *1997, based on U.S. Census Bureau,* "Money Income in the U.S: *1995."*

CURRENT SITUATION

Economic Gains

As the list of CEOs at the nation's 500 largest companies confirms, white men still run corporate America. But in the last 30 years African-Americans have made progress in their quest to join the country's business elite. Some gains, of course, were inevitable given the fact that until the civil rights movement, there were virtually no high-ranking black executives. "We really had nowhere to go but up," says Morgan State's Hill.

Today, the situation is somewhat different. At many of the nation's biggest corporations, African-Americans are near the very top of the corporate totem pole, including Kenneth Chenault and Lloyd Ward, the presidents of American Express and Maytag. Other corporations, among them General Motors, Walt Disney and Morgan Stanley, have African-Americans in top-level slots. According to Richard Parsons, president of entertainment giant Time Warner, "people of color are achieving corporate positions that their parents never dreamed of reaching, and in unprecedented numbers."[25]

But according to many blacks, the fact that some African-American executives have managed to climb most of the way up the corporate ladder should not be taken as a sign that racism has been eliminated from the boardroom. For one thing, none of the big corporations has ever been run by a black person. "You'd think over the last 30 years someone would have made it to the top" says Collins, author of the recent book *Black Corporate Executives.* In addition, Collins notes, since the 1970s, there have always been a few black executives who were touted as the next CEO. "But all of them were moved to less important positions or they left," he says.

Many black executives who cut their teeth in large corporations have gone on to start their own businesses. Some just want to go it alone. Others go into business for themselves, at least in part, because of the frustration they felt in largely white corporate America. Alexander started her own business because she was tired of being mistreated and taken for granted while at the same time working diligently. "I thought: 'I've made so much money for [my white boss] over the years, why shouldn't I do it for myself?' " she says.

Alexander is far from alone. The number and size of black-owned businesses have grown significantly in the last few decades. According to *Black Enterprise* magazine, the 100 largest black-owned companies generated $14.1 billion in revenue in 1996. In 1973, the top 100 produced less than a half-million.[26]

Still, as with African-American

executives, the success of black-owned businesses, while notable, is not staggering. For instance, if the top 100 black businesses today merged into one company, it would only be the 83rd-largest corporation in the United States as ranked by annual revenue. [27]

The Asset Gap

While a significant disparity in income exists between whites and blacks, the difference in total worth is even more profound. In 1993, the median net worth of the average white household was $45,740; the average black household was worth only $4,418.

Even among households with equal income levels, net worth among African-Americans is still much lower. According to the new book *America in Black and White* by scholars Stephan and Abigail Thernstrom, the asset gap, even among high-earners, largely is determined by inherited wealth. They write that "only within the past few decades have any but a handful of black people had the opportunity to acquire substantial property; few of their parents and grandparents, living under slavery and then Jim Crow, bequeathed significant estates to their descendants." [28]

The impact of the asset gap is significant, scholars say. For instance, it is not uncommon for young middle-class whites to ask their parents for financial help for everything from their education to buying their first home. This option is available to far fewer black people. "It puts you at a disadvantage early on," Hill says. It also contributes to segregation, since many black professionals do not have the financial backing to afford as expensive a house as their white counterparts.

Not having the assets to buy a nice house, or any house, tends to make the net-worth disparity self-perpetuating. That's because a house, for most middle-class people, is the primary asset. And for those African-Americans who own a home, it is more likely to be a greater source of total wealth than having a house is for whites. According to 1991 statistics, the house makes up 63 percent of the total wealth of the average black homeowner compared with 41 percent for the average white homeowner, who is more likely to have other financial assets. [29] (*See graph, p. 91.*) ■

"In 1993, the median net worth of the average white household was $45,740; the average black household was worth only $4,418."

OUTLOOK

Guarded Optimism

A recent CNN/*Time* magazine poll showed that only 18 percent of black teens think that the problems faced by African-Americans today are caused by whites. Similarly, only 23 percent said that they had ever been the victim of discrimination. [30]

Some scholars say that statistics like these confirm their optimism about the future. Children, they say, are not as hobbled by America's segregated past as are their parents. "If you go to a suburban mall and look at groups of kids, you'll see a girl from India, three WASPs, a Jew and two blacks," says the University of Pennsylvania's Anderson. "That's the future."

But, Anderson and others point out, middle-class blacks are struggling with their children's willingness to mix with whites. "On one hand, they know it's good to have all different kinds of friends," he says. "But on the other, they feel their kids should know what it means to be black — so that you know where it comes from when you're kicked."

How best to raise black children in today's America is part of a larger question that middle-class African-Americans are asking: How far should I assimilate? The question is different for blacks than it has been for many other groups. Long after the Civil War and Emancipation, the idea of African-American assimilation was absurd to both blacks and whites, although for different reasons. But the advent of the civil rights movement and the rise of the black middle class make the proposition much less unrealistic.

Some, like Reynalds, say that the death of Jim Crow and the birth of economic opportunity will slowly push blacks into the mainstream. One particularly telling sign of this change, he argues, is that younger blacks have turned their backs on government as the prime engine of opportunity. "Young folks tend to look to

At Issue:

Is affirmative action still necessary?

yes

Hilary Shelton

Deputy Director, Washington bureau, National Association for the Advancement of Colored People

Opponents of affirmative action have distorted the meaning of the principle, rewritten history and clearly ignored present realities in their eagerness to eliminate present programs. Since the end of slavery, African-Americans, as well as other ethnic minority groups and women, have struggled for economic justice, an equal opportunity to enter the workplace to earn equal pay and equal access to higher education.

Dr. Mary Frances Berry, U.S. Commission on Civil Rights chairperson, has stated: "Some progress in job opportunities for African-Americans was made during World War II and beyond. But it was limited. In grocery and department stores, clerks were white and janitors and elevator operators were black. Generations of African-Americans swept the floors in factories, while denied the opportunity to become higher paid operators on the machines."

The reality of life in America before affirmative action included thousands of towns and cities in which the police departments and fire departments were all white males. . . .

Detractors of affirmative action use the battle cry of "merit" over any racial or gender considerations. They seem to forget there were no merit standards for employment for white males who occupied the best jobs. . . . Men with the privilege of white skin, whether their granddaddies ever owned slaves or not, whether they were early or late immigrants, had the good-job pie all to themselves.

To be sure, women and minorities have been the major beneficiaries of affirmative action over the past three decades. Few realize, however, that white males are also beneficiaries. Before affirmative action, the "old-boys' network" way of doing things prevailed.

Because of affirmative action, fairness is now the rule, guaranteeing more opportunities for white males as well as minorities and women to compete for jobs. Indeed, the purpose of affirmative action has always been to create an environment where merit can prevail.

On July 19, 1996, President Bill Clinton delivered an address on affirmative action at the National Archives in Washington, D.C., while standing in front of the original U.S. Constitution. He said:

"If properly done, affirmative action can help us come together, go forward and grow together. It is in our moral, legal and practical interest to see that every person can make the most of his [or her] life. In the fight for the future, we need all hands on deck, and some of those hands still need a helping hand."

no

Gerald Reynalds

President, Center for New Black Leadership

Race-based affirmative action policies harm many of their intended beneficiaries, as well as better-qualified white and Asian competitors. For example, data from elite public colleges clearly demonstrate that double standards in admissions policies have harmed many of the black beneficiaries of preference policies. College administrators are quick to point out any increase in minority enrollment. However, they never mention that a disproportionate number of these students never graduate. . . .

By shielding blacks from unfettered competition in college admissions, contracting and employment, proponents of preference polices have placed too many middle-class blacks in a protective cocoon. Many of these blacks have no incentive to work hard enough to meet or exceed "real world" standards since they are not penalized for a substandard performance. Preference policies also cheapen the accomplishments of those blacks who meet or exceed the same standards met by whites and Asians.

Recently President Clinton implied that Gen. Colin Powell owed his success to racial-preference policies. President Clinton is not alone. Many supporters of preference policies believe that the tremendous gains achieved by the black middle class are due, in large part, to preference policies and that these policies are still needed. They are wrong. The data do not support the assertion that preference policies were the primarily cause behind the growth of the black middle class. In fact, the data suggest that the groundwork for the growth of the black middle class was in place prior to the implementation of racial preference policies.

The confluence of black migration from the South to the North, a strong work ethic, enhanced employment opportunities, the enactment and enforcement of anti-discrimination statutes and improved educational opportunities enabled black strivers to reach the middle class. Racial preference policies merely accelerated the advancement of those blacks who possess middle-class values. These policies have never been prerequisites for advancement.

For much of our history black Americans lived under a racial caste system. Prior to the civil rights revolution, one's chances of economic, social and political advancement were not determined by talent, initiative and industry. The prospects of the majority of blacks were severely limited by state-sponsored segregation and a hard-core white racism. However, racial discrimination is no longer an insurmountable obstacle for black Americans. My grandmother use to argue that because of racism, blacks had to be twice as good their white competitors. While the level of racism has waned substantially, the need to strive for excellence has not.

Are Black Conservatives on the Rise?

Thomas Sowell once joked that if you put all African-American conservatives in one room there wouldn't be enough people for a game of pinochle.

Sowell, the much-quoted Hoover Institution scholar, would have plenty of card players to sit down with nowadays. In the last decade, the number of black conservatives in the public eye has jumped dramatically. From Supreme Court Justice Clarence Thomas and Rep. J.C. Watts, R-Okla., to talk-show host Armstrong Williams and anti-affirmative action crusader Ward Connerly, more and more black conservatives are entering the limelight.

Indeed, Alan L. Keyes, a Harvard-educated radio talk show host and former Foreign Service officer, ran for the GOP presidential nomination in 1996. Another black Republican, retired Gen. Colin Powell, is considered his party's front-runner for the 2000 presidential nomination, although he has said he's not interested.

These new faces come at a time when black support for the Democratic Party endures. Since the Great Depression of the 1930s, the vast majority of blacks have voted for Democrats in presidential and congressional elections. Today, fewer than 10 percent of all African-Americans identify themselves as Republicans. Black Republicans hold just one seat in Congress (Watts). Furthermore, as of 1997, only 11 of the 550 African-Americans in state legislatures were members of the GOP. [1]

Conservatives explain these statistics by arguing that there is a tremendous pressure within the black community to conform politically. "Black America is a one-party system," says Shelby Steele, another black research fellow at Hoover and author of the best-selling book on affirmative action *The Content of Our Character*. "Black conservatives are immediately labeled as 'Uncle Toms' and as traitors to their race," he says.

The "one-party system," as Steele labels it, is perpetuated by more than just loyalty to race. It is built, he says, on adherence to an overriding belief. "As a black man, I am judged on [my attitude about] one issue: whether victimization is black America's biggest problem. If I say 'yes,' it's OK. If I say 'no,' I'm a black conservative, period."

The reality, Steele and others say, is that African-Americans are much more conservative than their Democratic political affiliation would indicate. Gavin Jackson, a human relations specialist at the Department of the Treasury and a self-described conservative, agrees. "I think black folks are inherently conservative," he says, "especially when you look at our attitudes toward religion, family and money."

Indeed, according to a 1996 poll commissioned by the Joint Center for Political and Economic Studies, a black-oriented think tank, 30 percent of all African-Americans identified themselves as "conservative." By contrast, only 31 percent of the blacks polled said that they were "liberal." [2]

Why, then, does the GOP fare so poorly with black Americans? The answer, according to black liberals, is tied directly to the hostility the Republican Party and conservatives in general have shown toward African-Americans and their priorities. "It is not even close to think that the assault on government that [House Speaker] Newt [Gingrich] and company are leading is in the interest of the vast majority of black people in this country," says famed civil rights activist Julian Bond. [3]

In addition, many black Democrats accuse the GOP of using wedge issues like affirmative action to scare white voters into supporting them. While this tactic has helped Republicans capture the Congress, they say, it has alienated African-American voters.

But black conservatives are optimistic about the growth of their movement. "It's going to keep expanding," Steele says. He and others compare the black community today with Jewish Americans, a traditionally liberal group that has begun to diversify ideologically. "During the 1980s, we started to see Jewish Republicans," Steele says. He predicts a similar trend in black America as the old, liberal mantras begin to ring hollow. "There's no other way for us to go," he says.

Yet some black conservatives are not convinced that the expansion of conservatism is inevitable. According to Gavin Jackson, the GOP can't just wait for African-Americans to come to them. "I think more black folks will vote Republican when [the GOP] focuses some attention on black issues."

[1] Stephan and Abigail Thernstrom, *America in Black and White: One Nation, Indivisible* (1997), pp. 302-303.

[2] *Ibid.*, p. 303.

[3] Quoted in Eric Alterman, "The Right Brothers," *The Nation,* March 4, 1996.

themselves more than the government," he says. "The folks wedded to government solutions tend to be older ones, and that's understandable since it was government that broke the back of Jim Crow."

If there is a problem, conservative African-Americans and others say, it is the influence of many black leaders, who are pushing for greater dependency on the government. According to Thomas Sowell, a fellow at the Hoover Institution: "Too many black 'leaders' today have a vested interest in the application of old myths. They are like Moses in reverse — leading their people back into the welfare state, to a self-imposed isolation from the growing opportunities all around them." [31]

But others are less sanguine, arguing that racism is still causing a lot of middle-class African-Americans to feel ostracized and angry. And, they say, these negative feelings multiply when whites show impatience with the lack of black progress. "You know, it's like, 'After 30 years, haven't we done enough for you people,' " says Collins of the University of Illinois.

Henderson agrees, arguing that attacks on affirmative action and other programs have left many well-to-do blacks suspicious of white America's motives. "Some people feel like refugees in their own country," he says. According to Henderson and others, blacks have done all they can to integrate into American society, and now just need to be welcomed.

"African-Americans are among the most patriotic of citizens, " Henderson says. "We ascribe to core American values and see ourselves as part of the mainstream of America." ■

FOR MORE INFORMATION

Hoover Institution, Stanford University, Stanford, Calif. 94303; (650) 723-1754; www.hoover.org. The Hoover Institution is a public-policy think tank that has attracted a large number of conservative scholars.

Joint Center for Political and Economic Studies, 1090 Vermont Ave., N.W., Suite 1100, Washington, D.C. 20005; (202) 789-3500; www.jointctr.org. This think tank researches issues that are of concern to black Americans.

Lincoln Institute for Research and Education, 1001 Connecticut Ave., N.W., Suite 1135, Washington, D.C. 20036; (202) 223-5112. The Institute studies issues that impact middle class African-Americans. Topics include education, employment and health.

National Association for the Advancement of Colored People (NAACP), 1025 Vermont Ave., N.W., Suite 1120, Washington, D.C. 20005; (202) 638-2269; www.nvi.net/naacp_washington_bureau/. The NAACP works for civil rights in all sectors of society. Efforts include lobbying, legal action and education.

National Urban League, 1111 14th St., N.W., Suite 1001, Washington, D.C. 2005-5603; (202) 898-1604; www.nul.org. This federation of affiliates is concerned with the welfare of African-Americans and other minorities.

Notes

[1] Kevin Merida, "Worry, Frustration Build for Many in the Black Middle Class," *The Washington Post,* Oct. 9, 1995.

[2] Cited in Stephan and Abigail Thernstrom, *America in Black and White: One Nation, Indivisible* (1997), p. 185.

[3] Ellis Cose, *The Rage of a Privileged Class* (1993), p. 1.

[4] For background, see "Intelligence Testing," *The CQ Researcher,* July 30, 1993, pp. 649-672.

[5] For background, see "Housing Discrimination," *The CQ Researcher,* Feb. 24, 1995, pp. 169-192.

[6] For background, see "Racial Tensions in Schools," *The CQ Researcher,* Jan. 7, 1994, pp. 1-24.

[7] See Connie Aitcheson, "Corporate America's Black Eye," *Black Enterprise,* April 1997.

[8] Quoted on "The NewsHour with Jim Lehrer," Nov. 12, 1996.

[9] Quoted in Eric Pooley, "Fairness of Folly," *Time,* June 23, 1997.

[10] Thernstrom, *op. cit.,* p. 211.

[11] Lisa Frazier, "Pr. George's is 62% Black, Study Finds," *The Washington Post,* Dec. 7, 1997.

[12] Quoted in Haya El Nasser, "In Cleveland, Dream Homes Displace Decline," *USA Today,* Oct. 23, 1997.

[13] Haya El Nasser, "Growing Middle-Class Isn't Fleeing to the Suburbs," *USA Today,* Oct. 23, 1997.

[14] See Carol Morello, "Controversial Measure Proves Difficult to Enforce," *USA Today,* Nov. 17, 1997.

[15] Quoted in Susan Page, "Race Panel Head Sees Progress, Backsliding," *USA Today,* Nov. 17, 1997.

[16] Thernstrom, *op. cit.,* p. 391.

[17] Doris Warriner, Joint Center for Political and Economic Studies, "African Americans Today: A Demographic Profile," 1996, p. 32.

[18] Thernstrom, *op. cit.* p. 80.

[19] *Ibid.,* p. 84.

[20] *Ibid.,* p. 192.

[21] For background, see, "Rethinking Affirmative Action," *The CQ Researcher,* April 26, 1995, pp. 369-392.

[22] *Ibid.*

[23] Pooley, *op.cit.*

[24] Warren P. Strobel, "Forum Finds No Consensus on Race Issues," *The Washington Times,* Dec. 4, 1997.

[25] Quoted in Roy S. Johnson, "The New Black Power," *Fortune,* Aug. 4, 1997.

[26] Cited in *Ibid.*

[27] *Ibid.*

[28] Thernstrom, *op. cit.* p. 198.

[29] Warriner, *op. cit.* p. 53.

[30] Christopher John Farley, "Kids and Race," *Time,* Nov. 24, 1997.

[31] Thomas Sowell, "Yes, Blacks Can Make It on Their Own," *Time,* Sept. 8, 1997.

Bibliography

Selected Sources Used

Books

Cose, Ellis, *The Rage of a Privileged Class,* HarperCollins, 1993.
Cose, a writer at *Newsweek*, tries to answer the question: Why are successful black professionals so angry? The answer, he says, is that many African-Americans who have "made it" still do not believe they are operating in a system that will fully reward them for their intelligence, education and effort.

D'Souza, Dinesh, *The End of Racism: Principles for a Multiracial Society,* The Free Press, 1995.
D'Souza, a fellow at the American Enterprise Institute, argues that civil rights advocates are fighting against a largely non-existent enemy. One reason, he says, is that fighting racism has become an industry, one that is self-perpetuating.

Shipler, David K., *A Country of Strangers: Blacks and Whites in America,* Alfred A. Knopf, 1997.
A journalist and Pulitzer Prize-winning author, Shipler looks at how Americans are dealing with the issue of race. By combining history and statistics with literally hundreds of anecdotes and stories, Shipler paints a picture of a nation and a people that are not close to achieving any kind of racial harmony.

Thernstrom, Stephan and Abigail, *America in Black and White: One Nation, Indivisible,* Simon & Schuster, 1997.
Stephan Thernstrom, a professor of history at Harvard University, and his wife Abigail, a fellow at the Manhattan Institute, have produced a sweeping portrait of black America as it was and is. The Thernstroms argue that blacks have made much more progress during the 20th century than is generally acknowledged. They also make the case that race relations are better than many people think.

Articles

Biskupic, Joan, "On Race, a Court Transformed," *The Washington Post,* Dec. 15, 1997.
Biskupic describes the transformation of the Supreme Court from "the salvation of civil rights advocates" to "a place to be avoided." The reason, she writes, is that Presidents Ronald Reagan and George Bush appointed justices who were generally less friendly to affirmative action and some other programs favored by the civil rights community.

El Nasser, Haya, "Growing Middle Class Isn't Fleeing to Suburbs," *USA Today,* Oct. 23, 1997.
El Nasser details a growing trend among middle-class blacks: suburban flight. Many African-Americans who can afford to live in the suburbs are choosing instead to move to inner-city areas, many of which have high crime and other problems. Some are lured by cheap land, an opportunity made even sweeter in certain cities through tax breaks and cheap loans. Other blacks found the largely white suburbs "isolating" and want to live with people of their own race.

Johnson, Roy. S, "The New Black Power," *Fortune,* Aug. 4, 1997.
Johnson's piece is the lead-off to several articles on African-Americans and business. He argues that while blacks have made substantial progress in the business world, both as corporate executives and entrepreneurs, "people of color still confront huge obstacles in the workplace."

Merida, Kevin, "Worry, Frustration Build for Many in the Black Middle Class," *The Washington Post,* Oct. 9, 1995.
Merida looks at middle-class black attitudes and discovers a surprising amount of anger and fear. Black professionals are plagued by the same problems that affect their white counterparts, such as the fear of being downsized out of a job. But African-Americans also say they have problems that are unique to minorities, like feeling devalued at work by their white colleagues.

Pooley, Eric, "Fairness or Folly?" *Time,* June 23, 1997.
Pooley does a good job of describing the players and dynamics in the debate over affirmative action. In particular, he focuses on Ward Connerly, the African-American businessman who successfully led the fight for Proposition 209, the California ballot initiative that eliminated the use of preferences at all state agencies and institutions.

Reports

Doris Warriner, "African Americans Today: A Demographic Profile," Joint Center for Political and Economic Studies, 1996.
This report from the black-oriented think tank contains a wealth of statistical data on the state of black America. Topics include education, income, wealth and political participation.

6 Environmental Justice

Mary H. Cooper

An impoverished area of southern Louisiana has become the latest battleground in the struggle for civil rights. Only this time the goal is not desegregation or affirmative action but the right to a clean environment.

The controversy in rural St. James Parish focuses on 3,000 acres of sugar cane and a $700 million plastics plant planned by a Japanese manufacturer. The fight pits Shintech Inc. and a cadre of local supporters against environmental activists and other residents who want no part of it.

"This is our *Brown v. Board of Education*, our line in the dirt," says Robert D. Bullard, executive director of the Environmental Justice Resource Center at Clark Atlanta University. "This community is already overburdened with toxic plants."

Indeed, the parish lies along a stretch of the Mississippi River between Baton Rouge and New Orleans that is so heavily industrialized it's known as "cancer alley." More than 120 chemical plants line the 120-mile river corridor, many of which have spewed thousands of tons of dioxin and other carcinogens into the air, water and soil for decades. The parish itself is already home to 11 fertilizer and chemical plants.

Bullard and other activists argue that it is no accident that so many toxic polluters have zeroed in on the region. Throughout the country, they say, poor and minority communities are disproportionately exposed to noxious industry byproducts. Siting the Shintech plant in St. James Parish, they contend, would amount to yet another instance of environmental racism, another example of a poor community not benefiting from the nationwide improvements in environmental quality over the past three decades.

From *The CQ Researcher*, June 19, 1998.

Since Bullard helped lead the call for environmental justice in the early 1980s, the movement has won high-level support. In 1994, President Clinton issued an executive order directing all federal agencies with a public health or environmental mission to make environmental justice an integral part of their policies and activities. "All communities and persons across this nation should live in a safe and healthful environment," the president's order declared. [1]

Since then, 19 federal departments, agencies and executive branch offices, from the Environmental Protection Agency (EPA) to the Federal Highway Administration, have been required to ensure that their policies do not have a disparate impact on poor and minority communities.

In February, EPA Administrator Carol M. Browner lent an even stronger endorsement to the environmental justice argument by issuing "interim guidance," or guidelines, for processing a rash of claims of environmental injustice, based on the 1964 Civil Rights Act. Title VI of the act, the country's basic civil rights law, prohibits discrimination based on race, color or national origin in programs or activities that are supported by federal funds.

The Environmental Justice Resource Center.

Among the agencies covered by the law are state environmental commissions, which issue permits to factories and other potential polluters. According to regulations issued under Title VI, an agency violates the law if its policies or activities have a discriminatory effect, even if there was no intent to discriminate. An agency found guilty of such civil rights violations would face the loss of federal funds and be required to implement costly mitigation programs.

When Shintech proposed building the plant in St. James Parish, residents opposed to the move, together with Bullard, the Tulane University Environmental Law Clinic, Greenpeace and other environmental justice advocates lodged a formal complaint against the project. Although the state Department of Environmental Quality had already cleared Shintech to begin construction, last September Browner ordered the agency to rescind one of the project's permits and launched an investigation into charges that the choice of the site amounted to environmental racism.

Shintech joins a growing list of companies whose expansion plans have run afoul of the environmental justice movement in recent years. Since the first lawsuit of this type was filed in 1979 against a waste-dump operator in Houston, activists have turned increasingly to the courts on behalf of poor and minority communities seeking protection from pollution. [2]

Although environmental justice advocates have successfully lobbied companies to change their siting plans in a number of U.S. communities, they finally won their first legal victory in April. A Nuclear Regulatory Commission (NRC) hearing board rejected plans to build a uranium-enrichment plant in a poor, minority community in northwestern Louisiana (*see p. 106*).

Residents of Sierra Blanca, Texas, are fighting a plan, recently approved by Congress, that would allow Vermont, Maine and Texas to dump their low-level nuclear waste at a facility to be built near their largely Hispanic community. And the EPA has agreed to study a claim of environmental racism brought by the Coeur d'Alene Indians in Idaho, who have asked the agency to designate a 1,500-square-mile area polluted by decades-old mine tailings as a vast Superfund site.

Another case has made it to the U.S. Supreme Court. Residents of Chester, Pa., a majority-black town in overwhelmingly white Delaware County, went to court to block construction of a waste facility in their community. Because there are already five such facilities in the town, and only two in the rest of the county, residents charged the decision to build yet another dump in their midst amounted to environmental racism. The court announced June 8 that it would decide whether activists can bring suits in federal court alleging environmental racism. The state claims such charges can only be filed with the EPA.

Environmental Justice Resource Center

Residents of Chester, Pa., went to court to block construction of a waste facility in their community. The Supreme Court agreed on June 8 to decide whether the activists can bring suit in federal court alleging environmental racism.

But Shintech has become what the company's controller, Richard Mason, calls the "poster child" of the environmental justice movement. He rejects the claims of environmental racism made against his company. "We did not choose that site because there were African-Americans there," he says. "We chose it because there was nobody there."

Not only is the planned location a mile and a half from the nearest residential areas, Mason says, but the company's other U.S. plant, in Freeport, Texas, has a good environmental record. "In the 24 years we have produced polyvinyl chloride (PVC) resin at the Texas plant, we have had three or four incidents, in which no one was injured and no remediation was required."

Shintech has promised to provide jobs and training, including opportunities for management positions, to local residents. "We've worked very hard to get to know the people there and understand their concerns," he says. "And a lot of those concerns are economic in nature."

Indeed, not all local residents are opposed to Shintech's plan. The St. James and Louisiana chapters of the National Association for the Advancement of Colored People (NAACP) are vocal supporters of the new plant, which they hope will bring jobs and economic development to a region that suffers 12 percent unemployment and where 44 percent of residents live in poverty. [3] "Poverty has been the No. 1 crippler of poor people, not chemical plants," Ernest L. Johnson, president of the Louisiana State Conference NAACP, said in a statement. "Also, the present mortality rate for African-Americans in St. James is less than the Louisiana state rate, despite the 11 previously existing petrochemical plants in the area." Johnson says an NAACP survey shows broad local support for the new plant. "Unequivocally, the residents of the 'affected community' want Shintech!"

But environmental justice advocates say jobs and other investments are inadequate tradeoffs for the health risks, noxious odors and sheer ugliness that many industrial and waste facilities impose on poor communities. "Citizens want control of their environment rather than money," says Robert Knox, acting director of EPA's Office of Environmental Justice. "The time is past when companies could come in and pay for new school buses or other amenities in exchange for locating in poor, minority communities. Everyone understands about environmental pollution now, and they are not going to accept that any more."

The Shintech case and the shift in policy that gave rise to it have created a growing backlash against the environmental justice movement. In March the Environmental Council of the States (ECOS), made up of the top appointed environmental regulators from the states, denounced the EPA's interim guidelines, claiming they were vague, detrimental to economic development and poorly devised because the state commissioners, who are EPA's partners in administering federal environmental laws, had no say in the guidelines. Furthermore, the state commissioners say the policy undermines the democratic process.

"Most decisions to locate industrial facilities are not made by bureaucrats but by locally elected officials," says ECOS member Russell J. Harding, director of the Michigan Department of Environmental Quality. "That is absolutely the way these decisions should be made in an elected democracy. The EPA guidance turns the process upside down by calling for us — the regulators who are unaccountable to local voters — to make those decisions. This is not right."

As this latest chapter in the struggle for civil rights unfolds, these are some of the questions being asked:

Do poor and minority populations suffer disproportionately from exposure to toxic materials?

"Poor and minority communities are where you find children with lead poisoning living near polluting industries, garbage dumps, incinerators, petrochemical plants, freeways and highways — all the stuff that other communities reject," says Bullard of the Environmental Justice Resource Center. "And the fact that the problem has existed for so many years seems to be still a matter of denial for a lot of people."

Statistics seem to confirm Bullard's view. A widely cited study of U.S. Census data by the NAACP and the United Church of Christ Commission for Racial Justice found that people of color were 47 percent more likely than whites to live near a commercial hazardous-waste facility. The study also found that the percentage of minorities was three times higher in areas with high concentrations of such facilities than in areas without them. Moreover, the study suggested that minorities' exposure to environmental toxins was getting worse. [4]

Environmental Justice Resource Center

Children play in a park across from a Shell Oil refinery in Norco, La.

The EPA found similar disparities in exposure to toxins depending on income and race. Ninety percent of the nation's 2 million farmworkers, the agency estimates, are people of color, including Chicanos, Puerto Ricans, Caribbean blacks and African-Americans. Of these, more than 300,000 are thought to suffer from pesticide-related illnesses each year. Even air pollution affects minorities disproportionately, according to EPA. The 437 counties and independent cities that failed to meet air-quality standards in 1990, for example, are home to 80 percent of the nation's Hispanics and 65 percent of African-Americans but just 57 percent of all whites. [5]

Some critics of the environmental justice movement say the stunning improvements in environmental quality brought by 30 years of anti-pollution legislation benefit everyone in the United States. They also claim that the remaining environmental threats do not necessarily impact poor or non-white Americans more than anyone else.

"Since toxic air emissions, pesticide runoffs and groundwater contamination cannot neatly select their victims by race or income, the inequities visited upon minorities afflict a great many others as well," writes Christopher H. Foreman Jr., a senior fellow at the Brookings Institution. "Indeed, the range of arguably significant environmental-equity comparisons is so broad that some doubtless cut the other way: Many Native Americans, for example, breathe cleaner air than urban Yuppies and live further from hazardous waste than New Jersey's white ethnics." [6]

Activists reject this reasoning out of hand. "Sure, everyone is exposed to some level of toxins," says the EPA's Knox, "but exposure is disproportionate in poor and minority communities. He points to a black neighborhood in Gainesville, Ga., that accounts for just 20 percent of the town's population but handles 80 percent of its waste. The predomi-

An Indian Leader Speaks Out for the Land ...

Most instances of environmental racism that come to public attention involve black or Hispanic communities trying to keep polluting factories, sewage plants or toxic-waste dumps out of their communities. But an older and much less visible struggle is being fought by remote Indian tribes that are trying to clean up water supplies contaminated by mine tailings. Since the mid-19th century, miners and mining company executives have scoured the West for gold, silver and other minerals. They have left behind vast deposits of waste rock, or tailings, containing toxic materials. Cyanide and other chemicals used to separate some ores from rock also are left behind, usually in holding ponds. Over the years, rainwater carries these pollutants into streams and rivers, where they can be carried for miles, killing fish and contaminating drinking water.

Native Americans' pleas for environmental protection were ignored for decades, but now Indians are gaining a voice in the environmental justice movement. In what could turn out to be the most sweeping federal cleanup of pollution from mining activities ever undertaken, the Environmental Protection Agency (EPA) in February agreed to study the feasibility of designating the entire Coeur d'Alene River basin in Idaho as a Superfund site. The decision came largely as a result of the efforts of Henry SiJohn, environmental leader of the 1,600-member Coeur d'Alene tribe, whose reservation lies along the southern banks of Lake Coeur d'Alene. Staff writer Mary Cooper interviewed SiJohn by phone from his home in Plummer, Idaho.

How long has pollution in the Coeur d'Alene River basin been a problem?

In the 1920s and '30s, we noticed that the water potatoes, which grow along the lake, began to have a strange, metallic taste. We used to drink water from the lake, but we haven't since then.

How did government authorities react to your complaints about the water pollution?

The situation was different then because we were Indians, and everything was done by the superintendents of the Bureau of Indian Affairs. They had charge of us on our reservation. They said we didn't have any voice, that we couldn't buck the state or the federal government. They wouldn't do anything for us.

Do you think minority communities like yours are exposed to more pollution than white Americans?

I'm afraid that's true. It seems we have embedded an undercurrent of racism here in America. The Indian people have been for the longest time put into a situation whereby they were considered people who were unfamiliar with things. They couldn't participate in politics until 1924, when Congress allowed American Indians to have the vote. But even that didn't help for a long time because we

nantly black town of Chester, Pa., accounts for 11 percent of Delaware County's population but has 70 percent of the county's waste facilities. "That's clearly disproportionate," Knox says. "And it's not atypical for the country as a whole."

Some business representatives reject the notion that factory owners even look for communities of any kind to site their facilities. They say that when petrochemical companies flocked to southern Louisiana early in the century, for example, they were drawn primarily by the fact that such a long segment of the Mississippi River was deep enough to enable oceangoing barges to transport large shipments of raw materials and finished products.

"No one lived near the Baton Rouge Exxon refinery, the oldest in Louisiana, when it was built in the early 1900s," says Dan S. Borné, president of the Louisiana Chemical Association in Baton Rouge. "It and other chemical plants were built in agricultural areas, and communities literally grew toward them because that's where the jobs were. What's inferred in this debate — that people of color are targeted for chemical plants simply because they're people of color — is repugnant and ridiculous."

Does President Clinton's 1994 executive order provide sufficient guarantees of environmental justice?

When President Clinton issued his 1994 environmental justice executive order, more than 10 years had passed since the first complaints of environmental racism gained public attention. In November 1992, in response to growing pressure to address the concerns of communities exposed to toxins, President George Bush created the Office of Environmental Equity within EPA to study the problem.

But it was not until Clinton's 1994 policy statement that the goal of environmental justice gained formal recognition at the federal level. "[E]ach federal agency shall make achieving environmental justice part of its mission by identifying and addressing, as appropriate, disproportionately high and adverse human health or environmental effects of its programs, policies and activities on minority populations and low-income populations," Clinton declared.

. . . An Interview with Idaho's Henry SiJohn

had to establish our tribal government as an entity in itself and prove to people we knew what we were doing. Then we had to do assessment screenings to determine the pollution in the river basin.

Is the government responding adequately to your requests now?

I wish the EPA would protect the environment, especially of Indian people, through the enforcement arm of their agency. I feel they have been neglectful of punishing people that are the perpetrators of this pollution. If the Indians were the polluters, the public would have gotten up in arms and demanded that the Indians pay. However, this isn't the case. And the federal government has not protected the Indian people or the environment to the point where they enforce the law.

Has President Clinton's support of environmental justice affected your dealings with EPA?

By good fortune, I feel optimistic, in that someone is getting to the president of the United States with this issue. I have a lot of faith in Vice President Al Gore and his staff. I feel they truly have the interests of the environment at heart. But they can't move without the Congress of the United States. Congress is for corporate America, and corporate America is the segment of society that has dug this hole for us, and I don't know if we can escape.

Has the environmental justice movement helped your cause?

Environmental justice advocates are trying to help, but they don't have any idea how to go about it. I feel they and the Clinton administration could do more if they would only take a stand and tell the perpetrators they're the guilty ones.

Industry is polluting the rivers of America. People need to understand the Indian philosophy of the cycle of life. Fish have to spawn, and the spawning beds have to be protected, so they can complete the cycle of life. Because people don't understand this, they jeopardize the species to the point where they're endangered, and then we have this big to-do with the Endangered Species Act. So we have a political response rather than a natural response. Things would be different if people let animals complete the cycle of life.

Do you think EPA will accept your request to clean up the Coeur d'Alene River basin?

I'm very optimistic. If America doesn't wake up and take hold of things, it's going to put us all in jeopardy. People need to realize they can't survive without the environment. That's where the Indian philosophical view comes in. It perpetuates the purity of the environment. Without the natural resources of fish, animals, birds and the like we can't live. We will starve.

The agencies were not only required to correct existing problems but also had to take steps to prevent environmental injustice from occurring in the first place. Clinton gave each federal agency a year to develop and submit its strategy for achieving environmental justice and another year to report on progress in implementing the strategy.

Even though the new policy directive does not change laws currently in force, environmental justice advocates say it strengthens both the 1964 Civil Rights Act and the 1969 National Environmental Policy Act, which calls for environmental information to be made available to citizens. "We have two important pieces of legislation on the books which, if used in tandem, can be very potent weapons against environmental racism," says Bullard, pointing to several instances in which plans to build polluting facilities in communities of color were rejected after Clinton issued his executive order.

"These decisions make a lot of states nervous because they haven't really enforced equal protection when it comes to permitting," he says. "They could even lose transportation dollars because environmental justice is not just incinerators and landfills. It's also construction of highways, which have definite impacts on low-income communities and communities of color."

According to Knox of the EPA, the president's executive order has already changed the way states are dealing with the issue. At least three states — Louisiana, Maryland and Oregon — have passed executive orders on environmental justice that mirror the president's policy in order to pre-empt possible complaints of environmental racism and the loss of federal funds for highway building and other state operations. "They did this as a result of the executive order," Knox says. "They want to look at problem areas in the states so they can get ahead of the problem and make recommendations to their governors."

But some civil rights activists fear the policy may tip the scales in favor of those who want to keep industry out of poor areas at all costs, even when vital job opportunities are at stake. "In light of the executive order, environmental justice requires balancing economic benefit with environmental risks," writes Johnson of the Louisiana NAACP. "It is critical that we not succumb to outside pressure by those who have otherwise failed to promote their ideologies and now use the 'environmental race card' for their own agendas."

Does the focus on environmental justice distract attention from bigger health problems in poor and minority communities?

Some observers suggest that by single-mindedly opposing industrial development in poor communities, environmental justice activists may be hurting the very people they purport to represent. "It's very common to meet people in St. James, both black and white, who say their great-great-grandfather lived here," says Mason of Shintech. "They also say they want to continue living here with their families but that there are no job opportunities that will allow them to stay. Because the base of employment there now is the parish government and the existing chemical plants, the only way to find a job is if someone quits, retires or dies."

Not only are poverty and joblessness more serious problems for most minority communities than pollution, critics say, but so are a whole range of health and social ills. "Hypertension, obesity, low birthweights, inadequate prenatal care, substance abuse and violence are only some of the forces that arguably deserve pride of place in the struggle to improve the lives and health of communities of color," writes Foreman of Brookings. "That such forces are more intractable and harder to mobilize around than a Superfund site or a proposed landfill must not deter communities from asking . . . hard questions about overall health priorities." [7]

Activists say it's false logic to draw distinctions between their quest for environmental equity and these other goals of poor, minority communities. "Environmental justice is also about health," Bullard says. "The No. 1 reason why children in these communities are hospitalized is not because of drive-by shootings. It's because of asthma." The incidence of respiratory diseases has increased, especially among children and the elderly, in areas of high concentrations of ozone and particulate matter, notably urban neighborhoods close to major roadways. [8]

Bullard also points to lead poisoning as an environmental threat to health in minority communities. "The No. 1 threat to kids is lead poisoning, and this, too, is an environmental justice issue because African-American children are three to five times more likely to be poisoned by lead than are low-income white children," he says. "That's the direct result of residential segregation, so housing is another environmental justice issue."

Even crime and illiteracy can be traced to environmental racism, in Bullard's view. "There is a direct correlation between lead poisoning and learning disabilities, aggressive behavior and kids dropping out of school," he says. "So if you look at the root of many of the problems facing minority communities, both physical and environmental, you'll see they are all about health. It's no longer just a matter of a chemical plant."

Knox of the EPA agrees that environmental pollution has far-reaching effects on the quality of life in poor and minority neighborhoods. "Some people say the fight against crime should take precedence over other issues in these neighborhoods," he says. "But environmental problems only exacerbate such problems as crime and asthma in minority communities. Just because a community is poor doesn't mean the people there should not breathe clean air, drink clean water and be able to eat fruit from their gardens. You would not expect to find the same environmental quality in South Central Los Angeles that you find in Beverly Hills, but that doesn't mean that the people in South Central L.A. should not have clean air, clean water and clean soil." ■

Environmental Justice Resource Center

Riverbank State Park was built on top of the North River Sewage Treatment Plant in West Harlem, N.Y.

BACKGROUND

Plight of the Poor

The poor have always suffered the health effects of inferior living conditions. Even before the Industrial Revolution unleashed the toxic byproducts of the manufacturing process in Europe and North America, serfs, slaves and farm laborers often lived amid farm animals in crowded, drafty hovels under unsanitary conditions that took a disproportionately heavy toll in the form of infant mortality and premature death among adults.

Industrialization added numerous new environmental threats to health and well-being that were borne overwhelmingly by the poor. As factories sprang up along the railroads and rivers in the center of towns and cities, wealthy families moved out of range of the smoke and foul odors they emitted. Lacking transportation or the money to move away from the industrial centers, poor factory workers had little choice but to live close to their places of work. Where factories sprang up in rural areas along rivers and other transportation corridors, new communities of workers and job-seekers grew up around them.

In the United States, race compounded poverty as a factor in determining exposure to industrial toxins. Beginning in the 1950s, when many black farmworkers moved to cities in the East and Midwest in search of better-paying jobs, they were drawn to downtown neighborhoods where housing was affordable and close to work. Hispanic immigrants also gravitated to low-cost, inner-city neighborhoods where manufacturing jobs could be found, or to farming communities in remote agricultural areas of the West — frequent sites of toxic-waste dumps and pesticide contamination.

Native Americans were exposed to inordinate levels of toxic waste by virtue of another historical phenomenon — the relegation of Indians to remote reservations, many of which were later found to harbor vast deposits of uranium, gold, silver and other minerals. Mine tailings exposed many tribes to toxic runoff that contaminated their water supplies.

Birth of a Movement

The environmental plight of poor and minority communities was not an immediate priority of the modern environmental movement, which took shape in the late 1960s. [9] The first Earth Day, held April 22, 1970, marked the start of a national campaign whose main legislative victories were the 1970 Clean Air Act, the 1972 Clean Water Act, the 1973 Endangered Species Act and the 1980 Superfund legislation (the Comprehensive Environmental Response, Compensation and Liability Act).

These basic environmental laws focused on reducing the sources of pollution but basically ignored the varying impact of pollution on different income or racial groups. The first official acknowledgement that poor, non-white Americans were disproportionately impacted by environmental degradation was a statement in the Council on Environmental Quality's 1971 annual report that racial discrimination adversely affects the urban poor and the quality of their environment. [10]

That discrete communities could be disparately affected by environmental degradation became clear in 1978, when 900 families living in the Love Canal neighborhood of Niagara Falls, N.Y., discovered that their homes had been built near 20,000 tons of toxic waste. Initially rebuffed in their calls for reparations, residents demanded, and eventually won, relocation benefits. Their struggle also helped galvanize public support for federal legislation to clean up hazardous waste — the 1980 Superfund law.

Race and income were not the main issues at Love Canal. Working-class and mostly white, the neighborhood nonetheless served as a model for communities trying to ward off environmental threats. The first largely minority community to take up the challenge was in Warren County, N.C., where residents in 1982 demonstrated against a state plan to dump 6,000 truckloads of soil laden with polychlorinated biphenyls (PCBs), a highly toxic compound similar to dioxin. More than 500 protesters were arrested, calling national attention to the issue. Although the landfill was completed as planned, the protesters won agreement from the state that no more landfills would be put in their county, the state's poorest. [11]

A series of reports on environmental threats to poor and minority communities followed the Warren County protest, helping galvanize the nascent movement for environmental justice. The General Accounting Office found in a 1983 study that three of four hazardous-waste facilities in the Southeast were in African-American communities. In 1987, the United Church of Christ issued a widely cited study showing that landfills, incinerators and other waste facilities were found disproportionately in or near poor or minority communities across the country. [12]

In 1990, Bullard published the first of his four books on the subject. Like most other early works on environmental justice, *Dumping In Dixie* focused on toxic wastes and their close association with black communities in the Southeast. Bullard also called attention to the fact that black Americans are far more likely to be exposed to lead than whites, and that Hispanics are more likely to live in areas with high soot pollution. In his efforts to help impacted communities, Bullard was joined by Benjamin Chavis Jr., former executive director of the NAACP, other civil rights groups as well as mainstream environmental organizations such as Greenpeace and the Sierra Club, whose Earthjustice Legal Defense Fund works with poor communities.

The Bush administration recognized the environmental justice movement's growing clout in 1990, when then-EPA Administrator William K. Reilly established the Environmental Equity Workgroup to study the issue. Two years later, the movement gained permanent federal status with the creation of EPA's Office of Environmental Equity.

Environmental Justice Resource Center

Residents claim that Fort Lauderdale's Wingate Incinerator, now contaminated and a Superfund cleanup site, spewed ash and soot for over 25 years on the mostly African-American Bass Dillard neighborhood.

Clinton's Policies

President Clinton took office in January 1993 promising to restore federal environmental protections that he said had eroded during the previous 12 years of Republican administrations. His newly appointed EPA administrator, Browner, declared that environmental justice would be a priority for the agency and renamed the Office of Environmental Equity the Office of Environmental Justice.

"Many people of color, low-income and Native-American communities have raised concerns that they suffer a disproportionate burden of health consequences due to the siting of industrial plants and waste dumps, and from exposure to pesticides or other toxic chemicals at home and on the job, and that environmental programs do not adequately address these disproportionate exposures," she said shortly after taking office.

"EPA is committed to addressing these concerns and is assuming a leadership role in environmental justice to enhance environmental quality for all residents of the United States. Incorporating environmental justice into everyday agency activities and decisions will be a major undertaking. Fundamental reform will be needed in agency operations." [13]

On Sept. 30, 1993, Browner established the National Environmental Justice Advisory Council (NEJAC), a 23-member group of representatives of environmental organizations, state and local agencies, communities, tribes, businesses and other interested parties to increase public awareness of the issue and help EPA develop strategies to ensure environmental equity. By rotating membership in NEJAC (pronounced "knee-jack," or "knee-jerk" by its critics) every three years, the agency is trying to involve as many interested parties as possible in the ongoing policy debate.

President Clinton elevated environmental justice to yet a higher plane with Executive Order 12898, which required each federal agency involved in public health or environmental matters to "make achieving environmental justice part of its mission," particularly as minority and low-income populations were affected. The order also directed Browner to create and chair an interagency working group on environmental justice to coordinate federal policies aimed at furthering environmental equity. ■

CURRENT SITUATION

Recent Cases

The cause of environmental justice has been advanced on several fronts since President Clinton's

Chronology

1960s *Job opportunities draw black workers to cities in the industrial East and Midwest and Hispanic farmworkers to agricultural areas of the West.*

1964
Congress enacts the Civil Rights Act, establishing the country's basic law to protect the rights of minority groups. Title VI of the law prohibits discrimination based on race, color or national origin under programs or activities supported by federal funds.

1969
The National Environmental Policy Act calls for information on pollutants to be made public.

1970s *The environmental movement produces major laws to curb pollution.*

April 22, 1970
The first Earth Day marks the start of a national campaign to improve environmental protection, starting with the Clean Air Act, passed the same year.

1971
The Council on Environmental Quality acknowledges that racial discrimination adversely affects the urban poor and the quality of their environment.

1972
Congress passes the Clean Water Act, requiring reductions in polluting runoff into the nation's waterways.

1978
Residents of the Love Canal neighborhood of Niagara Falls, N.Y., discover that their homes sit atop a toxic-waste dump. They demand, and eventually win, relocation benefits, establishing a model for later action by poor, minority communities.

1979
The first lawsuit claiming environmental racism is filed against a waste-dump operator on behalf of a poor community in Houston.

1980s *Environmental justice movement takes off.*

1980
The Comprehensive Environmental Response, Compensation and Liability Act creates the Superfund to pay for the identification and cleanup of severely polluted sites.

October 1982
More than 500 protesters are arrested after trying to block a landfill being created for soil laced with polychlorinated biphenyls (PCBs) in Warren County, N.C., the poorest county in the state. The landfill project goes ahead, but the state agrees to build no more landfills there.

1983
The General Accounting Office finds that three of four hazardous-waste facilities in the Southeast are in black communities.

1987
The United Church of Christ issues a study showing that landfills, incinerators and other waste facilities are sited disproportionately in or near poor or minority communities.

1990s *Environmental justice gains federal support.*

November 1992
President George Bush creates the Office of Environmental Equity within the Environmental Protection Agency (EPA).

1993
Newly appointed EPA Administrator Carol M. Browner renames the Office of Environmental Equity the Office of Environmental Justice and promises to promote environmental protection for all Americans.

Feb. 11, 1994
President Clinton issues Executive Order 12898 directing all federal agencies with a public health or environmental mission to make environmental justice an integral part of their policies.

Sept. 10, 1997
The EPA delays permission for Shintech Inc. to build a new plastics plant in St. James Parish, La., a highly industrialized, largely African-American area.

Feb. 5, 1998
Browner issues "interim guidance" to provide a framework for processing claims of environmental injustice, based on Title VI of the Civil Rights Act.

June 8, 1998
The U.S. Supreme Court agrees to decide whether lawsuits alleging environmental racism can be brought in federal court.

Fighting for Environmental Justice . . .

The ongoing controversy over plans by Shintech Inc. to open a new plastics plant in St. James Parish, La., is among the most visible environmental justice cases. The following are some of the other notable battles being waged around of the country:

Sierra Blanca, Texas — Residents of this West Texas community, located in the 10th poorest county in the nation, fought construction of a low-level nuclear-waste facility outside the town. The facility would be the final repository for radioactive wastes from hospitals and research facilities in Texas, Maine and Vermont. Opponents complained that Sierra Blanca already is home to a large sewage sludge dump and said its selection as a dumping ground for nuclear waste amounted to environmental racism against the area's predominantly Hispanic population. Residents called on Congress to reject the three-state compact authorizing the facility. *(See "At Issue," p. 111.)* They lost their battle April 1, when the Senate approved the House-passed plan after adding amendments requiring an environmental review of the proposed site and barring other states from dumping radioactive wastes there as well.

Brunswick, Ga. — Contamination from lead, mercury, polychlorinated biphenyls (PCBs) and other toxins around an inactive LCP Chemicals-Georgia Inc. plant led to a $40-million, EPA-directed cleanup of this industrial area several years ago. Afterwards, the agency led a detailed area study, called the Brunswick Initiative, which failed to turn up other pollution threats to neighboring communities. But an environmental justice group called Save the People rejected the study's findings. The group and many residents of a mostly black community adjacent to another chemical plant, owned by Hercules Inc., claim that their yards are contaminated by toxaphene, an insecticide that Hercules manufactured until it was banned two decades ago.

Oak Ridge, Tenn. — Residents of the predominantly black neighborhood of Scarboro attribute a range of diseases in their community to the nearby Department of Energy (DOE) Y-12 nuclear weapons plant. The federal Centers for Disease Control and Prevention is investigating a possible link between the plant and respiratory illnesses in Scarboro. The DOE has offered to pay for health assessments but has not yet taken responsibility for any illnesses reported, some of which are the subject of pending litigation.

Houston, Texas — Three decades ago, the Kennedy Heights neighborhood was built over abandoned oil pits once owned by Gulf Oil. Today residents of this African-American community claim that leakage of oil sludge into their water supply is responsible for at least 60 cases of serious diseases found there, such as cancer and lupus, as well as hundreds of other lesser health complaints. In a lawsuit brought against Chevron, which bought out Gulf Oil, plaintiffs claim a corporate document slating the contaminated site for "Negro residential and commercial development" proves that environmental racism is at the root of their medical problems. Chevron denies that the incidence of disease in Kennedy Heights is high enough to prove a link with oil contamination. [1]

Huntington Park, Calif. — After four years of community opposition, the operator of a concrete recycling plant was forced to close it. Similarly, black and Hispanic residents of South East Los Angeles are organizing to get rid of the growing number of recycling facilities in their part of the city. Glass-recycling ventures spew ground glass into the air, residents say, aggravating asthma and other respiratory diseases and killing trees. Metal crushers at car- and appliance-recycling plants cause walls of neighboring houses to crack and release tiny fragments of oil and metal that contaminate the soil. [2]

Pensacola, Fla. — The Escambia Treating Co. ran a wood-treating facility here for 40 years, depositing highly toxic dioxin into the soil and prompting a $4 million Superfund cleanup of the site. Residents of the primarily low-income, black neighborhood adjacent to the site objected to the cleanup, saying it exposed them to an even greater health threat by bringing toxins to the surface. A local activist group, Citizens Against Toxic Exposure,

1994 executive order. Activists cite three cases that they say set legal precedents that will help reduce the incidence of environmental racism.

In northwest Louisiana in May 1997, a citizens' group blocked plans by a German-owned firm, Louisiana Energy Services, to build the first private uranium-enrichment plant in the United States. After nearly seven years of opposition, Citizens Against Nuclear Trash persuaded the Nuclear Regulatory Commission (NRC) to deny the company the required license based on evidence that race had played a part in site selection.

"The communities around that site are 97 percent black," says Bullard, who drafted a social and economic analysis of the area for the NRC. "The company didn't consider the fact that these people live off the land as subsistence hunters, fishermen and

. . . From New Jersey to California

convinced the Environmental Protection Agency (EPA) to test the soil and, as the results proved compelling, pay for the relocation of all 358 households around the site, which is expected to cost $18 million. [3]

Newark, N.J. — A section of the city's East End, known as Ironbound, lies in one of the most polluted areas of the country. It is home to a garbage incinerator that serves all of Essex County and a sewage-treatment plant serving 33 municipalities and 1.5 million people. The area also contains the now-closed Diamond Alkali plant, which once produced Agent Orange, the defoliant used in the Vietnam War. The area is thought to have among the highest concentrations of dioxin in the world. When Wheelabrator Technologies tried to build a $63 million sewage sludge treatment facility there, Ironbound's residents claimed that the placement of yet another waste plant in their community, home to many poor Portuguese immigrants, blacks and Hispanics, would constitute environmental racism. The Ironbound Committee Against Toxic Waste persuaded the state Department of Environmental Protection to deny the plant's final permits. [4]

Environmental Justice Resource Center

Responding to public health concerns in a black neighborhood in Anniston, Ala., Monsanto has begun buying out residents and relocating them.

Anniston, Ala. — In the low-lying industrial and residential neighborhood of Sweet Water, production of toxic PCBs had been going on since the 1930s. In 1996, the Alabama Department of Public Health declared Sweet Water and the adjacent community of Cobb Town a public health hazard. Monsanto stopped producing PCBs at the facility in 1971, eight years before EPA banned the chemical, a known carcinogen in laboratory animals. The company also began buying out residents and relocating them, even before agreeing with the state to do so and clean up the polluted areas. But the Sweet Valley-Cobb Town Environmental Justice Task Force charges Monsanto with environmental racism against the black communities by knowingly releasing PCBs from the plant after the environmental threat became apparent in the late 1960s. About 1,000 residents have sued the company.

Coeur d'Alene, Idaho — Silver mining came to the pristine area around Lake Coeur d'Alene in the 1880s. By the 1920s, members of the Coeur d'Alene Indian tribe began noticing that the water and root vegetables had taken on a metallic taste. Ignored by the mining companies and governmental officials for decades, the 1,600-member tribe finally convinced the EPA in February to consider declaring the entire Coeur d'Alene River basin a Superfund site. If the agency adds the site to its list — which is strongly opposed by local businesses in this recreational area — it will become the largest federal cleanup ever undertaken, covering an area of 1,500 square miles including the Idaho Panhandle and part of western Washington, where mine tailings have also polluted the Spokane River. [5] *(See story, p. 100.)*

[1] See Sam Howe Verhovek, "Racial Tensions in Suit Slowing Drive for 'Environmental Justice,' " *The New York Times,* Sept. 7, 1997.

[2] See David Bacon, "Recycling — Not So Green to Its Neighbors," posted on EcoJustice's Web page, www.igc.org, July 28, 1997.

[3] See Joel S. Hirschhorn, "Two Superfund Environmental Justice Case Studies," posted on Ecojustice's Web page, *op. cit.*

[4] See Ronald Smothers, "Ironbound Draws Its Line at the Dump," *The New York Times,* March 29, 1997.

[5] See Michael Satchell, "Taking Back the Land That Once Was So Pure," *U.S. News & World Report,* May 4, 1998, pp. 61-63.

farmers whose water comes from wells. That plant would have been slam-dunk, in-your-face racism."

The company appealed the ruling, but a three-judge NRC panel rejected the appeal. Not only was there evidence that racial discrimination had played a role in the siting process, the judges ruled, but also that the NRC staff had failed to consider the plant's environmental and social impact on the surrounding community, as required by the executive order as well as by the 1969 National Environmental Policy Act.

"This was the first environmental justice case that we actually won in court outright," Bullard says. It was also the first time a federal agency had used President Clinton's executive order to deny a license or permit.

In Flint, Mich., last year, environmental justice activists succeeded in delaying the issuance of a permit for a power plant sited in a mostly black neighborhood. The case began after the Michigan Department of Environmental Quality issued a permit to Genesee County to build a cogeneration electric power plant fueled in part by wood scraps from building construction and demolition, which might have been contaminated with lead-based paint. The permit allowed lead emissions from the plant of 2.4 tons a year. The Flint chapter of the NAACP and other plaintiffs sued the department, charging that the surrounding community was already overburdened by lead contamination and that by issuing the permit the state had violated its mandate to protect the health of all citizens.

In response, the department reduced the allowable level of lead emissions, but the plaintiffs proceeded with the suit, charging the department with practicing racial discrimination in issuing the permit in the first place. According to Director Harding, the department agreed to comply with additional demands but refused to settle the case because the plaintiffs would not drop their charges of racial discrimination.

Both sides claimed a victory of sorts from the judgment, handed down on May 29, 1997, by Circuit Judge Archie Hayman. Plaintiffs won an injunction against future permits, pending the state's performance of risk assessments to be paid for by applicants and the holding of broader public hearings when applications for toxic facilities are made. They also won recognition that compliance with air-quality standards under the Clean Air Act does not necessarily mean that a community is not adversely affected by air pollution.

For its part, the state claimed vindication on the racial discrimination charges. "The judge said there was no racial discrimination," Harding says. "In fact, he complimented my agency, saying our overall environmental regulatory system was sufficiently protective, though he directed the agency to do more initial determinations of environmental impact."

Environmental Justice Resource Center

The Southwest Network for Environmental and Economic Justice staged a protest in Phoenix, Ariz., in 1995.

In Chester, Pa., residents complained that their predominantly African-American city had become the main waste dump for all of largely white Delaware County. In 1996, after the Pennsylvania Department of Environmental Protection issued a permit to Soil Remediation Services Inc. to build yet another waste facility in the city, Chester Residents Concerned for Quality Living sued the agency for racial discrimination in its permitting process.

Their suit, *Chester Residents Concerned for Quality Living v. Seif,* was the first filed against a state agency under Title VI of the 1964 Civil Rights Act, which prohibits agencies that receive federal funds from practicing racial discrimination, either deliberately or by effecting "policies or practices [that] cause a discriminatory effect."

On Nov. 6, 1996, U.S. District Judge Stewart Dalzell dismissed the suit for technical reasons. On Dec. 30, 1997, however, the 3rd Circuit Court overturned the lower court, allowing the citizens' group's suit to proceed. The ruling also set an important legal precedent by enabling a low-income and minority community to pursue a charge of environmental racism regardless of whether the discrimination was deliberate. The Supreme Court has agreed to hear the case, addressing the question of whether lawsuits alleging environmental racism can be brought in federal court.

Pressure on EPA

The Circuit Court's ruling in the Chester case did not, however, elaborate on the question of evidence needed to mount a successful environmental justice suit against a state agency. [14] With the proliferation of charges of environmental racism in the 1990s, the EPA has come under increasing pressure to clarify the procedures for dealing with such cases. According to Knox of EPA's Office of Environmental Justice, the agency has received 49 complaints based on Title VI alone, about 20 of which are now under investigation. "EPA had to respond to a backlog of complaints," he says. "The agency had to do something to respond to this, so we issued guidelines to help identify who could bring claims and what constitutes a disparate impact on a community."

The backlogged complaints include the one in Louisiana brought against Shintech, which proposed in September 1997 to build a state-of-the-art plant to produce PVC, used to make a range of consumer products, such as plumbing pipes and shrink-wrap food wrapping. On May 23, 1997, the Louisiana Department of Environmental Quality issued three air permits for the facility. But on Sept. 10, in response to a citizens' petition, EPA Administrator Browner took the agency's first formal action on the environmental justice issue.

She canceled one of the firm's permits and directed the state agency to take environmental justice into greater consideration when reissuing the permit. In addition, she ordered further investigation of charges that the choice of St. James Parish for the plant site amounted to environmental racism. "It is essential the minority and low-income communities not be disproportionately subjected to environmental hazards," Browner wrote in her decision.[15]

The Shintech case is also the test case for the EPA's interim guidance, or guidelines. Browner issued the guidance on Feb. 5, 1998, in the wake of the Chester ruling, seeking to clarify the conditions under which a decision to issue a permit violates Title VI. The guidance describes a five-step process by which EPA must identify the affected population, primarily on the basis of proximity to the site in question, determine the race or ethnicity of the affected population and decide whether the permitted activity will impose an "undue burden" on the community. The agency will then identify any other permitted facilities in the vicinity that may compound the community's environmental threat.

S.C. Delaney/Environmental Protection Agency

Residents of Wagner's Point, a working-class enclave in South Baltimore, link the abnormally high cancer rates in their neighborhood to emissions from a nearby wastewater treatment plant, an oil refinery and other industrial sites.

If EPA determines that the community is impacted at a "disparate rate," the permit recipient may mitigate the environmental impact by offering other benefits to the community. Shintech, for example, has promised to spend about $500,000 for job training and small-business development in St. James Parish.

State environmental officials quickly identified what they saw as numerous flaws in the EPA's guidance, however, and asked the agency to rescind the guidance and draft a new policy together with the states. Fourteen state attorneys general and the U.S. Chamber of Commerce endorsed the environmental officials' request. "We believe the guidance is vague," says Robert E. Roberts, executive director of ECOS. "It speaks of mitigating or justifying 'disparate impacts' but doesn't make clear what such an impact is. So for those of us who have to carry out the policy, it's very difficult to know what the policy is."

Knox defends the guidance language and suggests that the state environmental officials are mainly concerned because they were left out of the drafting process. "The states are upset because they thought they should be sitting at the table," he says. "We think the guidance should work out pretty well."

Roberts says the state officials' exclusion is more than a matter of pique. "The fact that the states weren't included is important," he says, "because the state environmental departments will be making decisions that will be the basis for any environmental justice complaints that arise. Because we weren't involved in helping to craft the approach to this issue, chances are we won't do it the way EPA wants it done. At some point, we're bound to make decisions improperly because we don't know what their perspective is."

Since ECOS voiced its objections to

the new guidance, EPA has set up a special committee responsible for implementing Title VI, which also includes several state environmental officials.

Aid for "Brownfields"

The EPA's latest attempt to promote environmental justice may prove to be a double-edged sword. For while the interim guidance is intended to make it easier for minority and low-income communities to protect themselves from environmental threats to their health, it may also weaken economic development in these communities by discouraging companies from building new, non-polluting facilities in their midst that could provide needed employment. EPA has led an effort to convert abandoned commercial and industrial sites into productive use.

Many of these so-called "brownfield" sites scare off investors, fearful of being held liable for potential lawsuits by users of the site. While the sites are polluted, they are not polluted enough to qualify for federally funded cleanup under the Superfund program. On Jan. 25, 1995, EPA launched a program to encourage investors to build non-polluting businesses on brownfield sites, which tend to be in urban areas in or near poor or minority communities. By the end of fiscal 1997, EPA had awarded $200,000 seed-money grants to 121 brownfield restoration projects.[16]

"A lot of brownfields are in environmental justice communities," says Knox of EPA. "These communities see brownfields as providing an opportunity to get involved in the siting process and address problems in the city, an opportunity for jobs and a chance to reverse the fiscal deterioration that has drained resources from their neighborhoods. Most of all, brownfields allow communities to get their vision involved in development because they have a seat at the table."

In Knox's view, furthering environmental justice goes hand in hand with brownfield development. "The interim guidance actually helps," he says. "By ensuring that environmental justice has to be considered in the permitting process and bringing affected communities to the table, we are educating residents so they can take over their own communities and bring in clean industries."

But state environmental officials predict the new guidance will be a killer for brownfield development. "The guidance enables anyone with a typewriter to stop a permit from being issued," says Harding, Michigan's environmental commissioner. "We're not opposed to environmental justice, but the guidance goes against getting brownfields going, especially in places like Detroit." Hit by widespread plant closings in the 1970s and '80s, Detroit and other Midwestern cities have many lightly polluted sites that qualify for brownfield development.

"Under the interim guidance, anybody who files an objection in an urban area can show a disparate impact," he says. "It makes it easy to make that showing and turns permitting into a nebulous process that can drag on for years."

Business representatives agree. "We're not saying there aren't concerns that need to be dealt with," says Borné of the Louisiana Chemical Association. "We are saying that with this interim guidance EPA is forever changing the landscape of development in this country. And you can forget about brownfield development because most brownfield sites are in minority communities."

Environmental Justice Resource Center

Residents of this African-American neighborhood built on top of the Agriculture Street Landfill in New Orleans are petitioning the EPA to relocate them from the area, now a Superfund site. Activists call this the "black Love Canal."

OUTLOOK

Impact on Business

Industry representatives predict that EPA's policy to promote environmental justice will harm more than just brownfield development. Mason says that charging Shintech with environmental racism sends a message to industry that may not be what the activists intended.

At Issue:

Would constructing a low-level radioactive nuclear-waste dump near Sierra Blanca, Texas, constitute "environmental injustice"?

yes

BILL ADDINGTON
Rancher, farmer and merchant, Hudspeth County, Texas

FROM TESTIMONY BEFORE THE HOUSE COMMERCE SUBCOMMITTEE ON ENERGY AND POWER, MAY 13, 1997.

I speak today on behalf of Save Sierra Blanca, our citizens group, and many people in West Texas who feel run over by the state and federal governments. These people are opposed to the forced placement of this risky radioactive-waste cemetery at Sierra Blanca near the Rio Grande River. . . .

Most of the people in Hudspeth County and Sierra Blanca are poor — the median annual income is $8,000. Seventy percent of the people are of Hispanic origin, like myself. This is the reason Texas "leaders" have focused on our county for the dump site since 1983. This appeared to be the political path of least resistance. But there is strong resistance locally, regionally and internationally. There are about 3,000 people and 1,300 registered voters in the county, and every one of them who was asked signed the petition against the dump. . . .

The siting of the Sierra Blanca dump by the state legislature was a violation of environmental justice and our civil rights. . . .

If the radioactive-waste dump is approved in Sierra Blanca, it is likely that additional radioactive and hazardous facilities will follow. Westinghouse Scientific Ecology Group has entered into an option agreement to lease 1,280 acres of land adjoining the proposed Sierra Blanca site for radioactive waste processing and storage, possibly including incineration. There is also a proposal for an additional sludge dump in the community. This concentrating of hazardous facilities in communities is a characteristic of environmental injustice.

The proposed radioactive dump site is geologically fatally flawed. It is in an earthquake zone, and there is a buried fault underneath the proposed trenches. . . .

The real reason for the compact is economic — to make it cheaper for nuclear power generators to bury their waste and shift their liability. It does not "protect Texas," as has been touted. . . .

Texas began negotiations with . . . Maine in 1988, and in 1992 passed the compact. Maine's and Vermont's legislatures have approved the compact. They failed to develop their own waste sites because of heavy opposition. Maine voters approved the compact by referendum, yet people in my home are not even heard or considered. We do not get to vote on the measure or placement of the dump like Mainers, who chose to dump on us, did.

no

SEN. OLYMPIA J. SNOWE, R-MAINE

FROM A SENATE FLOOR SPEECH, APRIL 1, 1998.

As the law requires, Texas, Vermont and Maine have negotiated an agreement that was approved by each state. . . . So, we have before us a compact that has been carefully crafted and thoroughly examined by the state governments and people of all three states involved. Now all that is required is the approval of Congress, so that the state of Texas and the other Texas Compact members will be able to exercise appropriate control over the waste that will come into the Texas facility. . . .

Opponents of the Texas Compact would have you believe that should we ratify this compact it will open the doors for other states to dump nuclear waste at a site, in the desert, located five miles from the town of Sierra Blanca, exposing a predominantly low-income, minority community to health and environmental threats.

The truth is that Texas has been planning to build a facility for its own waste since 1981, long before Maine first proposed a compact with Texas. That is because whether or not this compact passes, Texas still must somehow take care of the waste it produces. . . .

The opponents of the compact would have you believe this issue is about politics. It is not about politics, it is about science: sound science. It is very dry in the Southwest Texas area, where the small amount of rainfall it receives mostly evaporates before it hits the ground. The aquifer that supplies water to the area and to nearby Mexico is over 600 feet below the desert floor and is encased in rock.

The proposed site has been designed to withstand any earthquake equaling the most severe that has ever occurred in Texas history. Strong seismic activity in the area is nonexistent. All these factors mean that the siting of this facility is on strong scientific grounds.

Our opponents say we will be bad neighbors if we pass this compact because the proposed site is near the Mexican border. In fact, the U.S. and Mexico have an agreement, the La Paz Agreement, to cooperate in the environmental protection of the border region. The La Paz Agreement simply encourages cooperative efforts to protect the environment of the region.

Any proposed facility will be protective of the environment because it will be constructed in accordance with the strictest U.S. environmental safeguards.

FOR MORE INFORMATION

Center for Health, Environment and Justice, P.O. Box 6806, Falls Church, Va. 22040; (703) 237-2249, www.chej.org. The center helps community-based groups fend off environmental hazards. It was founded by a former resident of Love Canal, N.Y., the community built near a toxic-waste dump.

Earthjustice Legal Defense Fund, 180 Montgomery St., Suite 1400, San Francisco, Calif. 94014; (800) 584-6460; www.earthjustice.org. Formerly known as the Sierra Club Legal Defense Fund, this nonprofit law firm is active in cases involving environmental justice.

Environmental Council of the States, 444 N. Capitol St. N.W., Suite 445, Washington, D.C. 20001; (202) 624-3660; www.sso.org/ecos/. A membership group representing environmental officials of the states and the District of Columbia, ECOS opposes the EPA's new rules for handling environmental justice complaints.

Environmental Justice Resource Center, Clark Atlanta University, 223 James P. Brawley Dr. S.W., Atlanta, Ga. 30314; (404) 880-6911. www.ejrc.cau.edu. Directed by Robert D. Bullard, a longtime environmental justice leader, the center helps communities protect themselves from pollution sources.

Greenpeace, 702 H. St. N.W., Washington, D.C. 20001; (800) 326-0959; www.greenpeace.org. This research and activist group has recently become involved in several cases involving complaints of environmental racism.

Office of Environmental Justice, U.S. Environmental Protection Agency, 401 M St. S.W., Washington, D.C. 20460; (202) 564-2515 or (800) 962-6215; es.epa.gov/environsense/oeca/oej.html. The OEJ coordinates EPA activities and provides technical assistance to communities threatened by environmental hazards.

"The message is, 'You're stupid if you try to move into a community with a significant number of African-Americans, or any other racial minority,' " Mason says. "We don't want to be in a community that doesn't want us there. But this policy will deprive many people of economic opportunity, and it's bad news for economic development in general."

Some critics predict that the EPA's policy is such a deterrent to industrial development and job creation that many companies will shift production overseas.

"In the long run, this is the best economic-development program for Mexico that's ever come down the pike," Borné says. "If EPA really wants to chase our industry over the border, then this is a first-class ticket. I already see how detrimental this policy is to economic development in my state."

EPA is still investigating the Shintech case. However it is resolved, supporters of the environmental justice movement are optimistic that more aggressive steps to combat environmental racism will pay off, not only for poor and non-white Americans but also in the development of cleaner manufacturing and waste technologies.

"The movement has moved beyond the siting of facilities," Bullard says. "It's bigger than that. It embraces the full question of prevention, health and employment. We're now asking if we really need more chemicals entering the waste stream, as opposed to changing production processes to protect health and the environment. A company that produces waste is a wasteful company. So it makes sense to reduce waste so we won't need as many facilities to dispose of this stuff."

Knox agrees with Bullard's assessment and argues that the struggle for environmental justice need not be adversarial because it will benefit everyone. "If this is to be the greatest industrial society of all time, industry has to be clean," he says. "But we all have to work together to make that happen. There's a role for everybody, including business and communities. We all have to sit at the table."

Bullard says pressure from low-income and minority communities that have lodged environmental racism complaints has already spurred manufacturers to develop and adopt cleaner production processes and products, including soy-based ink for newspapers, recycled paper for packaging and pesticide-free fruits and vegetables.

"But I think the biggest impact of the environmental justice movement has not come yet," Bullard says. "That is consumers who are selective and educated about what they will buy and what they won't buy. Creating educated consumers who will start punishing companies that hurt the environment and rewarding those that adopt environmentally sound business practices will be the last civil rights battle." ■

Notes

[1] Executive Order 12898, "Federal Actions to Address Environmental Justice in Minority Populations and Low-Income Populations," Feb. 11, 1994. For background, see "Cleaning Up Hazardous Wastes," *The CQ Researcher*, Aug. 23, 1996, pp. 752-776.

[2] In *Bean v. Southwestern Waste Management*, residents of a predominantly black subdivision in Houston charged that Browning-Ferris Industries had practiced environmental discrimination by choosing their community to site a municipal solid-waste landfill. They lost the case.

[3] For background, see "Jobs vs. Environment," *The CQ Researcher*, May 15, 1992, pp. 409-432.

[4] Benjamin A. Goldman and Laura Fitton, *Toxic Wastes and Race Revisited,* Center for Policy Alternatives, National Association for the Advancement of Colored People and United Church of Christ Commission for Racial Justice, 1994.

[5] U.S. Environmental Protection Agency, Office of Environmental Justice, *Serving a Diverse Society,* November 1997. For background, see "New Air Quality Standards," *The CQ Researcher*, March 7, 1997, pp. 193-217.

[6] Christopher H. Foreman Jr., "A Winning Hand? The Uncertain Future of Environmental Justice," *The Brookings Review*, spring 1996, p. 24. Foreman's new book, *The Promise and Peril of Environmental Justice,* is due to be published by the Brookings Institution in the fall.

[7] *Ibid.*, p. 25.

[8] See American Lung Association, "Health Effects of Outdoor Air Pollution," 1996.

[9] For background, see "Environmental Movement at 25," *The CQ Researcher*, March 31, 1995, pp. 283-307.

[10] See Environmental Protection Agency, Office of Environmental Justice, *Environmental Justice 1994 Annual Report: Focusing on Environmental Protection for All People,* April 1995.

[11] See Robert D. Bullard, *Unequal Protection* (1994), pp. 43-52.

[12] General Accounting Office, *Siting of Hazardous Waste Landfills and Their Correlation with Racial and Economic Status of Surrounding Communities* (1983); United Church of Christ Commission for Racial Justice, *Toxic Wastes and Race in the United States* (1987).

[13] Quoted in EPA, *Environmental Justice 1994 Annual Report, op. cit.,* p. 3.

[14] See Andrew S. Levine, Jonathan E. Rinde and Kenneth J. Warren, "In Response to Chester Residents, EPA Releases Environmental Justice Rules," *The Legal Intelligencer*, Feb. 18, 1998.

[15] See Paul Hoverten, "EPA Puts Plant on Hold in Racism Case," *USA Today*, Sept. 11, 1998.

[16] See "New EPA Report Lists Positive Effects of Agency Superfund Reform Efforts," *Hazardous Waste News*, Feb. 16, 1998.

Bibliography

Selected Sources Used

Books

Bullard, Robert D., *Dumping in Dixie: Race, Class and Environmental Quality,* Harper Collins, 1996.
A leading activist in the environmental justice movement examines the enforcement of environmental-protection laws in the Southern United States, where poor, mostly black communities are commonly chosen as sites for waste dumps and incinerators.

Bullard, Robert D., ed., *Unequal Protection: Environmental Justice and Communities of Color,* Sierra Club Books, 1994.
This collection of essays describes how communities of poor and non-white Americans are disproportionately exposed to toxic wastes and other environmental hazards.

Szasz, Andrew, *EcoPopulism: Toxic Waste and the Movement for Environmental Justice,* University of Minnesota Press, 1994.
The author describes the environmental justice movement's evolution from grass-roots activism to federal policy. By focusing on pollution prevention rather than cleaning up polluted sites, the movement is changing the focus of environmental policy.

Articles

Arrandale, Tom, "Regulation and Racism," *Governing,* March 1998, p. 63.
The Environmental Protection Agency's decision to overturn a state-issued permit to build a plastics plant near a poor, minority community in Louisiana last fall does not further the goal of environmental justice, the author writes, because it will discourage industry from bringing jobs to the very communities that are hardest hit by unemployment.

Hampson, Fen Osler, and Judith Reppy, "Environmental Change and Social Justice," *Environment,* April 1997, pp. 12-20.
The authors apply the tenets of environmental justice to global environmental issues, including global warming. Developed nations, which have contributed the most to this problem, should help devise solutions that reduce economic inequality between rich and developing nations, the authors contend.

Northridge, Mary E., and Peggy M. Shepard, "Comment: Environmental Racism and Public Health," *American Journal of Public Health,* May 1997, pp. 730-732.
The authors call for further study of the disparate impact of environmental hazards on poor, non-white communities and a broad public health initiative, similar in scope to the anti-smoking campaign, to prevent and remove toxins from these communities.

Parris, Thomas M., "Spinning the Web of Environmental Justice," *Environment,* May 1997, pp. 44-45.
This collection of Internet addresses provides a wealth of sources, including Environmental Protection Agency (EPA) reports and non-governmental studies, on efforts to combat pollution that affects poor and minority communities.

Sachs, Aaron, "Upholding Human Rights and Environmental Justice," *The Humanist,* March-April 1996, pp. 5-8.
The author reviews the international movement for environmental justice that took off after the 1988 murder of Chico Mendes, a Brazilian rubber tapper who fought for the rights of rain forest inhabitants against cattle barons who were clearing the forests for grazing land.

Schoeplfle, Mark, "Due Process and Dialogue: Consulting with Native Americans under the National Environmental Policy Act," *Common Ground,* summer/fall 1997, pp. 40-45.
The 1969 National Environmental Policy Act provides standards for informing Indian tribes of environmental hazards and taking steps to protect themselves from pollutants.

Reports and Studies

Goldman, Benjamin A., and Laura Fitton, *Toxic Wastes and Race Revisited,* Center for Policy Alternatives, 1994.
This update of a 1987 report on the racial and socioeconomic characteristics of communities with hazardous-waste sites finds that poor and minority communities are even more disproportionately exposed to toxins than before, despite the growth of the environmental justice movement.

National Environmental Justice Advisory Council, *Environmental Justice, Urban Revitalization and Brownfields: The Search for Authentic Signs of Hope,* December 1996.
An EPA advisory committee finds that the development of brownfields — abandoned industrial sites that are not polluted enough to warrant federal cleanup under the Superfund program — is an important contribution to the goal of environmental justice.

U.S. Environmental Protection Agency, Office of Environmental Justice, *Serving a Diverse Society,* November 1997.
This pamphlet summarizes the adverse impact of air pollution, pesticides, agricultural runoff and other environmental hazards on communities of color and suggests steps communities can take to minimize exposure.

7 Income Inequality

MARY H. COOPER

By most people's standards a salary of $750,000 is almost beyond comprehension. But last year that was just the appetizer for Walt Disney Co. CEO Michael Eisner. By exercising his stock options, Eisner boosted his take to an astounding $575 million — more than a million dollars a day. And while Eisner's case is extreme, it is hardly unique. Earnings for top executives in 1997 rose by as much as 21 percent. [1]

But rank-and-file workers didn't fare as well. They only received 3 percent raises, on average.

The U.S. economy has rarely been in better shape. The current recovery, now entering its eighth year, has created so many new jobs that unemployment fell to 4.6 percent in February, its lowest level in 24 years. [2]

A tight labor market usually fuels a round of inflation, as workers demand higher wages and manufacturers pass on the labor costs to the consumer. But not this time. Inflation stands at a mere 1.6 percent. Interest rates also are low, enabling businesses and consumers to borrow cheaply. And the stock market continues to set new records, bringing unexpectedly high returns to investors.

There's just one flaw in this glowing picture. While Eisner and other Americans are reaping benefits from the long period of prosperity, many others are falling behind. Moreover, it's the least well-off who are losing out, while those who are already prosperous are benefiting the most. As a result, the income gap — the difference in income between the richest and the poorest Americans — is widening. At the same time, the number of people in the middle class — the traditional objective of working Americans — is actually shrinking.

The picture was not always so bleak for the nation's have-nots.

From *The CQ Researcher*, April 17, 1998.

Reuters/Peter Morgan

Walt Disney Co. CEO Michael Eisner took home $575 million last year.

"Looking at income growth over the postwar period, we saw income rising at all levels," says Elizabeth McNichol, a director at the Center on Budget and Policy Priorities. "But that's not what is happening now. Income at the low end is falling, while it's increasing a lot at the high end, and the middle is flat or dropping. It's not like one group is doing just a little better than the other."

In analyzing Census Bureau data, the center found that the income of the richest Americans increased by 30 percent from the late 1970s to the mid-'90s, while the poorest saw their incomes shrink by 21 percent. Americans occupying the middle range experienced a paltry 2 percent gain in income. Because the inflation-adjusted data do not include annual incomes over $100,000, the figures actually understate the breadth of the income gap. [3]

There are a number of reasons for the growing disparity in income. The decline in manufacturing during the 1980s eliminated thousands of high-wage, blue-collar jobs, which were replaced with largely low-paid jobs in the expanding service sector. Labor unions, which had won high wages for industrial workers throughout the postwar era, lost their clout as factories closed and unions were kept out of many service workplaces. At the same time that the earning potential of low-skilled workers waned, rapid technological advances increased demand for better-skilled workers. This trend also widened the income gap between high school and college graduates.

Black Americans are disproportionately represented at the bottom of the income distribution, as they always have been. Thirty years ago, when the Kerner Commission submitted its landmark report on the roots of civil disorders in the United States, it concluded, "Our nation is moving toward two societies, one black, one white — separate and unequal." A recent update of that report found that black Americans are still locked out of economic prosperity. [4]

"The main problem is that poverty has increased since the Kerner report," says Fred R. Harris, a former Democratic U.S. senator from Oklahoma and Kerner Commission member, who co-authored the update. "We have more poverty and a greater percentage of poor people than we did 30 years ago, while the wealth and income gaps have widened."

Like other low- to middle-income workers, black Americans have suffered from the disappearance of industrial jobs. But poor black residents of the country's central cities have been especially disadvantaged by the migration of businesses to the suburbs. "The new jobs are out in the suburbs, where it's hard for central-city people to get to, and the ones in the city are low-paying service jobs," Harris says.

Technological changes also have left many black Americans particularly ill-prepared for today's high-wage jobs. "These jobs have high requirements for skills and education," Harris says. "So we've seen another kind of gap emerge between people with high school or college edu-

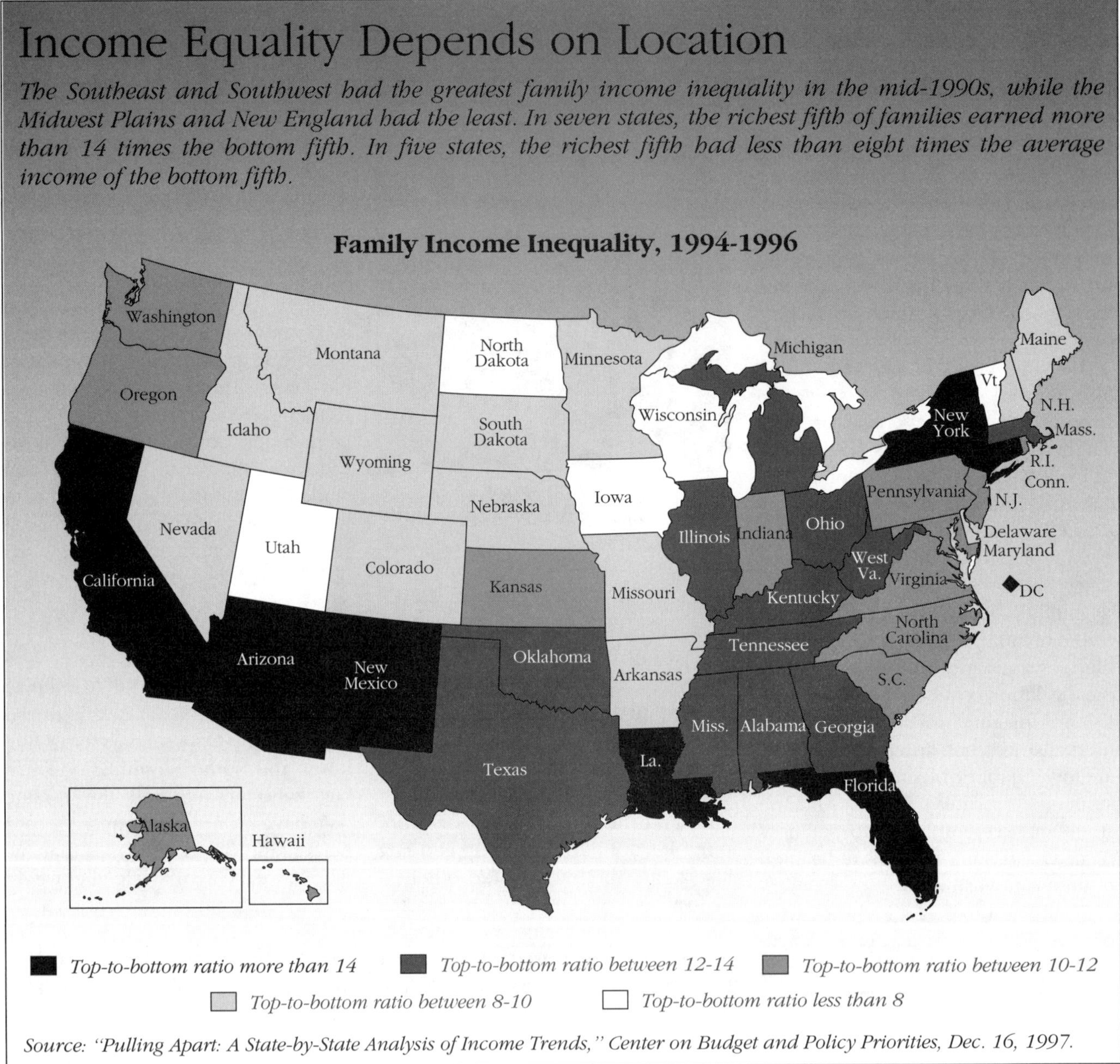

Income Equality Depends on Location

The Southeast and Southwest had the greatest family income inequality in the mid-1990s, while the Midwest Plains and New England had the least. In seven states, the richest fifth of families earned more than 14 times the bottom fifth. In five states, the richest fifth had less than eight times the average income of the bottom fifth.

Source: "Pulling Apart: A State-by-State Analysis of Income Trends," Center on Budget and Policy Priorities, Dec. 16, 1997.

cations and those without, and this is a huge and growing gap."

At the other extreme of the income spectrum, rising stock prices have boosted the investment income of shareholders, who are mostly higher-income Americans. According to the center's analysis, average investment income received by the wealthiest 5 percent of families rose 56 percent, adjusted for inflation, between 1979 and 1994, averaging more than $51,000 per household in 1996 alone. Here too, because the Census data do not include capital gains, the actual total-income figures are probably considerably higher.

Further skewing income distribution toward the wealthiest Americans is the widespread corporate practice of rewarding top executives with stock options, which enable recipients to buy shares at a set price for a specified period. As the stock market has boomed, so too has the value of the options available for executive compensation.

"CEOs are cashing in on the bull market," says William Patterson, director of the AFL-CIO's office of investment. "And that's based less on their good works or their own particular merits than on the enormous amount of capital that has entered the stock market in the last five years."

Some analysts say the gap in living standards is more accurately measured by including not just household income but net worth — a household's accumulated wealth minus outstanding debts. "The distribution of wealth is even more skewed than the distribution of earnings," says Alan B. Krueger, a labor economist at Princeton University and former chief economist at the Labor Department. For example, Bill Gates, the 41-year-old chief executive of Microsoft, who topped last year's *Forbes* 400 list of the richest Americans, is worth an estimated $40 billion. "That's equivalent to the combined net worth of the bottom 40 percent of U.S. households," Krueger says. "Even when you account for the fact that the bottom 18 percent have no net worth, 40 percent is a lot of people. In a democracy, one needs to be worried about that kind of concentration of wealth."

The Clinton administration points to signs that the ever-widening income gap may recently have reversed course. According to *The 1998 Economic Report of the President*, household income has grown across the income spectrum since 1993, with the greatest improvement going to the poorest households. The report points optimistically at a reduction in the poverty rate from 15.1 percent in 1993 to 13.7 percent in 1997, a development that has been especially beneficial to black Americans, whose poverty rate is at the lowest level ever. [5]

Some economists agree that today's strong economy may have stopped the income gap from widening. "The income gap is still there, in fact it's worse than it was as recently as 1980," says Richard Freeman, an economist at Harvard University. "But it hasn't widened all that much in recent years, and now it's leveled off. There's even some evidence that the very bottom is coming up as well. So it's safe to say that income inequality may have gotten better."

The latest economic data seem to confirm the optimists' views. The Labor Department reported in March that wages for the lowest-paid workers reversed their downward course last year and rose by 1.6 percent to $260 a week, the biggest increase since the government began collecting such data in 1979. [6]

But any narrowing of the income gap seems unlikely to bite into the fortunes of Gates and other tycoons. "The momentum of prosperity in the United States suggests that the income gap will start to narrow, but not at the expense of the very, very rich, the 1 percent of the income distribution who are raking in megamillions on this incredible stock market," says Allen Sinai, chief economist at Primark Decision Economics in Boston. "But, on average, the lower end of the income distribution is picking up speed."

If the optimists are right, low unemployment is finally helping workers who have not shared in the current recovery. "The economy is dipping into unskilled workers and the lowest end of the compensation pool in a significant way because there's a shortage of workers everywhere," Sinai says. "General prosperity is doing its thing, raising the pay of ordinary workers."

Just how long the current recovery will last is, of course, a matter of speculation. Economic turmoil in Asia may yet slash demand for U.S. goods and services and tip the economic balance once again into recession. But even if the recovery continues to boost average incomes, the wide disparity in Americans' incomes is likely to persist.

As economists watch the impact of burgeoning economic growth on the income gap, these are some of the questions being asked:

Does the income gap matter?

Income inequality in the United States is at an all-time high. But because of advances in health care, agriculture and other factors that contribute to the overall standard of living, some experts say the United States is now enjoying a period of prosperity that has a far greater impact on all Americans' living standards than the persistent income gap.

"[I]t is true that, by some measures, there has been a recent increase in income inequality in the United States," writes Christopher C. DeMuth, president of the American Enterprise Institute for Public Policy Research, a conservative think tank. "But it is a very small tick in the massive and unprecedented leveling of material circumstances that has been proceeding now for almost three centuries and in this century has accelerated dramatically. In fact, the much-noticed increase in [income] inequality is in part a result of the increase in real social equality." [7]

DeMuth cites the general availability of food, shelter and clothing, medical advances, the replacement of social class with intellectual ability as the key to success and the reduction of workplace discrimination against women as trends that have contributed to our society's unprecedented prosperity. "One implication of these trends is that in very wealthy societies, income has become a less useful gauge of economic welfare and hence of economic equality," he writes. [8]

This view reflects the economic adage "a rising tide lifts all boats," which suggests that economic growth makes life better for everyone in society by making the kinds of advances DeMuth describes available throughout society. But other experts maintain that the income gap is clear evidence that the benefits of today's booming economy are not being enjoyed by all.

"It is correct to look at a lot of

Today's Rich Are Really Rich

Income inequality is hardly a secret in American society. Poor workers who are struggling to get by on the minimum wage, currently $5.15 an hour by federal law, are bombarded by television advertisements hawking luxury cars, cruise vacations and other amenities that only the wealthy can afford. They root for athletes who take home millions of dollars a year and are entertained by actors and musicians whose annual incomes are hundreds of times higher than their own meager wages. Adding insult to injury, the rich are getting a lot richer. It took a net worth of $475 million to get on the annual *Forbes* 400 list of the wealthiest Americans last year, up from $415 million in 1996. [1]

But the truly rich Americans — the megamillionaires — are less visible than the mere millionaires who populate Hollywood and the sports arenas. As one might expect, they are typically old white men, such as William Hewlett, 84, co-founder of Hewlett Packard (net worth $4.1 billion) and Metromedia founder John Kluge, 83 ($7.8 billion). Talk-show hostess Oprah Winfrey was the only black person in *Forbes'* rankings last year, and she placed a lowly 343rd, with a net worth of only $550 million.

But the technology boom has added younger blood, and a lot more money, to the top of the heap. The richest man in America is Microsoft co-founder William Henry Gates III, who at 41 has already amassed a fortune of about $40 billion — more than the gross national product of many countries. Another Microsoft founder, Paul Gardner Allen, 44, ranks third at $17 billion. Of the richest 25 Americans, seven made their fortunes in high technology.

But there are other roads to riches. Many who made the list were simply in the right place at the right time and inherited their wealth, such as the widow and four children of Wal-Mart founder Sam Walton, who share the family fortune of $32 billion. William Wrigley ($2.5 billion) got rich from the family chewing gum empire, while liquor magnate Edgar Bronfman Sr. ($3 billion) took over Joseph E. Seagram & Sons from his father. John Richard Simplot amassed his $3.3 billion growing potatoes — and later producing microchips. [2]

Reuters/Ian Hodgson

Microsoft co-founder Bill Gates is worth an estimated $40 billion.

What do they do with all their wealth? Most, of course, make more by investing their fortunes. And if the stock market continues its current upward spiral, the multibillionaire club can only multiply. Others buy land — lots of it. Media mogul Ted Turner (net worth $3.5 billion) has acquired hundreds of thousands of acres of pristine forest and prairie throughout the Mountain West.

The super-rich also give some of their money away, if for no other reason than the fact that the Internal Revenue Service rewards philanthropy by excluding donated funds from taxation. But wealth and generosity do not always go hand in hand.

Bill Gates may be the richest man in America, but he has given away a relatively paltry $100-$500 million to date, according to a recent listing of America's 100 leading philanthropists. [3] Compare that with the generosity of retired publisher Walter Annenberg, who has donated more than $1 billion, nearly a third of his $3.8 billion fortune, or Paul Mellon, who has given away almost all of his $1.2 billion oil and banking inheritance. (Turner's pledge last year of $1 billion to the United Nations isn't included in the listing because it only considered disbursed contributions.)

Granted, Annenberg and Mellon are in their 90s, while Gates has a wife and child to support. In fact, Gates is not alone among tycoons who, to date, have not distinguished themselves as great philanthropists. Only 61 of the people who made the *Forbes* 400 list also made the *American Benefactor* 100 list.

---

[1] See "The 400: The Average Net Worth of the Forbes Four Hundred is $1.6 billion," *Forbes*, Oct. 13, 1997, pp. 181-250.

[2] "The Top 25," *Forbes*, Oct. 13, 1997, pp. 152-166.

[3] Dan Rottenberg, "100 Most Generous Americans," *The American Benefactor*, fall 1997, pp. 42-68. For background, see "The New Corporate Philanthropy," *The CQ Researcher*, Feb. 27, 1998, pp. 169-197.

things, such as medical advances, but clearly a very important determinant of well-being is the wage rate people command," Krueger says. "And a large income gap is cause for concern."

Some critics also dispute DeMuth's assertion that the non-wage benefits of industrial development help everyone. "The whole point of the surge in inequality is that the benefits are far from equally enjoyed," says Jared Bernstein, an economist at the liberal Economic Policy Institute. "It's pretty meaningless to say don't worry about it if the gains themselves are unequally distributed." A wealthy American, for example, can buy the latest medical treatment, even if it isn't covered by health insurance, while many poor workers cannot afford even the most basic health coverage. "With medical care, the further you are down on the income scale, the less access you have to the system, especially to quality health care," Bernstein says.

Even the recent narrowing of the income gap fails to convince some economists that the boom is having a significant impact on the poorest Americans. "The gap grew considerably during the 1980s, stabilized in the 1990s and last year incomes at the bottom grew a bit more than they did in the middle," Krueger says. "But the gap that opened in the 1980s was only slightly reduced. So to the extent that one was concerned about the income gap before, one should still be."

Prosperity Boosts CEOs, Not Workers

The booming economy boosted corporate profits by 50 percent from 1990 to 1995 and added more than $1 million to the average CEO's pay, but layoffs of workers increased by more than a third and their pay decreased slightly.

Winners

Investors and CEOs

Corporate Profits: 1990 — $176 billion; 1995 — $264 billion

Average CEO Pay: 1990 — $1.9 million; 1995 — $3.2 million

Losers

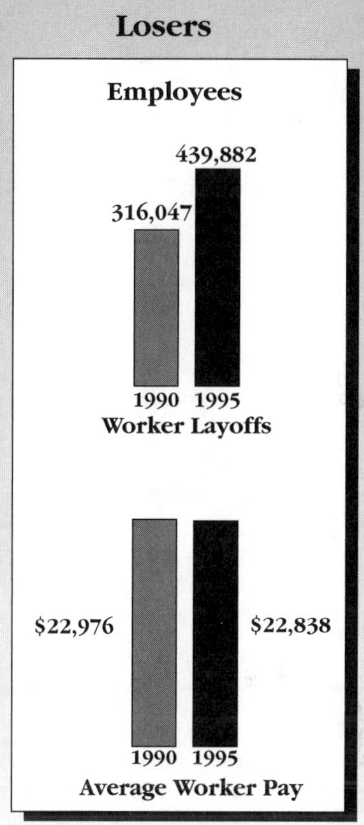

Note: Dollar amounts are in constant 1990 dollars.

Sources: United for a Fair Economy, from Business Week, *April 22, 1996; Bureau of Labor Statistics and Challenger, Gray and Christmas*

Supply-side economists, who support the notion that the benefits of economic growth "trickle down" to the lowest income levels, say the income gap is not the most important measure of well-being. "A capitalist economy over time produces an affluent society, a society with a high level of average income," writes Irving Kristol, an American Enterprise Institute fellow and co-editor of *The Public Interest*, a conservative magazine. "In such a society, income inequality tends to be swamped by even greater social equality." Kristol observes that all Americans wear blue jeans and buy expensive cars on installment. "In all of our major cities, there is not a single restaurant where a CEO can lunch or dine with the absolute assurance that he will not run into his secretary," he writes. "If you fly first class, who will be your traveling companions? You never know." [9]

But this view does not take into account the persistent failure of some groups in the population to benefit from the general prosperity. "It's just not so for a lot of people, especially people who are locked in the poorhouse in the central city," Harris says. "Today 14.4 million Americans have incomes at less than half the poverty threshold, which is an increase over 1995. So there are more poor people today, and people who are poor are poorer, so it's much harder for them to get out of it. And poverty is more concentrated in the central cities, and thus among African-Americans and Hispanic-Americans."

Wages Rose for Top Earners, Fell for Poor

Wages fell at least 5 percent for the lowest wage earners in the United States from 1979 to 1989 but rose for the top 25 percent.

Wage Growth, 1979-1989

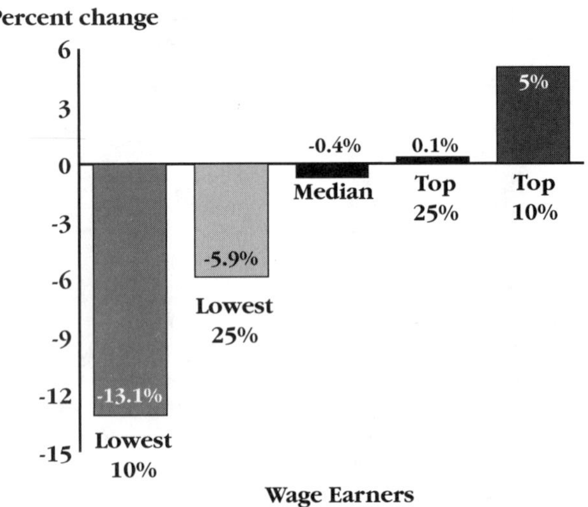

Note: Wages are in constant 1982-1984 dollars.

Sources: The Milton S. Eisenhower Foundation and The Corporation for What Works, The Millennium Breach: Richer, Poor and Racially Apart, *March 1, 1988.*

Is racism a leading cause of income disparity in the United States?

The civil rights movement of the 1960s and early '70s led to changes in public policy that have greatly improved the lot of black Americans over the past 30 years. The number of African-Americans who have been elected to public office has risen dramatically, as has the number of black business owners, white-collar employees and high school graduates. Laws barring racial discrimination and affirmative-action policies in college admissions and hiring have helped more and more black Americans to join the middle class.

But beginning in the 1980s, efforts to combat racial discrimination came under attack, culminating in the recent bans on affirmative-action rules in the California and Texas state-university systems. As a result, admissions offers to black and Hispanic students for next fall's freshman class at the University of California at Berkeley, the First class chosen without affirmative-action rules, fell by more than half over last year. [10]

Supporters of affirmative action say its erosion has resulted in a worsening of living standards among black and Hispanic-Americans that is closely linked to the deepening income gap. The Eisenhower Foundation's recent update of the Kerner Commission report, for example, points out that while overall unemployment in the United States fell to 4.6 percent in February, it still stands at 9.9 percent for African-Americans. While 11.2 percent of white teenagers are unable to find jobs, teen unemployment is more than three times higher among black teens. The median income of black and Hispanic-Americans is still just over half that of non-Hispanic, white Americans. And more than three-quarters of poor people live in central cities today, up from about half in the late 1960s. [11]

"This concentrated poverty certainly involves race, because of segregation of housing and schools, which is happening once again," Harris says. "Families in the inner city, where poverty is concentrated, have a really difficult time breaking out. Shut off from contact with people in the middle class, those who are left behind don't have contact with the institutions or people to help them get out of poverty."

Harris stops short of blaming income inequality on racial discrimination alone. But, he says, "it has been very much involved with it. We've knocked down the legal and political barriers of discrimination, but we still have a great deal of institutional discrimination. There's no question that we've made enormous progress with regard to race — many African-Americans are middle-class people and officials," he says. "But that does not mean that we should give up on affirmative action."

Not all black commentators agree that racial discrimination plays a significant role in income inequality. "If race were at the bottom of it, then why aren't all blacks suffering equally?" asks Robert L. Woodson Sr., chairman of the National Center for Neighborhood Enterprises. "The biggest income gap today is not between black and white people," he says, "but between upper-income blacks and low-income blacks."

Woodson says most black teachers in the Washington, D.C., public school system send their children to schools outside the system, but oppose adoption of a voucher program that would allow other black parents to do the same. "So poor black kids are being disadvantaged in a system controlled by other blacks. They are suffering at the hands of their own people."

Even Woodson concedes that institutional discrimination still contributes to inequality in America. Citing a recent survey finding that two out of five blacks applying for mortgage loans from 75 institutions faced stiffer requirements to qualify than did whites, he says, "institutional discrimination plays some role in income disparity. But it's not the dominant role."

Income is not the sole measure of racial inequality, however. "When you talk about racial disparities, it's really important to move beyond income and look at wealth, because that is where the disparity is the greatest," Bernstein says. In 1993, he notes, the median net worth of white families was $45,740, more than 10 times the $4,418 net worth of African-American families. "Regardless of where you think racial discrimination is today, the cumulative history of discrimination has resulted in huge disparities in wealth between minorities and whites."

Tax Cuts Benefited Rich, Not Poor

Taxes for the poorest 20 percent of the population rose 10 percent from 1980 to 1990, while taxes for the richest 5 percent were reduced by about 13 percent.

Changes in Tax Rates

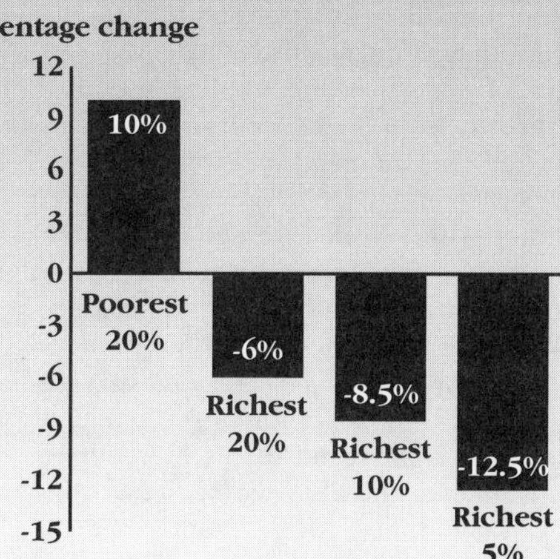

Sources: The Milton S. Eisenhower Foundation and The Corporation for What Works, The Millennium Breach: Richer, Poor and Racially Apart, *March 1, 1998; Congressional Budget Office*

Should the government do more to reduce income disparity?

Through policies ranging from the progressive income tax to the minimum wage, the federal government has long interfered in the free market in an attempt to reduce the extremes of wealth and poverty. Tax rates that increase with income ensure that the rich pay the greatest percentage of their income in taxes, while laws guaranteeing workers a minimum wage and the earned-income tax credit are attempts to buoy the disposable incomes of the poorest workers.

But some of these safeguards were eroded during the 1980s as the Republican administration of Ronald Reagan adopted a supply-side approach toward managing the economy. By reducing tax burdens, especially those of investors and business owners, policy-makers reasoned, the economy would grow faster, producing more jobs and raising incomes at the middle- and lower-income levels as well.

The 1986 Tax Reform Act and other changes in the 1980s did, in fact, lower the burden of taxation on the wealthy. But other initiatives eroded the "safety net" of social programs designed in the wake of the Great Depression to raise the living standards of the poorest Americans. At the same time, low-wage workers saw their incomes actually fall as inflation reduced the value of the minimum wage, which was left unchanged from 1981 to 1990.

Policies adopted since 1990 have reversed some of the economic policies of the '80s. The minimum wage, for example, has been increased four times, twice during the Bush administration and twice during the Clinton administration. But the overriding concern of balancing the federal budget has meant that government programs designed to aid the poor have not been strengthened. Some programs, notably Aid to Families with Dependent Children (AFDC), have been cut back even further under the 1996 Welfare Reform Act. [12]

Supporters of the law say it will help boost earnings at the low end of the income spectrum by forcing current welfare recipients to work and eventually go off the welfare rolls. "Along with family disintegration," says Woodson of the National Center for Neighborhood Enterprises, "policies that discourage work, such as welfare, are among the leading factors contributing to income inequality."

Although the most recent data show a slight reversal in the trend toward greater income disparity, many analysts say the federal government should do more to reduce the wage gap. "The minimum

Gender Gap Adds to Income Inequality

The gender gap — the difference in earnings between men and women — is a persistent contributor to income inequality in the United States. American women make only 74 cents for every dollar earned by men, although the gap has narrowed by five cents over the past two decades, according to the AFL-CIO. [1]

For years, wage discrimination against female workers was attributed to lack of education and training. Because many women went directly from high school or college to marriage and life as full-time homemakers and mothers, they tended to have less formal job training than men. When they finally entered the work force, often in their late 30s or 40s, women also lacked the years of service — and annual raises — their male counterparts had built up.

The 1970s and '80s saw a rapid increase in the number of women in the work force. The loss of high-paying manufacturing jobs, the decline in union representation and rampant inflation had all reduced men's earnings in this period, forcing many married women to seek employment. At the same time, young women began entering graduate schools in increasing numbers, preparing them for high-paying jobs in law, medicine and business.

But even after women began entering the work force in large numbers, the gender gap remained stubbornly high. Female business-school graduates, many now in their 30s and 40s, complain repeatedly of a corporate "glass ceiling" preventing them from ever attaining top management jobs. Today women hold only 3 percent of the top six executive positions at the country's biggest companies, and only a few have become chief executive officers. [2]

Most workers, male or female, lack the education and training that would enable them to aspire to top positions. But women throughout the work force claim that men routinely receive higher pay for similar work. According to the Census Bureau, the average income of college-educated, white, female managers is $38,800, or $17,100 less than that of white males of the same category. The gender gap is less conspicuous among African-Americans: Black female managers earn $31,000, which is $10,000 less than African-American males. But the racial divide is clear, even at this highly skilled level. [3]

Perhaps reflecting wage inequality, a recent survey found that 56 percent of working women were unable to save part of their paychecks or even keep up with their bills. The vast majority of women polled — 91 percent — said laws should be strengthened to ensure equal pay for equal work. [4]

"There is still a glass ceiling preventing women from gaining access to leadership positions in both corporate and government jobs," writes Kate Bronfenbrenner, director of labor education research at Cornell University's New York School of Industrial and Labor Relations. "Even more damaging, however, is the pervasiveness of the 'sticky floor,' the combination of forces which confine the majority of women to low-wage occupations." [5]

Working women are beginning to strike back at sexual discrimination that still pervades the workplace. According to polling data and a new study by the AFL-CIO, women in unprecedented numbers are taking an active role in bringing unions to their job sites to achieve wage parity as well as pension and health-insurance coverage and such family-related benefits as day care and elder care. While unions have weakened in male-dominated manufacturing industries as a result of downsizing and outsourcing over the past two decades, union representation has begun to pick up again with health-care and social-service providers, hotels and other service establishments where women make up the majority of employees. [6]

As part of a campaign to boost the numbers further, the AFL-CIO recently named April 3 Equal Pay Day, estimating that it takes until April of the following year for women to catch up with the earnings received by their male counterparts the year before.

---

[1] "Today's Working Women Are Organizing Unions in Escalating Numbers," press release of the American Federation of Labor and Congress of Industrial Organizations, March 19, 1998.

[2] See Kirstin Downey Grimsley, "MBA No Ticket to Top for Women," *The Washington Post*, March 24, 1998. For background, see "The Glass Ceiling," *The CQ Researcher*, Oct. 29, 1993, pp. 973-960.

[3] See Julianne Malveaux, "Women, Blacks See Between the Bottom Lines," *Los Angeles Times*, July 6, 1997.

[4] Peter D. Hart Research Associates, Inc., conducted the survey from Jan. 31-Feb 4, 1997 for the AFL-CIO.

[5] Kate Bronfenbrenner, *Lifting as They Climb: The Promise and Potential of Organizing Women Workers*, AFL-CIO, March 18, 1998.

[6] For background, see "Labor Movement's Future," *The CQ Researcher*, June 28, 1996, pp. 553-576.

wage should be increased again," says Bernstein of the Economic Policy Institute. "For nine years we allowed inflation to erode the value of the minimum wage, and those years correspond quite neatly to the time when the bottom was beginning to really fall out. Raising it again would help lift the fortunes of those at the bottom, who've lost the most."

Opponents to further increases in the minimum wage argue that they would spark inflation and harm small-business owners. "Small-business owners were just hit with a minimum-wage increase last year, and they can't afford another one," said Jack Faris, president of the National Federation of Independent Business. "Every time there's a minimum-wage hike, more small-business owners are forced to lay off employees, pass costs on to consumers or not hire new employees." [13]

Faris also argues that the minimum wage does not keep low-wage workers out of poverty. "In reality, 84 percent of employees whose wages would be hiked either live with their parents or another relative, live alone or have a working spouse," he said. "By increasing the minimum wage, low-skilled employees are priced out of the market, denying them an opportunity to get a job and gain valuable experience."

Tax policy is another tool that could be used to narrow the income gap. Tax reform proposals now before Congress, such as the flat tax and the national sales tax, would fall more heavily on the poor than the current income tax. [14]

In a book soon to be published, author Steve Brouwer argues that the most effective step the federal government could take to reduce income inequality would be to institute a new tax on wealth. "If we had a Congress and a president who were willing to promote the interests of the vast majority of Americans," he writes, "we could recapture some of the accumulated wealth that has been transferred to the rich over the last two decades." [15] An annual wealth tax of 3 percent on the richest 1 percent of Americans, he estimates, would add $250 billion a year to the Treasury's coffers.

Labor economist Krueger focuses on education, not fiscal policies, as the ultimate solution to income inequality. "The reason the income gap expanded in the 1980s was the demand for more skilled workers," he says. "And the best way to narrow the gap would be to increase the skills of workers." In his view, training programs should be targeted to women coming off welfare, displaced workers and other people who are most likely to benefit from them. "The group that is most difficult to help is out-of-school youth," he says. "We also need to develop new initiatives to help these disadvantaged people."

While emphasizing the need for government intervention to boost the incomes of the poor, Freeman suggests that middle-income workers would benefit the most from corporate decisions to make stock options and other investment opportunities available to all workers, not just executives.

"Making profit-sharing schemes and stock options more widely available throughout the work force would take care of most workers," he says. "If it's good for executives, it's good for workers. This is an extraordinarily positive thing that can happen without government intervention." ■

"The reason the income gap expanded in the 1980s was the demand for more skilled workers. And the best way to narrow the gap would be to increase the skills of workers."

— Alan B. Krueger
Labor economist
Princeton University

BACKGROUND

Postwar Prosperity

The Great Depression still serves as the bench mark for measuring economic misery in the United States. By the mid-1930s, average incomes had dropped by almost a third, and unemployment approached 25 percent. [16] New Deal legislation funneled large amounts of federal dollars into employment and welfare initiatives. By 1940, the U.S. economy was well into recovery, and incomes, at least for whites, had returned to their pre-Depression levels.

Unemployment was all but wiped out when the United States entered World War II. Workers who were not in the armed services were employed in wartime industrial production. Black workers, however, were largely excluded from all but low-wage, menial jobs.

The United States emerged from World War II as the only industrial power that had been left relatively unscathed from the war and was thus in the best position to profit from demand for manufactured goods both at home and abroad. This circumstance produced an economic boom that boosted the incomes of Americans of all earning levels. High-paying manufacturing jobs enabled men with high school educations to buy a car, a house and the myriad other accoutrements that went with membership in the growing middle class. High manufacturing wages also meant that two-income families were a rarity, as most married women stayed at home.

In 1949, as the postwar boom gathered steam, only a fifth of families were in the lowest earnings quintile, or lowest 20 percent. Almost half of these were comprised of the elderly and the small number of families headed by women, whose incomes were limited by the lack of widespread retirement or welfare benefits. The lowest quintile also included a quarter of all white families and half of all black families, who lived in the mainly rural Southeast, the poorest region of the country at the time. Children actually fared better than families: Only 15 percent were in the lowest quintile, though these included almost half of all black children.

Not surprisingly, the typical family in the top income quintile was headed by a middle-aged man in a professional job somewhere other than the Southeast. But in pre-suburban America of 1949, fully 30 percent of the families living in central cities belonged in the top quintile.

By the end of the 1950s, the "Ozzie and Harriet" economy had produced further improvements in income distribution. Despite three recessions, the Korean War and three periods of inflation, the decade also was marked by a fall in poverty from 32 percent to 22 percent of the population and a 43 percent rise in median family income. The portion of total income going to the lowest quintile even rose slightly during the 1950s, from 4.5 percent to 4.9 percent. Greater access to higher education, technological developments and increased efficiency all contributed to greater productivity, the main engine of income growth over the decade. Incomes also rose as farmworkers left the countryside for higher-paying jobs in city factories and offices.

The 1960s saw an even more dramatic narrowing of the income gap, in part as a result of the civil rights movement, President Lyndon B. Johnson's "War on Poverty" and other efforts to end racial discrimination — a major contributor to income disparity. Helped by favorable economic conditions — mainly continued rising productivity and low inflation — these policies helped reduce unemployment to as low as 4.4 percent in 1963 and raise incomes by 38 percent over the decade. Unemployment among black men fell twice as fast as among white men, providing a strong boost to black family incomes. The share of total income going to the bottom quintile again grew, to 5.6 percent, while the percentage of people in poverty fell by almost half; by the end of the 1960s, it stood at 12 percent.

By the end of the 1950s, the "Ozzie and Harriet" economy had produced further improvements in income distribution. Despite three recessions, the Korean War and three periods of inflation, the decade also was marked by a fall in poverty from 32 percent to 22 percent of the population and a 43 percent rise in median family income.

The end of the '60s also marked the end of the steady gains in income growth and income distribution, however. The economic boom and low unemployment had begun to fuel inflation, which President Richard M. Nixon — following the Keynesian model — tried to brake in 1971 by introducing wage and price controls. Inflation failed to drop, however, even in the face of a recession, resulting in the first of a series of bouts of stagflation — inflation accompanied by sluggish economic growth. This development was to help reverse the postwar narrowing of the income gap.

Energy Crises

But even more damaging to income disparity were the energy crises of the 1970s. Caused by a cutback in crude oil exports by the Organization of Petroleum Exporting Countries (OPEC) following the 1973 Arab-Israeli War, the first oil shortage resulted in a tripling of oil prices. As the price increase rolled through the economy, prices for all other goods rose, causing consumers to curtail purchases. As businesses cut back on production, unemployment rose as well, and income growth came to a halt. From 1973 to 1975, median family income fell below the 1969 level.

Worsening the slowdown in income levels was an abrupt fall in productivity growth. Although it had slowed in the late 1960s, it was not until the energy crisis struck that pro-

Chronology

1950s *A postwar economic boom lifts the incomes of all Americans.*

1950
Only a fifth of American families — a quarter of all whites and half of all blacks — are in the lowest earnings quintile. Almost half of the poor are elderly and families headed by women.

1959
Twenty-two percent of Americans live in poverty, down from 32 percent at the beginning of the decade, and median family incomes are 43 percent higher than they were in 1950.

1960s *Racial discrimination continues to exclude many African-Americans from enjoying the fruits of a booming economy, but the income gap overall continues to narrow.*

1968
The Kerner Commission's landmark report on the roots of civil disorders describes a growing income gap between black and white Americans.

1969
The burgeoning economy and President Lyndon B. Johnson's "War on Poverty" help raise the median family income by 38 percent over 1959 and cut unemployment, especially among black men. The share of the nation's total income going to the bottom quintile of families grows to 5.6 percent of the total.

1970s *The energy crisis brings America's postwar boom to a halt, widening the gap between rich and poor.*

1973
Following the Arab-Israeli War, the Organization of Petroleum Exporting Countries (OPEC) imposes an oil embargo, resulting in a tripling of oil prices.

1975
Inflation and business closures stall family income growth.

1979
Median family income remains below the level of 1973, while inflation continues to rise.

1980s *The decline in manufacturing eliminates thousands of high-paying, blue-collar jobs.*

1980
A second energy crisis raises oil prices fourfold. Unemployment stands at 7.5 percent.

1981
Republican President Ronald Reagan begins his eight years in the White House, marked by cuts in benefits for the poor and tax breaks for the wealthy.

1984
The Reagan administration's anti-inflation drive pushes unemployment up to more than 9 percent. Median family income is 6 percent below the 1973 level and poverty has risen to 14.4 percent of the population.

1990s *A prolonged recovery begins to slow the gap in incomes.*

1990
The first of two increases in the minimum wage during the administration of Republican President George Bush takes effect, marking the first increase since 1981.

1993
Democratic President Bill Clinton takes office. A tax increase on the wealthy results in a slight decrease in the share of income going to the richest Americans, but this group continues to receive a higher share than in 1973.

1996
The Welfare Reform Act forces welfare recipients to find work. The minimum wage is increased from $4.25 to $4.75 an hour.

Sept. 1, 1997
The minimum wage is increased again, to $5.15 an hour. Walt Disney Co. CEO Michael D. Eisner receives $575 million in compensation for the year, mostly from stock options.

Feb. 10, 1998
The 1998 Economic Report of the President declares that "since 1993, living standards for all Americans are on the rise, especially for those at the bottom of the income distribution."

March 1, 1998
An update of the Kerner Commission report finds that income and wealth inequality is greater than it was three decades ago.

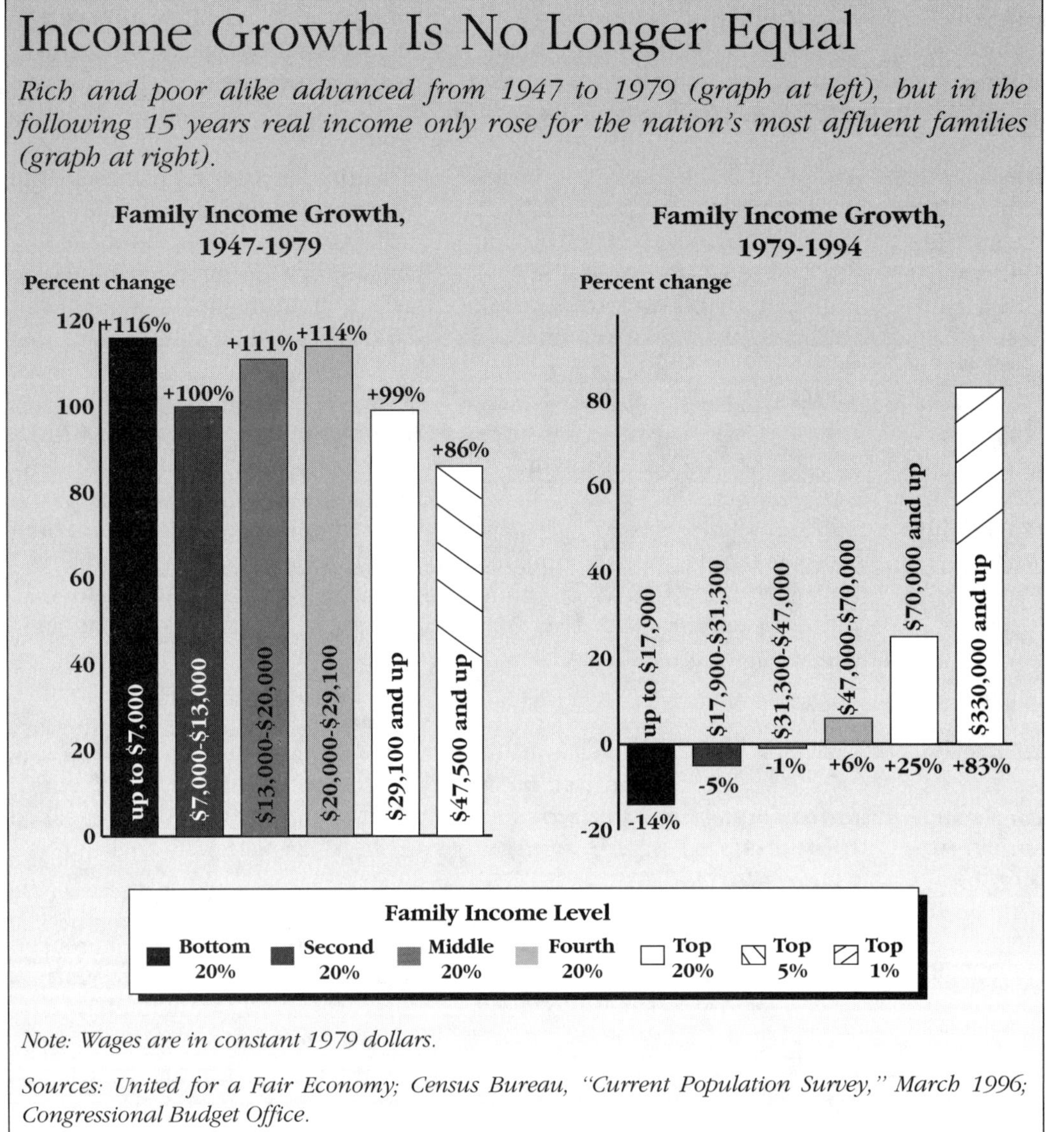

Income Growth Is No Longer Equal

Rich and poor alike advanced from 1947 to 1979 (graph at left), but in the following 15 years real income only rose for the nation's most affluent families (graph at right).

Note: Wages are in constant 1979 dollars.

Sources: United for a Fair Economy; Census Bureau, "Current Population Survey," March 1996; Congressional Budget Office.

ductivity growth fell below 1 percent a year, a level it would not exceed for the next eight years. Meanwhile, growing competition from other industrial countries that had rebuilt their war-torn economies into export-driven powers depressed demand for U.S.-made products, further eroding income growth in the United States.

Stagnant productivity proved so entrenched that efforts by Presidents Gerald R. Ford and Jimmy Carter to reduce unemployment failed to result in significant income gains. By 1979, unemployment had fallen more than two percentage points to 4.2 percent, but median family income remained below the level of 1973, before the first energy crisis began to take its toll. Inflation, meanwhile continued to rise, as wage and price increases outpaced productivity growth.

Incomes suffered further with a second energy crisis, in 1980. This time OPEC raised crude prices fourfold, following the halt of oil production by Iran after the 1979 overthrow of the shah. By late 1980, inflation exceeded 11 percent, while unemployment stood at 7.5 percent, producing an economic debacle that helped scuttle Carter's re-election bid and usher in the free-market policies of President Reagan.

Upon taking office in 1981, the Reagan administration launched a tough monetary policy aimed at bringing down inflation. Though the policy quickly paid off, it also helped raise unemployment to more than 9 percent. By 1984, a decade after the first energy crisis unfolded, median family income had fallen by 6 percent. The progressive narrowing of the income gap of earlier decades reversed course. The trend intensified with the Reagan administration's cuts in welfare programs, such as AFDC, which increased the portion of the population living in poverty.

A clear sign of the growing income inequality was the fall in the portion of total income going to the lowest quintile of families. In 1984, this group received 4.7 percent of total income, down almost a full percentage point from the 1973 level. At the same time, the percentage of people in poverty rose from 11.1 percent to 14.4 percent. A leading culprit in the spread in poverty was, of course, unemployment, which reduced the income of low-skilled workers and also contributed to a rise in the number of families headed by women.

Manufacturing industries, the source of much of the rise in blue-collar income levels throughout the postwar period, were especially hard hit in the early 1980s, eroding the earlier gains made by this group of workers.

The Shrinking Middle

Another phenomenon that appeared in the wake of the energy crises was the shrinking of middle-class incomes. While earlier periods had seen a rise in the middle class, the years 1973 to 1984 brought a reversal in that trend. The percentage of families with incomes over $50,000 rose slightly, from 14.9 percent to 15.6 percent, while the proportion of families earning less than $20,000 rose from 32.1 percent to 36.4 percent. As a result, the percentage of families in the middle of the income spectrum, which had represented just over half the population, declined from 53 percent to 47.9 percent.

Middle-income jobs became scarcer for several reasons. Squeezed by higher energy costs and growing competition from abroad, many large U.S. companies shut down factories in the heavily unionized industrial centers of the Midwest and shifted production to lower-wage, nonunion areas of the South, or overseas. As a result of this "outsourcing," the portion of the work force employed by the 500 largest U.S. corporations has fallen from 20 percent to just 10 percent since the 1950s. [17] Many of the lost jobs were highly paid union positions, and many of the workers who were displaced from them had to work for lower wages.

Another way U.S. businesses tried to maintain their competitive advantage during the 1980s and '90s was by paring back operations, keeping only the most profitable enterprises, and hiring fewer workers to do the job. Corporate "downsizing" has been accompanied by a fall in union representation. "A harsh new world of work has emerged: Average workers are accustomed to declining wages, while the top managers who instituted the new 'lean and mean' production standards expect extraordinary growth in their compensation," Brouwer writes. While workers' wages rose just 16 percent from 1989 to 1995, he calculates, corporate profits rose 23.3 percent and CEO salaries jumped 54 percent in 1996 alone. "Once again," he writes, "millions of employees had nothing to show for their efforts: Wages went up 3 percent, lagging just behind inflation." [18]

Demand for more highly skilled workers widened the income gap still further. The decline of manufacturing industries over the past two decades has been accompanied by a shift toward service industries, many of which require highly skilled workers, and toward low-wage retail businesses. College graduates with specific training in such areas as computer technology, engineering and management have continued to experience real income gains in the 1990s. But low-skilled workers, especially those who have not completed high school, have seen their wages drop. [19] ■

CURRENT SITUATION

Clinton's Policies

President Clinton came to office in 1993 promising to reverse many of the policies introduced during the previous 12 years, when Republican Presidents Reagan and George Bush occupied the White House. Clinton launched his presidency with a campaign to make health insurance available to all Americans, restore greater progressivity to the income tax code and raise the minimum wage — all steps aimed at improving living standards for middle- and lower-income Americans and narrowing the income gap.

But Clinton's policy agenda has become less ambitious over the past five years. Buoyed by a Republican majority in both houses of Congress since 1995, opponents eviscerated some of his more ambitious proposals, such as universal health insurance. Others, notably welfare reform and last year's budget agreement that promised to balance the budget, became law because they matched longstanding Republican goals.

The 1993 budget law, which barely won passage by Congress, imposed a tax increase on the wealthy, including upper-income beneficiaries of Social Security, and provided tax credits for the working poor. This law attacked the income gap at the upper end and resulted in a slight decrease in the share of after-tax income going to the top 20 percent of families from 49.9 percent in 1992 to 49.3 percent in 1994. The share of after-tax income received by the wealthiest 1 percent of families fell from 12.1 percent to 11.4 percent over the same period, even as their share of pretax income rose. But even after these changes, the share of after-tax income going to the top 20 percent of the population in 1994 was much higher than in 1974. [20]

The administration's tax policies have done much less to reduce income inequality since the Republican Party took control of Congress in 1995. The budget agreement signed on Aug. 5, 1997, provided far less tax relief to low- and middle-income families than it did to the wealthiest taxpayers. According to Citizens for Tax Justice, the richest 1 percent of Americans will receive a third of the benefits from the law's tax cuts once they go into effect, more than the benefits that will be received by the bottom 80 percent of the population.

"The tax provisions of the budget agreement consequently will accentuate the already-large disparities in the distribution of income," concludes an analysis of the law by the Center on Budget and Policy Priorities. "High-income families — the one group whose average after-tax income has risen sharply since the 1970s — will ultimately be the principal beneficiaries." [21]

Some analysts see risk in the Clinton administration's emphasis on economic growth over investments in social welfare, as reflected in the budget agreement. "The United States has taken a big gamble that full employment will continue," says Freeman, who sees this as the biggest difference between the United States and Europe, where generous social welfare programs help compensate for the region's high unemployment. "The United States' answer to problems at this point is to put all our hope in jobs. We have tremendously reduced the safety net, so that the fraction of out-of-work people actually getting unemployment compensation today is really small. We're counting on full employment," he says, "and we're betting that we can get former welfare recipients jobs. The problem is, they'll lose them in the next recession."

Impact of NAFTA

Another policy area that many analysts say affects income distribution is trade. The North American Free Trade Agreement (NAFTA), signed by President Bush on Dec. 17, 1992, was strongly supported by President Clinton, who won congressional approval of the agreement in 1993. [22] By removing barriers to trade among the United States, Canada and Mexico, he and other supporters promised, the agreement would spur demand for American goods and stimulate job creation for American workers.

But free trade also has negative effects. By facilitating the sale of cheap imports to U.S. consumers, free trade can hurt U.S. manufacturers and strengthen their hand in holding down wages for American workers. "Trade policy has a big impact on jobs in the United States as well as wages," Bernstein says. "But the benefits of free trade — and there are some — have been the exclusive focus in the policy debate. Only recently has Clinton started to acknowledge that there are losers, too. Free-trade policy has resulted in non-college-educated workers who have lost jobs in industries that compete with imports. We should pursue a trade policy that's mindful of those who are hurt."

Reuters/Steve Grayson

Superstars like Michael Jordan have raised incomes for athletes to the stratosphere.

Minimum Wage Increases

Perhaps the most effective policy change supported by the Clinton administration has been a series of increases in the minimum wage. Following two increases in 1990 and 1991 during the Bush administration — the first since 1981 — the federal minimum wage was increased from $4.25 to $4.75 an hour on Oct. 1, 1996, and again, to $5.15, on Sept. 1, 1997. "Even with the increases, the minimum wage hasn't kept pace," says Harris of the Eisenhower Foundation. "The increases have helped a little, but we're still way behind in terms of purchasing power compared with earlier times because the minimum wage hasn't kept up with inflation."

Clinton supports a further increase in the minimum wage introduced March 19 by Sen. Edward M. Kennedy, D-Mass., and Rep. David E. Bonior, D-Mich. The Fair Minimum Wage Act would raise the minimum wage to $5.65 an hour in 1999, and then to $6.15 in 2000. Conservatives and business representatives oppose the legislation as a threat to the current economic recovery.

"Although wage differences have widened over the past 20 years, such bad economic policy as a mandated minimum wage for workers serves only to exacerbate this problem," writes D. Mark Wilson, labor economist at the Heritage Foundation, a conservative think tank. "President Clinton's proposal to raise the minimum wage, moreover, works against the efforts of Congress to address the problem of moving unskilled Americans

At Issue:

Do American workers lack the necessary skills to qualify for better-paying jobs?

Richard W. Judy and Carol D'Amico
Senior research fellow and senior fellow, Hudson Institute

From* Workforce 2020: Work and Workers in the 21st Century, *A 1997 update of* Workforce 2000 *(1987), The Hudson Institute.

yes

One of *Workforce 2000's* important contributions was to identify an emerging shortage of skilled workers in the American economy. The book foresaw a gap between the qualifications of workers and the changing job mix of the American economy.

Can a "skills gap" exist? In one sense, no: A free labor market tends to equilibrate the supply and demand of various kinds of labor. But in a second, perhaps more important sense, there can be a skills gap. *Workforce 2000* argued presciently that America's productivity (and hence its standard of living) would rise significantly only if its work force came to be much better educated and much more highly skilled. *Workforce 2000* also stated that major public and private efforts would be needed to bring about those improvements. In other words, *Workforce 2000* raised a normative concern about a mismatch between the skills that might be available and those that would be most desirable; it did not predict imbalance in the labor market.

Is the American economy changing so rapidly that the skills of today's work force will be obsolete early in the 21st century? Must new entrants into the work force require vocational skills that are much more sophisticated than those of today's jobholders? To answer these questions, we compare the Bureau of Labor Statistics projections for future employment (by occupational category) with information contained in the Department of Labor's *Dictionary of Occupational Titles*, which describes skills needed to work in various occupations. . . .

Whether we look at language, mathematics or reasoning, [the data] tell essentially the same story: 99 percent of the jobs in decline require skills at Level 3 or lower [with Level 6 the highest skill level]. By contrast, much job growth will be in occupations requiring skills rated at Level 4 or higher; for example, over 30 percent of expanding jobs will require reasoning skills at Level 4 or above. In short, shrinking occupations overwhelmingly require modest skills, but high skills are called for by a significant component of the expanding occupations. The words of *Workforce 2000* still ring true: "The fastest-growing jobs require much higher math, language and reasoning capabilities . . . while slowly growing jobs require less." If anything, the case is stronger today than when those words were written in 1987.

Jared Bernstein
Economist, Economic Policy Institute

From testimony before the House Education and the Workforce Subcommittee on Oversight and Investigations, Oct. 29, 1997.

no

Like its predecessor, *Workforce 2020* paints an unrealistically rosy scenario of the future of work. The analysis overestimates the acceleration in technology and its impact on the economy, the increase in the demand for skilled workers and the quality of the current labor market conditions. This last point is central because [the authors'] overly optimistic view of the present generates an unrealistic view of the future. . . .

My view is that we have less a skill deficit in our present and future economy than a wage deficit, caused by the unleashing of market forces and the erosion of worker protections. Strengthening labor market institutions that have been allowed to erode is the way forward. . . .

Workforce 2020 argues that there has been (and will continue to be) a growing mismatch between workers' skills and employers' skill demands. This story leaves the impression that the U.S. work force has been growing less well-educated over time. Of course, the opposite is the case. . . . Yet this fact by itself does not prove *Workforce 2020* to be incorrect. The book argues that while the work force's skills are growing, they are not growing fast enough.

This is a testable hypothesis. If [the authors] are correct, then the wages of high-skilled workers should be rising, as they are bid up by employers who seek this scarce resource. . . . Instead of having their wages bid up, the real hourly wages of both male and female young college graduates fell by about 10 percent [from 1989 to 1996]. . . . [T]he wage offers to new college graduates with engineering and computer degrees have also been falling. . . .

Workforce 2020 correctly points out that with increased deregulation and expanded trade, an increasing share of the work force will be fighting an uphill battle in the face of unleashed market forces. Historically, labor market institutions such as labor unions, minimum wages, anti-discrimination enforcement and workplace safety protocols have protected those workers whose bargaining power has been severely diminished.

Strengthening these vital labor market institutions is the best way to address the wage deficit, so that future growth can be shared by all workers.

from welfare to work. It is an uncompassionate mandate that gives some low-wage workers an increase in their earnings while depriving others of the opportunity to earn anything at all." [23]

The Strong Economy

For the first two years of the Clinton administration, the income gap continued to widen, one of the few blemishes on an otherwise rosy economic record. Finally, last year came the statistics the policy-makers were waiting for.

"Since 1993, living standards for all Americans are on the rise, especially for those at the bottom of the income distribution," proclaimed the Council of Economic Advisers' *1998 Economic Report of the President*. "The poverty rate fell to 13.7 percent in 1996, from 15.1 percent in 1993; the poverty rate for black Americans is at a historical low, and in 1997 unemployment among blacks fell to its lowest rate since 1973. Since 1993, household income has grown in each quintile of the income distribution, with the largest percentage increase going to the poorest members of our society. Maintaining a full-employment economy is essential if this progress is to continue." [24]

But to some analysts, finding good news in the Census statistics is merely grasping for straws. Indeed, considered over the longer term, last year's improvements in income inequality pale in comparison to the devastating trends of the past several decades. "Since the Kerner Commission's report 30 years ago, actual poverty, in numbers and as a percentage of the population, is up," Harris says. "Thirty years ago, 12.8 percent of the population, or 25.4 million people, were in poverty. Today it's 13.7 percent, or 36.5 million people."

Poverty also is worsening among the most vulnerable members of society, children. "In 1994, half the kids under 6 years of age were living at or below the lower half of the poverty line, and that is twice what it was 20 years earlier, in 1974," Harris says. "In addition to more poverty today, poor people are poorer now than they were before."

If income inequality is the main focus of concern about the economy, the latest statistics are actually more alarming than in the earlier years. For while the widening of the income gap halted in 1993 at the lower end of the income spectrum, it proceeded even faster at the high end. According to one survey, average compensation of the top executives at the biggest U.S. companies was $8.7 million last year, an increase of 37.8 percent over 1996. Salaries and bonuses accounted for $2.1 million of the total, making for a hefty 12.3 percent pay increase — compared with the 3.5 percent average increase for workers. But the bulk of executive compensation came from stock options. [25]

In light of the huge pay increases granted executives, some economists point with irony to recent attempts by U.S. corporations to gain special exemptions from immigration rules so that they can hire foreign skilled workers for jobs they claim Americans are unqualified to perform. [26] "There's no scarcity of skilled American workers," says Freeman of Harvard. "They just don't want to give skilled workers wage increases. What if we turned that around and said that because top executives are pulling in these huge pay increases we should declare an executive shortage? I don't hear anyone saying we should be importing business leaders. It's just incredible chutzpah on the part of executives."

Other economists are less concerned about the rise in incomes at the top, even the use of stock options as a principal source of compensation. "This is one of the reasons the market has done so well," says economist Sinai, who sees stock options and other stock plans as useful incentives for workers as well as executives. "They keep down costs and foster an ownership mentality among workers. More and more publicly listed companies are selling company stock at discount to employees because they're a very big incentive to be more productive."

Despite the recent evidence of improvement on the income front, labor economist Krueger is concerned about the long-term stagnation of earnings among middle-income workers. "The strong economic growth is starting to reach the bottom, which is a very good development, though it doesn't reverse the fall of the 1980s," he says. "Meanwhile, the middle has experienced falling real wages, which is one reason average wage growth has been so subdued in the 1990s. In the last year or so, that has come to a halt, which is a good sign. But one year does not an era make." ■

OUTLOOK

Fear of a Downturn

With compensation at the top of the income spectrum based so heavily on the stock market and wage growth dependent on continued low unemployment, the prospects for further narrowing of the income gap are clearly tied to the business cycle. As long as the current economic boom continues apace, creating jobs and spurring confidence in the stock market, the income gap could well continue to narrow.

But recovery has always been followed by recession, and many experts predict that the next downturn will erase last year's progress toward income equality. "The only things helping narrow the income gap a little is today's tight labor markets, recent increases in the minimum wage and low inflation," says Bernstein of the Economic Policy Institute.

In his view, underlying trends in the workplace and the economy at large make it unlikely that all income groups will benefit equally as they did before the 1980s. "The structural problems are still very much in place, and if and when labor markets loosen up a bit, I'm afraid we'll be back where we were a couple of years ago."

With inflation and unemployment at bay, there have been few public complaints about the income gap. But because welfare programs have been eliminated or cut back in recent years, some analysts predict the next downturn will unleash a torrent of criticism of the political leadership's handling of the economy. "Full employment makes everybody feel good," Freeman says. "The trouble will surface when and if we run into a recession, and then it will hit with a vengeance because the safety net will have vanished. Then we'll see a big movement to deal with the problem of income inequality."

But optimists believe that changes in the global economy may help break the traditional cycle of boom and bust in the U.S. economy, or at least mitigate its impact on incomes. "I believe that the general prosperity we're enjoying today will go on, fed by technological breakthroughs and a global economy that buys more and more from the United States," Sinai predicts. "The conditions for ordinary Americans are the best in decades and will stay that way. And while I don't really think the wealth gap will change, the income gap definitely has turned, so the situation is no longer so negative for ordinary working Americans and the working poor." ■

FOR MORE INFORMATION

American Enterprise Institute for Public Policy Research, 1150 17th St. N.W., Washington, D.C. 20036; (202) 862-5846; www.aei.org. The institute's Economic Policy Studies division examines trends in employment, earnings and income in the United States. Published materials tend to minimize the impact of income inequality in the face of rising overall living standards.

Census Bureau, Housing and Household Economic Statistics, Washington, D.C. 20233; (301) 763-08550; www.census.gov. This division collects and analyzes income data and other economic, social and demographic statistics and publishes a periodic survey of incomes.

Center on Budget and Policy Priorities, 820 1st St. N.E., Suite 510, Washington, D.C. 20002; (202) 408-1080; www.cbpp.org. This research group analyzes federal, state and local government policies affecting low- and moderate-income Americans.

Economic Policy Institute, 1660 L St. N.W., Suite 1200, Washington, D.C. 20036; (202) 775-8810; www.epinet.org. This research organization analyzes income distribution and other economic data. Its published materials emphasize the negative impact of the income gap on American workers' living standards.

Notes

[1] See Tim Smart, "An Eye-Popping Year for Executive Pay," *The Washington Post*, March 22, 1998. For background, see "Executive Pay," *The CQ Researcher*, July 11, 1997, pp. 601-624, and "Fairness in Salaries," *The CQ Researcher*, May 29, 1992, pp. 457-480.

[2] The unemployment rate crept back up to 4.7 percent in March. For background, see "Jobs in the '90s," *The CQ Researcher*, Feb. 28, 1992, pp. 169-192.

[3] Kathryn Larin and Elizabeth C. McNichol, *Pulling Apart: A State-by-State Analysis of Income Trends*, Center on Budget and Policy Priorities, Dec. 16, 1997.

[4] The Milton S. Eisenhower Foundation and The Corporation for What Works, *The Millennium Breach: Richer, Poorer and Racially Apart*, March 1, 1998. For background, see "The Black Middle Class," *The CQ Researcher*, Jan. 23, 1998, pp. 49-72.

[5] *The 1998 Economic Report of the President*, Council of Economic Advisers, Feb. 10, 1998.

[6] See Jacob M. Schlesinger, "Wages for Low-Paid Workers Rose in 1997," *The Wall Street Journal*, March 23, 1998.

[7] Christopher C. DeMuth, "The New Wealth of Nations," *Commentary*, October 1997, pp. 23-24.

[8] *Ibid.*, p. 25.

[9] Irving Kristol, "Income Inequality without Class Conflict," *The Wall Street Journal*, Dec. 18, 1997.

[10] See Rene Sanchez, "Black, Hispanic Admissions Plunge at 2 Calif. Campuses," *The Washington Post*, April 1, 1998. For background, see "Rethinking Affirmative Action," *The CQ Researcher*, April 28, 1995, pp. 369-392.

[11] Eisenhower Foundation, *op. cit.*, p. 10.

[12] For background, see "The Working Poor," Nov. 3, 1995, pp. 969-992, and "Welfare Reform," *The CQ Researcher*, April 10, 1992, pp. 327-350.

[13] From a March 19, 1998, NFIB press release.

[14] For background, see "IRS Reform," *The CQ Researcher*, Jan. 16, 1998, pp. 25-48, and "Tax Reform," *The CQ Researcher*, March 22, 1996, pp. 241-264.

[15] Steve Brouwer, *Sharing the Pie* (1998), p. 157.

[16] Unless otherwise noted, information in this section is based on Frank Levy, *Dollars and Dreams* (1987), pp. 45-61.

[17] Brouwer, *op. cit.*, p. 48.

[18] *Ibid.*

[19] See Daniel H. Weinberg, "A Brief Look at Postwar U.S. Income Inequality," U.S. Census Bureau, June 20, 1996, available on the Census Web page at www.census.gov.

[20] See Isaac Shapiro and Robert Greenstein, "Trends in the Distribution of After-Tax Income: An Analysis of Congressional Budget Office Data," Center on Budget and Policy Priorities, Aug. 14, 1997.

[21] *Ibid*, p. 8.

[22] For background, see "Rethinking NAFTA," *The CQ Researcher*, June 7, 1996, pp. 481-504.

[23] D. Mark Wilson, "Increasing the Mandated Minimum Wage: Who Pays the Price?" *Backgrounder*, The Heritage Foundation, March 5, 1998.

[24] Council of Economic Advisers, *op. cit.*, available on the White House Web page at www.whitehouse.gov.

[25] See Adam Bryant, "Flying High on the Option Express," *The New York Times*, April 5, 1998.

[26] See "High-Tech Labor Shortages," *The CQ Researcher*, April 24, 1998.

Bibliography

Selected Sources Used

Books

Brouwer, Steve, *Sharing the Pie: A Citizen's Guide to Wealth and Power in America*, Henry Holt, 1998.

This soon-to-be-published volume blames a rightward shift in American politics since 1980 for what the author describes as a steady decline in the living standards of most Americans.

Judy, Richard W., and Carol D'Amico, *Workforce 2020: Work and Workers in the 21st Century*, Hudson Institute, 1997.

The sequel to an earlier Hudson study on workplace trends warns that technological advances will continue to create demand for skilled workers and recommends bigger investments in primary and secondary education as well as job training.

Levy, Frank, *Dollars and Dreams: The Changing American Income Distribution*, Russell Sage Foundation, 1987.

This analysis of Census data shows how social and economic changes, as well as public policies, have affected the distribution of income and wealth in the United States during the postwar period.

Wolff, Edward N., *Top Heavy: The Increasing Inequality of Wealth in America and What Can Be Done about It*, Twentieth Century Fund, 1995.

The author, an economics professor at New York University, describes the unprecedented shift in income from lower- and middle-income Americans to the wealthy over the past decade and a half.

Articles

Burtless, Gary, "Worsening American Income Inequality: Is World Trade to Blame?" *Brookings Review*, spring 1996, pp. 26-31.

While liberal trade with developing countries undoubtedly hurts the job prospects of low-skilled American workers, writes the Brookings economist, the widening income gap is more closely related to other changes, such as deregulation, increased immigration, a low minimum wage and the weakening of unions.

DeMuth, Christopher C., "The New Wealth of Nations," *Commentary*, October 1997, pp. 23-28.

Social and economic advances have produced the highest standards of living in history throughout the developed world, writes the president of the American Enterprise Institute. These advances benefit everyone, all but erasing the significance of remaining disparities in income and wealth.

"The 400: The Average Net Worth of the Forbes Four Hundred is $1.6 Billion," *Forbes*, Oct. 13, 1997, pp. 181-250.

As evidence that the rich are getting richer, it took a net worth of $475 million to get on the list of the 400 richest Americans last year, up from $415 million in 1996.

Fox, Justin, "Manage Your Stock Options," *Fortune*, Dec. 29, 1997, pp. 167-173.

Stock options have thus far been used mainly to boost compensation to top executives, but more and more companies are beginning to offer stock option plans to other workers as well.

Mishel, Lawrence, Jared Bernstein and John Schmitt, "The State of American Workers," *Challenge*, Nov. 21, 1996, p. 33.

Despite the fall in unemployment and the steady growth of full-time jobs in the 1990s, most workers' real wages have fallen during the current recovery. As a result, income inequality between the richest Americans and the rest of the population continues to grow.

Rottenberg, Dan, "100 Most Generous Americans," *The American Benefactor*, fall 1997, pp. 42-68.

Each of the 100 biggest contributors to charity has given away $20 million or more over their lifetimes, about half of it during the past 10 years. But the list does not mirror the *Forbes* 400 list of the richest Americans, as some of the wealthiest people prefer to hang on their riches.

Reports and Studies

Larin, Kathryn, and Elizabeth C. McNichol, *Pulling Apart: A State-by-State Analysis of Income Trends*, Center on Budget and Policy Priorities, Dec. 16, 1997.

According to this analysis of Census data, since the late 1970s the average, inflation-adjusted incomes of the poorest families with children fell more than 20 percent. At the same time, the average incomes of rich families grew by almost 30 percent. As a result, the income gap between the richest and poorest American families has widened significantly.

The Milton S. Eisenhower Foundation and The Corporation for What Works, *The Millennium Breach: Richer, Poorer and Racially Apart: A Thirty-Year Update of the National Advisory Commission on Civil Disorders*, March 1, 1998.

This update of the 1968 Kerner Commission report on civil disorders finds that income and wealth inequality is even greater than it was three decades ago, especially for African-American residents of the nation's inner cities.

8 Diminishing Diversity of Language

DAVID MASCI

Japanese Prime Minister Keizo Obuchi sent shock waves through Japan early this year when he released his government's goals for the new century. Some of the proposals — such as increasing immigration levels and shortening the school week — were understandably controversial in a country that is resistant to change.

But it was one recommendation in particular — to make English the nation's official second language — that dominated newspaper headlines for days.

AP/Chien-Min Chung

The ubiquitous golden arches and modern architecture of a McDonalds outlet clash with traditional Chinese symbols in downtown Beijing. Many fear that the encroaching predominance of English around the world could erode the world's diversity of languages and cultures.

"Achieving world-class excellence demands that all Japanese acquire a working knowledge of English," the report said, suggesting that the alternative was to be left behind in the global race to prosperity. [1]

Obuchi's bow to English is just the latest indication that it is becoming the world's *lingua franca*. Around the globe, from classrooms to boardrooms to diplomatic soirees, English is increasingly the language of choice. Even in France, known for its resistance to foreign influence, Prime Minister Lionel Jospin recently uttered what amounted to linguistic heresy by acknowledging that the French must learn English, as it is likely to be the world's language someday. [2]

An estimated 20 percent of the world's 6 billion people now speak English at some level of proficiency. But many linguists and observers of global affairs expect a dramatic increase in the percentage of English-speakers in coming decades as the benefits of using English become more obvious.

"English is already the global language, and it is only going to grow as more and more young people learn it," says Richard H. Schlagel, a professor of philosophy at the George Washington University.

According to Schlagel and other experts, the new century will see English supplant many other tongues as the language of everyday discourse. For example, they predict, in a hundred years someone in Germany will be more likely to hear English spoken on the street than German. Those who envision the triumph of English argue that the Internet and other mass media are helping to create the need for a global language. In addition, they say, globalization in general will continue to increase pressure for linguistic standardization.

"Economic, cultural and other barriers are eroding all over the world, making the necessity of cross-border communication greater," says John Brough, a professor of philosophy at Georgetown University. "English is the common language people will use."

But some experts say that English is unlikely to replace other major languages, even if it remains the most widely spoken tongue on the planet. "The world is too culturally diverse to accommodate only one language," says Donna Jo Napoli, chairman of the Linguistics Department at Swarthmore College in Pennsylvania.

Napoli and others contend that what language people speak is not just a question of convenience. Other factors, such as politics and culture, also help determine whether someone will continue speaking their native tongue. "Languages like Italian or French are so tied to who and what we are that people will not give that up," she says.

In addition, Napoli and others say, a shift in the world's geopolitical balance would most likely mitigate the global impact of English. For instance, they say, the growing economic and political power of China could make Mandarin a more appealing common language in other countries, especially in Asia.

But while scholars are debating the present and future impact of English around the world, a fight is brewing over the status of the language in the country with more English-speakers than any other: the United States. Some observers worry that millions of immigrants and their children are not attaining fluency in English because businesses and, more important, the U.S. government are providing services to them in their native languages.

"The government has gotten itself into the translation business by providing bilingual services in the voting booths, the classrooms and elsewhere," says Jim Boulet Jr., executive director of English First, a group in

---

From *The CQ Researcher*, November 17, 2000.

Springfield, Va. "This just encourages people to retain their native languages at the expense of English."

Boulet argues that designating English as the official language of the United States would send a clear, strong message to newcomers that English is the nation's language and, as such, needs to be mastered. That's important, he says, because the nation's current policy of encouraging Americans to speak different languages will only sow division and discord in a country that is already very heterogeneous.

"Do we really need to generate more differences than we already have?" Boulet asks, adding that multilingual societies, such as Yugoslavia, often fragment and fall apart.

But others say that Boulet is fighting a problem that doesn't exist. "Immigrants who come to the United States want to learn English, and they do," says Cecilia Muñoz, vice president for policy at the National Council of La Raza, the nation's largest Latino advocacy group. [3]

In addition, Muñoz says, studies show that the grandchildren of newcomers only learn English and not the language of their grandparents' country of origin.

Declaring English as the nation's official language would only be interpreted as inhospitable by new arrivals, Muñoz and others say. "It sends a very negative message to immigrants," she says. Besides, she adds, bilingualism should be encouraged since having knowledge of more than one language is very helpful in today's increasingly global economy. [4]

Debates over language also are raging in other countries. In France, Italy, Poland and other European nations, the increasing inclusion of English and other foreign words in native vocabularies has sparked an organized backlash. While some linguists sympathize with such opposition, few believe that languages can be shielded from outside influences. Indeed, many experts argue that new, foreign words inject energy and vigor into a language.

The World's Top 10 Languages

Chinese and English are the most widely spoken languages in the world.

Native Language	No. of Speakers (in millions)
Chinese	1,200
English	460
Hindi	430
Spanish	300
Arabic	200
Portuguese	168
Russian	130
Japanese	125
Bengali	120
German	117

Source: The New York Times 1998 Almanac

Meanwhile, many languages once spoken by small groups of indigenous peoples in Australia, Africa and in the Americas have become extinct, and thousands more are in danger. In a number of cases, efforts are under way to save some of the threatened languages, but experts warn that the vast majority will die out if more isn't done quickly.

As technology and globalization bring the world's peoples ever closer together, here are some of the questions experts are asking about the role of language:

Will English become a truly global language?

When Pope John Paul II arrived for his historic visit to the Middle East last April, he spoke to his hosts not in Arabic or Hebrew, but in English. Likewise, when Air France pilots request permission to land at Charles de Gaulle Airport outside Paris, they do so in English, not in their native French.

English has increasingly become the world's most common language, and for more than just world leaders and airline pilots. In a host of spheres ranging from business to academia, English is now the language of choice.

Even those who don't speak English recognize and exploit its importance. For instance, when Italy's then-Prime Minister Massimo D'Alema addressed a conference on Jan. 15, he stood under a huge banner emblazoned with his party's slogan: "I Care," it read, in English. The fact that D'Alema doesn't speak English did not stop him from trying to use the language to send a message to Italian voters.

The popularity of English is largely due to the economic, cultural and political dominance of the United States. Much of the film, television and music that people watch or listen to is in English. In addition, it is the language of one-quarter of the world's periodicals and a majority of scientific and technical journals. English also is the language used on more than 75 percent of all Internet sites. [5]

Today, according to recent estimates, more than 1.5 billion people around the globe speak English with varying degrees of fluency. A little more than a quarter of that group, or about 460 million people, speak English as their native tongue in countries such as the United States, the United Kingdom and Australia. [6]

An additional 375 million people use English as a second language in their native countries. While they may speak their nation's indigenous tongue at home, they turn to English to communicate with their countrymen, often at work. [7] English is also

English Around the World

More than 400 million people speak English as their mother tongue, while about 375 million use it as their second language, mainly in countries once ruled by England or the United States, such as India and the Philippines. The largest group — about 750 million people — uses English for business or other purposes in countries that have no tradition of the language, such as Germany and Japan.

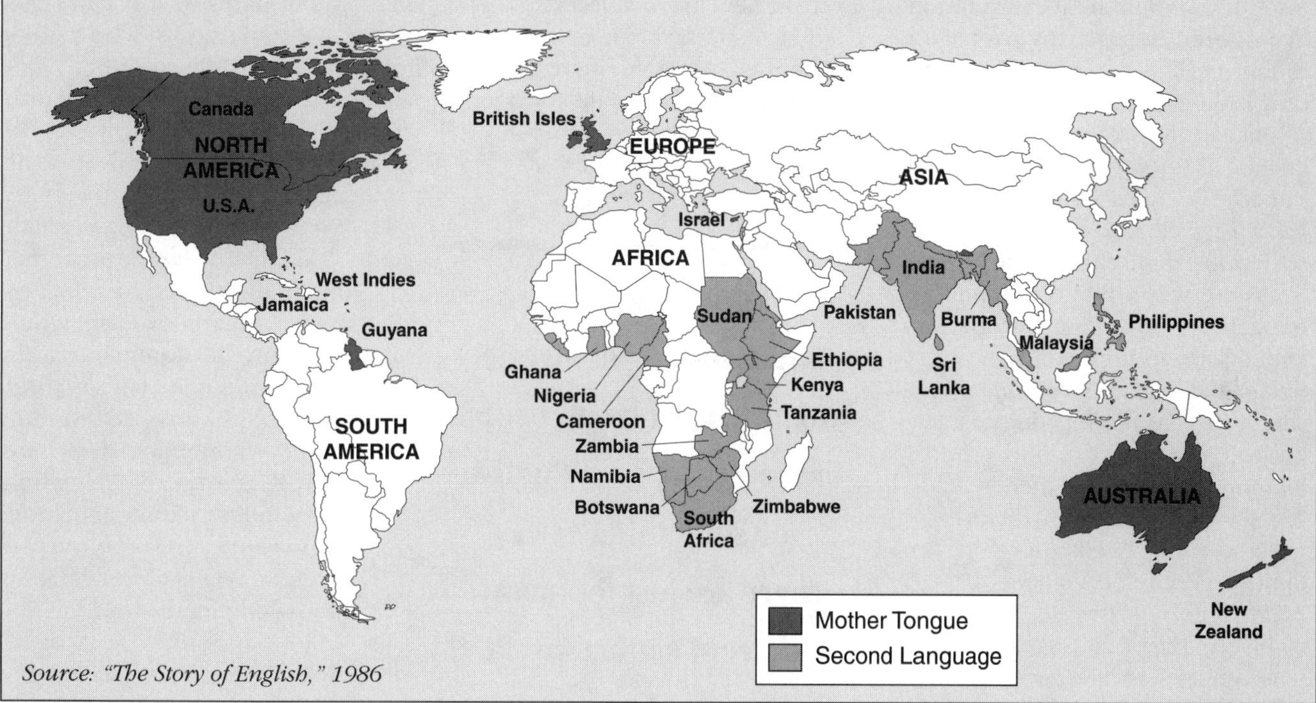

Source: "The Story of English," 1986

commonly used as a second language in countries that were once ruled by England or the United States, including India, Nigeria and the Philippines.

By far, the largest number of English-speakers — roughly 750 million people — use English to communicate with people outside their own cultures. People in this group can range from a Tokyo businessman to a hotel proprietor in Greece. This group is likely to grow, as an estimated 1 billion people are currently trying to learn English. [8]

According to many language experts, the trends are unmistakable: English is achieving a linguistic dominance hitherto unknown in the world. "It's well on its way to becoming the global language, if it isn't there already," says Georgetown's Brough.

He envisions a time in the not-too-distant future when almost everyone in the world will be speaking English. "In the coming century, most people will eventually speak English fluently and use it in their everyday lives," he says. Some people "may not entirely give up French or German or whatever their native tongue is, but English will probably be what they use most."

Schlagel at George Washington University takes Brough's argument a step further and predicts that English will essentially eliminate the perceived need to know other tongues. "One hundred years from now, almost everyone will be using English for everything," he says. "People will learn other languages only as a luxury."

According to Brough and Schlagel, English is likely to solidify and expand its dominant position as a result of globalization and the information-technology revolution. On one hand, globalization is increasingly standardizing economic, political and cultural forces, making linguistic standardization inevitable. "We're living through an age of global integration of cultures," Schlagel says, "and as a consequence the desire and need for a common language is strong and getting stronger."

In addition, he says, the Internet and other recent telecommunications innovations, which allow people to contact anyone, anywhere — easily and cheaply — are helping to drive the trend toward globalization. "As cultural barriers continue to erode and technology makes communication easy, people need one language so they can speak with each other across borders," Schlagel says.

But other experts say that while English is the most widely spoken language in the world today, it is unlikely to replace native tongues. "I don't see a time when there will be one language used by all people of the world, be it English or something else," says Napoli at Swarthmore. "There are just too many people and too many different cultures to fit into one language."

Instead, Napoli says, English will be like Latin was in Europe during the Middle Ages — a *lingua franca* for certain segments of society in certain circumstances.

"There was a time when all educated people in Europe spoke Latin to their colleagues but something else at home," she says. "Likewise, educated people around the world are learning English, but there's a big difference between learning and using English for certain purposes and using it for everything."

Indeed, Napoli and others say, while many obscure languages currently spoken by small groups of people may disappear in the coming decades, more widespread tongues — like German, Arabic and Mandarin Chinese — are unlikely to be replaced any time soon. "I don't see these big languages, like French or Italian, dying out, if only for political reasons," says Naomi Baron, a professor of linguistics at American University.

Language is so tied to culture and national feeling that people will resist giving up their native tongue, Baron says, even if they do learn to speak English for their jobs. "Look at the former Yugoslavia," Baron says. "They created Serbo-Croatian when they created the country. But now that they've broken up again, the Serbs are back to speaking Serb, and the Croats are speaking Croat."

In addition, the information-technology revolution ultimately may not be a boon to English, Barbara Wallraff argues in *The Atlantic Monthly*. She notes, for example, that 44 percent of all Internet users speak a language other than English at home and that non-English speakers are the fastest-growing group of new Internet users. [9]

In fact, she says, the Internet may actually help preserve language diversity by offering the means for people with the same language to band together. "The Internet," she writes, "besides being a convenient vehicle for reaching mass audiences such as, say, the citizenry of Japan or Argentina, is also well suited to bringing together the members of small groups — for example middle-class French-speaking sub-Saharan Africans." [10]

"I don't see a time when there will be one language used by all people of the world, be it English or something else. There are just too many different cultures to fit into one language."

—Donna Jo Napoli
Chairman of the Linguistics Department, Swarthmore College

Finally, say those who dispute the inevitability of global English, there is no guarantee that the same factors driving the spread of English today will be in place in 20 or 40 or 60 years.

"Depending on what happens economically or politically in the coming century, who's to say we all won't be speaking Mandarin Chinese?" Baron asks. "The rise of English is really due to the dominance of Britain in the 19th century and the United States in the 20th," she says. "We don't know who's going to be on top in the future."

Even a smaller geopolitical shift could knock English down a few pegs on the global linguistic scale, according to some observers.

"If something as earth-shaking as the Internet had been developed in, say, Japan, perhaps English would not now be dominant to the extent that it is," Wallraff writes. "Future technology may well originate elsewhere. In the rapidly advancing field of wireless communications devices, for example, Scandinavia is already the acknowledged leader." [11]

Should English become the official language of the United States?

Efforts to establish English as America's national language are almost as old as the Republic. The huge influx of immigrants from Germany in the late 18th and early 19th centuries, for instance, led to the widespread fear that German would eventually replace English as our native tongue. Many Americans at the time called for Congress to make English the official language of the United States.

More recently, the arrival of tens of millions of Spanish-speakers from Latin America has revived the debate. Indeed, during the past decade, there has almost always been at least one piece of legislation being considered in the House of Representatives or Senate that would make English the country's official language.

The outgoing 106th Congress was no exception. In the House, Rep. Bob Barr, R-Ga., introduced a bill that would have codified English as America's national language. Another would have accomplished the same goal through a constitutional amendment. A number of other bills also introduced in the 106th Congress would have required all government business to be conducted in English and banned bilingual ballots and bilingual education.

Supporters of such efforts argue that the nation's governing institutions need to make clear that the United States is one people with one language. They are troubled by the current policies of the federal and state governments that accommodate non-English-speaking immigrants by offering them services in Spanish, Chinese and a host of other languages.

"The government has gotten into the business of encouraging linguistic divisions by offering bilingual ballots, bilingual government forms and bilingual education," says Boulet of English First.

Boulet is particularly troubled by President Clinton's Aug. 11 signing of Executive Order 13166, which mandates federal agencies to strengthen services to non-English speakers. "This basically requires every agency in the government to provide services in any language that anyone speaks," Boulet says. "We've turned language into a civil right, creating a linguistic entitlement."

Proponents of "English-only" laws charge that by protecting bilingualism, Clinton and others are encouraging newcomers to "get by" without learning proper English. This policy, they claim, will impede efforts to integrate new arrivals into American society. "The motive to learn English is already strong among immigrants," says Jorge Anselle, vice president for education at the Center for Equal Opportunity, a research group concerned with issues of race, ethnicity and assimilation. "When we repeatedly accommodate them in their native language, we're sending out the wrong message: That their first impulse is incorrect and that we're going to make it as easy for you not to learn English as we can."

According to Anselle, recent government policies on language reflect a "paradigm shift" in thinking about new immigrants. "We've turned our motto, 'E Pluribus Unum' — which means 'Out of many, one' — on its head," he says. "The old ways, of assimilating immigrants by Americanizing them, are now considered bad. The thought is that we need to work to preserve their differences, which includes saving their language."

The danger of "preserving differences" — especially in language — is that Americans will stop thinking of themselves as one people, sowing division among different groups, Boulet says. "History shows us that linguistic divisions ultimately lead to other kinds of divisions," he says. "I mean, when you build these multilingual, multicultural societies you find yourself with the kinds of dilemmas they have in places like the Balkans or Canada. Is that what we want?" [12]

Instead, Boulet and Anselle say, the government needs to send a very different message to non-native English-speakers. "We need to let them know that we have a common language and a common culture and that these things are important," Anselle says.

"Don't we already have enough differences without working to create more?" Boulet asks. "Is it so much to ask those who come here to respect our linguistic tradition and learn English?"

Opponents of a one-language policy agree that immigrants need to learn English. "No one is disputing the fact that English is our common language, least of all immigrants," says Delia Pompa, executive director of the National Association for Bilingual Education. "They come here wanting to learn English because they understand it's the coin of the realm."

But making English our official language isn't going to help anyone master the language, Pompa and others say. "Why do we need a law to tell us what we already know," says Elizabeth Salett, president of the National MultiCultural Institute, which promotes diversity. "It would be a response to a crisis that doesn't exist."

Opponents of English-only policies say studies show that non-English-speaking immigrants generally want to learn English. In addition, they point out, surveys show that the grandchildren of immigrants speak only English and not the language of their grandparents' country of origin.

The only thing an English-only policy will accomplish, they claim, is to make some immigrants feel excluded from their new homeland. "We would be sending a negative message to people who come here, a message that's not welcoming," says Muñoz at the National Council of La Raza.

In addition, Muñoz argues, "English-only" policies are unnecessarily cruel to people who have just arrived and may not have mastered the nation's language, rules and customs. "Not communicating to people what they need to know in their native tongue is foolish and counterproductive," she says. "It's not as if keeping them in ignorance is going to shame them into learning English."

Pompa agrees. "I don't think passing an English-only law will stifle people's desire to speak in their own language," she says. "People will do what they want, what they feel comfortable with."

Furthermore, English-only opponents say, it's in the national interest

Echoes of "One" Language?

According to linguist Joseph H. Greenberg of Stanford University, almost all of the major language categories contain languages in which a "tik"- or "dik"-like word signifies the concept of one or finger or point. In English, the word is "digit" or "digital."

Language Family	Form	Meaning
Niger-Kordofanian	"Dike"	One
Nilo-Saharan	"Tek" "Dek" "Tok"	One
Khoisan	Absent	--
Afro-Asiatic	"Tak"	One
Dravidian	None	--
Indo-European	"Deik"	To point
Uralic-Yukaghir	"Otik"	One
Altaic	"Tek"	Only
Chukchi-Kamchatkan	Unclear	--
Eskimo-Aleut	"Tik"	One
Sino-Tibetan	"Tik"	One
Austric	"Tik" "Ting"	Hand, arm
Indo-Pacific	"Dik"	One
Australian	Absent	--
Amerind	"Tik"	Finger, one
Na-Dene	"Tikhi"	One

Source: Merritt Ruhlen, On the Origin of Languages

to encourage people to retain their native language and pass it on to their children. "We live in an increasingly global economy, which makes having a multilingual population desirable," Salett says.

Finally, opponents dispute the contention that encouraging immigrants and their descendents to retain their language of origin will lead to a fragmented society. "In other developed countries, especially in Europe, bilingualism is encouraged," Muñoz says, "and it's fine." ■

BACKGROUND

Rise of Language

Many cultures have tried to explain the emergence of language. According to the ancient Hebrews, God originally endowed humanity with one language. But mankind's hubris and ambition prompted the creator to punish his people by dispersing them around the globe and imbuing them with many different tongues. To the Acoma tribe of New Mexico, the goddess Iatiku created different languages to discourage people from arguing with each other.

Scientists believe that language usage probably first occurred in Africa, sometime between 500,000 and 1 million years ago.[13] The earliest speakers were hominids known as *Homo erectus*, immediate predecessors of *Homo sapiens*, or modern humans. The first efforts at vocal communication by *Homo erectus* were primitive, with few words and very limited grammar. But over the course of tens of thousands of years, their vocabulary undoubtedly expanded and a grammar developed.

Most recent paleontological evidence suggests that our immediate ancestors — *Homo sapiens* — first ventured out of Africa roughly 50,000 years ago. Within 10,000 years humans had spread to Europe, Asia, and even Australia. [14] As humanity fanned across the globe, people broke into different ethnic groups. Likewise, the new groupings developed different languages that are the linguistic ancestors of the thousands of languages that people speak today.

Scholars have grouped the world's languages into 21 broad categories, each with various subgroups. [15] For instance, most of the tongues spoken in Western Europe as well as in parts of Western and Southern Asia are derived from the Indo-European category. This language root was spread to Europe by invaders from India. One of the Indo-European languages, Latin, in turn became the basis for French, Italian, Spanish and even Romanian.

No one is sure whether the world's languages originated from one or multiple sources. Many language anthropologists argue that it is impossible to know, since a language evolves too quickly to trace its origins back tens of thousands of years. Indeed, they say, words change so fast that it is generally impossible to discern a language's roots more than about 5,000 years in the past. [16]

But some experts argue that languages do leave enough clues to their origins to make it possible to dig deep into their past, certainly further back than 5,000 years. "Certain items in language are extremely stable, like personal pronouns or parts of the body," said Joseph H. Greenberg, a professor of anthropology at Stanford University. [17] Greenberg has classified the world's language categories into four "supergroups," including one, Euroasiatic, which links languages as disparate as Portuguese and Japanese.

Greenberg believes that he also may have found words in most of the world's languages that harken back to a single mother tongue. For instance, in almost all major language families, he notes, words related to the concept of one, such as the number "one" or a single finger, or digit, have the sound of "tik" or "dik." [18]

It is generally believed that written language first appeared in around 3500 B.C. among the Sumerians in Mesopotamia (now Iraq). In its earliest form, the first writing used primitive pictures to convey concepts, like fish or bread. As time went on, the pictures became more abstract, eventually taking on phonetic qualities; thus, the signs came to represent actual spoken sounds that, when taken together, formed words. [19]

The Sumerians wrote on soft clay tablets with a wedge-shaped stylus. Today their writing is known as "cuneiform," after the Latin *cuneus*, for "wedge." Like most writing today, Sumerian was organized into horizontal rows that were read from left to right and top to bottom. [20]

But cuneiform writing differs from most modern writing systems in a very important respect: It has no alphabet. Instead, Sumerians and later users of cuneiform relied on literally hundreds of written signs to communicate. [21]

The first alphabet was created sometime after 2000 B.C. by one of the tribes of Semites living in what is today Israel, Jordan and Lebanon. While scholars are unsure which of the early Semitic alphabets came first, one of them (created by the

Languages on the Web

More than a quarter of a billion people around the world use Web sites that offer language translation and other services. Here are some of the most popular sites: [20]

The Endangered Language Fund:
http://sapir.ling.yale.edu/~elf/index.html

Ethnologue: Languages of the World:
http://www.sil.org/ethnologue

The Human Languages Page:
http://www.june29.com/HLP

Native American Languages:
http://www.mcn.net/~wlelman/langlinks.htm

Teaching Indigenous Languages:
http://jan.ucc.nau.edu/~jar/TIL.html

Kualono Hawaiian Web Site:
http://www.olelo.hawaii.edu/OP/orgs/apl

Babelfish Web Translator:
http://doc.altavista.com/help/search/babel_tool.shtml

Phoenicians) was passed onto the ancient Greeks in the early 8th century B.C. Over the next three centuries, the Greeks used Phoenician letters to develop the world's first modern alphabet, complete with vowels.

The Greeks, in turn, passed their system of writing onto the Etruscans, a group living in Tuscany in Italy. It was from the Etruscans that ancient Romans acquired the alphabet they would eventually use to create written Latin, which is the basis for the lettering system used today in English, Spanish and other European languages.

A Violent Birth

Like many great developments in history, the evolution of the English language was driven as much by violence and bloodshed as by any other factor. In fact, the birth of English can be traced back to a series of invasions in the 5th century A.D., when Angles, Saxons and Jutes crossed the North Sea from Denmark and northwestern Germany and conquered much of the British Isles. The three tribes each spoke a dialect of low German that eventually formed the nucleus of what would become English.[22]

At the time, Britain was home to groups of Celts, who had spent three centuries under Roman rule. Many spoke local Celtic languages or the Latin of Rome. But within a hundred years of the first Germanic invasions, the Celts had been driven from most of the island, remaining only in what is today Cornwall, Wales and western Scotland.

The new tribes took almost nothing from the Celtic language as they settled in Britain. Instead, the German dialects these groups spoke were gradually fused together into a new Germanic tongue — Anglo-Saxon or Old English. It became even more distinctive after 597 A.D., when St. Augustine arrived from Rome and began converting the tribes to Christianity. Soon, a large infusion of Latin — the language of the Roman Catholic Church — was finding its way into the Anglo-Saxon vocabulary.

Archive

Elizabethan playwright William Shakespeare made great contributions to the development of modern English by helping to standardize the usage of certain words. He also was the first writer known to use hundreds of new terms, such as "dislocate," "premeditated" and "submerged."

In the 8th century, a new band of invaders — the Norsemen, or Vikings, from Scandinavia — began raiding and then settling in Britain. For a time, it looked as though the Vikings would conquer the Angles, Saxons and Jutes and replace Old English with their Scandinavian language. But Alfred, a king in southwestern England, rallied the English and defeated a large Viking army at the battle of Ethandun in 878.[23]

King Alfred's victory over the Vikings confined them to northern and eastern parts of the island and literally saved the English language. In an effort to unite the tribes against future Scandinavian incursions, Alfred encouraged a sense of common culture and language among them. Schools began teaching in English rather than Latin, and a host of books were translated into English.

Still, the Scandinavian invasions did leave a linguistic mark. Today, for example, words like sky, skull, egg and leg and the pronouns they, their and them are derived from the language of the Vikings.

Modern English

The third major invasion to influence the English language came in 1066, when William, Duke of Normandy, conquered Britain after defeating an English army at the Battle of Hastings. The Normans were originally Vikings who had conquered a part of northern France hundreds of years earlier and established a kingdom there. By the time William and his men crossed the English Channel in 1066, the one-time Scandinavians spoke French.

The Normans did not turn England into a French-speaking land, although that was their intention. Instead, they unintentionally changed English, giving it much French vocabulary and grammar. By 1200, less than 150 years after Hastings, Old English had been transformed into what is today known as Middle English.

Chronology

500,000B.C. to 1B.C.

Humans develop first spoken and then written language.

500,000 B.C.
Some scientists believe the predecessors of modern humans, Homo erectus, began using a primitive form of language at or before this time.

50,000 B.C.
Modern humans, Homo sapiens, begin spreading from Africa throughout Eurasia and other parts of the world. Different groups settle down and eventually create different languages.

3500 B.C.
The first written language appears in Mesopotamia.

2000 B.C.
Semitic tribes create the first alphabet.

800 B.C.
Phoenicians pass on their system of letters to the Greeks, who use it to create the first modern alphabet, complete with vowels.

1A.D. to 1500

The languages of several primitive Germanic tribes develop into modern English.

449
Angles, Saxons and Jutes migrate from northwest Germany and Flanders to Britain. Within a generation, native Celts are driven to western fringes of the island.

6th Century
The invaders' Germanic dialects fuse together to become the dominant language of England, known today as Old English or Anglo-Saxon.

597
St. Augustine arrives in England and begins converting the people to Christianity. The new religion adds many Latin words to Old English.

750
Viking invaders begin landing in Britain. Soon, the newcomers are threatening to conquer the Germanic tribes and displace their new language.

878
King Alfred the Great defeats the Vikings at the battle of Ethandun, saving the English and their language.

1066
William, Duke of Normandy, conquers England, bringing many French-speakers to the island. Soon, this influence begins changing the English language.

1200
Old English gives way to Middle English, the language of Geoffrey Chaucer.

1386
Chaucer begins work on *The Canterbury Tales*, a masterpiece of Middle English poetry.

1500 to Present

Modern English emerges. British colonization spreads the language around the world.

16th Century
Printing brings new ideas from the Renaissance in southern Europe to England. The influence of Latin, Greek, Italian and other languages has profound impact on English. By century's end, people speak what will become known as modern English.

1592
Shakespeare begins writing plays. His work helps standardize and expand the English vocabulary.

1604
First English dictionary is published.

1611
Standard King James English translation of the Bible is published.

1755
Dr. Samuel Johnson publishes his famous Dictionary of the English Language.

1776
The 13 British colonies in North America declare independence, creating the United States.

1828
Noah Webster publishes first dictionary of American English.

20th Century
The United States supplants Great Britain as the largest and most powerful English-speaking nation. American political, economic and cultural power cements English as the world's lingua franca.

2000
About 1.5 billion people speak English at some level of proficiency, more than any other language in the world.

Is There a "Language Instinct"?

Many animals use sounds to communicate. Some cry out to warn others of danger. Others growl, bark or honk to intimidate competitors. Certain birds can even mimic human words and short sentences. Some researchers think advanced primates can be taught simple sign language.

But only the human brain enables man to string together sounds to communicate complex thoughts, most scientists say. Moreover, some researchers claim that the ability to communicate complex ideas is instinctive, not something we need to learn.

"Language is not a cultural artifact that we learn in the way we learn to tell time or how the federal government works," writes Massachusetts Institute of Technology psychology Professor Steven Pinker in his best-selling book, *The Language Instinct: How the Mind Creates Language*. "Instead, it is a distinct piece of the biological makeup of our brains." [1]

Like the spots on a leopard, the "language instinct" is encoded in our genes, Pinker and others claim, along with basic linguistic principles. For instance, basic rules of grammar, such as the use of singular and plural or the formulation of questions are not learned, but inherited, they say, which is why all languages share much of the same basic structure.

The language instinct is what allows a child to pick up a language or languages very easily, without much instruction from elders. It helps to explain why children talk long before they can play a musical instrument or even skip rope. [2]

"A preschooler's tacit knowledge of grammar is more sophisticated than the thickest style manual or the most state-of-the-art computer-language system," Pinker writes. [3] The same cannot be said for skills like "baking or brewing," which need to be learned, according to Charles Darwin. [4]

But some scientists and language experts dispute the notion that there is proof of a language instinct. According to Geoffrey Sampson, a professor of computer science at the University of Sussex in England and author of *Educating Eve: The Language Instinct Debate*, language is probably largely "culturally acquired" and not innate. "There may be some small predetermined structure for language [in the brain], but it is minimal," he wrote.

Indeed, he says, every argument put forth by Pinker and others in favor of the language instinct "doesn't really hold up when subjected to scrutiny." Moreover, he contends that the world's languages are not structurally similar, as Pinker and others claim. "There really are no common properties in language," Sampson argues. "For every one they point to, there are languages that have different ones."

In addition, he disputes a study Pinker points to as evidence that specific language skills are genetically acquired. To bolster their arguments, Pinker and others have pointed to a family that has inherited an inability to understand grammar. Pinker argues that the family's grammar gene must have mutated and sees their deficiency as proof of a direct genetic link to language ability.

But, Sampson claims, the family in question had a host of mental handicaps and, upon further examination, actually did have some grasp of grammar. "It turns out that these people can and do apply linguistic rules," he says. "It also turns out that they had a general inherited mental deficiency that had nothing to do with language at all."

Some scientists also disagree with the generally held idea that language is unique to human beings. E. Sue Savage-Rumbaugh, a professor of biology at Georgia State University, argues that bonobos (chimpanzee-like African primates) are fully capable of making and understanding language. Using a keyboard consisting of 400 symbols, she says she can carry on a conversation with her primate test subjects.

The only obstacle to bonobos creating humanlike language, Savage-Rumbaugh claims, is their lack of the kind of vocal tract that allows humans to form words. "If you talk to apes and point to little symbols, they learn to understand language just as I'm talking to you," she said. [5]

---

[1] Steven Pinker, *The Language Instinct: How the Mind Creates Language* (1994), p. 18.

[2] Jack Chambers, "Plipping' Through Language," *The Globe and Mail*, Dec. 11, 1999.

[3] Pinker, *op. cit.*, p. 19.

[4] Quoted in Charles Darwin, *The Descent of Man* (1874), pp. 101-102.

[5] Quoted in "Bonobo Study Suggests Animals Communicate," *Minneapolis-St. Paul Star-Tribune*, Jan. 19, 2000.

The merger of Germanic Old English, or Anglo-Saxon, with Latin-based French created a uniquely new language that allowed its users great latitude of expression. The new tongue's great subtlety and sophistication is reflected in the works of Geoffrey Chaucer, whose *Canterbury Tales* (written in the late 14th Century) exhibits dazzling wordplay.

But Middle English was only a linguistic bridge. By 1500, the language was changing dramatically. Once again, English owed its evolution to an invasion. This time though, the culprits were not marauders or conquerors, but ideas. The invention of printing in the middle of the 15th century brought the humanism of the Renaissance in Italy north to England. For the first time, texts in Greek and Latin, as well as Italian, French and Spanish, became commonly available, adding thousands of new words to the English language. Many of the works were quickly translated into

Native American Languages at Risk

When Columbus arrived in the New World, an estimated 300 Native American languages were spoken. More than 500 years later, linguists now say the number has dwindled to 175.

Speakers	Number	Where Spoken	Examples
Still spoken in homes by children	20	Mostly in New Mexico and Arizona	Navajo, Western Apache, Hopi, Zuni, Havasupai-Hualapai
Still spoken by parents and elders	30	Montana, Iowa, Alaska	Crow, Cheyenne, Mesquakie, Jicarilla Apache
Spoken only by elders	70	California, Alaska, Oregon, Maine, Washington	Tlingit, Passamaquoddy, Winnebago, Comanche, Yuma, Nez Perce, Kalispel, Kakima, Makah
Spoken by fewer than 10 elders	55	California, Iowa, North Dakota	Eyak, Mandan, Pawnee, Wichita, Omaha, Washoe

Source: The Cambridge Encyclopedia of Language; Global Reach; University of Alaska; U.S. Census Bureau

English, further accelerating the changes taking place.

By the time William Shakespeare began writing in the early 1590s, people were speaking an early version of modern English. The fact that many people can still read and understand Shakespeare's original plays and the King James Bible (translated into English in the first decade of the 17th century), is a testament to the similarity of English then and now.

The new language that emerged from the English Renaissance was strengthened and expanded by the literature of the day, by such great writers as Edmund Spenser and John Milton and the translators of the King James Bible. Shakespeare himself used almost every English word existing at the time and made up many new ones.

At this time, English began to become standardized. In 1604, the first English dictionary appeared, defining 2,500 "hard" words. A century and a half later, in 1755, Samuel Johnson's famous *Dictionary of the English Language* was published, defining 40,000 words. Meanwhile, Daniel Defoe, Jonathan Swift and other writers proposed academies and boards to oversee the language and prevent it from being corrupted by outside influences. [24]

But "outside influences" were part of England's stock in trade, driven by economic and political expansion around the world as well as close to home. Rule over Scotland and Ireland brought with it new English dialects and the creation of new words. More far-flung colonies in North America, the Indies and Australia also contributed. Soon after Johnson published his dictionary, the Scottish poet Robert Burns began writing verse in English. And in 1828, Noah Webster published his first *American Dictionary of the English Language*. English was no longer the sole province of the English.

By the beginning of the 20th century, the United States had become the most populous and powerful English-speaking nation. As a result, America became the primary locus of the English language.

Like its proper cousin across the Atlantic, American English has been influenced by the tongues of many other cultures. Hundreds of Native American words, from moose to kayak, have passed into the language. Immigrants have also added innumerable words and phrases, from the Yiddish of Eastern European Jews to the many words brought by millions of German immigrants. ■

CURRENT SITUATION

Erosion of Linguistic Diversity

In the middle of the Amazon, in Belem, Brazil, Denny Moore is in a race against time. Moore, a linguistic

Keeping Up With Internet-Speak

The computer revolution has sparked many important changes in our lives, including the language we use. "We are already using the vocabulary and conceptual framework of computers when we speak," says Richard H. Schlagel, a professor of philosophy at the George Washington University, including such ubiquitous words as "download," "virtual" and "cyber."

Moreover, the increasing popularity of e-mail has created hundreds of new terms recognized by the on-line community and beyond. Many on-line "words" are no more than abbreviations that have become commonplace. "A lot of this is about speed," says Donna Jo Napoli, a professor of linguistics at Swarthmore College in Pennsylvania.

How many of the new "e-words" will enter the broader vocabulary? Not many, according to Kathleen Ferrara, associate professor of linguistics at Texas A&M University. "The majority of these words won't last," she said. [1]

Still, many common words, including scuba (self contained underwater breathing apparatus) and wow (wonder of wonders), began as shortcuts or acronyms.

Here are some of the more popular abbreviations and terms currently being used on-line:

AYT - Are you there?
BTW - By the way.
CUL - See you later.
F2F - Face to face.
ISP - Internet service provider.
JAM - Just a minute.
ICCL - I could care less.
LOL - Laughing out loud.
Me-mail - E-mail for egomaniacs.
OTOH - On the other hand.
POTS - Plain old telephone service.
RAM - Random access memory.
Snail-mail - Old-style letter sent through the postal service.
YYSSW - Yeah, yeah, sure, sure, whatever.

1 Quoted in Leah Beth Ward, "Internet Age Spawns New Words," *The Dallas Morning News*, Sept. 20, 2000.

anthropologist, is trying to catalog and analyze the languages of Brazil's indigenous tribes. "Brazil has 41 languages with fewer than 50 speakers, and a lot of those only have two or three surviving speakers," he said. [25]

Halfway around the world, in Russia, Johanna Nichols is in a similar race. Nichols, a professor of Slavic languages at the University of California at Berkeley, is trying to assemble a Chechen-English dictionary. She fears that decades of Soviet cultural and political domination, coupled with the recent Russian invasions, will turn the language of Chechnya into a relic of the past. "If the [Chechen] language isn't recorded soon, one day it may only exist symbolically," she said. [26]

Moore and Nichols are two of the foot soldiers in the battle to preserve language diversity. It is, many experts say, a battle that they and others are losing.

About 6,700 languages are currently spoken around the world. But linguists estimate that within 100 years, as many as 95 percent of the tongues will either be extinct or moribund, only spoken by a few experts or elders but unknown by younger generations. [27]

Still, there have been a few success stories. For instance, millions today speak Hebrew, a language that until the 19th century was used almost exclusively by Jewish religious scholars. Welsh and Gaelic have also made strong comebacks in Wales and Ireland, respectively.

But according to many experts a huge number of languages are on the verge of extinction. "Right now, we're in a state of absolutely, unprecedented crisis," says Michael Krauss, a professor of linguistics at the University of Alaska at Fairbanks. "I don't think the vast majority of languages currently spoken will survive this century."

According to some estimates, a language disappears every two weeks. Already, 90 percent of the 250 aboriginal languages spoken in Australia are extinct or moribund. Of the 72 languages spoken by native peoples of Alaska and Siberia, 56 are disappearing. And 82 of the 100 to 150 indigenous languages spoken in the Amazon region are headed for extinction. [28]

Language erosion is even accelerating in the United States. Of the 300 languages spoken by Native Americans at the time of European colonization, only about 175 survive. Of these, 135 are threatened and may die out within a generation or two.

Some Native American languages are already very close to extinction. For instance, only about 10 people currently speak and understand Yuchi, the language of the Creek Indians of northeast Oklahoma. "In a few more years, there won't be anybody left to teach it," said Henry Washburn, a 74-year-old Creek who still speaks the language of his ancestors. [29]

Language experts point to a number of reasons for the rapid decline of language diversity. For one thing, they say, access to new information technologies encourages people who speak rare languages to learn their region's dominant tongue. "People today want to watch television or listen to the radio, and they can't do that if they speak these smaller languages," says Peter Ladefoget, a professor of phonetics at the University of California at Los Angeles (UCLA). "They have to learn the *lingua franca*, and after a while it becomes commonplace to speak it at home," he says. "And as soon as a mother stops speaking her language to her children, that language is in trouble because soon only the old speak it."

Krauss agrees, arguing that for indigenous peoples around the world, "television is like cultural nerve gas: It's painless and odorless, and they wake up no longer functioning in their native language."

Another factor, Ladefoget says, is that governments often encourage "monolingualism" as a means to unify a country's population. "Governments find it much more convenient if everyone speaks the same language, so naturally they urge people to do so."

Similarly, he says, corporations and businesses discourage linguistic diversity, since having a host of different languages in one area makes commerce much harder. "Those who speak the big languages like Spanish or Portuguese or English have economic control over people's lives in their hands," Krauss says. ■

Rescue Efforts

Efforts are being made to save some languages from extinction. In some cases, experts like Moore and Nichols are trying to preserve many languages before they are lost forever. "Documenting a language is at least something," Krauss says. "We can try to revive it later, like we did with Hebrew."

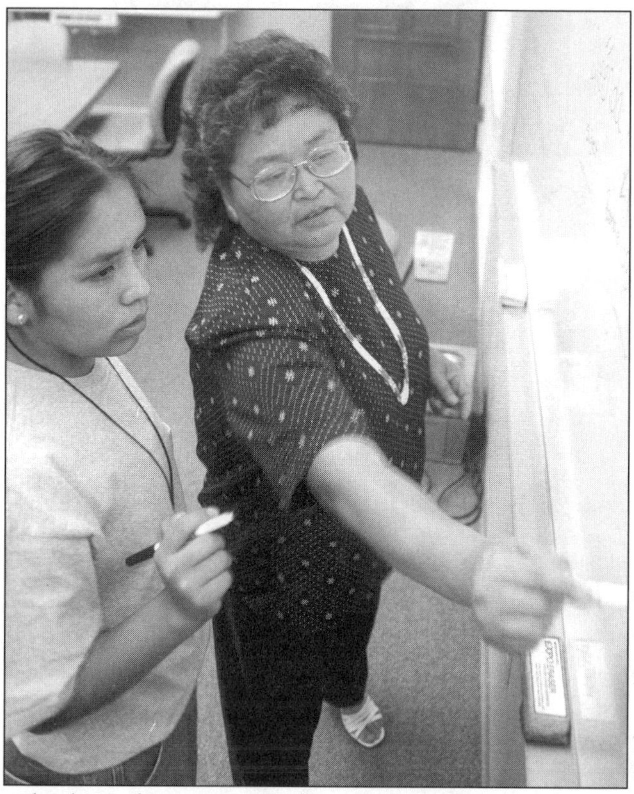

AP Photos/Guy Jacobs

Glenda Mark practices translating her Navajo language into English, with the help of her teacher Barbara Howard at New Mexico's Newcomb High School in Shiprock. Of the 300 languages spoken by Native Americans at the time of the European colonization, many are extinct and only 40 are expected to survive another generation or two.

More important though, are efforts to get native speakers to keep their endangered tongues alive among their own people. Washburn, for instance, is trying to pass Yuchi onto children in his tribe. In New Zealand, many Maori children attend nursery schools staffed by elders and conducted in the Maori language.

It's important that these efforts succeed and are duplicated around the world, Swarthmore College's Napoli says, because the loss of language diversity would culturally "impoverish" humanity. "Different languages are beautiful," she says. "They make life interesting."

Beyond the aesthetic value of living in a world with many different tongues, there are practical reasons to preserve every language, many linguists say. For one thing, Krauss claims, each language is in essence a library of facts about the world, as seen by those who speak it.

"Every language has imbedded within it exquisitely detailed knowledge of people's experience with their environment," he says, such as which plants in the jungle have medicinal value.

In addition, Krauss and others say, loss of each language ultimately means loss of a culture, of an entire way of thinking. "What we think, what we believe and our whole identity is wrapped up in our language," American University's Baron says. "So when you lose a language, you lose a whole cultural identity."

Baron also claims that linguistic diversity contributes to better understanding of how the mind works, because language is unique to the human brain. "The scope of language diversity aids our understanding of our cognitive ability," Baron argues. "But if you only have, say, Indo-European languages and not African or Turkic languages, you have a very skewed view of how the mind creates language."

But others view the possible loss of language diversity with less alarm. "Having all of these different languages isn't *per se* enriching," George Washington University's Schlagel says. "This isn't like losing endangered species of animals: There's probably nothing you can say or express in these smaller languages that you can't say or express in a big language like English or Spanish."

In addition, Schlagel and others say, small tribes or groups lose one language and learn another for a reason. "Learning these big languages gives people access to information and education that they never had before," Ladefoget says. "It's paternalistic to tell these people that they have to keep their original language. If it's important to them, they'll make the effort to keep it."

But, Krauss says, there's another way to look at the problem. "We need to shake off the feeling that indigenous people can't learn the dominant language and keep their native tongue at the same time," he says. "That's ludicrous."

Anti-English Backlash

In September, 100 scholars in Italy joined forces to sign a petition against what they termed the "linguistic contamination" of Italian. Their complaint: The language of Dante and Petrarch is being infused with too many words in English and other languages. For example, in the latest edition of a popular Italian dictionary, 4,000 of the 100,000 listed words — 4 percent of the total — were foreign. [30] Half of the linguistic gatecrashers were English.

Many of the new words, such as "e-mail" or "chat-line" — have come to Italy via the Internet, a medium created and largely dominated by Americans. (*See box, p. 144.*) Others, though, like "new age," "gay" and "pet therapy," reflect the reach and impact of U.S. culture in general. [31]

"Learning these big languages gives people access to information and education that they never had before. It's paternalistic to tell these people that they have to keep their original language. If it's important to them, they'll make the effort to keep it."

—Peter Ladefoget
Professor of Phonetics
University of California at Los Angeles

"Components of English are making their way into native languages around the world," American University's Baron says. "This will change these languages, but they will survive."

But like the petition signers in Italy, critics in other countries also are not taking changes in their native languages lightly. French officials in the Academie Francaise have long been fighting to keep English out of the glorious language of Moliere and Balzac.

In Poland, a recent law prohibits the use of foreign words for business or advertising unless accompanied by Polish translation. The law imposes stiff fines on violators and creates a language council to monitor compliance.

"We simply want to keep the language free from pollution and to send out a signal to people that their culture is being protected despite the increasing influences from outside," says Iwona Sledzinska-Katarasinska, the Polish legislator who introduced the bill. [32]

According to Jay Jasanoff, a professor of linguistics at Harvard University, the backlash against English is understandable. The opponents of English "don't want their cultures submerged by an American cultural wave," he says. "I would do it, too, if I were them."

But many others argue that efforts to keep language "pure" are counterproductive and futile. "These attempts never work," says Roberto Severino, a professor of Italian at Georgetown University. "The French have been trying to protect their language for years, and their efforts have had little or no effect."

Swarthmore's Napoli agrees that laws designed to preserve a language defy linguistic gravity. "Language is like clothing: It's a convention that changes all the time," she says. "So no matter what law they pass, the language will ignore it and go on changing."

Indeed, Severino says, it's only natural that a language would take

At Issue:

Should non-standard English, such as Ebonics and Spanglish, ever be used in the classroom?

CAROLYN TEMPLE ADGER
SENIOR RESEARCHER, CENTER FOR APPLIED LINGUISTICS

WRITTEN FOR THE CQ RESEARCHER, NOVEMBER 2000

yes

How students and teachers talk in classrooms depends on what they're doing and who they are. They draw from a repertoire of features and styles to adjust to the shifting communicative demands of classroom activities — from the more formal speech of lectures and reports to the less formal interaction among lab partners to informal chats after class. This is the classroom equivalent of the natural language shifting that occurs in the workplace, the home and social settings. Adjusting speech reveals a fine-tuned human sensitivity to shifting social scenes and settings.

No one speaks the same way all the time. Like all speakers, students whose dialects include non-standard features shift along a dialect continuum to accommodate changes in formality. When the occasion demands more formal speech, students use more standard features. For instance, a student might tell a lab partner, "It ain't no oxygen left," to explain why a candle is flickering in a closed container, but tell the whole class, "There wasn't any oxygen left." In both cases, the student demonstrates an understanding of the subject matter. However, demanding that students always use a highly formal style won't produce that kind of language.

Our speech also shows our social identity. Given the natural predisposition toward group affiliation and the tensions that surround ethnicity and class, it's easy to understand why attempts to outlaw vernacular dialects or "correct" students' speech have always failed. Perhaps if instructors would precisely identify the contrasts between vernacular and standard dialects it would more effectively strengthen students' command of standard English as a second dialect.

Should non-standard English ever be used in the classroom? Yes, when speakers and settings combine to produce appropriate and natural occasions for using such a variety. Language is the backbone of education: Students learn through writing and reading, and through talking with teachers and peers. Forbidding a significant portion of their language competence would silence them. It would prevent them from interacting with their peers and teachers, depriving them of a rich opportunity for learning.

Further, deriding the language of students' communities negates the community. Rather, perhaps, the curricula should be organized to support language development for all students, including increasing proficiency in standard English and academic language.

BY JIM BOULET JR.
EXECUTIVE DIRECTOR, ENGLISH FIRST

WRITTEN FOR THE CQ RESEARCHER, NOVEMBER 2000

no

What is really behind the notion that African-American children should be taught in Ebonics or that the mixture of Spanish and English known as "Spanglish" belongs in the classroom? The answer is a combination of misguided education theory along with battles over status and political clout.

The *New Republic* admitted that "Ebonics did not really take off until the late 1980s, when black parents saw that new waves of immigrants were receiving federal funds for bilingual language education." (The Oakland School Board admittedly passed its 1996 Ebonics resolution as a step toward applying for federal bilingual education funds.)

A 1990 *Sacramento Bee* article entitled "The Department of Spanglish?" reported that students insisted that the Department of Spanish at the University of California at Davis teach both Chicano Spanish as well as correct Spanish.

How did we get here? Ask the folks who invented bilingual education programs.

A 1995 article in the National Clearinghouse for Bilingual Education's *Directions in Language & Education* argued that: "[b]uilding a positive self-concept in children and developing a healthy attitude toward schooling rests on valuing what the children bring with them from home — including the non-English language."

Education Professor Lisa Delpit similarly claims that any suggestion that Ebonics is bad English is "to suggest that something is wrong with the student and his or her family." Spanglish education is justified in the same manner.

All forms of bilingual education are based on a hotly debated notion of "language transfer." Bilingual-education advocate Steven Krashen explains that language transfer occurs when: "bilingual programs . . . supply subject matter knowledge in the students' primary language, [making] the English the students hear and read much more comprehensible."

Unfortunately for the children involved, this theory defies the proven success of immersion techniques, which Berlitz schools have used successfully for much of the 20th century.

Further, teaching in Ebonics did not help students at Normandie Elementary School in Los Angeles, Calif. Students there showed a drop in reading and language skills despite the school's embrace of Ebonics education.

Advocates of Ebonics or Spanglish education forget that while the academic literature believes that these dialects are just as good as correct English, the job market vehemently disagrees. Lifelong unemployment or underemployment seems a much worse fate than a "D" on an English test.

on foreign words to describe new, foreign influences. "When you import a new concept or machine, you often import the words for that concept or machine," he says. "Since so many new ideas and machines, like computers, come from America, it's natural that so many new words are English."

UCLA's Ladefoget agrees, adding: "Languages are always absorbing new words — always have and always will." And, he says, exchanges of words and influences are usually beneficial and enriching. "Should we give the Italians back piano forte and andante?" he asks. "Of course not. Words like this keep our language alive and give it vigor." ■

OUTLOOK

New Informality?

The history of language is about change. And if there is one point on which language experts agree, it is that languages will continue to evolve. Beyond that, prognostication becomes difficult.

"Predicting the course of language over long periods is about as easy as predicting the weather," wrote Steven Pinker, a psychology professor at the Massachusetts Institute of Technology and author of the 1994 best-seller *The Language Instinct*. Still, some experts say they have spotted trends that presage a sea change in the way we write and speak.

In particular, some say, language is becoming less formal. "Beginning around World War II, there has been a tendency for written English to become increasingly like casual speech," says American University's Baron. "We are using contractions and much less formal vocabulary, and we are paying much less attention to spelling and grammar."

She traces the decline in formality to a number of factors, including the increased influence of popular culture via radio, film and television. She also blames what she sees as a change in educational philosophy that came about in the 1960s.

"Around that time, educators began making self-expression and creativity the priority in the teaching of writing," she says. "They became more concerned with what you were saying rather than how you were saying it."

"Television is like cultural nerve gas: It's painless and odorless, and [people] wake up no longer functioning in their native language."

— Michael Krauss
Professor of Linguistics
Univ. of Alaska at Fairbanks

Baron believes that e-mail may be accelerating the trend toward informality. "E-mail communication is so much sloppier that I feel as though, in the next 10 years, we may see English becoming less structured and more carefree," she says. "I could see us going back to something like the situation we had in the 15th or 16th centuries, where there were some notions of punctuation or spelling, but people basically did what they wanted."

Similarly, some scholars worry about the spoken word. "Our language is being eroded," George Washington University's Schlagel says. "We've contaminated our speech with words like 'like' and 'no problem,' which merely detract from our point and make us appear stupid."

Like Baron, Schlagel blames much of the problem on television and other technologies of the Information Age. "Television and the like have come along and changed everything, reducing our speech to the lowest common denominator," he says. "Just listen to what they are saying and how they're saying it and you understand why it is ruining our speech."

By contrast, Schlagel says, people in days past had a richer and more formal sense of their language. "If you just look at the letters of the 19th century, the language used was so uncluttered and beautiful."

But other linguists dispute the notion that language is undergoing a major sea change due to technology. "Language always changes, but any kind of radical change is most unlikely," says Don Ringe, a professor of linguistics at the University of Pennsylvania.

UCLA's Ladefoget agrees, arguing that there is little evidence that language "is changing any faster or slower than it did before," since new technologies are always emerging that alter language somewhat. "Yes, there are more information outlets than ever before," he says. "But the rate of change per person is roughly the same because we have many more people than ever before." In other words, new information technologies may carry a greater linguistic punch than previous ones, but the strength of their impact is diluted by increases in population.

As Ringe puts it, "You may watch TV, but you don't talk to the guy on TV. At the end of the day, you interact with your neighbors."

Ringe also argues that 19th-century letters can't be used to show that speech has become less formal. "Writing was more formal in those days than it is today," he says. "But that's not the way people spoke to each other."

FOR MORE INFORMATION

Center for Applied Linguistics, 4646 40th St. N.W., Suite 200, Washington D.C. 20016; (202) 362-0700. www.cal.org. The center serves as a clearinghouse on the application of linguistics to practical language problems, such as bilingual education and the teaching of English as a second language (ESL).

English First, 8001 Forbes Pl., Suite 102, Springfield, Va. 22151; (703) 321-8818; www.englishfirst.org. The organization seeks to make English the official language of the United States.

Linguistic Society of America, 1325 18th St. N.W., Suite 211, Washington DC 20036; (202) 835-1714; www.lsadc.org. The society is the professional organization for academics and others interested in the scientific analysis of language.

National Council of La Raza, 1111 19th St. N.W., Suite 1000, Washington, D.C. 20036; (202) 785-1670; www.nclr.org. The council, an advocacy group for Latinos, opposes efforts to make English the nation's official language.

National MultiCultural Institute, 3000 Connecticut Ave, N.W. Suite 438, Washington D.C. 20008; (202) 483-0700; www.nmci.org. The institute encourages understanding and communication among people of various backgrounds.

U.S. English, 1747 Pennsylvania Ave. N.W. Suite 1100, Washington, D.C. 20006; (202) 833-0100; www.us-english.org. The organization promotes English language education for all immigrants and advocates English as the official language of the U.S.

Notes

[1] Quoted in Kathryn Tolbert, "Japanese Wringing Their Hands Over Nation's Poor English Skills," *The Oregonian*, Feb. 6, 2000.

[2] Ben MacIntyre, "Must France Now Swallow 'le Cheeseburger'?" *The Times of London*, Oct. 3, 1998.

[3] For background, see Nadine Cohodas, "Language Help Crucial to Hispanic Voters," in "Electing Minorities," *The CQ Researcher*, Aug. 12, 1994, pp. 697-720.

[4] For background, see Craig Donegan, "Debate Over Bilingualism," *The CQ Researcher*, Jan. 19, 1996, pp. 49-72.

[5] John Thor Dahlburg, "English is in the Air for Carrier," *Los Angeles Times*, April 1, 2000.

[6] The British Council.

[7] *Ibid.*

[8] *Ibid.*

[9] Barbara Wallraff, "What Global Language?" *The Atlantic Monthly*, November 2000.

[10] Quoted in *Ibid.*

[11] Quoted in *Ibid.*

[12] For background, see Mary H. Cooper, "Quebec Sovereignty," *The CQ Researcher*, Oct. 6, 1995, pp. 873-896.

[13] Steven Roger Fischer, *A History of Language* (1999), p. 44.

[14] Jared Diamond, *Guns, Germs and Steel* (1997), p. XX.

[15] Quoted in Nicholas Wade, "What We All Spoke When the World was Young," *The New York Times*, Feb. 1, 2000.

[16] *Ibid.*

[17] Quoted in *Ibid.*

[18] *Ibid.*

[19] Diamond, *op. cit.*, pp. 218-222.

[20] *Ibid.* p. 218.

[21] Hugh Thomas, *World History* (1996), p. 41.

[22] Robert McCrum, William Cran and Robert MacNeil, *The Story of English* (1986), pp. 60-64.

[23] Ted Anthony, "English: One Tongue for the New Global Village," The Associated Press, April 8, 2000.

[24] McCrum, Cran and MacNeil, *op. cit.* pp. 128-136.

[25] Quoted in Michael Astor, "Linguist Looks to Spoken Record to Provide Clues," *Los Angeles Times*, June 11, 2000.

[26] Quoted in Sam Bruchley, "Linguist Looks to Save Chechen Tongue from Extinction," *Los Angeles Times*, March 26, 2000.

[27] Guy Gugliotta, "Saying the Words That Save a Culture," *The Washington Post*, Aug. 9, 1999.

[28] Cited in *Ibid.*

[29] Quoted in *Ibid.*

[30] Desmond O'Grady, "Purists Say Addio to English Words," *Sydney Morning Herald*, Sept. 23, 2000.

[31] *Ibid.*

[32] Quoted in Kate Connolly, "Poland's Language Police Wage War on 'Polglish'" *The Guardian*, Sept. 4, 2000.

Bibliography

Selected Sources Used

Books

Crystal, David, *Language Death*, Cambridge University Press, 2000.
Crystal, one of the world's foremost authorities on language, examines the reasons why so many languages are dying and offers a prescription for preserving fading tongues.

Fischer, Steven Roger, *A History of Language*, Reaktion Books, 1999.
Fischer, director of the Institute of Polynesian Languages and Literature in New Zealand, charts the history of communication, from the prehistoric era to the modern age. He also examines the birth and development of the study of language.

McCrum, Robert, William Cran and Robert MacNeil, *The Story of English*, Viking, 1986.
Famed broadcast journalist MacNeil and his co-authors trace the history of English, from its humble beginnings among Germanic marauders in the 5th Century A.D. to its status today as a global language. The book is particularly good in its examination of the various dialects that have developed as English-speaking peoples have settled more and more of the world.

Pinker, Steven, *The Language Instinct: How the Mind Creates Language*, William Morrow, 1994.
Pinker, a professor of psychology at the Massachusetts Institute of Technology, presents a forceful argument in favor of the theory that language is not a learned skill, but something innate to human beings. According to Pinker, the "language instinct" is encoded in our genes just like other traits.

Articles

Anthony, Ted, "English: One Tongue for the New Global Village," The Associated Press, April 8, 2000.
Anthony explores how and why English has become the world's dominant language. He concludes that "in a world sewn together like never before, with common destinies and common dangers, English has become a crucial thread of connection."

Connolly, Kate, "Poland's Language Police Wage War on 'Polglish.'" *The Guardian*, Sept. 4, 2000.
Connolly explores Poland's efforts to stave off the infiltration of English words into the native language.

Fox, Justin, "The Triumph of English: To Compete Globally, More and More European Businesses are Making English Their Official Language," *Fortune*, Sept. 18, 2000.
According to Fox, many businesses in Europe and elsewhere have taken to using English as their in-house language. He predicts that soon, all executives "will sound like they're from California."

Gugliotta, Guy, "Saying the Words That Save a Culture," *The Washington Post*, Aug. 9, 1999.
Gugliotta examines some of the efforts under way to save endangered, indigenous languages.

Hotz, Robert Lee, "A Scalpel, a Life and Language," *Los Angeles Times*, Jan. 24, 2000.
Hotz gives a good overview of what neural and cognitive researchers have learned about how the brain processes language.

King, Robert D., "Should English Be the Law?" *The Atlantic Monthly*, April, 1997.
King ponders the possibility of making English the official language of the United States and concludes that it would only create divisions where none really exist. "Benign neglect is a good policy for any country when it comes to language, and it's a good policy for America," he writes.

Ruane, Michael E., "An Instant Language Packed With Meaning," *The Washington Post*, Dec. 14, 1999.
The article examines the new terms and words being created as a result of the increasing popularity of the Internet.

Sampson, Geoffrey, "Collapse of the Language Nativists," *The Independent*, April 9, 1999.
Sampson, a professor of computer science and artificial intelligence at the University of Sussex, argues that Steven Pinker's arguments in *The Language Instinct* are flawed. Language is not instinctual, but is largely learned like many other skills, Sampson claims.

Wallraff, Barbara, "What Global Language?" *The Atlantic Monthly*, November, 2000.
Wallraff, a language specialist and senior editor at *The Atlantic Monthly*, argues that English isn't fated to become the world's *lingua franca*. She contends that many factors cited by English-language triumphalists, such as the Internet, may actually work to preserve the viability of other languages.

9 Debate Over Immigration

David Masci

Hail a taxi, drop off dry cleaning, buy a lottery ticket at the local 7-Eleven. Chances are good that an immigrant from Ghana, South Korea, Mexico or some other faraway nation served you. Indeed, there's a good chance programmers from India or China wrote some of the software in your computer.

Across the country, in towns and cities alike, the United States, more than ever before, is a nation of immigrants.

"It's amazing how things have changed since the 1970s, how many people there now are in this country who were not born here," says Steven Moore, an economist at the Cato Institute, a libertarian think tank.

In the last 30 years the United States has absorbed the biggest wave of immigrants since the turn of the century, when millions arrived at Ellis Island in search of a better life. Today, more than 25 million Americans are foreign born — nearly 10 percent of the population. [1]

And that's good for the economy, according to Federal Reserve Chairman Alan Greenspan, who says the pools of skilled and unskilled workers created by high levels of immigration have greatly contributed to the nation's prosperity.

"As we are creating an ever more complex, sophisticated, accelerating economy, the necessity to have the ability to bring in . . . people from abroad to keep it functioning in the most effective manner increasingly strikes me as [sound] policy," he told lawmakers on Capitol Hill in February. [2]

Greenspan's comments were just the latest salvo in the continuing debate over immigration, a debate that is older than the country itself.

From *The CQ Researcher,* July 14, 2000.

CQ Photo/ R. Ellis

Newly naturalized Americans take the citizenship oath during a federal court ceremony. The Immigration and Naturalization Service processed 1.2 million citizenship applications in 1998.

More than 200 years ago, for instance, Benjamin Franklin pronounced recent arrivals from Germany as "the most stupid in the nation. Few of their children speak English, and through their indiscretion or ours, or both, great disorders may one day arise among us." [3]

But to immigration boosters like Greenspan, immigrants' work ethic and motivation make them cornerstones of America's economic prosperity.

"We're getting a lot of the best and brightest from other countries, and of course these people benefit the U.S. economy because they are driven to improve their lots," says Bronwyn Lance, a senior fellow at the Alexis de Tocqueville Institution, which works to increase understanding of the cultural and economic benefits of legal immigration. Lance and others say immigrants are more likely to start businesses — from corner grocery stores to giant computer companies — than native-born Americans are. Even newcomers with little education aid the economy, immigration boosters say, taking undesirable jobs that employers can't fill with native-born Americans.

Opponents of expanded immigration counter that the United States doesn't need a million newcomers each year to ensure a strong economy. Most immigrants aren't well-educated entrepreneurs but "poorly educated people who take low-skilled jobs for little money," says Dan Stein, executive director of the Federation for American Immigration Reform (FAIR), which opposes high immigration levels. In Stein's view, immigration largely benefits employers by providing a cheap and plentiful labor force. Moreover, he says, the newcomers take Americans' jobs and suppress wage levels.

Immigration opponents also reject the argument that immigrants are willing to do the jobs that most Americans won't do. In parts of the country with few immigrants, low-wage jobs still get done, and by native-born people, says Mark Krikorian, executive director of the Center for Immigration Studies.

"Employers could find Americans to do these jobs if they wanted to, but they'd have to provide training and raise wages to do so," Krikorian says. Immigrants are simply an easier and cheaper alternative for businesses, he and others maintain.

Finally, opponents point out, high immigration levels are overcrowding the United States, especially in urban areas, and preventing immigrants already here from assimilating into American society.

"The way we're going now we won't turn these people into Americans, and without assimilation we will increasingly be beset by ethnic conflicts," says John O'Sullivan, editor-at-large at the conservative *National Review* magazine and a noted expert on immigration.

Still, immigration supporters argue, today's newcomers, like those who sailed into New York Harbor in the past, come because they want to be Americans.

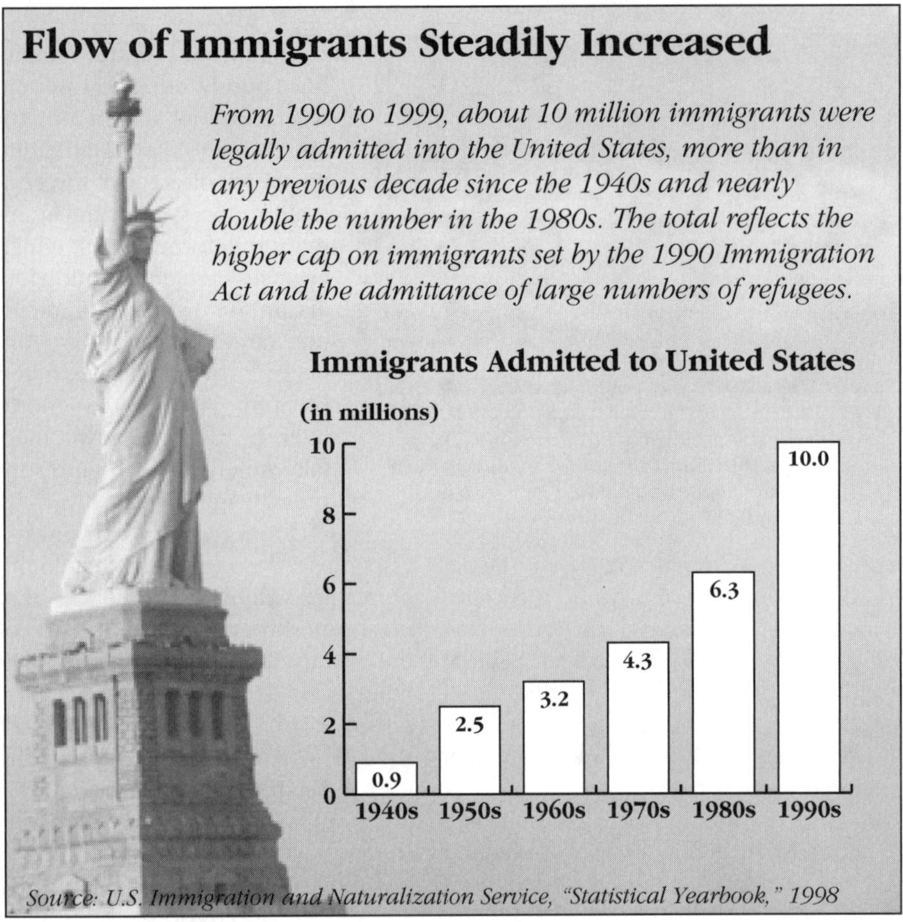

"We've always been afraid that new immigrants aren't assimilating and becoming American," Moore says. But immigrants are attracted to the United States for more than job opportunities. "America is more than a country, it's an idea with concepts like freedom," he says. "Most new immigrants buy into this idea. That's one of the reasons they want to be here."

Not all immigrants, of course, are here legally. While there is wide disagreement about how many newcomers the nation should admit, most experts favor taking at least some steps to block the estimated 300,000 or more illegal immigrants who come to the United States annually. Many support beefing up the U.S. Border Patrol, the enforcement arm of the Immigration and Naturalization Service (INS), and some call for greater use of a rarely enforced provision of the 1986 immigration law that punishes employers who knowingly hire illegal immigrants. [4]

Proponents of employer sanctions argue that some form of "internal enforcement" is necessary to catch the thousands who slip by border police. "The way things are right now we're sending a message to illegal aliens that once they get into the country they don't have to worry about getting caught," Krikorian says. This encourages more people to try to enter the U.S. illegally, he says.

Opponents of employer sanctions argue, however, that instead of discouraging illegal aliens, sanctions merely force them to take jobs with employers who are more likely to exploit them.

"In many cases, all we do is push people to take jobs for less pay and with unsafe working conditions," says Cecilia Muñoz, vice president for policy at the National Council of La Raza, the nation's largest Latino advocacy group. Moreover, Muñoz adds, if employer sanctions did work, many businesses, especially in the service sector, would find themselves without workers.

"Many industries rely on [undocumented] labor," she says, pointing out that illegal aliens are ubiquitous on farms and construction sites and other sectors of the economy that depend on low-skilled workers willing to do grimy, often back-breaking labor.

But immigrants are not just an important source of low-skill, low-wage labor. Skilled workers from abroad are also in demand, mainly in the high-technology sector, and controversy is raging over how many should be issued so-called H-1B visas and admitted on a temporary basis. Current laws permit up to 115,000 H-1B workers, which employers say is not enough. [5]

Those who favor expanding the H-1B program argue that it is needed to offset the drastic labor shortage facing high-tech companies. They see the importation of highly educated and skilled workers from overseas as an unfortunate but necessary step in their efforts to stay competitive in a fast-changing and cutthroat industry. "Our colleges and universities are gearing up to turn out more people qualified to do this kind of work, and so we don't see [H-1B visas] as a long-term solution," says Harris Miller, president of the Information Technology Association of America (ITAA). "But right now, we simply don't have enough people to fill all of the jobs available."

Norman Matloff, a professor of computer science at the University of

California at Davis, challenges that claim. "There are plenty of people right here for these jobs," he says, contending that high-tech firms would rather import well-educated workers from overseas at lower salaries than go to the trouble of recruiting and training Americans.

As the United States enters a new millennium, here are some of the questions being asked in the debate over how many newcomers the United States should admit:

Crackdown Increased Arrests Along Border

The flow of undocumented immigrants across the 2,000-mile U.S.-Mexico border has persisted despite Operation Gatekeeper, a renewed Border Patrol enforcement effort that began in 1994. Apprehensions increased at traditional entry points, such as San Diego and El Paso. But officials say the crackdown has pushed more people to sneak across the border in remote areas.

Apprehensions of Undocumented Immigrants

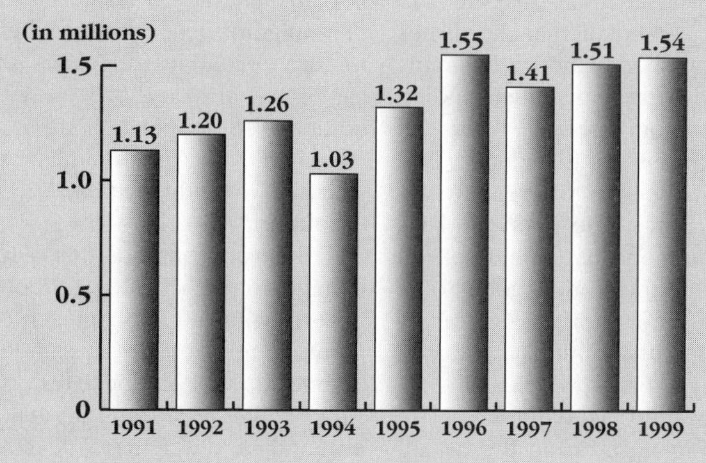

Source: U.S. Immigration and Naturalization Service

Does the United States admit too many immigrants?

During the 1990s, the United States took in nearly 10 million foreigners, almost double the number that came during the 1980s and more than in any previous decade. [6]

For many Americans the large number of newcomers and the prospect of millions more is disquieting. "We've already got gridlock from sea to shining sea," says FAIR's Stein. "So, of course, people are asking themselves how many new people does this country really need?"

But for the Cato Institute's Moore, the surge in immigration has largely been a blessing, one he hopes will continue. "Over the last 20 years, we've let in more than 15 million people, and it's been a stunning success story," he says.

In fact, Moore and other immigration proponents credit immigrants with playing a key role in the American economy's stellar performance in the past decade. "If we want to keep this phenomenal economic growth rate up," the de Tocqueville Institution's Lance says, "then we'd better keep letting in immigrants because they are helping this economy."

Immigrants aid the economy, Lance and other experts say, because they tend, almost by definition, to be highly motivated and hard working. "This is a self-selected group of people," Moore says, "because the very act of leaving your home country and taking a risk to come here means that you're probably ambitious and likely to succeed."

Indeed, proponents say, studies show that immigrants start more small businesses than the native population. And while many are modest "mom and pop" operations, others are at the leading edge of the new economy. For instance, one out of every four new businesses in Silicon Valley is founded by an entrepreneur of Indian or Chinese origin. [7]

In addition, immigration proponents argue, immigrants are stoking the economic flames by taking hard-to-fill jobs. "Immigrants offer us a ready supply of hard-working people to fill niches in the labor market in vital ways, be it picking crops or making our food, driving taxis, caring for our children or building our buildings," Moore says.

La Raza's Muñoz agrees, adding: "I don't think people realize how many important jobs are done by immigrants and what would happen if they all went away."

What would happen, Muñoz, Moore and others contend, is that many industries, especially in the growing service sector, would grind to a halt as the people who washed the dishes or cleaned the offices disappeared. "So many important parts of the economy have become very dependent on immigrants," Moore says.

But Stein says there is a downside to importing workers who are mainly poorly educated with few or no skills. "All we're doing is importing a huge pool of cheap labor, which helps employers but keeps wages low for Americans," he says

The great need, Stein notes, is for people with a lot of education and skills. "Our future lies in improving productivity by providing our own people with training and education, not importing low-wage labor," he says.

Moreover, says the Center for Immigration Studies' Krikorian, immigrants are not irreplaceable in certain segments of the economy. "Anyone who imagines that the fruit won't get picked or that the dishes won't get washed without immigrants has a fundamental misunderstanding of market economics," he says. "All of this service work gets done in the parts of the country where there are few immigrants," he says, "and it's done by Americans. The question isn't whether the work is going to be done, but who's going to do it?"

Krikorian and others say that instead of importing workers to fill vacancies, the United States should be focusing on training the unemployed here. "If we lost immigration as a source of workers, employers would seek to increase the labor pool by increasing wages," he says. "They would also look to communities with higher unemployment rates — more marginal elements of the population — like those on public assistance, ex-convicts or the handicapped."

But opposition to immigration extends beyond its economic impact. Many argue that the nation's population is already too high and that admitting close to a million people annually is going to cause intolerable crowding in some areas. Indeed, the Census Bureau predicts the nation's population will rise from the current level of 270 million to more than 400 million by 2050.

"More than 70 percent of this growth is going to come from immigration," says Tom McKenna, president of Population-Environment Balance, a grass-roots organization that advocates population stabilization to protect the environment. "Think about how crowded our cities are now, and then think about what it will be like with twice the number of people."

Immigration opponents also claim that the nation needs to reduce current immigration levels to allow the nation to absorb the tens of millions of newcomers who are already here. In particular, they say, a steady stream of immigrants will overwhelm efforts to turn recent arrivals into Americans. "When you have these high numbers of people coming in year after year, you can't assimilate them so easily," says the *National Review*'s O'Sullivan.

O'Sullivan contends that a lull in immigration would allow schools and governing institutions to teach immigrants English and give them an appreciation for American history and values. "We are a transnational society, and in order to work together effectively we must maximize our common cultural sympathies," he says. "If every ethnic group retains its own cultural sympathies, it will be hard for us to work together as one people."

But immigration supporters say that concerns about assimilation are as old as the Republic and just as overblown now as they were in the 18th century. "People who come here want to be American," Lance says. "Very few would run the gauntlet to get here unless they wanted to become part of this country."

Lance and others point out that — just as with previous groups — today's immigrants are quickly integrating into American society and losing their ties to their country of origin. "Look at the Hispanic kids who grow up here," she says. "They don't speak Spanish or don't speak it well. They're American now." [8]

In addition, proponents doubt that continued immigration is going to turn the United States into an overcrowded country like China or India. "The numbers [McKenna] uses assume that the birth rate among immigrants will stay constant for succeeding generations," Muñoz says, noting that recent arrivals have more children than native-born Americans. "But data show that the children of immigrants have far fewer children than their parents."

Should the Immigration and Naturalization Service crack down on employers who knowingly hire illegal immigrants?

Not long ago, the INS conducted a series of raids against undocumented aliens working in the onion fields of Vidalia, Ga. Within days of the action, five members of the state's congressional delegation — including both U.S. senators — had fired off a letter to Attorney General Janet Reno complaining that the agency she supervises had shown a "lack of regard for the farmers." [9] The letter had the desired effect. The INS stopped arresting undocumented pickers, and the onion crop made it to market.

Similarly, in other parts of the country complaints from local and national politicians have prompted the INS to back off. "This is very ironic," Krikorian says. "Congress passed [the Immigration Reform and Control Act of 1986] making it illegal to employ illegal aliens and then basically told the INS not to enforce it."

The law, which made it a crime to knowingly employ undocumented workers, imposed fines on employers caught using illegal aliens and even authorized jail time for repeat offenders. [10]

But the employment-related provisions of the 1986 act have not worked. According to the INS, there are 5 million illegal aliens in the United States, an estimate that many immigration experts believe to be low. In addition, at least 300,000 are believed to enter the country each year. Many industries in the United States rely heavily upon undocumented workers, from the meatpacking plants of the Midwest to the restaurants and garment factories of New York City. "It's very clear to me that we're not sufficiently enforcing the law at all," says Rep. Lamar Smith, R-Texas, chairman of the House Judiciary Subcommittee on Immigration.

In some places, the local economy is largely supported by the labor of illegal aliens. Thomas Fischer, who until recently headed the INS in Georgia and three other Southeastern states, estimates that one out of every three businesses in Atlanta employs undocumented workers. "I'm talking about everything from your *Fortune* 500 companies down to your mom-and-pop businesses," he says.

For supporters of tough controls on illegal immigration, the presence of so many undocumented workers in so many industries represents a major failure in immigration policy. "The INS is making no effort whatsoever to fight the ever-increasing presence of illegal immigrants in this country," says Peter Brimelow, author of *Alien Nation*, a best-selling 1995 book that argues for stricter controls on immigration. According to Brimelow, a senior editor at *Forbes* and *National Review*, the INS' abrogation of duty has led to "the development of a huge illegal economy that is growing."

The solution, Brimelow and others say, is stricter enforcement of the sanctions already on the books. "They're absolutely necessary, because without them many employers feel free to hire illegal immigrants," Krikorian says.

Giving employers a green light to bring in undocumented workers has a snowball effect that leads to even more illegal immigration, Krikorian claims. "As long as people in other countries know that they can get jobs easily here, regardless of their status, they will keep coming," he argues. "Once they get in, there is little to fear since employment laws are basically ignored."

Moreover, Stein says, "Once someone hires illegal aliens they have a competitive advantage because their labor costs have dropped." That forces competitors to follow suit, leading to an even greater demand for illegal immigrants and fewer jobs for citizens or legal residents. "It's a vicious cycle."

But opponents of employer sanctions argue that they are not being enforced for a good reason: They don't work. "When they've tried to enforce employer sanctions in one area or another, they haven't reduced illegal immigration," says Frank Sharry, executive director of the National Immigration Forum, a think tank that favors increased immigration.

Sharry argues that sanctions only drive immigrants further into the underground economy. "The only thing employer sanctions do is push illegal immigrants from decent employers into the hands of unscrupulous employers," he says. "They push them down into the shadier parts of the economy, but not out of it."

Opponents of sanctions also argue that sanctions are unfair to employers, many of whom don't know they've hired illegal aliens. "Many illegal immigrants are hired unwittingly, because they forged the right documents," says Lance of the de Tocqueville Institution. "Only a minority of employers knowingly hire illegal immigrants, so imposing sanctions would get many of them in trouble for a good-faith mistake."

Cato's Moore agrees, adding: "Businesses should not be responsible for being immigration policemen." Such a system "would lead to great discrimination against foreigners — regardless of their status — because businesses would automatically wonder whether a foreign worker was illegal and worth the risk of hiring."

Moore and Muñoz are among those who say that illegal immigration should be controlled at the border, not at the office or factory. "We need to put more people and resources at the border," Muñoz says. "It can work if we put our minds to it."

But supporters of sanctions say that relying on the Border Patrol to stem the flow of illegal immigration is close to meaningless without "internal enforcement" since, by its own

AP Photo/Robert Lahser

A billboard near Gastonia, N.C., reflects fears that America is taking in too many newcomers. Nearly 10 million were admitted in the 1990s, the highest level in history.

Most Recent Immigrants Come From Latin America, Asia

More legal immigrants came from Mexico in 1998 than any other country, in part because U.S. immigration law grants preference to relatives of recent immigrants, a policy known as "family reunification." Although no individual African countries made the Top 15 list, the United States admitted more than 40,000 Africans in 1998.

The Top 15 Countries of Origin for U.S. Immigrants, 1998

Rank	Country	Number Entering United States Legally
1.	Mexico	131,575
2.	China	36,884
3.	India	36,482
4.	Philippines	34,466
5.	Former Soviet Union	30,163
6.	Dominican Republic	20,387
7.	Vietnam	17,649
8.	Cuba	17,375
9.	Jamaica	15,146
10.	El Salvador	14,590
11.	South Korea	14,268
12.	Haiti	13,449
13.	Pakistan	13,094
14.	Colombia	11,836
15.	Canada	10,190

Source: U.S. Immigration and Naturalization Service

estimate, the patrol only catches one in three people trying to cross into the United States. (*See sidebar, p. 162.*)

Moreover, 40 percent of all illegal immigrants initially enter the United States legally, but stay longer than the time allowed on their visa. "There's no way to stop visa overstays because they came in a perfectly legal manner," Krikorian says.

Should the number of H-1B visas be increased?

Michael Worry has a problem. The CEO of Nuvation Labs, a 30-person Silicon Valley software-engineering firm, said he is constantly grappling with a shortage of employees. "We've had positions go unfilled for months at a time," he said. [11]

So Worry has done what many others in similar positions have done — hired workers from abroad, many admitted only on a temporary basis. In fact, one-third of his workers are temporary foreign employees.

For years, Worry and others in the information-technology industry have complained of an almost crippling shortage of skilled workers. "The number of jobs in our industry has grown so fast that our colleges and universities just can't keep up with demand," says ITAA's Miller. "We have no choice but to look abroad."

Miller says there is already a huge gap between the number of jobs and qualified workers in the information-technology industry. Industry estimates of the shortage run as high as 800,000. [12] In addition, according to a recent Cato report, the demand for skilled high-tech jobs is expected to grow 150,000 per year over the next five years. [13]

Like many high-tech companies, Nuvation tries to bring in qualified workers from abroad using H-1B visas, which require applicants to have a bachelor's degree and allow a stay of up to six years.

But firms that fill vacancies with H-1B visa holders complain that the program is much too limited to fill their needs. "The demand for high-tech workers is clearly outpacing the number of people that can currently be brought in" under the H-1B program, says Rep. Smith.

In the current fiscal year, which ends Sept. 30, the INS can issue up to 115,000 H-1B visas. But pro-business groups point out that demand is so great that the agency already has issued its quota for the year. Moreover, under existing law, the number of H-1B visas issued will drop to 107,500 next year and 65,000 the year after that.

High-tech companies and others have vigorously lobbied Congress to substantially increase the number of H-1B visas, and several bills are under consideration, including one sponsored by Smith that would lift the cap on H-1Bs for the next three years. The House Judiciary Committee approved that measure on May 18. Another measure sponsored by Sen. Spencer Abraham, R-Mich., that would increase the number of available visas to 195,000 for the next three years won the approval of the Senate Judiciary Committee on March 9.

Supporters of expanding the H-1B program are confident that an increase will become law this year, especially since the idea has the backing of the White House and numerous members of Congress from both parties. "The time is right for this, and I'm fairly optimistic that we'll be able to work something out," Miller says.

But opponents of an increase — including many labor unions and some Democrats in Congress — argue that they are unnecessary and harmful to American workers. They say that companies clamoring for more temporary foreign workers are not taking advantage of the domestic labor force.

"Just call any employer of programmers in any city — large or small — and they'll tell you that they reject the overwhelming majority of job applicants without even giving them an interview," the University of California's Matloff says. For instance, he says, Microsoft rejects all but 2 percent of the applicants for technology jobs. "Now, how can they do this when they claim they're so desperate for workers?" he asks.

The real reason employers want more H-1Bs is they don't want to find and train skilled U.S. workers, Matloff says, although there are many highly qualified Americans who only need to have their skills updated. "These companies don't want to take the time and spend the money it takes to hire and train domestic workers," he says. "I think many of them are afraid that they'll lose someone after they've trained them."

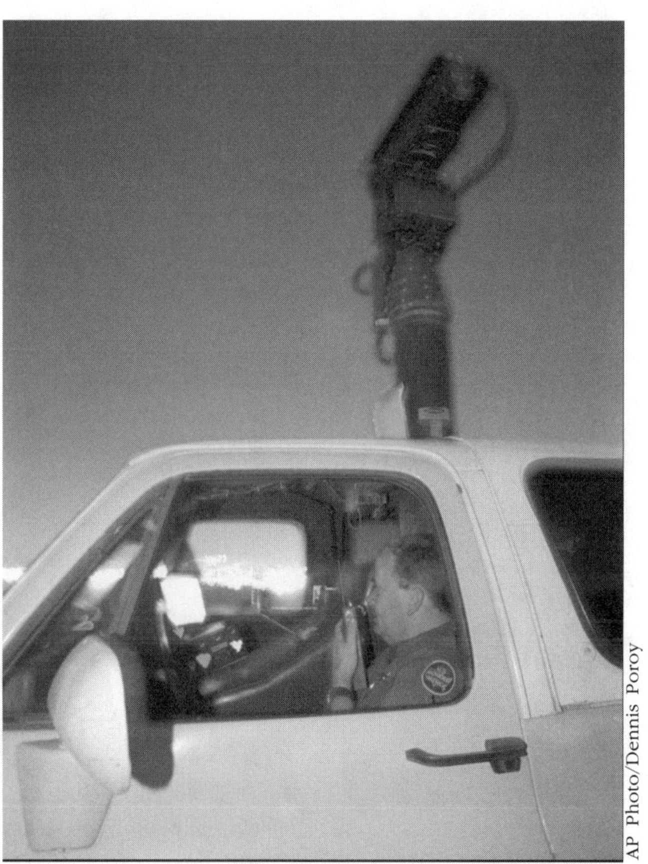

AP Photo/Dennis Poroy

A U.S. Border Patrol agent watches for illegal immigrants to cross the border from Mexico into the U.S. Arrests have risen since the 1994 launch of "Operation Gatekeeper," a renewed effort to crack down on illegal entries.

In addition, opponents say, temporary visas allow companies to keep industry wages low. "If there were a labor shortage in one industry or another, wages would naturally rise and workers would shift into this area," says David A. Smith, director of public policy at the AFL-CIO. "But H-1B visas distort the market by bringing in outside workers, and that holds down wages."

Matloff points out that 79 percent of H-1B visa holders make less than $50,000 per year. While such a pay level is above the national average, it is considered low for skilled high-technology workers. "This is the kind of industry where if you're any good, you make at least $100,000 a year," he says.

Finally, opponents argue, H-1B visas give employers too much leverage over these temporary workers, because many are desperate to get permanent work status and need the company's assistance to do so. According to the *National Review*'s O'Sullivan, "employers say that they will help them get a green card, but in the meantime, 'you belong to us.' " Since the process can take up to five years, O'Sullivan and others argue, an H-1B visa can often lead to a form of indentured servitude. "This whole aspect of the system is open to terrible abuse," he claims.

Instead of expanding the H-1B program, critics say business and the government should focus on training and hiring domestic workers for high-tech jobs. "H-1B visas prevent us from doing what we need to generate a long-term supply of skilled labor that we're eventually going to need in this industry," the AFL-CIO's Smith says.

But H-1B supporters counter that high-tech companies really are facing a skilled labor shortage. They note that the unemployment rate within the information-technology industry is generally much lower than the already low national rate of 4 percent. "Look, our colleges and universities simply can't keep up with demand," Miller says.

Moore agrees. "It's vital that we have access to these highly skilled workers in order to maintain our competitive edge," he says. "We're getting the cream of the crop from developing countries like India. It's sort of a form of reverse foreign aid, a gift from the rest of the world to the U.S."

In addition, supporters say, the information-technology industry is already doing much to train new and existing employees to keep up with industry changes. "We're already the leader in spending on worker training," Miller says. "We spend 60 percent more than the financial-services industry or more than $1,000 per year, per employee."

H-1B supporters also dispute the notion that they are trying to bring in temporary workers to permanently replace domestic talent in order to drive down wages. "The law requires that we pay these people the prevailing wage, so they are well compensated for what they do," Miller says. ■

BACKGROUND

The Latest Wave

The foundation of the current immigration system dates back to 1965, when Congress overhauled the rules governing who could and couldn't enter the United States. Since 1920, immigration quotas had largely favored Northern Europeans over people from other parts of the world. The quotas, coupled with the impact of the Great Depression and World War II, markedly reduced immigration into the country.

CQ Photo

CQ Photo

Vice President Al Gore, left, and Texas Gov. George W. Bush, candidates for this year's presidential election, both favor raising the number of skilled foreign workers admitted to the United States on H-1B visas.

From 1930 to 1950, fewer than 4 million newcomers arrived in the United States, less than half the number in the first decade of the 20th century. The heated debates that had accompanied the great waves of immigration in the late 19th and early 20 centuries faded, replaced by smaller questions, such as whether to allow refugees from Europe to emigrate after World War II. "Immigration didn't even really exist as a big issue until 1965, because we just weren't letting that many people in," author Brimelow says.

In 1965 the landscape changed. The quota system was replaced by one that gave preference to immigrants with close relatives already living in the United States and to those with special skills needed by American industry. The law, which took effect in 1968, set an overall annual cap of 290,000 immigrants — 170,000 from the Eastern Hemisphere and 120,000 from the Western Hemisphere.

The 1965 law dramatically changed the face of immigration. Until the late 1960s, most immigrants came from Europe. Thereafter, the majority of newcomers hailed from the developing world — nearly half from Latin America. Initially, the country took in many refugees escaping communist regimes in Cuba and Indochina. In the late 1970s and '80s, a large group of immigrants came from Central America, where a number of brutal wars were raging. [14] But the largest number of newcomers — fully 20 percent of all immigrants between 1968 and

Chronology

1920-1964 ***After decades during which tens of millions of people emigrated to the United States, a new, restrictive immigration policy substantially limits the number of newcomers who can settle in the country.***

1921
Congress passes The Quota Act, which establishes a new system of national-origin quotas favoring Northern Europeans over immigrants from Southern Europe and elsewhere.

1924
Congress passes the Johnson-Reed Act, which stiffens the national-origin quotas established three years earlier. The law also creates the U.S. Border Patrol to combat illegal immigration.

1930
The coming decade will see immigration drop to roughly 500,000, down substantially from the more than 8 million who emigrated to the United States during the first decade of the 20th century.

1942
Workers from Mexico and other nations are admitted to work temporarily in the United States, mainly in California's agricultural industry, under an initiative later called the Bracero program.

1952
The McCarran-Walter Act retains the national-origins quota system.

1954
The U.S. government institutes "Operation Wetback" to stem the increase in illegal immigration. The program is successful.

1964
The Bracero program ends.

1965-1980 ***The civil rights movement prompts Congress to end racially restrictive immigration quotas. The new law leads to a large influx of immigrants from Latin America and Asia.***

1965
Congress passes the Immigration and Nationality Act Amendments, which remove racial quotas and substantially increases the number of immigrants allowed entry into the United States each year.

1968
Immigrants from the Western Hemisphere, previously admitted freely into the United States, are subjected to quotas, largely in response to a surge in illegal immigration after the 1964 expiration of the Bracero program.

1980
The annual number of legal immigrants entering the country surpasses a half-million.

1981-2000s ***An increase in legal and illegal immigration prompts Congress to change the system.***

1986
The Immigration Reform and Control Act makes many illegal aliens eligible for permanent residence and establishes sanctions against employers who hire illegal workers.

1990
Congress passes the Immigration Act, which raises the immigration ceiling to 700,000 a year and grants preferences to relatives of U.S. residents or citizens and to aliens with high-demand work skills.

1992
Patrick J. Buchanan makes curtailing legal and illegal immigration one of the cornerstones of his bid for the Republican presidential nomination.

1993
Some 880,000 legal immigrants arrive in the United States.

1994
Californians pass Proposition 187, which denies social services to illegal aliens. The initiative is later struck down in the courts.

1996
Congress passes the Illegal Immigration and Immigrant Responsibility Act, which toughens border enforcement and streamlines deportation procedures.

1998
Immigrant voters, particularly Latinos, prove crucial in a host of congressional and gubernatorial elections.

2000
GOP presidential candidate George W. Bush proposes splitting the Immigration and Naturalization Service into two separate agencies — one to guard the border and the other to process legal immigrants.

America's Changing Demographics

Fifty years ago, the population of the United States was 89 percent white and 10 percent black. Latinos, Asians and other minority groups constituted a mere sliver of the demographic pie. Thanks to immigration, everything has changed.

Today, more than one-quarter of Americans are not white — more than double the percentage in 1950. Hispanics now account for 12 percent of the population and are about surpass African-Americans as the nation's largest minority. Asians, though only making up 4 percent of the U.S. population, are the nation's fastest-growing minority group.

Fifty years from now, America will look even more different. According to the U.S. Census Bureau, slightly more than half of the anticipated 400 million residents will be white. Fully one-fourth of the nation will be of Latin American descent. And there will be almost as many Asians as there are African-Americans.

Some immigration experts warn, however, that census projections can be misleading. "There are a lot of assumptions built into the data that may not be correct," says Jeff Passel, a demographer for the Urban Institute, a social policy think tank in Washington, D.C. "It's really impossible to know these numbers."

The numbers can get tricky because, for instance, no one knows how many new immigrants will enter the United States in the future. In addition, it's difficult to predict what the birth rates will be among various immigrant groups.

More important, Passel says, the Census Bureau's projections assume that today's racial categories will remain the same. "One hundred years ago," he says, "Americans didn't think of Italians, Jews and other immigrants from Southern and Eastern Europe as white. Now, obviously they do." Future racial categories may be much broader, incorporating Hispanics and Asians into the same racial group, for instance. "In 50 years people may not make distinctions between, say, Hispanics and whites, just like they don't between Italians and whites today," Passel says.

The blurring of racial distinctions may be nudged along by high rates of intermarriage between new immigrant groups and other Americans. Third-generation Asian-Americans marry outside their race more than 40 percent of the time, according to the National Immigration Forum. Similarly, third-generation Latinos marry non-Hispanics about one-third of the time.

"All of this mixing across racial lines is going to make these categories very fuzzy," Passel says, adding that fuzziness will allow these new groups to more easily integrate into American society, just as newcomers a century ago have done today.

But other experts are much more concerned about coming demographic changes. "Our ethnic component is part of what makes the United States what it is, and that's going to be radically altered," says Peter Brimelow, a *Forbes* magazine editor and author of *Alien Nation*, a 1995 book that makes a case against allowing high levels of immigration.

It's foolish, Brimelow contends, to assume that a society that is no longer dominated by one racial group — whites, in the case of the United States — will be able to avoid tremendous tensions. "I don't think multiracial societies work — period," he says. "Our differences are irrepressible."

He fears that a United States with large racial blocks could undergo the same ethnic tensions that have troubled countries like the former Yugoslavia. Some pockets of the country, he says, could diverge so greatly that they will become de facto independent states. "I think parts of the country are going to be as different as different parts of the world are today," Brimelow says.

But many immigration experts say such concerns are unfounded. They believe that new immigrants will do much as their predecessors did — work very hard to become part of American society while retaining pride in their heritage.

"People think that cities like [Los Angeles] are going to be so Mexican that they'll secede from the union," says Frank Sharry, executive director of the National Immigration Forum. "But L.A. is going to be Mexican in the same way that Boston is Irish or Milwaukee is German."

1993 — came from impoverished Mexico.[15]

In the wake of the 1965 law, the United States also began grappling with illegal immigrants, also mainly from Mexico. The number of undocumented aliens entering the United States increased dramatically from the mid-1960s to the mid-'80s, in spite of beefed-up Border Patrol efforts. The number of illegal aliens apprehended at the border reflects the increase. In 1965 fewer than 100,000 undocumented aliens were stopped, but by 1985 the number had exceeded 1.2 million.[16]

Many of the illegal aliens had for decades been accustomed to crossing the southern border for agricultural work and then returning to Mexico at the end of the picking season. In fact, for more than two decades the United States had allowed migrant pickers into the country legally. But the so-called Bracero program was discontinued in 1964, prompting many to begin crossing the border illegally.

In 1986, Congress moved to stem illegal immigration by passing the

Immigration Control and Reform Act. IRCA attacked the problem by using a carrot-and-stick approach. On one hand, the act granted a general amnesty to all undocumented aliens who could prove that they had been in the United States before 1982. But it also imposed monetary sanctions against employers who knowingly hired undocumented workers. Repeat offenders risked prison.

Four years later Congress moved to overhaul the system governing legal immigration, passing the Immigration Act of 1990. The new law increased the number of aliens allowed to enter from roughly 500,000 each year to 700,000. It also set new country-based quotas in an effort to alter the impact of the 1965 law, which had heavily favored immigrants from Latin America and Asia. Newcomers from other countries, especially from Europe, received a greater share of the entry visas. In addition, more visas were set aside for workers with special skills.[17]

The decade that followed the 1990 act saw the largest influx of immigrants in U.S. history, with nearly 10 million newcomers arriving on America's shores. Most still came from Latin America (particularly Mexico) and Asia. But a substantial number came from Eastern Europe in the wake of the Soviet Union's collapse and the breakup of Yugoslavia.

Congress took one more stab at reforming the rules governing legal and illegal immigration in 1996. But efforts to lower levels of legal immigration stalled after running into tough opposition from business groups and others. Instead, the new law focused on curbing illegal entry into the United States by beefing up the Border Patrol and streamlining deportation procedures.[18]

Family Reunification

The rules governing legal immigration are often criticized for being everything from misguided to contradictory. "It's actually worse than the tax code because there's absolutely no real rationale behind it," Brimelow says. "It's just a collection of accidents."

But others say the current system actually works quite well, especially given the number of people who emigrate to the United States each year. "We have a very well-regulated immigration system," La Raza's Muñoz says. "It actually does work."

The cornerstone of the current system revolves around family reunification. Roughly two-thirds of all immigrants who enter the United States legally each year are sponsored by a close relative. Of these, around 75 percent are either the sponsor's spouse or child.

The idea behind family reunification is that people already living in the United States should be able to live with their close relatives, even if they are not legal residents. "Doesn't your neighbor José have the right to live with his wife Maria?" Muñoz asks. "That's the question people need to ask when they think about family reunification."

Few people would answer "no" to Muñoz's question. But many immigration experts say that while family reunification is important, it is given too much weight in the current system. For his part, Brimelow says family reunification takes legal immigration "out of the realm of public policy and turns it into a civil rights issue, giving certain people a right to immigrate."

Brimelow and others would like to see a much greater share of visas issued to necessary and skilled workers. "An employment-based system would benefit this country much more than one that stresses family ties," he says.

Even the National Immigration Forum's Sharry, who favors the current high levels of family-based immigration, supports an increase in employment-related visas. "Employers need to be able to sponsor a greater number of people each year," he says. "The existing numbers are much too low."

AP Photo/Kathy Willens

A state labor investigator interviews a 15-year-old Chinese immigrant, at left, working in a New York City garment factory. Many recent immigrants take low-wage jobs, which critics contend can lower the wage scale for other Americans.

Armed Ranchers Aid Agents . . .

Every day, thousands of Mexicans, Central Americans and others illegally cross into the United States along its southern border. The U.S. Border Patrol last year apprehended more than 1.5 million undocumented immigrants. It expects to catch even more this year.

Still, for each one caught entering illegally, at least two others sneak through. "It's clear that we're not doing nearly enough to secure our borders," says Gregory Rodriguez, a fellow at the New America Foundation, a think tank in Washington, D.C.

Reuters Photo/Daniel Aguilar

U.S. Border Patrol agents search undocumented Mexican migrants in California's Calexico Desert.

A major reason the border is so porous, Rodriguez and others contend, is that the Border Patrol is woefully understaffed. More than 9,000 agents guard the country's northern and southern borders. That's roughly double the number of personnel as in 1993. Still, says Mark Krikorian, executive director of the Center for Immigration Studies, the Border Patrol could easily use another 10,000 people in the field.

A recent University of Texas at Austin study estimates that the Immigration and Naturalization Service's enforcement arm needs 16,000 agents to effectively guard the 2,000-mile border with Mexico. [1] Agency officials have tried to add 1,000 personnel per year, as mandated by Congress in a 1996 law. *(See "Background," p. 158.)*

But the Border Patrol's efforts to boost its size have been slowed by the lure of other opportunities. "They've been training a lot of people, but there's been a lot of turnover as well," Krikorian says. "They've lost a lot of people to organizations like the Houston Police Department because Border Patrol agents are a good catch since they have the most rigorous training of anyone in the federal government."

Indeed, as of last year, 40 percent of all Border Patrol agents had been on the job two years or less. [2] "A lot of the people on the border right now are young and inexperienced," says Tamar Adler, a policy analyst at the American Friends Service Committee.

Soldiers and Ranchers

For many who live along the southern border, the Border Patrol's current force is simply not enough. For example, in a recent poll, 89 percent of Arizona residents indicated that they favor using the military to help patrol

Currently, the INS can issue up to 140,000 employment-related visas — known as green cards — per year. Unlike H-1B and other temporary work visas, a green card gives an immigrant permanent status. The rules allow no more than 9,800 work visas to be given to people from any one country, to ensure a certain amount of ethnic diversity. The INS also issues an additional 50,000 green cards each year by lottery, attracting 7 million applicants. [19]

The low number of permanent work visas makes it difficult for employers to sponsor workers from abroad. According to Sharry and others, this leads many businesses to turn to illegal immigration. "If you're a restaurant owner and you need people and can't sponsor someone, of course you're going to turn to undocumented workers," he says.

There are other ways for immigrants to enter the United States. For instance, the country can take in tens of thousands of refugees per year. The number, 78,000 in FY 2000, is determined each year by the president and Congress. [20]

And, of course, many foreigners enter or remain in the country illegally. The INS estimates that around 300,000 people per year move to the United States without proper documentation. Few are ever detected and fewer still deported.

"The dirty little secret of our system in this country is that once you get here you can stay if you want to," Moore says. "It's like lawyers say: Possession is nine-tenths of the law." ■

CURRENT SITUATION

Election Issue?

Like many issues, immigration comes and goes from the political agenda. In 1996, for instance, GOP presiden-

. . . In Patrolling Porous U.S. Border

the border.[3]

Some border residents have even taken matters into their own hands, policing their property and arresting undocumented immigrants caught trespassing. Over the last two years, Arizona ranchers Roger and Donald Barnett have captured about 3,000 illegal aliens and turned them over to the Border Patrol.

Some have accused the Barnetts, who use rifles and dogs for their searches, and other ranchers of "hunting" human beings. "It's illegal for citizens to detain other people — regardless of their status — unless they are breaching the peace," Adler says. "This is vigilante activity, plain and simple."

But the Barnett brothers defend their actions. "They're on my land, they're trespassing and I have a right to protect my property," said 57-year-old Roger Barnett, who owns a 22,000-acre ranch along the Mexican border near Douglas, Ariz.[4]

Others say neither military nor civilian action is the solution. Krikorian and others advocate giving the Border Patrol more of the tools it needs to adequately do the job. In addition to more agents, Krikorian favors erecting more physical barriers in areas where the flow of illegal aliens is heavy.

He also believes that those apprehended repeatedly should be imprisoned as a deterrent for them and those who would follow in their footsteps. "Right now, you have to be caught 10 or 15 times before you face prosecution," Krikorian says. "As things stand, everyone just gets an air-conditioned ride back to Mexico and a chance to try again."

And try again, they do. Many undocumented immigrants are willing to cross long stretches of desert and other rough terrain in order to enter the United States. Such determination has put some aliens at terrible risk. Since October, the Border Patrol has found 217 undocumented aliens dead near the border. Most had either drowned or died of thirst in the desert. Agents rescued more than 1,000 others in imminent danger during the same period.

To reduce the number of deaths, the Border Patrol has stepped up its efforts to train agents in lifesaving techniques. The agency also is putting up warning signs along those parts of the border considered the most dangerous to cross — either because of long stretches of desert or dangerous waterways.

The high number of deaths along the border is "unacceptable," said Doris Meissner, commissioner of the Immigration and Naturalization Service, which oversees the Border Patrol. "We want to reduce the number of deaths and increase safety on both sides of the border," she said at a June 26 press conference.[5]

---

[1] William Branigin, "Border Patrol Being Pushed to Continue Fast Growth," *The Washington Post*, May 13, 1999.

[2] *Ibid.*

[3] Tim McGirk, "Border Clash," *Time*, June 6, 2000.

[4] Quoted in William Booth, "Emotions on the Edge," *The Washington Post*, June 21, 2000.

[5] Quoted in Michael A. Fletcher, "Lifesaving on the Border," *The Washington Post*, June 27, 2000.

tial candidate Bob Dole ran advertisements in California blaming the state's many illegal immigrants for high crime, poor schools and other social ills. Dole's ads came on the heels of congressional passage of a number of immigration-related measures, including a stricter deportation law and a welfare-reform bill that denied benefits to legal immigrants.

Four years later, the terrain is much different. Congress is no longer trying to get tough with immigrants and instead is working on legislation to increase the number of visas for high-skilled foreign workers. Meanwhile, a coalition of Republican and Democratic policy-makers, including Jack Kemp and former HUD Secretary Henry G. Cisneros, has formed to push for a relaxation of immigration laws.[21]

Most analysts say the changing political winds are largely due to the economy. The United States is in the middle of the longest economic expansion in its history — with high rates of growth, very low unemployment and (until recently) a booming stock market. In a period when many Americans feel more financially secure than ever before, traditional fear that immigrants will threaten jobs or cause societal upheaval is fading.

Not surprisingly, polls show a growing acceptance of immigrants by the public. According to a Gallup Poll taken last year, 44 percent of Americans favor restricting immigration, down from 65 percent in 1995.[22]

The change in attitude has not been lost on the political establishment. Both presumptive nominees in this year's race for the presidency seem to support the status quo, speaking in positive terms about recent immigrants and their contributions to America's economy and society. Vice President Al Gore has said that immigration has made the country "not only culturally richer, but also spiritually stronger."[23]

Gov. George W. Bush, R-Texas, has expressed similar sentiments. He even stated that he might have entered the country illegally himself in search of

Foreign-Born Americans on the Rise

The percentage of the U.S. population comprised of foreign-born adults and their children is expected to surpass 25 percent by the middle of the century. That nearly equals the level attained during the late 1800s following a massive influx of Germans and Irish.

Immigrants and Their Children in the U.S.

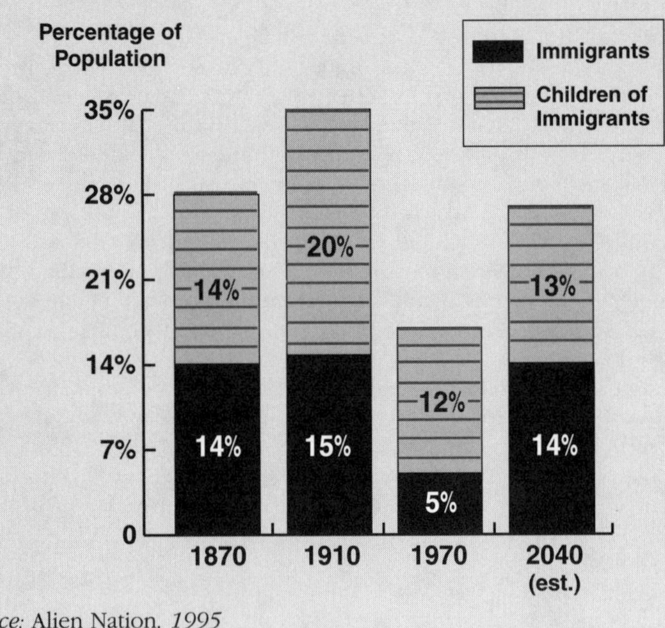

Source: Alien Nation, *1995*

work had he been born poor in Mexico. Bush has also proposed breaking the INS into two separate agencies with an eye toward improving services to legal immigrants.

Neither candidate has called for any major initiatives aimed at increasing or decreasing immigration levels, although both support expanding the H-1B visa program to allow in more skilled workers. In addition, Gore said he supports restoring benefits to legal immigrants that were taken away by Congress as part of the 1996 Illegal Immigration and Immigrant Responsibility Act. Bush has yet to state his position on the issue.

But, aside from these relatively narrow proposals, immigration is unlikely to emerge as a big issue in this year's presidential race, many experts say. "This is not national issue like education or health care, and I don't see that changing in the coming months," says James Thurber, a professor of political science at American University.

Thurber and other experts say most Americans really don't care very much about immigration right now. "Look," Krikorian says, "the bottom line is that the economy is too good and unemployment too low for many people outside the Beltway to be thinking about this very much."

The National Immigration Forum's Sharry, however, thinks that immigration might be "the sleeper issue" of the year. "The fastest-growing group of new voters is immigrants and so, of course, Bush and Gore are going to try to address issues important to these voters, including immigration," he predicts.

Sharry believes that each candidate will try to use immigration as a way of attracting Latino and other minority voters in states that are thought to be strongholds for their opponents. "I think Bush will try to pin Gore down in California by appealing to Latinos, and Gore will do the same in Florida, which is likely to go to Bush."

For example, Sharry says, "I could see Bush trying to address illegal immigration by saying that he would sit down with the president of Mexico and work out a solution." Sharry also believes that Bush might stress his pro-immigrant stance as a way of appealing to moderate white voters who might still be scared that he is too conservative. "He could propose a bunch of pro-immigrant initiatives to show that he's not a mean Republican," Sharry says.

The issue might also rise if Patrick Buchanan receives the Reform Party's nomination and becomes a serious candidate, in the same way the party's founder, H. Ross Perot, did in 1992. Buchanan has long opposed most legal immigration and has vowed to put the military on the U.S.-Mexico border to stop illegal immigration.

"Buchanan could really force this if he works it right," Brimelow says. "If he sold this as a jobs issue, it might fly." ■

OUTLOOK

Focus on the Economy

There is a commonly held belief among immigration opponents and boosters alike that when the eco-

At Issue:

Should illegal immigrants be permitted to remain in the United States if they have been here for several years?

FRANK SHARRY
Executive director, National Immigration Forum

WRITTEN FOR *THE CQ RESEARCHER*, JULY 2000

"Vicente" and his wife are from Latin America and graduated from U.S. colleges in the early 1980s. They stayed on and led exemplary lives. He works in customer service for a technology company; she does marketing for a direct-mail firm. Their three U.S.-born children are all-star Little League players.

There's only one hitch: Mom and Dad are in the United States illegally. They missed the 1982 cutoff for the previous legalization program.

Then there is "Blanca." She graduated from high school with top honors but found her hopes of attending college dashed because she does not have proper immigration papers. Her family fled persecution and civil war in El Salvador, but inequitable treatment under successive administrations has kept her parents in legal limbo.

Three legalization measures pending before Congress would enable some 750,000 people in situations like these to live and work in the United States legally. The proposed bills, all of which enjoy bipartisan support, would:

• Update an immigration law provision that allows undocumented immigrants of good moral character who have resided and worked in America since before 1986 to remain permanently;

• Correct for past unequal treatment among groups of similarly situated Central American and Haitian refugees; and

• Restore Section 245(i) of the immigration code to allow those on the verge of gaining permanent status to remain in the United States to complete the paperwork process.

Enactment of the three measures is both the right thing and the smart thing to do. It will correct past mistakes that have unfairly kept immigrant families in bureaucratic limbo, stabilize our work force at a time of growing labor shortages and keep families together.

As President Ronald Reagan said when he signed the legalization provisions of the 1986 Immigration Reform and Control Act, offering permanent legal status to those already rooted in our communities "will go far to improve the lives of a class of individuals who now must hide in the shadows, without many of the benefits of a free and open society. Very soon many of these men and women will be able to step into the sunlight and, ultimately, if they choose, become Americans."

It's time to revive our great heritage as a nation of immigrants and reward those who have already proven to be valued and positive members of our country by enacting these targeted measures this year.

yes

DAN STEIN
Executive director, Federation for American Immigration Reform

WRITTEN FOR *THE CQ RESEARCHER*, JULY 2000

Politicians perpetually talk about the need to control illegal immigration. But because the talk is rarely backed with action, about 6 million illegal aliens now reside in the United States. Now, some in Congress are suggesting illegal immigration once again be rewarded by granting amnesty to millions of brazen law violators.

What sort of signal does this send? It tells people we will do little to stop them and even less to deport them if they decide to bypass the legal immigration process. It tells them we will grant them legal status if they have the fortitude to stick it out for a few years. Is it any wonder the illegal immigrant population equals the population of Massachusetts?

The last amnesty in 1986 — which Congress pledged would never be repeated — legalized some 3 million people and cost taxpayers an estimated $78 billion.

Today, immigration enforcement has virtually collapsed. And despite the fact that financial institutions manage to run millions of electronic verifications every day, the government has yet to develop a system that can even authenticate a job applicant's right to work and live in the United States. Consequently, the availability of jobs and generous social services continues to attract illegal immigrants.

Another amnesty would tell the world that the United States literally is unable to control its borders. Such an admission inevitably would force a reappraisal of the validity and purposes of the meaningless immigration quotas now on the books.

Illegal immigration also inflicts economic injury on Americans in the lower half of the wage structure. Numerous studies show that immigration, especially illegal immigration, results in wage loss for Americans who must compete against illegal immigrants.

While amnesty proponents argue that legalization will give illegal aliens more bargaining leverage, even this questionable merit is likely to be short-lived. Another amnesty is guaranteed to set off an even greater influx of illegal immigration as people perceive this to be our way to deal with the problem periodically.

Amnesty is not the answer. The only way to stop illegal immigration is to link aliens' ability to immigrate with their willingness to play by our rules. Encourage those here illegally to return to their home countries through incentives and get control of our borders — only then would any discussion of an amnesty and reward program be responsible.

no

nomic growth slows or stops, so will support for letting immigrants into the United States. "Immigration is always driven by the economy — is always a big issue when the economy is poor and a non-issue when it's doing well," says Cato's Moore, who favors continued high levels of immigration.

"Only when this economy goes south and your job is threatened will an atmosphere of fear and insecurity take over," he says. "When it's José who is competing with you, most people will say, 'Things would be fine if only we could keep José and his kind out of the country.' "

Immigration opponent Stein of the Federation for American Immigration Reform agrees that the last decade of high economic growth has left the immigration debate withering on the vine. But unlike Moore, Stein approaches the prospect of an economic downturn with anticipation, not worry.

"In the current heady, narcotic trance this country's in, there's a detachment from reality about immigration," he says. "But when the economy comes down to Earth, this issue will come to the fore, and there will be a backlash."

Stein believes that when the American people actually turn their attention to immigration, they will demand substantial reductions in the number of people allowed entry each year. "I think the public really wants a breather for at least 20 if not 30 or 40 years," he says.

The *National Review*'s O'Sullivan concurs, arguing that Americans "will come to see that we need to reduce it at least for a while, so that we can absorb the people we already have." O'Sullivan doesn't "see us closing the doors, but bringing it down to the level it was in 1950s, when we let a quarter of a million people in each year."

Others also predict a backlash when the economy slows, but not against continued high levels of immigration. "Instead of doing something about immigration, we'll stick it to the immigrants themselves when things slow down," Krikorian says. "That's what we've done in the past."

Krikorian sees the potential for another Proposition 187 — the 1994 California ballot initiative that denied social services to illegal immigrants. "The reason Proposition 187 passed wasn't because people really favored it. They were pissed off at our immigration policy, and it was the only way they could register their opposition."

"Sticking it to the foreigners" is the easy way for policy-makers to assuage the public's concern about immigration without actually doing anything about it, he says. "We'll continue to propose these anti-immigrant measures instead of sensible restrictions on immigration because too many powerful groups have an interest in keeping things as they are," he says.

Krikorian and others blame both major political parties for wanting to preserve the immigration status quo. GOP support parallels that of big business, which favors high levels of immigration in order to maintain a steady supply of both unskilled and skilled labor. Democratic support for immigration stems from its connection to various ethnic groups — largely Asian and Hispanic — that favor higher levels.

But others say a backlash, in any form, is unlikely for a number of different reasons. According to the de Tocqueville Institution's Lance, newcomers will continue to be welcome because the American people have come to accept high immigration levels as almost a permanent condition.

"If you look at the past 10 years, it seems that the pendulum has really swung in favor of immigration," she says. "Sure, we may have moments — especially during recessions — when there is a fear of foreigners, but unless there is a major catastrophe, like a war or a depression, I don't think the American people will seriously question" current immigration policies.

Sharry agrees. "I think the premise is that immigration is a good thing

"Sure, we may have moments — especially during recessions — when there is a fear of foreigners, but unless there is a major catastrophe, like a war or a depression, I don't think the American people will seriously question current immigration policies."

— Bronwyn Lance, Senior Fellow, Alexis de Tocqueville Institution

and will increasingly be viewed as a crucial part of our economy," he says. Besides, Sharry says, the economy is unlikely to take the kind of nose-dive that would actually prompt people to rethink immigration policy.

"I think the economy's going to stay relatively strong for the foreseeable future," he predicts, "and this will lead not only to a preservation of the current system but to an expansion of it." ■

FOR MORE INFORMATION

Alexis de Tocqueville Institution, 1611 N. Kent St., Suite 901, Arlington, Va. 22209; (703) 351-0090; www.adti.net. The institution works to increase public understanding of the cultural and economic benefits of immigration.

Center for Immigration Studies, 1522 K St., N.W., Suite 820, Washington, D.C. 20005; (202) 466-8185; www.cis.org. The center conducts research on the impact of immigration.

Federation for American Immigration Reform (FAIR), 1666 Connecticut Ave., N.W., Suite 400, Washington, D.C. 20009; (202) 328-7004; www.fairus.org. FAIR lobbies in favor of strict limits on immigration.

National Council of La Raza, 1111 19th St., N.W., Suite 1000, Washington, D.C. 20036; (202) 785-1670; www.nclr.org. La Raza monitors legislation and lobbies on behalf of Latinos in the United States.

National Immigration Forum, 220 I St., N.E., Washington, D.C. 20002; (202) 544-0004; www.immigrationforum.org. The forum advocates and builds public support for pro-immigration policies.

U.S. Immigration and Naturalization Service, 425 I St., N.W., Suite 7100, Washington, D.C. 20536; (202) 514-1900; www.ins.usdoj.gov. The INS, part of the Department of Justice, administers and enforces U.S. immigration and naturalization laws.

Notes

[1] Data provided by the U.S. Census Bureau. For background, see Charles S. Clark, "The New Immigrants," *The CQ Researcher*, Jan. 24, 1997, pp. 49-72.

[2] Greenspan testified before the Senate Committee on Banking, Housing and Urban Affairs on Feb. 24, 2000.

[3] Quoted in John Micklethwait, "The New Americans," *The Economist*, March 11, 2000.

[4] For background, see Kenneth Jost, "Cracking Down on Immigration," *The CQ Researcher*, Feb. 3, 1995, pp. 97-120.

[5] For background, see Kathy Koch, "High-Tech Labor Shortage," *The CQ Researcher*, April 24, 1998, pp. 361-384.

[6] Figures provided by the Immigration and Naturalization Service.

[7] Micklethwait, *op. cit.*

[8] For background, see David Masci, "Hispanic Americans' New Clout," *The CQ Researcher*, Sept. 18, 1998, pp. 809-832.

[9] Quoted from Douglas Holt, "INS Is Scaling Back Its Workplace Raids," *Chicago Tribune*, Jan. 17, 1999.

[10] Mary W. Cohn (ed.), *Congressional Quarterly Almanac* (1986), p. 61.

[11] Quoted in Karen Cheney, "Foreign Aid: Hiring Abroad Can Ease Your Labor Woes," *Business Week*, April 24, 2000.

[12] Micklethwait, *op. cit.*

[13] Suzette Brooks Masters and Ted Ruthizer, "The H-1B Straitjacket," CATO Institute, March 3, 2000.

[14] For background, see David Masci, "Assisting Refugees," *The CQ Researcher*, Feb. 7, 1997, pp. 97-120.

[15] For background, see David Masci, "Mexico's Future," *The CQ Researcher*, Sept. 19, 1997, pp. 817-840.

[16] Figures cited in Peter Brimelow, *Alien Nation* (1995), p. 34.

[17] Kenneth Jost (ed.), *Congressional Quarterly Almanac* (1990), p. 482.

[18] Jan Austin (ed.), *Congressional Quarterly Almanac* (1996), p. 5-3

[19] Micklethwait, *op. cit.*

[20] Mary H. Cooper, "Global Refugee Crisis," *The CQ Researcher*, July 9, 1999, pp. 569-592.

[21] Steven Greenhouse, "Coalition Urges Easing of Immigration Laws," *The New York Times*, May 16, 2000.

[22] Figures cited in Mike Dorning, "Acceptance of Immigration on the Rise," *Chicago Tribune*, April 3, 2000.

[23] Quoted in *Ibid.*

Bibliography

Selected Sources Used

Books

Brimelow, Peter, *Alien Nation: Common Sense About America's Immigration Disaster*, HarperPerennial, 1996.

Brimelow, a *Forbes* magazine senior editor, makes what many consider a strong case for a restrictive immigration policy. He argues that unless the flood of newcomers to America's shores is halted or at least curtailed, the United States will become a nation of ethnic fiefdoms, each pulling in a different direction. If present trends continue, Brimelow writes, "Americans themselves will become alien to each other."

Smith, James P., and Barry Edmonston (eds.), *The Immigration Debate*, National Academy Press, 1998.

This collection of essays by immigration experts examines the fiscal, economic and demographic effects of the recent wave of newcomers to the United States. In particular, the book discusses whether immigrants add to or detract from the economy.

Articles

Cheney, Karen, "Foreign Aid: Hiring Abroad Can Ease Your Labor Woes," *Business Week*, April 24, 2000.

Cheney examines the current debate over H-1B visas, which allow high-skilled workers to enter the United States on a temporary basis.

Cooper, Mary H., "Immigration Reform," *The CQ Researcher*, Sept. 23, 1993.

A slightly dated but valuable overview of immigration-related debates that still are relevant today. Particularly valuable is Cooper's examination of the economic impact of immigration.

Kempner, Matt, "The Big Wink: Undocumented Latino Workers Are So Vital to Georgia's Economy That Those in Charge Look the Other Way," *The Atlanta Journal*, Jan. 23, 2000.

Kempner examines the impact of illegal immigration in Georgia and finds that many industries are heavily dependent upon undocumented workers.

Koch, Kathy, "High Tech Labor Shortage, *The CQ Researcher*, April 24, 1998.

Staff writer Koch examines the debate surrounding the perceived shortage of workers in the high-technology industry and details the drive to allow businesses to bring in more high-skilled foreign workers on a temporary basis.

Micklethwait, John, "The New Americans," *The Economist*, March 11, 2000.

This superb series of articles explores the economic, political and cultural impact of the most recent wave of immigration on the United States. Micklethwait acknowledges the many challenges associated with absorbing millions of foreigners, many of whom are poor and speak little or no English. Still, he argues that immigrants, with their energy and drive, will make the United States a more prosperous nation.

Samuelson, Robert J., "Ignoring Immigration" *The Washington Post*, May 3, 2000.

Samuelson, a columnist for *The Washington Post*, advocates dramatically changing the nation's policy on legal immigration. He proposes admitting better-educated immigrants instead of the low-skilled people who make up the lion's share of newcomers each year.

Stern, Marcus, "A Semi-Tough Policy on Illegal Workers; Congress Looks Out for Employers," *The Washington Post*, July 5, 1998.

Stern argues that even though Congress has shown a great willingness to pass laws aimed at curtailing illegal immigration, many lawmakers defend businesses in their districts that use undocumented workers.

Reports and Studies

Lance, Bronwyn, Margalit Edelman and Peter Mountford, "There Goes the Neighborhood — Up: A Look at Property Values and Immigration in Washington, D.C.," Alexis de Tocqueville Institution, January 2000.

Evidence in this report counters the commonly held belief that property values fall when large numbers of immigrants move into an area. Indeed, the de Tocqueville researchers found that property values actually rise.

Masters, Suzette Brooks, and Ted Ruthizer, "The H-1B Straitjacket: Why Congress Should Repeal the Cap on Foreign-Born Highly Skilled Workers," The Cato Institute, March 3, 2000.

The authors, both attorneys, make the case for expanding the H-1B temporary work visa program. They argue that the current shortage of skilled foreign workers is forcing high-tech companies to move their operations overseas.

10 Hispanic-Americans' New Clout

DAVID MASCI

It was a real fiesta, complete with a mariachi band and spicy Mexican food.

For Antonio Villaraigosa, it was a hard, almost bitter defeat. "I put everything I had into this race," a visibly tired Villaraigosa said soon after finding out that he had been narrowly defeated in his bid to become the first Latino mayor of Los Angeles in almost 150 years. "I don't have anything left." [1]

But Villaraigosa's despair over his June 6th, 2001, loss to white city councilman James K. Hahn belies a deeper trend that is changing the political landscape in Los Angeles. With Hispanics now accounting for nearly half of the city's residents, most political analysts predict that L.A. will soon have a Latino mayor. "I think this is the last election of the old guard," said Peter Dreier, a professor of political science at L.A.'s Occidental College.[2]

Indeed, Latinos are poised to play a more active political role on the national scene. Already, the number of Latino officials around the country has jumped dramatically, from 3,128 in 1984 to 5,191 in 1998.[3] And every recent administration, Republican or Democrat, has picked Hispanics as cabinet secretarys and for other high level posts.

This new political clout mirrors the rise in the nation's Latino population—up from just over 12 million in 1984 to more than 35 million today, according to recently issued figures from the 2000 census.[4] In California, the nation's most populous state, Latinos are poised to become the state's largest ethnic group, outnumbering both whites and blacks, in the next few years. Other major states, like Texas, Florida and New

AP Photo/RichPedroncelli

York, also have large and growing Hispanic populations.

Moreover, Hispanics are also rapidly moving into the nation's suburbs and its middle class; for the first time, there are now more than 1 million Latino-owned businesses nationwide.

Until recently, however, demographic and even economic clout hasn't always translated into commensurate political power for Latinos. Many were not citizens or legal residents and hence were ineligible to vote. Even among Hispanic citizens, voter turnout traditionally has been low.

But lately things have been changing. Efforts to cut health and other benefits to Latinos who are legal residents of the United States have led millions to apply for citizenship, making them eligible to vote. In California, for instance, the number of Hispanics registered to vote has jumped from 1.3 million in 1994 to well over 2 million today.

In addition, the efforts to deny benefits to immigrants as well as bruising debates over affirmative action and bilingual education have politically galvanized many Latinos who might otherwise have stayed home on election day. "We're starting to see more and more Latinos turn up at the polls and seeing them better educated about the issues," says Ingrid Duran, assistant director of the National Association of Latino Elected and Appointed Officials.

So far, the increased political participation has translated into gains for the Democratic Party. Indeed, in the last presidential election, GOP candidate George W. Bush received 35 percent of the Hispanic vote, more than the dismal 20 percent garnered by Bob Dole in 1996, but still less than what President Ronald Reagan received in 1984.[5]

Democrats predict that Latinos will largely stick with their party in the future. To begin with, they say, Republicans have largely alienated Hispanics by pushing an anti-immigrant agenda that includes cutting benefits to illegal and legal immigrants and supporting efforts to do away with affirmative action and bilingual education. "The GOP have been immigrant bashers, and they've driven Latinos into the arms of the Democratic Party," says Rep. Xavier Becerra, D-Calif.

In addition, Democrats say, their party is much more in tune with the aspirations and needs of most Latinos, especially on issues like education, health care and immigration. Democrats are even confident that they can win over Latino voters on issues traditionally thought to be GOP strengths, like business development and crime. "Those stereotypes that we are hostile to small business or soft on crime don't wash anymore," says Ed Kilgore, political director of the Democratic Leadership Council (DLC).

But Republicans say that they can win a sizable share, if not a majority, of the Latino vote. GOP strategists point to a host of Republican candidates, from former Los Angeles Mayor Richard Reardon to George W. Bush, who as governor of Texas success-

From *The CQ Researcher.*
Originally published September 18, 1998.
Introduction updated by David Masci, August 23, 2001.

Latino Population Is Growing Rapidly

*The nation's Hispanic population increased 29.6 percent from 1990-97 — four times as fast as the overall U.S. population — due to high birth rates and rising immigration levels. The number of Hispanics is expected to increase 23.6 percent from 1997-2005. There were 29.2 million Hispanics in the United States in 1997, or 11 percent of the population.**

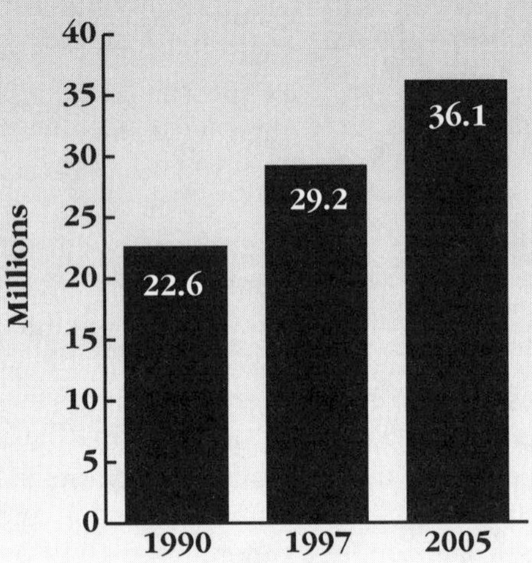

* *Total does not include the estimated 3.8 million residents of Puerto Rico.*

Source: "Latino Education: Status and Prospects," National Council of La Raza, July 1998, U.S. Census Bureau

fully wooed a majority of Latino voters and had an 80 percent approval rating among Hispanics in his state.

GOP strategists argue that Reardon, Bush and other Republicans have succeeded in communicating the party's pro-family, pro-economic opportunity message to a growing number of Hispanics, who are traditionally very conservative, especially on social issues. "You look at family issues, crime, business development—we have the message that is most in line with their thinking," says Lorenzo Lopez, a special assistant on Hispanic affairs at the Republican National Committee (RNC).

Whether Republicans draw more Latino votes in future elections or not, it is clear that the party is more focused on winning over Hispanics than it was four years ago. Indeed, many in the GOP, including Bush, have distanced themselves from their party's traditional opposition to bilingual education.

Ironically, Latinos are divided in their feelings about bilingual education. For instance, a 1998 ballot measure eliminating bilingual learning from California's schools—known as Proposition 227—was approved by voters with the support of about 40 percent of the state's Hispanics.

Opponents of bilingual education see Latino support for Prop. 227 as a sign that Hispanics, especially those with children in school, are turning away from bilingual programs because they are failing. "Many parents with children in bilingual programs are frustrated, not because they're being taught in Spanish, but because they are not learning English," says Eric Stone, director of research for U.S. English, an organization that advocates making English the nation's official language.

Indeed, say Stone and others, many children with limited or no English proficiency are kept in bilingual programs for six or more years, leaving them woefully unprepared for life in an English-speaking country. "Immigrant parents understand that English is necessary for advancement in this country," he says.

Finally, opponents point to early studies that suggest that Hispanic children in California are performing better in school since Proposition 227 was passed and implemented.

But supporters of bilingual education say that most Latinos still favor Spanish in the classroom until children are proficient in English. They claim that many Hispanics voted for Prop. 227 because they are angry with the poor overall performance of California's schools, not bilingual education per se.

In addition, supporters argue, most Latinos know that bilingual education is not a substitute for learning English but a tool that helps students while they're being taught their new nation's tongue. "The truth is that bilingual education is working for most kids," says Oscar Sanchez, executive director of the Labor Council for Latin American Advancement, a Hispanic trade union group. Sanchez points out that before the widespread introduction of bilingual learning in the late 1960s, Latino kids had a much higher dropout rate than they do today.

According to Sanchez and others, the battle against bilingual education is part of a larger war against Latinos retaining any of their culture. Indeed, he argues, many Americans expect Latinos to assimilate and forget about where they came from.

Advocates of cultural retention, like Sanchez, argue that it is good for Latinos to keep not only their language but also their cultural heritage. Latinos are different from European immigrants, they argue, in that they are not crossing an ocean to come to America and, in many cases, are returning to lands once ruled by Mexico or Spain. In addition, they say, Hispanic children need to be taught the history and traditions of their ancestors in order to give them an identity and greater sense of self-worth.

But others disagree, arguing that Hispanics, like all other immigrants past and present, need to work to adopt the language, culture and traditions of their new country. Any other road will lead to ethnic separatism, they say. "Immigration is a compact between the host country and the newcomer: We welcome you into our home and you, in turn, learn our language, mores and begin identifying with your new family," says Linda Chavez, president of the Center for Equal Opportunity.

By the middle of the next century, Hispanics are likely to make up a quarter of the nation's population, and the extent to which they feel welcomed in their new country could significantly affect America's future.

As scholars, politicians and others continue to look at this growing community, similar questions over political loyalties and social integration have arisen since many of the same issues confronted the community in the past. The remainder of this issue, written in 1998, focuses on these key questions to give a valuable perspective on where the Hispanic American community has come from. Here are some of the questions they have been asking:

Will Latino Democrats remain loyal to the Democratic Party?

When Speaker of the House Newt Gingrich, R-Ga., rose to address a July meeting of the League of United Latin American Citizens (LULAC), the nation's largest Hispanic group, he was greeted with polite but muted applause. In spite of his recent support for Puerto Rican self-determination and restoration of some public benefits denied to legal immigrants, many Latinos still regard the Speaker with suspicion.[6]

But the tepid welcome was not just directed at Gingrich. Latinos generally have not been happy with Republican support for measures to deny benefits to immigrants as well as GOP opposition to bilingual education and continued high levels of immigration. In California, home to more than half of all U.S. Hispanics, Republican Gov. Pete Wilson's support for Prop. 187 has cost the GOP tremendously with the Latino community, both in and out of state. For example, since 1984, the GOP's share of the Latino vote in presidential elections has fallen from over 40 percent that year, to under 20 percent in 1996.

At the same time, the number of registered Hispanic voters has increased dramatically. For instance, from 1992-1996, the number of Latinos registered to vote rose 30 percent, to 6.6 million, and 75 percent of the new voters registered as Democrats.[7]

In addition, Latinos are concentrated in almost all of the key electoral vote-rich states needed to win the presidency, including California, Texas, Florida and New York. "In California, which is a keystone in any presidential strategy, Latinos are not just the swing vote, they are a big part of the vote," says Roberto Suro, a reporter at *The Washington Post* and author of a recent book on Latinos, *Strangers Among Us*. Indeed, President Clinton won California, Florida and New York in his successful 1992 and 1996 races, in part due to Latino support.

The current disconnect between many Latino voters and the GOP represents a great threat to Republicans. Unless they begin to regain Latino support, the GOP could be severely handicapped in future national elections.

Indeed, Democrats know that solid Latino support in the near future could help keep a Democrat in the White House and even allow the Democrats eventually to retake control of Congress. "We recognize the importance

AP Photo/Frank Wiese

A police line separates demonstrators for and against Proposition 187 in Los Angeles, Calif., in August 1996.

Most U.S. Hispanics Are Mexican-Americans

Nearly two-thirds of the nation's Hispanics were Mexican-Americans in 1996. Two-thirds were American citizens, and 62 percent were U.S.-born.

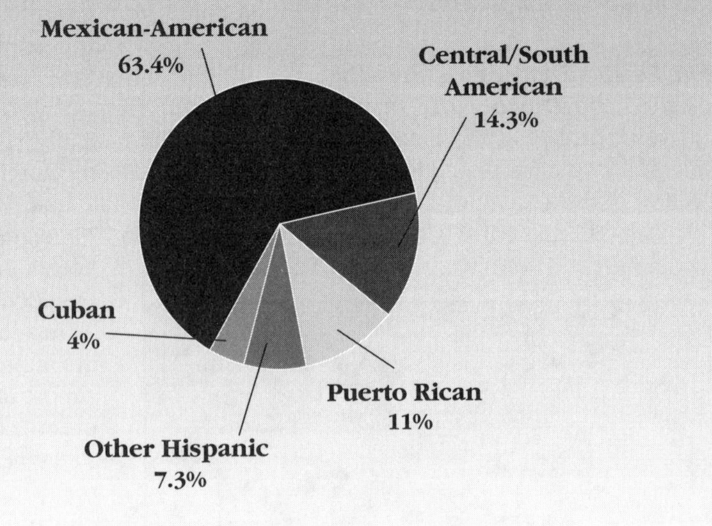

Sources: Latino Education: Status and Prospects, National Council of La Raza, July 1998, U.S. Census Bureau

of this community," says the DLC's Kilgore, "and we're not going to take a single vote for granted."

Kilgore and other Democrats see several reasons why Latino voters generally feel more comfortable with their party than with the GOP. Above all, they say, many Hispanics believe that Republican initiatives to limit immigration, bilingual education and benefits for recent arrivals have unfairly targeted Latinos and are inherently racist. "Republicans in general have really been anti-Latino," says Sanchez of the Labor Council for Latin American Advancement. "There's no other way for us to look at what they've done."

Sanchez acknowledges that some Republicans, like Gingrich, have begun reaching out to Latino voters in recent months. But so far, they argue, kind GOP words have not been matched by much action. "Republicans need to go beyond the rhetoric," says Duran of the Latino officials' association. "It's nice of them to welcome us to their party, but they need to change their anti-Latino policies."

In addition to the perceived Republican hostility, Democrats say their party's message and agenda is more in line with Latino aspirations. "When you look at the profile of the Hispanic voter — very upwardly mobile, obsessed with education, concerned about crime and a belief in an active government — you are increasingly looking at the profile of the Democratic Party," Kilgore says.

But Republicans counter that Latino aspirations are actually more in line with the GOP. "Hispanics are in tune with our pro-family, pro-business message," says the RNC's Lopez. Chavez of the Center for Equal Opportunity agrees. "There is a confluence of interests between them," she says.

The real problem, Republicans say, is not the message but the way it is being conveyed. "In the past, we failed with Latino voters because we didn't explain our positions well on things like Proposition 187, and the Democrats were able to demagogue us on that," Lopez says. The GOP needs to become more effective at showing Latinos that they have much more in common with the Republicans than with Democrats, he says.

For instance, Lopez and Chavez point out, the GOP's positions on moral and family issues are generally in line with the Latino community. "Hispanics are very family-oriented," Chavez points out. "So on issues like homosexuality or handing out birth control in schools, they feel the same way that most Republicans do."

And, Lopez says, when it comes to family policy, the GOP puts its money where its mouth is. For example, he says, Republicans in Congress recently pushed through a $500 per child tax cut. "This really helps Latinos, who generally have larger families than others," he says.

At the same time, Republicans say, the rapid increase in the number of Latino entrepreneurs means that more and more Hispanics will embrace the party's opposition to what it considers excessive regulation and high taxes. "Latinos are bothered by red tape and an intrusive government just like other small-business men are," Chavez says.

Such predictions make the DLC's Kilgore chuckle. "If they still think they're the party of small business, they're living in the past," he says. Sanchez agrees, adding that "everyone knows that under Clinton businesses in this country have done very well."

Even on family values, where Kilgore admits there may be some differences of opinion, Democrats consider their agenda much better suited to Hispanics due to the party's emphasis on tolerance. "Given a choice between a [Republican] ideology that's intolerant and one that's tolerant, [Latinos] will choose tolerance, even if they're not always comfortable with everything we stand for, like gay rights."

Thanks to Latinos, Spicier English

Spanish has been a part of American English for centuries. Early settlers began picking up Spanish words and phrases almost from the start of the nation's long expansion. In the South, for instance, areas like Florida and Louisiana were, at times, under Spanish rule. And the American Southwest and West were part of Mexico until the Mexican-American War changed the boundaries in 1848.

Today, the huge influx of Hispanic immigrants into the United States is once again adding to the country's language. Much of this change reflects the immense popularity of Latino food, music and other cultural offerings. Anglos — the name given to non-Hispanic whites — find themselves ordering *fajitas* and listening to *Tejano* music with increasing frequency.

New and old Spanish words and phrases that have spiced up American English include:

bronco — a Mexican-Spanish word for wild or rough.

enchilada — popular filled and baked tortilla; also slang for "everything," as in "The whole enchilada."

gringo — derogatory word to refer to an outsider, usually an American. Word may be a derivative of "green grows," a song American troops supposedly sang during the war with Mexico.

guerrilla — unorthodox style of fighting developed by Latin Americans.

incommunicado — increasingly popular way to say "not available."

loco — a 19th-century Mexican word originally used to describe a weed that made horses "crazy."

macho — derived from a Mexican-Indian word that originally meant "to be known."

maquiladora — a foreign-owned factory in Mexico near the U.S. border.

mañana — Spanish for "tomorrow."

salsa — Spanish for sauce made of tomatoes (a Mexican word), onions and chilis (a Mexican-Indian word); also refers to a style of Latin American music.

tobacco — 16th-century Spanish word.

tornado — from the Spanish word *tronada*, for thunderstorm.

Sources: Merriam Webster's Collegiate Dictionary, *Earl Shorris,* Latinos: A Biography of the People.

According to Kilgore and others, the Democrats should be able to keep a very high percentage of the Hispanic vote in coming elections. "If we stick to our message of economic optimism and an emphasis on families, education and equal opportunity, they should stay a solidly Democratic voting group."

Sanchez agrees. "Hispanics are a natural constituency for the Democratic Party," he says. "So as long as they continue to cultivate us and not take us for granted, they should reap enormous benefits come Election Day."

But, Republicans point out, they are already eroding that support. For instance, on the same day that Gingrich received a lukewarm reception before LULAC, another party leader, Gov. Bush, received a rousing ovation from the group. Bush is likely to be re-elected in November with half or more of the Hispanic vote. His brother Jeb, who is married to a Mexican-American, is running for the governor's mansion in Florida. He, too, is expected to win the election, thanks in no small part to his popularity with Florida Hispanics. Other Republicans who have recently gotten or are expected to get a sizable portion of the Latino vote include New York City Mayor Rudolph Giuliani, Michigan Gov. John Engler and Sens. Pete V. Domenici, R-N.M., and John McCain, R-Ariz.

According to Lopez, the Bush brothers, Giuliani and McCain prove that the GOP can do well among Latinos if they reach out to them. "A lot of Latinos, especially the young, are becoming disenchanted with the Democrats because they haven't really done much for them," he says.

As a result, Lopez argues, the Latino community won't automatically be wedded to the Democratic Party in the future. "You know, Latino voters are much more savvy than most people think. Democrats just can't show up anymore, say a few words in Spanish, eat a taco and expect to automatically get their vote."

Is bilingual education losing support in the Latino community?

It was only a matter of time before California, the state that has already held controversial referenda on everything from property taxes to affirmative action, finally got around to asking its voters to pass judgment on bilingual education. The initiative, sponsored by Silicon Valley millionaire Ron Unz, gives a preference to English-language teaching, allows bilingual programs only in schools where parents actually request them and strictly limits the amount of time a student can spend in a non-English class. [8]

One Name, Many Communities

When author Earl Shorris asked a Mexican-American woman named Margarita Avila how he should write about her ethnic community, she replied: "Just tell them who we are, and that we are not alike."

Shorris assumed that Avila was referring to Hispanics when she said "we," but she surprised him and explained that she meant "Mejicanos." [1]

Shorris' anecdote speaks volumes about Latinos. Not only did Avila distinguish between Mexicans and other Hispanics, but she saw differences within the Mexican-American community itself. Indeed, Mexican-Americans from Texas refer to themselves as Tejanos. In California and elsewhere, most Americans of Mexican descent call themselves Chicanos.

All of this goes to show that Latinos are not a homogeneous group. They come in every shade of skin color, from pale white to black. And they can trace their ancestry all over the globe. Some have largely European or African blood in their veins. Many others are at least partly from indigenous Indian stock. A few even hail from Asia. The majority are a mixture of different ethnicities.

Nor do they come from one country or even one part of Latin America. Many, like Avila, are originally from Mexico. Others come from Cuba, Puerto Rico and the Dominican Republic in the Caribbean. Still others are from Central or South America. All have different traditions, history and culture that they are proud of and think unique.

What they do largely share is a language, Spanish, although dialects abound. To a lesser extent, Latinos also share the same faith, Roman Catholicism. But that is changing. A large and growing number of Latinos have become Protestants, converted by missionaries in Latin America or after their arrival in the U.S. Most of these Protestant Latinos are Evangelical Christians. A small number of Hispanics also are Jewish.

Like Asian-Americans (another heterogeneous community) Latinos have been grouped together due to misunderstanding and convenience. Many whites (called "Anglos" by Latinos) and blacks just assumed that all immigrants from Latin America were the same, regardless of where they came from. "There's been this tendency to lump us all together into one big group," says Felix Gutierrez, senior vice president of the Freedom Forum Pacific Coast Center, in San Francisco.

Pressure to identify Latinos as a single, definable group has also come as voting-rights remedies, affirmative action and other programs designed to aid minorities have become commonplace. In fact, the word "Hispanic" was chosen by the U.S. Census Bureau in 1980 in order to classify all Spanish speakers and their descendants. "Latino" has come into widespread use more recently as an alternative that is more acceptable to the community itself.

But most Latinos do not prefer either word. Instead, they tend to refer to themselves by their country of origin: They are Bolivian, Salvadoran or Cuban.

The majority of Latinos in the United States, about 63 percent, are from Mexico. Mexican-Americans have settled predominantly in those states that were once part of Mexico: California, Texas, New Mexico, Colorado, Nevada and Arizona. Indeed, some Americans of Mexican descent can trace their family history in the United States back many generations, having lived in Texas, New Mexico or California before Mexico was forced to hand over the northern half of its territory to America in 1848.

The second-largest group of U.S. Latinos, about 12 percent, is from Puerto Rico. Puerto Ricans have largely settled in the New York City area. Because Puerto Rico has been a U.S. territory for 100 years, all people born in Puerto Rico are American citizens, giving them a unique status among Latino arrivals.

Cuban-Americans are another unique community, but for a different reason. Many were well-educated, middle-class professionals when they came to the United States in the early 1960s, not the usual "tired" and "hungry" immigrants that often seek refuge on America's shores. These Cubans, who now comprise 8 percent of the nation's Latino population, left their homes to escape Fidel Castro's communist revolution. Some (though not their children) still dream of returning to the land of their birth. But since Castro remains in power, they must be content to wait in their communities in southern Florida and, to a lesser extent, New Jersey.

Immigrants from the Dominican Republic are relatively recent arrivals in the United States. Most have come in the last two decades and have settled in the Northeast, especially New York.

About 12 percent of America's Hispanics come from Central and South America. Many of the Central Americans, from El Salvador, Honduras and Nicaragua, arrived in the 1980s fleeing terrible civil wars. A large number have settled in southern Florida. Others have moved north to Eastern cities like New York and Washington, D.C. There are fewer South Americans, although growing communities of Colombians, Bolivians and Brazilians have sprung up in the last decade.

[1] Earl Shorris, *Latinos: Biography of the People* (1992), p. XV.

When Unz first began campaigning for what would become Proposition 227, many analysts predicted that the debate would degenerate into the kind of racially charged slugfest that had characterized earlier statewide initiatives limiting affirmative action and benefits to illegal immigrants. And indeed, many Latinos and others in the education and civil rights communities characterized Unz and his allies as everything from anti-immigrant to racist.

But the debate over Prop. 227 didn't entirely mirror those earlier battles.

Throughout the campaign, polls often showed a majority of Latinos in favor of the initiative. And a number of prominent Hispanic leaders in California — notably Jaime Escalante, the high school math teacher profiled in the film "Stand and Deliver" — supported the proposition.

On June 2, 1998, Prop. 227 passed by a comfortable margin. And although a majority of Latinos voted against it, a sizable minority, about 40 percent, supported the initiative.

Why are Hispanics in California split over a program that was designed to help their children?

No one denies that California's bilingual education program, and those in other states as well, were established with good intentions. Bilingual education, which aims to help English-deficient children keep up in other subjects while they learn their new nation's language, was first instituted in California by then Gov. Ronald Reagan (R) in 1967. At that time, educators were grappling with high dropout rates among Hispanic students, and it was thought that the program might help acclimate them to the educational system and keep them in school.

Today, the question of what to do with limited-English-proficiency students is more pressing than ever. For example, California has about 1.4 million students with limited or no English ability — about one-quarter of all children enrolled in its schools. About 70 percent of them are Latinos, most Mexican-American. [9]

Few people advocate the "sink or swim" method employed with many immigrant children earlier in our history. But those who oppose all or most bilingual education argue that a growing number of Latinos, especially those with children in school, are realizing that teaching their children in Spanish — especially for lengthy periods — can jeopardize their ability to master English.

"Look, the reason there has been this backlash in California is that parents are noticing that their kids are not learning English as quickly as they should be," says Nina Shokraii, an education policy analyst at the Heritage Foundation. "You're seeing parents in other states like New Mexico and Colorado saying the same thing: 'We want our children taught in English, not their native tongue.'"

Part of the problem with bilingual education, Shokraii says, is that students are often kept in Spanish classes for years while receiving little or no English instruction. "In some places, students spend six or seven years in Spanish-only classes," says Stone of U.S. English. Indeed, in California, only 6 percent of students in bilingual classes are deemed ready each year to make the leap to English-only education.

At the same time, Shokraii, Stone and others argue, Latino parents desperately want their children to be fluent in English and as quickly as possible. "A lot of immigrants who come here want to live the American dream, and they know that that's impossible without English," Shokraii says.

And yet, Shokraii and others claim, the educational establishment as well as Latino advocacy groups in places like California are wedded to the notion that bilingual education is what Hispanic children need. "There is a real disconnect between the ethnic leadership and the rank-and-file on this," says Charles Glenn, a professor of education policy at Boston University and the author of *Educating Immigrant Children*.

Opponents of bilingual education claim that many Latino parents are beginning to take matters into their own hands. For instance, 70 mostly Mexican-American families in Los Angeles removed their children from a city elementary school in 1996 after administrators refused to place them in English instruction.

Two weeks after the boycott began, the school changed its policy. [10] "The notion of parents publicly boycotting a school for weeks because the school was refusing to teach their children English just seemed very extreme," says Unz, who claims that the incident inspired him to begin the campaign for Prop. 227. [11] Similar boycotts have taken place in a number of other cities in the Southwest.

But supporters of bilingual education argue that opponents are unfairly trying to paint Spanish instruction as a replacement for learning English. They point out that bilingual education is not meant to keep children in a linguistic ghetto. "Who is against children learning English fluently?" asks Sanchez of the Labor Council for Latin American Advancement. "No one. This is not an either/or thing."

"The whole point of bilingual education is for children to learn [other subjects] at their current level while also learning English," Duran says. "The idea that the 'English-only' people have — that you can learn it in a year — is ridiculous." Without bilingual education, Duran and others say, children will fall years behind in other subjects.

While Sanchez concedes that there may be isolated cases where bilingual learning "goes on too long," leading parents to become upset, in most cases children benefit from having some instruction in Spanish. "You look at most kids in bilingual programs, and they are able to easily shift between the two languages," he says.

Supporters also point out that many Latino parents are frustrated with poor, underfunded schools and may be taking their legitimate anger out on bilingual education. Indeed, nationwide, Latinos underperform students in other groups, including African-Americans. "When people are angry, they tend to blame the easiest thing," Sanchez says, "and in this case that's often bilingual education."

Lisa Navarette, a spokeswoman for La

Spanish-Language TV Taps $350 Billion Market . . .

Every morning, millions of Latinos across the country start their day with "Despierta America" ("Wake Up, America"). Like "Good Morning America" or "Today," "Despierta America" offers viewers news, weather, sports, celebrity interviews and features on everything from cooking to doing your taxes.

But there are differences. First, of course, the show is in Spanish. Indeed, it is one of the most popular offerings on Univision, the nation's largest, most-watched Spanish-language network. But the program's Latin flavor extends beyond the language. For instance, the set is decorated more like a Mexican hacienda — with earth-colored walls and bright Latin American murals — than the staid, book-lined sets of traditional morning shows. In addition, the program's hosts are much more lively, exuberant and spontaneous than, say, "Today's" Matt Lauer or "Good Morning America's" Lisa McRee. Often, they will break into loud fits of laughter or an unrehearsed dance routine.

"Despierta America," with its American format and Latino flavor, has been a tremendous success. On some days in Los Angeles, only "Today" gets higher ratings. The popularity of shows like "Despierta America" has led to predictions that Spanish-language television has a bright future in the United States.

AP/Univision

The Univision soap opera "Esmeralda" gets higher ratings than "Seinfeld" and "ER" in Miami, Fla.

While the three biggest English-language networks in the United States (ABC, CBS and NBC) have been losing viewers since the 1970s, Univision has experienced strong growth. Since 1992, the network's audience has increased at an annual rate of 14 percent. Today, Univision is the fifth-largest network in the United States, behind the Big Three and Fox but ahead of Viacom's UPN and Time Warner's WB.

Los Angeles-based Univision is the 800-pound gorilla of Spanish-language broadcasting in the United States, with over 80 percent of the U.S. Spanish television market. During prime time, Univision often has more than 2 million viewers. Univision's only real competitor to date is Miami-based Telemundo, which has about 18 percent of the American Spanish-language television market.

In many ways, the soap operas, news and talk shows seen on Univision and Telemundo are similar to those on English-language networks — but they are not carbon copies of American television. For instance, the soaps (or *telenovelas*) tend to have moral messages intertwined with the usual steamy plots. In addition,

Raza, agrees. "I look at the Prop. 227 vote as a referendum on the California school system," she says. "So it's no wonder so many Latinos voted for it."

Finally, supporters of bilingual education point out that before Spanish-language instruction was available for Hispanic students, the dropout rate was astronomically high. "People forget that the Latino dropout rate used to be 80 percent before bilingual ed.," Navarette says. "Today it's 30 percent — not good, but a lot better."

Will encouraging Latinos to retain their language and culture hamper their ability to integrate into American society?

During a soccer match in Los Angeles last February between the U.S and Mexican national teams, something happened that many would have thought unthinkable in the United States. As the U.S. national anthem began to play, most of the more than 91,000 fans in the L.A. Coliseum started to boo or blow horns, drowning out the song entirely. After the game, a barrage of bottles, cans and Spanish epithets rained down on the U.S. team. [12]

Speaking of the largely Mexican-American crowd after the game, U.S. player Alexi Lalas said: "I'm all for roots and understanding where you come from and having respect for your homeland, but tomorrow morning all those people are going to get up and work in the United States and live in the United States and have all the benefits of living in the United States." [13]

Lalas was asking, in essence: These immigrants and their children may live here, but do they think of themselves as Americans? Some observers worry that at least for some Latinos, the answer is "no." The reason, they say, is that the idea of the melting pot — a place where all peoples slowly adopt a common culture — is being replaced by a new ideal, the mosaic, where everyone keeps their native culture and adopts some American values.

Most Latino-watchers agree that Hispanics behave much like other newcomers to the United States. "They want to learn English, to succeed, to become American," Chavez says. The problem, as she sees it, is that there

. . . But Its Future Remains Uncertain

much of the programming, including the *telenovelas*, comes from Latin America, especially Mexico.

Recently, Univision has begun replacing its imported shows with home-grown fare, including "Despierta America," which replaced a Mexican spinoff of "Sesame Street." And Telemundo has announced that it will soon begin airing newly produced Spanish-language versions of hit American TV shows like "Jeopardy" and "Mad About You." [1]

The consensus on Wall Street and elsewhere is that Spanish-language television is an industry with tremendous untapped potential. According to Jessica Reif, a stock analyst for Merrill Lynch Global Securities, networks like Univision are "tapping into the fastest-growing segment of the population that is incredibly attractive to advertisers and who are becoming bigger and better consumers." [2]

The statistics seem to back up Reif's assessment. After all, there are already some 30 million Latinos in the United States with more than $350 billion in buying power. Moreover, high birth rates and continued immigration will greatly expand the number of Spanish-speakers in the country. Indeed, the number of U.S. Hispanics will likely double in the next 20-25 years. Moreover, Latinos tend to be fiercely loyal to brands they like, making them model consumers.

And the business community has noticed. Recently Sony, cable giant Telecommunications Inc. (TCI) and a number of other investors ponied up more than $500 million to purchase Telemundo. The new owners plan to invest heavily in buying and developing new shows for the network, which is generally thought to have had a lackluster programming schedule as compared with Univision. [3]

Meanwhile, CBS recently began an all-Spanish-language news station on cable. In addition, Univision and The Home Shopping Network are starting a home-shopping channel for Spanish-speakers. And, TV Azteca, a Mexican company, plans to create another Spanish-language network to compete with Univision and Telemundo.

But there may be clouds on the horizon. Some analysts, among them Pepperdine University research fellow Gregory Rodriguez, say that within two generations Latinos will have largely assimilated into American culture, making them just as comfortable in English as in Spanish, if not more so. "People who watch Spanish-language TV are new immigrants," says Linda Chavez, president of the Center for Equal Opportunity. "If you know English, you'll watch mainstream media because it's better."

For Univision and Telemundo, the challenge is to keep English-speaking viewers who could switch to English-language media. Given the cost of mounting a whole roster of first-rate programs, that will not be easy. Already, some of Univision's key audience — young men and women — is slipping away from the network. According to a recent study from Nielsen Media Research, Univision recently lost 6 percent of its young female viewers and a whopping 26 percent of its young males. [4]

[1] Andrew Pollock, "The Fight for Hispanic Viewers; Univision's Success Story Attracts New Competition," *Broadcasting and Cable*, Jan. 19, 1998.

[2] Quoted in David Tobenkin, "Univision vs. Telemundo," *Broadcasting and Cable*, Oct. 6, 1997.

[3] Marla Matzer, "Telemundo Agrees to be Acquired by Sony, Liberty," *Los Angeles Times*, Nov. 25, 1997.

[4] Robert La Franco, "All in la Familia," *Forbes*, March 23, 1998.

are forces in U.S. society, especially in our educational institutions, that are encouraging Latinos to cling to their native culture, almost to the exclusion of their new one. "There is an aggressive ethnic promotion going on in the Mexican-American and other communities," she says.

For example, Chavez and others say, in California, Texas and the other Southwestern states, many Mexican-American students are taught primarily about the history of Mexico, not the United States. "You are more likely to hear about a famous Mexican leader than about Washington or Lincoln," she says.

This is not the way immigrant children were once taught. "Our public schools were the melting pot, where students learned to be Americans, where they learned to think of U.S. culture as their culture," she says. These methods, Chavez says, need to be brought back into the classroom.

Stone of U.S. English agrees. "We have to focus on what unites us as Americans, rather than on ethnic identity and [Latinos'] status as oppressed minorities."

Opponents of this new multicultural model cite several reasons why much of the educational establishment has adopted it as the best way to educate immigrant children. "The education blob has gotten it into their heads that what is essential for immigrant children is that they feel good about themselves," says Boston University's Glenn. "Of course, there's no evidence that any of this actually works. And it goes against what most immigrant parents want: teach my child English, to be an American and to read and write."

But Chavez thinks the problem is greater than just some misguided educational theory. "Many of the cultural elites in this country are anti-American," Chavez says. "They don't appreciate American values and culture and don't think they should be transmitted to newcomers." In other words, many who run educational and other institutions do not believe that most American traditions are worth imparting to immigrants.

But many argue that Chavez and others wrongly assume that Latino immigrants will be just like their

European predecessors when it comes to assimilation. "You can't compare the Hispanic experience in this country with that of Europeans," argues the Post's Suro, "because Latinos have been here all along."

Felix Gutierrez, executive director of the Freedom Forum's Pacific Coast Center in San Francisco, agrees that the European immigrant model doesn't hold up for Latinos when it comes to assimilation. "We live in conquered territories, not a land we crossed an ocean to get to," he says, referring to the fact that much of the American Southwest and West were once part of Mexico. As a result, Gutierrez and others say, Latino immigrants in places like Texas, California and New Mexico are, in a sense, returning to places that were once their own. Moreover, other Hispanics were there when Americans arrived and never left. "In the case of my family, we didn't come to the U.S., the U.S. came to us," Gutierrez says.

Hence, Gutierrez and others argue, it is more understandable that Latinos would cling to their native culture and traditions. "We are a proud people with a rich history, a history that has always existed here," says Raul Yzaguirre, president of La Raza.

Another reason Latinos might cling to their roots a little more than others before them is that in today's interconnected world, it's easier to keep in touch and to visit the "old country" than it was for Europeans 100 or 150 years ago. "Ultimately, we will not lose our culture or Anglicize our names because we have closer contact with Cuba, Mexico, Puerto Rico or wherever we came from," Yzaguirre says. [14]

Advocates of deep cultural retention also argue that Hispanic children have a greater need to keep connected to their native traditions than other young people because of the discrimination and rejection they face. "It gives a child an identity, something they need because [Latinos] are not fully accepted here," Sanchez says.

But retaining your native language and a sense of where you came from, does not preclude you from being an American, Sanchez and others argue. "We think of ourselves as Americans first and then Mexicans or whatever second," Yzaguirre says. He and others say that so long as Latinos are welcomed in the United States, cultural retention will not stand in the way of love of their new country. "People are afraid of these things leading to separatism," says Elizabeth Salett, president of the National Multicultural Institute. "But as long as people are included in our system, there'll be no separatism."

So what happened at the Los Angeles soccer match? "I don't condone it, but maybe when you are harassed by immigration authorities, even if you're a citizen or a legal immigrant, you get frustrated and angry," Sanchez says.

And, he points out, it was not the first time Americans showed disrespect for one of their nation's symbols. "Look at the kids who burned the American flag or spit on American soldiers during the Vietnam War," he says. ■

BACKGROUND

Spanish Heritage

People were speaking Spanish in the territory that would become the United States long before the English language was ever heard on these shores. In the 16th century, the Spanish built settlements throughout the Southwest, a legacy that lives on in the names of many American cities in the region, from San Francisco to Santa Fe.

For centuries, the cultures of English- and Spanish-speaking America existed largely apart, separated by huge tracts of wilderness. But westward expansion from the English-speaking United States, beginning in the late 18th century, brought the two cultures increasingly into contact and conflict. In 1848, the United States defeated Mexico in a brief, bloody war. Mexico was forced to give up the territory that would become California, Texas and the rest of the American Southwest.

For Mexicans living in the conquered land, life was not easy. Although the United States offered them citizenship (an offer many refused), anti-Latino discrimination was widespread and often harsh. Still, the expansion of the railroads westward and the need for workers brought more Mexicans into what had been their country during the second half of the 19th century. By 1900, 500,000 Mexicans were living in the United States. [15]

Immigration from Mexico continued at a steady pace until World War II, when a severe labor shortage led the United States to establish a guest worker program for Mexicans. From 1942 until the program finally expired in 1964 more than 4.8 million Mexicans came to the United States, many temporarily. [16]

Mexicans were not the only Latinos coming to the United States after World War II. During the 1950s and '60s, a wave of Puerto Rican migration to the Northeast, particularly New York City, occurred. Unlike Mexicans and others in Latin America, Puerto Ricans were already citizens, since the island had been acquired by the United States following the Spanish-American War of 1898.

In the early 1960s, other groups of Latinos migrated to the United States. Cuban refugees fleeing the communist regime of Fidel Castro settled

Chronology

1800s *English- and Spanish-speaking America collide, leading to war and conquest.*

1848
The United States acquires California and the Southwest from Mexico after the Mexican-American War.

1898
Puerto Rico becomes an American territory following the Spanish-American War.

1900-1930s

Hard economic times and new laws slow immigration from Mexico.

1900
There are 500,000 people of Mexican descent living in the United States.

1928
The U.S. Border Patrol is formed to stem illegal immigration from Mexico.

1929
The Great Depression begins.

1940s-1960s

Economic expansion after World War II leads to an influx of Latino immigrants, first from Mexico and then from elsewhere in Latin America.

1941
The United States enters World War II.

1942
In an effort to alleviate a wartime labor shortage, the U.S. initiates a guest-worker program, which allows Mexicans to work in the country.

1959
Fidel Castro seizes power in Cuba, prompting many on the island to flee to the United States.

1965
President Lyndon B. Johnson signs the Immigration and Nationality Act, opening the door to more legal immigrants from Latin America.

1968
Congress passes the Bilingual Education Act, providing funds for bilingual programs around the country.

1970s-1980s

The size of the Latino community in the United States grows dramatically through immigration and high birth rates.

1975
The Voting Rights Act is extended to include Latinos.

1980
The U.S. Census Bureau reports that there are 12 million Hispanics in the United States.

1984
President Ronald Reagan wins more than 40 percent of the Latino vote.

1986
Congress passes the Immigration Control and Reform Act, which allows millions of illegal immigrants to apply for legal residency.

1990s-2000s

Latinos begin to gain political and economic power.

1990
The U.S. Census Bureau reports that there are 22.6 million Hispanics living in the United States.

1994
California voters approve Proposition 187, which denies basic services to illegal immigrants.

1996
Republican presidential candidate Bob Dole wins about 20 percent of the Latino vote.

February 1998
Antonio Villaraigosa becomes the second Latino Speaker of the California state Assembly, replacing Cruz Bustamonte.

June 1998
California approves Proposition 227, dramatically scaling back bilingual education.

2006
Latinos are projected to become the nation's largest minority.

2050
Hispanics are expected to comprise a quarter of the U.S. population.

primarily in the Miami area. By the end of the decade, people from the Dominican Republic began arriving in New York City, a migration that continues to this day.

Latino Influx

Since the mid-1960s, the overall rate of Latino immigration to the United States has grown rapidly. The impetus for these increases has come in part from a 1965 change in immigration law. Under the Immigration and Nationality Act, the longstanding preference for newcomers from Europe was replaced with a racially neutral policy. As a result, the door was opened to Latinos not only from Mexico but also from the Caribbean and South and Central America.

Today, according to the latest estimates from the Census Bureau, 29.7 million Latinos reside in the United States, or 11 percent of the nation's population. If the present rate of growth continues, Hispanics will become the nation's largest minority by 2006, surpassing African-Americans, who make up 12.8 percent of the population. [17]

Already, there are more Hispanics than blacks in U.S. public schools. Indeed, the 10.5 million Latinos under age 18 outnumber African-Americans in the same age group by 35,000. [18]

Demographic projections even further into the future show that Latinos will comprise nearly a quarter of the nation's population by 2050. The growth will be fed in part by continuing immigration from Latin America and the Caribbean. In addition, high birth rates among Latinos already in the United States will also add greatly to these numbers. Indeed, between 1990-1996, Latina women had 106.3 births per thousand compared with 65.6 births per thousand for whites and 79.6 for blacks. [19]

"This is clearly a huge demographic undertaking for our nation," says Suro of *The Washington Post*. He and others predict that absorbing this new population will cause a certain amount of collective tension. "I don't see how it can be avoided," he says.

Of course, the dramatic demographic projections could be altered by a change in the nation's immigration policy, which fuels much of the growth of the Latino population, both legal and illegal. In fact, almost half of the nation's 12 million Latinos are foreign-born. Reducing the level of legal immigration and cracking down on illegal entry into the United States would significantly slow Hispanic population growth.

Polls show that a majority of Americans currently favor reducing levels of legal and illegal immigration. "There is a feeling among some people that this is going too far," Chavez says. Nowhere is this attitude better reflected than in Rogers. Ark., a town that has seen its Hispanic population grow dramatically in the last decade. "I'm not a racist," says Rogers resident Jason Riggins. "I just don't want to be outnumbered in my own country." [20]

According to Suro, such attitudes will spread once the current economic expansion comes to an end. "The issue will really come to a head when the unemployment rate hits 6 percent nationwide," he says.

But many observers, Suro included, say it would be a mistake to stop or reduce immigration. Indeed, they argue, immigrants helped the United States reach its eighth consecutive year of economic growth. "This large expansion of immigration has come at the same time we had this unprecedented economic expansion," he says. ■

CURRENT SITUATION

Climbing the Ladder

The nation's growing Latino population has embraced the American dream. Like immigrant groups before them, Hispanics are striving to "make it" in America with a drive and ambition that seems especially prevalent in newcomers.

Even the poorest new arrivals from Mexico and elsewhere in Latin America aspire to the middle class. Since 1980, for example, the number of Latino middle-class households in Los Angeles has tripled, to 450,000. [21]

Indeed, more than half of all native-born Hispanic families in the United States own their own home, according to Gregory Rodriguez, a research fellow at Pepperdine University. Among foreign-born Latinos, the percentage of home ownership was lower — about one-third — but still impressive. Not surprisingly, the most common surname of new home buyers in Los Angeles County is Garcia. [22]

More broadly, recent data from the Center for the Study of Latino Health at the University of California, Los Angeles, show that Hispanics have a higher rate of male participation in the labor force than whites and blacks. At the same time, Latinos were the least likely group to use public assistance. [23]

Another important and positive indicator is the phenomenal growth in the number of Latino businesses. Nationwide, the number of Hispanic enterprises has nearly doubled in the last five years. In states like California and Texas, where Hispanics make up a sizable minority, Latino business

Latinos Lagged in High School Completion

Less than 60 percent of U.S. Latinos completed high school in 1995. Latinos' completion rate decreased about 6 percent from 1989-1995, while the rates for whites and African-Americans increased slightly.

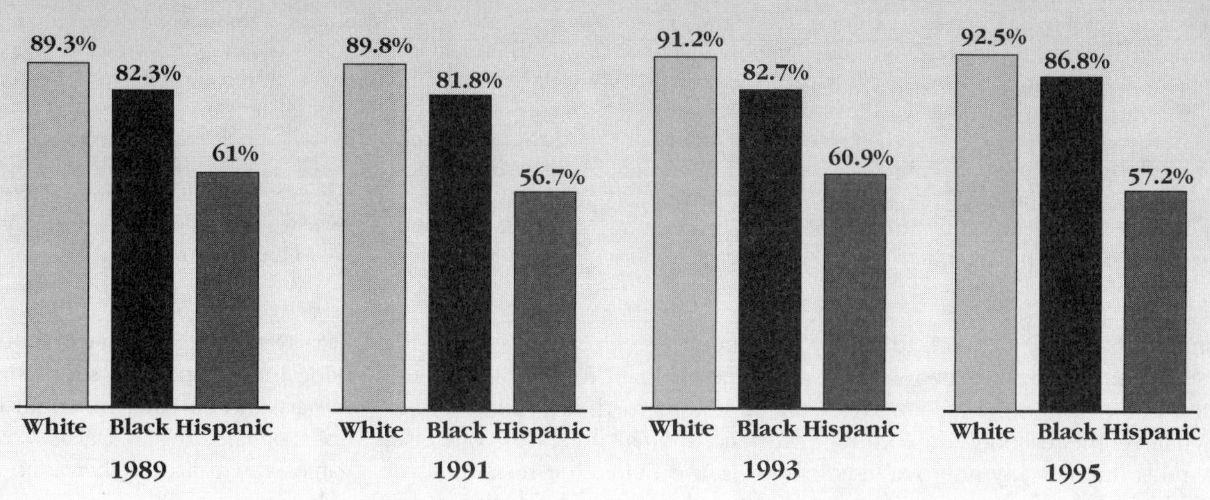

Sources: "Latino Education: Status and Prospects," National Council of La Raza, July 1998; National Center for Education Statistics, June 1996; "Educational Attainment in the United States," Census Bureau, March 1995.

start-ups are responsible for a substantial share of economic growth.

Latino buying power also is growing and becoming an increasingly important part of the national economy. Currently, Hispanics spend over $350 billion annually, up 65 percent since 1990. This number is increasing by about $2 billion per month.[24] As a result, more and more businesses are paying attention to Latinos and marketing products and services directly to the community through Spanish-language TV and other media. *(See story, p. 176.)*

Dropout Dilemma

In spite of their impressive economic gains, Latinos are lagging behind in the classroom. According to the Department of Education, the overall dropout rate for Latino children is 30 percent, four times higher than the 7.7 percent dropout rate for whites and nearly three times the 12.6 percent dropout rate of blacks.[25]

Moreover, in 1996 only 61 percent of Latino youth completed high school, compared with 92.6 percent for whites and 86 percent for blacks.[26] Even among Hispanic students who do receive a high school diploma, only 34.9 percent go on to college; by comparison, 43.7 percent of white high school graduates enroll in an institution of higher learning.[27]

Perhaps even more troubling than the current statistics themselves are recent trends.

"It's disheartening to see that while whites and blacks have made improvements in dropout rates, for Hispanics it has been getting worse," Suro says.

Many Latino observers believe these statistics bolster an unfair stereotype of Hispanics as largely unconcerned about learning. "There is belief in the broader culture that Latinos don't care about education, but that's not true," says La Raza's Navarette.

Much of the real problem, Navarette and others argue, lies with outside forces. In addition to the language barrier that many face, Latino children are often forced to make do with woefully underfunded and substandard schools. "There's a history of neglect when it comes to educating the Latino community," she says, adding that the "most schools are failing us."

Sanchez agrees. "Unfortunately, most education policies in this country have been geared to whites and, to a lesser extent, blacks," he says. "Meanwhile, Latinos have been left out in the cold."

Another problem is that many Latino young people may have to drop out of school, even if they are performing well. "Often, there is an

Bilingual Education: An Old Debate

The controversy surrounding bilingual education is as old as the Republic. Throughout American history, pockets of students in different parts of the country have received instruction in tongues other than English. Beginning in the 18th century, children were taught in a variety of foreign languages, including German, French, Greek, Dutch and Swedish. Often these bilingual schools were located in isolated rural areas where members of a particular ethnic group had clustered together.

Then, as now, many English-speaking Americans opposed bilingualism as a threat to national cohesion. Benjamin Franklin, for one, complained bitterly that German immigrants threatened the culture of English-speaking America. More than a century later, President Theodore Roosevelt, pushed for schools around the country to adopt an English-only policy to ensure, as he put it, that we did not become a nation of "hyphenated Americans."

Moreover, the patriotic fervor that accompanied World War I led to a drive to remove foreign languages, especially German, from any classrooms that were still teaching them. Still, bilingual education was never as widespread as it is today. Most immigrant children arriving in the United States were taught in English.

Rapid urbanization in the 19th and 20th centuries guaranteed that a majority of newcomers would live with or near native-born people as well as immigrants from other lands. And English was often seen as the glue that would hold these new Americans together.

economic necessity to work to support the family, and so people are forced out of school," Sanchez says.

Whatever the reason, Latinos know they must dramatically improve their level of educational attainment if they hope to ultimately succeed in the United States. "In an economy that values education as much as ours does, it's troubling where we are now," Suro says.

And the problem won't just be for Latinos, Gutierrez says. "When you think about the number of Latino students today and the greater number there will be tomorrow and the percentage of workers who will be Latino, you realize that this isn't just a Latino problem, it's an American problem." ■

OUTLOOK

In or Out?

For the most part, observers are at least cautiously optimistic about Hispanics becoming an accepted and integral part of the American social fabric, as immigrant groups did before them.

Some say that Latinos will succeed, in part, due to their willingness to work harder than almost anyone else, be it in the fields, the restaurant, or the board room. "The Latino work ethic has helped and will continue to help us survive," Navarette says. Indeed, Latinos are showing an uncanny ability to move from low-skill, low-wage jobs to business ownership.

But while few observers question Latinos' willingness to work and their drive to succeed, some Americans do wonder whether this fast-growing community will fully integrate into the national society or remain apart.

Part of the answer to this question may already be found in the substantial rate of intermarriage between Latinos and other Americans. Currently, roughly one-third of all Hispanics marry non-Latinos, usually whites. By contrast, only 6 percent of African-Americans wed someone outside their race. [28]

Significantly, the intermarriage rate is higher now than it was a decade ago, indicating that in the future, a majority of Hispanics will marry non-Latinos. "The rate of intermarriage is a very important, very healthy thing because it shows that this idea that we'll be a separate community is not supported by the facts," says La Raza's Yzaguirre. "When you see us marrying [non-Hispanics], supporting the military and all other American institutions or cheering at Dallas Cowboys games, you realize that there is no danger of balkanization."

At the same time, Yzaguirre and others say, while Latinos are and will be as American as anyone else, they will be different than Irish, Italians or other Europeans who have come before. "We will keep more of our language and traditions than they did," he says.

Gutierrez of the Pacific Coast Center agrees, adding that the pressures for cultural retention will come not just from the Latinos themselves but from the broader society. "[Hispanics] will be coming of age a multicultural, multilinguistic America that is very different from the Anglo-dominated country of the past," he says. "We will be the model for the new American, one who is comfortable in more than one culture."

But others, while not disagreeing that Latinos will hang on to more of their native culture longer than previous groups of immigrants, argue that it will be impossible to keep as much as they want and at the same time be American. Rep. Becerra sees Latinos only retaining what is truly important to them, like their language or cuisine. "The tent is only so big, and so we'll have to leave

At Issue:

Is bilingual education losing support in the Hispanic community?

JORGE AMSELLE
Vice President for Education, Center for Equal Opportunity, Washington, D.C.

WRITTEN FOR THE CQ RESEARCHER, SEPTEMBER 1998.

yes

Support for bilingual education has long been a litmus test for the Hispanic left. For three decades politicians and ethnic activists have taken the concerns of Hispanic parents for granted and assumed their unwavering support for these bilingual programs. Any doubts raised about the effectiveness of bilingual education was repeatedly met with dismissive statements like: "They used to hit us for speaking Spanish in school," and "We just need to spend more money on these programs."

Initially, the Latino community embraced bilingual education, which promised to save Hispanic children from scholastic failure. This early support was largely based on the lack of alternatives. Even today, too many Hispanic parents face a choice between bilingual education or no help at all for children who lack English proficiency.

However, as bilingual education programs are increasingly exposed as the fraud they truly are, Latino support for them is decreasing rapidly. In 1998 nearly 40 percent of California Latinos voted to eliminate their bilingual programs, despite a multimillion-dollar advertising effort against the proposal. My organization conducted its own polling of Hispanic parents in 1996, and over 80 percent wanted their children taught in English, not Spanish.

There are several reasons why it has taken nearly three decades for Hispanic opposition to bilingual education to finally reach the national spotlight. The primary cause is that all of the national Hispanic advocacy organizations wholeheartedly support bilingual education as the only acceptable method of educating Hispanic children. Parents who approach these groups for help in fighting bilingual programs are rebuffed.

Also, for many Hispanic parents the only source of information about their children's education is their school's bilingual education teacher — often more interested in preserving his or her job than in providing accurate, non-biased information to parents. But these trends are changing as parents are looking elsewhere for help. Parents in New York City turned to the Catholic Church in their fight against bilingual programs while parents in Los Angeles were aided by a local Episcopal priest and community activist.

Latino communities are breaking away from the molds their traditional advocates have forced them into and forging their own grass-roots coalitions with religious and sometimes even conservative organizations. This is leaving groups like the Mexican American Legal Defense and Educational Fund and the National Council of La Raza increasingly on the fringes of the Hispanic community.

LAURA FERREIRO
Communications Associate, Mexican American Legal Defense and Educational Fund (MALDEF)

WRITTEN FOR THE CQ RESEARCHER, SEPTEMBER 1998.

no

The country focused its gaze on California last June, as voters decided on an initiative that proposed to replace bilingual education programs in the state with English immersion. The initiative received a tremendous amount of media coverage, but little was learned about what bilingual education offers to students.

Before the election, inaccurate polls showed that a majority of Latinos supported the initiative. But when Election Day came around, two out of three Latinos voted against it. Despite this fact, the passage of the initiative led to the misperception that the Latino community no longer supported bilingual education. Conservative groups jumped on this bandwagon and seized the opportunity to announce that Latino political leaders and advocates who supported bilingual education were self-serving and out of touch.

But those who work directly with parents and children in the Latino community have a different story to tell. They can tell you about Latino parents who appear before school boards, pleading with them not to end their bilingual education programs. They can tell you about high school students who reaped the benefits of bilingual education programs, speak and write both English and Spanish fluently and are worried that recent immigrant students will not receive the same benefits if bilingual education were to end. They can tell you about the flood of calls Latino civil rights organizations received after the election from concerned parents wanting to know how to keep their children in bilingual education programs. And educational experts, Latino and otherwise, will tell you that bilingual education, when implemented properly, is the most effective way of teaching limited-English-proficient students.

Although the media spotlight has recently been on California, there are many flourishing, successful bilingual education programs throughout the country. In Dade County, Fla., home of the nation's fourth-largest school district, parents showed overwhelming support for the school board's plan to increase bilingual teaching for all students earlier this year. Miami residents view the ability to speak more than one language as a great business asset. And the same holds true in many states throughout the country.

Latino parents realize the importance of learning English, but also of learning other core academic subjects during the English-learning process that is done best through bilingual education teaching methods. They want their children to receive a solid education and excel in both English and Spanish.

some stuff behind," he says.

Still others argue that the European model, in which Latinos would lose much of their original culture and take on more American traits, is the only way Hispanics will truly be accepted in the United States. "If we don't fully commit ourselves to assimilation, we'll be in trouble," Chavez says. She is "cautiously optimistic" that Latinos will follow the assimilationist path because they will recognize that it is in their best interest. "I think we are seeing the error of our ways, when we followed those who preached ethnic separatism," she says, referring to academic and Latino advocacy communities, which encourage cultural retention.

But *The Washington Post's* Suro believes that Latinos will forge a new ethnic path in the United States. "Latinos will not follow the straight line of assimilation that characterized the European experience," he says. "Neither will they hold onto the sense of permanent aggrievement that characterizes the black experience."

Still, Suro worries that a portion of America's Latinos may find themselves in the situation now faced by the black underclass. "We have 30 percent of our community living below the poverty line," he says. "If this kind of poverty persists, we will pay a terrible social price." ■

FOR MORE INFORMATION

Center for Equal Opportunity, 815 15th St. N.W., Suite 928, Washington, D.C. 20005; (202) 639-0827; www.ceousa.org. This research organization focuses on issues of race, ethnicity and assimilation and opposes bilingual education and affirmative action.

League of United Latin American Citizens, 1133 20th St. N.W. Suite 750, Washington, D.C. 20036; (202) 408-0064; www.lulac.org. The league works for political, economic and educational rights for Hispanics.

Mexican American Legal Defense Fund, 1518 K St. N.W. Suite 410, Washington, D.C. 20005; (202) 628-4074; www.maldef.org. The fund provides assistance to Mexican-Americans and other Latinos in areas ranging from voting rights to immigration and supports affirmative action and bilingual education.

National Council of La Raza, 1111 19th St. N.W. Suite 1000, Washington, D.C. 20036; (202) 785-1670; www.nclr.org. La Raza studies issues of interest to Latinos and offers technical assistance to Hispanic community organizations.

Notes

[1] Quoted in Beth Shuster and Dan Moran, "Even for a Loser, Future Holds Plenty of Possibilities," *The Los Angeles Times,* June 7, 2001.

[2] Quoted in Rene Sanchez, "In LA, an Old Guard Victory," *The Washington Post,* June 7, 2001.

[3] Martin Kasindorf, "Latinos Tap into Expanding Political Power," *USA Today,* March 19, 1998.

[4] D'Vera Cohn, Shifting Portrait of U.S. Hispanics," *The Washington Post,* May 10, 2001.

[5] Thomas Edsall, "Census a Clarion Call for Democrats, GOP," *The Washington Post,* July 8, 2001.

[6] Dan Balz, "Gingrich Pitches GOP to Latinos, Hoping to Heal Divisions," *The Washington Post,* July 2, 1998.

[7] Guy Gugliotta, "Democrats Hope to Translate Latino Distrust of GOP into Votes," *The Washington Post,* Jan. 5, 1998.

[8] Rosalie Pedalino Porter, "The Case Against Bilingual Education," *The Atlantic Monthly,* May 1998. For background, see Craig Donegan, "Debate Over Bilingualism," *The CQ Researcher,* Jan. 19, 1996, pp. 49-72.

[9] Betsy Streisand, "Is it Hasta la Vista for Bilingual Ed?" *U.S. News & World Report,* Nov. 24, 1997.

[10] *Ibid.*

[11] Quoted on National Public Radio's "Morning Edition," Jan. 5, 1998.

[12] Bill Plaschke, "Star Spangled Banter," *Los Angeles Times,* Feb. 17, 1998.

[13] Quoted in Grahame L. Jones, "This is Much Worse than Trash Talking," *Los Angeles Times,* Feb. 16, 1998.

[14] For background, see David Masci, "Castro's Next Move," *The CQ Researcher,* Dec. 12, 1997, pp. 1093-1116.

[15] For background, see Rodman D. Griffin, "Hispanic Americans," *The CQ Researcher,* Oct. 30, 1992, pp. 929-952.

[16] *Ibid.*

[17] Steven A. Holmes, "Hispanic Population Moves Closer to Surpassing That of Blacks," *The Washington Post,* Aug. 7, 1998.

[18] Barbara Vobejda, "Hispanic Youths Outnumber Blacks," *The Washington Post,* July 15, 1998. For background, see Kenneth Jost, "Rethinking School Integration," *The CQ Researcher,* Oct. 18, 1996, pp. 918-941, and Susan Phillips, "Racial Tensions in Schools," *The CQ Researcher,* Jan. 7, 1994, pp. 1-24.

[19] Figures cited in National Council of La Raza, *Latino Education: Status and Prospects* (1998), pp. 6-7.

[20] Quoted in "Immigrant Influx," *The NewsHour with Jim Lehrer,* Feb. 16, 1998.

[21] Figures cited in "The Keenest Recruits to the Dream," *The Economist,* April 25, 1998.

[22] Figures cited in "Enter the Garcias' Own Party," *op. cit.*

[23] "The Keenest Recruits to the Dream," *op. cit.*

[24] *Ibid.*

[25] National Council of La Raza, *op. cit.*, p. 48.

[26] *Ibid*, p. 49.

[27] *Ibid*, p. 73.

[28] "The Keenest recruits to the Dream," *op. cit.*

Bibliography

Selected Sources Used

Books

Jones-Correa, Michael, "Between Two Nations: The Political Predicament of Latinos in New York City, Cornell University Press (1998).
Jones-Correa, an associate professor of government at Harvard University, examines the political life of Latinos in the New York City area. He finds that political participation among these communities is low, in part because of fear that they will lose touch with their homelands if they become too involved in their new country's affairs.

Shorris, Earl, *Latinos: A Biography of the People*, W.W. Norton (1992).
Shorris takes an exhaustive look at the Latino community in the United States, from Mexican-Americans in Texas to Puerto Ricans in New York. Hispanics defy categorization, he argues, because they are not really one community, but many.

Suro, Roberto, *Strangers Among Us: How Latino Immigration is Transforming America*, Knopf (1998).
Suro, a staff writer at *The Washington Post*, argues that it is misguided to compare Latino immigration with the waves of largely European newcomers who arrived in the United States in the past. Hispanics, Suro says, come from nearby and no longer have the economic opportunities in agriculture and, especially, manufacturing enjoyed by their immigrant predecessors.

Articles

Bronner, Ethan, "Bilingual Education is Facing Push Toward Abandonment," *The New York Times*, May 30, 1998.
Bronner chronicles the shift in attitude concerning bilingual education. No longer hailed as a "humane and sound" way to teach immigrant children, bilingual learning is increasingly being rejected by recent arrivals as well as native-born citizens.

Chavez, Linda, "Our Hispanic Predicament: Lack of U.S. Assimilation Despite Economic Progress," *Commentary*, June 1998.
Chavez, president of the Center for Equal Opportunity, argues that the United States will become a balkanized country if it continues to encourage Hispanics to retain their culture and language.

Donegan, Craig, "Debate Over Bilingualism," *The CQ Researcher*, Jan. 19, 1996.
A slightly dated but thorough examination of the various arguments for and against bilingualism in the United States.

"Enter the Garcias' Own Party," *The Economist*, Aug. 15, 1998.
The article argues that Latinos and the GOP have more in common (like family values) than past election results would suggest. It argues that Republicans who work for the Latino vote should be able to reap substantial benefits come Election Day.

Gugliotta, Guy, "Democrats Hope to Translate Latino Distrust of GOP into Votes," *The Washington Post*, Jan. 5, 1998.
Gugliotta details Democratic plans to solidify their already strong support within the Latino community.

Kasindorf, Martin, "Latinos Tap into Expanding Political Power," *USA Today*, March 19, 1998.
The article gives a good overview of growing Latino electoral power and argues that the community's political strength is finally beginning to match its demographic size.

"The Keenest Recruits to the Dream," *The Economist*, April 25, 1998.
This piece examines the economic, political and cultural status of Latinos and concludes that this rapidly growing minority has tremendous potential to succeed on all levels in the United States.

Porter, Rosalie Pedalino, "The Case Against Bilingual Education," *The Atlantic Monthly*, May 1998.
Porter, director of the Institute for Research in English Acquisition and Development, makes a strong case against the continuation of bilingual learning, arguing that teaching children in Spanish retards their educational development and segregates them from the rest of the school.

Streisand, Betsy, "Is it Hasta la Vista for Bilingual Ed?" *U.S. News & World Report*, Nov. 24, 1997.
Streisand gives a good overview of the debate over bilingual education that preceded the vote on Proposition 227 in California this year.

Reports and Studies

Fisher, Maria, Sonia M. Perez, Bryant Gonzalez and Jonathan Njus, *Latino Education: Status and Prospects*, The National Council of La Raza, July 1998.
This report, issued by the nation's premier Latino-advocacy group, examines all aspects of Hispanic educational achievement. The results are not encouraging. Latino children have lower test scores and higher dropout rates than their black and white peers.

11 The New Immigrants

CHARLES S. CLARK

The bustling mall, with a tire store at one end and a variety store at the other, seems typical of shopping centers in affluent American suburbs — save one key detail: Almost all the shops and restaurants display neon signs in Vietnamese. Restaurants advertise *pho*, a traditional Asian noodle soup; travel agents specialize in trans-Pacific flights and currency transfers; nightclubs blare the latest pop hits in Saigon; and posters in video stores promote sexy Asian film stars.

Welcome to Eden Center in Falls Church, Va., just outside Washington. The site that just a decade ago housed a quintessentially American retail arcade — complete with a paint store, greeting card shop and ice cream parlor — is now said to be the largest Vietnamese shopping center in the United States.

"I'd like to take credit, but it really just happened by itself," says owner Norman Ebenstein, of Boca Raton, Fla. "It just grew bigger, the place became a meeting center, so we sort of fell into the plan."

Today, 70 percent of the customers at the 250,000-square-foot shopping center are Asian, Ebenstein says. He credits his success to his tenants, and their "homogeneous, hard-working, family-oriented society."

Ebenstein "gets a kick" out of his involvement in Vietnamese small business. He flies the South Vietnamese and American flags in the parking lot. He and the merchants are erecting Oriental archways at the center's entrance, and they built a replica of a landmark clock tower in Saigon. Ebenstein also contributes to Vietnamese charities, organizes checkers tournaments for Asian senior citizens and joins in celebrations of Vietnam's Armed Forces Day.

Eden Center reflects the dramatic impact of immigrants in modern America, an impact that affects both the new arrivals and long-time residents. In the 1990s, Americans who grew up in a historically white, Anglo-Saxon society are having to adjust to a Polish-born chairman of the Joint Chiefs of Staff, John Shalikashvili; to Spanish-language editions of *People* magazine on Seven-11 shelves; and to Buddhist temples and Islamic mosques rising in their communities. [1]

From *The CQ Researcher*, January 24, 1997.

Thomas J. Colin

Today's America contains nearly 23 million foreign-born residents, or about 8.4 percent of the population, and about 32 million residents whose primary language is not English. Los Angeles, the Census Bureau says, is now about 40 percent foreign-born, while 88 percent of its Monterey Park neighborhood is Asian and Hispanic.

The impact of immigration is not spread evenly across the country, notes George Vernez, director of the Center for Research on Immigration Policy at the RAND Corp. For example, most Cubans stream to Miami; people from the Caribbean and Central America flock to New York City; and Asians make Seattle a prime destination. California is home to fully 45 percent of the nation's Mexican immigrants, which strains California schools because Mexicans tend to have lower education levels than other immigrants.

Though earlier historical periods have seen as much or more immigration, many of today's immigrants differ from their 19th- and early 20th-century counterparts. The classic stories of American immigrants have focused on the "tired and poor," but many modern immigrants are well-educated and even wealthy — witness the 12,000 Chinese technicians working in Silicon Valley computer firms or the well-heeled Iranian expatriots so visible in Beverly Hills.

Over the past three decades, Asians, Latinos and Caribbean immigrants have outpaced the numbers of Irish, Italian and Eastern European immigrants so familiar at the turn of the century, sometimes prickling racial tensions among native-born Americans. And Hispanics and Asians, in particular, have become politically more influential, as evidenced by the important political races in 1996 that turned on the Latino vote (*see p. 202*) and by the current concern over Asian involvement in President Clinton's campaign financing. (*See story, p. 192*)

"Political loyalty has dropped in weight due to globalization, the end of the Cold War and the rise of the United Nations," says Harvard University sociologist Nathan Glazer, author of the forthcoming book *We Are All Multiculturalists Now*. "The world of today's immigrants has two main differences from the immigrants' world of the 1920s. One is the rise of the welfare state that offered a safety net for immigrants, having replaced the [modest] private welfare efforts of the 1920s that prompted many immigrants to give up and return home. Secondly, the whole thrust toward Americanization in language and culture that used to be common in this country has weakened."

Saigon in the Suburbs

Flying the U.S. and South Vietnamese flags, sprawling Eden Center in suburban Falls Church, Va., boasts dozens of shops and restaurants catering to Vietnamese-Americans.

Thomas J. Colin

Thomas J. Colin

Perhaps because of their daily encounters in the new "melting pot," many Americans have grown weary of high immigration, viewing it as a drain on jobs and government social spending. Indeed, an NBC News/*Wall Street Journal* survey of 2,000 Americans in December found that 72 percent want the number of immigrants reduced, a huge increase from the 33 percent who wanted reductions in 1965. For several years now, states and the federal government have been planning cutbacks in welfare, health and education benefits for immigrants both legal and illegal. [2]

The new immigrants have not stood by idly. Taking advantage of newly streamlined procedures at the Immigration and Naturalization Service (INS), thousands who have been in the country the required five years have been applying for citizenship. "Since welfare reform," says Vilay Chaleunrath, executive director of the Indochinese Community Center in Washington, D.C., "there's been a surge of applications, especially among the elderly, who used to think they would one day go back and die in the old country."

In 1996, an estimated 1.1 million people took the citizenship oath, up from an average of only 200,000 in the early 1990s. The increase in part reflects newly eligible illegal aliens who won amnesty following the 1986 Immigration Reform and Control Act. The INS predicts 1.7 million applications in fiscal 1997.

"Naturalization builds bridges between new immigrant groups and the existing society, much as labor unions, political parties and public schools have done in the past," says INS Commissioner Doris Meissner. [3] That's one reason that Hungarian-born billionaire George Soros last September set up his $50 million Emma Lazarus Fund to help immigrants become citizens.

The rush to citizenship, however, is not welcomed by all. In her recent book, *Americans No More: The Death of Citizenship,* journalist Georgie Anne Geyer blasts immigrants and government policies that encourage immigrants to view citizenship as an opportunity for economic benefits rather than civic responsibility.

Indeed, she says, immigrants take naturalization about as seriously as "joining a health club." And, she told a Senate panel, Americans seem reluctant to assert their national identity. If not countered, she warns, the trend "will destroy America as we have known it and substitute a very different country, one that is spiritually incoherent, humanly conflict-ridden and economically hobbled." [4]

John Fonte, a visiting scholar at the American Enterprise Institute, denounces immigrant demands for ethnic-group rights, such as multicultural education and bilingual ballots. "Today we face a crisis of citizenship," he told the Senate panel. "Our goal should be Americanization, stated clearly without apology and without embarrassment. . . . Americanization does not mean giving up our ethnic traditions, customs, cuisine or birth languages. It means patriotic assimilation." [5]

Finally, a perception that immigrants tend to vote Democratic has led some

Republicans in Congress to charge that the Clinton administration's INS was partisan and even corrupt in its efforts to streamline the naturalization process so that new citizens could vote in the last elections *(see p. 200)*.

Immigration supporters — including many who belong to the Republican Party, which is split over immigration — argue that new immigrants traditionally have been among the most patriotic Americans and that all they want is help in making the transition. Some accuse immigration "restrictionists" of veiled racism and xenophobia, of scapegoating immigrants for many social ills.

John Kromkowski, president of the National Center for Urban Ethnic Affairs, challenges the notion of a fixed and superior American identity. "America itself is a history of changes, of developments, not of static categories," he says. "The nativists are out of touch with the real situation and the process. And their whole anti-immigrant hysteria has recently done what the League of Women Voters never could do: produce record voter registration and citizenship."

Today, says a 1993 Ford Foundation study, "America's story is no longer one simply of 'coming to America.' It is also an account of the places where immigrants settle and how those already there change." [6]

As policy-makers and everyday citizens consider the nation's immigration policies, these are some of the questions being asked:

Are immigrants doing enough to fit into American life?

"There is a central American culture that goes beyond our legal institutions," writes former State Department official Francis Fukuyama. "America was founded with liberal political institutions, but it is the sectarian nature of American Protestantism that set the cultural tone." [7]

How newcomers fare at picking up on this "cultural tone" is the focus of much anxiety among Americans who look askance at the immigration influx from places such as Latin America and the Caribbean. "Successful" societies value education, says Massachusetts Institute of Technology international studies Professor Lawrence Harrison, citing Western Europe, North America, East Asia and Australia as examples. In Latin America, by contrast, "the tradition has been a focus not on the future, not on progress, but on the present, or on the past. Work has been seen as a necessary evil, importantly informed by the slavery experience. Education is something which has been made available principally to the elite. . . . Merit plays a relatively unimportant role in how people get ahead. Connections — family — are much more important. . . . The idea of fair play is not well-developed." [8]

Immigrants from such societies, the argument goes, inevitably produce the kind of tensions that arose, for example, in Mount Kisco, N.Y., recently, when citizens complained that Latino day laborers who gather every morning in parking lots were too often publicly intoxicated. "We want our town back," longtime residents wrote to the local paper. [9]

Complaints are not limited to whites. "A for-sale sign in our neighborhood causes panic," writes an African-American of the arrival of Hispanic immigrants in South-Central Los Angeles. "We know who will get that house. There will be 20 to 30 people living in it, they will keep goats, they will grow corn in their front yard, they will hang their wash on the front fence." [10]

Critics such as Geyer cite examples of immigrant crime, singling out the Middle Eastern terrorists convicted of the 1993 World Trade Center bombing, or Ethiopians who seek to import the practice of female genital mutilation. *Forbes* magazine writer Peter Brimelow, himself a U.S.-naturalized Briton, warns of the day when America is no longer majority white. "This unprecedented demographic mutation," he writes of current immigration levels, is creating an America in which people are "alien to each other." [11]

What has disappeared, says Daniel A. Stein, executive director of the Federation for American Immigration Reform (FAIR), "is the old immigrants' idea that you would never go home, that you were so proud to learn English that you would be insulted if someone spoke your old language. Immigrants are no longer grateful to be here."

It is the high level of immigration itself that prevents many immigrants from assimilating, adds Yeh Ling-Ling, founder of the Diversity Coalition for an Immigration Moratorium, in San Francisco. "In schools in places like Monterey [Calif.], many immigrants are surrounded only by other immigrants while they receive bilingual education and multiculturalism. I get calls from immigrants saying they're angry at the ethnic activists who tell them, 'You'll never be an American. Your yellow skin will never turn white.' "

According to an Urban Institute report, the number of immigrants who told 1990 census takers that they "don't speak English well" totaled about half the population of Miami, a fifth of New York and a third of Los Angeles. [12]

Polls, however, show that immigrants do not see themselves so ghettoized. Fifty-eight percent of immigrants who have been in the U.S. less than 10 years report that they spend time with "few or none of their fellow countrymen," according to a May-June 1995 *USA Today*/CNN/Gallup survey. An identical 58 percent felt it is important to blend into American culture, compared with only 27 percent who said it was important to maintain their own culture. (Surprisingly, a higher portion of native-born Americans — 32 percent — said the immigrants should maintain their own culture.)

Studies show that many of the most visible immigrant enclaves are con-

Naturalizations on the Rise

During the 1990s, the number of immigrants who became naturalized American citizens skyrocketed. Several factors caused the rise, including efforts to deny public assistance to non-citizens and the large group of illegal immigrants who became eligible for citizenship through the 1986 amnesty law.

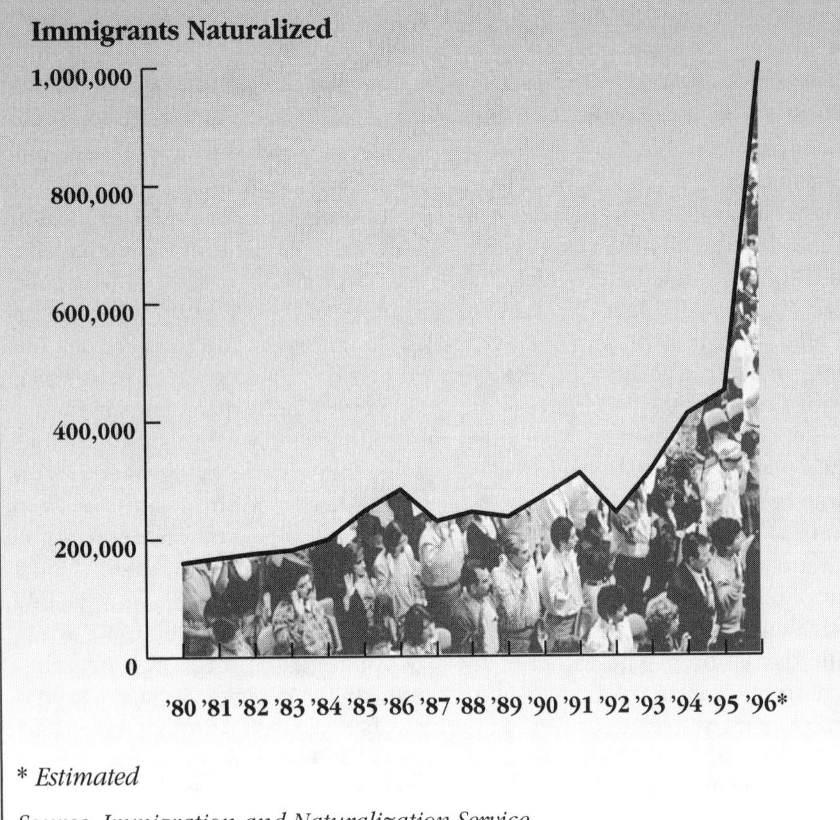

* *Estimated*

Source: Immigration and Naturalization Service

stantly turning over, with new arrivals replacing veterans who acquire education and skills that permit them a better job and housing. The 1995 annual housing survey by the Federal National Mortgage Association (Fannie Mae) found that 55 percent of immigrants who are renters are more likely to see themselves as foreigners temporarily living in America; among immigrants who own a home, the percentage with that feeling drops to 41. The Commerce Department, meanwhile, recently reported that the number of Hispanic-owned businesses jumped 76 percent from 1987 to '92. [13]

"Walk into any Latino neighborhood and you see all the American icons, from Dallas Cowboys posters to the New York Yankees to rock and roll," says Raul Yzaguirre, president of the National Council of La Raza, the nation's largest Latino civil rights group. "Hispanics are learning English faster than previously, and there are 50,000 waiting for night classes in Los Angeles alone. Latinos are hard-working and patriotic, and in the armed forces they win more medals proportionately than their numbers."

Rather than generalizing about a whole continent and culture, Yzaguirre adds, critics should understand that persistent Hispanic poverty has to do with job discrimination, which he says has been documented time and again in controlled studies.

Other immigrants' spokesmen stress the importance to transplants of maintaining their self-esteem by staying in touch with their cultural roots, even if that means disguising it. "Concealing one's real emotional feelings was particularly useful while dealing with the white majority," wrote a Japanese immigrant woman in 1981. "To show a 'good face' as a representative of the Japanese in general insured greater acceptance by the majority society." [14]

Critics of new immigrants, says Frank Sharry, executive director of the National Immigration Forum, a lobbying and research group, "overlook that there's a tremendous desire to belong, to participate, to embrace America, to love it and wrestle with it while maintaining one's own sense of identity. This is a good thing. Citizenship is a classic example of how dynamic and vibrant American democracy is. But in the public mind, it is largely the Latino population that seems not to have embraced America the way average Joes want them to."

But Linda Chavez, president of the Center for Equal Opportunity and a critic of ethnic lobbies that cry racism, says "the first generation that is born here is the dividing line. If they fully take part in American life, then all is fine, and it is not impossible for the country to absorb large numbers of immigrants. Unless you're too old, you must learn English to take part. The foreign-language newspapers that many immigrants read are too concentrated on news from the old country."

Speaking foreign languages creates barriers, she adds, which produce frustration among Americans that leads to the anti-immigrant backlash and the debate over English as the official language.

The language debate, though often discussed in the context of government administration and official documents, has an emotional undercurrent relating to political domination.[15] Recently retired Rep. Toby Roth, R-Wis., one of the leaders of the official-English legislation movement in Congress, told a press conference in December that new Americans were some of his biggest supporters because they see learning English as the key to economic opportunity. "One tells me that Spanish is the language of bellhops and busboys, while English is the language of doctors and lawyers," he says.

Yzaguirre finds such views "suggestive of the offensive, ugly-American attitude that has gotten us in trouble all over the world. We've got to stop having America be the world's most linguistically ignorant country."

Dennis Gallagher, executive director of the Refugee Policy Group, acknowledges that there are limits to how much new immigrants should assert their native cultures. "My [Indian-born] wife is appalled by the garish show some Hindu groups make in building temples in prominent places in the United States, some of which would be extreme even in their own countries," he says. But, Gallagher adds, having a group of 100,000 Iranians, some of whom succeed or fail only within boundaries of that community, is not a threat to our overall society. They won't get us to learn Farsi. They're a part of America now.

"Immigrants bring different attitudes and values and perceptions of who the good and bad guys are in international affairs," he adds. "That's both the benefit and cost of diversity. We're getting more frightened of that. We shouldn't be, because in the longer term, it makes us stronger."

Immigration and Naturalization Service/Rick Kenney

Attorney General Janet Reno administers the oath of citizenship to 3,000 new citizens at a 1995 ceremony at the U.S. Air Arena in Maryland, near Washington, D.C.

Should immigrants be permitted to hold dual citizenship?

"American citizenship is more precious than any other status a man or woman can have," recently retired Sen. Alan K. Simpson, R-Wyo., told the Senate Judiciary hearing in October. "Not only does it guarantee membership in the society that offers the most political and civil liberty of any nation . . . and the opportunity to participate in choosing the government and therefore in crafting the laws that will help shape its future — in addition, it provides the immense emotional satisfaction of being part of a nation with a very special and wonderful history."[16]

Given the allure of U.S. citizenship, Simpson and others question an increasingly common practice among immigrants: dual citizenship. Commonplace among Britons who emigrate to the United States and American Jews who move to Israel, dual citizenship in recent years has become popular among Central American and Asian immigrants as well, in part due to advances in worldwide mass communication. In New York City, seven of the 10 largest immigrant groups come from countries that permit it, said Linda Basch, author of a 1985 book on transnationalism. "Many people live an existence that's transnational," she wrote. "They have families in both places. They invest in both places. They get involved in politics in both places."[17]

By law, the United States does not recognize dual citizenship, says an INS spokesman, though the Supreme Court has ruled that a foreigner need not renounce foreign citizenship to apply for U.S. citizenship. When a qualified immigrant takes the oath of U.S. citizenship, the State Department notifies the government of his native country, and it is up to that government to determine whether to revoke citizenship.

Critics question the loyalty of dual citizens, warning of wartime defections and the risk of the proverbial "fifth column" of espionage agents. They point to dual citizens who have become pawns in international aggression, as in the late-1930s, when Adolf Hitler cited the presence of German nationals in Czechoslovakia as a pretext for launching an invasion.

"Dual nationality with Britons or Israelis at least involves a shared cultural legacy," says Stein of FAIR. "But now, with immigration from neighboring countries such as Mexico and Latin America, it involves huge income differentials and claims to ancestral territory" within the United States.

Efforts to discourage dual citizenship have put new pressure on immigrants who have been willing to forgo such privileges as government employment opportunities and security clearances in order to maintain links with their

Clinton Troubles Over Campaign Finance . . .

Foreign money. Immigrants' money. Money from citizens with foreign-sounding names. Such distinctions have been blurred by the current controversy over foreign money contributed to U.S. political campaigns. Among many of America's immigrants, the issue has brought a discomfiting feeling that they are regarded with new suspicion.

"In the last few weeks," President Clinton told a post-election press conference on Nov. 8, "a lot of Asian-Americans who have supported our campaign have come up to me and said, 'You know, I'm being made to feel like a criminal.' " Their reports of harassing calls from reporters and "disparaging comments" about people with Asian last names prompted Clinton to "remind" the public that "our country has been greatly enriched by the work of Asian-Americans. They are famous for working hard for family values and for giving more than they take."

Reuters

Democratic fund-raiser John Huang

Since then, however, the press, Clinton's Republican opponents and his own fund-raising officials have documented a growing array of apparent violations of U.S. campaign finance law and custom, most involving Asian-Americans, Indonesians, Thais and Chinese.

The scandal broke during the final weeks of the election with news reports that a Democratic fund-raiser named John Huang, an Indonesian-American, had raised what eventually was estimated at $3.4 million from Asian-Americans, some $1.2 million of which had to be returned because the true donors were apparently foreigners. Huang's previous employment as a mid-level Commerce Department official and with the Lippo Group, an Indonesian financial conglomerate, provoked suspicion that his fund-raising and dozens of visits to the White House might constitute illegal lobbying on behalf of Indonesian interests.

The story expanded with reports that $140,000 had been raised during a Democratic fund-raiser held last April at a Los Angeles-area Buddhist temple attended by religious devotees of modest means. Many of the donations had to be returned when it was ascertained that they were actually from non-citizens. [1]

Then came reports that a Chinese-American entrepreneur from Torrance, Calif., Johnny Chung, had given $366,000 to the Democratic Party and had made 49 visits to the White House over two years, sometimes bringing Chinese business leaders with him. [2]

Next, there were problems at the legal defense fund set up to raise money for President Clinton's defense against the sexual harassment case filed by Paula Corbin Jones. Fund officials revealed that they were returning some $400,000 raised by Little Rock, Ark., restaurateur Charles Yah Lin Trie, a friend of Clinton, because the money had come from non-citizens, mainly followers of a Buddhist sect leader. Trie was later shown to have made numerous visits to the White House, including one in which he escorted a Communist Chinese arms dealer to meet with Clinton, apparently without the president's knowledge. [3]

Soon after, it was revealed that Pauline Kanchanalak, a legal, non-citizen U.S. resident originally from Thailand, had brought five business associates to a White House coffee to meet the president after having given some $253,000 to the Clinton campaign. The money was later returned when it came out that it belonged to her mother. [4]

Though the Clinton campaign was able to delay the most embarrassing disclosures until after the election (in part by using a public relations strategy that dismissed the charges as racism and Asian-bashing), the damage is still being determined. Besides an internal review by the Democratic National Committee (after which it made a confession of laxness), a probe is under way by the Justice Department (including the FBI). And in February, the Senate Government Affairs Committee is set to open hearings on fund-raising abuses of the 1996 campaign, just as Congress as a whole is under pressure to take up campaign finance reform. [5]

The impact of the disclosures on Asian-Americans, meanwhile, has already been dramatic. "The image of Asian-Americans has been tarnished by a perception that they are foreigners and are illegally participating in campaign finance," says Stewart Kwoh, executive director of the Asian Pacific American Legal Center of Southern California, an immigrant-advocacy group. "The media coverage has been one-sided. Only 10 or 12 contributions have had to be returned out of thousands given legally by Asian-Americans.

"I'm not saying the alleged improprieties are not serious, or that they don't need investigating," Kwoh continues. "But the press has not been reporting the other ways in which Asians participate politically, such as our voter registration drive," he adds. "The public has not tuned into the fact that Congress [in the early 1970s] permitted campaign donations from permanent residents and from

native land. "My wife is not quite comfortable giving up her ties [to India] because of tax advantages and the loss to her identity," Gallagher says. "Even some of our non-xenophobic but well-traveled friends tell her that after 25 years, what's so bad about having to make up your mind? And she could probably get her Indian citizenship back

. . . Put Spotlight and Suspicions on Asian-Americans

foreign subsidiaries that earn money here. Overall, Asian companies gave less than European and Canadian subsidiaries, but reporters didn't care. They knew that the scandal about 'the yellow peril' would attract more readers."

The suggestion that the scandal was fueled by an age-old fear of inscrutable Asians was picked up by columnist Russell Baker, who ridiculed "Fu Manchu's latest incarnation" in an age of globalized trade. [6]

But many observers see genuine cultural differences that have contributed to the problem. "This idea of racism is ludicrous," says Daniel A. Stein, executive director of the Federation for American Immigration Reform (FAIR). "These are orchestrated transactions by people outside the country. The way things are done in Japan and China is antithetical to the tradition of openness in the United States. Clinton needs to reread George Washington's farewell address, where it says be vigilant about pernicious foreign influences."

Similarly, efforts by Clinton and other Democrats to paint the issue in racial terms strike many as a diversion. "Clinton will do anything to deflect discussion from what is really an old-fashioned corruption scandal that people can understand," says Linda Chavez, president of the Center for Equal Opportunity.

Chavez acknowledges, however, that many Asian cultures view the giving of gifts to high officials as a sign of respect. "A lot of the Asians are probably mystified at what they have done wrong," she says, "and this is the kind of thing that immigrants learn during the assimilation process. But Clinton himself knows the rules of the game. If he really wants to be sensitive to Asians, he should make sure they know them, too."

Kwoh, however, says that what traditions of gift-giving exist in Asian cultures are hardly different from American campaign finance laws, which permit unlimited donations of soft, or unregulated, money and allow millionaires to fund their own rise to power. "I personally believe in campaign finance reform across the board, but it shouldn't come from scapegoating Asians," he says, citing a remark made by former independent presidential candidate Ross Perot. In a jab at Clinton fund-raiser Huang, the Texas billionaire asked an audience, "Wouldn't you like to have someone named O'Reilly out there?" [7]

"Asians are not going to change their last names," Kwoh promises.

Francey Lim Youngberg, executive director of the Congressional Asian Pacific American Caucus Institute, worries that the press' focus on the Asian money connection will "be to the detriment of the Asian-American community because it comes at a time when we are coming of age politically, with more Asian candidates running for office than ever before. I am scared it will have a chilling effect on participation because it has now evolved into a witch hunt for anyone who is connected to someone who's mentioned in one of the media's stories."

The Clinton administration, meanwhile, argues that no one has found evidence that any Asian or Asian-American donor won a quid pro quo in terms of policy changes. At his press conference, Clinton pointed out that many Asian-Americans vote Republican, and that Republicans have their own campaign-finance and foreign-money issues to confront. (Indeed, last month, Rep. Jay C. Kim, R-Calif., who is the first Korean-American in Congress, saw his campaign treasurer indicted following a four-year FBI investigation into fraud involving money allegedly funneled from five South Korean companies. [8])

In January, the DNC announced it would no longer take money from resident non-citizens and U.S. subsidiaries of foreign companies.

As for press coverage of Asians, several newspapers, as preparations were under way for Clinton's second inauguration, have been reporting on Asians both here and abroad who have been jockeying for inaugural tickets. They see it as a chance to get their photo taken with Clinton, a proven reputation enhancer for doing business in Asia. [9]

Tom McCarthy, deputy bureau chief of the *Los Angeles Times* in Washington, who has managed the paper's campaign finance stories, disagrees with the charge that Asian-American donors have been unfairly singled out by reporters. "It is apparent why we have written about the donors we have," he says. "As a normal part of the process, we methodically scrub all campaign finance reports. We see some perennial names and some new ones. Not a lot of people give sums as high as $250,000, so we don't have a lot of discretion as to who we contact. What you do in journalism is follow the money."

---

[1] *The Washington Post*, Dec. 6, 1996.

[2] *Los Angeles Times*, Nov. 28, 1996.

[3] *The New York Times*, Dec. 19, 1996.

[4] *The Washington Post*, Dec. 27, 1996.

[5] See "Campaign Finance Reform," *The CQ Researcher*, Feb. 9, 1996, pp. 121-144.

[6] Russell Baker, "Yellow Peril's Return," *The New York Times*, Dec. 7, 1996.

[7] *Philadelphia Inquirer*, Oct. 30, 1996.

[8] *Los Angeles Times* [Washington edition], Dec. 4, 1996.

[9] See *The Wall Street Journal*, Dec. 27, 1996.

later if it were withdrawn when she became an American."

"But it's not a trivial thing, psychologically," he adds. "She told me when we married that she had to give up a lot when she moved here, and now has to give up that last remaining link to home. Americans don't seem to understand. Their nationalism is so strong, they don't seem to respect it in other countries."

The legal arguments against dual citizenship, says Douglas Klusmeyer, editor of the *Stanford Humanities Review,* "more often than not are red herrings. The modern trend in international law and in state practice has been to acknowledge that in today's mobile world, the phenomenon of dual citizenship is simply going to increase." Moreover, says Klusmeyer, who testified before the Senate panel, banning it in the United States will simply perpetuate a fiction, because "if their countries of origin are willing to issue new passports, there's no way you can stop it."

The country whose dual citizenship policy raises the most concern is Mexico. In December its Parliament voted to allow dual citizenship so that Mexicans who naturalize in the United States could still go back to Mexico to own property and get a Mexican passport, but not to vote. This move was alarming to some Americans, particularly those in Southern California who worked on the 1994 measure passed by California to halt public benefits to immigrants (since blocked by courts). The fear is that dual citizenship openly encourages Mexicans to move to the U.S. and try to influence U.S. policy toward Mexico. Latino college students and the occasional state legislator often talk of banning English in parts of the United States gained from Mexico under the 1848 Treaty of Guadalupe Hidalgo.

"This is not immigration, this is colonization," Stein says. "If at some point down the line Mexico were to decide to run its [boundary] across parts of the southern United States, which side of the conflict would these dual nationals fall on? The Mexican mythology that the Americans stole their land," Stein adds, "means that a time could come when Southern California will say we need a regional Hispanic council and then become as fragmented and confused as the Weimar Republic" was in Germany.

The large number of Mexican immigrants in the Southwest gives new credence to the theory of Mexican irredentism known as the "reconquista," agrees historian David M. Kennedy. "There is no precedent in American history for these possibilities. No previous immigrant group had the size and concentration and easy access to its original culture that the Mexican immigrant group in the Southwest has today."[18]

Such theories are "crazy," says La Raza's Yzaguirre. "Even if there were too many Mexican-Americans in the Southwest, I know of no serious movement that talks about seceding. Being American is one of the most prized attributes — there has never been a Mexican-American turncoat in U.S. history."

Are Americans doing enough to ease the transition of new immigrants?

In New York City, 90 percent of the 45,000 cab drivers are foreign-born. So last year, when the city's Taxi and Limousine Commission was looking to boost the industry, it decided to provide new business opportunities for immigrants. For the first time since 1937, it increased the number of licensed cabs, adding 400 "medallions" to the 12,000 coveted plaques already in use.

"Many drivers in the past put their kids through college by owning a medallion," says Allan Fromberg, the taxi authority's assistant commissioner for public affairs. "But today it means more because it also means freedom, whether from religious persecution or an absence of economic opportunity. We're proud to have a part in it."

In the hotel industry, Marriott International Inc. has been leading a trend toward stabilizing corporate work forces by offering day care and social service referrals to the Bosnian, Chinese and Mexican immigrants who staff its cleaning and kitchen crews.[19]

The federal government aids immigrants with money provided by the 1982 Job Training Partnership Act and by State Legalization Impact Assistance Grants, as well $262 million annually for bilingual education programs for Asian and Hispanic students.

On the religious front, the Council of Jewish Organizations in Brooklyn recently launched its Business Outreach Center to help ethnic small businesses. And the Catholic Legal Immigration Network (CLINIC) has long provided legal aid, mentoring and training to indigent immigrants. "In many ways, the human condition is that of an immigrant," says John Swenson, executive director of migration and refugee services for the U.S. Catholic Conference. "Yes, some national limits on immigration are reasonable, but Catholic social policy emphasizes what is necessary for the preservation of individual dignity, even for illegal immigrants."

Public schools have an interest in being effective for immigrants, says Michael A. Resnick, senior associate executive director of the National School Boards Association. "Immigrants are an investment because the chances are they will be here the rest of their lives. Many of them come from countries with higher poverty rates and are illiterate even in their native language. And they require help not just with language transition problems but also with the larger cultural context. Some children from Mexico, for example, sometimes stay home for several weeks during the Christmas season because they're not used to having just a week off."

According to the 1995 Fannie Mae survey, 35 percent of immigrants say that native-born Americans are warm and welcoming, while 14 percent say they are cold and negative.

And just as there are extremes of antisocial immigrants, there are examples of home-grown misbehavior. South Asian newcomers settling on Staten Island, N.Y., for example, were recently greeted with graffiti reading "Indians go home. Leave or Die."[20] And in Houston, a Vietnamese immigrant was beaten to death by skinheads.

To accuse average Americans of xenophobia, however, is unfair, says Yeh of the diversity coalition. "In Minnesota or Iowa, where immigration numbers are low, Americans will help newcomers, even if they don't speak English," she says. "But in a high-impact state like California or New York City, most people think immigration has made life worse. You don't have an obligation to adopt your neighbor's children. It's a burden. And if there are high numbers, it doesn't matter what color the people are. People in Oregon, Idaho and Montana are getting up in arms about the high numbers of white Californians coming to their states."

Immigration restriction advocates also argue that offering generous social services merely makes the United States a magnet for immigrants who are either illegal or too numerous. FAIR's Stein believes that America does not have to have a diverse society if it doesn't want to. "If we as a nation choose to believe it's better, more productive of human happiness not to be, then it's our own business.

"Most Americans don't see why we have immigration," he says. "They're told by *The Wall Street Journal* that it's a free lunch, but then they're told that immigrants are getting on welfare. How far can we stretch it without social turmoil? We could admit Moslems or Buddhists at rates that would overwhelm us, but why? Would it be the same country? I won't pass judgment on whether it would be for better or for worse, but it *would be* different. The old ties that bind are easy to ignore when the economic pie is growing, but the test is in periods of crisis."

The same arguments against racial and ethnic diversity "were made early in this century against Jews, Italians and Greeks, who were even called 'blacks' then because of their dark hair," Chavez says. "But I don't disagree that we have to have an American common culture and that the largest part of it is not merely European but in fact English. People adjust to it."

Such talk of preserving American culture is fine, "but which culture?" asks Gregory Fossedal, chairman of the Alexis de Tocqueville Institute, a pro-immigrant think tank in Arlington, Va. "When I drive along Wilson Boulevard in Arlington and see it teeming with hard-working Koreans and Vietnamese, I see the teamwork of new Americans. No one has established that difficulties are economic or culturally due to immigrants. There may be cultural limits, but we don't know where those limits are, and they would be at least three-to-five-times the current immigration levels because we handled that amount in the past with the Irish and Italians."

If immigration critics "can find an America that doesn't include these foreign influences," Fossedal says, "I'd like to see it."

Reuters Photo/HO

Newly arrived European immigrants were sent to the processing facility at Ellis Island, N.Y.

BACKGROUND

A Nation of Immigrants

"Once I thought to write a history of the immigrants of America," wrote renowned Harvard University historian Oscar Handlin. "Then I discovered that the immigrants *were* American history." [21]

INS records show that since 1820, the earliest year records were kept, fully 60.7 million immigrants have come to America, plus uncounted others who came illegally. [22]

This vital component of the American society has been expressed in an array of metaphors — mosaic, rainbow, kaleidoscope, melting pot, simmering cauldron, necklace of varied stones and "jazz ensemble, with each member improvising as an individual but having to play together under the agreed-on framework of a song." [23]

From the beginning of the Republic, most new Americans had a strong romantic sense of themselves as a unique, fresh slate of a nation. As French writer J. Hector St. John de Crevecoeur put it: "He is an American, who, leaving behind him all his ancient prejudices and manners, receives new ones from the new mode of life he has embraced, the new government he obeys and the new rank he holds. He becomes an American by being received in the broad lap of our great Alma Mater. Here, individuals of all nations are melted into a new race of men, whose labors and posterity will one day cause great changes in the world." [24]

Founding Fathers' Nationalism

Yet the Founding Fathers were overwhelmingly British in their outlook, and were hardly what today might be called world citizens. It was Thomas Jefferson who insisted on the five-year residency requirement for citizenship, and Benjamin Franklin who worried that German immigrants were arriving at such rates that they were "shortly to be so numerous as to Germanize us instead of us Anglifying them." [25] (Indeed, *The Federalist Papers* were published in German as well as English, and a 1794 proposal from some German settlers in Virginia to have federal laws translated into German was defeated in committee by just one vote.)

The Founding Fathers were careful to equip the president, under the 1798 Alien and Sedition Act, with the power to deport immigrants deemed dangerous to security. Colonists "held the view that somehow the good people had come here and the bad people had stayed home in Europe," says Yale University historian John Morton Blum. [26]

In the early 19th century, famed French political writer Alexis de Tocqueville marveled at America's capacity for absorbing foreigners: "As they mingle, the Americans become assimilated," he wrote. "They all get closer to one type." But precisely because de Tocqueville is cited by American immigration enthusiasts, immigration critic Brimelow argues that de Tocqueville actually hated many of the immigrants he saw in America, blaming them for an urban riot and calling them part of a "rabble more dangerous even than that of European towns. [They carry] our worst vices to the United States without any of those interests which might counteract their influence." [27]

Rising Hostility

By the mid-19th century, when the Irish potato famine had brought more than a million new immigrants to the U.S., hostility toward them was formalized in the political party that took the name Know-Nothings. With the slogan "Nationalize, Then Naturalize," the group wanted to impose a 25-year waiting period for the foreign-born to become citizens, and it wanted Catholics (most of the Irish) prohibited altogether.

After running Millard Fillmore unsuccessfully for president in 1856, the Know-Nothings prompted Abraham Lincoln to comment: "As a nation, we began by declaring that 'All men are created equal.' We now practically read it 'All men are created equal, except negroes.' When the Know-Nothings get control, it will read 'All men are created equal, except negroes, and foreigners, and Catholics.' " [28]

As the Civil War approached, the subsequent debates over slavery, black citizenship and the 14th Amendment prompted soul-searching comments among members of Lincoln's Cabinet, one of whom acknowledged that they themselves enjoyed citizenship by a mere "accident of birth." The language amending the Constitution in 1868 would read: "All persons born or naturalized in the United States and subject to jurisdiction thereof, are citizens of the United States and of the State wherein they reside."

The phrase "subject to the jurisdiction thereof," modern interpreters argue, was inserted to exclude self-governing American Indians (who would become U.S. citizens by statute in 1924) and to exclude the children of diplomats who happened to be born while their parents resided in the United States. It would figure in current-day debates over the citizenship status of children born in the U.S. to illegal aliens. [29] (*See "At Issue," p. 201.*)

In the latter 19th century, the waves of immigration continued at such a pace that in 1886, when the French government presented Americans with the world's largest statue to celebrate the American Revolution, they quickly converted the Statue of Liberty to a celebration of America's "open gates." Its famous poem by Emma Lazarus, a wealthy German Jew —"Give me your tired, your poor, your huddled masses yearning to breathe free" — is gently mocked by some modern-day descendants of immigrants, who point out that many of those masses were actually brimming with pluck and marketable skills. [30]

Fear of Foreigners

The phrase "the melting pot" was first popularized in a play written and produced in 1908 in Washington, D.C., by an immigrant named Israel Zangwill. The plot, which revolved around a Russian Jew and a Russian Christian who fall in love in New York City, included such universalist dialogue as: "East and west, and north and south, the palm and the pine, the pole and the equator, the crescent and the cross, how the Great Alchemist melts and fuses them with his purging flame!" [31]

Such transcendental ideals, however, were resisted by a prominent Jewish-American philosopher, Horace Kallen, who thought it more realistic to speak of "cultural pluralism." He wrote of "a federation or commonwealth of national cultures . . . a democracy of nationalities, cooperating voluntarily and autonomously through common institutions . . . a multiplicity in a unity." [32]

The issue was of no small consequence in the first decades of the 20th century. Statesmen such as Theodore Roosevelt and Woodrow Wilson expressed worry over the loyalties of what already were termed "hyphenated Americans." Roosevelt warned against becoming "a tangle of squabbling nationalities," and Wilson argued that "a man who thinks of himself as belonging to a particular national group in America has not yet become an American." [33]

Chronology

1800s *U.S. gains reputation as world's most welcoming immigrant society.*

1845-1849
Ireland's potato famine sends more than a million Irish immigrants to the United States.

1886
President Grover Cleveland dedicates Statue of Liberty, a gift from France.

1898
Supreme Court rules in *United States v. Wong Kim Ark* that a man born in California to Chinese parents is a U.S. citizen.

1900s *The white Anglo-Saxon Protestant establishment grows concerned about open immigration by Irish, Italians, Greeks and Jews.*

1908
Opening of Israel Zangwill's play "The Melting Pot" in Washington.

1910
Census shows 13.5 million Americans out of a total population of 92 million are foreign-born.

1920s-1950s

Growing concern about immigration leads to restrictions.

1924
Congress tightens immigration, implementing quotas that favor Northern Europeans.

1941
Japanese attack on Pearl Harbor prompts U.S. to hold Japanese-Americans in internment camps.

1952
Immigration and Nationality Act limits non-Western Hemisphere immigrants and gives preference to high-skill workers.

1960s-1970s

Government "Great Society" programs lay groundwork for aid to immigrants.

1965
Immigration and Nationality Act Amendments increase immigration, invite more non-Europeans and stress family unification.

1972
Congress passes Ethnic Heritage Studies Programs Act.

1980s *Debate over high immigration levels produces compromise legislation.*

1980
Refugee Act calls for refugees to be processed separately from immigrants and offers social services.

1986
Immigration Reform and Control Act gives amnesty to illegal aliens, who in early 1990s will become eligible for citizenship.

1988
Immigration amendments promote diversity by allowing visas for countries that have sent few immigrants to the U.S. in recent years.

1990s *Efforts to streamline citizenship processing cause controversy.*

1990
Immigration Act (IMMACT) streamlines citizenship process for 4 million eligible citizens.

1994
Census reports that 22.3 million Americans are foreign-born. Jordan Commission on Immigration Reform recommends reducing number of immigrants. California voters pass Proposition 187 ("Save Our State") in November, denying school and health benefits to non-citizens including children; courts later block its implementation.

August 1995
Immigration and Naturalization Service (INS) launches Citizenship USA drive.

Aug. 1, 1996
House votes 259-169 to declare English the official language of the federal government.

September 1996
Financier George Soros sets up $50 million fund to help immigrants become citizens. President Clinton signs continuing resolution containing immigration bill beefing up border security. Congress holds hearings on whether INS and Vice President Al Gore sought to pressure INS to speed naturalizations to create Democratic voters.

Dec. 4, 1996
Supreme Court agrees to hear *Arizonans for Official English v. Arizona* on whether government services must be in English.

Should the Test for U.S. Citizenship Be. . .

Question: *A proper test for aspiring citizens should be (choose one):*

a) a solemn ritual that inculcates deep patriotic feelings;

b) a routine indicator that the applicant has mastered a minimum of American civics.

For a decade now, the Immigration and Naturalization Service (INS) has required every foreign-born person seeking U.S. citizenship to pass a written test. (In earlier decades, the tests were less formal, with administering attorneys merely requiring the applicant to write a few dictated sentences as proof of some knowledge of English.)

Today's test, typically comprised of a dozen questions drawn from nearly 300 that the INS has available, is a factually oriented review of Civics 101. It has simple queries about political history, the structure of the U.S. government and the design of the American flag. To prepare test takers, the INS publishes paperback books, such as "Citizenship Education and Naturalization Information," "United States History: 1600-1987" and "U.S. Government Structure."

Due in part to variations in how the test is administered in each of the 33 INS districts, it has become the object of political feuding between those who consider the questions laughably shallow and those concerned that new immigrants not be tripped up over challenges that are beyond the ken of many native-born citizens.

Journalist Georgie Anne Geyer, in her recent book bemoaning what she views as the "death of citizenship" in this country, sees the test as part of a general laxness she calls "the great American citizenship dumb-down." To the question, "Name one benefit of being a citizen of the United States," a thoughtful would-be citizen, she says, might reflect on French writer Hector Saint John de Crevecoeur's 18th-century notion of the American "who is a new man, who acts upon new principles."[1] Instead, she notes, the answers the INS accepts focus on such personal benefits as "vote for the candidate of your choice, travel with a U.S. passport, serve on a jury, apply for federal employment opportunities."

Other critics complain that only 5-10 percent of the test takers fail, largely, they argue, because local test officials in the districts sometimes spoonfeed applicants the answers. "We try to administer the test in line with the applicant's capacity," an assistant INS district director in Puerto Rico told two researchers from the Center for Equal Opportunity.[2]

"There is an overemphasis on memorization, which is one-dimensional, and the facts are not presented in context," says center President Linda Chavez. "But the test shouldn't be a Ph.D. dissertation."

Finally, many observers object to reports that the INS conducts some citizenship tests in Spanish, Thai or Vietnamese. "It is sad that they would give the test in multiple languages," says Yeh Ling-Ling, founder of the Diversity Coalition for an Immigration Moratorium, in San Francisco. "Why become a citizen if you can't speak the language of the land? They should make the test tougher, because now people call it a joke."

Proposals to require more of test takers are resisted by Dennis Gallagher, executive director of the Refugee Policy Group in Washington, D.C. "The critics ought to go out to some high school that has lower-middle-class whites and give them the test, and see how many of them know the name of the vice president," he says. "You can't impose on immigrants higher standards than you impose on your own people who already speak good English."

Indeed, surveys of average American students show startling gaps in their knowledge of civics. Results of a "grade-school-level" questionnaire given to 500 college seniors by the

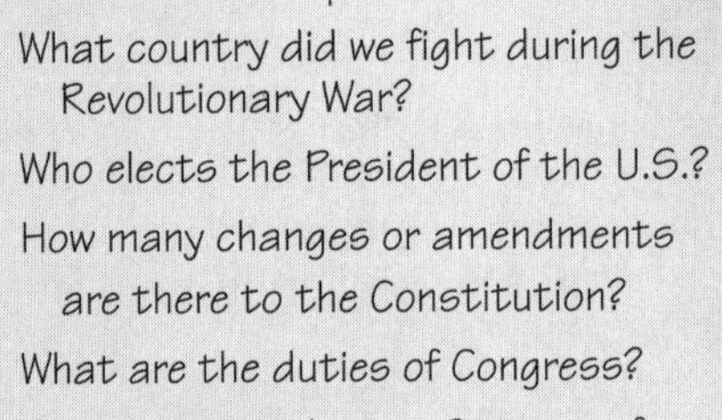

Sample Naturalization Questions

What do the stripes on the flag mean?

What country did we fight during the Revolutionary War?

Who elects the President of the U.S.?

How many changes or amendments are there to the Constitution?

What are the duties of Congress?

Can you name the two Senators from your state?

Who becomes President if both the President and Vice President die?

Can you name the 13 original states?

Who said, "Give me liberty or give me death?"

Which countries were our Allies during World War II?

Who helped the Pilgrims in America?

Name one amendment which guarantees or addresses voting rights?

Which President freed the slaves?

During the first decades of the 20th century, America was home to a (then and still) unequalled proportion of foreign-born residents — mainly Irish, Italians, Greeks and European Jews. Many of them were seeking what Jewish writer Irving Howe called "an interval of equilibrium." For Russian Jews, this meant "a structure of values neither strictly religious or rigidly secular" for use in adapting American ideas, style, manners and language to be "transformed by their ab-

. . . a Patriotic Ritual or a Routine Drill?

Roper Center for Public Opinion Research last year showed that only 44 percent correctly answered such questions as, Which political party is currently in the majority in Congress? and How many United States senators are there?

One proposal now under debate would eliminate the test for any applicant with a U.S. high school diploma or anyone who has passed a course in U.S. history or political science at any American college or INS-approved facility. [3]

Defenders of offering the test in foreign languages point out that by law, the INS permits it only for applicants who are at least 50 years old and who have been in the United States for at least 20 years. (Those at least 55 years old need only to have been in the country 15 years.)

About 90 percent of those who take the test pass on the first try, according to a 1992 survey by the Los Angeles-based National Association of Latino Elected and Appointed Officials. Of the test takers, 49.5 percent described the test as very easy, 28 percent as somewhat easy and just 25 percent as hard. Fully 97 percent of those surveyed thought the questions were fair.

Complaints that the citizenship test should be more standardized around the country were first addressed in the early 1990s. Following a set of streamlining procedures passed as part of the 1990 Immigration Act, the Educational Testing Service (ETS), in Princeton, N.J., was asked to create a uniformly worded set of questions that test givers can choose from. At the same time, however, the INS agreed to contract out about a quarter of its citizenship testing to six private firms, including ETS and American College Testing. Some offer courses in how to pass the test, charging up to $215, and many boast a 98 percent pass rate.

"Many of the outside groups that are administering the test or are working closely with the INS on regulations are the same organizations that reject Americanization, work hard at obliterating all distinctions between citizens and non-citizens and promote multicultural separatism," complains American Enterprise Institute scholar John Fonte. [4]

One licensee, Florida-based Naturalization and Assistance Services Inc., last year was the target of television news exposés that captured test proctors on videotape coaching paying applicants as to which questions would be on the company-administered test. A subsequent INS investigation resulted in the company losing its contract (a decision it is challenging in court), and the INS rethinking its policy of hiring outside firms to conduct tests.

Rep. Lamar Smith, R-Texas, chairman of the Judiciary Subcommittee on Immigration and Claims, is planning oversight hearings early this year that will focus, in part, on the conduct of citizenship test licensees. It's part of an overall look at charges that the INS in the Clinton administration has accelerated the naturalization process to create more Democratic voters. "We will ask very probing questions on whether the INS had begun to investigate Naturalization and Assistance Services before the news media called attention to it," Smith spokesman Allen Kay says.

David Rosenberg, INS director of program initiatives, explains that the reason for the variations in different INS districts is that the decision to qualify someone for citizenship is a judgment call made by an immigration official after a face-to-face interview and a separate oral test for spoken English. "There is no requirement that a certain number of the civics questions be answered," he says. "The test is just one tool."

The INS is seeking to develop a new, more standardized test, Rosenberg adds, working with the Center for Applied Linguistics and soliciting suggestions from the public. "We are not saying that the test is either too hard or too easy. We're focusing on what people use. I mean, to ask which was the 49th state is a test of whether the applicant completely read the study book, but is it really something that all Americans must know?

"We would like to get at something more substantive, such as the concept of government limited by the people," he says. "But the written test was never envisioned as a knowledge test — imagine the language sophistication that would be needed."

Rosenberg envisions the ideal test as one that encourages the "minimum knowledge needed to participate in the body politic so one can become part of the mainstream and not be open to demagoguery." At this stage, he says, "it doesn't have to be more than a basis on which to build."

But still, the test does represent "our stamp of approval," Rosenberg adds, which is one reason the INS sponsors a public television series called "Cafe Crossroads," a sort of "adult Sesame Street" for the basics of American civic life. "The INS feels an obligation not just to test the applicants, but a duty to help them prepare."

1 Georgie Anne Geyer, *Americans No More: The Death of Citizenship* (1996), p. 3.

2 John J. Miller and William James Muldoon, "Citizenship for Granted: How the INS Devalues Naturalization Testing," Center for Equal Opportunity Policy Brief, October 1996.

3 Arnold Rochvarg, "Reforming the Administrative Naturalization Process: Reducing Delays While Increasing Fairness," *Georgetown Immigration Law Journal*, Vol. 9, No. 3, summer 1995, p. 128.

4 Testimony at hearings before Senate Judiciary Subcommittee on Immigration and Claims, Oct. 22, 1996.

sorption" into Yiddish culture. [34]

The blending, however, was not always smooth. A contemporary observer described the new arrivals at the dock as "hirsute, low-browed, big-faced persons of obviously low mentality. . . . They simply look out of place in black clothes and stiff collar, since clearly they belong in skins, in wattled huts at the close of the Great Ice Age." [35] And in the infamous Red Scare of 1920, Attorney General A. Mitchell Palmer raided immigrant homes looking for anarchists and Bolsheviks, arguing that Fourth Amendment bans on search and seizure did not apply to foreigners. [36]

In the 1920s, with the U.S. Congress having enacted a crackdown on unchecked immigration, the rise of presidential candidate Al Smith, a New York Democrat and the first Catholic to run nationally, became an emblem of the country's divisions over immigration. Influential columnist Walter Lippmann was moved to comment: "Here are the new people, clamoring to be admitted to America, and there are the older people defending their household gods. The rise of Al Smith has made the conflict plain, and his career has come to involve a major aspect of the destiny of American civilization." [37]

Ethnic Pride

Mainstream culture, meanwhile, clearly celebrated the superiority of native-born Americans. As author Sanford Ungar argues, patriotic lyrics by early-20th century songwriter George M. Cohan contained a gentle jab at naturalized citizens: "This is my country; *land of my birth*. This is my country, the greatest on Earth." [38]

Many immigrants would compensate by becoming superpatriots, among them Sol Feinstone, a Lithuanian Jew who came to America in 1902. Working his way up in New York City sweatshops, he became a chemist and then a real estate investor. The fortune he amassed allowed him to become a philanthropist and major collector of books and 18th-century manuscripts relating to the American Revolution. He would found a well-known library in Washington Crossing, Pa. [39]

As second and third generations were launched, however, there arose a new phenomenon of ethnic pride. In the oft-quoted words of immigration historian Marcus Lee Hansen, "What the son wishes to forget, the grandson wishes to remember." [40] The post-World War II period brought popular ethnic novels and Broadway plays (such as "Fiddler on the Roof" and novels by Philip Roth and Saul Bellow), while the 1960 election of Irish-Catholic John F. Kennedy, one historian wrote, "reinvigorated the idea that being an American also meant being a member of one ancestral group or another." [41]

By the 1970s, Democratic Rep. Roman Pucinski of Chicago was holding hearings on ethnicity, criticizing the tendency to "homogenize 200 million human beings into a single monolith, instead of recognizing that America is a magnificent mosaic, made up of many cultures." [42]

In 1972, Congress enacted the Ethnic Heritage Studies Programs Act, and the Ford Foundation and other philanthropic groups began giving out ethnic-studies grants. The American Jewish Committee and the U.S. Catholic Conference began serving as mediators in tensions between ethnics and American blacks. By 1988, when Greek-American Michael S. Dukakis became the first major ethnic candidate in modern times to seek the presidency, his campaign theme song was Neil Diamond's "Coming to America."

Modern immigrants and their descendants were not only proud of their ethnic identity, but — unlike their predecessors — they could count on government policies designed to help them along. "The civic incorporation of newcomers," wrote the late Barbara C. Jordan, chair of the 1994 U.S. Commission on Immigration Reform, "is an essential part of immigration policy."

As Jordan later told a congressional hearing, "It was immigration that taught us that, in this country, it does not matter where you came from, or who your parents were. What counts is who you are." [43] ■

CURRENT SITUATION

Immigration Politics?

Last fall, thousands of new Americans gave up foreign allegiances by taking the citizenship oath in courtrooms, sports stadiums and even historic sites such as Mount Vernon, George Washington's stately Virginia home. By law, each candidate must be at least 18 years of age; have lived in the U.S. legally for five years; be of good moral character; be able to speak, read, write and understand ordinary English words and phrases; and be able to demonstrate knowledge and understanding of the fundamentals of U.S. history and principles of government. Also required are $95, two photos and a fingerprint card.

In return, citizenship bestows on citizens the right to vote, serve on a jury, hold office, apply for government jobs that require security clearance, bring immediate relatives to the U.S. without a waiting period and travel abroad for an unlimited period of time.

For years, applicants have found themselves thwarted by INS backlogs. In 1994, the wait for citizenship processing was 390 days in the Detroit district, 360 days in San Francisco and 300 days in Milwaukee, according to the National Immigration Forum.

When Meissner, a veteran INS official, appeared at her confirmation hearings in 1993, she and a bipartisan group in Congress agreed that the agency should seek ways to reduce its backlog. Following a 1995 report on "Reengineering the Naturalization Process," the INS added 1,000 new staffers. At the same time, the National Performance Review, the government efficiency effort led by

At Issue:

Should children born to illegal immigrants in the United States be denied birthrights to U.S. citizenship?

yes

REP. ELTON GALLEGLY, R-CALIF.

FROM TESTIMONY BEFORE A JOINT HEARING OF THE HOUSE JUDICIARY SUBCOMMITTEE ON IMMIGRATION AND CLAIMS AND THE SUBCOMMITTEE ON THE CONSTITUTION, DEC. 13, 1995.

Since 1991, I have sponsored legislation to amend our Constitution to abolish automatic citizenship to children born in this country to illegal alien parents. . . . I have long championed this change to the 14th Amendment because it is my belief that our current law encourages widespread illegal immigration and costs American taxpayers billions of dollars each year.

I expect that opponents of this change in our citizenship law will decry this proposal as radical. However, far from being radical, such restrictions on citizenship are the norm around the world. Only a handful of countries — Argentina, Canada and Mexico — still grant automatic birthright citizenship. . . .

Nearly every nation in Europe, Africa and Asia does not permit automatic citizenship to children of illegal immigrants. In fact, both the United Kingdom and even Australia, a country which shares a long immigration tradition similar to ours, both repealed their U.S.-style citizenship policies during the 1980s. My proposed amendment is much more limited. It would confer automatic citizenship to children of legal residents as well as citizens, denying it only to children of illegal alien parents.

This change in our citizenship laws is long overdue, as there are a growing number of women who illegally enter the United States for the sole purpose of giving birth to an American citizen. . . . [T]hese children are eligible for federal, state and local benefit programs, and having a child is a virtual guarantee against deportation. In addition, under our current legal immigration system, the citizen child can sponsor [his] illegal parents, or any other close relative, for permanent resident status. . . .

Some will argue that the reform would violate the spirit of the 14th Amendment. That amendment was drafted after the Civil War to guarantee that recently freed slaves did not lose their citizenship rights based on action by the states. When that amendment was enacted in 1868, there were no illegal immigrants in the United States because there were no illegal-immigration laws until 1875.

Other advocates of maintaining the status quo argue that reforming citizenship policies would create a permanent subclass of residents, as is found in some parts of the world. I reject that analogy because our nation continues to encourage assimilation and citizenship of those who are here legally. Our proposal only aims at illegal immigrants.

no

REP. LUIS V. GUTIERREZ, D-ILL.

FROM TESTIMONY BEFORE A JOINT HEARING OF THE HOUSE JUDICIARY SUBCOMMITTEE ON IMMIGRATION AND CLAIMS AND THE SUBCOMMITTEE ON THE CONSTITUTION, DEC. 13, 1995.

Should we deny citizenship to an entire group of people — people born in America? Let me answer by quoting a Republican. A Republican leader who also had to consider whether we should deny citizenship to an entire group of people, born in America. A Republican leader who faced a decision — how to respond to a Supreme Court that wanted to deny those rights.

How did that Republican leader respond to the idea that America should deny citizenship to an entire group of people? He said that idea, quote, "does obvious violence to the plain, unmistakable language of the Declaration of Independence. It leaves the Declaration assailed, and sneered at, and construed, and hawked at, and torn — till, if its framers could rise from their graves, they could not at all recognize it."

That Republican was Abraham Lincoln. The idea was Justice Roger Taney's *Dred Scott* decision — which denied the right of citizenship to all blacks, merely because they were black. Our greatest president answered that idea with courage. And because he did, the 14th Amendment was born, and America became a greater, stronger nation. That Republican, faced with exclusion, chose unity. Lincoln took a stand — a stand that our nation should not abandon the words of the Declaration of Independence . . . that "We hold these truths to be self-evident, that all Men are created equal."

Now, the proposals before this committee make a very different declaration: that today "We hold these truths to be self-evident, that all Men — except those born to non-citizens — are created equal." The proposals that we consider today suggest that where Lincoln chose brotherhood, we should choose division. . . .

Lincoln was right: Denying citizenship to an entire group of people at our whim leaves the Declaration of Independence assailed. It leaves the Constitution frayed. And it steals from the American people a principle that is at the foundation of what makes our nation great — a commitment to equality.

Unfortunately, this stab at the heart of the Constitution and the Declaration of Independence is wrapped in rhetoric concerning a serious national problem. Sponsors of these proposals want us to believe that by punishing children, our nation's immigration problems will somehow magically disappear. Unfortunately, absolutely no evidence exists that supports these claims. . . .

FOR MORE INFORMATION

Federation for American Immigration Reform, 1666 Connecticut Ave. N.W., Suite 400, Washington, D.C. 20009; (202) 328-7004; www.fairus.org. Founded in 1979, FAIR is a national advocacy group that works for "new and realistic approaches to immigration law and border security."

National Council of La Raza, 810 First St. St. N.E., Suite 300, Washington, D.C. 20002; (202) 785-1670; www.nclr.org. La Raza, the nation's largest Hispanic civil rights group, monitors legislative and regulatory policies affecting Hispanics and provides technical assistance in such areas as language, housing, community development and immigration.

National Immigration Forum, 220 I St. N.E., Suite 220, Washington, D.C. 20002; (202) 544-0004; www.immigrationforum.org. Founded in 1982, this coalition of 200 organizations promotes "fair and generous immigration policies in the United States."

Vice President Al Gore, became interested. In August 1995, the INS launched "Citizenship USA," a centralized paperwork-tracking center that President Clinton called "the most ambitious citizenship effort in history." As the election drew nearer, Gore stepped in to further "cut red tape" after hearing complaints from immigrant groups that INS "incompetence" might deprive thousands of aspiring citizens of a chance to vote in the 1996 elections.[44]

Republican political strategists, however, became wary that the Clinton administration was seeking to pad the electoral rolls with new immigrants, who, they believe, tend to vote Democratic. The accelerated efforts became the subject of political accusations. "Aren't you outraged that Vice President Gore with his staff would push the INS to naturalize as many people as possible?" presidential candidate Bob Dole thundered last fall. He accused the INS of rushing through over a million applicants "so they could be ready for the election, even if they have criminal records."[45]

In late October, the INS released a review saying it had found no evidence that applicants with criminal records had had their background checks waived. But after the elections, current and former INS employees told a House panel that FBI background checks had been skipped for more than 10,000 applications.[46] The INS again reported that it had tightened procedures but that it had not waived checks for anyone. Attorney General Janet Reno rejected a Republican request for an independent counsel to look into the INS.

David Rosenberg, the INS director of program initiatives, said the issue was not a new policy instituted by the Democrats but problems with the existing policy. The FBI, he said, partly because it was short-staffed following the move of its fingerprint center to West Virginia, fell behind in processing citizenship applications, but that only 2 percent of the year's applications were affected. When critics refer to criminal "rap sheets" they must be careful, he added, because not all charges against someone resulted in a conviction, and while a homicide conviction automatically disqualifies one for citizenship, a drunken-driving offense might not, depending on the circumstances.

Still, Rosenberg says, the INS is double-checking all the cases in question, using an outside auditor. "None of this was political or a last-minute election-year policy," he says. "Yes, there are always local pressures from community groups who have political intent, but from a social and governmental standpoint, it is still a positive thing to try to get people to become citizens and exercise suffrage."

Ethnics for Democrats

The Republican assumption that immigrants vote Democratic seemed to have been partially borne out in the November elections. Republicans took a beating in many high-immigrant areas, and 72 percent of Latino votes went Democratic. (Democrats took only 43 percent of the Asian vote, however.) Most notable was the defeat of conservative Rep. Robert K. Dornan, R-Calif., by Loretta Sanchez, the daughter of Mexican immigrants, by less than a thousand votes.

"I don't want to be the first person in history, man or woman, House or Senate, to be voted out of office by felons, by people voting who are not U.S. citizens, who are felons or children or people not allowed to vote," Dornan told C-SPAN in early December after demanding a recount and filing a fraud complaint with House officials. Orange County records studied by the National Immigration Forum showed that voter registration went up by 9,000 among Latinos, and by 7,000 among Vietnamese, but down 17,000 among whites. Approximately the same changes were recorded for voter turnout, a clear sign of immigrant impact on Dornan's race.

The Republicans brought it on themselves, says the forum's Sharry. "If you stand in line at the naturalization bureau, the name on all the immigrants' lips is [Republican California Gov.] Pete Wilson," he says. "He and lots of GOP politicians after him have used the language issue, bilingual education and citizenship to blur the line between legal and illegal immigrants. He tried to ride the tiger of Proposition 187, but the GOP ended up in the tiger's belly," referring to the 1994 ballot referendum that would have cut off public health and welfare aid to all California immigrants. "Immigrants felt attacked, and feared government was after them," Sharry says, "so they did what people in a democracy do — they expressed power at the ballot box.

"What's wrong with this picture?" he asks. "Nothing. Most immigrants seem to have voted for Clinton, but party affiliation is up for grabs. Our polls show the Cubans went mostly for Dole. Immigrants don't just vote on the immigration issue; they're concerned about crime, education and jobs, and tend to be socially conservative. The Democrats benefited this time only."

Chavez, a Republican, said the "GOP made a big mistake by going hog wild on immigration. But Pete Wilson is a smart politician who had an uphill battle, and immigration gave him an issue that he had hoped would take him national. He's not a racist. He probably wanted to walk the line but attracted some folks who are motivated for the wrong reasons. It's an old problem of being a politician."

A Changed Congress?

The recently departed 104th Congress passed an immigration bill in 1996 that sponsors originally had hoped would include broad language reducing legal immigration. But a coalition of immigrant advocacy groups and business interests blocked it. Instead, the legislation only provides new funding for a border fence between the U.S. and Mexico and new INS inspectors. [47]

Though many in the new Republican-controlled Congress are wary of taking on immigrant issues because of their 1996 losses, several are talking of changing the law on the birthright of babies born to illegals. And the effort begun in the House last year to declare English as the nation's official language is expected to be renewed.

Clinton, meanwhile, is hoping to use executive authority to block some of the provisions of last year's welfare reform bill that halt aid to legal immigrants. Wilson, in a reversal, recently announced that he would allow children of legal immigrants to still get some public welfare and health benefits.[48] ■

OUTLOOK

Weaving New Fabric

In November, the New York state Legislature passed a bill requiring every public and private school in the state to teach about the devastation inflicted on the Irish by the 19th-century potato famine, including discussion of charges that British agricultural and trade policies deliberately caused the tragedy. [49]

That demonstration of political clout by a well-entrenched ethnic group was followed the next month by a sign of coming immigrant clout. Shanghai-born computer mogul Charles B. Wang announced that he was giving nearly $25 million to establish an Asian-American cultural center at the State University of New York at Stony Brook to create a little "touch of home" for students from Asia.

The Census Bureau, meanwhile, forecasts 9 million new immigrants to the U.S. this decade, the most since the 1900s.

Will we all get along? The Ford Foundation study says it will take leadership in bridge-building by teachers, clergy, social workers and police. And it recommends shared activities such as sports and public festivals, which "create opportunities for interaction and improve the general level of tolerance. Festivals often reduce tension because they celebrate symbols of diversity, such as food and dance, that do not directly threaten day-to-day American beliefs about culture and identity," the study says. [50]

In California, trade analyst and demographer Joel Kotkin notes that 20 percent of the marriages are interracial, and that nearly half of the Mexican-Americans intermarry. [51] "No nation in history had proved as successful as the United States in managing ethnic diversity," historian Lawrence Fuchs said. "No nation before had ever made diversity itself a source of national identity and unity." [52]

Harvard's Glazer recommends that policy-makers "concentrate on a few problems, such as the language issue, and not focus on the general resistance to assimilate. As a country, we made political errors," he said. "We allowed language rights in voting, which became mere rallying points for militants, and we allowed foreign languages to become the way to get federal money. We should withdraw from our errors, even though that creates the impression that we're anti-immigrant. They were only mistakes."

FAIR's Stein warns that "we're changing into a country that lacks a coherent civic culture. There's more to civic life than cuisine. We must balance immigration with the natural desire to remain a family as defined by natural boundaries. We have to reassert our national and religious identity out of civic defense. That means building a sense in immigrants that there's a country worth dying for. Being an American is a set of core virtues, and values. It is not ethnically defined."

To Chavez, "There is such a thing as American exceptionalism, with the hegemony of our vibrant pop culture. We're a wonderful country, but we risk losing that. We have enormous problems in crime, the family, city decay."

Many of the perceptions of the problems, however, have to do with fear of the unknown and preconceived notions. In 1992, the American Jewish Committee surveyed Americans on their perception of the social standing of 58 ethnic groups. At the top of the ladder were Germans, Irish and Scandinavians, followed by Italians, Greeks, Poles, Russians and Jews. Yet the lowest score went to a fictional group the researchers created and named the Wisians." Fully 39 percent of Americans believed that Wisians as a class were not doing well. [53]

"New immigrants have always been hated, and xenophobia and insecurity are hardly new," says Gallagher of the Refugee Policy Group. "We're in one cycle now, and it will lift over the years. But the danger is, once we start to legislate against some of the negative things about immigration, the laws become harder to change later, even if public attitudes have changed." ∎

Notes

[1] See "Asian Americans," *The CQ Researcher,* Dec. 13, 1991, pp. 945-968, and "Hispanic Americans," *The CQ Researcher,* Oct. 30, 1992, pp. 929-952.

[2] See "Cracking Down on Immigration," *The CQ Researcher,* Feb. 3, 1995, pp. 97-120; "Illegal Immigration," *The CQ Researcher,* April 24, 1992, pp. 361-384; and "Welfare, Work and the States," *The CQ Researcher,* Dec. 6, 1996, pp. 1057-1080.

[3] National Conference of State Legislatures, *America's Newcomers: An Immigrant Policy Handbook,* September 1994, p. 57.

[4] Testimony before the Senate Judiciary Subcommittee on Immigration, Oct. 22. 1996.

[5] *Ibid.*

[6] Ford Foundation, "Changing Relations" (1993), p. 4.

[7] Manhattan Institute and Pacific Research Institute, *Strangers at Our Gate: Immigration in the 1990s* (1994), p. 76.

[8] Senate Judiciary hearing, *op. cit.*

[9] *The New York Times,* Dec. 1, 1996.

[10] Terry Anderson, "The Culture Clash in South-Central L.A." *Los Angeles Times,* May 29, 1996.

[11] Peter Brimelow, *Alien Nation* (1995), p. xix.

[12] National Conference of State Legislatures, *op. cit.,* p. 60.

[13] *The Wall Street Journal,* July 11, 1996.

[14] Quoted in National Endowment for the Humanities, "A National Conversation: How We Act in Private and in Public," 1994.

[15] See "Debate Over Bilingualism," *The CQ Researcher,* Jan. 19, 1996, pp. 49-72.

[16] Senate Judiciary hearings, *op. cit.*

[17] Quoted in *The New York Times,* Dec. 30, 1996.

[18] David M. Kennedy, "Can We Still Afford to be a Nation of Immigrants?" *The Atlantic Monthly,* November 1996, p. 58.

[19] See "Low-Wage Lessons," *Business Week,* Nov. 11, 1996, p. 109.

[20] See Juan F. Perea (ed.), *Immigrants Out! The New Nativism and the Anti-Immigrant Impulse in the United States* (1997), p. 13.

[21] Quoted in National Conference of State Legislatures, *op. cit.,* p. 49.

[22] Sanford Ungar, *Fresh Blood: The New American Immigrants* (1996), p. 98. Ungar is dean of the School of Communications at American University.

[23] National Endowment for the Humanities, *op. cit.*

[24] Arthur M. Schlesinger Jr., *The Disuniting of America* (1991), p. 1.

[25] Perea, *op. cit.,* p. 18.

[26] Interviewed in *Los Angeles Times,* June 12, 1994.

[27] Brimelow, *op. cit.,* p. 213.

[28] Schlesinger, *op. cit.,* p. 9.

[29] See House Judiciary Committee hearings, Dec. 13, 1995.

[30] Column by A.M. Rosenthal, *The New York Times,* Dec. 3, 1996.

[31] Arthur Mann, *The One and the Many: Reflections on the American Identity* (1979), p. 100.

[32] Schlesinger, *op. cit.,* p. 13.

[33] *Ibid.,* pp. 12, 69.

[34] Irving Howe, *World of Our Fathers* (1976), p. 169.

[35] Kennedy, *op. cit.,* p. 52.

[36] Ungar, *op. cit.,* p. 107.

[37] Mann, *op. cit.,* p. 131.

[38] Ungar, *op. cit.,* p. 106.

[39] David J. Fowler, *Guide to the Sol Feinstone Collection of the David Library of the American Revolution* (1994).

[40] Schlesinger, *op. cit.,* p. 16.

[41] Mann, *op. cit.,* p. 5.

[42] *Ibid.,* p. 37.

[43] Statement to House Judiciary Committee hearings, Dec. 13, 1995.

[44] Dick Kirschten, "The Politics of Citizenship," *Government Executive,* January 1997, p. 36.

[45] Quoted in *National Journal,* Nov. 30, 1996, p. 2622.

[46] *The Washington Times,* Dec. 13, 1996. The House panel was the Government Reform and Oversight Subcommittee on National Security, International Affairs and Criminal Justice.

[47] *CQ Weekly Report,* Dec. 14, 1996, p. 3397.

[48] *Los Angeles Times* [Washington edition], Dec. 23, 1996.

[49] *The New York Times,* Nov. 21, 1996.

[50] Ford Foundation, *op. cit.,* p. 56.

[51] Manhattan Institute and Pacific Research Institute, *op. cit.,* p. 92.

[52] Schlesinger, *op. cit.,* p. 79.

[53] National Conference of State Legislatures, *op. cit.,* p. 51.

Bibliography

Selected Sources Used

Books

Brimelow, Peter, *Alien Nation: Common Sense About America's Immigration Disaster,* Random House, 1995.
A British-born, U.S.-naturalized, conservative writer for *Forbes* and *National Review* magazines lays out his ideological and historical case for curbing immigration.

Chavez, Linda, *Out of the Barrio: Toward a New Politics of Hispanic Assimilation,* Basic Books, 1991.
The president of the Center for Equal Opportunity criticizes Hispanic ethnic lobbies in the United States that pursue a separate culture and government benefits.

Geyer, Georgie Anne, *Americans No More: The Death of Citizenship,* Atlantic Monthly Press, 1996.
A longtime syndicated columnist in international affairs outlines her case that promiscuous immigration policies and what she sees as a lax approach to processing citizenship applications pose disturbing questions about the future of the country.

Mann, Arthur, *The One and the Many: Reflections on the American Identity,* University of Chicago Press, 1979.
A University of Chicago historian offers this historical overview of the forces that shaped the American immigrant experience, offering a paradigm for group affiliation in the United States that leaves room for ethnic loyalty while creating an American whole.

Perea, Juan F. (ed.), *Immigrants Out!: The New Nativism and the Anti-Immigrant Impulse in the United States,* New York University Press, 1997.
A University of Florida law professor assembled these interdisciplinary essays providing history and analysis of political and behavioral issues that the authors regard as nativistic and xenophobic, including the official English movement.

Schlesinger Jr., Arthur M., *The Disuniting of America: Reflections on a Multicultural Society,* Whittle Direct Books, 1991.
A noted historian now at the City University of New York surveys the literature and history of the American "melting pot," asking whether the 'E Pluribus" is in danger of overshadowing the "unum."

Ungar, Sanford J., *Fresh Blood: The New American Immigrants,* Simon & Schuster, 1995.
A journalist and foreign affairs analyst now the dean of American University School of Communications traces his own Eastern European ancestry, interviews dozens of immigrants across the United States and argues that many of the tensions involving new American immigrants result from misunderstanding.

Reports

Bouvier, Leon, *Embracing America: A Look at Which Immigrants Become Citizens,* Center for Immigration Studies, 1996.
A demographer for a Washington-based research and policy group examines the numbers and trends within different immigrant nationalities to determine which factors—education and language skills, for example—make residents more likely to seek citizenship.

Ford Foundation, *Changing Relations: Newcomers and Established Residents in U.S. Communities,* 1993.
A multidisciplinary team of scholars from the State University of New York examined which programs and approaches are best for integrating new immigrants into the American mainstream, emphasizing the responsibilities both of immigrants and native-born Americans.

Manhattan Institute and Pacific Research Institute, *Strangers at Our Gate: Immigration in the 1990s,* 1994.
Two conservative think tanks teamed up to collect these essays, debating statements and data advancing the argument for slowing the current rate of immigration to the United States.

National Conference of State Legislatures, *America's Newcomers: Am Immigrant Policy Handbook,* September 1994.
This anthology of articles assembled by the immigrant policy division of a state legislatures group examines federal, state and local programs designed to ease the transition of new immigrants.

National Endowment for the Humanities, *A National Conversation on American Pluralism and Identity,* 1994.
As part of NEH Chairman Sheldon Hackney's "conversation starter" series to promote American discourse, this packet provides essays, quotations, histories and provocative questions surrounding immigration, ethnicity, race and patriotism.

12 Native American's Future

MARY H. COOPER

To the somber thump of a cottonwood drum, eight young men and women filed into the dusty schoolyard. The men's bodies were striped with paint, red ocher symbolizing the blood of the Earth, white to ward off evil spirits. The men wore headdresses with majestic rams' horns, the women colorful dresses. Facing North, South East and West, they began dancing to the rasp of gourd rattles and the drum's slow cadence.

For centuries, the Havasupai Indians of northwest Arizona have performed the ram dance to conduct the spirits of their dead relatives to the next world. But today the sacred ceremony has become more than just a funeral rite. It is a vital teaching tool in the 650-member tribe's fight for cultural survival. On a recent afternoon, the dancers performed for a hushed audience of children and elders alike. Afterwards, everyone, including a non-Indian visitor, joined hands in a circle dance for peace.

"We use any occasion we can to dance before our tribe because our customs and language will die with us if we don't teach them to the next generation," says Matthew Putesoy, a dancer and member of the tribal council. "People from other tribes are surprised when they hear our kids speak because their kids speak English only. Our young people all speak Havasupai."

The Havasupais' concerns are shared by American Indians across the country. "I wasn't raised on the 'rez,' so I don't speak the language except for a few words," says Sen. Ben Nighthorse Campbell, R-Colo., a Northern Cheyenne and the only Native American in Congress. "But most tribes are trying to record their songs or dances and compiling dictio naries to preserve their languages."

From *The CQ Researcher,* July 12, 1996.

Barbara Sassa-Daniels

To many observers, economic survival is an even more pressing concern for the country's 2.1 million Indians. They not only have the highest unemployment and poverty rates of any group in the United States but also the nation's worst disease rate. (*See story, p. 212.*)

But Americans seem indifferent to their plight, Indian leaders say, pointing to recent cuts in funding for the Bureau of Indian Affairs (BIA), which operates most housing, education and welfare programs on reservations. Even with the nation's Indian population growing at some 4 percent annually in recent years, Congress cut funding for Indian programs by $160 million in fiscal 1996, down 9 percent from BIA's $1.7 billion 1995 budget. And while President Clinton proposed restoring the 1995 spending levels for fiscal 1997, House and Senate budget committees have recommended even deeper cuts for BIA — as much as $193 million below the 1995 level. These cuts follow a 20-year decline in funding for Indian affairs. [1]

"American Indians have always been underfunded and short-changed," says Ada E. Deer, a member of Wisconsin's Menominee tribe, who as assistant Interior secretary for Indian affairs heads the BIA. "This country was built on the land and the resources that were ceded to the government by the tribes. If the tribes had been allowed to develop in a more just way, we would not have some of the problems we have. But Congress doesn't understand or acknowledge the obligation of this country to the native peoples. This country can send a man to the moon, and we're talking about spending billions of dollars for space programs. We should be able to invest a few billion more in Indian tribes to address this historic injustice."

Congressional budget-cutters say Indians should share the burden of balancing the federal budget. For example, in addition to funding the BIA, the Interior appropriations bill now before Congress also funds a number of major, non-Indian programs, including the National Park Service, the Forest Service and many museums and cultural institutions. "It's probably safe to say that all of these groups are going to be treated fairly equally, because no one can get an increase over 1996 without someone else getting a decrease," says Sen. Slade Gorton, R-Wash., chairman of the Senate Interior Appropriations Subcommittee and an outspoken advocate of cutbacks in Indian programs. "And I don't propose to close national parks or the Smithsonian." [2]

Indian advocates say their programs are legally protected because they are cited in scores of treaties between various tribes and the U.S. government. Though Congress granted Indians U.S. citizenship in 1924, they also are considered members of sovereign nations. "Indians are not a minority group," says Gwen Carr, a Cayuga who chairs the National Urban Indian Policy Coalition, a Chicago organization that represents Indians who live off reservations. "Indians are a distinct political entity, the only group of

"If We Could Develop Our Land . . .

It's an eight-mile hike down Havasu Canyon to the village of Supai, Ariz. The narrow switchback down the canyon wall eases into a winding, rocky descent among towering ocher cliffs toward the Colorado River. Pack horses carrying mail and supplies share the trail.

The clear blue waters of Havasu Creek mark the town limits. A narrow footbridge leads to the main street, a dusty road bordered by a 600-year-old irrigation ditch funneling precious water from the creek to the fields. A sign warns riders not to gallop in town. The road leads past the office where tourists pay their visitation fees, an elementary school and the administrative office of the Havasupai Tribe's seven-member council.

With no access to motor vehicles, Supai is the most remote village in the lower 48 states. While its location clearly distinguishes the 650-member Havasupai tribe from the other 551 federally recognized tribes in the United States, the problems the council members addressed recently could be heard almost anywhere in Indian country.

"The Havasupai people have been living here a long time," says Tribal Chairman Wayne Sinyella. "We've also been struggling a long time." Known as the Guardians of the Grand Canyon, the Havasupai once occupied hundreds of square miles of territory extending from the Grand Canyon southward about 80 miles, as far as present-day Flagstaff. But like other tribes across the country, the Havasupai lost most of their homeland to settlers and cattle ranchers after the mid-1800s. They suffered a major blow to their heritage after Teddy Roosevelt, awed by the Grand Canyon, declared the area a national park in 1903 and had the Indians driven out of the Colorado River basin — the Havasupai into adjacent Havasu Canyon. "The Forest Service bulldozed our homes, filled our wells and chased us out," Sinyella says. "Finally, this is where we ended up."

Supai village once served as a summer refuge where the tribe grew corn, melon, beans and other crops. These they stored for use during the winter months, when they moved to the plateau above to hunt. The tribe's seasonal migrations ended, Sinyella says, "when the government insisted on our kids going to school." After a nine-year struggle to regain part of their aboriginal homeland, the Havasupais received 124,000 acres under the 1974 Grand Canyon Enlargement Act. "This was a fraction of what we claimed to be our aboriginal territory," Sinyella says.

"The Havasupai people have been living here a long time. We've also been struggling a long time."

— Tribal Chairman Wayne Sinyella

Deprived of most of their winter hunting and gathering lands, they also suffered a radical change to their traditional way of life. Today only a few families live on the plateau, where the tribe grazes its horses and cows. Tribal members occasionally travel there to gather pine nuts and medicinal herbs or to hunt deer and rabbits. But most of the tribe now live permanently in Supai, close to the school and clinic as well as the small tourist hotel and rustic cafe.

Apart from territorial restrictions, the tribe's biggest concern, as it is throughout most of Indian country, is the impact of federal budget cuts on Indian programs. The 1975 Indian Self-Determination and Education Assistance Act (Public Law 93-638), dubbed "638," turned the administration of federal education, health, housing, law enforcement and other Indian programs over to the tribes that choose to manage them. The Havasupai run all the federal programs they participate in, except for law enforcement, which the Bureau of Indian Affairs (BIA) administers.

While 638 was welcomed by tribes as a means of achieving some independence from Washington, it was accompanied by progressive cuts in funding for Indian programs. The

people [in the U.S.] who have two governments. There are treaties that were made between American Indians and the federal government, so there is a government-to-government relationship, just like the one between the United States and Italy or any other foreign country."

Gorton dismisses the notion that tribal sovereignty makes Indians immune to budget cuts. "These are peculiar treaties because they are clearly the law of the land, but they can also be abolished by Congress at will," he says. "It's not like a treaty with Russia or Great Britain, where it's between two equal sovereigns." Such views have made Gorton a leading champion of non-Indian property owners, who challenge tribal claims to water and hunting and fishing rights that conflict with their own property rights.

Tribes across the country feel their very survival is threatened by what they see as an increasingly hostile attitude toward Indians by a government that seems to have forgotten its

. . . We Could Become More Self-Sufficient"

Havasupai receive $168,000 a year to run all their programs, or about $255 for each member of the tribe. (The tribe says the state of Arizona's total contribution is $4,000 a year.) "Allocations from BIA are very low," Sinyella says. "Congress approves dollars to the central office of BIA, but by the time every dollar comes down through the area offices to the tribes, we get only a few cents. We need more dollars to operate social services, senior citizens' program, education and housing. The list goes on and on."

Federal funds are crucial to the Havasupai because tourism is their only other source of income. Each year, about 25,000 visitors hike, ride horses or fly in by helicopter to see the spectacular waterfalls below Supai that have earned the tribe its designation as the "people of the blue-green water." The tribe was concerned that its fragile desert habitat was being harmed by the flow of tourists. But that concern has been replaced by a new worry: A devastating flood in 1991 and two later floods have all but destroyed the fragile falls, threatening the tribe's sole independent income base.

"We want Congress to change restrictions that say we can't harvest timber or mine or even issue public hunting permits on our land."

Desperate for an alternative, the tribal council tried to set up a casino in Williams, population 2,500 and 100 miles away — the closest town. "The plan was to set aside eight to 10 acres of city property," Sinyella explains. "The tribe would then go to the federal government to have the land converted to a reservation and later apply to the governor to negotiate a gaming compact." Negotiations were progressing with the town government, but Arizona Gov. Fife Symington rejected the proposal, refusing to discuss it with the tribe, and the deal fell through early this year.

Now the tribe is seeking to have restrictions lifted on its use of reservation lands on the plateau, the only part of the reservation that is accessible by car. "We want Congress to change restrictions that say we can't harvest timber or mine or even issue public hunting permits on our land," Sinyella says. "We'd also like to build up on top, maybe a motel, a restaurant, an RV park and a gas station. Our people need jobs, and these things could help meet the essential needs of our community. If we could develop and improve our land, we could become more self-sufficient instead of depending only on the BIA year after year."

The Havasupai Tribe's isolation is not all bad, tribal members concede. For one thing, young people have been largely spared exposure to urban gangs that have plagued other reservations. For another, it has been easier for tribal elders to pass on their language and culture to the next generation. Like other Indian children of his generation, Sinyella was taken from his family at an early age to attend school far from home, speak English and renounce his traditions. Sinyella and other Havasupai children were sent to school at Fort Apache, hundreds of miles away. "We were there for nine months a year for six years," he says. "Our parents became strangers to us. When we weren't speaking English, we spoke Apache. I didn't want this to happen to my kids."

Today children attend an elementary school in Supai, and all of them speak Havasupai. After the eighth grade, however, they must go on to high school in Kingman or Flagstaff, where most live with relatives. Far from home, as many as two-thirds drop out before obtaining a diploma. Despite the lack of employment opportunities in Supai, young people tend to return to the reservation to live. "Most young people come back to the reservation after school," Sinyella says. "Very few stay out for more than a year."

debt to the country's "first people." Some tribes see economic development — fueled by revenues from gambling operations — as the key to their survival. Since the 1988 Indian Gaming Regulatory Act (IGRA) allowed the nation's 552 tribes to set up casinos and other gambling operations on their reservations, 220 Indian casinos have cropped up in 26 states.

Indeed, gambling is by far the most lucrative industry in Indian country, and a few Indian casinos have been spectacularly successful. The Foxwoods Casino Resort in Ledyard, Conn., operated by the tiny Mashantucket Pequot Tribe, amassed profits of $319 million last year.[3] But Indian gaming has come under increasing attack in states that oppose gambling on moral grounds or already have non-Indian casino operations that don't want competition from the Indians.

Some Indians see the opposition to Native American gaming as yet another expression of racism by a society that can't come to grips with its bloody past. "It's very, very difficult for people to deal with successful Indians," says Marjorie Mitchell Bear Don't Walk, a Flathead and director of the Indian Health Board, a clinic in Billings, Mont. "Has Congress reacted to Donald Trump in the same way? I don't think so. We're being punished if we're successful in the free-market system."

Opponents of Indian gambling won an important victory March 27, when the U.S. Supreme Court ruled that Florida's Seminoles could not force the state to allow them to launch casino operations. While the ruling did not jeopardize existing Indian gaming operations in other states, it effectively placed a moratorium on new ones in states that oppose Indian gambling.

Most tribes, however, probably could not profit from gambling even if they could open casinos. Reservations typically are located in isolated areas far from the large population centers that gaming enterprises need to flourish. Some tribes rely entirely on tourism: The Havasupai run a small hotel to house visitors who hike, ride or helicopter into the canyon to visit the spectacular waterfalls along Havasu Creek. Other tribes, such as the Oneidas of Wisconsin and the Mississippi Band of Choctaw Indians, are entering the mainstream economy by setting up factories on their reservations that employ both Indians and non-Indians.

"Native American people want to be contributors to this society just as much as anyone else," says Oneida Chairman Deborah Doxtator. "We don't want a handout. But we also need to be given the means to bring ourselves up by our bootstraps. We're willing and able, but we've not always had the opportunities in front of us in a viable way."

As Indians look for ways to prosper in the American economy while protecting their unique heritage, these are some of the issues they face:

Do Indian tribes depend too heavily on aid from the federal government?

Many tribes on remote reservations with no tourist attractions or other economic enterprises depend almost entirely on government assistance to run their schools, health clinics, tribal governments and other institutions. These reservations are often the most severely afflicted with unemployment, alcoholism, crime and a pervasive sense of hopelessness.

"The single group of people who have had the most systematic and longest-lasting welfare system are at the same time the group of people who are most despairing, most out of the mainstream, generally speaking have low educational attainments and a very high percentage of unemployment."

— Sen. Slade Gorton, R-Wash.

Some critics of federal Indian policy say it's to blame for the desperate living conditions in many Indian communities. One thing is certain: No other issue sparks such heated exchanges between Indian advocates and their opponents.

"The single group of people who have had the most systematic and longest-lasting welfare system are at the same time the group of people who are most despairing, most out of the mainstream, generally speaking have low educational attainments and a very high percentage of unemployment," says Sen. Gorton. "So that association is absolutely clear. When you're deprived of the ability to make your own decisions, you're not very likely to do the kinds of things that are necessary to improve your condition. The fact that the system has gone on longer and is more pervasive [among Indians] than any place else and that its failure has been overwhelming simply can't be argued by anyone."

"It's not dependency that has fomented those things," counters Carr of the Urban Indian Policy Coalition. "It's genocide." Carr agrees with Gorton that the government is to blame for the misery in Indian country. But where the senator sees paternalistic welfare handouts as the culprit, she blames a long history of betrayals. "Picture the Jewish people being in concentration camps for the past 200 years, and ask them if that's about the welfare state," Carr says. "I don't think so. It's much deeper and much uglier than that."

But even on reservations where residents depend almost entirely on government programs, the recent federal budget cutbacks are being seen as a boost for Indian self-reliance. "Some

Indian people are looking at the cutbacks as a blessing in disguise," says Tom Arviso Jr., managing editor of *Navajo Times* in Window Rock, Ariz. "They say we've become too complacent, that we're too dependent on the government and that now we need to get off our butts and start working and taking care of things on our own."

The Navajos are the second-largest tribe in the country, counting some 300,000 members, about 250,000 of whom live on the vast reservation overlapping parts of Arizona, New Mexico and Utah. The Navajos have few prosperous enterprises. Like the Hopi, whose reservation lies inside Navajo lands, the Navajos have rejected gaming on moral grounds. They are hoping instead to enhance their small tourist industry by building hotels and restaurants to draw more visitors to the reservation's natural and archaeological treasures, such as Canyon de Chelly, Chaco Canyon and Monument Valley.

Like other rural tribes, the Navajos also view the revival of their traditional livelihood as a way out of their current problems. "We need to go back to farming and livestock and stop depending so much on buying food at the supermarket and using the microwave," says Arviso. "We need to start growing our own traditional foods again, like corn, melons and squash, and taking care of our water and livestock so we can fend for ourselves like we used to. We've gotten too far away from that kind of lifestyle."

While self-sufficiency remains a widely accepted goal, Indian advocates point to significant obstacles. Few people realize, for example, that the federal government holds reservation lands in trust for the tribes. Since they don't own the land and thus can't use it for collateral for loans, tribes often cannot obtain credit as easily as non-Indians to start up their own businesses.

"Indian people generally have said that they would welcome the same opportunities that anybody else has to develop factories or to build jobs, and if they did they probably wouldn't need so much government help," says Sen. Campbell. "The fact of the matter is, they can't do it. If you're in an Indian tribe and you want to build a factory on the reservation, you can't get the investment capital to do it because you have nothing you can put up for collateral."

Given such obstacles, Campbell and other advocates remind budget-cutters of the events that placed Indians in their current desperate straits. "If you gave back all the lands that were taken by force or subterfuge from Indian people long ago, they would be very happy to give up any government subsidies or programs," Campbell says. "In lieu of that, Indians feel they have a special right to earn whatever they can through 20th-century America's normal system of business. But at the same time, the government has a trust responsibility to them."

AP/Michael Okoniewski

The casino opened by Wisconsin's Oneida tribe in 1991 has provided revenue for investments in a hotel, convenience stores and a printing plant.

Is gambling the Indians' best hope for economic development?

Since Congress passed the Indian Gaming Regulatory Act in 1988, gambling has become an important source of revenue for many tribes. Operations ranging from one-room bingo halls to glitzy casinos generated $3.4 billion in gross earnings for tribes in 1994. [4]

Supporters of Indian gaming say it is by far Native Americans' most promising avenue to prosperity. "Gaming has had the broadest impact on economic development for the tribes and has produced the greatest amount of revenue on a broad basis for the tribes that are engaged in it," says Tom Acevedo, a member of the Confederated Salish and Kootenai Tribes in Montana and executive director of the National Indian Gaming Commission.

The IGRA requires tribes to invest their gaming profits in tribal services. After meeting its obligations under the act, the Foxwoods casino in Connecticut distributes $200,000 annually to each of the tribe's 200 adult members. [5]

But opponents of gambling point to the phenomenal success of Foxwoods and other casinos as proof that gambling is socially destructive. They cite nationwide data showing that about a quarter of casino and state lottery prof-

Health and Social Problems Plague Native Americans

If health statistics provide a reliable barometer of a group's well-being, Indians are at the very bottom of the ladder in American society. No group fares worse than Indians on a number of health indicators, according to the federal Indian Health Service, which serves recognized tribes and Alaska Natives.

The death rate among Indians from alcoholism is four and a half times that of the total U.S. population; from tuberculosis, three and a half times higher; from accidents and from diabetes mellitus, about one and a half times higher. Suicide and homicide also claim a disproportionately high number of Indians. [1]

Ever since Europeans first introduced whiskey to the New World, alcoholism has exacted a huge toll among Indians. Although the death rate among Indians from alcoholism has fallen by half since the early 1980s, it continues to plague Indian communities, even on reservations where tribal councils have banned alcohol altogether. Some scientists have suggested that a genetic anomaly explains Indians' susceptibility to alcoholism, a theory that may soon be tested by genetic mapping. [2]

But many Indians reject this theory and attribute alcoholism and most other health and social problems among Indians to their mistreatment by U.S. society. "Because there is institutional racism against Indians in this country, we have needed to comfort ourselves with food, alcohol and drugs," says Marjorie Mitchell Bear Don't Walk, executive director of the Indian Health Board of Billings, Mont. "If you are constantly told that you are no good, how can you be good? If you put other people down, you teach them not to be self-sufficient, you teach them that they are not capable of taking care of themselves. And yet the very people who do that don't want to support Indians by paying taxes to fund Indian programs."

Bear Don't Walk's outpatient clinic is one of 34 urban facilities established under the 1976 Indian Health Improvement Act to provide health care to non-reservation Indians or those who do not qualify for federal Indian programs because their tribal affiliations are not recognized by the government. Not being officially considered a Native American is blamed for contributing to alcoholism among Indians wherever they live. "My dad was a full-blood Little Shell Chippewa who was born and died without ever being a legal Indian in the eyes of the United States government," she says. "How do you think he felt about himself? My dad was stabbed to death when he was drunk."

Alcoholics don't always die of liver disease, but often succumb to suicide and accidents. "My experience of being around alcoholics my whole life and directing this facility for 10 years is that alcoholics who survive alcoholism will become diabetics," says Bear Don't Walk. Obesity, another persistent health problem among Indians, also is a contributing factor in diabetes. "My grandparents probably never ate more than 5 percent of what we eat today," says Bear Don't Walk. "The natural foods that they ate and the exercise they got are extremely different from what is socially acceptable for our way of life today."

Indian women, Bear Don't Walk says, die from alcoholism at 10 times the rate of non-Indian women, of diabetes at triple the rate and of cervical cancer at twice the rate of non-Indian women. "We have more than a 50 percent chance of having gall bladder problems and diabetes," she says. "Indian women are now drinking at the same rate as Indian men, and some studies show that of childbearing-age women, one in four is giving birth to children with fetal alcohol syndrome or other effects of the mother's alcohol abuse."

Poverty contributes not only to disease but also to social problems within the Indian community. Per capita income in 1989 among Indians was $8,284, compared with $14,420 for the total U.S. population, the Census Bureau reported in its 1990 survey. Nearly a third of Indians live in poverty, more than twice the overall U.S. poverty rate. And unemployment on some reservations exceeds 50 percent, especially those far from towns and job opportunities.

But proximity to urban centers is a mixed blessing for many reservations. Like young people in poverty-stricken inner cities across the country, Indian youth are falling prey to gang violence. "We've got stabbings, shootings, beatings and deaths every weekend, and most of them go unreported," says Tom Arviso Jr., managing editor of *Navajo Times* in Window Rock, Ariz. Although alcohol is banned on the Navajo reservation, he says, "Most of the time alcohol and drugs are involved."

Most of the gang activities are introduced by Indians or non-Indians from major cities such as Albuquerque or even from smaller towns, such as Gallup, N.M., and Flagstaff, Ariz., that lie just outside the vast reservation's borders. "The reason gangs take hold is that there's not a whole lot for our young people to do," Arviso says. "Without jobs, young people wander because they have too much idle time. It's really scary because we've all been touched in one way or another by the gang violence. Loved ones are killed needlessly, and our young people are killing themselves for no reason. It's hurting us and our culture."

[1] Indian Health Service, *Trends in Indian Health — 1995*, p. 5.

[2] See Rick Weiss, "Discovery May Be Brewing in Search for Genetic Link to Alcoholism," *The Washington Post*, July 1, 1996.

its come from just 5 percent of all players, evidence that gambling is addictive. [6] "There's very little socially redeeming about gambling," says Sen. Gorton. "The social pathology — the family breakup, the welfare created by widespread organized gambling — is an extremely serious problem. I'm relatively indifferent as to who gets the profits from it, so my concentration isn't on Indian gambling, though at the present time most of the expansion is through Indian tribes."

Some Indian tribes have resisted the economic lure of gambling for some of the same reasons cited by non-Indian critics. "There are a lot of tribes who have done quite well using Indian gaming to better themselves, but here on the Navajo reservation we turned it down," says Arviso. "Just last week our council voted for the second time against legalizing gaming. We feel there are better ways to generate revenue.

"Gaming just creates more problems," Arviso adds. "Alcoholism and drug abuse would go up, and people would be [throwing away] their money. The general belief is that it would be a large negative."

In comparison with Las Vegas or Atlantic City, Indian gambling is a small-stakes industry. Indian casinos raked in less than 10 percent of the $40 billion in U.S. gambling revenues in 1994. Like their non-Indian counterparts, most highly profitable Indian gaming operations are near population centers. "But those in the Midwest or the West — where the populations are small — are doing very modestly," says Acevedo. "So while gaming is a plus for them, it clearly isn't answering all their needs."

Some tribes that have prospered from gaming are investing their profits in new enterprises. Wisconsin's Oneidas, whose reservation encompasses part of Green Bay, found themselves in the same financial bind as other tribes. "We have properties, but they're in trust status with the government," says tribal Chairman Doxtator. "So they cannot be encumbered for bonding or financing purposes."

But the Oneidas, blessed by their urban location, have been able to develop a wide variety of new businesses using the revenues earned from a bingo hall that opened in 1976 and, since 1991, a casino. "Gaming has taken away a lot of the development barriers that we've run into over the years," Doxtator says. "It's a very quick source of revenue that has given us the leverage to do things that we could not do before." The tribe now runs a 301-room Radisson Hotel at the local airport, a chain of convenience stores and a small printing plant.

"This country was built on the land and the resources that were ceded to the government by the tribes. . . . But Congress doesn't understand or acknowledge the obligation of this country to the native peoples."

— Ada E. Deer, Assistant Interior Secretary for Indian Affairs

The Wisconsin Oneidas have been so successful that they are currently negotiating to buy some of the tribe's aboriginal lands near another Oneida reservation in New York state. The tribe also is branching out into off-reservation ventures. The Wisconsin Oneidas now own a one-third interest in a local bank, making them the first tribe with a federally chartered financial institution. In mid-June, the tribe broke ground on a new $6.9 million plant on the reservation that will produce computer chips for automatic car-door openers, medical devices and other electronic equipment. The joint venture between Oneida Nation Electronics and Plexus Corp., a high-technology firm based in Neenah, Wis., will employ almost 400 Indians and non-Indians from the Green Bay area.

A few tribes have managed to establish a foothold in their local economies without the benefit of gaming revenues. With little to offer but their members' labor, the Mississippi Band of Choctaws attracted a General Motors electronics assembly plant to their reservation outside Philadelphia, Miss. (The tribe later set up a riverboat gambling operation as well). The Salish and Kootenai Tribes co-manage a privately owned hydroelectric dam that has generated revenues enabling the tribes to invest in other businesses on and off their Montana reservation. But these are the exceptions. "Each of these enterprises has worked for those individual tribes," says Acevedo, "but they don't have the same general impact that gaming has had for all the tribes that are engaged in it."

Are Indians today victims of widespread discrimination?

Few Americans would challenge the

notion that Indians have long been victimized. From the time Columbus landed in the New World, whites seeking gold, farmland or simply a new homeland established their claims at the expense of the continent's original inhabitants. Even after the United States was founded, official policy continued to discriminate against Indians, who reluctantly ceded their ancestral lands before the inexorable push westward. Decimated by new diseases, vanquished during decades of Indian Wars, deprived of their traditional hunting way of life and confined to infertile reservation lands, Indians died by the hundreds of thousands in the first two centuries of U.S. history.

Many American Indians say the victimization continues unabated. Less apparent than the outright massacres of the past, critics say, the federal government's Indian policy today is still based on a form of racism that relegates Indians to the bottom rungs of the country's social and economic ladder. "The history of Indian-American governmental relations is full of betrayal, bloodshed and tears," says Carr of the Urban Indian Policy Coalition. "The Indian people represent collectively this country's shame. The entire BIA is dedicated to having Indians not be successful. So they keep them in a corner, out of sight, to manage them."

BIA head Deer says the Clinton administration is trying to change things. "Government policy is moving away from paternalism toward self-determination and self-governance," Deer says. But she agrees that racism still permeates American views of Indians. "There's always been an underlying racism in this society," she says. "This was the attitude from day one. Many tribes met the settlers with peace and friendship, but this was not reciprocated. The country still does not want to recognize our history, and we need to."

Racism directed against Indians continues to crop up in the society at large. "The Freemen that just left Jordan ranch [in Montana] in mid-June refer to Indians as prairie niggers, and this attitude is not limited to extremists," says Marjorie Bear Don't Walk. "People in Billings call the local K-Mart the Crow-Mart as a putdown because there are a lot of [Crow] Indians there. As a people, we have suffered racism since Columbus landed. The laws of this country are founded on racist attitudes from Europe. Racism today is a fact of life for us."

Bear Don't Walk says racism toward Indians is far more prevalent in the West, but others disagree. "You should go up to Connecticut" if you want to see racism, says Herb Becker, director of the Justice Department's Office of Tribal Justice. "It's not necessarily region-peculiar anymore."

Becker sees anti-Indian racism in the Northeast springing directly from the phenomenal success of the Mashantuckets' casino. "I'm a firm believer that non-Indians just can't stand to see Indians prosper." He says recent actions in his home state of New Mexico back up his claim. In compliance with the 1988 gaming act, Republican Gov. Gary E. Johnson signed compacts with a number of tribes allowing them to open casinos. But last summer the state Supreme Court ruled the agreements were invalid because they had not been ratified by the Legislature. When some tribal leaders refused to close their casinos, claiming that Indian gaming falls under federal jurisdiction, the state court ruled that no one in New Mexico could operate casino-type gaming.

"The Supreme Court ruled that gaming as a matter of public policy is illegal," says Becker. "But this was a blatant lie. In New Mexico you've got horse racing, you've got parimutuel betting, you've got every fraternal organization with slot machines and card rooms. They said that just so they could try to shut off tribal gaming." Becker concludes that racism is at the heart of the decision. "You still have racism in the South, of course, but it's no longer institutional," he says. "That has been replaced by institutional racism against Indians in the West and other places where tribes are successful." *

Critics of Indian gaming adamantly deny that racism colors their views. "Racism doesn't have anything to do with it," says Sen. Gorton. "It has to do with the feeling that gambling itself is highly socially undesirable." The senator backs a bill now before Congress that would establish a special commission to study the impact of gambling, including state lotteries and both Indian and non-Indian casinos, on players' behavior, on local crime patterns and on local and state economies. ■

BACKGROUND

Early Treaties

In the four centuries since Columbus' "discovery" of the Western Hemisphere in 1492, the indigenous peoples of what became the United States were nearly wiped out through war, starvation, disease and U.S. policies that many call genocidal. [7]

Today, federal relations with Indian tribes are based on treaties that were drawn up by the British during Colonial times and later by the U.S. government. [8] During the Colonial period, as European settlers competed for lands, they negotiated at least 175 treaties with tribes and tribal alliances, such as the powerful Iroquois confederacy in the North and the Creek confederacy in the South.

Under Article II of the U.S. Constitution, treaties must be ratified by a

* New Mexico's Indian gaming operations are running pending the outcome of a court challenge to the shutdown.

Chronology

1800s

Settlers, ranchers and prospectors push westward, forcing Indians to abandon much of their aboriginal territory.

Aug. 13, 1868
The last Senate-ratified Indian treaty is signed, with the Nez Perce Tribe of Idaho, bringing the number of ratified Indian treaties to 370. Three years later, Congress abolishes the ratifying process as a means of dealing with tribes.

1887
The General Allotment Act forces Indians to accept non-Indian ownership of reservation lands under a system that permits the federal government to purchase and resell reservation parcels not claimed by Indians under the law's terms.

1900-1950s

Goals of federal Indian policy shift between forced assimilation and exclusion of Indians.

1905
U.S. Supreme Court upholds Indian treaty rights in *United States v. Winans.*

1924
Indians are granted U.S. citizenship.

1934
The Indian Reorganization Act ends the allotment policy and provides funding for economic development on reservations.

1945
Over the next 15 years, some 12,000 Indians are "terminated," as the federal government rescinds official recognition of their tribes and removes 2.5 million acres of Indian land from protected status.

1960s-1980s

Self-determination becomes the watchword of federal Indian policy.

July 7, 1970
President Richard M. Nixon denounces termination policies and promises federal assistance to help Indians achieve greater autonomy.

1973
Two Indians die and an FBI agent is wounded during a shootout between federal agents and followers of the militant American Indian Movement (AIM) who had occupied the village of Wounded Knee on the Pine Ridge Reservation in South Dakota.

1975
The Indian Self-Determination and Education Assistance Act enables tribes to elect to administer federal education, health and other Indian programs. In *Antoine v. Washington* the U.S. Supreme Court rules that treaty rights hold for U.S.-tribal agreements signed after formal treaty-making ended.

1978
The Indian Child Welfare Act allows tribes to have limited authority to prevent adoption of Indian children by non-Indians.

1988
The Indian Gaming Regulatory Act (IGRA) allows tribes to negotiate compacts with their state governors to operate casinos. The same year House Concurrent Resolution 331 reaffirms "the constitutionally recognized government-to-government relationship with Indian tribes."

1990s

Indian rights are challenged by cuts in the funding of federal Indian programs and efforts to curtail Indian gaming.

April 29, 1994
President Clinton holds an unprecedented White House conference with more than 300 tribal leaders to hear their grievances.

1995
Amid growing resistance to Indian gaming, the New Mexico Supreme Court rules that existing gaming compacts are illegal and orders the casinos shut down. In December, Sen. John McCain, R-Ariz., introduces a bill that would shift authority away from BIA headquarters in Washington to area offices to give tribes greater influence over BIA decisions.

March 27, 1996
The U.S. Supreme Court challenges the IGRA by ruling in *Seminole Tribe of Florida v. Florida* that the tribe cannot force the state government to negotiate an agreement allowing it to open casino operations in Florida.

Not All Native Americans Are Indians

The term Native American is widely used today to describe the tribal peoples, or Indians, who were the original inhabitants of what is now the United States. But they are not the country's only Native Americans.

The aboriginal people of Alaska are Native Americans, too. They include three distinct groups: Indians, Aleuts and Eskimos. Like the ancestors of the Indians who populate the rest of North and South America, the ancestors of Alaska's Indians are believed to have migrated from Asia between 20,000 and 35,000 years ago, crossing the "land bridge" then connecting Siberia and Alaska (now the Bering Strait). Like Indians in the lower 48 states, Alaska's Athabaskan and coastal Indians live in tribes and speak languages that are distinct from the other Alaskan aboriginal peoples. [1]

The Aleuts crossed the land bridge later, though still in prehistoric times, and traditionally inhabited western Alaska and the Aleutian Islands. As many as 80 percent of the Aleuts died from disease and violence after coming in contact with Russian fur traders in the mid-1700s. Alaska's Eskimos, or Inuit, arrived still later and settled along the coasts and riversides as far north as the Arctic Ocean. Like the Aleuts, Eskimos traditionally lived in family units, or clans.

All three groups of Alaska's Native Americans have fared better than their counterparts in the lower 48 states. Under the 1971 Alaska Native Claims Settlement Act, these groups received collectively $1 billion in cash and 44 million acres of land rich in natural resources. They established regional corporations, in which all Native Alaskans are entitled to shares, to develop timber and oil industries and fisheries in Alaska, and to invest outside Alaska. [2]

Native Hawaiians comprise another distinct group of Native Americans, a title many disdain because of their turbulent relations with the United States. Descendants of Polynesians who sailed thousands of miles to settle in the Pacific island chain between 1,000 and 1,500 years ago, Native Hawaiians first came into contact with Europeans in 1778, when Captain James Cook landed. Some 90 percent of the island's 300,000 inhabitants soon died from diseases they contracted from the newcomers.

Hawaii was a sovereign country with a constitutional monarchy until a coup backed by American businessmen in 1893 overthrew the government. It became a U.S. territory in 1900. In 1959, Hawaii became the 50th state. Despite numerous laws aimed at improving their lot, many Native Hawaiians continue to live in severely impoverished conditions.

[1] See Jack Utter, *American Indians* (1993), pp. 14-17.

[2] See "From Fur-Trading to Portfolios," *The Economist*, May 25, 1996, p. 31.

two-thirds majority of the Senate. Article VI further states that treaties are binding on the states and others as "the supreme law of the land." U.S. treaties with Indian tribes, many of which predated the Constitution itself, were subsequently considered to be Article II treaties. As such, they had the same legal force as treaties with other countries, and were filed with the State Department.

But after the War of 1812 assured American sovereignty, Indian tribes lost their value as military assets, and treaty-making slowed. The last Senate-ratified Indian treaty was signed Aug. 13, 1868, with the Nez Perce tribe of Idaho, bringing the number of ratified Indian treaties to 370. At the same time, resentment toward the treaty-making process was building in the House of Representatives, which was responsible for funding the Indian programs emanating from treaties approved by the Senate.

In 1871, Congress abolished the constitutional treaty-making process with Indians. The law expressly refrained, however, from challenging the legal status of existing Indian treaties: ". . . [N]othing herein contained shall be construed to invalidate or impair the obligation of any treaty heretofore lawfully made and ratified with any such Indian nation or tribe." [9]

When Native Americans speak of treaty rights, they often take pains to note that they are not referring to rights that were given to them by the federal government, but rather to rights they retained for themselves in exchange for land they handed over to the United States. The U.S. Supreme Court upheld this interpretation in 1905 in *United States v. Winans,* noting that "the treaty was not a grant of rights to the Indians, but a grant of rights from them." [10] By the same token, Indian reservations are by law not a kind of ghetto to which tribal members are to be confined, but rather a small portion of a treaty-making tribe's ancestral homeland that it "reserved" for its exclusive domain.

Because westward expansion continued well into the 20th century, Indian tribes were forced to continue negotiating reductions in their land holdings with the federal government long after formal treaty-making ended in 1871. Subsequent Indian pacts, called "agreements," were subject to approval by both houses of Congress and generally were attached as riders to appropriations bills covering funding for Indian programs. Almost 100 such agreements were ratified by Congress. The last Indian land agreement, with the Wiminuche Band of Southern Ute Indians in Colorado, was approved in 1913.

After 1913, all future agreements between the federal government and Indian tribes were treated by Congress as any other initiative in the legislative process. But in its 1975 ruling in *Antoine v. Washington,* the Supreme Court declared that traditional treaty rights pertain to Indian agreements concluded after 1871 as well. "Once ratified by Act of Congress, the provisions of the agreements become law, and like treaties, the supreme law of the land." [11]

Indians Pushed Out

As a matter of political reality, however, Indian treaty rights were largely forgotten whenever they blocked other national policy goals. Since the early 1800s, Indians have been at the mercy of the policy pendulum: Successive generations of lawmakers have tried to solve the "Indian problem" by conflicting programs aimed either at segregating Indians or assimilating them into the larger society.

Beginning in the early 1800s, waves of settlers moved westward into Indian country. To make way for them, tribes were forceably relocated from 1817 until the mid-1880s. The first to go during this so-called "removal era" were virtually all the Eastern tribes, including the Delaware, Seminole and Cherokee, who were pushed west of the Mississippi and forced to relocate in Oklahoma, then considered to be of no interest to white settlers. By the 1880s, more than 40 tribes were in Oklahoma.

Even as it was relocating Indians far from white society, however, Congress in 1819 began appropriating money for a "Civilization Fund" run by missionaries. Its aim: to convert Indians to Christianity.

After the United States extended its territory to the Pacific Ocean under the 1848 Treaty of Guadalupe Hidalgo, westward expansion moved still deeper into Indian country, triggering the Indian wars of 1860-1880. Treaties were made and broken as successive waves of ranchers, prospectors and other newcomers took over Indian lands.

Forced Assimilation

During the last half of the century, efforts to assimilate Indians gave rise to Indian boarding schools, where children were forced to live away from their families, speak English and adopt American dress and customs.

Further changes in Indian life were carried out under the 1887 General Allotment Act, which ended Indians' communal ownership of reservation lands. The act forced Indians to adopt the European model of land ownership, allotting 160 acres to every reservation family head. The parcels were not actually owned, however, but were to be held in trust by the federal government.

In addition, the act permitted surplus lands within reservations to be sold by the government to non-Indians, with the proceeds to be used for the tribes' benefit. As a result of the allotment policy, which continued into the 1930s, more than half the people living within the boundaries of many reservations today are non-Indians.

Indians were granted U.S. citizenship in 1924. But the policy of forced assimilation proved a dismal failure for most Indians. Confined to marginal lands, deprived of the buffalo that had been slaughtered by non-Indians during the westward expansion, Indians were beset by poverty, alcoholism and disease. The federal government finally acknowledged the failure of forced assimilation in 1928.

Allotment Policy Ends, Termination Begins

In another policy about-face, the 1934 Indian Reorganization Act ended allotment, provided funding for economic development on reservations and restored some degree of tribal self-governance. Concluding that the federal government had failed as an effective administrator of Indian affairs, Congress also that year gave the states a greater role in administering some Indian programs.

Barely a decade later, however, federal Indian policy again shifted, this time ushering in the so-called termination period of 1945-1960. Tribes occupying valuable lands, such as the Klamath who lived in Washington's timber forests and the Agua Caliente of Palm Springs, Calif., were among more than 100 tribes that were "terminated." In other words, they were deemed no longer qualified to own reservation land or receive benefits reserved for Indians.

In addition to making valuable land available to non-Indians, termination reduced the federal government's welfare burden and enabled it to physically relocate Indians to cities where they were expected to blend into the dominant society. By 1962, some 12,000 Indian people had lost official recognition, while some 2.5 million acres of Indian land were removed from protected status. [12]

Self-Determination

Termination gave way to self-determination as a major goal of Indian policy after 1960. Presidents John F. Kennedy (1961-63) and Lyndon B. Johnson (1963-69) called for investments in economic development on reservations. The 1968 Indian Civil Rights Act further prohibited states from assuming jurisdiction over Indian lands without obtaining tribal consent.

President Richard M. Nixon (1969-74) went furthe rthan any of his predecessors in denouncing termination and in supporting Indian autonomy while continuing federal assistance programs. "Self-determination among the Indian people can and must be encouraged," Nixon proclaimed July 7, 1970. "This, then, must be the goal of any new national policy toward the Indian people." [13] With presidential support, Congress passed a number of laws in the 1970s to strengthen Indian self-determination.

Key legislation of this period included the 1975 Indian Self-Determination and Education Assistance Act (Public Law 93-

638), which Indians often refer to as 638. By funneling federal monies directly to tribes through contracts and grants, 638 encourages tribal councils to assume control over school, health, housing, law enforcement and other programs formerly administered by federal agencies. In this way, the federal government grants tribes some autonomy in much the same way as it does other localities.

The self-determination movement continued through the 1970s and '80s, with several Supreme Court decisions strengthening Indian sovereignty. The movement reached a climax in 1973 when a group of Indians led by Russell Means of the militant American Indian Movement (AIM) occupied the village of Wounded Knee, S.D., on the Pine Ridge Reservation. Two Indians died and an FBI agent was critically wounded in the shootout with federal agents ending the 71-day siege. AIM, which had been founded to help Indians who had been displaced to cities, lost much of its support among Indians after Wounded Knee.

Though President Ronald Reagan (1981-89) reaffirmed his support for Indian self-determination and economic development, budget cuts during his administrations reduced federal spending for Indian programs. Still, Indian tribes obtained a congressional statement of support for their unique status in U.S. society. A House resolution adopted Oct. 4, 1988, reaffirmed "the constitutionally recognized government-to-government relationship with Indian tribes which has been the cornerstone of the nation's official Indian policy." It also acknowledged the government's "need to exercise the utmost good faith in upholding its treaties with the various tribes."

Indian Gaming

In 1988, the same year that the House reaffirmed tribal rights, Congress also passed legislation defining conditions under which Indians could engage in gambling operations. Gaming not only became the most promising source of revenue for many tribes but also "by far the most politically charged economic issue in Indian country during this final decade of the 20th century," according to Professor Jack Utter of the Center for Indian Bilingual Teacher Training at Prescott (Ariz.) College. [14]

"If you gave back all the lands that were taken by force or subterfuge from Indian people long ago, they would be very happy to give up any government subsidies or programs. In lieu of that, Indians feel they have a special right to earn whatever they can through 20th-century America's normal system of business."

— Sen. Ben Nighthorse Campbell, R-Colo.

Although many tribes traditionally engaged in various forms of gambling, it was not until 1979, when the Seminoles opened a commercial bingo operation, that any tribe operated profitable gambling halls. Consistent with its support of Indian self-determination, the Reagan administration endorsed Indian gaming. As many tribes across the country followed the Seminoles' lead, however, conflicts erupted among state, federal and tribal governments over jurisdiction over the new gambling operations.

The issue was at the center of a landmark dispute between California and the Cabazon Band of Cahuilla Mission Indians, who ran a gambling operation on their reservation 20 miles east of Palm Springs. A federal court ruled in *California v. Cabazon* — and the U.S. Supreme Court affirmed — that tribes could legally engage in forms of gambling that were not expressly prohibited by the state in which the tribe is located.

The Supreme Court further held that because all state gaming regulations fall under civil law — under which Indian tribes cannot be held accountable — states are required under federal law to enter into negotiations with tribes to establish mutually acceptable regulations of Indian gaming operations. The states can only refuse to negotiate compacts for types of gambling that they expressly prohibit under criminal law.

To establish a regulatory framework for Indian gaming, Congress passed the 1988 Indian Gaming Regulatory Act. The law defines three classes of

Indian gambling. Class I, including traditional Indian games, are under the exclusive jurisdiction of tribes. Class II games, comprising bingo, lotto, pull tabs and some card games, are allowed on Indian lands if they are conducted in a state that allows them for any other group. Only two states, Hawaii and Utah, prohibit all gambling. The tribes share regulatory jurisdiction over Class II gaming with the National Indian Gaming Commission, created under IGRA.

Class III gaming includes all other forms of gambling, primarily the games found in casinos, such as slot machines, roulette, blackjack and any electromechanical versions of games such as video poker and video bingo. Horse and dog racing also fall into this category. A tribe can offer Class III gaming only after it has negotiated a compact with the state stipulating the size and type of gaming facilities. Because of resistance to Indian gambling either from the non-Indian gambling industry or citizens who oppose gambling on moral grounds, some state governments have refused to negotiate compacts for Class III gaming. In several cases, as a result, tribes have sued their states for failing to negotiate with them in "good faith," as the law requires. ■

CURRENT SITUATION

Clinton's Policy

Continuing a policy outlined by President George Bush (1989-93), President Clinton early in his term championed tribal sovereignty and Indian self-determination. He appointed Deer, a Menominee, to head the BIA. "President Clinton said he wanted a government that looked like America," says Deer. "So here I am, the first woman to serve in this position. And I'm not doing things in the way they've been done in the past."

On April 29, 1994, Clinton and his top officials listened to the concerns of more than 300 tribal leaders invited to air their grievances at an unprecedented White House conference on Indian issues. Following the meeting, Clinton ordered the heads of 15 federal departments and agencies to consult directly with tribes when dealing with Indian issues "in order to ensure that the rights of sovereign tribal governments are fully respected." [15]

"This is the first time that any administration has taken the time and energy to put together a procedures document for each one of its resource agencies that deals with Indian tribes," says Jim Pace, a spokesman for the Interior Department's Office of American Indian Trust. The office was set up in 1991 by the Bush administration as a separate entity from BIA to strengthen the federal government's trust responsibility toward Indian tribes. "The procedures are dynamic," Pace says, "in that the agencies can change them as they need to, to make sure they're meeting the needs of the tribes."

The policy of tribal self-determination also is changing the way tribes receive federal support. Deer says that about 55 tribes to date have chosen to take advantage of this new approach by signing self-governance compacts with the federal government that enable them to receive federal monies in block grants, which they then spend according to their particular needs. "In the past, a lot of control and decision-making were exerted by the federal government," she says. "But now there is much more flexibil-

Ceremonial dancers from Arizona's Havasupai tribe performed this year at the SuperBowl and the Arizona Indian Festival, both in Phoenix.

ity. Government policy is moving toward self-determination."

The Clinton administration also has tried to increase funding for Indian programs. "This administration has submitted the largest budget request for the BIA ever, and that was the $1.9 billion budget request for fiscal 1997," says Deer. "This reflects the sensitivity of the administration in trying to meet the longstanding needs in Indian country. Also under this administration, 12 new tribes have been recognized."

The administration is not without critics among Indians, however. Urban Indian activist Carr faults the president for failing to defend Indian programs from the budget ax. "I think he's a decent man who's in a lousy job and has to make incredibly unpleasant decisions," she says. "Because American Indians are a segment of the population that is not a huge voting bloc, we are at the mercy of the whims of someone else's conscience. The monies that they cut from the budget are not going to balance the budget. What they're going to do is create starvation, disease and despair in people who have had more than a bellyfull of all those things."

Program Cuts

The administration's advocacy of Indian rights lost momentum after Republicans won control of both houses of Congress in the November 1994 elections. As balancing the budget became the overriding priority for Congress, spending for Indian programs fell dramatically. The fiscal 1996 budget for BIA programs totaled $1.6 billion, a decrease of $160 million from the year before.

Budget cutbacks are taking a heavy toll on the tribes. A 4 percent annual increase in the school-age population on reservations, for example, means that education programs can't keep up with the need. "The per student allocation of the bureau is about $3,000, which is about half that of the public schools," says Deer, who notes that Indian child welfare protection services, law enforcement and family services are among the programs that have suffered as a result of budget cuts. "Cutting these funds is like blaming the victim. It gets really tedious. As President Nixon stated back in 1970, by any socioeconomic indicator, Indians and Alaska Natives are at the bottom of the ladder. The funding that has been approved will not enable the tribes to get over this. I don't even know if it will maintain the status quo."

Although the Clinton administration requested $1.8 billion in BIA funding for fiscal 1997, there is little support in Congress to boost spending for Indian programs. Despite charges from the White House that the fiscal 1997 appropriations bill for the Interior Department would violate Indian rights by eliminating services promised in treaties, the House on June 20 passed a $12.3 billion spending bill that includes $239 million less than Clinton requested for BIA.

There is little indication that the Senate will augment the bureau's budget. "Basically, we'll have a freeze," says Sen. Gorton, who chairs the Appropriations Subcommittee overseeing Interior Department funding. "We'll have the same amount of money for 1997 as for 1996 for the Interior Department, and out of that total I've got to fund almost all of the Indian programs, as well as national parks and monuments, the Bureau of Land Management, the National Forest Service, energy conservation and all of our cultural institutions."

The conflict over funding Indian programs is pitting a Republican-dominated Congress against a Democratic White House. But Indian policy is not a strictly partisan issue. The most vocal advocates on both sides of the debate over Indian rights in Congress — Arizona Sen. John McCain, an Indian supporter, and opponent Gorton — are both Republicans. And the lone Indian member of Congress, Campbell of Colorado, was elected in 1992 as a Democrat but switched to the Republican Party in March 1995 because he supported the GOP call for a constitutional amendment to balance the budget.

Lawmakers on both sides of the budget debate agree on the need to restructure the oft-criticized BIA. Citing a General Accounting Office finding released May 3 that government auditors were unable to account for an astounding $2.4 billion held in trust accounts for Indian tribes, McCain charged the agency at a recent hearing with "theft from the Indian people. I'm afraid the BIA's approach has been as bad as the land-grabbing policies of the past by which United States agencies separated Indians from their lands. This time-weary way of handling Indian assets has got to stop." [16]

In December, McCain introduced a bill that would shift authority away from BIA headquarters in Washington to area offices in order to give tribes greater influence over bureau operations.

Tribal Sovereignty

At the same time that Indian tribes are suffering program cutbacks at the hands of Congress, they are facing a mounting challenge from states over the extent of tribal sovereignty.

The U.S. Supreme Court handed a number of states a key victory in their quest to limit the ability of tribes to start gaming operations. On March 27, the court ruled in *Seminole Tribe of Florida v. Florida* that states cannot be sued in federal court for refusing to engage in good-faith negotiations with Indian tribes over opening casinos. The 5-4 ruling challenges the 1988 IGRA, which granted tribes the right to sue recalcitrant states over this issue.

The *Seminole* decision does not

At Issue:

Should Congress make it easier for non-Indians to adopt Indian children?

REP. GERALD B.H. SOLOMON, R-N.Y.
FROM TESTIMONY BEFORE THE SENATE INDIAN AFFAIRS COMMITTEE, JUNE 26, 1996

yes

As some of our sociologists and social workers negatively portray adoption and adoptive families, it is up to those of us who work with personal experience of adoption to relay its importance to the formation of our children and the strengthening of the family. . . .

It is up to those of us who have been adopted not only to share our stories with others but to speak out in favor of the adoption decision. My support has grown out of my fundamental view that every human life is precious and that every person deserves the right to life and a happy home.

I, myself, was blessed to be adopted by a generous stepfather and raised in a loving family. For these reasons, I wholeheartedly supported recent adoption legislation in the House, HR 3286. This bill makes adoption an option for families of all income levels by offering a $5,000 tax credit while also streamlining the process for interracial cases. This groundbreaking legislation will decrease the backlog of children in foster care and help find caring homes for all children. This legislation is extremely important in reforming adoption regulations. In the limited legislative schedule we have remaining, we must finish work on this bill to allow for the soonest relief for American families.

I am here today to also offer my full support for reform of the Indian Child Welfare Act to add to this adoption legislation. The Indian Child Welfare Act was passed in 1978 in response to a terrible problem within the Indian community; the high numbers of Indian children being placed in foster care and the breakup of many Indian families because of the unwarranted removal of their children by non-tribal public and private agencies. . . .

The problem that the act was created to correct, namely the inordinate number of Indian children in foster care, has actually risen since its enactment because of the increased authority the act can give an Indian tribe.

There have been cases of parents being blocked from adopting children because the Indian Child Welfare Act allows retroactive registration even after the biological parents have given up all legal rights to the child. . . .

This legislation is extremely important to the families of this country, Indian and non-Indian. Adoption plays a vital role in strengthening the family unit and protecting the values of this great nation. We must remember that the best interests of the children must be paramount in all child custody proceeding. Congress must work diligently to remove barriers to adoption and provide a sense of security to adoptive parents and children that their adoptions will be permanent.

SEN. DANIEL K. INOUYE, D-HAWAII
FROM TESTIMONY BEFORE THE SENATE INDIAN AFFAIRS COMMITTEE, JUNE 26, 1996

no

The removal of Indian children from their families and tribal communities has deep roots in this country. From the very beginning of our history as a nation, deliberate efforts by Europeans to "civilize" and "Christianize" the inhabitants of this country were directed at Indian children. . . .

These attitudes have also served to promote the removal of Indian children from their homes and place them in adoptive homes. . . . The adoption of Indian children became popular at a time when there was a decline in healthy, white children available for adoption by childless couples. Religious groups also encouraged their members to become foster or adoptive parents to Indian children. The Latter-day Saints placement program removed as many as 2,000 Hopi and Navajo children every year from their reservations, placing them in Mormon homes throughout the country.

In the early 1970s, the erosion of Indian family life received extensive publicity. Surveys conducted in 1969 and 1974 by the Association on American Indian Affairs disclosed the shocking disparity in placement rates for Indian and non-Indian children. These surveys revealed that over 25-35 percent of all Indian children were separated from their families and placed in foster homes, adoptive homes or institutions. . . .

The Indian Child Welfare Act was a reform measure enacted by the Congress in 1978 to combat "the wholesale separation of Indian children from their families" and tribal communities. With the passage of the act, federal law required that preference by given to Indian families, and Indian foster care and group homes in the placement of Indian children by state and private social service agencies. The act authorized an Indian tribe to intervene on behalf of a child in court proceedings that involve child custody matters and the placement of Indian children. . . .

Despite its shortcomings, the Indian Child Welfare Act serves as a ray of hope and promise to Indian people striving to retain their heritage and pride in a pluralistic society. The law was enacted by Congress to secure a long-overdue protection for Indian children. Tribal leaders have been resisting the removal of their children for over two and a half centuries. For each time an Indian child is taken from their ranks, their very existence as a culturally distinct people is diminished, and this nation's first Americans are threatened to the point of extinction.

I believe that it is time that Washington hears from Indian country on this matter that is of such critical importance to their efforts to preserve Indian families. After all, it is their children that will be affected by any amendments to the act.

FOR MORE INFORMATION

Bureau of Indian Affairs, Interior Department, Main Interior Bldg., 18th and C Sts. N.W., Washington, D.C. 20240; (202) 208-3711; www.doi.gov/bureau-indian-affairs.html. The main agency involved in federal Indian policy administers programs benefiting federally recognized tribes, mostly on reservations.

National Congress of American Indians, 1301 Connecticut Ave. N.W., Washington, D.C. 20003; (202) 466-7767; www.ncai.org. The largest advocacy group representing Indians monitors legislation and regulations and provides information on member tribes.

National Indian Gaming Commission, 1441 L St. N.W., 9th floor, Washington, D.C. 20005; (202) 632-7036; www.nigc.gov. Created under the 1988 Indian Gaming Regulatory Act, the commission oversees the management of casino gambling operations run by Indian tribes.

National Urban Indian Policy Coalition, 4753 N. Broadway, Suite 1126, Chicago, Ill. 60640; (312) 784-0808. The coalition represents the interests of non-reservation Indians, who comprise more than half the Indian population and who do not qualify for most government support programs.

jeopardize existing gaming compacts, but it does call into question tribes' ability to open new casinos as the law allows. "The question is, in the long run, when some of these compacts have to be renewed, whether *Seminole* will impact them," says gaming commission Director Acevedo. "For those tribes that have not compacted with states, the ruling in effect acts almost like a moratorium on new gaming operations."

Because the 1988 law allows tribes to turn to the Interior Department for help when they run into obstacles with states over gaming, the Supreme Court ruling effectively left the issue in the hands of Interior Secretary Bruce Babbitt. But hostility to Indian gaming runs high in states that could prove influential in the November presidential election, such as Florida and California. For this reason, observers agree that it is highly unlikely that Babbitt will force the issue until after the election.

Meanwhile, states'-rights advocates welcomed the Supreme Court ruling. "I think it is entirely wrong to tell a state, whether it's Washington or Florida, that it cannot control the gambling within its boundaries," says Gorton. "I'm opposed to the expansion of Indian gambling because I'm opposed to the expansion of all gambling unless it's the decision of the people of an entire state that they want to go ahead with the activity. Under those circumstances, obviously I approve of the Supreme Court decision."

Gorton is at the center of another challenge to Indian rights in his home state of Washington, where the Lummi tribe is contesting the rights of non-Indian homeowners on their reservation to have unlimited access to reservation water. As a result of the allotment policies that enabled non-Indians to purchase reservation land, about half the residents of the Lummi Reservation are non-Indian homeowners. When the tribe dug a large well close to these private properties, the homeowners complained that the Lummis were threatening their water supply.

The homeowners cannot sue the tribe, however, because it is protected by the Indians' longstanding right to sovereign immunity. "It is the feeling of the non-Indians that what the Indians want to do is to make their property close to worthless, buy it at distressed prices and drive them off the reservation," says Gorton, who advocates abolishing Indian rights to sovereign immunity. "I believe that Indian self-determination and sovereignty are totally appropriate to the extent that they apply to the affairs of the members of the tribe," he says. "I do not believe that they should grant them special rights against their non-Indian neighbors, who can't vote in their elections and who aren't members of their tribe."

States won another concession June 20, when the House granted them more power to collect taxes on all Indian-run businesses. Under current law, tribes may buy land outside reservations and place it in trust with the government, thus shielding any businesses opened there from retail sales taxes. The new measure, an amendment to the $12.3 billion Interior appropriations bill for fiscal 1997, would require tribes to agree with states on tax collection before the land could be placed in trust. [17] The measure has long been sought by states such as New York, where Republican Gov. George E. Pataki plans to begin this summer taxing sales at gas stations and convenience stores run by the Senecas and other tribes. [18]

Another challenge to Indian sovereignty now before Congress would restrict the authority of tribes to intervene in the adoption of Indian children by non-Indians. (*See "At Issue," p. 221.*) A measure passed May 10 by the House to provide a tax credit of up to $5,000 to defray adoption expenses would also prohibit officials from making race the determining factor in adoption decisions. This would overturn a provision of the Indian Child Welfare Act, enacted in 1978 to halt longstanding adoption practices that handed as many as a third of Indian children over to non-Indian parents. [19]

Calling the measure "well-intended but misguided," McCain promised to try to keep the restriction on tribal authority out of the adoption measure when it goes to the Senate floor. "Nothing is as precious as our children," he said. "This is as true for Indians as for non-Indians." [20] ■

OUTLOOK

Taking Control

Many experts on Indian policy see the assault on tribal sovereignty by Congress and the states as a threat to Indians' ability to survive. Joseph Kalt, director of Harvard University's Project on American Indian Economic Development, believes that sovereignty is the key to economic development on reservations. "Our research says quite clearly that the successful tribes, which have broken their institutional dependency on the federal government, have done it in a two-step process of first asserting and taking control of their own sovereignty, and second, backing that up by building their own institutions of government," Kalt says.

Kalt compares Indian lands to Eastern Europe. "The countries like Hungary and the Czech Republic, which got out early from under the Soviet umbrella and are succeeding now, were able to establish the rule of law," Kalt says. "The story is the same in Indian country, where we keep finding that sovereignty precedes economic development."

To thwart current moves to erode tribal sovereignty, many Indian advocates are calling for greater participation by tribal members in local and national politics. "There should be more Indians here, or none at all," says Sen. Campbell. "One [Native American in Congress] is the wrong number; I can't do enough because I don't have the resources. There are 1.3 million enrolled Indians in this country, and anthropologists say there may be as many as 15 million Americans who have Indian ancestry that are not on a [tribal] roll. I can't very well say I speak for all Indians because they're not alike."

Campbell may have company after this fall's elections. At least three Indians are running on the Democratic ticket for the House — Bill Yellowtail, a Crow from Montana, Joe Bowen, an Upper Skagit from Washington state, and Georgianna Lincoln, an Athabaskan from Alaska.

Meanwhile, younger Indian leaders are gaining experience in tribal government with an eye toward higher office. "This is definitely the way we are going to have to go," says the Oneidas' Doxtator, who at 35 is thought to be the youngest female tribal leader in the country. "I'm not at the point of entering national politics just yet, but I do have that as a goal down the road for myself. That's the way we're going to be able to help America know and understand what our issues are on a political level." ■

Notes

[1] See "How to Succeed, How to Fail," *The Economist,* April 6, 1996, pp. 25-31.

[2] For a critical view of Gorton's record on Indian affairs, see Paul Shukovsky, "Sincerely Yours," *Common Cause Magazine,* fall 1995, pp. 22-23.

[3] See Howard Rudnitsky, "Big Chief Kerzner," *Forbes,* April 22, 1996, pp. 176-180.

[4] From testimony by Associate Deputy Attorney General Seth P. Waxman at hearings before the Senate Indian Affairs Committee held May 9, 1996.

[5] See Bruce Upbin, "Indian Chief," *Forbes,* May 20, 1996, pp. 179-180.

[6] See Blaine Harden, "Gambling Study Clears Senate Hurdle," *The Washington Post,* May 11, 1996. See also "Gambling Boom," *The CQ Researcher,* March 18, 1994, pp. 241-264.

[7] For background, see "Native Americans," *The CQ Researcher,* May 8, 1992, pp. 385-408.

[8] Unless otherwise specified, material in this section is based on Jack Utter, *American Indians* (1993).

[9] *Ibid.,* p. 46.

[10] *Ibid.,* p. 50.

[11] *Ibid.,* p. 54.

[12] *Ibid.,* p. 256.

[13] *Ibid.,* p. 257.

[14] *Ibid.,* p. 134.

[15] The White House, "Memorandum for the Heads of Executive Departments and Agencies," April 29, 1994.

[16] McCain, chairman of the Senate Indian Affairs Committee, spoke June 11, 1996, at the committee's hearing on Indian trust fund management.

[17] See Allan Freedman, "House Passes Interior Bill, But Difficulty Lies Ahead," *Congressional Quarterly Weekly Report,* June 22, 1996, pp. 1748-1749.

[18] See Raymond Hernandez, "Reservations May Be Taxed on Some Sales Outside Tribes," *The New York Times,* May 5, 1996.

[19] See Lori Nitschke, "Panel Votes to Delete Limits on Tribal Role in Adoptions," *Congressional Quarterly Weekly Report,* June 22, 1996, p. 1767. See "Adopting Native American Children," in "Adoption," *The CQ Researcher,* Nov. 26, 1993, pp. 1033-1056.

[20] Utter, *op. cit.,* pp. 258-259.

Bibliography

Selected Sources Used

Books

Bordewich, Fergus M., *Killing the White Man's Indian: Reinventing Native Americans at the End of the Twentieth Century*, Doubleday, 1996.
The author, who spent much of his childhood on Indian reservations, challenges white society's myths about Indians as mindless victims or inhuman savages to examine their place in modern U.S. society.

Gattuso, John, ed., *Insight Guides: Native America*, Houghton Mifflin, 1994.
Introduced by an insightful overview of American Indian history, this tour guide of Indian country describes the culture and history of individual tribes of North America.

Matthiessen, Peter, *Indian Country*, Penguin, 1979.
A noted naturalist and author cites 10 tragic episodes of encroachment by whites on Indian lands that reflect mainstream society's threat to Indian culture.

Utter, Jack, *American Indians: Answers to Today's Questions*, National Woodlands Publishing Co., 1993.
A professor at the Center for Indian Bilingual Teacher Training at Prescott (Ariz.) College offers an excellent review of legal, cultural and social issues facing Indians today.

Articles

"The Native — and Not So Native — American Way," *The New York Times Magazine,* Feb. 27, 1994, pp. 45-52.
Two articles point out differing approaches to economic development. In "The Apaches," Eric Eckholm describes a tribe that is trying to survive by combining traditional enterprises with assembly shops. In "The Pequots," Francis X. Clines shows how a small Eastern tribe has struck it rich with casinos.

Reno, Janet, "A Federal Commitment to Tribal Justice Systems," *Judicature*, November-December 1995, pp. 113-117.
The U.S. attorney general reviews the history of U.S.-Indian relations in the area of law enforcement and the courts in an issue of the magazine dedicated entirely to the Indian tribal court system.

Shukovsky, Paul, "Sincerely Yours," *Common Cause Magazine*, fall, 1995, pp. 22-23.
With his campaigns to defend non-Indian property rights and reduce funding for many Indian programs, Sen. Slade Gorton, R-Wash., has earned a reputation as the one of the most ardent critics of Indian sovereignty in Congress.

Van Biema, David, "Bury My Heart in Committee, " *Time*, Sept. 18, 1995, pp. 48-51.
Many of the country's poorest Indians, such as the Pine Ridge Oglala Sioux, live on remote reservations with few employment opportunities. They faced even greater destitution last fall as Congress cut funding for Indian programs.

Reports and Studies

Cornell, Stephen, and Joseph P. Kalt, *Reloading the Dice: Improving the Chances for Economic Development on American Indian Reservations,* Harvard Project on American Indian Economic Development, March 1992.
The authors examine the myriad obstacles to economic development in Indian country and conclude that success depends on three factors: sovereignty, effective governing institutions and a realistic economic plan that harnesses each tribe's particular assets.

Indian Health Service, U.S. Department of Health and Human Services, *Trends in Indian Health 1995.*
The Indian Health Service, set up in 1954 to provide health care to members of recognized tribes, publishes statistics that provide a barometer of health in Indian country. Indians are far more likely to suffer from alcoholism, diabetes and a number of other diseases than other Americans.

National Indian Gaming Association, *A Historical Review of Gaming in the United States,* April 1994.
An advocacy group presents an overview of both Indian and non-Indian gambling in the United States and assess the impact of Indian gaming on the industry as a whole.

Walke, Roger, *Indian Issues in the Second Session of the 104th Congress*, Congressional Research Service, Feb. 23, 1996.
The author, an analyst at the Library of Congress' research branch, found that more than 340 bills introduced during the current session of Congress have provisions that would affect Indian tribes.

13 Women in Sports

JANE TANNER

Notre Dame University basketball star Ruth Riley led the Fighting Irish women's team to its first national championship this spring, clinching the final against Purdue after making two free throws with 5.8 seconds left in the game. Not surprisingly, she is a sought-after speaker throughout basketball-crazed Indiana.

In the lobby of Notre Dame's basketball arena, a poster features Riley next to men's basketball standout Troy Murphy. The poster is in a trophy case with awards, basketball shoes and other memorabilia. This year, for the first time, the contents of the trophy case are split evenly between a male and female player, Riley and Murphy.

"If there's something of Troy's, there's something of mine matching," Riley says.

Reuters/Gary Brady

Notre Dame's Ruth Riley received the most valuable player award after scoring 28 points against Purdue in the NCAA Women's Basketball Championship on April 1 in St. Louis. Notre Dame won 68-66.

Women athletes are getting equal billing elsewhere on campus as well. The university bookstore, which once sold only men's basketball team jerseys, now sells jerseys for women and girls with Riley's number 00. And, thanks to a generous donor, both the men's and women's basketball teams recently got identical, new locker rooms. Riley was surprised. "They've always had a lot of stuff for guys," she says. "It's starting to equal out a bit."

But, in fact, Notre Dame may be moving faster than most colleges to equalize spending between male and female sports, partly because its women's teams are so successful. Besides the success of women's basketball, the women's soccer team was ranked No. 1 until it lost in the national semifinals. In addition, with its generous alumni and national appeal to broadcasters and sponsors, Notre Dame has the wherewithal to boost women's sports programs.

Advocates for equal treatment of women's sports say the progress made at Notre Dame reflects the changing landscape on many campuses across the nation. Thanks to a landmark 1972 law known as Title IX, public secondary schools and colleges cannot discriminate against girls or women in their sports programs. *

In addition to boosting excitement about women's college basketball, the 1972 law has helped spur interest in women's sports among broadcasters. For instance, for the first time, broadcasters are bidding to carry the National Collegiate Athletic Association (NCAA) women's basketball finals, beginning in 2003. CBS offered $200 million for the rights to broadcast the women's basketball finals and a package of other college sports for 11 years. That's nearly seven times higher than what ESPN has been paying. [1]

Meanwhile, the Big East tournament game this spring between top-ranked Notre Dame and No. 2 Connecticut "was the highest rated and most-watched women's basketball game in ESPN2 history," the network says. [2]

This year's graduating crop of female players, including Riley, is considered the most talented ever — another indication that the nearly 30-year effort to equalize sports opportunities for girls and women is bearing fruit. With great anticipation, coaches from the Women's National Basketball Association (WNBA) selected from this rich pool of seniors last month during the league's fifth draft season.

Last year, about 41 percent of the nation's 6.5 million high school athletes were girls, up from just 7.4 percent in 1971, according to the National Federation of State High School Associations. [3] A General Accounting Office (GAO) study found that from 1981 to 1999, the number of women playing college sports skyrocketed 81 percent, from 90,000 to 163,000, while male participation edged up only 5 percent. [4]

From *The CQ Researcher*, May 11, 2001.

* Title IX refers to Title IX of the Education Amendments of 1972.

Women's Teams Increased Dramatically

The number of college teams for women nearly doubled between 1981 and 1999, thanks mainly to Title IX. Although there are 300 more women's teams than men's, males still outnumber females in college sports, 232,000 vs. 163,000, largely because of 70,000 male football players.*

Number of College Teams by Gender

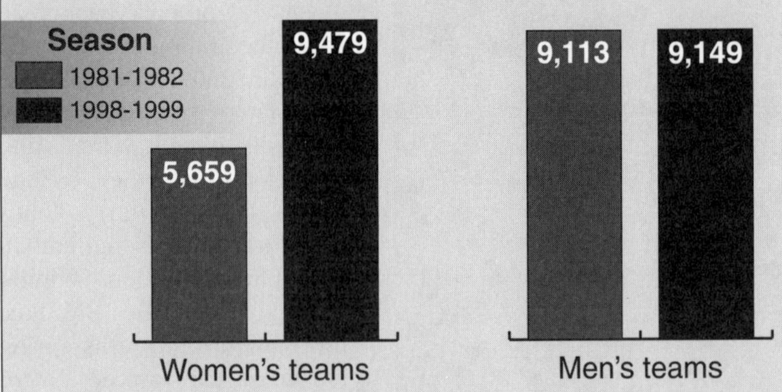

** Title IX refers to Title IX of the Education Amendments of 1972, which prohibits gender discrimination in secondary school and college sports.*

Source: General Accounting Office

At the 2000 Summer Olympics, a record 42 percent of the athletes were female, with women for the first time entering such previously all-male domains as weightlifting and pole-vaulting. Women's wrestling may be added to the 2004 Olympic lineup. Professional leagues of women's basketball and fast-pitch softball — established five years ago — are still going, although neither is profitable yet. And a professional women's soccer league was launched this spring.

Women are making other advances in professional sports. NASCAR driver Shawna Robinson plans to compete in six Winston Cup races this year, more than any woman in the past two decades. [5] And tennis star Venus Williams' jaw-dropping, $40-million, five-year endorsement deal with Reebok last December was seen by many as a watershed event, signaling irreversible progress for women's sports.

"There is no question the size of this contract is a positive breakthrough for women's sports," said Donna Lopiano, executive director of the Women's Sports Foundation. "Whenever you break a barrier [or] shatter a glass ceiling, you can't go back. It's one thing to have given women the opportunity to play. But it's a whole other thing to give them economic equity." [6]

Mary Jo Kane, head of the Tucker Center for Research on Girls & Women in Sport at the University of Minnesota, is elated, but cautious. "Compared to before Title IX, our cup runneth over," she says. "But compared to parity, we still lag behind."

There also have been casualties of the landmark 1972 law. The percentage of women coaching female college teams has dropped to an all-time low of 45.6 percent, even as the number of women coaching men's teams has remained stagnant — about 3.5 percent — for decades. [7] Salaries for female coaches, with some exceptions, are far lower than those for men. In Division I — the college league with the largest programs — women's teams get only 32.8 percent of the overall budget for coaches' salaries. [8]

In recent years, Title IX complaints have shifted from limited opportunities for women to participate in sports to grievances about the need for equal scholarship money, playing fields and other aspects of practice and competition. Many high school districts are being sued by parents demanding more opportunities for younger girls. And women are suing to open up traditionally male contact sports, like football and wrestling.

Meanwhile, in perhaps the biggest boost for women's sports in Title IX history, the U.S. Supreme Court refused to hear an appeal in a case that found Brown University guilty of discriminating against female athletes.

Even opponents of the landmark civil rights law agree that the court sent a strong message to universities and secondary schools that it supports gender equity in sports. Possibly more important, the decision is considered validation of the common measure of Title IX compliance, known as proportionality. The rule holds that the number of female varsity athletes should closely mirror their percentage of the female undergraduate population.

Men's sports advocates charge that proportionality imposes a quota system that is gutting men's sports by forcing colleges to either cut teams or cap the size of squads. But proportionality proponents question whether such direct trade-offs are necessary. They argue that if bloated programs for powerhouse sports like men's football and basketball were trimmed, the need to drop other men's sports would be alleviated.

Plus, the GAO study found that most universities have been able to add women's teams without cutting men's.

Opponents of proportionality are encouraged by President Bush's opposition to it. They are lobbying him to appoint someone sympathetic to their views to head the Department of Education's Office of Civil Rights (OCR), which enforces Title IX. Feminists worry about a change in OCR leadership, but hope current case law will prevent a drop-off in enforcement.

As sports officials and women await the new head of the OCR, these are some of the questions being asked about women in sports:

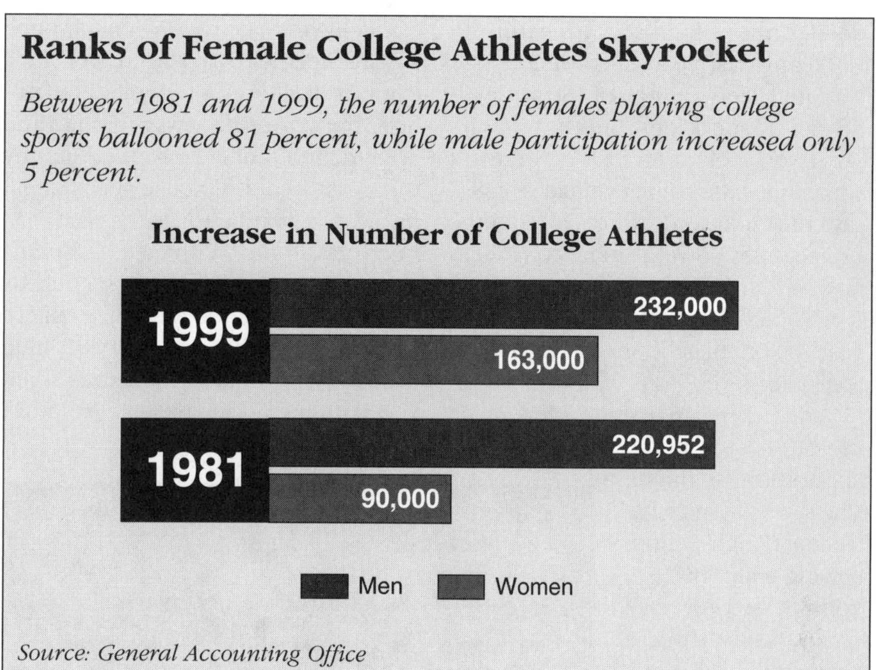

Are colleges playing numbers games with Title IX compliance?

Opponents of Title IX enforcement complain that in order to comply with the law, colleges are adding women's teams and subtracting from male varsity teams, through cuts or caps on the number of players. Such actions amount to a quota system that is detrimental to men's teams, they say.

Meanwhile, coaches for the newly created women's teams sometimes find themselves scrounging around for squad members, because the new teams often don't reflect the athletic interests of female students.

But women's sports advocates say shifts in sports offerings are long overdue and that women's interests will grow over time. The process wouldn't be so painful now, they argue, if universities had addressed the issue decades ago, rather than having to be pressured into it now.

The proportionality measure is by far the most controversial aspect of Title IX. It requires that the percentage of varsity athletes who are female must be the same as the percentage of female undergraduates on campus.

"Participation quotas have been created by bureaucrats and upheld by the courts," said Kimberly Schuld, policy director of the Independent Women's Forum, a conservative advocacy group. [9] "The result has been drastic cuts in male athletic opportunities in order to demonstrate adherence to the law. This is not fighting discrimination against women, it is enforcing quotas against men."

But Title IX advocates point out that universities are not legally bound to cut men's programs. They can use two other measures to reach compliance: a continuing history of expansion for women's athletic programs or accommodation of girls' and women's interests.

"When they call it a quota, it is so untrue," says Ray Yasser, a University of Tulsa law professor who has filed Title IX cases against schools around the country. "I've told school districts that they can reach compliance by creating a history of continuing improvement or just accommodating the interests [of women athletes] when they find them."

But opponents point to women's rowing as evidence that Title IX enforcement constitutes a quota system. To quickly boost the head count of female athletes, many universities are rushing to add female crew teams, which can have 90 or more members per team — the closest equivalent to a football team. The typical college football team has upwards of 103 players on its roster.

"We always figured it was the natural counter sport to football because you have to have at least 50 women to field a team," says Wendy Davis, crew coach at the University of Minnesota, which added the team last year.

Today there are 122 college-level women's varsity crew teams, up from 43 in 1981. [10] But women's crew coaches are struggling to find rowers.

Rowing not only requires expensive equipment but also, of course, a suitable lake or river nearby. And, unlike women's soccer, with its huge, nationwide grass-roots infrastructure reaching down to elementary grades, rowing has only a miniscule supporting infrastructure, located in scattered geographic pockets, from which to recruit college team members. Indeed, only 34 high schools had rowing teams last year, according to the National Federation of State High School Associations.

"If you look at football or women's soccer, the base of the pyramid is huge," says Brett Johnson, a spokesman for the United States Rowing Association. "Right now, it's an inverse pyramid in rowing. It will probably be quite a few more years before there is any catching up at the junior level."

Arizona is an extreme example of the stretch some schools must make. The state doesn't have a single high school rowing team, but Arizona State University (ASU) is adding a women's crew team next year, just to meet Title IX requirements. The team will row in a two-mile channel created in a dry desert river bed. "If you add rowing, it gets you closer to your OCR numbers," says Bill Kennedy, ASU's assistant athletic director. "We're as thin as we're going to get on the men's side, so we're looking to add women."

Sometimes coaches must go to extremes to fill their women's crew team slots. Minnesota's Davis, who also coached at Yale and Stanford, scouts for castaways from women's basketball, track and volleyball. Coaches pass along names of strong, tall female players who won't make their cuts but who could be trained to row. Crew coaches entice young women with scholarships. Davis posts recruiting flyers in women's restrooms. "At Stanford, we went dorm room to dorm room looking for athletic-looking females," she says.

Michigan State rowing coach Bebe Bryans recruited a star rower in a campus building stairwell. She noticed the student's powerful build and approached her. "I stopped in my tracks and said, 'Excuse me, I don't know where you're going, but you need to come with me,'" Bryans said. [11] University of Massachusetts coach Jim Dietz recruited a tall, fit waitress — who had played high school lacrosse and basketball — at a restaurant near campus. [12]

AP Photo/Dan Loh

Bowdoin College, foreground, rows against Robert Morris College during the Dad Vail Regatta in Philadelphia last May. Women's crew has grown in popularity, as universities create new teams in order to comply with federal gender-equity rules in their sports programs. A single crew team can boost a university's female-athlete total by up to 90 women.

But often recruiting is the easy part. Getting rowers to stay on the team is more difficult, thanks to the grueling workouts. After Minnesota launched its crew team last fall, the roster dropped from 100 to 45 in the first month. Drake University's team hit the water last season with 30 members but had only nine members — just enough to fill a single shell — for the end-of-season championship. [13]

"You're artificially creating numbers," complains University of Minnesota wrestling coach Jay Robinson. "The university goes out, and at a cost of millions [decides] we're going to have a rowing team, when there's not one rowing team in this state. Girls get scholarships who've never rowed before."

Women's rowing coaches acknowledge rowing often is added simply to boost numbers. "Yes, it's an easy way out," says longtime crew coach Jan Harville at the University of Washington. "You can add the numbers in one fell swoop.

"But the root of the discussion is not so much, is this fair?" she continues. "A lot of athletic departments dragged their feet with regards to gender equity, and now they are stuck dealing with the numbers game."

Plus, she says, crew teams' large rosters mean more women will get sports opportunities. "Rowing is a great sport for women, even if you have to do some education," Harville says. "The students are going to benefit. I think that's great."

The rise in women's crewing, however, isn't lifting men's boats. At many schools, women's rowing has been elevated to varsity status while men's crew teams remain only clubs. "You can't have a new men's team," Robinson says, "because if you did you'd be right back where you started."

The University of Michigan added varsity women's rowing but left its men's team at club status, even though the men's team had raised the money to build the boathouse that both teams share. "It is something that hurts men's rowing," Johnson says. "They are caught on the other side of Title IX. University of Michigan has the money to make men's rowing a varsity sport, but in order to stay in line with the numbers, they can't."

In fact, men's wrestling has taken the biggest hit under Title IX, losing 171 teams and 2,600 participants. Next on the chopping block has been men's tennis, losing 84 teams and men's gymnastics, dropping 56 teams. Opponents of Title IX concede that in some cases — such as gymnastics and tennis — the cuts are due to waning interest in the sports.

Can professional women's leagues survive?

A slew of women's professional sports leagues was created in the last five years, including basketball, fast-pitch softball, hockey and football. A pro soccer league began this spring and a volleyball league starts next year.

So far none is profitable. The WNBA dribbles into its fifth season this summer thanks only to financial aid from the men's National Basketball Association (NBA). The Women's Pro Softball League (WPSL) also is bleeding red ink. Last season, it had only four teams.

Will they survive the decade? "It comes down to [whether they will] eventually be in the black," says Rayla Allison, a Title IX attorney and WNBA advisory board member.

While men's professional leagues all had many years to develop into profitable businesses, she points out, "In today's society, the public expects a professional team to launch and, in just a few years, have sold-out events and major TV coverage and corporate sponsors."

Former WNBA Detroit Shock coach and basketball Hall-of-Famer Nancy Lieberman-Cline agreed that the WNBA needs more time. "If our barometer is our brothers at the NBA, they've been building their fan base for 54 years; we've been building [ours] for four. Are we going to get to that level? Absolutely." [14]

Yet, she conceded, "If we're in the same place in 10 years, I'll give you a different answer."

Experts say the climate is right for professional women's sports. "There is something that has substantially changed in the American market overall," says Ellen Staurowsky, a sociology professor at Ithaca College. "Title IX has created a much greater appreciation for female athletes in general. We have a consumer market that has been encouraged from a very early age to at least consider women sports as something they would watch, something they would buy into."

"Compared to before Title IX, our cup runneth over. But compared to parity, we still lag behind."

— Mary Jo Kane
Director, Tucker Center for Research on Girls & Women in Sport, University of Minnesota

Smith College economics Professor Andrew Zimbalist adds: "Clearly, women's sports are not as popular as men's sports, and we don't know that they ever will be. But there is a popularity out there, and it's growing and it's significant."

However, Zimbalist worries that the centralized ownership of the women's leagues doesn't provide a viable business structure. The WNBA, WPSL and new Women's United Soccer Association (WUSA) all are centrally owned enterprises rather than a confederation of individually owned teams, as in men's professional sports.

Women players are hired and paid by central offices. In some cases, players have been assigned to teams by central management, rather than through drafts or competing team offers. "They've been developed paternalistically, and I think inefficiently," Zimbalist says. "That deprives the fans of the sense of legitimacy in the competitive process."

Since the turn of the century, he explains, men's league sports have evolved into a system in which teams competitively recruit players during the off-season. That's when teams re-shuffle their players based upon decentralized decisions and team strategies. "Fans really glue onto this off-season process," Zimbalist says.

With the women's leagues, the centralized structure also keeps player salaries low and discourages the best talent, complains Zimbalist, who is a consultant to the NBA players union and has worked informally with the WNBA players union. WNBA player salaries average $55,000, compared with $2.4 million for the average NBA player. "A decent athlete might ask herself: Why should I spend 30 hours a week and undermine a good college education in order to eventually earn $60,000 a year for five years?"

But WNBA President Val Ackerman says the league probably wouldn't exist if it operated with independent owners. By avoiding bidding among teams and having the league pay players' salaries, she says, "We have been able to better manage our player costs. Young sports leagues aren't in a position to have their teams bid for talent."

Women Moving Up in Pro Sports

Kim Ng studied public policy at the University of Chicago. But the varsity softball player's passion was sports, and after graduation in 1990 she won an internship with the Chicago White Sox. Among her duties: holding a radar gun to track the speed of pitches.

Along the way, Ng learned about arbitration and contract negotiations while also typing in data from scouting reports. The internship soon turned into a full-time job, and Ng quickly moved up to assistant director of baseball operations.

In 1997 she signed on with the American League as director of waivers and records, approving all player transactions in the league and assisting general managers in interpreting and applying Major League rules. After 14 months, she was tapped by the New York Yankees, where she is assistant general manager. Ng, 34, is one of only two woman among 30 assistant general managers in baseball.

Few woman in professional sports can match Ng, who works to improve the Yankees' roster by analyzing the club's strengths and weaknesses and making changes through trades, waiver claims and free agents.

"When I go out and say I work for the Yankees, people say, 'Are you in ticket sales?' or, 'Oh, you're in PR,' " Ng says.

While it still takes some hunting, it's easier to find women in key positions nowadays than in years past. Amy Trask is chief executive of the Oakland Raiders, the only woman to head a National Football League team. Three NFL teams, the Miami Dolphins, St. Louis Rams and Tennessee Titans, have female chief financial officers. Mary Ellen Garling became the first woman to head a men's league when she was named in 1999 as executive director and commissioner of Arenafootball2, the newest indoor league.

Courtesy of ESPN

ESPN announcer Pam Ward was the first woman to call a college football game on TV.

Last November, Pam Ward made history when she did play-by-play for ESPN2's cablecast of a University of Toledo-Bowling Green University football game. It was the first time a woman called a college football game on national TV. The next month she called the NCAA Division III football championship. "Some people were staring with big eyes," Ward recalled.[1]

Studies show that off-the-field opportunities for women are rising. *USA Today* reporter Rudy Martzke reviewed media network sports divisions and found women held 19.5 percent of on-air positions — 81 of 335 sportscasters.[2]

The Center for the Study of Sport in Society at Northeastern University notes there were 24 female vice presidents with National Basketball Association teams in 1999 (13 percent of NBA vice presidents), up from four in 1993.[3] The NFL had 10 female vice presidents in 2000 (7 percent), also compared with four in 1993. Major League Baseball had nine female veeps last year (5 percent), versus only one in 1994.

For some women in the media, there hasn't been enough progress. "I think there's a glass ceiling that's so overwhelming in the business that it's ridiculous," says Leba Hertz, president of the Association for Women in Sports Media and an assistant sports editor at *The San Francisco Examiner*. "They bring women into departments to a certain level, and then it just stops."

Martzke agrees. "Though the number of women sportscasters might appear sizable," he wrote, "a generous portion are reporters and analysts on low-profile sports."

Hertz attributes the lockout to "the old-boys network." Her association has expanded its internship and scholarship programs to help more women enter the field.

That dovetails with Ng's plan for improving women's prospects. "The most important thing for us as women is to get into the entry-level jobs and flood this market so you increase the pool of candidates past the entry-level jobs," she says.

Ng says female fans will play a role. As a little girl in the late 1970s, she was a rabid Yankees fan who collected baseball cards and clipped out articles on the team. Today's girls who are sports fans will be tomorrow's sports business employees, she says. "If girls are fans, they learn about the game, and they may consider a career in sports."

Trask, who first worked for the Oakland Raiders during law school internships, advises against playing up the gender issue. "Don't make an issue out of being the only woman if you don't want other people to make an issue out of it," she said.[4] "I just choose to push forward — as they say in football, lower your shoulder and gain some yards."

---

[1] Quoted in Michael Hiestand, "Play-by-Play Announcing Isn't Gender-Specific at ESPN," *USA Today*, Nov. 29, 2000.

[2] Rudy Martzke, "Aiming for More Air Time: Debate Picks up on Women's Place in Sportscasting," *USA Today*, Sept. 7, 2000, C1.

[3] Center for the Study of Sport in Society at Northeastern University.

[4] Quoted in Pamela Kramer, "Women to Watch," women.com

Staurowsky agrees that the current structures may be the only way to launch women's leagues, due to the enormous costs involved. For instance, all but a fraction of the cost of the women's softball league has been financed by a single wealthy Minneapolis family—John and Sage Cowles of Cowles Media Co. They have lost more than $20 million, according to WPSL CEO John Carroll. And media giants, including Time Warner Cable and Discovery Communications, have invested $64 million in the women's soccer league startup.

Ackerman won't release WNBA revenue and expense figures, but she says that the league is still working toward a break-even point, and that players' salaries and benefits last year totaled about $12 million. The NBA finances any shortfalls, along with individual NBA team owners with women's teams in their cities. Each chips in coaches' salaries and at least $250,000 annually to market the women's teams. Many NBA team owners spend much more.

Most of the WNBA's revenues come from corporate sponsors, who kicked in $40 million in 1998, the latest figures available from the Chicago-based IEG Sponsorship Report. So far, the league doesn't have big television contracts. In fact, the women round up television advertisers on their own and share the revenues with broadcasters. Eventually, they need to reach the point where broadcasters pay them for the right to carry their games.

"National television is the secret to success," Ackerman says. "That's what sponsors are attracted to."

Fifteen previous attempts to create women's basketball leagues failed. The most recent casualty, the American Basketball League, only lasted from 1996 to 1998, unable to compete against the WNBA, with its formidable NBA largesse.

The women's softball league is struggling for footing. This summer it is replacing its regular season with a two-team tour of fast-pitch champions — exhibitions pitting its players against Olympic gold medal winners. When the league resumes next year, it will be restructured into 14 markets, this time in smaller cities like Akron, Ohio, and Rockford, Ill. Under its previous contract with sponsor AT&T Wireless Services, which pitched in $3 million for three years, the women played in larger cities like Atlanta, where games drew as few as 300 spectators.

But the league may also get a boost from Major League Baseball. In an effort to increase baseball's appeal to females, the men's league is negotiating with women's softball, with an eye toward crafting a women's tour sponsorship relationship this summer.

Despite all the obstacles, the WPSL's Carroll is optimistic about the future of women's leagues. "The great opportunity of sports is in the women's arena," he says. "There's a saturation in men's sports. This is the millennium of women."

Do female athletes who pose for sexy photographs diminish women's accomplishments in sports?

Female athletes are popular sex symbols these days. They are striking provocative poses in everything from mainstream *Rolling Stone*, *Sports Illustrated*, *Esquire* and *Gentlemen's Quarterly* to racy publications like *Gear* and *Maxim*. The photos have spurred heated debate over whether such exposure detracts from women's gains on the playing fields or is a sign that muscular, athletic women are finding greater acceptance.

Volleyball star and aspiring Ladies Professional Golf Association (LPGA) player Gabriella Reece was featured in a January *Playboy* spread. Brandi Chastain, famous for jubilantly whipping off her jersey after nailing a penalty kick to win the 1999 Women's World Cup, later posed for *Gear* wearing nothing but soccer cleats and holding two strategically placed soccer balls. Runner Nnenna Lynch posed suggestively for *Maxim's* September issue in a skimpy red dress.

The list goes on. The Olympic gold medal U.S. women's ice hockey team posed for Rolling Stone in 1999. They appeared to be naked but for ice skates and an American flag loosely draped over their midsections. Just before the 2000 Summer Olympics, *Sports Illustrated* featured swimmer Jenny Thompson, an Olympic gold-medallist, wearing a tiny swimsuit bottom and red boots, her fists covering her bare breasts.

That photo especially infuriated women's sports advocates. "Since the World Cup, we talked about great women athletes, the next generation of Title IX, but, instead, *Sports Illustrated* kicks off its pre-Olympics coverage with Jenny Thompson on the beach in a tight fitting red bottom," complains Kane.

"I have no problem about women showing off muscles and the results of their training and what it takes be an athlete," she adds, "but I don't think these photos [are seen] as 'My god, she has a beautiful body.' Come on. You can show off your muscles without taking your shirt off. Let's be honest, this is about soft pornography."

Kane isn't alone in denouncing the provocative photos. "Today's trend of marketing female athletes as if they were selling 1-900 numbers raises questions, particularly for the female athletes who were on the front lines a quarter century ago seeking equity," wrote Jill (J.R). Labbe, a newspaper columnist and former college volleyball player. "The sweat and the hours spent to build credible athletic programs was for what? So that at the dawn of a new millennium, female athletes could take their clothes off for America?" [15]

Yet, athletes like Olympic high jumper Amy Acuff, who posed nude for *Rolling Stone* and created a 2000 calendar of nude track and field athletes, defends the exposure. "I think it's about time that the media started celebrating the female athletic form instead of the female form in all its various other sickly manifestations, such as surgically enhanced and anorexic," she says.

Even some detractors concede that point. "We're seeing healthy strong women with muscles rather than waif-like models like Kate Moss, who starve themselves to death to get that look," said Roberta Nuff, a psychology professor at Texas Women's University "But it's still objectification of the female body." [16]

Reece said in an article accompanying the *Playboy* photographs that they weren't about sex. "I don't think of the images as sexual," she wrote. [17] "Our goal was to shoot the body as a form. They're more of a statement that a woman can be really powerful, really feminine, really natural and really confident and just put it out there. No big deal. I'm not trying to say, 'Check me out.' "

Kane's response: "I think it is not too far-fetched of me to assume that men who are the consumers of *Playboy* and other men's magazines are not terribly interested in women's strength and power, physical or otherwise. They are interested in seeing women's bodies as objects of sexual desire. So maybe Reece is not saying 'Check me out,' but I bet those who produce *Playboy* are saying exactly that to their readers."

Acuff, 25, who is training for the 2004 Olympics, says cultural standards vary. The most repressive societies insist that women cover-up, she points out, citing the way female athletes had to cover their legs and stomachs when last fall's track-and-field Grand Prix finals were held in the Persian Gulf country of Qatar. "In the burning heat they had to wear long tights and bodices," she says.

"In some countries in the Middle East, it's obscene for women to show their mouths," she adds.

AP Photo/Eric Risberg

U.S. soccer player Brandi Chastain raised eyebrows when she celebrated her team's overtime win against China in the 1999 Women's World Cup final by taking off her jersey.

Stacy Dragila, Olympic gold medallist and world record pole vaulter, posed for Acuff's track calendar, which raised money for athletes and a children's charity to honor Florence Griffith-Joyner. However, she later regretted posing as she did, in thigh-high stiletto boots and body paint, proudly holding a pole at her side.

Her husband went ballistic, she recalls. He told her that men see the photos in sexual terms regardless of how tasteful or artistic. "I've done a lot to promote young girls in the sport, and he said, 'If you want to portray that image and keep that image clean, you can't be doing stuff like this, because it's definitely over the border,' " Dragila recalls.

But provocative publicity, some argue, can increase athletes' commercial viability and boost other pursuits. For instance, Staurowsky says, Reece's volleyball playing days are over and she is trying to jump start her career with the LPGA.

Such photos also are meant to distance female athletes from the stereotypical lesbian athlete, she suggests. "Sexualized images of female athletes make women's sports more acceptable" to mainstream fans, she says.

Some athletes argue that posing nude helps bring legitimate attention to women's sports. In Australia, the Matildas soccer squad produced a 1999 nude calendar to raise the team's profile. Player Sarah Cooper, speaking at a conference in Australia last fall entitled "Sex Sells? Women in Sport," said after the calendar was published attendance jumped from a few hundred spectators to 5,000 to 10,000. "If people were only inter-

Chronology

1900s-1940s

Women overcome Victorian expectations and prove their mettle in sports competitions, but objections continue.

1900
Women compete in golf and lawn tennis at the Paris Olympics — the first time women compete in the Olympics.

1914
American Olympic Committee opposes participation by females except in floor exercises, where they wear long skirts.

1920
Female swimmers are first American women to win full Olympic status.

1927-1932
Tennis champ Helen Wills Moody wins eight times at Wimbledon.

1930s
Some colleges add women's basketball programs, but then cancel them.

1932
Mildred "Babe" Didrickson becomes top U.S. female athlete of her time with three track and field Olympic medals and later a celebrated golf career.

1970s-1980s

Rise of civil rights activism and feminism spark a power struggle in the male-dominated sports establishment.

1972
Congress passes Title IX of the Education Amendments, outlawing sex discrimination by universities and high schools that receive federal funds.

1973
Billie Jean King defeats Bobby Riggs in "Battle of the Sexes" tennis match.

1974
Little League baseball admits girls, two years after a 12-year-old Hoboken, N.J., girl goes to court for the right to play.

1982
Demise of the Association for Intercollegiate Athletics for Women, formed in 1971 to challenge the male-dominated National Collegiate Athletic Association, triggers a long-term decline in the number of female coaches.

1984
U.S. Supreme Court narrows the scope of Title IX by ruling in *Grove City College v. Bell* that the law applies only to programs that directly receive federal aid.

1988
Congress passes Civil Rights Restoration Act over President Ronald Reagan's veto, striking down a 1984 court decision that restricted Title IX enforcement in sports.

1990s

U.S. Supreme Court boosts women sports at colleges; women's professional sports leagues are launched.

1992
High court lets students sue for monetary damages in gender-discrimination cases against high schools and colleges. Female athletes at Brown University file landmark suit.

1997
Anita DeFrantz, an attorney who was a bronze medal winner in rowing in 1976, is the first woman to become an International Olympic Committee vice president. Professional leagues are launched in women's basketball and fast-pitch softball. Brown University appeals to the U.S. Supreme Court after lower court rules for the female athletes.

1998
Supreme Court refuses to hear Brown's appeal in what is considered a boost to Title IX enforcement.

2000s

Progress for female athletes continues, but not without disappointments

October 2000
A former Duke University female place-kicker who was kicked off the football team wins a $2 million discrimination suit against the school. The number of female coaches of women's teams at universities hits all-time low of 46 percent.

January 2001
National Women's Law Center reaches settlements with 25 universities it accused of short-changing women on scholarship funding. This signals a new trend: complaints against schools to equalize resources, not just participation opportunities.

ested in the calendar, how do we explain the increased interest in the team on the field?"[18]

However, Australian Women's Soccer Association CEO Warren Fisher said that while the first calendar brought attention, another would damage the team's credibility.[19]

Matildas player Amy Taylor disagreed. "I don't think it's degrading or demeaning if it is done properly," she said. "And no one has the right to take that choice away from us."[20] ■

BACKGROUND

For Men Only

At the start of the 20th Century, Victorian notions of feminine frailty prevailed, and women's limited athletic endeavors were permitted by the male-dominated establishment. Popular athletic competitions were for men, with the exception of socially acceptable women's sports played by the upper crust. Indeed, the first U.S. female Olympians in 1900 were seven women who competed in golf and lawn tennis. Their uniforms were long garments covering their bodies from male onlookers.[21]

During the next few decades, women's opportunities progressed unevenly. In the 1920s, some colleges formed women's athletic programs, but soon many were withdrawn. The specter of females in shorts performing for male audiences drew sharp criticism. Many women's basketball programs were jettisoned by the end of the decade. An indication of the prevailing attitude toward women's athletics was the 1930 Amateur Athletic Union women's basketball championship — it featured a beauty contest.[22]

During World War II, women's baseball enjoyed a short-lived career. Teams owned by Major League Baseball (MLB) or by league entities served as a substitute for the men's league while men fought overseas. But at the end of the war, MLB funding was pulled, and the women's league disintegrated, Staurowsky says.

Through the early 1970s, college sports remained largely for men. Norma V. Cantú, who headed the Department of Education's Office of Civil Rights (OCR) under former President Bill Clinton, often cited the fate of double gold medal Olympic swimmer Donna de Varona as an example of the times. The 17-year-old effectively was forced to retire in 1964 after high school, since there were no college swimming teams for women at the time. Meanwhile, fellow gold medal swimmer Don Schollander headed to Yale University on full scholarship.

Title IX to the Rescue

In 1972, Title IX of the Education Amendments outlawed gender discrimination at schools receiving federal funds, eventually spurring an overhaul of college and high school athletics.

But the legislative triumph resulted in several negative consequences, including a massive reduction in female coaches. For instance, the Association for Intercollegiate Athletics for Women (AIAW) — a sister organization to the NCAA — created an environment in which 90 percent of women's team coaches were women. But in 1981, the NCAA, citing Title IX, began offering women's tournaments to compete with the AIAW, and in 1984 the AIAW folded.

In addition, many universities combined men's and women's athletic departments, which were largely — and continue to be — headed by men. In 1972, 90 percent of women's team coaches were female; now about 46 percent are.

And, while the GAO says 72 percent of colleges have found ways to add women's sports without dropping men's teams, some colleges have chosen to cut minor sports, like men's wrestling, in order to more closely balance male and female participation.[23]

Nonetheless, opponents of Title IX enforcement have mounted vigorous challenges. In 1984, the Supreme Court ruled in *Grove City* [Pa.] *College v. Bell* that Title IX only applied to specific school programs that received direct federal aid. Since athletic programs didn't, 64 discrimination complaints were dropped.

Four years later, that decision was reversed when Congress passed the Civil Rights Restoration Act, declaring that programs throughout schools receiving federal funds must comply with the anti-gender-discrimination law. The high court gave the law another boost in 1992, when it ruled that students can sue for monetary damages in these cases.

That same year, in a bellwether case, female athletes at Brown University sued the school under Title IX. A federal district judge and appellate panel largely sided with the students, rejecting Brown's plan for remedying discrimination. The Ivy League university appealed to the Supreme Court. In April 1997, the court declined to hear the appeal.

Under a final agreement between Brown and the plaintiffs, Brown agreed to keep the proportion of female athletes within 3.5 percent of the proportion of female undergraduates. However, Brown officials say a key question remains: Is the ratio of male and female undergraduates a fair yardstick to measure athletic equity? "Wouldn't the pool of male and female undergraduates interested in playing sports be a better barometer?" asks Mark Nickel, head of Brown's news service.

Brown gave up the court fight, but Nickel says the issue could be resurrected if the same challenge comes up in another appellate district. Meanwhile, the Supreme Court's response is viewed by proponents and opponents alike as a sign that current enforcement of Title IX stands.

"U.S. colleges and universities took the April 1997 decision as a clear message that they must act decisively to support gender equity," wrote Smith College's Zimbalist. [24]

Number of Female Coaches Declined

The number of females coaching college women's teams has plummeted to an all-time low as a result of Title IX. To comply with the 1972 gender-equity law, many universities combined men's and women's athletic departments, which continue to be largely headed by men. Meanwhile, the number of women coaching men's teams has remained at about 3 percent for decades.

Percentage of Female Coaches of Women's Teams

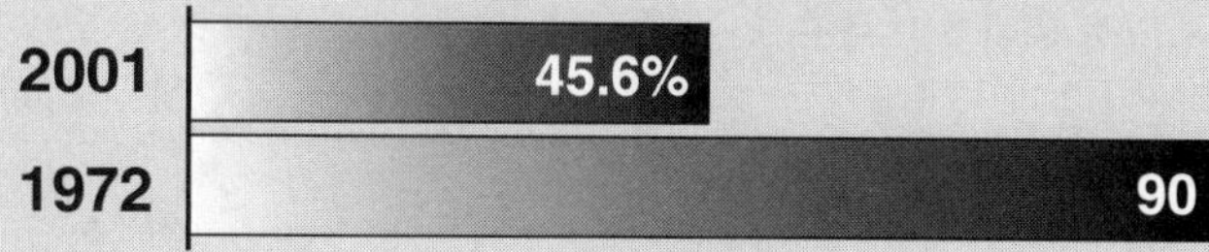

Source: R. Vivian Acosta and Linda Jean Carpenter, "Women in Intercollegiate Sport: A Longitudinal Study— Twenty-Three Year Update, 1977-2000," Brooklyn College, March 2000.

Storming the Barricades

Since the Brown University case, lawsuits have emerged to expand women's opportunities in sports that have been male bastions. Last October, a federal jury awarded $2 million in punitive damages to a former female Duke University student who was cut from the football team.

Heather Sue Mercer had joined the team in 1994 as a walk-on place-kicker. She kicked a game-winning field goal during a spring intra-squad competition. The next fall, she was placed on an inactive roster. She tried out again, but was cut. Mercer claimed she was treated differently because she's a woman. During closing arguments in the case last winter, Duke lawyer John Simpson said the university had given her many unique opportunities to try out and practice with the team, but in the end she didn't have strength or skill on par with male place-kickers. [25]

The university is appealing the punitive damage award. Meanwhile, Mercer, who works for Charles Schwab Co. in New York City said she'll use the jury award for a scholarship fund for girls who want to be place-kickers. "I think it will open the eyes of universities to the abilities of women to do things that they never imagined could be done," said Mercer's lawyer. [26]

In 1998, 14-year-old Jennifer Radzik, a wrestler, was the first girl to participate in the summer wrestling camp held at the United States Military Academy at West Point. But the organization Trial Lawyers for Public Justice had to first threaten the academy with a discrimination lawsuit to open the way for Radzik.

Initially, Radzik's entire high school wrestling team planned to attend the camp near her home in Cornwall-on-Hudson, N.Y. The team's boys got in, but Radzik, the only female, was rejected. "First, they told me that Jennifer couldn't attend because they'd need a separate dorm room and a female coach for her," her father said. [27] "Then, they said that boys' egos would be crushed if they lost to a girl, and finally they said that wrestling simply wasn't an appropriate sport for girls."

Officials at West Point say events unfolded differently. Spokesman Mike D'Aquino says when Radzik initially contacted the academy, the person who handled the request didn't understand the rules. "The policy has always been that it's an open camp," D'Aquino says. He adds, however, that Radzik is the only female to attend wrestling or other traditional boys' camps there.

Radzik, now 16, says the experience toughened her. "I learned you have to go after what you want because it's not going to come to you."

In 1999, world-class wrestler Jenny Wong spent part of her freshman year practicing with the University of Wisconsin's men's wrestling team. The university allowed her to participate in a previously all-male program after the Trial Lawyers for Public Justice, again, threatened suit. (*See story, p. 237.*)

Robinson, the college wrestling coach, says women shouldn't encroach on men's sports. "They want the best of both worlds; they want to be able to cross over, but men can't cross over," he says. "If there's no men's volleyball team, men can't go out for the women's team. If we are going to be fair here, if we're truly going to be equal, let's have one basketball team, one football team. Do women want that? No."

Robinson says cases like Wong's and Radzik's simply prove a lack of demand among women for sports like wrestling. "There is not enough interest in having many women's wrestling teams," he says. "Is Jenny being discriminated against? No, there's not enough interest."

AP Photo/Gerry Broome

Heather Sue Mercer won $2 million in damages from Duke University as the result of a sex discrimination lawsuit. A federal jury ruled that the place-kicker was cut from the team solely because of her gender.

But Trial Lawyers Executive Director Arthur Bryant says women should get more opportunities to swing the pendulum in their direction even by invading men's territory. "The current reality is a situation where men already have more than their fair share of opportunities to participate," Bryant says.

Equalizing Resources

For most of the 1990s, most legal cases and OCR complaints pushed for women's participation. Those challenges still arise, but in the last few years the focus of confrontations has shifted to equalizing resources for men's and women's sports. Now the spotlight is on equality in areas such as recruiting, scholarships, equipment, playing fields, coaching staffs and practice schedules. The scope is drilling down to nitty-gritty details such as tutoring, trainers, lockers and uniforms.

"To comply fully with Title IX, ultimately it will be necessary for schools to provide nearly equal support in all areas of intercollegiate athletics," Zimbalist wrote. [28]

Athletic scholarships also have been under intense scrutiny. Just after the Supreme Court refused to hear the Brown University case, the National Women's Law Center went after the 25 Division I universities that spent the smallest percentage of their overall athletic scholarship funds on females. Among colleges targeted were University of Colorado, where 39 percent of the athletes were women but they received only 31 percent of the $3 million in 1996 scholarship spending, and Northeastern University, where women constituted 48 percent of athletes but received only 38 percent of scholarship money.

In response to the complaints, the OCR clarified its scholarship policy, stating that men's and women's scholarships should be in line with gender-participation rates, with a gap of no more than 1 percent. In other words, if women make up 42 percent of a university's athletes, they should receive no less than 41 percent of the scholarship funds but no more than 43 percent.

Legitimate factors could allow exceptions, such as scholarship athletes switching schools at the last minute or differences between in-state and out-of-state tuition for recruits. In the case of the 25 universities targeted by the Law Center, 15, including Colorado and Northeastern, agreed to increase scholarship money for females. Several others already increased women's scholarship funding, and the rest convinced the OCR that they had reasonable cause to exceed the gap. ■

CURRENT SITUATION

Widening Gap

Today, the controversy over scholarship money persists. A 2000 *Chronicle of Higher Education* survey found 36 of 321 Division I schools in compliance on scholarships, but 175 institutions were giving women more than the OCR standard. Some colleges spend more on women because men's sports attract more players who participate without scholarships. [29]

When Women Wrestle

The 48-member men's wrestling team at Lock Haven University in Pennsylvania contains two surprises: Sara McMann and Jenny Wong.

The two women participate in the same tough drills as the men and practice against them. "It's a real advantage to practice against the guys," says McMann, a junior. "They are so much stronger." Usually.

At the Penn State University Open last December, McMann, competing in the 133-pound weight class, won her first match against a man. "It's a rare occasion when they beat a man at that level," says Carl Poff, Lock Haven's wrestling coach. "It shows you how far women have come in the sport."

Typically, the pair only competes against men in open tournaments, which have looser rules than interscholastic leagues. Instead, McMann and Wong, a sophomore, train for national and world-wide women's competitions. McMann is first in the country in her weight class; Wong is third nationally among 114-pounders.

Courtesy of Lock Haven University

Sara McMann (dark hair) wrestles for Pennsylvania's Lock Haven University, one of several dozen small schools where women practice with the men's team.

Lock Haven is among several dozen small universities that allow women to practice with men's teams. Only seven colleges have women's wrestling teams, but others are considering it, says Doug Reese, who coaches the women's and men's wrestling teams at the University of Minnesota at Morris. In 1994, Morris was the first university to offer varsity women's wrestling. The other women's teams were established since 1999.

Girls wrestling has mushroomed. In 1985, only six girls were on high school wrestling squads, according to the National Federation of State High School Associations. By 1990, the number had jumped to 132 at 21 high schools. Today, 2,474 girls wrestle at 734 schools, but only Hawaii and Texas offer state-sanctioned tournaments for girls. The 2004 Olympics in Athens likely will offer competition in women's wrestling for the first time.

What is the draw for girls? "They usually had a boyfriend or father or brother who wrestled," Reese says. "They like something a little more challenging and physical, and that it's an individual sport." Reese says it does not take a male physique to wrestle, and that girls can do it well with the right training and technique.

In high school, girls regularly go up against boys in tournaments. Jen Radzik, a 16-year-old at Cornwall Central High School in New York, wrestles on the boy's team. Last year, she finished with six wins and six loses. This season she was 2-1 when she dropped out because of illness. Two years earlier, she threatened a discrimination suit when a summer wrestling camp initially refused to admit her.

McMann became interested in wrestling from watching her older brother's practices and matches. When she was a ninth-grader, she and her best friend decided to try out for the boys' team. The friend's father said, no, but McMann went ahead. "At first, coach was worried," she recalls, "but he saw how dedicated I was."

In 1998, her senior year, she won the first U.S. Girls High School National Championship. This spring, McMann, a theater major who wants to be an actress, is training for the Women's Wrestling World Championships.

Poff has integrated McMann and Wong into his team. "The guys on my team love the sport, and Jen and Sara love the sport. They've won the respect of the men because of their work ethic."

The two live near campus with several wrestling teammates, including senior Rob Weikel. He says at first it was hard to adapt to women on the team, but now the men look past gender. "I think it's definitely different, but as long as they are motivated to do the sport, it's fine," Weikel says.

Still, things don't always go smoothly. When McMann won a match against a male wrestler, Poff says, "I was very happy for Sara, but at the same time felt badly for the young man who was defeated."

Even McMann was uneasy. "I kind of felt bad because I knew what that guy was going to hear," she says. "But I have to have good training, so I didn't feel bad enough that I'm not going to do it anymore."

But the survey revealed a widening resource gap for females at different types of colleges. Universities where television contracts and post-season play make men's football and basketball programs profitable tend to boost women's sports funding, while schools with unprofitable men's programs don't. At the University of Arkansas at Fayetteville, which has profitable football and basketball teams, women's softball coach Carie

Dever-Boaz said she felt like a "spoiled kid with her daddy's credit card." But at University of Arkansas at Pine Bluff, which has a money-losing football team, women's basketball players get one warm-up shirt while the men get two warm-up suits and three other shirts to wear during pre-game drills. [30]

"Ultimately, the gap means that the gender-equity revolution has come much more slowly to the institutions outside the top six Division I conferences," Welch Suggs wrote in the *Chronicle* report. [31]

High schools also are being brought to task for unequal resources. This year, many California high schools switched the girls' soccer season from winter to spring after complaints were filed with the OCR that girls were playing in winter mud and rain in the northern part of the state.

In December, U.S. District Judge Anne Conway ruled that two Central Florida high schools violated federal law because the girls softball teams play on substandard off-campus fields, while boys play on lighted fields on the schools' campuses. [32]

Around the same time, *The Orlando Sentinel* found that girls were treated poorly in many schools. Among the deficiencies cited: Girls played on fields without lights, no fixed restrooms and no lockers, while boys teams had all three. At Leesburg High School, girls play softball in a city park, while boys play at a former Major League Baseball spring training facility. [33]

The National Women's Law Center joined a private law firm in a class action lawsuit — set for trial in August — against the Michigan High School Athletic Association. The suit claims the association isn't providing enough opportunities for girls, specifically ice hockey and water polo tournaments.

Reuters Photo/Jerry Lampen

Stacy Dragila became the first woman to win an Olympic gold medal for pole vaulting at the 2000 Olympic Games. Women's pole vaulting made its Olympic debut during the games in Sydney, Australia. Dragila later posed provocatively for a calendar showing women's track-and-field athletes in racy poses, but later regretted it, saying that it didn't set a good example for young girls.

Athletic association officials say there's not enough interest. Statewide there are eight girls ice hockey teams and 14 girls water polo teams at 740 high schools. The association sponsors a tournament only if 64 schools offer a sport for two years.

Law center attorney Neena Chadhry says a tournament would prompt creation of teams. "Really, a tournament is what you are striving for," she says. "By having a tournament, you sanction the sport, by not doing that, we claim they are discriminating."

The lawsuit also challenges the scheduling of girls' seasons. Girls play basketball, for instance, in the fall instead of winter in Michigan, one of four states where girls and boys don't play basketball at the same time. Chaudhry claims it hurts Michigan girls in college recruitment because most NCAA scouts prospect for talent during winter.

"Our claim is that not even one boys' sport is out of season, and lots of girls' sports are in the non-traditional seasons," Chaudhry says. "If, for instance, you saw half the boys' sports in the wrong season and half of girls' sports in the wrong season, that wouldn't be a problem. But, as it stands, girls are bearing the burden of these non-traditional seasons."

Michigan Athletic Association attorney Edward Sikorski says schools voted, and the majority picked the playing season time slots. He says high schools shouldn't make decisions based on college recruiting, but instead should focus on opportunities for the entire student body. "High schools are not farm clubs for Division I college," Sikorski says. "The philosophy of interscholastic high school athletics is to give the most kids the most experience you can." Only a tiny percent of high school athletes will end up in Division I athletics, he pointed out.

The association also plans to argue that it's not subject to Title IX enforcement because it receives no

At Issue:

Should women be able to participate on men's teams?

MARCIA D. GREENBERGER
CO-PRESIDENT, NATIONAL WOMEN'S LAW CENTER

WRITTEN FOR THE CQ RESEARCHER, APRIL 2001

yes

Of course, most women and men will play on single-sex teams. But when, for example, there is no women's team in a sport and a woman has the ability to make the men's team, she should be allowed to play. It's only fair, and in fact the law can require it. For example, in a much publicized recent lawsuit, Duke student Heather Sue Mercer tried out and made her school's football team as a placekicker, only to be told that she should watch from the stands with her boyfriend. A jury said that Heather, whom even a former Redskins kicker, Mark Moseley, described as talented, deserved to play.

Heather is not alone. More than 3,000 girls nationwide play ice hockey, more than 2,000 wrestle on high school teams, about 4,000 compete on weightlifting teams, over 1,200 play high school baseball and more than 800 play football. Many of these girls have to play on boys' teams in order to play at all.

But allowing a woman to play on a male team will not, by itself, resolve the inequities in athletics faced by most girls and young women. Despite the dramatic increase in the number of female athletes since 1972, the playing field for women is far from level. Although women are over half of the undergraduates in our nation's colleges, there are 232,000 male athletes compared to only 163,000 women.

In Division I colleges, male athletes receive twice as much of total athletic budgets as female athletes (67 percent to 33 percent), with school dollars going to such "essentials" as housing football players in hotels the night before home games, chartered jets for away games and mahogany-paneled offices for football coaches. In contrast, female athletes too often are still treated like second-class citizens. The Atlanta Journal & Constitution recently highlighted the unfairness young women face at one Georgia high school: The boys' baseball field was described as a "mini-stadium, spectacularly manicured, with a Wrigley Field-like brick backstop behind home plate," box seats, brick dugouts with lights, brick concession stands and permanent restrooms. On the other hand, the girls' softball field is a "bare-bones" field enclosed by a chain-link fence, with temporary bleachers, open dugouts topped with Fiberglass sheets, a former football ticket booth for a concession stand, no lights and "two foul-smelling portable toilets."

Unfortunately, these disparities occur across the country. Women have proven that they can excel in any sport if given the opportunity. Our country owes its young women no less.

LEO KOCHER
HEAD WRESTLING COACH AND ASSOCIATE PROFESSOR, UNIVERSITY OF CHICAGO
BOARD MEMBER, NATIONAL COALITION FOR ATHLETIC EQUITY

WRITTEN FOR THE CQ RESEARCHER, APRIL 2001

no

Today's Title IX policy interpretation by the Department of Education creates an overwhelming legal and financial incentive for schools to senselessly eliminate tens of thousands of college male sports opportunities. In comparison to this very real consequence, the issue of a female on a male wrestling team pales in significance.

Nevertheless, the two issues are related in one important respect: They both reflect how the rush to "level the playing field" in our schools has tilted the field against boys. Why are rules that are designed to create equity only applied in one direction?

For instance, under the current system, "fairness" is served by females joining male teams, but not vice versa. And, for a female to be on a team, she does not have to be better than males who get cut from that team. Both these operative assumptions are based on the premise that females do not have "their fair share" when it comes to sports.

But consider: Are male dancers denied their fair share because collegiate dance programs are more than 85 percent female? Females have majority status in almost every category of high school extracurricular activity — verbal arts, music, student government, etc. — and no one blinks an eye. Yet in the only area where males show more interest — sports — discrimination against females is assumed. Unfortunately this kind of thinking has allowed our Education Department to do some awful things to male athletes.

In the Title IX gender wars, females litigating their way onto male teams is a relatively minor issue. However, the cultural environment that supports that phenomenon — and promotes the prevailing view that females are shortchanged and males are privileged — is a major issue. It has led to policies, laws and funding decisions that ignore the desperate needs boys are facing.

The fact is, boys are 80 percent of those on Ritalin, have a 50 percent greater chance of flunking, commit five times as many suicides and are currently only 44 percent of college students.

Christina Sommers' *The War Against Boys*, should be at the top of the reading list of our senators and congressmen. The 2000 book meticulously documents how advocates who don't represent the views of the overwhelming majority of Americans accrue power and resources with a bogus spin about the neglect of girls — a spin that also blinds us to the downward spiral of today's boys.

federal funding. But the plaintiffs argue that Title IX applies to the association because the association runs high school sports tournaments. If high schools opt out of the association, their teams cannot participate.

Fewer Female Coaches

The percentage of females coaching women's college teams is at an all-time low of 45.6 percent, according to a long-term study by retired college professors Vivian Acosta and Linda Jean Carpenter, who have tracked the numbers since 1977. [34]

When Title IX was enacted, 90 percent of university women's teams had female coaches. Since 1998, men have been hired for 80 percent of the new women's team coaching jobs, the study said. In addition, the percentage of female assistant coaches for women's teams is declining, from 60.5 percent in 1996 to 58.1 percent last year.

Meanwhile, women haven't been successful in crossing over to men's teams. The percentage of females coaching men's athletics has been just under 2 percent for the last three decades.

The NCAA provides slightly different numbers that nonetheless reveal a diminished role for female coaches. An NCAA study shows even fewer female coaches for women's teams, 42.3 percent, but a marginally higher number of women coaching men's teams, 3.4 percent. [35]

"It's not a concern that men are coaching women, but that the door is not open both ways," says attorney Allison. "Men have access and are recruited to coach woman, but women do not have access, nor are they recruited to coach boys and men."

Women's Basketball Coaches Association retired CEO Betty Jaynes predicts no improvement. "Women coaching men is never going to happen," she says. "We've been trying to get administrations to interview female coaches, but they've said it would be detrimental in recruiting. Females would not be able to recruit male athletes. [But] they haven't done any research on it; they are just giving you an opinion."

But it's an opinion that determines hiring, she says.

University of Arizona Athletic Director Jim Livengood says perceptions play a role. Some basketball players may think they won't have as good a chance to make the NBA if they're not playing under a coach who already has sent players to the NBA, he says. "I don't know that the door is closed," Livengood says. "At the same time I don't know that it is necessarily wide open."

Coaches are largely hired by men, and men generally hire men, observers say. "Their circle of influence is men," says Laurie Garrison, a spokeswoman for the National Association of Collegiate Directors of Athletics (NACDA). "Men are going to get recommendations about men." Of 321 athletic directors in Division I overall, 26 are women, according to NACDA. Those numbers include only women who oversee both men's and women's programs, not women who lead women's sports only.

Cheryl Levick, athletic director at Santa Clara University and former chair of the NCAA's committee on women's athletics, says new strategies are needed to increase the ranks of female coaches. "When I talk to female athletes, they are pursuing business or law school," she says. "They have lofty goals and they aren't just interested in coaching. We need to come up with ways to entice females to get into coaching."

Among the disincentives: generally low salaries compared with other career opportunities, understaffing of assistant coaches and long hours that may discourage women with children.

Division I head coaches of women's teams on average bring home about $44,614 a year, while assistant coaches make $25,927, according to a *Chronicle of Higher Education* study based on information gathered under the 1996 Equity in Athletics Disclosure Act. [36] The women's teams average salary is skewed by sky-high salaries for high-profile coaches, such as University of Connecticut women's basketball coach Geno Auriemma, who makes $590,000.

On the men's team side, Division I coaches make an average $72,332, while assistant coaches take home $39,830. Zimbalist says men's salaries are elevated by forces of male camaraderie. "There is, in effect, a closed circle of male athletic directors and basketball coaches who serve artificially to inflate and to validate each others' worth," Zimbalist wrote. [37]

Livengood disagrees, but says revenue-generating potential impacts salaries. At Arizona, the men's basketball coach makes about $550,600 a year (though his contract stipulates that about $200,000 each year in speaking fees and sponsorships go back to the university). Arizona's women's basketball coach makes only $125,000. The financial success of the men's basketball program, which has sold out a 14,536-seat arena for years, supports a dozen other sports programs, Livengood says. "If we got rid of that, we'd have a tough time keeping all the sports we have."

The Justice Department is taking note of men's and women's pay disparities. Its Civil Rights Division has been researching the issue for evidence of employment discrimination, but is not conducting a formal investigation, says spokeswoman Cristine Romano. "We're taking a look at the research that's already out there to determine what more, if anything, is warranted," she says, adding that there isn't much existing detailed research. So, far, the Justice Department has issued no findings.

Beyond salaries, women's teams have fewer assistant coaches to help carry the workload, Levick says. Division I women's teams averaged 7.6 assistant coaches, while men's teams averaged 12.3, the Chronicle revealed.

Levick is lobbying for more enticements for women, such as child-care benefits or nannies for road trips. University of Tennessee women's basketball coach Pat Summitt has brought her 10-year-old son, Tyler, and his nanny along on many road trips. Joan Cronan, Tennessee's women's athletic director, says she tries to create a family-friendly environment, although the university doesn't provide child-care benefits. "I guess I've always wanted to have my cake and eat it too," she says. "If a woman wants to be married and have children, we help them do that." ■

OUTLOOK

Bush's Plans

Opponents of Title IX enforcement hope the tide will turn in their favor with George W. Bush in the White House. During a campaign speech, then-candidate Bush said: "Title IX has opened up opportunities for young women in both academics and sports, and I think that's terrific. I do not support a system of quotas or strict proportionality that pits one group against another. We should support a reasonable approach to Title IX that seeks to expand opportunities for women, rather than destroying existing men's teams." [38]

Some speculate that Bush will soon appoint a like-minded person to head the Title IX enforcement in the Department of Education.

Specifically, Title IX enforcement opponents want to eliminate the proportionality test used to measure compliance. "With the new administration, we hope for changes in the OCR's interpretation of equity in sports," says Schuld of the Independent Women's Forum. "We have been shut out for eight years, but now we feel like we have a voice at the table. I'm very optimistic."

Although some Title IX advocates worry about potential personnel changes in Washington, others think existing case law will prevent much re-interpretation of the law.

"We would be very surprised if OCR tried to tamper with long-standing policies that virtually every court in this nation has upheld as consistent with the statute and with Congress' intent in passing Title IX," said Verna Williams, director of educational opportunities at the National Women's Law Center. [39]

Schuld disagrees. "I think they are grasping at straws," she says. "The case law is in its infantile stage. It's not so set in stone and not so historically established."

Bush is expected to begin intense interviews later this spring for the position of OCR chief, but White House spokesman Ken Lisaius declines to comment further.

Speaker of the House J. Dennis Hastert, R-Ill., a former wrestling coach who has vehemently opposed Title IX policy, is expected to influence the issue. "I know he is very interested in the OCR," says John Feehery, a Hastert spokesman.

Sen. Paul Wellstone, D-Minn., also a former wrestling coach, in 1998 had tried to protect men's teams. He introduced a bill requiring universities planning to drop a sport or reduce its funding to first to show the cost of the sport within the overall athletic budget. But he quickly pulled the bill and apparently doesn't plan to raise the issue again. "We have absolutely no intention to make changes to Title IX this year or at any time in the future," says Allison Dobson, a Wellstone spokeswoman.

Whatever happens, women's sports advocates intend to keep pressing for more opportunities and equal resources. Litigators say most future cases will target gender inequities in high schools.

"I expect there will be more high school cases, in terms of opportunities to play, facilities, coaching, uniforms, equipment and practice times," says Bryant of Trial Lawyers for Public Justice. "Colleges have been more alert to the problem and addressing it faster than high schools." ■

Notes

[1] Rudy Martzke, "CBS has $200M women's NCAA bid," *USA Today*, Feb. 20, 2001, p. C1.

[2] "UConn-Notre Dame Does Well for ESPN2," *The New York Times*, March 8, 2001, p. C18.

[3] National Federation of State High School Associations, "1999-2000 Athletics Participation Survey."

[4] "Intercollegiate Athletics: Four-Year Colleges' Experiences Adding and Discontinuing Teams," U.S. General Accounting Office, March 2001, p. 4.

[5] David Poole, "Kranefuss Comes Back With Woman As Driver: Robinson's 6-Race Deal

Could Become Full Time," *The Charlotte Observer*, March 15, 2001, p. C2.

[6] Quoted by Greg Couch, "Venus' Sky-High Deal: Will Williams' $40M Contract Raise the Bar for Female Athletes?" *Chicago Sun-Times*, Dec. 22, 2000.

[7] "The NCAA Minority Opportunities and Interests Committee's Biennial Study of the Race Demographics of Member Institutions' Athletics Personnel," National Collegiate Athletics Association, March 27, 2000, p. 100. For a study showing a lower percentage, see R. Vivian Acosta and Linda Jean Carpenter, "Women in Intercollegiate Sport: A Longitudinal Study — Twenty-Three Year Update, 1977-2000," Brooklyn College, March 2000, p. 5.

[8] Welch Suggs, "Uneven Progress for Women's Sports," *The Chronicle of Higher Education*, April 7, 2000, chart, p. A57.

[9] Kimberly Schuld, "Title IX Athletics: Issue In-Depth: Background and Analysis of Government Policy Governing Sports in Schools," *Independent Women's Forum*, June 2000.

[10] GAO, *op. cit.*, Table 3, p. 12.

[11] Quoted by Barbara Carton, "You Don't Need Oars in the Water to Go Out for Crew: Colleges Have Plenty of Money For Tall, Muscular Women; 'No Experience Necessary,'" *The Wall Street Journal*, May 14, 1999, p. A1.

[12] *Ibid.*

[13] Randy Peterson, "Drake Team Numbers Dwindle: Rowers Cite Lofty Expectations," *The Des Moines Register*, April 19, 2000, Sports, p. 5.

[14] Quoted by Sheila Mulrooney Eldred, "WNBA Makes Stop in N.O. League Faced with Questions About Future," *The Times-Picayune*, Oct. 29, 2000, p. A1.

[15] Jill Labbe, "Hot Shots Skin-baring Photos Do Female Athletics No Favors," *The Fort Worth Star-Telegram*, Sept. 17, 2000, editorial page.

[16] *Ibid.*

[17] *Playboy*, January 2001.

[18] Quoted in Megan Doherty, "Women Athletes' Forum on Sex Selling Sport," *Canberra Times*, p. 79.

[19] *Ibid.*

[20] *Ibid.*

[21] Richard L. Worsnop, "Gender Equity in Sports," *The CQ Researcher*, April 18. 1997, p. 344.

[22] *Ibid.*

[23] GAO, *op. cit.*, p. 16.

[24] Andrew Zimbalist, *Unpaid Professionals: Commercialism and Conflict in Big-Time College Sports* (1999), p. 58.

[25] Quoted by Vicki Cheng, "Duke University ordered to pay female kicker $2 million," *The News & Observer*, Oct. 13, 2000.

[26] *Ibid.*

[27] Quoted in Trial Lawyers for Public Justice newsletter, *Public Justice*, summer 1998, p. 11.

[28] *Ibid.*, pp. 69-70.

[29] Suggs, *op. cit.*, p. A56.

[30] *Ibid.*, p. A57.

[31] *Ibid.*

[32] Lynne Bumpus-Hooper, "9 Schools Discriminate Against Girls: A Survey Shows the Area High Schools Violate Title IX, the Federal Provision that Bans Gender Bias," *The Orlando Sentinel*, Dec. 26, 2000, p. A1.

[33] *Ibid.*

[34] Acosta, *op. cit.*, p. 5.

[35] NCAA, *op. cit.*, p. 100.

[36] The Equity in Athletics Disclosure Act was passed in 1996 and requires all coeducational institutions receiving federal funds to report participation figures and spending on men's and women's sports annually.

[37] Zimbalist, *op. cit.*, p. 83.

[38] Quoted in Kay Hawes, "New view of Title IX?" *The NCAA News*, Feb. 12, 2001.

[39] *Ibid.*

FOR MORE INFORMATION

Center for the Study of Sport in Society, Northeastern University, 716 Columbus Ave., Suite 161 CP, Boston, Mass. 02120; (617) 373-4025; www.sportinsociety.org. The center produces the "Racial and Gender Report Card," analyzing the demographics of players, coaches and key administrators in college and professional sports.

National Collegiate Athletic Association, 700 W. Washington St., Indianapolis, Ind. 46206; (317) 917-6222; www.ncaa.org. The NCAA is the governing body for men's and women's programs at most four-year colleges. It produces news reports and studies on participation in college sports.

National Federation of State High School Associations, P.O. Box 690, Indianapolis, Ind. 46206: (317) 972-6900; www.nfhs.org. The federation represents governing bodies for sports at the secondary school level and accumulates statistics on participation and offerings.

National Women's Law Center, 11 Dupont Circle, N.W., Suite 800, Washington, D.C. 20036; (202) 588-5180; www.nwlc.org. Founded in 1972 to protect women's rights, the nonprofit has been involved in numerous Title IX legal challenges and produces reports on females in sports.

Tucker Center for Research on Girls & Women in Sport, University of Minnesota, 203 Cooke Hall, 1900 University Ave., S.E., Minneapolis, Minn., 55455 (612) 625-7327; www.tuckercenter.org

Women's Sports Foundation, Eisenhower Park, East Meadow, N.Y. 11554; (800) 227-3988; www.womenssportfoundation.org. Founded in 1974 by former tennis star Billie Jean King, the foundation promotes sports activities for girls and women and produces reports and articles and advocates for female athletics.

Bibliography

Selected Sources Used

Books

Andrew Zimbalist, *Unpaid Professionals: Commercialism and Conflict in Big-Time College Sports*, Princeton University Press, 1999.
Zimbalist, an economics professor at Smith College, concludes that college sports is a commercialized industry that runs counter to educational goals. He predicts that equity complaints will force equality.

Articles

Bumpus-Hooper, Lynne, "9 Schools Discriminate Against Girls: A Survey Shows the Area High Schools Violate Title IX, the Federal Provision That Bans Gender Bias," *Orlando Sentinel*, Dec. 26, 2000.
The newspaper's survey of 49 area high schools alleges gender-equity violations, including poorer facilities for women than boys.

Carton, Barbara, "You Don't Need Oars in the Water to Go Out for Crew: Colleges Have Plenty of Money for Tall, Muscular Women; 'No Experience Necessary,' " *The Wall Street Journal*, May 14, 1999, p. A1.
Carton outlines the rise of women's rowing on college campuses, not because of a ground swell of interest but as a way to comply with Title IX.

Couch, Greg, "Venus' Sky-High Deal: Will Williams' $40M Contract Raise the Bar for Female Athletes?" *Chicago Sun-Times*, Dec. 22, 2000.
Sex sells as evidenced by tennis beauty Anna Kournikova's popularity among corporate sponsors despite the fact she has never won a tournament, Couch writes. But Venus Williams' prowess attracted the largest endorsement deal.

Doherty, Megan, "Women Athletes' Forum on Sex Selling Sport," *Canberra Times*, Oct. 15, 2000, p. 79
Doherty asks the central question: "Olympic medals or nude calendars. What will we remember most about sportswomen?" Then, she goes on to offer various points of view from athletes and sports administrators. Some say the nude photos degrade women's sports, but others say it has brought positive attention.

Navarro, Mireya, "Women in Sports Cultivating New Playing Fields," *The New York Times*, Feb. 13, 2001.
Navarro chronicles women's burgeoning sports careers, but says they are far from achieving parity.

Reilly, Rick, "Bare in Mind," *Sports Illustrated*, Sept. 4, 2000.
Columnist Reilly attacks feminists and argues that the sexy photos of star female athletes serve to highlight their accomplishments and empowerment.

Suggs, Welch, "Uneven Progress for Women's Sports: A Chronicle survey finds gains at big-time football powers, struggles at the 'have-nots,' " *The Chronicle of Higher Education*, April 7, 2000, pp. A52-57.
In its annual gender-equity analysis, the Chronicle reports women's sports are growing, but at schools without revenue-producing football and basketball teams the gap between men and women is widening.

Report and Studies

Acosta, R. Vivian, and Linda Jean Carpenter, *Women in Intercollegiate Sport: A Longitudinal Study — Twenty-three Year Update 1977-2000*, Brooklyn College, 2001.
The study reports good and bad news: Participation is up for women, who now have more teams to choose from, but the number of females coaching women's teams has dropped to an all-time low.

National Collegiate Athletic Association, *The NCAA Minority Opportunities and Interests Committee's Biennial Study of the Race Demographics of Member Institutions' Athletics Personnel*, March 27, 2000.
A study shows that the number of African-American female coaches has only risen slightly, a shortfall that the NCAA is attempting to address.

National Federation of State High School Associations, *1999-2000 Athletics Participation Summary*, 2000.
The survey contains data on participation in sports from 1971 to 1999-2000. Last year, girls accounted for 40.9 percent of high school athletes, compared with 7.4 percent in 1971.

Schuld, Kimberly, *Independent Women's Forum, Title IX Athletics: Issue In-Depth: Background and Analysis of Government Policy Governing Sports*, June 2000.
The report concludes that Title IX policies have led to drastic cuts in male athletic opportunities and advocates policy changes to reflect levels of interest in athletics by all students.

U.S. General Accounting Office, *Intercollegiate Athletics Four-Year Colleges' Experiences Adding and Discontinuing Teams*, March 2001.
The independent watchdog agency for Congress reports that women's athletic participation in the past two decades at universities grew at more than twice the rate of their undergraduate enrollment growth while men's participation more closely matched their growth.

14 Gay Rights

KENNETH JOST

Holly Puterbaugh and Lois Farnham have lived a quiet, loving life together for 28 years. But up until last July a cloud of uncertainty hung over them because their relationship was unrecognized in law.

"If we were in a car accident on the way home," Puterbaugh explained, "there's no guarantee that I'd be able to go see her, to sit with her, because I'm not 'family.' "

For the past three years, the two Vermont women have fought a legal battle to change that. They joined two other same-sex couples in an historic lawsuit that forced the state legislature to pass a law recognizing "civil unions" with essentially the same rights as heterosexual marriage — including property rights, insurance coverage, and child custody.

Puterbaugh, who teaches mathematics at the University of Vermont, and Farnham, a school nurse supervisor, were among many Vermonters who took advantage of the new law on the day it went into effect: July 1.

"I think it's about time, after 27½ years," Farnham told reporters outside the South Burlington town clerk's office. "It's nice after all this time to call Holly my spouse."[1]

Gay rights advocates hailed the Vermont law. The measure "represents a sea change in the entire framework in which gay and lesbian rights are fought," says Beatrice Dohrn, legal director of the New York-based Lambda Legal Defense and Education Fund.

Anti-gay rights groups opposed the law, but agreed that it had broader implications than giving legal rights to same-sex couples. "This isn't just about them wanting their rights," said John Paulk, who handles homosexuality issues for Focus on the Family, a Colorado-based Christian organization. "What they want is societal approval and sanction of homosexuality."

Originally published April 14, 2000.
Updated by Kenneth Jost,
December 8, 2000.

AP Photo/Toby Talbot

The three couples who sought the right to same-sex marriage in Vermont are Holly Puterbaugh and Lois Farnham, front, and rear, from left, Stacy Jolles and Nina Beck and Stan Baker and Peter Harrigan.

Same-sex marriage is one of several gay rights issues that have risen to the top of the national agenda over the past year. Gay rights advocates have been pressing their efforts to modify or repeal the military's "don't ask, don't tell" policy on homosexuality ever since the murder of a young soldier believed to be gay at an Army base in Kentucky in July 1999. They renewed their arguments in March with the release of a Defense Department report that found evidence of widespread harassment of gay and lesbian servicemembers *(see p. 256)*.

Vice President Al Gore, campaigning as the Democratic presidential nominee, vowed to repeal the policy, if elected. Texas Gov. George W. Bush, the Republican nominee, said he favored the existing policy.

Gore also called for passage of federal legislation to prohibit job discrimination due to sexual orientation. Gay rights groups have won passage of anti-discrimination legislation in 11 states and some 165 municipalities, but have failed to get a federal bill through either the House or the Senate. Bush opposed such legislation *(see p. 257)*.

Meanwhile, the U.S. Supreme Court acted on a closely watched New Jersey case testing whether the Boy Scouts of America can enforce a policy of barring open homosexuals as leaders. The New Jersey Supreme Court ruled that the policy violated the state's anti-discrimination law. But the high court sided with the Boy Scouts in July, holding that the New Jersey ruling infringed on their First Amendment rights *(see p. 255)*.

In addition, some school districts are contending with the issue whether to allow high school students to form so-called "gay-straight alliance" clubs. Proponents say the clubs help promote tolerance and combat harassment of gay and lesbian students. Critics say they promote homosexuality. *(See story, p. 260; "At Issue," p. 259.)*

In Vermont, the state Supreme Court forced the legislature's hand by ruling that lawmakers had to allow same-sex couples either to marry or to form a "domestic partnership" or some alternative relationship.[2] The decision in *Baker v. State* was based on a provision in the Vermont constitution and therefore could not be appealed to the U.S. Supreme Court, which cannot override a state court's interpretation of state law.[3]

The legislature quickly turned to the issue in January, the month after the state high court's ruling. Most lawmakers rejected marriage for same-sex couples and turned instead to a bill allowing homosexuals to form a "civil union" with essentially all the legal rights of marriage. The

Laws Prohibiting Discrimination

Legislation prohibiting discrimination in private employment based on sexual orientation is in force in 11 states, the District of Columbia and some 124 municipalities and counties. Similar federal legislation has failed in the House and Senate.

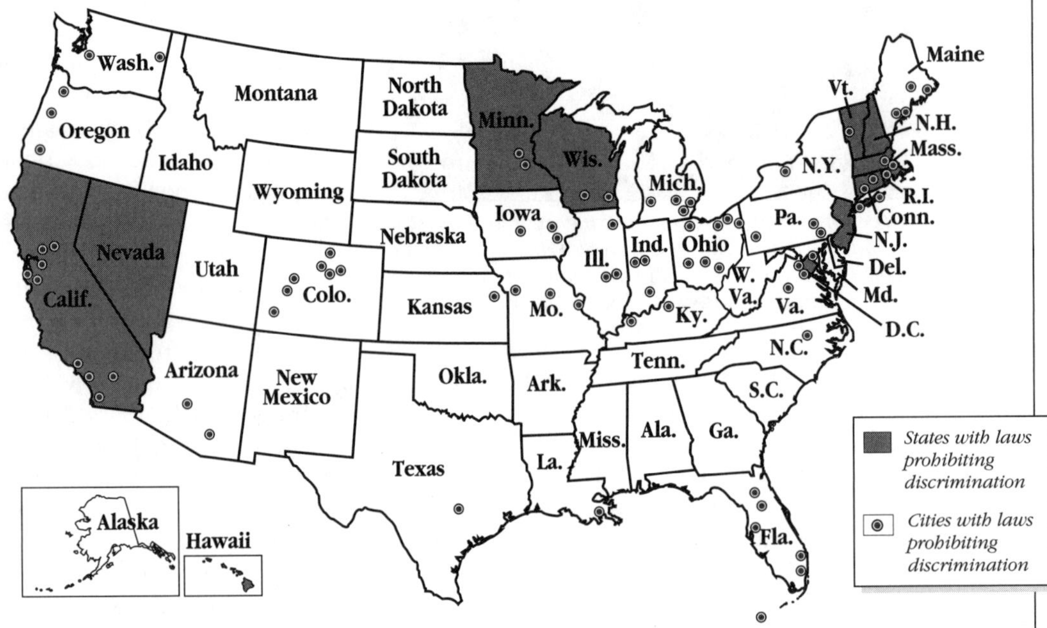

Source: Wayne van der Meide, "Legislating Equality: A Review of Laws Affecting Gay, Lesbian, Bisexual, and Transgendered People in the United States," National Gay and Lesbian Task Force

Vermont House of Representatives narrowly approved the bill in March; the more liberal state Senate followed suit in April; and the state's Democratic governor, Howard Dean, signed it into law on April 26.

Opponents had mounted a strong lobbying campaign against legal recognition for homosexual couples. "I disagree with the concept that they're entitled to the same things that heterosexual couples are entitled to," said Michele Cummings, president of the ad hoc lobbying group Take It to the People. "We do not believe that benefits should be awarded on the basis of sexual activity."

Nationally, social conservative advocacy groups make similar arguments. "If you say two men constitute a marriage, you are creating a counterfeit," says Robert Knight, director of cultural studies for the Family Research Council. "Homosexual relationships are not a facsimile of marriage. They are entirely different."

Gay rights advocates, however, contend that the reasons for refusing to recognize same-sex relationships are outdated. "Our social context of marriage has changed so much," says Paula Ettelbrick, director of the family law project of the National Gay and Lesbian Task Force (NGLTF). "It's really about economic benefits and the support systems that government provides to family. It's much less about being a proper procreative form or having a male head of household."

The opposing advocacy groups also clashed on the role of the courts in dealing with the issue. "We feel that it needed to be taken to the people, that five judges shouldn't make that decision for all of us," Cummings said.

"The very reason for being of the judicial branch of government is to protect the rights of the minority against the majority," countered Susan Murray, a Burlington lawyer and one of the attorneys for the three same-sex couples in the Vermont case. "If we waited for the majority to grant rights that they're not interested in thinking about granting, it would take a heck of a longer time."

The Vermont measure represents a major victory — both substantively and symbolically — for the gay rights movement. But one leading gay rights advocate says the new civil unions recognized under the law can also be viewed as a "second best" status. "The glass is still at least half-empty," says William Rubenstein, a law professor at UCLA. "No same-sex couple can be married anywhere in the United States."

Rubenstein, formerly director of the American Civil Liberties Union's national lesbian and gay rights project, says gay rights advocates have comparable records in other areas. "There has been enormous progress in the last 30 years, but alongside that is there still an enormous amount of work to go," he says. Only a minority of states have enacted anti-discrimination laws, he notes, while some 19 states have refused to repeal anti-sodomy laws once widely used to prosecute homosexuals for consensual sexual behavior *(see map, p. 250)*.

Nonetheless, a *Newsweek* poll last spring showed that Americans are becoming more comfortable with homosexuality. In 1998, 54 percent said homosexuality was a sin compared with 46 percent today.

Critics and opponents, however, accuse the gay rights movement of fostering legal and social changes that they say are undermining traditional morality.

"When you have corporations promoting open homosexuality, when you have ordinances on the books of many cities adding sexual orientation to civil rights laws, you are well on the way to suppressing dissent on the issue," Knight says. "But like any good activist, they say they are never satisfied. Just a few years ago they were demanding tolerance. Now they're demanding gay marriages and homosexual curriculums in the schools. That's quite an advance, particularly for such a tiny segment of the population."

The debate — part political, part legal, part cultural — continued as gay rights groups held a major march in Washington in April to highlight their agenda *(see p. 258)*. Here are some of the issues they and their opponents are debating:

Should same-sex relationships be legally recognized?

Over the past five years, attorneys Murray and Beth Robinson talked to dozens of church and civic groups in Vermont as they made the case for legal recognition of same-sex relationships. Audiences were skeptical initially, Murray recalls, but most meetings ended with greater sympathy for their position.

"If we can talk to Vermonters about the tangible benefits that married couples obtain simply by obtaining a marriage certificate, fair-minded Vermonters sit back and say, 'Wow, I've never thought of it that way; of course, gay couples deserve that,' " she says.

By the time Vermont lawmakers took up the issue in March, a poll — commissioned by the Vermont Freedom to Marry Task Force — found that most people supported allowing homosexual partners either to marry (30 percent) or to form "civil unions" (25 percent). Only 40 percent opposed either legal recognition for same-sex couples.

Across the nation, however, same-sex marriage still draws fire. National polls consistently show solid majorities opposed to homosexual marriages. [4] And Congress and some 30 states have passed laws to block recognition of same-sex marriages.

Gay-rights advocates view the government's refusal to recognize same-sex relationships as outright discrimination. "The issue is not so much marriage, it's a denial of equal benefits," Ettelbrick says. "That's the constitutional problem. That's where the state most fundamentally treats same-sex partners differently."

Opponents, however, insist that recognizing same-sex relationships would lead to myriad practical problems. "Marriage is about more than the two individuals involved," the Family Research Council's Knight says. "It's how kinship develops and family names are passed down and the generations are linked and property is distributed and where new life is created."

Advocates of same-sex marriage say legal recognition would benefit homosexuals as well as society at large. "Same-sex marriage is good for gay people and good for America," writes Yale Law School Professor William Eskridge Jr., "and for the same reason: It civilizes gays, and it civilizes America." [5]

Eskridge argues that recognizing same-sex marriage would encourage the broad social trend toward tolerance for homosexuality while reducing promiscuity among homosexuals, especially gay men. Other gay-rights advocates, however, back away from any such claim.

"I see the issues as different," UCLA's Rubenstein says. "There's the question of legal recognition, and there's the question of sexual practices."

Indeed, some gay-rights advocates are less than enthusiastic about marriage for homosexual couples. Ettelbrick, for example, has previously denounced marriage as a "patriarchal" institution. "I don't think marriage should be the only way that we describe or support families," she says. "Good public policy will accept and provide economic support for people who are caring for each other whether they're married or not." [6]

In any event, opponents are unconvinced that recognizing same-sex marriage would reduce the incidence of multiple sexual partners among homosexuals. "That is a disingenuous argument," says Lynn Wardell, a law professor at Brigham Young University in Provo, Utah. "I'm waiting to see the evidence."

Given the strong opposition to same-sex marriage, gay-rights organizations began working in the 1980s for a less ambitious goal: winning workplace benefits such as health insurance for same-sex couples. On that front, there has been what Ettelbrick calls "tremendous success." Thousands of employers, including many of the country's biggest businesses, today allow unmarried employees — homosexuals as well as heterosexuals — to designate their partners for health insurance coverage.

Anti-gay-rights groups, however, also object to domestic partnerships — though perhaps not as fiercely. "If you want the benefits of marriage, you have to meet the qualifications," Knight says, "the first of which is that

Military Discharges for Homosexual Conduct

President Clinton was forced to back away from a post-election promise to lift the strict Pentagon ban on homosexuals and in 1993 fashioned a compromise known as "don't ask, don't tell." Despite the seeming liberalization of the policy, the number of servicemembers discharged for homosexuality has increased since 1993 along with the reported incidence of anti-gay harassment.

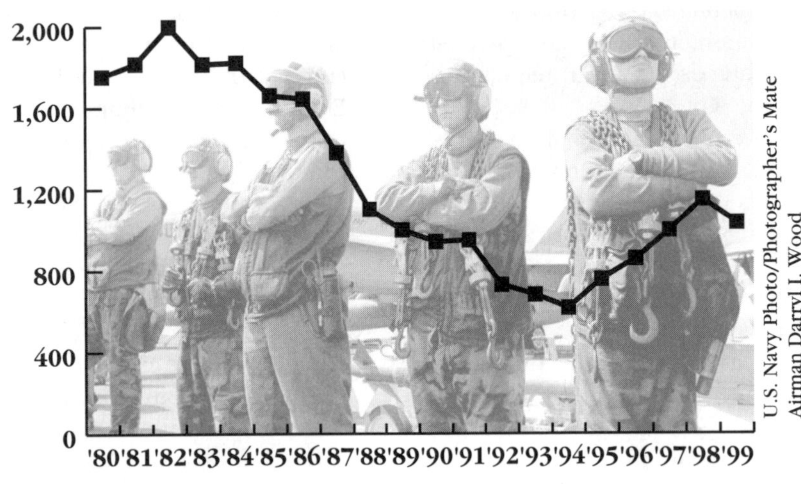

Source: Department of Defense

you have to open your life to a person of the opposite sex and make a lifelong commitment."

Wardell agrees, though he says he would allow some recognition for same-sex couples — for example, in hospital visitation. "Hospital visitation ought not depend on a marital relationship," he says.

Vermont's civil union law goes further than any previous law or employer policy in providing same-sex couples the rights enjoyed by heterosexuals. The Family Research Council called the measure "nothing short of an endorsement of 'same-sex marriage.' "

For her part, though, attorney Murray said the law does not go far enough. "Marriage, of course, is the only thing that gives gay and lesbian couples true equality," she says. "This is a very good bill, but it is a first step, not the end of the road."

Should the military's "don't ask, don't tell" policy be changed?

Pfc. Barry Winchell suffered through four months of taunting, harassment and anti-gay epithets from fellow soldiers at Fort Campbell in Kentucky before his murder on July 5, 1999. Two soldiers have been convicted in the killing: Pvt. Calvin Glover, who shattered Winchell's skull with a baseball bat, and Spec. Justin Fisher, who gave Glover the bat.

Gay-rights groups, however, believe the real culprit in the Winchell case is the Army itself — for tolerating anti-gay harassment — as well as the military's "don't ask, don't tell" policy — for forcing homosexual servicemembers to conceal their identities in order to serve their country.

"There is no safe haven for military members to turn to if they are harassed or threatened," says Michelle Benecke, co-director of the Servicemembers Legal Defense Network (SLDN). "How many people have to be harassed or murdered before people take this problem seriously?"

SLDN says that despite the seeming liberalization of "don't ask, don't tell," the number of service members discharged for homosexuality has increased since 1993 along with the incidence of anti-gay harassment. (*See graph.*) Winchell's murder did prompt the Defense Department to adopt more explicit anti-gay-harassment policies. But the "don't ask, don't tell" policy remains in effect, seven years after its adoption as a compromise of sorts following President Clinton's failure to win support for lifting the ban on homosexuals in the military altogether.

The Winchell episode did renew debate in Washington and across the country over the military's policy. But some opponents of homosexuals in the military say that the harassment issue has been exaggerated, and they remain convinced that homosexuality is "incompatible" with military service — just as Congress declared in 1993 in a Defense Department authorization bill that Clinton signed into law.

"There are no doubt incidents in which drill sergeants and platoon leaders have used derogatory language, and they're wrong," says Robert Maginnis, a retired Army lieutenant colonel and now director of national security and foreign affairs at the Family Research Council. "But I don't think that it's part of the dominant culture."

Maginnis calls Winchell's killing "a terrible situation." But he discounts SLDN's statistics on anti-gay harassment and considers the new anti-harassment policy an overreaction.

"Why are we getting so bent out of shape about a group of people that we've decided ought to be excluded?" he asks.

Gay-rights advocates continue to regard "don't ask, don't tell" as unfair to gay and lesbian servicemembers. The policy "discriminates against lesbian, gay and bisexual servicemembers," Benecke says. "Gay people are kicked out for saying and doing the same thing straight people do every day."

In addition, Benecke and other critics say the policy is bad for the military at a time when the services are having difficulty recruiting and retaining personnel. "This law is forcing commanders to kick good people out of the military," she says.

Supporters of the policy continue to defend the restrictions on open expressions of homosexuality as necessary to protect the rights of straight servicemembers forced to live with fellow soldiers and sailors in close quarters.

"You're talking about the privacy rights of straights as well as gays," says Charles Moskos, a professor of sociology at Northwestern University in Evanston, Ill., and an adviser to the administration at the time of the policy's adoption. "It might be that in the future people won't mind," he says, "but that's not the era we live in right now."

Maginnis cites other reasons for opposing homosexuals in the military, including the risk of sexually transmitted diseases and what he says is an adverse effect on the morale of individual units. "When we throw the ingredient of sex in, whether it's heterosexual or same-sex attraction, it undermines the confidence and trust we must have in these teams," he says.

Gay-rights advocates say they want the military to honor the "don't ask, don't tell" policy by ensuring that commanders do not investigate servicemembers suspected of being homosexual and that they crack down on anti-gay harassment. In the long term, though, they believe the policy should be replaced by one that permits homosexuals to serve openly.

"Ultimately, this law should be replaced with a principle of nondiscrimination where everyone is evaluated according to their merit rather than a characteristic that has nothing to do with their performance," Benecke says.

Maginnis, on the other hand, wants to reinstitute an outright ban on service by homosexuals — the policy that he says is prescribed by law but circumvented by the Clinton administration's regulations. "The law is very clear: it's an exclusion policy," Maginnis says. The administration, he says, "has forced something on the military that is not in the best interest of the service."

Moskos, however, sees no better alternative than the current policy. "It's much like what Winston Churchill said about democracy," Moskos says. "It's the worst system possible, except for any other."

Are additional laws needed to prohibit discrimination on the basis of sexual orientation?

Dwayne Simonton claimed in a federal civil rights suit that his co-workers at the Farmingdale, N.Y., post office mercilessly ridiculed him because of his homosexuality. A federal judge in June 1999 found their conduct "offensive" but dismissed Simonton's sexual-harassment lawsuit. The reason: The federal Civil Rights Act does not prohibit discrimination on the basis of sexual orientation. [7]

Gay-rights advocates have been pushing for two decades for passage of laws to prohibit discrimination against homosexuals in the workplace, in housing and in public accommodations. "There's a tremendous amount of individual bias against gay people," says Beatrice Dohrn, legal director for the Lambda Legal Defense and Education Fund. "Some people want us to continue having second-class status."

Polls show that a substantial majority of Americans — more than 80 percent — believe that homosexuals should not be discriminated against in the workplace. (*See poll, p. 254.*) But efforts to enact anti-gay-discrimination laws have fallen short in Washington and in most state capitals in the face of a swirl of arguments raised by conservative advocacy groups.

They warn of a parade of horribles that would result, in particular, from a proposed federal law, the Employment Non-Discrimination Act (ENDA): job quotas, heavy-handed federal enforcement, invasive questioning about employees' sexual orientation and intrusions on the religious liberties of faith-based employers. Most broadly, opponents say the law would undermine traditional morality and give "special rights" to a group that neither needs nor deserves special legal protections.

ENDA "requires the federal government to abandon its commitments to the traditions of marriage and family and to declare that all sexual preferences are equally valid," says a Family Research Council position paper. The bill "affords special protection to a group that is not disadvantaged," the paper continues. "Homosexuals, as a group, outpace most other Americans economically and educationally, and no one can dispute their political power and savvy."

Lobbyists insist the opponents are exaggerating or misstating the provisions of the federal bill. "This is a very modest piece of legislation," says Winnie Stachelberg, political director of Human Rights Campaign (HRC), a gay-rights organization. "All it would say is you can't be fired from your job for sexual orientation — because of a factor that has nothing to do with your job performance."

Sixteen States Still Have Anti-Sodomy Laws

Anti-sodomy laws historically have been used to prosecute homosexuals for oral and anal sex, although they also typically apply to heterosexuals. The laws are rarely enforced today but are still used, according to gay-rights advocates, to deny employment and child custody and visitation rights to gays. Supporters say that even if the laws are rarely enforced, they help to safeguard the legal and moral status of the family and to contain sexual conduct that is a factor in sexually transmitted diseases.

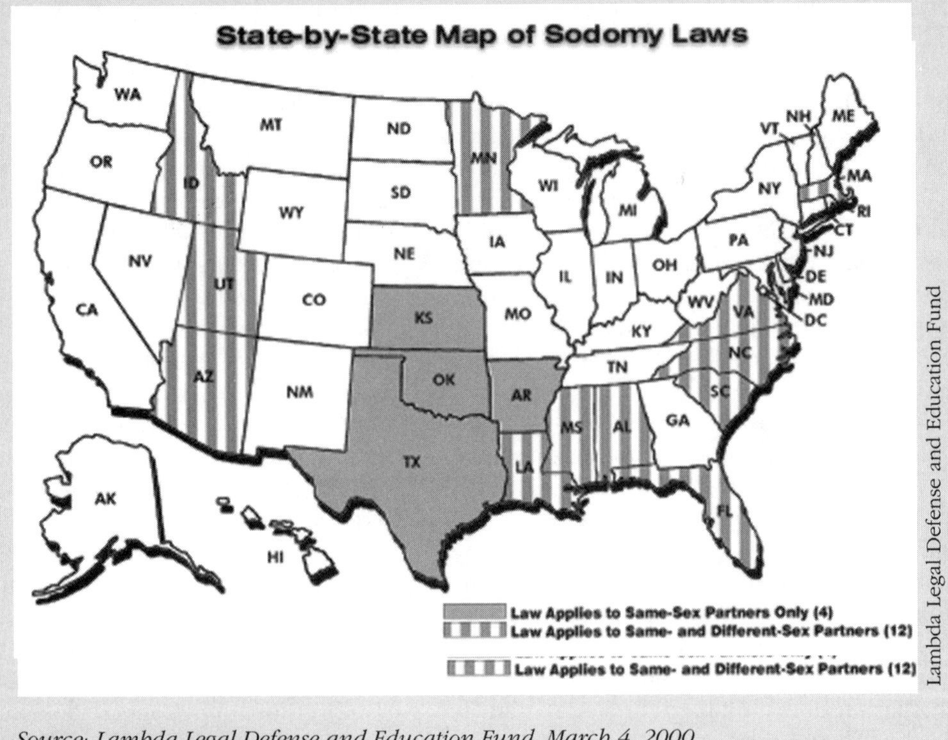

Source: Lambda Legal Defense and Education Fund, March 4, 2000

Opponents acknowledge that the bill bars the use of quotas or preferences for homosexuals. But they contend that administrative enforcement and litigation will pressure employers into adopting such schemes anyway. "Employers will be forced to learn more about their employees' sex lives," the Family Research Council warns, "in order to defend themselves against possible lawsuits."

Supporters of the bill dismiss such fears as groundless. "I don't think there's any reason to believe that having laws [in some states] has injected all sorts of sexual-orientation questions into the workplace," Dohrn says. "The laws provide an incentive for employers to leave the subject out." In any event, the notion of quotas is "kind of ridiculous," she says. "There is no way in the world to count how many people are gay."

Opponents also warn that the bill could force religious organizations to hire homosexuals despite religious convictions against homosexuality. They acknowledge the bill includes an exemption for religious organizations but say it does not extend to individuals and might not apply to some church-sponsored social services. Supporters again say the warnings are off base. The bill "has a religious exemption so big you could push the National Cathedral through it," Dohrn says.

Despite the failure of the federal bill, some 11 states, the District of Columbia and 124 municipalities and counties have passed gay-rights measures — almost all of them with employment-discrimination provisions. Gay-rights advocates say, somewhat regretfully, that the laws have not generated the kind of rush of litigation that opponents have warned about.

"The laws are underused, and that's because using them is an expensive, uphill battle," Dohrn says. "Coming out is still a dangerous proposition in many parts of the country, and litigating against your employer is always a risky proposition."

Congress has had only one recorded vote on the federal bill: in the Senate in September 1996. The measure failed 49-50, with one senator absent. The vote was largely symbolic since the House would have had no time to act on the measure late in the session. Since that time, Stachelberg says, the Republican leadership in the House and the Senate has kept the bill "bottled up."

The Family Research Council's Knight acknowledges that more states and municipalities are likely to pass such laws, though he doubts Congress will. But he also sees a likely backlash. "You're going to see more of these laws challenged," he says. "People will say you shouldn't create a sweeping new category" for civil rights laws.

But Dohrn thinks the movement

to enact such laws will continue. "It's remarkable how many people think that discrimination on the basis of sexual orientation is already illegal," she says. "Eventually, the law will conform to people's expectations about the law." ■

BACKGROUND

Birth of a Movement

Homosexuals were largely invisible, politically unorganized and legally vulnerable from the founding of the United States until the early 20th century. When homosexual subcultures started becoming more visible, the social pressures against homosexuality turned into legal strictures with expansively written "crime-against-nature" laws.

The legal crackdown on homosexuals increased from the 1920s through the decades after World War II. Ironically, the crackdown spawned the gay-rights movement, as homosexuals organized first to protect themselves from prosecution and then to demand legal recognition and equal rights. [8]

The legal crackdown on homosexuality was multifaceted. Under the 1917 Immigration Act, the government barred "sexual perverts" from entering the country, much as a 1921 Army regulation permitted exclusion for "sexual perversion." Homosexual organizations were shut down through the use of disorderly-conduct laws. Gay bars found their licenses suspended or revoked. Most dramatically, homosexuals were subject to criminal prosecution for sodomy, lewd conduct or other offenses. On the eve of World War II, Yale's Eskridge writes, "a homosexual with an active social life had a good chance of spending time in jail." [9]

The pursuit of homosexuals intensified after World War II, when Eskridge estimates that as many as 100,000 gays per year, mostly men, were arrested for consensual sexual behavior. Some states moved to bar homosexuals as teachers or as lawyers. Thousands of soldiers and sailors were discharged on grounds of homosexuality, proven or suspected.

The crackdown finally engendered resistance — and the first stirrings of the gay-rights movement. The leading resistance group was the Mattachine Society, formed in Los Angeles in 1951. Taking its name from a medieval Italian court jester who expressed unpopular truths from behind a mask, the group vowed to unify homosexuals and to assist "our people who are victimized daily as a result of our oppression." [10]

The Mattachine Society and the Daughters of Bilitis — the first lesbian organization, founded in San Francisco in 1955 — both adopted assimilationist strategies. Mattachine wanted to educate homosexuals and heterosexuals alike to an "ethical homosexual culture," while the Daughters advocated "a mode of behavior and dress acceptable to society."

The non-confrontational approach combined with liberalizing trends in politics, law and society to produce some tangible gains. Illinois became the first state to decriminalize sodomy in 1961. The California Supreme Court acted to protect gay bars from arbitrary closures, and the U.S. Supreme Court limited the Post Office's power to censor male physique magazines.

The number of gay organizations increased in the 1960s — from 15 in 1966 to nearly 50 three years later — and the groups became both more visible and more aggressive. [11] Then in 1969, two days of disturbances touched off by a police raid at a dilapidated — and unlicensed — gay dance bar in New York City gave new impetus and militancy to the gay-rights movement. [12] Plainclothes officers ordered patrons out of Greenwich Village's Stonewall Inn on June 28 and loaded three men dressed as women into paddywagons. When the crowd threw cans and bottles, the police retreated and reinforcements arrived to clear the streets.

The next night, as hundreds of protesters gathered, the mood was camp rather than revolution. But a milestone had been reached. Gay people, author Eric Marcus writes, "were finally pushed to the point where they'd had enough, and they fought back." A month later, activists in Greenwich Village organized what they called the city's "first gay-power vigil.

"Do you think homosexuals are revolting?" a leaflet asked, capturing the movement's new sense of pride and militancy. "You bet your sweet ass we are," it answered in capital letters. [13]

Successes and Setbacks

The gay-rights movement made fitful advances over the next two decades. Anti-sodomy statutes were repealed or invalidated in many states, while a few states and many municipalities prohibited discrimination against homosexuals. But social conservatives — the so-called New Right — responded with lobbying and citizen initiatives to block gay-rights measures or in a few cities to repeal ordinances already enacted.

The Supreme Court also dealt the movement a setback, upholding state anti-sodomy statutes. Meanwhile, same-sex marriage made no headway in the courts, although some cities enacted domestic partnership laws. And the Pentagon actually toughened its policy on homosexuality, explicitly excluding homosexuals from the military. [14]

The movement's broadest success came in eradicating sodomy laws. Connecticut followed Illinois' lead in repealing its anti-sodomy statute in 1971. By 1992, similar laws had been repealed in some 19 other state legislatures and nullified by court rulings in four others.

Nonetheless, the U.S. Supreme Court in 1986 voted 5-4 to uphold the constitutionality of enforcing sodomy statutes against private, consensual homosexual conduct. Writing for the majority in *Bowers v. Hardwick*, Justice Byron White said Georgia's law could be justified on the basis of "the presumed belief of a majority of the electorate in Georgia that homosexual conduct is immoral and unacceptable."

Gay-rights advocates began winning enactment of anti-discrimination laws at the local level in the 1970s and then in a handful of states in the '80s. Generally, the laws prohibited discrimination in government or private employment on the basis of sexual orientation; some also barred discrimination in housing or public accommodations.

Opponents succeeded in several cities in overturning ordinances through the referendum process — notably in Miami-Dade County, Fla., in a 1977 campaign led by pop singer Anita Bryant and fueled by conservative religious groups. At the state level, opponents succeeded in stalling bills or — for example, in California in 1985 — in persuading the governor to veto a measure approved by lawmakers. Despite the difficulties, by 1992 gay-rights laws were on the books in seven states and some 90 municipalities — mostly large cities or university towns.

Advocates of same-sex marriage made no headway before the 1990s. A few couples brought suits, but courts rejected their constitutional claims almost out of hand. None of the major gay and lesbian organizations supported their efforts. The community was, in fact, divided on the issue, with many gay and lesbian activists viewing marriage as the kind of hierarchical institution that the movement should seek to displace.

In the 1980s, gay-rights groups did support the emerging effort to win workplace equality through recognition of domestic partnerships. The San Francisco Board of Supervisors passed a domestic partnership bill in 1981, but it was vetoed by then-Mayor Dianne Feinstein. A year later, Berkeley, Calif., became the first city to enact such an ordinance. By 1991, another two dozen cities had followed suit — including San Francisco.

Gay-rights advocates suffered one clear setback — in the military. Regulations dating back to World War II had prohibited service by homosexuals, but they were often ignored. Pentagon officials began rewriting the regulations in the late 1970s, under President Jimmy Carter; the revamping was completed in the first year of President Ronald Reagan's administration in 1981.

The new regulations reiterated the description of homosexuality as "incompatible with military service" but expanded the definition to include anyone who "engages in, desires to engage in or intends to engage in homosexual acts."

As author Randy Shilts put it, "The military had, in effect, banned homosexual thoughts." [15] The new regulations were more rigorously enforced: nearly 17,000 servicemembers were discharged for homosexual conduct during the 12 years of Reagan's and George Bush's presidencies.

"A Seat at the Table"

Despite continuing resistance, the movement made remarkable strides in the 1990s, legally and politically. Gay rights became a focus of national debate for the first time during the 1992 presidential election. The Clinton administration and the Democratic Party aligned themselves for the rest of the decade with many of the issues on the gay-rights agenda.

Still, there were setbacks: the "don't ask, don't tell" policy; Congress' failure to pass a gay civil-rights law; and the adoption of defense of marriage laws by Congress and a majority of states.

Clinton signaled his support for the cause by appearing at a 1992 Los Angeles fund-raiser organized by gay activists. [16] The Clinton campaign netted $100,000 — and the gay community showed it could flex its considerable financial muscle to further its aims. For his part, Clinton said gay Americans represented "a community of our nation's gifted people that we have been willing to squander." He pledged to undo the Pentagon's policy, crack down on anti-gay hate crimes and include an HIV-positive speaker at the Democratic National Convention.

In office, Clinton proved unable to deliver on his promises. Most dramatically, his effort to open military service to homosexuals fell short in the face of a strong backlash from military leaders, members of Congress from both parties and the public. [17]

Clinton was forced to back away from a post-election promise to lift the ban on homosexuals by executive order and then fashioned a short-term compromise — soon known as "don't ask, don't tell." Gay servicemembers derisively termed it "don't tell, don't touch."

Congress kept at the issue, however, and eventually approved a provision in the Defense Department authorization that codified the ban on homosexuals

Chronology

Before 1945

Homosexuals are politically unorganized, legally vulnerable.

1945-1970

Initial stirrings of gay-rights movement.

1951
Mattachine Society is founded in Los Angeles to provide support for male homosexuals. Four years later, Daughters of Bilitis is founded in San Francisco as first U.S. lesbian organization.

1961
Illinois becomes first state to remove penalty for consensual homosexual relations between adults.

June 1969
Police raid on the Stonewall Inn, a popular gay bar in New York City, becomes defining moment for modern gay-rights movement.

1970s

Gay rights becomes national issue, but gains are limited.

1977
Miami-Dade County, Fla., adopts ordinance prohibiting discrimination against gay men and lesbians; ordinance overturned by referendum six months later.

1979
First national gay-rights march held in Washington.

1980s

Gay rights advances, but social conservatives stiffen opposition; AIDS becomes an epidemic.

1981
Wisconsin becomes first state to bar discrimination against homosexuals in employment, housing and public accommodations.

1984
Berkeley, Calif., becomes first city to provide domestic-partner benefits for gays and lesbians.

1986
U.S. Supreme Court upholds state laws against consensual homosexual sodomy.

1990s

Gay-rights movement combines political clout and legal initiatives to make significant gains against continuing resistance.

1992
Democratic presidential candidate Bill Clinton promises support for several gay-rights proposals; after his election, Clinton repeats vow to end military policy excluding gays.

1993
Congress forces Clinton to accept "don't ask, don't tell" policy on gays in military; Hawaii Supreme Court says state must justify law prohibiting same-sex marriages; third gay-rights march on Washington.

1994
Massachusetts becomes first state to outlaw discrimination against gays in public schools.

1996
Colorado initiative prohibiting legal protections for homosexuals nullified by Supreme Court.

July 5, 1999
Pfc. Barry Winchell is beaten to death by a fellow soldier after being taunted for being gay; Defense Secretary William Cohen announces policy against harassment of gays a month later.

Aug. 4, 1999
New Jersey Supreme Court says Boy Scouts' exclusion of gays violates state civil rights law.

Dec. 20, 1999
Vermont Supreme Court says state must allow same-sex couples to enjoy legal benefits accorded to heterosexuals.

2000s

New decade opens with gay-rights issues high on political, legal agendas.

Apr. 25, 2000
Vermont legislature gives final approval to law permitting "civil unions" for same-sex couples; law takes effect July 1.

Apr. 30, 2000
Hundreds of thousands join Millennium March on Washington for gay rights.

June 28, 2000
U.S. Supreme Court upholds Boy Scouts' policy of excluding gays.

Fall 2000
Democrat Al Gore and Republican George W. Bush differ on gay rights issues in presidential campaign.

How Americans Feel About Gay Rights

Public opinion polls indicate solid majority support for giving homosexuals "equal rights in terms of job opportunities." Most Americans, however, believe that sexual relations between two adults of the same sex are "always wrong," though the disapproval rate has fallen significantly in the last decade.

- Do you think homosexuals should have equal rights in terms of job opportunities? In 1996, Yes — 84%
- Do you think homosexuals should be accepted into the armed forces? In 1996, Yes — 66%
- Do you think homosexuals should be hired as elementary school teachers? In 1996, Yes — 60%
- Do you think sexual relations between two adults of the same sex is always wrong, almost always wrong, wrong only sometimes or not wrong at all?

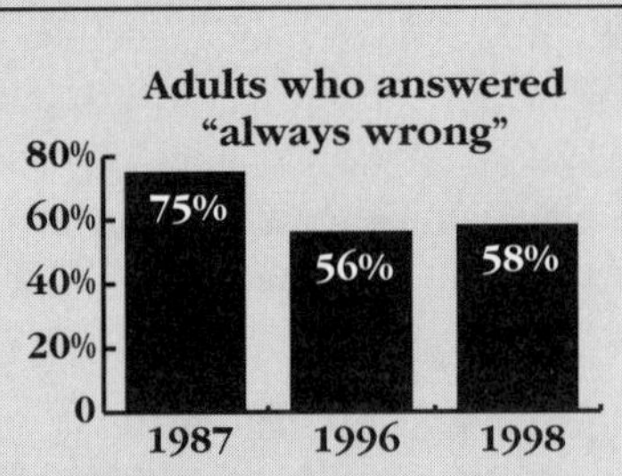

Source: Alan Yang, "From Wrongs to Rights, 1973-1999: Public Opinion on Gay and Lesbian Americans Moves Toward Equality," National Gay and Lesbian Task Force, 1999

while leaving intact the administration's decision not to ask recruits about their sexual orientation and not to initiate investigations except after receiving "credible information" of homosexual conduct. Clinton signed the bill.

The administration was also unable to win support for a gay civil rights bill or special federal penalties for anti-gay hate crimes. The 1990 Hate Crime Statistics Act, signed by President George Bush, does include anti-gay offenses as one category in an annual data compilation by the Justice Department.[18]

Gay-rights advocates continued to press their efforts both in Washington and before state and local legislative bodies. By the end of the decade, the number of gays was still increasing, two states had domestic-partnership schemes and the number of states with anti-sodomy statutes had dwindled to 19.[19]

Opponents tried to thwart gay-rights advocates with initiatives in several states aimed at blocking state or local governments from enacting laws to prohibit discrimination on the basis of sexual orientation. Colorado voters approved such a measure in 1992, but voters in three other states rejected similar initiatives: Idaho and Oregon in 1994 and Maine in 1995.

Then in 1996, the U.S. Supreme Court appeared to bar the tactic by ruling that the Colorado initiative violated the U.S. Constitution's Equal Protection Clause. The law had no rational basis, Justice Anthony Kennedy wrote in *Romer v. Evans*. It was, instead, a "status-based enactment" born out of "animosity toward homosexuals."[20]

The Hawaii Supreme Court's ruling on same-sex marriages in 1993 provoked a similar but stronger backlash. Opponents lobbied Congress and state legislatures to pass laws aimed at barring recognition of same-sex marriages. Congress cleared the federal Defense of Marriage Act on Sept. 10, 1996, just two months before the presidential election.[21]

The measure — which Clinton signed almost surreptitiously at 12:50 a.m. on Sept. 21 — said that states were not obligated to recognize same-sex marriages from other states and defined marriage for purposes of federal law as a union between people of opposite sexes. By decade's end, 30 states had similar laws — including Alaska and Hawaii itself, where voters approved constitutional amendments to ward off recognition of homosexual marriages. ■

CURRENT SITUATION

Debating "Civil Unions"

The Vermont Supreme Court's ruling in the same-sex marriage case touched off a wide-ranging debate from one end of the state to another. Most Vermonters — lawmakers and citizens alike — appeared to oppose marriage for homosexual couples. But with little maneuvering room

Court Upholds Boy Scouts' Rights to Exclude Gays

James Dale became a Cub Scout at age 6 and graduated to Boy Scouts 4 years later. He went on to earn 30 merit badges and achieve scouting's highest honors: Eagle Scout and the Order of the Arrow.

As a young man, Dale wanted to continue as a Scout leader, to give something back to an organization he believed in. But Dale's local Boy Scouts council in Monmouth, N.J., summarily expelled him in 1990 after it learned from a newspaper story that Dale is gay.

Dale challenged the expulsion in a high-profile legal dispute with the Boy Scouts of America (BSA) that pitted anti-discrimination principles against freedom of speech and association. He won a ruling from New Jersey courts that the action violated the state's law against discrimination on the basis of sexual orientation in "public accommodations." But the U.S. Supreme Court overruled that decision, holding that the Boy Scouts had a First Amendment right to enforce their policy of excluding homosexuals.

Dale's attorneys said the case, *Boy Scouts of America v. Dale,* was important not only for Dale but also for gay youths generally. "Gay youths need the same opportunity for socialization and fun and community service as their non-gay brothers and sisters do," said Evan Wolfson, senior attorney with the Lambda Legal Defense and Education Fund.

But BSA national spokesman Greg Shields said homosexuality is inconsistent with Scouting. "The Boy Scouts of America have long taught traditional family values based on the Scout oath and law," Shields says. "The Boy Scouts of America believe that an acknowledged homosexual would not be a role model for those values."

Dale came out as a homosexual while attending Rutgers University in Newark, N.J. While co-president of the gay and lesbian student organization, he attended a seminar in July 1990 on psychological and health needs of homosexual teenagers. The local newspaper ran a story on the seminar along with Dale's picture and a caption identifying his role in the gay organization.

Days later, the Monmouth Boy Scouts council sent Dale a letter that revoked his membership. When Dale asked for a reason, BSA officials responded by saying the organization "specifically forbids membership to homosexuals." Two years later, Dale sued the Scouts under New Jersey's "Law Against Discrimination."

The Boy Scouts had won five similar cases after courts decided that states' civil rights laws did not apply to private membership organizations. A lower court in New Jersey reached the same conclusion in Dale's case. But in August 1999 the New Jersey Supreme Court unanimously ruled that the BSA is a "public accommodation" for purposes of the state's civil rights law and that forcing the organization to accept homosexuals as leaders would not violate its First Amendment freedom of speech or association.

In two rulings in the 1980s, the U.S. Supreme Court did uphold the enforcement of state civil rights laws to require private organizations — the Jaycees and the Rotary Club — to admit women.[1] In a concurring opinion in the Jaycees case, however, Justice Sandra Day O'Connor mentioned the Boy Scouts as an example of an organization that might have a First Amendment right to select its members without running afoul of anti-discrimination laws.

In arguments before the high court, the Scouts' lawyer, George Davidson, defended the policy. "This case is about the freedom of a voluntary association to choose its own leaders," Davidson said. Wolfson countered that the Scouts were asking the court to "specially excuse" it from New Jersey's civil rights laws.

Wolfson insisted that the Scout oath and law — requiring scouts to be "morally straight" and "clean" — had "literally nothing" to do with homosexuality. But Justice Anthony M. Kennedy appeared skeptical. "Who is better qualified to determine the expressive purpose of the Boy Scouts: the Boy Scouts or the New Jersey courts?" he asked.

The court divided along conservative-liberal lines in its 5-4 ruling backing the Scouts on June 28, the final day of the 1999-2000 term. Writing for the conservative majority, Chief Justice William H. Rehnquist said application of the New Jersey law would burden the Scouts' "freedom of expressive association."

"The forced inclusion of an unwanted person in a group infringes the group's freedom of expressive association," Rehnquist wrote, "if the presence of that person affects in a significant way the group's ability to advocate public or private viewpoints."

Writing for the four liberal dissenters, Justice John Paul Stevens disagreed that admitting Dale would burden the Scouts' message. "It is plain as the light of day that neither one of these principles, 'morally straight' and 'clean,' says the slightest thing about homosexuality."

Ruth Harlow, deputy legal director of the Lambda Legal Defense Fund, called the ruling a "hollow, Pyrrhic" victory for the Scouts. "The Boy Scouts have fought long and hard for something that has marginalized the institution," Harlow said.

Dale himself, who had moved to New York and was working as an advertising director for a magazine for people who are HIV-positive, was disappointed both with the ruling and with his beloved Scouts. "The Boy Scouts are making themselves extinct," Dale told reporters, "and it's a very sad thing."

---

[1] The cases are *Board of Directors of Rotary International v. Rotary Club of Duarte* (1987) and *Roberts v. United States Jaycees* (1984). O'Connor's concurring opinion came in the Jaycees case.

under the high court's ruling, the legislature inexorably moved toward approving a "civil union" bill giving gay and lesbian couples rights broader than homosexuals can enjoy in any other state.

The plaintiffs' lawyers — Robinson, Murray and Mary Bonauto of Boston-based Gay and Lesbian Advocates and Defenders (GLAD) — based their case on a provision of the Vermont Constitution known as the common-benefits clause. It provides that government is "instituted for the common benefit, protection and security of the people . . . and not for the particular emolument or advantage of any single person, family or set of persons."

They argued that a law allowing only heterosexual couples to enjoy all the legal benefits of marriage violated that provision. The state's lawyers offered one principal rationale for limiting marriage to heterosexuals: the government's interest in promoting the link between procreation and child-rearing.

In his 45-page opinion for the court, Chief Justice Jeffrey Amestoy pointed out that many heterosexual couples marry "for reasons unrelated to procreation." In addition, he noted that "a significant number of children" are now being raised by same-sex couples and that the state legislature had actually removed legal barriers for same-sex couples to adopt and raise children.

With the state's main argument rejected, Amestoy concluded: "We hold that the State is constitutionally required to extend to same-sex couples the common benefits and protections that flow from marriage under Vermont law."

Nationally, gay-rights advocates were enthused about the ruling. "This decision marks the start of a tremendous sea change that will surely improve life for lesbian and gay families," Lambda's Dohrn declared. On the opposite side, the Family Research Council called the decision "dangerously wrong" because it would "force the people of Vermont to support what is essentially a sin registry."

Opinion was similarly divided in Vermont.[22] A statewide poll conducted a month after the court's ruling found 38 percent in favor of the decision and 52 percent opposed. A near majority — 49 percent — favored a constitutional amendment to overturn the decision, with 44 percent opposed.

In the legislature, the House took first crack at the issue. The Judiciary Committee sent to the House floor a detailed bill establishing "civil union" status for homosexual couples with virtually all the benefits and responsibilities of marriage. The bill declared the state's "strong interest in promoting stable and lasting families, including families based upon a same-sex couple." After lengthy debate, the House passed the measure on March 16 by a narrow margin: 76-69.

The Senate passed a comparable bill, 19-11, on April 19 on a mostly party line vote, with Democrats in favor and all but two Republicans opposed. That bill went back to the House, which gave final legislative approval to the measure on April 25. Gov. Howard Dean, a Democrat, signed the bill the next day with no public ceremony, unusual for a major piece of legislation. "The healing process now begins," he told reporters later.

The state drew national attention when town clerks began issuing civil union licenses on July 1 — some to Vermont couples and others to couples from out of state. The issue continued to divide Vermonters through the fall. Opponents of the legislation mounted a "Take Back Vermont" campaign aimed at defeating Dean and electing Republicans to the legislature. Dean won re-election — gaining a 50 percent majority in a three-way race — but Republicans captured control of the House. An exit poll by Voter News Service found that 49 percent of voters were enthusiastic or supportive of the legislation, while 48 percent were either opposed or angry.

"Disturbing" Harassment

Anti-gay harassment is pervasive and widely tolerated in the U.S. military. That is the conclusion not only from gay-rights groups but also from the Pentagon itself.

A survey of some 71,500 servicemembers conducted by the Defense Department's Office of Inspector General and released on March 24 found that 37 percent had witnessed or experienced serious forms of anti-gay harassment, and 80 percent had heard offensive speech or jokes or derogatory names or remarks about homosexuals during the past year. Most of the harassment was not reported up the chain of command, the survey found, and no action was taken in three-fourths of those cases where senior officers were informed.[23]

"The report shows that military leaders must do more to make it clear that harassment based on sexual orientation violates military values," Defense Secretary William Cohen said.

Gay-rights groups took satisfaction from the report. "This is the first time that the Pentagon has realized that it has a serious problem on its hands," said C. Dixon Osborne, co-director of the Servicemembers Legal Defense Network. But they also called for stronger action.

"Nothing is going to change until the uniformed military leadership, from the Joint Chiefs of Staff on down, send clear and unambiguous signals that this type of harassment will not be tolerated," said HRC Communications Director David Smith.

Opponents of military service by homosexuals questioned the survey's findings, noting that the report itself acknowledged that individual respondents were not randomly selected. "You can't paint the entire military with these results," the Family Research Council's Maginnis says. "That's political spin."

The survey's results suggested the limitations of the military's efforts to date to translate the "don't ask, don't tell" policy into actual practice. Most of the servicemembers surveyed — 57 percent — said they had received no training on the policy. About half — 54 percent — said they understood the policy, but only one-fourth of those correctly answered three questions designed to test their knowledge.

The military had already moved to make training in the policy universal. The Pentagon announced on Feb. 1 that every member of the armed forces would undergo training by the end of the year to prevent anti-gay harassment. [24] The hourlong training session is to include a slide presentation along with role-playing exercises and pamphlets. One of the slides reads, "Zero Tolerance for Harassment."

Reporters who watched some of the early training sessions observed instances of puzzlement among servicemembers taking part. At Fort Campbell — where Winchell was killed — an officer asked whether a gay soldier should be reported for asking another soldier on a date. "No, it's just associational behavior," the training officer, Maj. James Garrett, answered. [25]

At Fort Meade, Md., outside Washington, one of the soldiers attending a training session also worried about harassment of straight servicemembers, according to *The Washington Post*. "If I'm in the shower, and somebody comes up and starts groping me," the Post quoted the solider as saying, "my first instinct is not to go to the commander. My first instinct is, 'You better get off of me.' " [26]

Cohen responded to the report by creating a high-level working group to draft an "action plan" to address anti-gay harassment. The group's report, issued on July 21, detailed 13 steps aimed at reducing harassment of gay servicemembers. The recommendations were mostly reiterations of existing policy, including providing universal training and holding commanders responsible for policy infractions. "Today's recommendations, if implemented, would be a very good start," Servicemembers Legal Defense Network co-director Benecke said afterward.

The Defense Department on the same day, however, announced that it had cleared Fort Campbell commanders of creating the climate that led to Winchell's murder in 1999. The report found that the general command climate was "favorable." The post's former commander, Maj. Gen. Robert Clark, moved to a Pentagon job in June.

Playing Politics

A week after Al Gore narrowly beat Bill Bradley in New Hampshire's Democratic presidential primary, the HRC Board of Directors met to consider making an endorsement in the race. Since both candidates had staked out pro gay rights positions, there was an argument to stay neutral. Nonetheless, with crucial primaries coming up in states with sizable gay voting blocs — California and New York — the board decided on Feb. 9 to back Gore.

"The vice president has toiled at our side over the last seven years," said President Elizabeth Birch. "We thought we better make a decision while it is valuable and relevant." [27]

The competition between Gore and Bradley for gay votes and the HRC's explicitly political calculation in supporting Gore indicated both the changing political climate on gay-rights issues and the gay and lesbian community's increasing political sophistication.

"This is a community to be dealt with, and it can't be taken for granted," says Human Rights Campaign's Stachelberg.

The climate is different in the Republican Party. Gov. Bush snubbed the gay Log Cabin Republicans by refusing to meet with its leaders, though he later met with a selected handful of gay GOP officeholders.

During the primaries, Bush backed the "don't ask, don't tell" policy on gays in the military and opposed civil rights legislation. And during the crucial South Carolina primary he appeared to back away from previous statements that he would have no problem with appointing homosexuals to administration positions. "An openly known homosexual is somebody who probably wouldn't share my philosophy," Bush said. [28]

The Republicans' control of Congress has helped bottle up gay-rights legislation in Congress. "It is terribly disappointing that we still can't get a hate-crimes bill that includes sexual orientation, and we can't get the Employment Non-Discrimination Act passed," Stachelberg says. "Those two bills remain blocked by the leadership in Congress." At the same time, lawmakers in both parties rushed to approve the Defense of Marriage Act in 1996 to try to ward off what they saw as the threat of same-sex marriage.

Gay-rights groups see the climate as more favorable at the state and local level. In an end-of-year review in December 1999, the NGLTF said pro-gay-rights bills outnumbered "unfavorable" bills during the 1999 state legislative season, and "favorable" bills progressed in several states farther than in the past, even if they were not enacted.

Still, the review pointed to only a handful of gay-rights measures actually enacted into law. The biggest victories came in California, where a new Democratic governor, Gray Davis, signed measures establishing domestic-partnership benefits for same-sex couples, prohibiting employment and housing discrimination on the basis of sexual orientation and protecting gay and lesbian students against discrimination. [29]

Vermont's civil union bill topped the gay-rights movement's accomplishments in 2000. In an offsetting defeat, however, Mississippi banned gay and lesbian adoptions, joining Florida as the only other state with a statutory ban.

Gore and Bush continued to diverge on some gay rights issues after winning their parties' nominations in the summer. Gore actively courted the gay vote and continued to tout his support for allowing gay servicemembers to serve openly and for passing the federal Employment Nondiscrimination Act. For his part, Bush generally avoided dealing specifically with gay rights issues. "Governor Bush believes in treating all individuals with dignity and respect," campaign spokesman Scott McClellan told *The Advocate*, a gay magazine. "He does not tolerate discrimination in any fashion." [30]

The parties' platforms directly clashed on the same-sex marriage issue. The GOP platform "supports the traditional definition of 'marriage' as the legal union of one man and one woman." The Democratic platform endorsed "the full inclusion of gay and lesbian families in the life of the nation," including "an equitable alignment of benefits." But Gore hedged on the issue. "I'm in favor of legal protections for domestic partnership, but I'm not in favor of changing the institution of marriage as it is presently understood — between a man and a woman," he told *The Advocate*. [31]

On election night, exit polls by Voter News Service indicated that 70 percent of self-identified gay and lesbian voters cast ballots for Gore, 23 percent for Bush, and 4 percent for Green Party candidate Ralph Nader. Using those figures, the *Washington Blade,* a gay newspaper, calculated that gay and lesbian voters provided Gore a margin of victory in at least four states — Iowa, Minnesota, New Mexico, and Wisconsin — and gave Bush his winning margin in one: New Hampshire. [32] ■

OUTLOOK

Marching in Washington

National gay rights advocates spent the early spring preparing for what they hoped would be a massive gathering of gay, lesbian, bisexual and transgendered people in Washington over the April 29-30 weekend.

Organizers said the "Millennium March on Washington" — the fourth national event of its kind and the first since 1993 — was aimed in part at showcasing the gay community's growing political clout. "We have to show to the world how many people we are, what our voting bloc is and what we bring to the table," explained Dianne Hardy-Garcia, executive director of the march.

The march was marred, however, by organizational missteps and disagreements within the gay community over political priorities. Many gay activists complained that the time and money being spent on the march — the event was expected to cost about $1.73 million and take in about $1.95 million — would have been better used at the state and local level. "Our folks need to be at home doing serious political work, not having a tchotchke sale on the mall," Rick Garcia, of Equality Illinois, told *The Washington Post.*

Hardy-Garcia, who is also executive director of the Lesbian and Gay Rights Lobby of Texas, dismissed the criticism. "There's nothing like coming to your national capital and realizing you're part of a larger movement," she said.

Some gay scholars as well as gay rights opponents predicted that the march would not surpass the numbers of the 1993 event, which drew an estimated 300,000 people. "There is no widely perceived need for a march on Washington right now," said John D'Emilio, a professor at the University of Illinois in Chicago and author of a history of the early gay rights movement. "Most of the areas of advocacy that have a prospect of success and most of the advocacy energy have been focused on state and local issues, not on Washington."

In the end, law enforcement officials estimated that the march — held on the National Mall on April 30 following a previous day of festivals and concerts — at about 200,000. President Clinton addressed the crowd by videotape. He urged the crowd to lobby Congress to pass the Hate Crime Prevention Act, which would impose extra penalties for violent crimes motivated by animosity based on sexual orientation among other categories.

The march appeared to have no immediate political impact, however.

At Issue:

Should high schools permit "gay-straight alliance" clubs?

Jim Anderson
Communications director, Gay, Lesbian and Straight Education Network

WRITTEN FOR *THE CQ RESEARCHER*

yes

Considerable media attention has been paid over the past few months, to gay-straight alliance (GSA) controversies in Utah, Louisiana and Orange County, Calif. In each instance, school boards either considered or took action to prevent students from exercising their federally protected right under the Equal Access Act.

While these battles and controversies have been intriguing, it is, perhaps, more interesting to consider the stories that have not made the news.

Little attention has been paid to the approximately 700 gay-straight alliances that are currently meeting in high schools from coast-to-coast. These school communities accepted or embraced the students and their efforts, and not as a result of judicial mandate. Instead, they recognized their professional, if not moral, responsibility to do so.

Should other high schools permit the creation of gay-straight alliances? To answer the question, we need to define gay-straight alliances and to discuss why students are forming them in such numbers. A gay-straight alliance is formed by lesbian, gay, bisexual and transgender (LGBT) students and their straight classmates. These students join together to support one another and to address concerns about the misinformation and ignorance that too often result in anti-gay harassment or violence at school.

Their concerns are well-founded. Studies by the federal Centers for Disease Control and Prevention (CDC) show that lesbian, gay and bisexual students are more than four times as likely as their heterosexual classmates to be threatened with or injured by a weapon while at school.

The Gay, Lesbian and Straight Education Network found similarly disturbing trends. In a recent national survey, we found that 61 percent of LGBT students experience verbal harassment, 27 percent physical harassment and 14 percent outright physical assault while at school.

This harassment and isolation may negatively affect students' self-esteem and school performance. Such experiences may explain why national mainstream organizations such as the American Counseling Association and the National Association of Social Workers have recently endorsed gay-straight alliances.

Every student is entitled to a supportive, safe and affirming learning environment. With this goal in mind, we urge schools not only to permit gay-straight alliances but also to encourage and foster their existence.

Peter LaBarbera
Senior analyst, Family Research Council

WRITTEN FOR *THE CQ RESEARCHER*

no

School districts should not allow the formation of gay-straight alliances on their campuses. These groups, where they already exist, have become de facto homosexuality booster clubs — causing unnecessary divisions and distractions and subjecting the entire student body to one-sided propaganda. Moreover, they are part of a movement that promotes radical identities and dangerous sexual practices to vulnerable, confused teens.

The gay-straight alliances are part of an ingenious strategy by pro-homosexuality and transsexuality groups like the Gay, Lesbian and Straight Education Network (GLSEN) to inject their unhealthy sexual and gender ideologies into the classroom. Students rally around the "rights" of gay, bi or even trans (transgender) classmates who, it is true, are ostracized and sometimes mistreated by their peers.

But while GLSEN and other groups have artfully "spun" the issue of youth homosexuality into one of "discrimination," it is really about behavior and parents' rights to guide their children's moral decisions.

In Massachusetts, taxpayers subsidize the formation of gay-straight alliances — there are now 185 — through state grants for GSA projects.

Across the country, educators are wasting valuable school time by allowing GSAs to promote extreme notions to the entire student body. Students rarely get to hear the other side of the debate, and they fear expressing their opposition to homosexuality because of the schools' politically correct embrace of homosexuality.

The National Education Association, the American Civil Liberties Union, GLSEN and their allies promote GSAs in the name of school "safety." But schools shouldn't promote homosexual identities to troubled kids when studies show that homosexual males have drastically shorter life spans. This is due to the risky sexual behavior that flourishes in the promiscuous "gay" world. At a March conference sponsored by GLSEN's Boston affiliate, speakers from the state's Education Department approvingly discussed "queer sex" acts to an audience made up mostly of students ages 14-21.

Parents must resist an agenda that uses schools' authority to confirm impressionable youth in harmful lifestyles. As one former homosexual has noted, "From every medical and health aspect — up to and including the probability of becoming infected with AIDS — it is tragic, even criminal, to lead a child into homosexuality because he or she showed some degree of confusion in adolescence."

Gay-Straight Club Divides California Community

Anthony Colin wanted to make his school in Orange, Calif., a better place for homosexual teenagers like himself. His efforts in founding a so-called gay-straight alliance club at El Modena High School have brought him national publicity and a local human rights award, as well as daily name-calling in school and a draining federal court battle with the local school board.

"I knew I was going to be facing a lot of opposition, but I didn't know just how far it would go," said Anthony, a 16-year-old sophomore. [1]

The controversy over the club — one of some 700 gay-straight alliances at high schools around the country — has divided the 2,000-student school and the community. Students opposed to the club appeared at an early school board meeting carrying signs that read, "Grades, Not AIDS."

Nationally, gay-rights groups and social conservatives sharply disagree over such clubs. Supporters say they are needed to give homosexual high school students a safe place to talk about issues affecting their lives and to promote tolerance among gay and straight students alike.

"Gay-straight alliances help one of most vulnerable populations feel a little safer, a little more accepted," says Kevin Jennings, executive director of the New York-based Gay, Lesbian and Straight Education Network (GLSEN).

"Gay youth are typically very unsupported in schools, unsupported in other aspects of their life, too," says Barbara Rienzo, a professor of health sciences at the University of Florida in Gainesville and co-author of a book on local gay-rights disputes. "Schools are one of the places where we could do a lot of things to intervene and help make schools a safe and healthy place for all youth."

But Robert Knight, director of cultural studies for the conservative Family Research Council, says the clubs promote homosexuality.

"Gay-straight school clubs are a method by which homosexuality is introduced into schools," Knight says. "This is dangerous because some kids are undoubtedly sexually confused and have intense feelings toward same-sex classmates, which is normal. They can be seriously damaged by taking their healthy emotional drives and detouring into homosexuality because they're told it's cool and that they have no alternative."

Anthony was moved to start the club by the killing of Matthew Shepard, the gay University of Wyoming student who was beaten, tied to a fence and left to die in October 1998. Anthony and high school senior Shannon MacMillan applied for recognition of the club to the school's principal, Nancy Murray, saying its mission was "to raise public awareness and promote tolerance by providing a safe

And a new controversy erupted in early May when the organizers of the march disclosed that they had not received about $750,000 due from the company that produced the festival. The FBI was called in to investigate.

As gay rights organizations prepared for the fall elections, Hardy-Garcia insisted that the movement was becoming a factor in political campaigns. "We're 5 percent of the vote, on par with the Jewish and Latino vote," she said. "We've seen politicians respond to that."

Still, the movement had no assurance of tangible progress even if the gay vote helped elect supportive candidates. Clinton received strong support from gay political groups, but was unable to get Congress to approve lifting the ban on gays in the military, barring discrimination against gays, or passing the gay hate crimes measure.

The November elections kept Republicans in control of Congress. And, as the presidential contest remained undecided, the race seemed certain to end with a backward step for gay rights advocates no matter who emerged as the winner. Bush had opposed most of the gay rights legislative proposals, while Gore seemed unlikely to have much political capital to push their agenda on Capitol Hill.

In state and local races, gay rights groups did claim victories for an increasing number of gay and lesbian candidates, including the first openly gay state legislators in Georgia and Michigan. But Maine voters rejected an initiative to prohibit job discrimination against homosexuals. And two more states — Nebraska and Nevada — adopted constitutional amendments aimed at prohibiting same-sex marriage.

Still, supporters and opponents acknowledge the gay rights movement's growing strength. "The gay rights movement has never been stronger, more influential, more diverse, more organized, or better prepared for anything than it is today," says Eric Marcus, a New York writer and author of a history of the gay rights movement.

From an opposing viewpoint, Knight, of the Family Research Council, credits the gay rights movement with "taking over" mainstream media and other organizations. "They have been successful at using what most Americans regarded as mainstream organizations to push a radical agenda," Knight says.

From its start, however, gay rights

forum for discussion of issues related to sexual orientation and homophobia."

Contrary to normal policy, however, school administrators had instructed principals in 1998 to forward applications for gay-student clubs to the school board for decision. The seven-member Orange Unified School District school board held an open forum on the issue in November 1999 and then voted unanimously to deny the application.

Board member Kathy Ward, author of the resolution to reject the application, said the club's mission intruded on the school's sex-education curriculum. "Sex-based discussions have no place in a school club," Ward said. Other board members were harsher. The application, William Lewis said, "asks us to legitimize sin."

Colin and club co-president Heather Zetin responded by suing the School Board under the Equal Access Act. The 1984 federal law requires schools to be evenhanded in allowing use of school facilities by student groups.

"When a school allows one non-curricular club to meet at school during non-instructional times, they have to allow all groups that want to meet," says Myron Dean Quon, a lawyer with Lambda Legal Defense and Education Fund in Los Angeles, who is representing the club.

In February 2000, U.S. District Judge David Carter agreed that the school board's action probably violated the law and issued a preliminary injunction allowing the club to organize and meet in school.

"Defendants cannot censor the students' speech to avoid discussions on campus that cause them discomfort or represent an unpopular viewpoint," Carter wrote in his 23-page ruling.

The club met several times in the remaining months of the school year, with as many as 50-60 members, according to Quon. But opposition from parents and school board members persisted. "Parents say that there are things they don't want their children exposed to in high school," board member Terri Sargeant said.[2]

In September, the school board agreed to settle the suit by reversing its decision to ban the club. As part of the settlement, the board adopted rules prohibiting student clubs from discussing sexual activity and creating a system to allow parents to object to a child's participation in any school group.

Quon said students were happy with the outcome. "We're happy the kids can go back to being regular school kids and not under such great public scrutiny," he said.

[1] Quoted in *The Orange County Register*, March 26, 2000, p. B1. For background, see *The New York Times*, Feb. 10, 2000, p. A20; *Time*, Feb. 21, 2000, p. 52.

[2] Quoted in *The Orange County Register*, Feb. 11, 2000, p. A19.

has been both a personal and a political struggle — a process of individual self-acceptance as well as collective mobilization. The gay community's growing visibility makes that process less difficult than in previous generations, but the process is no less important. "These marches are like rites of passage," Hardy-Garcia says. "There's nothing like being somebody from Lubbock, Texas, and being on the mall with hundreds of thousands of people and realizing you're not alone."

"The direction has been positive for a long time," Marcus says. "And there's no reason at this time to believe that we won't continue to make progress as long as gay and lesbian people come out and as long as those who love us support us in ever greater numbers." ■

Notes

[1] Background and quotes drawn from *The Boston Globe*, Dec. 21, 1999, p. A28; *USA Today*, June 28, 2000, p. 1A; *The Washington Post*, July 2, 2000, p. A3.

[2] For background, see Richard L. Worsnop, "Gay Rights," *The CQ Researcher*, March 5, 1993, pp. 193-216; and Richard L. Worsnop, "Domestic Partners," *The CQ Researcher*, Sept. 4, 1992, pp. 761-784.

[3] The text of the decision can be found on the Web site of the National Gay and Lesbian Task Force: www.ngltf.org.

[4] See Alan Yang, "From Wrongs to Rights: Public Opinion on Gay and Lesbian Americans Moves Toward Equality," National Gay and Lesbian Task Force, 1999, p. 14. In the most recent poll cited, 29 percent of those surveyed in 1998 said marriages between homosexuals should be "recognized as legal by the law."

[5] William N. Eskridge Jr., *Gaylaw: Challenging the Apartheid of the Closet* (1999).

[6] For opposing views, see Thomas B. Stoddard, "Why Gay People Should Seek the Right to Marry," OUT/LOOK, *National Gay and Lesbian Quarterly*, No. 6 (fall 1989), and Paula L. Ettelbrick, "Since When Is Marriage a Path to Liberation?", *ibid.*, reprinted in Suzanne Sherman (ed.), *Lesbian and Gay Marriage: Private Commitments, Public Ceremonies* (1992), pp. 13-26.

[7] For background, see Sarah Glazer, "Crackdown on Sexual Harassment," *The CQ Researcher*, July 19, 1996, pp. 625-648.

[8] Background drawn from Eskridge, *op. cit.*

[9] *Ibid.*, p. 43.

[10] See Barry D. Adam, *The Rise of a Gay and Lesbian Movement* (rev. ed.) (1995), pp. 67-68. For background on the post-World War II decades, see John D'Emilio, *Sexual Politics, Sexual Communities: The Making of a Homosexual Minority in the United States, 1940-1970* (1983) and Dudley Clendinen and Adam Nagourney, *Out for Good: The Struggle to Build a Gay-Rights Movement in America* (1999).

[11] See Paul Varnell, "Stonewall: Get a Grip," *The Windy City Times*, June 10, 1999. The article appears on the Independent Gay Forum's Web site: www. indegayforum.org.

[12] Account drawn from Eric Marcus, "Stonewall Revisited" (www.indegayforum.org). The article was written for the defunct gay magazine *Ten Percent* to mark the 25th anniversary of Stonewall in 1994.

[13] Cited in Clendinen and Nagourney, *op. cit.*, p. 30.

[14] Background and data drawn from William B. Rubenstein, Lesbians, *Gay Men and the Law* (1st ed.) (1993).

[15] Randy Shilts, *Conduct Unbecoming: Gays and Lesbians in the U.S. Military* (1993), p. 380.

[16] Account drawn from Clendinen and Nagourney, *op. cit.*, pp. 566-573. The authors note that Clinton's appearance was covered the next day in both *The New York Times* and, on the front page, in *The Washington Post.*

[17] For background, see Kenneth Jost, "Hate Crimes," *The CQ Researcher*, Jan. 8, 1993, pp. 1-24.

[18] See *1993 Congressional Quarterly Almanac*, pp. 454-462.

[19] See Wayne van der Meide, *Legislating Equality: A Review of Laws Affecting Gay, Lesbian, Bisexual, and Transgendered People in the United States*, Policy Institute of the National Gay and Lesbian Task Force (1999) (www.ngltf.org).

[20] See Kenneth Jost, *The Supreme Court Yearbook, 1995-1996* (1996), pp. 34-38.

[21] See *1996 Congressional Quarterly Almanac*, pp. 526-529.

[22] Some background drawn from *The New York Times*, Feb. 3, 2000, p. A1. The two major opposing advocacy groups in Vermont have Web sites: www.vtfreetomarry.org; www. takeittothepeople.org.

[23] See Office of the Inspector General, Department of Defense, "Military Environment with Respect to the Homosexual Conduct Policy," Report No. D-2000-101, March 16, 2000 (www.dodig.osd.mil). Reaction drawn from *The New York Times*, March 25, 2000, p. A1; *The Washington Post*, March 25, 2000, p. A1.

[24] See *The New York Times*, Feb. 2, 2000, p. A15.

[25] Reported in *The New York Times*, Feb. 14, 2000, p. A1.

[26] *The Washington Post*, March 26, 2000, p. C3.

[27] The Associated Press, Feb. 10, 2000.

[28] Quoted in *The New York Times*, March 19, 2000, p. A24.

[29] Christina L. Lyons, "Adoption Controversies," *The CQ Researcher*, Sept. 10, 1999, p. 782.

[30] *The Advocate,* July 4, 2000.

[31] The full interview was published on *The Advocate's* Web site: www.advocate.com.

[32] *The Washington Blade,* Nov. 10, 2000, p. 24.

FOR MORE INFORMATION

American Family Association, P.O. Box 2440, Tupelo, Miss. 38803; (662) 844-5036; www.afa.net. Founded by the Rev. Donald Wildmon in 1977, it opposes same-sex marriage and "the movement to normalize homosexual behavior."

Family Research Council, 801 G St., N.W., Washington, D.C. 20001; (202) 393-2100; www.frc.org. The council opposes legal recognition of same-sex relationships, legislation to prohibit discrimination on the basis of sexual orientation and military service by homosexuals.

Gay, Lesbian and Straight Education Network, 121 W. 27th St., Suite 804, New York, N.Y. 10001; (212) 727-0135; www.glsen.org. The organization promotes non-discrimination policies and helps support high school-based "gay-straight alliance" clubs.

Human Rights Campaign, 919 18th St., N.W., Suite 800, Washington, D.C. 20006; (202) 628-4160; www.hrc.org. The organization is a political campaign and lobbying organization working for lesbian and gay equal rights.

Independent Gay Forum, www.indegayforum.org. The forum comprises a group of generally conservative-leaning gay writers, academics, attorneys and activists described as in favor of equality for homosexuals but "dissatisfied" with the current discussion of gay-related issues.

Lambda Legal Defense and Education Fund, Inc., 120 Wall St., Suite 1500, New York, NY 10005-3904; (212) 809-8585; www.lambdalegal.org. The legal center handles a wide array of gay-rights litigation, including employment discrimination, parenting issues, HIV- and AIDS-related discrimination, military and immigration.

National Center for Lesbian Rights, 870 Market St., Suite 570, San Francisco, Calif. 94102; (415) 392-6257; www.nclrights.org. The legal center handles various lesbian-rights issues, with special emphasis on child custody and same-sex adoption issues.

National Gay and Lesbian Task Force, 1700 Kalorama Rd., N.W., Washington, D.C. 20009; (202) 332-6483; www.ngltf.org. The task force, founded in 1973, works for civil rights for gay, lesbian, bisexual and transgendered people.

Servicemembers Legal Defense Network, P.O. Box 65301, Washington, D.C. 20035-5301; (202) 328-3244; www.sldn.org. The organization assists U.S. servicemembers affected by the military's policies on homosexuality.

Bibliography

Selected Sources Used

Books

Adam, Barry D., *The Rise of a Gay and Lesbian Movement* (rev. ed.), Twayne Publishers, 1995.
Adam, a professor of sociology at the University of Windsor, Ontario, relates the rise of gay and lesbian movements in the United States and around the world. The book includes chapter notes, a list of works cited and a three-page bibliography.

Button, James W., Barbara A. Rienzo and Kenneth D. Wald, *Private Lives, Public Conflicts: Battles over Gay Rights in American Communities*, CQ Press, 1997.
Three University of Florida professors examine local conflicts over gay-rights laws and the impact of those struggles on local schools.

Clendinen, Dudley, and Adam Nagourney, *Out for Good: The Struggle to Build a Gay Rights Movement in America*, Simon & Schuster, 1999.
The authors sympathetically trace the rise of the gay-rights movement from the Stonewall Inn riots in 1969 through the late 1980s. The book includes a three-page bibliography. Clendinen is an editorial writer and Nagourney a political reporter for *The New York Times*.

D'Emilio, John, *Sexual Politics, Sexual Communities: The Making of a Homosexual Minority in the United States, 1940-1970* (2d ed.), University of Chicago Press, 1998.
D'Emilio, a professor of gender and women's studies at the University of Illinois in Chicago, traces the early history of the gay-rights movement from the 1940s to the formation and increasing assertiveness of gay-rights groups in the 1950s and '60s. The book was originally published in 1983; the 1998 edition includes a new preface and afterword.

Eskridge, William N. Jr., *Gaylaw: Challenging the Apartheid of the Closet*, Harvard University Press, 1999.
Eskridge, a law professor at Yale, traces the history of anti-gay legislation and enforcement in the United States and examines the advance of gay rights along with the continuation of anti-gay inequities in the law. The book includes several appendices and detailed notes.

—, *The Case for Same-Sex Marriage: From Sexual Liberty to Civilized Commitment*, Free Press, 1996.
Eskridge expanded his unsuccessful representation of a Washington, D.C., gay couple's effort to legally marry into a comprehensive argument for permitting same-sex marriage based on history, law and morality. The book includes detailed source notes, an appendix of court cases, and a 19-page bibliography.

Magnuson, *Are Gay Rights Right?: Making Sense of the Controversy*, Multnomah Press, 1990.
The Minneapolis trial lawyer mounts a sharp attack on what he calls the homosexual-rights movement on grounds of religion, morality, law, and public health.

Marcus, Eric, *Making History: The Struggle for Gay and Lesbian Equal Rights, 1945-1990, An Oral History*, HarperCollins, 1992.
Author Marcus presents first-person accounts by some 50 people who figured in the history of the gay-rights movement since World War II.

Rubenstein, William B., *Cases and Materials on Sexual Orientation and the Law* (2d ed.), West Publishing, 1997.
This law school casebook includes court decisions, statutory provisions and other materials on the full range of gay-rights issues. Rubenstein is an acting professor at UCLA School of Law. The first edition of the casebook was published as *Lesbians, Gay Men and the Law.*

Shilts, Randy, *Conduct Unbecoming: Gays and Lesbians in the U.S. Military*, St. Martin's Press, 1993.
Shilts, a *San Francisco Chronicle* reporter until his death from AIDS in 1994, recounts the largely unacknowledged history of homosexuals in the U.S. military in order to mount a strongly argued attack on the then-existing ban on gay or lesbian servicemembers. The current "don't ask, don't tell" policy is not covered. The book includes detailed source notes and a four-page bibliography.

Articles

Leland, John, "Shades of Gay," *Newsweek*, March 20, 2000.
The cover story in this package of articles on gay-related issues depicts increased tolerance for homosexuals in schools, churches, offices, family life, and politics and government. The story notes a new Newsweek poll that for the first time found that less than a majority of those surveyed — 46 percent — believe homosexuality is a sin.

Reports and Studies

Yang, Alan, "From Wrongs to Rights, 1973-1999: Public Opinion on Gay and Lesbian Americans Moves Toward Equality," National Gay and Lesbian Task Force, 1999.
The report, based on opinion polls over the past decade or longer, finds increasing support for gay rights on a range of issues although most Americans continue to oppose same-sex marriage and believe homosexual relations wrong. Yang is a Columbia University researcher.

15 Boys' Emotional Needs

SARAH GLAZER

As Americans try to fathom the recent tragedy at Columbine High School, two points of view often surface:

To some experts on adolescence, Dylan Klebold and Eric Harris were young men in whom evil triumphed despite apparently normal, loving families.

But to a growing number of professionals, the horror the pair unleashed in Littleton, Colo., reflected the difficulty inherent in growing up male in America.

"It's a national boy crisis, and the two boys in Littleton are the tip of the iceberg," says William Pollack, a clinical psychologist at Harvard Medical School. "And the iceberg is *all* boys."

Two weeks before the April 20 rampage, Pollack predicted on the "Oprah Winfrey" show that American boys were under so much pressure that an outburst of violence could occur at any time. [1] "The way we bring boys up makes it impossible for them to talk about" the kinds of humiliation Eric Harris and Dylan Klebold apparently suffered, he says. "It either boils over or turns into a depressive, ongoing crisis."

The monosyllabic teenage boy wired to his computer or video game is a familiar fixture in American middle-class homes today. Indeed, the "strong, silent type" that evolved from the fictional cowboy hero who rode the range alone still occupies a position of admiration in America's individualist tradition.

But recently several child specialists have been arguing that millions of normal teenagers employing the automatic "I'm fine" response to almost any emotional difficulty "have us all fooled," writes Michael Gurian, a family therapist in Spokane, Wash.

From *The CQ Researcher*, June 18, 1999.

CQ/Douglas Graham

Most boys, even apparently normal boys, are far from fine, Gurian argues in his 1998 book, *A Fine Young Man*.

"We are dealing with adolescent males experiencing post-traumatic stress," Gurian writes, referring to the "millions of our adolescent males" who have experienced the trauma of parents' divorce, failures in school or unsuccessful relationships. [2]

In America's increasingly atomized suburban culture, teenage boys are leading lonely lives, experts like Gurian say. Compared with other societies around the world, they say, America creates too little opportunity for boys to bond with older relatives in their extended family and to receive the moral development that results from connections with beloved uncles and grandfathers.

What boys do have "are peers and their TV and their computers," Gurian says. "The tragedy is when they have so little of their extended family, they put everything into the love of their peers. When their peers reject them and humiliate them, they don't have emotional and moral resources to face that."

Gurian writes that boys' difficulty in dealing with emotional traumas stems from an "inherent intellectual fragility in the male brain system." [3] Young boys start out with a disadvantage when it comes to expressing emotions, Gurian argues, in part because they tend to be less verbal than girls, and words are an important way of expressing feelings.

Other experts say it's not so much a matter of male intellectual inferiority but of society's emotional miseducation of boys. Social pressure to act manly and hide emotions, imposed early in childhood, ultimately leads to lonely men — and in some cases dangerous ones.

"I think of Dylan Klebold and Eric Harris as over-conformists — not deviants at all — to traditional notions of masculinity that say, 'We don't get mad; we get even,'" says Michael Kimmel, a professor of sociology at the State University of New York at Stonybrook.

Schoolmates of Harris and Klebold have said the pair endured years of harassment from fellow students, particularly athletes. Columbine students called them "dirt bags" and often threw things at them at lunchtime, a student wounded in the assault told reporters. In their methodical carnage, the boys appeared to single out star athletes and others who had scorned them. [4]

If widespread suffering among American men seems to be a largely hidden phenomenon, some psychologists say, there's a simple explanation: Just as men typically refuse to ask for directions when driving, they rarely ask for help in emotional crises. "Boys are not socialized in a way that gives them the kind of emotional repertoire that will keep them out of trouble," says child psychologist Michael Thompson. "But they make us pay."

Thompson's book, *Raising Cain: Protecting the Emotional Life of Boys*, published just days before Littleton erupted, argues that "our culture is railroading boys into lives of isolation, shame and anger." Thompson and his co-author, Harvard University psychologist Dan Kindlon, question the cost to boys of suppressing their emotional life "in service to rigid ideals of manhood." [5]

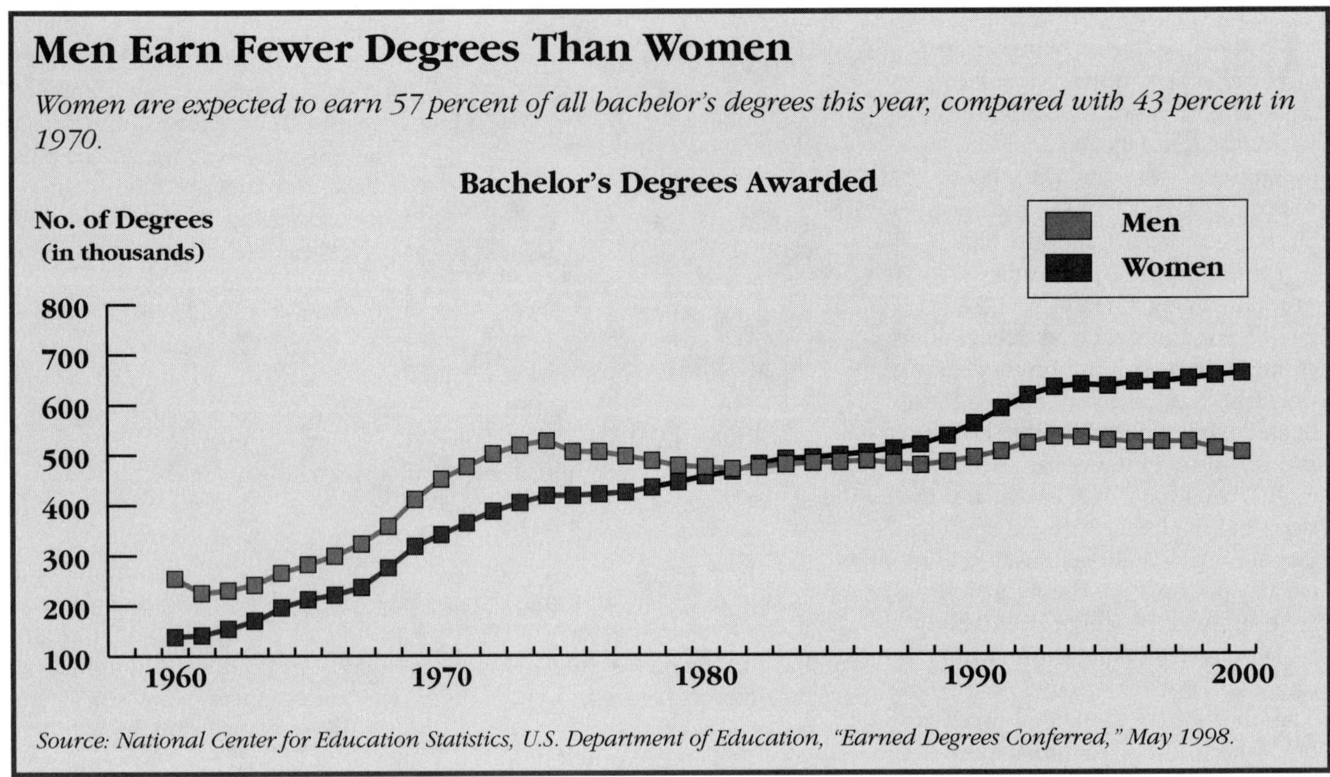

"Rejected, aggressive kids are a danger to us," Thompson says. "They've been hurt, they're resentful and then they become angry and explosive. If you don't reach them, if they're not in touch with parents or any other adult, they can be quite dangerous."

The new concern about boys follows a decade in which books, studies and news articles proclaimed that adolescent girls were suffering a loss in self-esteem and academic achievement, in part because teachers gave them less attention than boys. But American girls have largely closed the achievement gap with boys, several experts say. Girls now compose the majority in colleges and graduate school, and they are flocking to math and science courses, historically an area of weakness for girls.

Today, it is actually boys who are suffering the most, as measured by school grades, test scores and emotional and learning disorders, say specialists who are concerned about boys. One disturbing indication is the increasing number of boys shunted off to special education classes, where they outnumber girls 3-to-1. Referrals of boys for attention deficit disorder (ADD) are surging.

In Kindlon's view, teenage boys' predominance in violence and self-destruction constitutes a public health "crisis." Boys account for some 1,600 of the almost 2,000 suicides committed by teens each year. Ninety percent of the teenage victims of homicide each year are killed by teenage boys. Male teens are also the victims in 70 percent of cases. Boys are two-and-a-half times more likely to die in car accidents than girls, much of it attributable to drunken driving, a risk-taking behavior that Kindlon closely links to emotional despair.

Some observers think the new concern about boys overstates the level of crisis. "I don't see where people are getting the idea that there's an explosion, an epidemic going on here," says Gwen J. Broude, a professor of psychology and cognitive science at Vassar College in Poughkeepsie, N.Y., and author of a recent article criticizing Pollack's and Gurian's books. [6]

"We've had eight school shootings" recently, Broude says. "There are about 35 million boys" in the United States. "That's not a very big percentage on which to base a theory."

Despite the emotional or learning problems linked to boys today, only between 1 and 4 percent of boys are in trouble, according to Broude, and more girls than boys suffer from some of the same disorders. Far more girls than boys, for example, suffer from depression. About 80 to 90 percent of the suicide attempts among young people are made by girls, Broude points out. Girls' attempts are less successful than boys' because they're more likely to overdose on pills while boys are more likely to use guns.

Broude is also skeptical of the psychologists' suggestions that boys would be happier if they adopted an emotional style more like girls, such as examining their inner emotional despair. Psychological research identifies obsessive rumination as a classic feature of depression, she notes. "Alarmist" psychologists, she says, are "suggesting boys should learn to ruminate. They're perfectly right: If boys do that they'll be just like girls — miserable."

While it's true that more girls than boys are diagnosed with depression, Gurian counters that boys' depression may be more "covert" — more likely to take the form of criminal activity, drug and alcohol use, irritability and aggressive behavior. "Like soldiers traumatized in wartime, these males act out," Gurian writes, noting that adolescent males comprise about 20 percent of the arrestees nationally.[7] Girls' unsuccessful suicide attempts may represent a cry for help, in contrast to boys' determinedly lethal methods, Kindlon suggests.

Girls Take the Most AP Tests

More girls took AP (advanced placement) tests in 1994 than boys in English, social studies and foreign languages. Girls are catching up in math and science.

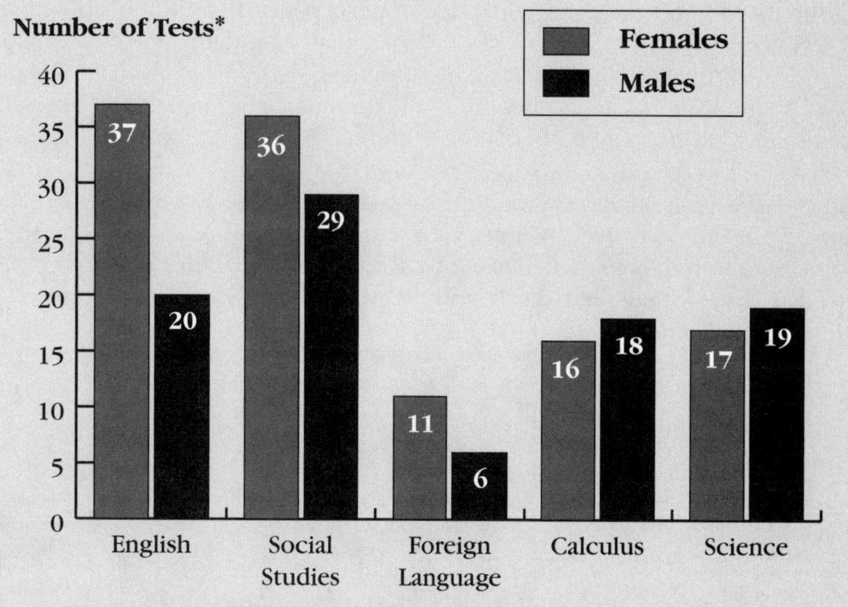

* *Per 1,000 11th- and 12th-grade students*

Source: "Selected Baseline Measures for Gender Equity," National Center for Educational Statistics, 1994

Christina Hoff Sommers, a resident scholar at the American Enterprise Institute, agrees that boys have been neglected in schools and have fallen behind girls academically after a decade of educators' efforts to render curricula and classrooms more girl-friendly.[8] But she is appalled by the contention that the Columbine violence reflects the condition of most American boys. She points to the heroic behavior of some of the male students who were caught in the shootings at Columbine High.

As symbols of American boyhood, Sommers asks, "Why not take the boy who threw his body over his sister and her friend, or the boy who, at great risk to himself, held the door open" to help other students escape the shooters? "The vast majority of boys behaved well and humanely. Look at those boys who were grieving and the boys who wrote songs," she says. "Those are our boys."

Boys are by nature a little more stoical than girls, Sommers argues. Just try to get your adolescent son to complete a homework assignment where he has to discuss his feelings about a work of fiction, she says. He'd rather memorize facts. Stoicism has been viewed as a virtue in many traditional societies, Sommers argues, and should be valued today for its traits of self-control and courage.

In the post-Littleton debate some experts have argued that the most salient feature of the tragedy was the sex of the shooters. Kimmel, for example, points out that violence and aggression are "the most intractable gender differences observed by social scientists" in males.[9] Across cultures, anthropologists have found, males are consistently the dominant sex, Kimmel notes.

Sommers agrees that boys are more aggressive than girls. "Where I part company with Kindlon and Kimmel is they tend to view masculinity as pathological," Sommers says.

While it is true that boys are less emotionally expressive than girls, Broude says, it's not necessarily a bad thing for boys' mental health. She points to research findings showing that traditionally masculine traits like independence and assertiveness are more likely to lead to good mental health than such feminine traits as emotional openness and sensitivity to others' needs.

The suggestion in the new wave of books about boys that seemingly normal boys are severely maladjusted poses the "danger of causing good parents of healthy boys to have nagging doubts about their own competence and about the well-being of their sons," Broude writes. The advocates for boys, she warns, "are in danger of seducing us into interpreting sex differences, where we find them, as personal deficiencies." [10]

"There's already a lot of anger at normal, healthy boys in our society," Sommers says, "and [equating Littleton with boyhood] is going to exacerbate it."

Harvard psychologist Robert Coles says there may be limits to understanding what happened in Littleton. "[P]sychology cannot explain the enormous variations of behavior, including the fact that millions of kids listen to the same rock music, or see the same videos that Harris and Klebold did and never commit murder. The greater mystery really is that most people don't act this way." [11]

As parents, educators and child-development experts focus on boys' needs, these are some of the questions being asked:

Does the U.S. education system shortchange boys?

Psychologist Michael Thompson knelt beside two females who he said had misbehaved in class. In a wheedling, almost pleading tone of voice, he asked one of them, "Why did you do that to her? How do you think that made her feel?" Thompson was role-playing to demonstrate the way elementary school teachers typically reprimand girls, and the two "girls" he addressed were actually the mothers of boys. Then he walked over to a father and towered over him to show the equivalent response to a disruptive boy student.: "Cut it out young man!" he said, his voice changing to a brusque command. "I don't want to see that in my classroom!"

The parents gathered at the 92nd Street Y in New York City responded with laughs of recognition. As Thompson pointed out afterwards, "It's hard not to discipline boys differently." But the harsher response boys get in even the most caring schools tends to color their experience of school in a more negative way than girls, Thompson contends.

From an early age, many boys get the signal that "school is rigged against them," in Thompson's words. For the average boy, who learns to read about a year later than the average girl and matures more slowly socially, the message that comes across is that school "is about sitting and words." The typical boy's response: " 'I'm not interested in any of that, and girls are better at it,' " Thompson said.

By school age, boys tend to be more physically active, restless and impulsive than girls. Boys' naturally higher energy level often gets them into disciplinary trouble at school, where males form the vast majority of disciplined students. "A girl can tolerate sitting and visual learning better than a boy can," Pollack says. "Some boys need five recesses a day, and when they wriggle in their chair their recess is taken away."

Boys' natural boisterousness is often misunderstood, critics say, by American schools' predominantly female teachers, who interpret normal boy behavior as discipline problems, attention disorders or learning disabilities. That may explain, at least in part, why three times as many boys as girls are enrolled in special-education classes, and why three quarters of the children taking Ritalin for ADD are boys, these psychologists suggest. [12]

While many cases of ADD are legitimate, Pollack writes, the almost 10-1 ratio of boys to girls diagnosed with the disorder raises the "possibility that many mild-to-moderate ADD cases are normal variants of boys' temperament that could be corrected by a properly trained, attentive adult." Diagnoses of ADD are often initiated by classroom teachers and school guidance counselors overwhelmed by chaotic, overcrowded classrooms. In a classroom properly designed for boys' temperament and energy levels, Pollack suggests, many of these behaviors would not even attract a teacher's attention. The typical boy with ADD may yell out impulsively, talk too much, act disorganized or be forgetful. But these behaviors are so close to those exhibited by emotionally healthy boys that it is often difficult even for trained professionals to make a diagnosis. [13]

Some research suggests that girls with learning disabilities fail to be diagnosed at the same rate as boys because girls tend to sit quietly in class even if they are having trouble learning. [14] "Boys get a lot more permission" to engage in disruptive behavior than girls, counters Heather

Reuters/Gary Caskey

The April shootings at Columbine High School in Littleton, Colo., reflected what some child-development experts say is the difficulty inherent in growing up male in America.

Why Are Boys Worse Students Than Girls?

It's a common observation among parents: Daughters want to please their teachers by spending extra time on projects, doing extra credit, making homework as neat as possible. Sons rush through homework assignments and run outside to play, unconcerned about how the teacher will regard the sloppy work.

Psychologists confirm some of these everyday parental observations about the different ways boys and girls respond to authority figures and other outside influences. University of Pennsylvania psychology Professor Beverly I. Fagot finds that girls are more influenced by teachers and other girls, whereas boys are influenced just by other boys. When boys are engaged in typical male behavior like playing with trucks or rough-and-tumble play, they are not affected at all by girls or teachers.

Psychology Professor Gwen J. Broude of Vassar College cites Fagot's research as an example of enduring sex differences. "Jerome Kagan, the developmental psychologist, once said boys try to figure out the task, and girls try to figure out the teacher," Broude observes. "Boys want to know how you do this; girls want to know what the other person wants from them. They want to please the other person."

Such differences in attitude may explain, in part, why females consistently make better grades in all major subjects. A study by the Educational Testing Service (ETS) notes that some people disparage grades as favoring students who are "nice" and "compliant." Yet grades are often the single best predictor of college grades, followed by tests. [1]

Increasingly schools are being urged by women's groups like the American Association of University Women (AAUW) to incorporate teaching approaches that are more amenable to girls. One such approach, "cooperative learning," encourages students to work together in groups on a project.

Harvard clinical psychologist William Pollack says cooperation is harder for boys. He describes a suburban public elementary school classroom he observed where the teacher's time was almost entirely consumed with disciplining the boys. Several boys were making a commotion together; one was calling out jokes; some had been sent out of the room to work by themselves because, in the words of the teacher, "Some kids just seem unable to fit into this more quiet team-based teaching." Pollack's conclusion: "I think the prevailing method in class that day was structured around the way girl students prefer to work, and that boys were at a disadvantage." [2]

For boys, difficulties with engaging in more quiet, "feminine" behaviors despite the best efforts of teachers may reflect enduring sex differences, suggests Broude. For example, the term "rough-and-tumble play" has been used to describe the distinctive play patterns of males in both primates and humans. In one study cited by Broude, preschool teachers were asked to praise and encourage cooperative play between boys and girls for two weeks. As long as the teachers continued to encourage the behavior, cooperative play among the boys increased. But as soon as the teachers stopped actively reinforcing cooperation, the children returned to their former distinctive girl and boy play patterns.

Some of the qualities traditionally associated with females, such as cooperation, may be more successful in the workplace than the individualistic skills associated with male achievement, according to Richard Lesh, a professor at the Purdue University School of Education. His research finds that some students who do poorly on math tests excel when given a real-life business case-study to solve. "Girls are often predisposed to enjoy working in groups, communicating with one another," he says. "Math is about communicating quantitative things at least as much as it is about following rules. Basically the people who do well on testing today are people who enjoy working by themselves on itsy-bitsy problems. Math tests test people who like to follow rules."

It's often puzzling to parents why otherwise well-behaved sons start acting up in the classroom to entertain their male peers even in the face of severe teacher disapprobation. It's almost a social verity that boys in groups tend to take an antisocial stance, observes child psychologist Michael Thompson, of Cambridge, Mass. "To prove that you're masculine you may need to do more bold, antisocial things to prove to your group you're a real guy," says Thompson. "That may mean disrespecting the culture — the adult aims in school."

Schools today increasingly set up a social system where girls are the good students, leaving boys with the "bad" territory, Thompson explains. "If girls are the student council leaders, the boys are going to be the negative leaders," Thompson says. "It's what most kids feel if they have a superstar older sibling: 'What can I do except excel in being a screw-up?' "

In the final analysis, it's not clear whether boys' more anti-authoritarian style hurts or helps them in the outside world. "Boys tend to be more troublesome to teachers," Lesh notes. "And troublesome kids are not going to get as good grades. But those troublesome kids are often precisely the ones that do well in life. People who succeed in business or the sciences are often people who like to break rules and think about things differently."

---

[1] Nancy S. Cole, "The ETS Gender Study: How Females and Males Perform in Educational Settings," 1997, pp. 18-19.

[2] William Pollack, *Real Boys; Rescuing Our Sons from the Myths of Boyhood* (1998).

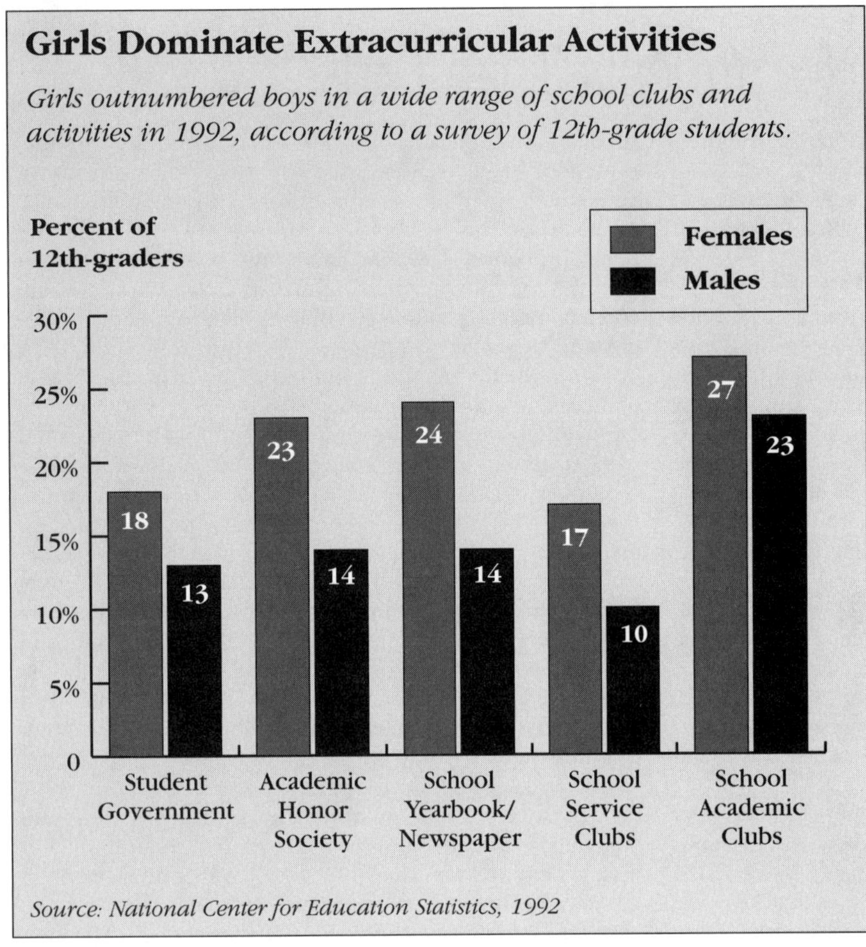

Johnston Nicholson, director of research for Girls Inc., which runs after-school programs for girls at 1,000 sites nationwide.

David M. Sadker, a professor of education at American University, suggests that the definition of learning disabilities is skewed toward problems that boys have — primarily reading — but neglects the problems girls have in areas such as spatial visualization, which is often crucial to understanding math.

Troubling statistics showing a declining proportion of boys entering college and graduate school may be traceable to the joyless experience of school for many boys in a female-dominated environment, Kindlon suggests. "Boys tend to get a worse image of themselves because they compete with someone better than them" — namely girls. "Too many boys give up on school too early."

The statistics confirm a dwindling interest in school on the part of boys. "Boys rather than girls are now on the short end of the gender gap in many school outcomes," concluded Providence College sociologist Cornelius Riordan. [15]

Enrollment in institutions of higher education now favors females. In 1995-1996, 55 percent of the nation's bachelor's degrees and 56 percent of the master's degrees went to girls. By comparison, in 1970, males outnumbered females receiving B.A.s 57 percent to 43 percent and M.A.s 60 percent to 40 percent. [16]

Boys seem to be lowering their expectations as well. In 1992, far more females than males among graduating high school seniors expected to attain a professional occupation by age 30. Girls usually outperform boys in reading and writing as early as the fourth grade. Girls have consistently obtained better grades and higher class ranks than boys. Eighth-grade girls were significantly more likely than boys to be in the highest quartile of self-reported grades and significantly less likely to have repeated a grade, according to a 1990 study. [17]

Boys are more likely to drop out of school, cut class, be suspended, be in trouble with the law and be placed in remedial math and English classes. Outside of school, boys appear less intellectual and studious than girls: They do less homework, work more at part-time jobs, read less for pleasure and watch more TV than girls. While in college, men spend more time than women partying, exercising, watching TV or playing video games. Consequently, says Riordan, they are less likely to graduate from college than women. [18]

In October 1998, the American Association of University Women (AAUW) reported that girls had leaped forward in math and science, two areas where they have traditionally lagged behind boys. Girls' enrollment in advanced math and science courses has increased significantly since 1990. For example, a higher proportion of females than males take algebra and geometry, and girls are more likely than their male counterparts to take both biology and chemistry. [19]

According to the Department of Education's National Center for Education Statistics, female high school students now take as many mathematics and science classes as males do, with the exception of physics. Growing numbers of females are also enrolling in advanced placement (AP) courses in mathematics and science. [20]

Despite these gains by girls, the AAUW report led its press release with the announcement that "a major new gender gap in technology has developed." [21]

Critics say the AAUW has seized on this issue because the argument that girls trail behind boys in school is essentially evaporating. Feminist organizations citing the low numbers of women in computer sciences and engineering are "searching for new areas of female victimization," in the words of AAUW critic Judith S. Kleinfeld, a professor of psychology at the University of Alaska, Fairbanks. Even the much-ballyhooed gap in computer-course enrollment is very small, according to Riordan: 25 percent of girls vs. 30 percent of boys. [22]

The AAUW report focused public attention on girls' tendency to sign up for courses in word-processing skills associated with secretarial work. "What we were saying is girls tend to enroll in data-processing coursework for the typing of the 21st century as opposed to the more technically based or programming courses," says Maggie Ford, president of the AAUW Educational Foundation, which produced the report. "Girls are reporting they're less comfortable [than boys] with computers; they tend to come to the classroom with less prior exposure to computers at home [and] they feel less skilled."

But psychologist Kleinfeld argues that girls' choices in this area may actually reflect higher professional aspirations than boys'. "You don't need to take a computer-science course in order to work with computers any more than you need to be a car mechanic to drive a car," Kleinfeld quipped in a recent article. "Besides, that more women prefer to be attorneys than cubicle-confined Dilberts hardly seems a social problem of great moment." [23]

"If anyone is getting shortchanged in schools, it's boys," Kleinfeld says. Boys' inferior verbal literacy should be of major national concern because reading is a skill that forms the foundation for later achievement, yet schools have paid little attention to remediating it, Kleinfeld says. Fewer boys than girls going to college could lead to the kind of social gulf African-American women already find as they search for compatible, well-educated mates, she warns.

Hales Franciscan High School

English teacher Matt Golden discusses Shakespeare with seniors at Hales Franciscan High School for boys in Chicago.

In addition, Kleinfeld says, "We need to be very concerned about what the new studies are showing us: Boys feel that schools are hostile to them, that teachers think the girls are smarter. The newest studies are showing that girls are the new Horatio Alger. They're the ones fingered for success, and the boys are feeling alienated."

As evidence, Kleinfeld cites several recent reports. A 1998 survey sponsored by the Horatio Alger Association found one-third of high school girls said they had gotten "mostly As" on their last report card compared with less than one-fifth of the boys. The students in the study were divided into three groups. Of the successful students (those doing well in school), two-thirds were girls. At the other end of the spectrum, 70 percent of the "alienated students" were boys. [24]

Similarly, a 1997 Metropolitan Life survey of 1,306 students and teachers found "teachers nationwide view girls as higher achievers and more likely to succeed than boys." The survey also found that "girls appear to have an advantage over boys in terms of their future plans, teachers' expectations, everyday experiences at school and interactions in the classroom." Of all groups, the survey found, minority boys are "the most likely to feel discouraged about the future and the least interested in getting a good education." [25]

Diane Ravitch, a senior fellow at the Brookings Institution and a former assistant secretary of Education in the Bush administration, says government-funded gender-equity programs aimed at making teachers more sensitive to girls have sent out a message of "repress the boys."

"As the mother of sons," she says, "I'm very happy they're no longer in school and too old to be affected" by what she calls a "frightening anti-male" atmosphere. "This is a very dangerous thing we've done," she says of the gender-equity programs.

Feminist organizations, which first raised alarms about the suppressed voices of girls in schools, respond with bafflement to the recent uproar of concern about boys and to the charge that anti-male sentiment has arisen in the wake of too much attention to girls. "I don't think advocating that women should be treated equally has ever implied that boys or men are suddenly painted as villains," says Patricia Ireland, president of the National Organization for Women (NOW). "I don't think the pendulum has gone anywhere near to equality for girls — much less over the line — to demonize young boys and in some way injure them in their education."

Adds the AAUW's Ford, "If there are negatives out there" from paying increased attention to girls, "we didn't see it in our work, and it's certainly not what our work is about."

Vassar's Broude says she's not at all convinced that schools have become such an uncomfortable place for boys. In fact for many boys, it's a welcoming place, she maintains. Although teachers do believe that girls are better behaved in the early grades, research indicates that in the later grades the pattern reverses, and teachers see masculine characteristics as indicative of intelligence, independence and success in school, according to Broude.

In addition, sometimes drops in self-esteem result when children get the opportunity to compare themselves to their peers in school and revise their inflated ideas of themselves, Broude maintains.

Questionnaires and interviews cited by Broude find that both boys and girls have high self-esteem in kindergarten, when they first enter school, that self-esteem falls for both sexes throughout the first few years of school and then recovers. Another dip in self-esteem occurs in seventh and eighth grade, when teenagers become especially sensitive to how they measure up against their age group. But Broude sees these hits to self-esteem as part of normal growing pains.

In her critique of Gurian and Pollack, Broude says the contention that boys are emotionally fragile can have dangerous consequences for child-rearing. That premise of fragility, she argues, underestimates the importance of fortifying children with resilience against hardship — and thus deprives them of the skills they need to weather adulthood. Besides, she notes, modern suburban American children enjoy one of the most comfortable lives imaginable in history. "If we buy into the fantasy that boys are china dolls," she warns, "we are in danger of making them just that."

American Association of University Women/Nicholas E. Waring

Girls appear to be overcoming their historical weakness in math better than boys are in language and writing skills.

Do boys and girls learn in different ways?

The public's current fascination with gender differences often blurs how small the differences are between girls and boys. In the most comprehensive study done to date, the Educational Testing Service (ETS) looked at data from more than 400 tests to determine gender differences.

Contrary to public opinion, ETS concluded that by 12th grade gender differences accounted for no more than 1 percent of all variation in scores on most tests. That's partly because boys' and girls' different areas of superiority tend to cancel one another out. At the same time, some intriguing differences in the intellectual strengths of boys and girls persist when the average boy is compared with the average girl. [26]

In the fourth grade, the ETS research showed, there are only small differences in scores between boys and girls, which become more pronounced as students move up through the grades. Girls' small advantage in writing and language skills gets larger between the fourth and eighth grades. Boys tend to gain on girls in math, science and geopolitical subjects between the eighth and 12th grades.

The classic work on sex differences, *The Psychology of Sex Differences*, concluded that four main sex differences are fairly well-established: Girls have greater verbal ability than boys; boys excel in visual spatial ability, boys excel in mathematics and males are more aggressive. [27]

The ETS study confirmed some of these differences. Among 12th-graders, girls tend to perform better on verbal and writing subjects while males perform better in mechanical and electronic areas. For example, on open-ended questions (as opposed to multiple choice) from advanced placement tests, females tended to do better if the response was written. Males tended to do better if the response was to produce a figure, such as a graph, or part of a figure to explain or interpret information. [28]

Yet girls appear to be overcoming their historical weakness in math better than boys have in language. While girls have reduced the familiar math and science gap in test scores to a quarter of what it was 30 years ago, boys have not closed the sizable gap in writing skills since 1960, according to ETS.

Those who argue that schools are failing boys point out that while high-achieving boys tend to attract the most attention, more boys than girls are clumped at the bottom of the academic ladder. This seeming paradox is explained by the fact that males tend to be more variable in performance than females, whether comparing cognitive, physical or behavioral traits. For example, the ETS study found that among 12th-graders, there are about five males for every four females below the 10th percentile and above the 90th percentile — more boys at the bottom and more at the top. [29]

But critics say the ETS study gives short shrift to an important area where girls still lag behind boys: the "high-stakes" tests like the Scholastic Assessment Test (SAT), required for college entrance, and the Graduate Record Exam (GRE), needed for entrance to graduate school. In 1998, female college-bound seniors scored an average of 496 on the math section of the SAT, 35 points behind the average male score of 531. Surprisingly, even on the verbal SAT, girls scored lower than boys, though by a much smaller margin. Girls averaged 502 compared with boys' 509. [30]

"My question to ETS is why are the girls doing so much worse on the tests that affect their lives?' asks Sadker of American University. Sadker and his late wife Myra authored several influential studies concluding that teachers give more attention in the classroom to boys than to girls. In a widely cited finding, they reported that elementary and middle-school boys called out answers more often than girls. When boys called out, teachers typically listened to the comment, according to the Sadkers. But when girls called out, they were usually corrected with comments like, "Please raise your hand if you want to speak." [31]

Sadker believes that the more intense spotlight experienced by boys in the classroom serves as a training ground for the high-stakes tests. "I think when you get more attention in the classroom, you have more confidence going into a test," he says. "Boys' performance on those tests is more aggressive, more risk-taking, more confident. One hypothesis I have is that boys perform better in stress situations," Sadker says. "They've been put on the spot to come up with the answer."

By contrast, girls treat multiple-choice tests more like social or classroom situations where they don't want to offend someone by claiming to know something that they don't, according to Sadker. He cites a study of a fourth-grade science test where the researchers added "I don't know" as one of the multiple-choice answers. Girls were four to five times more likely than boys to answer "I don't know" an answer for which they got no credit.

Brookings' Ravitch suggests the boys' superior performance on the SAT may lie in the fact that a broader range of female than male students take the test. For example, among African-Americans, girls taking the test outnumber boys 2-to-1, Ravitch notes. The predominance of girls in every ethnic group except for Asian-Americans suggests they represent a wider range of talents, including those at the low end of the ability scale, than the college-bound boys, who represent a self-selected group of excelling students.

But Sadker argues that in some sense women, who do better than men, "aren't believing the grades." They are believing the SATs. He sees a straight line from the classroom atmosphere, where boys aggressively shout out answers, and the workplace, where women earn less money than men with the same level of education.

"Part of what goes on in the classroom is a laboratory for life," Sadker maintains. "Women who sometimes do extraordinarily well on report card grades in school report to me 20 or 30 years later they don't understand what happened. They see guys get promoted, make higher salaries."

His explanation is that in the classroom the boys have learned how to have a "public voice." They've learned how to claim credit for their ideas in public meetings and how to demand a raise from the boss. By contrast, Sadker says, "The women haven't learned that unlike school, there isn't a quiz on Friday; you don't get smiles and pats on the back for being quiet in class."

Women's lack of assertiveness in the workplace, Sadker suggests, may explain in large part why women still earn significantly less than men with the same education. According to government statistics, a full-time working woman with a B.A. earns $13,237 less than a man with an equivalent education. A woman with an M.A. still earns $16,741 less than a male with the same degree. [32]

Ravitch dismisses Sadker's hypothesis that there's a link between classroom neglect of females and women's lower earnings. "I wouldn't trust any research he produces because I've never seen the replication of his research and its relevance to achievement," she says. "I think the kind of [teachers] calling-on [boys] he talks about is reprimand. And reprimand does not produce higher achievement." As for women's lower wages in the workplace, Ravitch says, some of the differential may result from choices women make to interrupt careers to have children and take lower-paying jobs.

In the last analysis, researchers on both sides of the debate agree that girls and boys are much more alike than they are different. Statistically, differences between genders on tests, for example, are dwarfed by the large amount of overlap in the male and female distribution along the achievement scale, ETS notes.

The leap forward of girls in math and science in recent years is one indication that differences formerly viewed as sex-linked are not as genetically predetermined as was once widely believed. "What we're seeing is girls' performance changing faster than the gene can travel," says Sadker.

"There's not a girls' style of learning; there's not a boys' style of learning. Boys and girls mostly learn the same way and mostly respond the same way," Ravitch maintains. "In any generalization, there's enormous overlap; there will be boys who are fine readers and writers and girls who are good in math and science." ■

BACKGROUND

Neglect of Girls

Rising concern about the neglect of girls in the classroom in the 1980s and early '90s sparked new efforts to interest girls in math and science and to test out more girl-friendly educational methods — including all-girls classes and schools.

In the early 1990s, research by Harvard psychologist Carol Gilligan described adolescence as a time when girls experience an erosion of self-esteem. [33] At adolescence, Gilligan reported, girls struggle to balance traditionally female traits like caring for other people against male traits like self-sufficiency, which she described as more highly valued by the wider society.

Gilligan's work gave credence to the proposition that "men and women are not necessarily the same, whether innately or through social conditioning and that their distinct ways of perceiving reality should be afforded equal value," writes St. John's University law Professor Rosemary C. Salomone. [34]

Gilligan's work was bolstered by the Sadkers' observations in the 1980s of hundreds of classrooms. The Sadkers reported that boys dominated discussions and were more likely to get attention from teachers. Whether praise or criticism, both kinds of teacher reactions helped boys' superior achievement, according to the Sadkers. [35]

Following closely on the Sadkers' research was a series of reports from the AAUW. A survey of 3,000 girls and boys ages 9-15 released in 1991 concluded that girls were far more likely than boys to suffer a loss of self-esteem and lose interest in math and science as they approached adolescence. [36]

In 1992, the AAUW released the report "How Schools Shortchange Girls." It reported that girls lagged seriously behind boys in math and science. The AAUW report seized prominent and enduring media attention. In a summary of the 1992 report, *The New York Times* reported that "School is still a place of unequal opportunity where girls face discrimination from teachers, textbooks, tests and their male classmates." [37]

Several scholars have criticized the 1992 AAUW report, noting that many of the girls' shortfalls the AAUW identified in 1992 had already been repaired by the time of their report. "The idea that the 'schools shortchange girls' is wrong and dangerously wrong," writes psychologist Kleinfeld in a critique of the AAUW report. "It is girls who get higher grades in school, who do better than boys on standardized tests of reading and writing and who get higher class rank and more school honors." [38]

Kleinfeld criticizes the AAUW report as one example of women's advocacy groups' effort "to intensify the image of women as 'victims' deserving special treatment and policy attention." In drawing attention to girls, Kleinfeld has argued, the AAUW drew attention away from the group scoring lowest on almost every educational measure — African-American boys.

In a recent paper, sociologist Cornelius Riordan argues that as early as 1980 and certainly by 1992, the year the influential AAUW report appeared, girls had already closed the gap they suffered in comparison with boys in the 1970s and in some areas had leaped ahead. By 1992, he writes, females "possess a clear and significant advantage on most central educational-outcome indicators, on average." [39]

For example, by 1992, women accounted for 54 percent of students receiving either a B.A. or M.A. degree. Among African-Americans and Hispanic-Americans, the gender gap in attaining higher education actually favored females in 1970 and has widened further in females' favor in the past two decades, Riordan reports. In 1972, more boys than girls were enrolled in college preparatory high

Chronology

1970s *Sex discrimination in education is prohibited. Separate-but-equal single-sex schools are ruled constitutional.*

1972
Congress passes Education Amendments including Title IX, prohibiting sex discrimination in any educational institution receiving federal funds.

1974
Congress passes Women's Educational Equity Act to enforce Title IX.

1977
In *Vorcheimer v. School District of Philadelphia*, the Supreme Court upholds the constitutionality of Central High School, an all-boys public high school, finding its sister school, Girls High, of equal quality.

1980s *Researchers express rising concern that girls are neglected in the classroom and are suffering a loss of self-esteem. Central High School is declared discriminatory by state court.*

1983
In *Newburg v. Board of Education*, a Pennsylvania state court rules that Girls High School offers an inferior education to all-boys Central High School and orders Central to admit girls.

1989
An article in *Educational Leadership* reports that boys receive more teacher attention than girls.

1990s *Reports publicizing girls' disadvantage in schools spark single-sex classes and girl-friendly approaches in schools. As trends show more girls succeeding in school, child specialists contend schools are shortchanging boys.*

1990
Harvard psychologist Carol Gilligan reports in *Making Connections* that private-school girls lose their self-confidence as they approach adolescence.

January 1991
American Association of University Women (AAUW) releases a survey concluding that girls are far more likely than boys to lose interest in math and science as they approach adolescence.

1991
In *Garrett v. Board of Education*, a district court in Michigan blocks the Detroit school district from opening three all-male academies for inner-city African-Americans. National Organization for Woman (NOW) joins suit charging the schools discriminate against girls.

1992
AAUW study reports that girls lag seriously behind boys in math and science.

1994
Congress reauthorizes the Elementary and Secondary School Education Act, containing provisions to encourage gender equity in schools.

June 1996
In *United States v. Virginia*, the Supreme Court requires all-male Virginia Military Institute to admit women. The landmark case sets specific conditions limiting single-sex education for schools that receive public funds.

Aug. 22, 1996
NOW and civil liberties groups file a complaint with the Department of Education charging that a new all-girls public school in Harlem is discriminatory. The department has not yet acted on the complaint.

1998
The AAUW releases a report concluding that girls are closing the gap with boys in math and science but that girls take less-advanced computer courses than boys.

April 1999
Psychologists Dan Kindlon and Michael Thompson publish *Raising Cain*, the latest of three books contending that American society is giving boys destructive emotional signals and that schools are failing boys.

April 20, 1999
Twelve students and a teacher are killed at Columbine High School in Littleton, Colo., after two teenage boys go on a shooting rampage and then kill themselves.

May 10, 1999
President Clinton holds a White House summit meeting with media and gun-making interests to discuss ways to counter youth violence.

May 20, 1999
In the most serious copycat event to follow Columbine, a 15-year-old boy in Conyers, Ga., opens fire on fellow students, wounding six.

All-Boys Schools Boast Impressive Results

Ten eighth-graders at the all-boys Nativity Mission School on New York's Lower East Side are critiquing one another's poetry recitations in preparation for their upcoming school poetry assembly.

"Through nights like this I held her again and kissed, her again and again," says José David "D.J." Estevez, 14, reciting the Chilean poet Pablo Neruda. The romantic sentiments evoke no giggles, smirks or elbow-poking from the other boys. Instead, they suggest ways to better convey the poem's tragicomic tone.

The attentive, serious mood of the class, in which boys speak without embarrassment of love and grief, is at odds with the fear often expressed by feminist opponents of all-boys' schools, who worry that boys will descend to a locker-room mentality without the civilizing influence of girls. National Organization for Women (NOW) President Patricia Ireland cites William Golding's *Lord of the Flies* — a novel about a group of boys stranded on a desert island who become terrifyingly savage — as the ultimate metaphor for what she believes can happen.

Yet boys at the predominantly Hispanic, Jesuit-run Nativity school, say that in contrast to the coed public schools they attended previously, it is socially acceptable to express the gentler emotions associated with the second sex, including affection for one another. Over lunch, George Figueroa, 13, notes, "If there were girls there, I'm sure people would be hesitant to recite poems about love and romance." At Nativity, he adds, "You get to act freely; you don't have to impress girls."

Nativity Mission School

Seventy-nine percent of Nativity Mission School students go to college.

"At coed schools, there's always a lot of jealousy," says Isaiah Parker, 14. "A lot of fights start over girls." That's one reason that in coed schools "boys are not close to each other," George says. By comparison, both boys say, the lack of girls makes it easier to concentrate on their studies.

Nativity Mission School was founded in 1971 to provide an alternative to the lure of the streets for boys from neighborhood families too poor to pay for traditional parochial schools, according to Father John "Jack" Podsiadlo, the director and acting principal. The students' parents, many of them on welfare, pay a fee of $35 a month in tuition.

The school's long-term success rate is impressive. Eighty-two percent of the boys who graduated from Nativity — which ends at eighth grade — between 1980 and 1993 went on to graduate from high school. In contrast, the high school dropout rate among Hispanic youth nationally is 42 percent. Seventy-nine percent of Nativity graduates went on to college, including such prestigious institutions as Cornell University, compared with only 54 percent nationally among Hispanic high school graduates. [1]

The high level of achievement attained by low-income, minority boys at schools like Nativity is the strongest piece of evidence favoring single-sex boys' schools, according to Cornelius Riordan, a professor of sociology at Providence College in Rhode Island. [2]

Based on his study of achievement-test scores, "There are clear differences in achievement" favoring single-sex schools for African-American and Hispanic-American children over coed schools, Riordan says. However, the achievement advantages of single-sex schools are limited to children who are disadvantaged by income, class, race or gender, Riordan has concluded.

"At the extremes, if you talk about affluent children, it doesn't matter if they're in small vs. large schools or coed vs. single-sex schools," Riordan says. "The thing that makes a difference is their home life. By contrast, the kid of low socio-economic status needs a good school because there's little growth going on at home."

Compared with students in coed schools, kids at single-sex schools talk back to their teachers less frequently, have fewer fights in class, cut classes less often and are more likely to come to class with paper and pencil, according to Riordan. Discipline problems are lower at single-sex schools because they have stricter school policies, and "better discipline creates better achievement," he says.

At Hales Franciscan High School, an African-American Catholic boys' school on the predominantly black South Side of Chicago, each caller is greeted with a recorded greeting by President Tim King announcing that "100 percent of our 1996, 1997 and 1998 students went to college." According to Derek Neal, an economics professor at the University of Chicago, a black or Latino child attending Catholic school in urban areas has an 88 percent chance of graduating on average, compared with a 62 percent chance from a public school. [3]

King believes Hales' all-male environment plays a crucial role in defining a positive male role for his students, the vast majority of whom are raised by mothers or grandmothers in the absence of fathers. Seventy percent of Hales' students receive some form of financial aid to help cover the tuition of $3,500, according to King. "We have to convince them they're valuable as boys, so they don't think the only way to be a young man is absent and not supporting a family economically," King says.

Most boys come to Hales from public schools where girls are typically at the top of the class and a boy who is doing well academically is branded a nerd. "Black kids think if they're talking articulately, they're 'talking white' and if they're doing well in school, they're acting white or like a girl," King says. "What happens at Hales is we take away the girls. It de facto has to be a male who's the No. 1 student," King says. "It doesn't become a negative thing to be smart. It liberates the student to be themselves, to be in the choir, to write poetry. Those things are not girl things anymore. Someone's got to do it, and it's going to be a male."

The 31 predominantly African-American Catholic schools in the United States, many of them single-sex, collectively send about 95-98 percent of their students to college every year, according to Vernon C. Polite, an associate professor of education at Catholic University in Washington.

Catholic single-sex schools are so different from a typical public school that it's hard to know how much is attributable to their being single-sex. The differences include small classes, high levels of discipline and dedicated teachers who provide after-school help. Polite thinks a major factor in Catholic schools' success is that children are not allowed to fall off the college preparatory track.

An American Association of University Women (AAUW) report concluded last year that although single-sex programs produce positive results for some students, "researchers do not know for certain whether the benefits derive from factors unique to single-sex programs or whether these factors also exist or can be reproduced in coeducational settings." [4]

"The same advantages that apply to those single-sex schools would apply in a coed school: lower student-teacher ratios, having more money, better programs," argues Ireland.

Yet Riordan is skeptical that the benefits he's found in single-sex education could be reproduced easily in coeducational public schools.

"The cultural norms of typical coed schools are anti-intellectual," says Riordan. "That's a dominant part of coed schools along with male sports. I see [the success of single-sex schools] as a parental choice, especially among families of low socioeconomic status. It's a recognition that once you're there, this is not a school with business as usual — where life is life with friends. There's a full recognition that this is an academic school."

It's hard to judge whether the success of Catholic boys' schools can be divorced from the strong religious values they inculcate. "Just having all boys together does not have positive results," says Polite. "In Catholic schools, there's religion and spiritual formation."

The California public school system, which has been experimenting with single-sex academies since 1996, has come up with mixed reviews for its all-boys academies. "For the boys the lack of pressure to impress the girls has enabled them to go wild," Jocelyn Lee, coordinator of the single-gender academy at Andrew Hill High School in San Jose, told the *San Jose Mercury News* in April. Disappointment with the boys' performance, compared with the improved grades and classroom participation at the all-girls academy at Andrew Hill, may force the program to close. [5]

"Some of the schools are not quite sure how to channel the energy positively, because they didn't realize how much energy an all-boys group brings to the classroom," says Amanda Datnow, associate research scientist at the Johns Hopkins Center for Social Organization, who is studying California's single-gender academies. "It may have as much to do with the teachers as the boys."

The West Coast's lack of a strong private boys schools tradition may partly explain why teachers report trouble handling all-boys' classes, Datnow suggests. On the other hand, "Boys will probably say, 'I'm getting more work done and my grades have improved.' "

Susan Condrey, former principal of the Single Gender Academies in Fountain Valley, said she was astounded by the positive change in the boys' behavior about three months after the new school started up. The boys were referred to the school for discipline problems; most come from low-income, Hispanic families.

"They stopped being cocky," according to Condrey. "They became gentler, softer, kinder. They weren't threatening and strutting the way they were when the girls were there. Their manners improved, they had a little more patience." As for achievement, she says, "These kids came from the lowest-performing school districts in the state. They just soared."

Condrey thinks Fountain Valley's focus on hands-on learning and student presentations may explain why boys at this school seem to have fared so much better than those at other California experimental schools. "I think boys don't sit still as easily as girls. And if you're going to stand up and lecture, you're not going to like the boys as well, especially if the class is being taught in the old ways."

---

[1] Philliber Research Associates, "Achievement Among Students of Nativity Mission," 1998, pp. 1, 3.

[2] Cornelius Riordan, *Girls and Boys in School: Together or Separate?* (1990).

[3] "Answered Prayer," *The Economist*, April 5-11, 1997.

[4] American Association of University Women Educational Foundation, "Separated by Sex: A Critical Look at Single-Sex Education for Girls," 1998.

[5] Anne Martinez, "Single-sex Classrooms Struggling," *San Jose Mercury News*, April 5, 1999, p. 1A.

school tracks; by 1992 there were already more girls in such programs.

In addition, Riordan's findings on girls' self-esteem run contrary to the premise in the AAUW reports that low self-esteem is linked to negative experiences in school. He reports that girls had higher self-esteem than boys in 1972 and 1980, when their educational expectations and opportunities were lower than boys. By contrast, by 1992, when girls expected to finish school with higher degrees than boys, their self-esteem was lower than boys'.

This suggests that self-esteem actually decreases with better education, possibly due to the "greater expectations and demands" that come with success in school, Riordan suggests. Paradoxically, African-Americans have consistently had higher self-esteem than whites despite inferior education and income, he notes. [40]

The Sadkers' research, too, has been the subject of stinging critiques by Kleinfeld and the AEI's Sommers. The Sadkers fail to substantiate the central premise of their research — that attention from a teacher is related to student achievement, Kleinfeld says. A major weakness of the research is that the conclusions depend on observers who may have their own biases, Kleinfeld says. Most classroom interaction studies in recent years have been conducted in math and science classrooms where females are suspected to be at a disadvantage as opposed to language classes, where they tend to excel, Kleinfeld notes, tipping the conclusions in favor of boys.

Promoting Gender Equity

The highly publicized findings of the Sadkers, Gilligan and the AAUW soon had an impact on the admissions offices of all-girls schools, which were seen as one way of remedying biases against girls, according to Salomone. In 1991, applications to schools belonging to the National Coalition of Girls Schools had increased by 21 percent over the previous year. The research findings on girls also stimulated a number of experiments in school districts around the country with single-sex math and science classes.

The findings about schools' neglect of girls sparked creation of a number of government-funded and school-based programs to increase attention to girls. The AAUW helped write provisions to promote gender equity into the Elementary and Secondary Education Act passed in 1994, such as a provision to require teacher training in gender equity and mandating gender-equitable teaching methods in high-poverty schools. The National Science Foundation initiated a $9 million program to interest girls in science.

While some women's groups credit these programs for girls' recent advances, other advocates say they are a drop in the bucket. "I can tell you in my experience, travels and readings, teachers are generally unaware they are biased" against girls, Sadker says. "I don't think they get the training. While there are a few federal programs, we're talking about minuscule funds," he says, estimating that only about 1 percent of America's 3 million teachers have been recipients of government-backed training in gender sensitivity.

Increasingly stringent high school graduation requirements for more years of math and science have probably done the most to boost female achievement in those subjects, according to Kleinfeld. In the 1980s, high school girls were far less likely than boys to take science and math. By 1994, females surpassed males in taking chemistry, algebra, geometry, pre-calculus and biology. Equal proportions of males and females take trigonometry and calculus. More males than females take AP math and science tests, but the proportion of females is increasing in that area. [41]

The growing tendency of women to seek advanced degrees might be a response to the fact that they need what Sadker calls an extra "insurance degree" to earn an income equivalent to men. Women who have earned a college degree make just $4,164 more than men with only a high school diploma. [42] These economics make it more attractive for a boy to get a job right out of high school, he suggests. "Girls are better students, but males have more options," says Sadker. "We have a good economy out there."

But Ravitch counters that the much publicized high-paid computer-industry jobs for high school graduates are still relatively rare, leaving most boys with only a high school education at a serious disadvantage in today's job market.

Women still receive a minority of doctoral degrees, particularly in math and science, but that gap is closing fast. In 1994, American women received 45 percent of all doctoral degrees, not counting foreign students. [43] ■

CURRENT SITUATION

Single-Sex Schools

When school districts began to experiment with single-sex schools in the early 1990s, civil rights and

At Issue:

Are parents, educators and others neglecting the emotional needs of boys?

Patricia Dalton
Clinical psychologist, Washington, D.C.

EXCERPTED FROM *THE WASHINGTON POST*, MAY 9, 1999.

yes

For all the unfathomable horror of the shootings . . . at Columbine High School, there was one thing that came as no surprise to me. It was boys who fired the guns in Littleton, Colo. Just as it was boys who fired the guns in the [other] school shootings. . . .

Because of legitimate concerns about gender discrimination, for years we tended to play down differences between boys and girls, even though research and common sense tell us they exist. . . . Most recently, as we've begun to acknowledge gender differences, we've focused our attention on girls. . . . Where does all this leave boys? . . .

The statistics that cross my desk are not encouraging. They suggest that boys may be the more fragile sex. Approximately three out of every four children identified as learning disabled are boys. Boys are much more likely than girls to have drug and alcohol problems. Four of every five juvenile court cases involve crimes committed by boys. Ninety-five percent of juvenile homicides are committed by boys. And while girls attempt suicide four times more often, boys are seven times as likely to succeed as girls — usually because they choose more lethal methods, such as guns.

While girls tend to internalize problems, taking their unhappiness out on themselves, boys externalize them, taking their unhappiness out on others. Boys have more problems than girls in virtually every category you can think of with the exception of eating disorders. The signs of depression my colleagues and I are likely to see in girls are typically straightforward — sadness, tearfulness and self-doubt. In boys, depression is generally hidden behind symptoms such as irritability, agitation and explosiveness. . . .

We all know that boys mature more slowly than girls, and that they reach the cognitive milestones essential for doing well at school later than girls do. Take reading, for example. Girls are usually ready to read earlier than boys. This means that average boys wind up feeling less successful, and learning-disabled boys can feel easily defeated. But what have schools done to accommodate these well-documented differences in rates of maturity? Very little. Schools, like researchers, have been concentrating on girls. . . .

There's no question in my mind that, in our haste to make up for the disadvantages that girls have historically suffered, we've tended to overlook the needs of ordinary boys. Like everyone else, boys of all ages need adults to love them, appreciate them and enjoy them, so that they can come to value and have faith in themselves.

REPRINTED WITH PERMISSION FROM THE AUTHOR.

Gwen J. Broude
Professor, Department of Psychology, Vassar College

WRITTEN FOR *THE CQ RESEARCHER*, MAY 1999.

no

The idea that we are neglecting the emotional needs of our boys is not supported by the statistics. Rather, evidence indicates that boys and girls face somewhat different life challenges. More important, adjustment problems are uncommon in both sexes. Proportions of children displaying behavioral and emotional difficulties typically range from 1 to 4 percent. Rather than pointing to the fragility of boys, these numbers dramatize the resilience of all of our children.

Boys do, however, display more aggressive behavior than girls. It is this male-biased tendency toward aggression that has been capturing the attention of the country, especially in light of the school shootings that we have witnessed over the last few years. All were carried out by boys. Male violence is not likely the result of the emotional neglect of our boys, as evidence indicates that with regard to amount of parent-child interaction, degree of warmth and nurturance displayed toward the child, encouragement of dependency and achievement, restrictiveness and disciplinary strictness, parents make no distinction between their sons and daughters.

Research indicates that the behavior of children is influenced by the age of the people with whom they are interacting. In the company of their peers, children display a variety of kinds of aggression, including threats, insults, teasing, physical assaults and competition. Slightly younger children elicit dominance on the part of older ones. This tendency for a child's behavior to be predicted by the company he keeps is found cross-culturally, indicating that human nature is at its foundation.

Given this effect, here is a radical proposal: How about ending the policy of housing children of the same age together for much of the day? Because our schools segregate children by age, we have come to think of the custom as natural and inevitable, but it is neither. Most children for most of history have grown up in the company of people of all ages. Such an upbringing is more likely to inhibit peer aggression, elicit helpfulness and expose children on a daily basis to a variety of adults engaged in a diversity of activities worth admiring and emulating. As a society, we are obsessed with the dangerous consequences of peer pressure for our children and especially adolescents, for whom peers are especially likely to trigger destructive behavior. What kind of insanity then provokes us to let adolescents spend much of their time in a society composed largely of peers?

women's groups opposed them as discriminatory. Ironically, these battles stymied single-sex experiments for girls as well as for boys from inner-city black neighborhoods. (*See story, p. 278.*) In several cases, the ACLU and NOW argued that the experiments violated the Equal Protection Clause of the 14th Amendment and Title IX of the Educational Amendments of 1972.*

Leading feminist groups fear that all-male schools could once again become bastions of male privilege. Marcia Greenberger, co-president of the National Women's Law Center, points to the inequities that existed into the early 1980s between Philadelphia's selective public all-boys Central High School and its sister school, all-girls Girls High. "We know when we're talking in a race context that separate is rarely if ever equal," Greenberger says. "And our history has shown that's been the case with respect to sex in institutions too."

Supporters of all-male schools find this fear laughable when it comes to talking about historically disadvantaged African-Americans. "I think we've always had all-male academies. We just call them prisons and reform schools," says Vernon C. Polite, associate professor of education at Catholic University in Washington, D.C., and editor of *African-American Males in School and Society*, to be published this fall.

With all-male schools, says Polite, "We're trying to overcompensate for social, pathological issues that affect this population significantly." According to Polite, who is African-American and Catholic, the 31 predominantly African-American Catholic schools in urban areas of the United States, many of them single-sex, collectively send about 95 to 98 percent of their students to college every year. He calls that record "phenomenal" considering that most of these graduates come from a population with just a 40 percent chance of going to college.

Here are some of the cases that have affected single-sex education:

• In 1977, in *Vorcheimer v. School District of Philadelphia*, the Supreme Court upheld an appeals court finding that Central High School and Girls High were of equal quality and therefore the schools were permissible under the Constitution.

• In a second challenge to Central, also brought by female students denied admission, a state court ruled in *Newburg v. Board of Education* in 1983 that the two schools were not equal when comparing such features as books in the school library, course offerings in math and average acceptance rates to colleges. Based on the new information, the court ordered Central to admit girls. The ruling was not appealed.

In the early to mid-1990s, the battle shifted to several efforts to found all-boys schools for minority boys.

• In 1991, in *Garrett v. Board of Education*, a district court blocked the Detroit School District from opening three all-male Afrocentric academies for at-risk students. The school district argued that the system was failing males, pointing out that only 39 percent of black males graduated from Detroit public schools compared with 61 percent of black females. The court found no evidence that the system was failing males because of the presence of females. The school board agreed to admit girls to the academies rather than risk the cost of future litigation it believed it could not win. According to St. John's Salomone, the case served as a powerful deterrent to other school systems considering similar programs for black males.[44]

• In a landmark Supreme Court case in 1996, *United States v. Virginia*, the federal government sued Virginia and Virginia Military Institute (VMI), alleging that VMI's all-male admissions policy violated the Equal Protection Clause of the 14th Amendment. The Supreme Court upheld the government's claim, requiring VMI to admit women. The opinion left open the door to single-sex schools under certain conditions.

• The most recent round of litigation began in 1996, when community School District 4 in New York City announced plans to establish an all-girls Young Women's Leadership School in East Harlem. Largely for black and Hispanic girls, the school opened in September 1996 with 50 seventh-graders. By 2000, it plans to expand through grade 12. Three groups — the New York chapter of NOW, the New York Civil Liberties Union and the New York Civil Rights Coalition — filed a complaint against the school with the Office for Civil Rights (OCR) at the Department of Education. As of June, the case remains under investigation by OCR.

School districts around the country attempting to experiment with single-sex education have shut down for fear of legal challenges, including separate middle-school classrooms for boys and girls in Irvington, N.J.[45]

It's not clear how many school districts currently have single-sex classrooms or schools because some have simply gone underground.

"I have no clue how many" there are, says Janice L. Streitmatter, a professor of educational psychology at the University of Arizona, Tucson, and author of *For Girls Only: Making a Case for Single-Sex Schooling*. "People are not willing to admit they have them. It's under a cloak of secrecy because people are afraid of Title IX."[46]

* The Equal Protection Clause states, "No state shall . . . deny to any person within its jurisdiction the equal protection of the laws." Title IX prohibits educational programs receiving federal funds from treating students unequally on the basis of their sex.

Nevertheless, the OCR has not been particularly active in cracking down on single-sex experiments, judging by its slowness in acting on the nearly three-year-old East Harlem girls' school complaint.

"I think the Office of Civil Rights has become uncomfortable with its whole position, so it's done nothing," says Salomone. ■

OUTLOOK

Chaos and Confusion

The range of proposals aimed at preventing future school shootings has exposed deep ideological divides in American society. Debates are likely to continue in the coming months over such solutions as tougher gun control, funding more mental health counselors at schools, stricter supervision over the culture of violence on the Internet and tougher discipline in schools.

Hundreds of school disciplinary actions in recent weeks to penalize students for wearing certain clothing, making jokes or other behavior reminiscent of the Columbine shooters have already roused the concern of the ACLU.

A student at a Wilmington, N.C., high school spent three days in jail this June after he used the phrase "The end is near" on his computer's background wallpaper. In Brimfield, Ohio, 11 high school students were suspended after contributing to an off-campus Web site about the Gothic subculture, which the Columbine shooters emulated.[47]

In the aftermath of the school shootings, some experts have been warning parents to be concerned if their children — like the Columbine shooters — play violent video games, spend hours on the Internet, seem to have few friends or appear to be social outcasts from the "right" school cliques. But as Harvard's Kindlon warns, if a separate school were established for all the boys who share attributes with the Columbine shooters, "That would be a pretty big school."

Pollack and Kindlon are among the psychologists who hope Columbine will force schools to pay more attention to taunting and social ostracism. But even those who advocate a larger therapeutic role for schools express a sense of discomfort with the new responsibility placed on untrained teachers to stop another Columbine at its roots.

"It's unfortunate that our schools have to do that," says Kindlon, but "that's the place society has decided we have to do our social engineering and socialization."

Skeptics worry about turning the classroom into a setting for therapy. "Those boys were evil," says Sommers of Klebold and Harris. According to newspaper reports, she notes, "They were given therapy; one had antidepressant drugs. Where they were ignored was in terms of ethics, character, discipline."

Sommers views proposals to encourage boys to vent their emotions as a misguided feminization of the culture away from such positive masculine attributes as self-control. "I think American children do not need to be encouraged toward narcissism and increasing self-awareness," she says. "They are the most self-aware children on the planet."

The last 25 years have seen a radical social revolution, argues psychologist Gilligan, as increasingly vocal women have redefined traditional gender roles in living, working and loving. Gilligan, who has recently shifted her research attention to preschool boys, argues that American society requires boys to suppress tender emotions— much as girls must suppress their inner selves at adolescence.

"We're not sure what we mean about masculinity" anymore, Gilligan told a group of parents at the 92nd Street Y in February. But the increasingly active presence of women in society signals "the end of patriarchy," she predicted.

Perhaps the inevitable result is a sense of chaos and confusion on the part of both men and women as they chart this new territory. As anthropologists say, it's hard to learn a new culture. ■

Notes

[1] Pollack appeared on "Oprah" to promote his book, *Real Boys; Rescuing Our Sons from the Myths of Boyhood* (1998). For background, see Kathy Koch, "School Violence," *The CQ Researcher*, Oct. 9, 1998, pp. 888-911.

[2] Michael Gurian, *A Fine Young Man* (1998), p. 24.

[3] *Ibid.*, p. 17. For background, see Charles S. Clark, "Sex, Violence and the Media," *The CQ Researcher*, Nov. 17, 1995, pp. 1017-1040.

[4] Michael D. Shear and Jacqueline L. Salmon, "An Education in Taunting," *The Washington Post*, May 2, 1999, pp. C1, C9.

[5] Dan Kindlon and Michael Thompson, *Raising Cain: Protecting the Emotional Life of Boys* (1999).

[6] Gwen J. Broude, "Boys will be boys," *The Public Interest*, summer 1999.

[7] Gurian, *op. cit.*, pp. 24, 25.

[8] Sommers' new book, *The War Against Boys*, is due to be published this year.

[9] Michael Kimmel, "Shooting Sheds Light on Problems Boys Face," letter to the editor, *The New York Times*, May 5, 1999, p. A32.

[10] Broude, *op. cit.*, p. 16.

[11] Quoted in Jay Tolson, "The Vocabulary of Evil," *U.S. News & World Report*, May 10, 1999, p. 22

[12] Pollack, *op. cit.*, p. 254.

[13] *Ibid*, p. 255.

[14] American Association of University Women (AAUW) Educational Foundation,

How Schools Shortchange Girls— the AAUW Report 1992 (1995), pp. 29-31.
[15] Cornelius Riordan, "Student Outcomes in Public Secondary Schools: Gender Gap Comparisons from 1972 to 1992," unpublished paper presented at annual meeting of the American Sociological Association, Aug. 21, 1998.
[16] National Center for Education Statistics, Department of Education, "Earned Degrees Conferred: Projections of Education Statistics to 2008," May 1998.
[17] Riordan, *op. cit.*, pp. 1-3.
[18] *Ibid*, pp. 3-4, 12.
[19] AAUW Educational Foundation, "Gender Gaps: Where Schools Still Fail Our Children," 1998.
[20] Judith Kleinfeld, "Student Performance: Males vs. Females," *The Public Interest*, winter 1999, p. 10.
[21] AAUW Education Foundation news release, "Technology Gender Gap Develops while Gaps in Math and Science Narrow, AAUW Foundation Report Shows," Oct. 14, 1998. Also see, "Gender Gaps: Where Schools Still Fail Our Children," *op. cit.*, pp. 10, 13, 14, 103.
[22] Riordan, *op. cit.*, p. 4.
[23] Kleinfeld, *op. cit.*, p. 13.
[24] The "State of Our Nation's Youth" survey covered 1,195 randomly selected high school students. The Horatio Alger Association is a nonprofit educational organization in Alexandria, Va., that gives out more than $1 million yearly in college scholarships.
[25] Kleinfeld, *op. cit.*, pp. 6, 18-19.
[26] Nancy S. Cole, "The ETS Gender Study: How Females and Males Perform in Educational Settings," 1997.
[27] E.E. Maccoby and C.N. Jacklin, *The Psychology of Sex Differences* (1974).
[28] Cole, *op. cit.*, p. 23.
[29] *Ibid*, p. 18.
[30] Educational Testing Service, "Profile of College-Bound Seniors," 1998.
[31] Quoted in AAUW Educational Foundation, pp. 118-119 (1995 paperback edition).
[32] U.S. Department of Education, "Outcomes of Education, Median Annual Income of Year-Round Full-Time Workers 25 Years Old and Over, by level of Education Completed and Sex: 1989 to 1997," 1998.
[33] Carol Gilligan, *In a Different Voice* (1982, 1993). See also Carol Gilligan et al., eds., *Making Connections* (1990), about self-esteem research at the Emma Willard School.
[34] Rosemary C. Salomone, "Single Sex Schooling: Law, Policy and Research," in Diane Ravitch, ed., *Brookings Papers on Education Policy*, 1999, p. 237.
[35] The Sadkers' observational research culminated in the book *Failing at Fairness* (1994).
[36] AAUW, "Shortchanging Girls, Shortchanging America" (January 1991)
[37] Susan Chira, "Bias Against Girls Is Found Rife in Schools with Lasting Damage," *The New York Times*, Feb. 12, 1992, p. A1.
[38] Judith Kleinfeld, "The Myth that Schools Shortchange Girls: Social Science in the Service of Deception," prepared for the Women's Freedom Network, 1998, pp. 1-2.
[39] Riordan, *op. cit.*, abstract page.
[40] *Ibid*, p. 10.
[41] Kleinfeld, "Student Performance: Males versus Females," *op. cit.*, p. 10.
[42] Based on 1997 statistics (the most recent available) from National Center for Education Statistics, "Outcomes of Education," Table 380. Male high school graduates in 1997 earned an average of $31,215 annually.
[43] Kleinfeld, "Student Performance: Males versus Females," *op. cit.*, p. 12
[44] Salomone, *Ibid*, p. 245.
[45] *Ibid*, p. 247.
[46] Janice L. Streitmatter, *For Girls Only: Making a Case for Single-Sex Schooling* (1999).
[47] Kevin Sack, "Schools Look Hard at Lockers, Shirts, Bags and Manners," *The New York Times*, May 24, p. A1. Also see, Anemona Hartocollis, "Joke Brings Suspension and Reversal," *The New York Times*, May 28, 1999, p. B3.

FOR MORE INFORMATION

American Association of University Women Educational Foundation, 1111 16th St., N.W., Washington, D.C. 20036-4873; (202) 728-7602; www.aauw.org. This arm of the AAUW, which represents 160,000 college graduates, has issued several influential reports calling attention to areas where girls lagged behind boys in school and where they have closed the gap.

Educational Testing Service, Communication Services, Mailstop 50-D, Rosedale Rd., Princeton, N.J. 08541; (609) 734-5050; www.ets.org. The ETS, which develops such major tests as the SAT, has published research examining boys' and girls' differing strengths on standardized tests.

International Boys' Schools Coalition, c/o University School, 2785 S.O.M. Center Rd., Hunting Valley, Ohio 44022; (216) 831-2200. The coalition represents some 170 private boys' schools and also funds and promotes research into boys' development.

National Center for Education Statistics, U.S. Department of Education, 1990 K Street, N.W., Washington, D.C. 20006; (202) 502-7300, nces.ed.gov/index.htm. The center is the source of statistics comparing the level of education achieved by men and women in the United States.

Bibliography

Selected Sources Used

Books

American Association of University Women Educational Foundation, *How Schools Shortchange Girls-the AAUW Report*, Marlowe, 1995.
The AAUW has released in book form its influential 1992 report, reporting that girls fall behind boys in higher-level mathematics and measures of self-esteem after 12 years of schooling. The report stimulated efforts nationwide to boost girls' self-esteem and their interest in math and science.

Gurian, Michael, *A Fine Young Man: What Parents, Mentors, and Educators Can Do to Shape Adolescent Boys into Exceptional Men*, Jeremy P. Tarcher/ Putnam, 1998.
Gurian, a family therapist, argues that millions of adolescent boys are suffering from a form of post-traumatic stress, which he traces largely to male brain systems that he says are more fragile than females', making it more difficult for boys to process emotional strains.

Kindlon, Dan, and Michael Thompson, *Raising Cain: Protecting the Emotional Life of Boys*, Ballantine, 1999.
Two psychologists charge that American culture is suppressing boys' emotional life "in service to rigid ideals of manhood." The authors cite high levels of adolescent suicide and drunk driving as well as learning problems in school as symptoms of a crisis.

Pollack, William, *Real Boys: Rescuing Our Sons from the Myths of Boyhood*, Random House, 1998.
American boys are being forced to separate from their mothers prematurely and to adopt an unwritten "Boy Code," where bravado must mask emotional vulnerability, argues a Harvard psychologist. When a boy falls short of this "ideal" myth of boyhood, Pollack writes, depression, anger and low self-esteem frequently result.

Articles

Broude, Gwen J., "Boys Will Be Boys," *The Public Interest*, summer 1999, pp. 3-17.
Challenging the grim profile of American boys' psychological plight presented by Pollack and Gurian, Vassar psychology Professor Broude argues that traditional male personality traits actually contribute to boys' mental health and that only a small percentage of boys suffer from mental and learning disorders.

Kleinfeld, Judith, "Student Performance: Males versus Females," *The Public Interest*, winter 1999, pp. 3-20.
University of Alaska psychology Professor Kleinfeld attacks the AAUW for making "misleading or false" claims in maintaining that girls are at the greatest disadvantage in school.

Koerner, Brendan I., "Where the Boys Aren't," *U.S. News & World Report*, Feb. 8, 1999, pp. 47-55.
This article reviewing the growing trend for women to outnumber men among college students suggests that higher salaries commanded by male high school graduates may partly explain their rush into the workplace.

Shear, Michael D., and Jacqueline L. Salmon, "An Education in Taunting," *The Washington Post*, May 2, 1999, p. C1.
This report on bullying is one of many articles that appeared after the Columbine shootings that explored the unforgiving social atmosphere of suburban schools.

Streisand, Betsy, and Angie Cannon, "Exorcising the pain," *U.S. News & World Report*, May 10, 1999, pp. 18-21.
As details about Columbine killer Eric Harris began to emerge, this was one of several articles that suggested the teenage shooters were not normal adolescents.

Tolson, Jay, "The Vocabulary of Evil," *U.S. News & World Report*, May 10, 1999, p. 22.
Tolson criticizes the flood of psychological explanations for the Columbine murders as contributing to a modern inability to see the massacre in terms of good and evil.

Reports and Studies

American Association of University Women Educational Foundation, *Gender Gaps: Where Schools Still Fail Our Children*, 1998.
In this follow-up to its 1992 report, the AAUW reports that the gap between girls and boys in math "appears to be diminishing."

American Association of University Women Educational Foundation, *Separated by Sex: A Critical Look at Single-Sex Education for Girls*, March 1998.
Despite the positive results shown in some single-sex settings, this report concludes that there is no evidence that single-sex education is better than coeducation.

Cole, Nancy S., *The ETS Gender Study: How Females and Males Perform in Educational Settings*, May 1997.
The Educational Testing Service (ETS) concluded that by 12th grade the differences between boys' and girls' performance are quite small in most subjects.

16 Roe v. Wade

SARAH GLAZER

The Supreme Court's decision last year striking down a Nebraska ban on so-called partial-birth abortion procedures has taken the steam out of one of the anti-abortion movement's most powerful issues. The Court's decision rendered invalid all of the 31 state bans and stalled the move to pass a similar ban in Congress. The decision was hailed as a victory by the pro-choice movement for upholding the principles of the Supreme Court's landmark 1973 *Roe v. Wade* ruling guaranteeing the right to an abortion. But the surprisingly slim 5–4 majority on the ruling means the judicial climate favoring *Roe* could be reversed if just one justice from the majority retires and is replaced by a justice sharing President George W. Bush's strongly anti-abortion views.

Just two weeks after the Supreme Court legalized abortion in 1973, women flooded into the first abortion clinic to open between Miami and Washington, D.C.

The Orlando, Fla., clinic stayed open seven days a week, 14 hours a day as it struggled to accommodate women from as far as five states away.

"It was like a dam had opened," recalled Susan Hill, who worked as a counselor at the clinic and now runs a chain of eight abortion clinics. "I wondered where the women had gone before. It was incredible."*

Roe v. Wade has brought about revolutionary social change in the 28 years since the landmark ruling was handed down.** The deaths that once resulted from abortions, many of them illegal, back-alley procedures, have virtually disappeared. Today, even the poorest women enter Hill's Mississippi clinic confident that they have a legal right to the procedure.

"A first-trimester abortion is now safer than having a shot of penicillin," said Richard Hausknecht, an obstetrician-gynecologist who helped start the first legal abortion clinic in New York City in 1970.

However, *Roe* also spawned the National Right to Life movement, including militant groups like Operation Rescue, which blocked access to clinics around the country. The movement has succeeded in passing laws restricting abortions in many states, throwing up hurdles that affect low-income women and teenagers in particular.[1]

"I think the pro-life movement is stronger than ever at the grass-roots level," said Judie Brown, president of the American Life League, a pro-life group based in Stafford, Va. "There is tremendous strength at the state level. What once might have been viewed as a woman's right is now being questioned seriously."

"In 1967, every state prohibited abortion. We think it would be good social policy to go back to that time," said Douglas Johnson, legislative director of the National Right to Life Committee. "The right to life has a foothold in the Constitution; the right to kill doesn't. We think [*Roe*] is of constitutional clay and ought to fall. And every year demonstrates the horrific human consequences."

Due to the influence of the Right to Life movement, many abortion-rights advocates say that even with *Roe* in place, much needs to be done. "Things haven't changed a whole hell of a lot since *Roe v. Wade*," said Hausknecht, a professor at Mount Sinai School of Medicine.*** "Poor women in the U.S. still have trouble getting access to abortions." He cited federal and state bans on Medicaid funding for abortions and private health insurers that won't pay for abortions.

"It's more difficult today for American women to get an abortion than at any time since the freedom to choose was established as a constitutional right," said Kate Michelman, president of the National Abortion and Reproductive Rights Action League (NARAL). "We now have somewhat of a pre-*Roe* state-by-state patchwork of laws," she said. More than half the states enforce at least one significant restriction on abortion, according to the Alan Guttmacher Institute (AGI), an abortion-rights research group.[2] *(See chart, p. 290.)* The mandatory restrictions include

- waiting periods typically ranging from 24–48 hours before women can receive the procedure;

*All interviews were conducted in 1997 unless otherwise indicated.

** The Supreme Court's 7-2 ruling on Jan. 22, 1973, described the right of a Texas woman to terminate her pregnancy as a "fundamental right" and struck down all state laws banning abortion. Abortion was illegal in Texas, and the woman, who used the pseudonym Jane Roe, had lacked the money to get a legal abortion elsewhere.

*** Hausknecht is also medical director at Danco Laboratories, the distributor of the abortion pill mifepristone, also known as RU-486.

From *The CQ Researcher*, November 28, 1997. Revised September 2001.

Abortions on the Decline

The number of legal abortions in the United States skyrocketed after the Supreme Court's 1973 Roe v. Wade *decision, then leveled off and declined from 1990 to 1997, the last year for which statistics are available.*

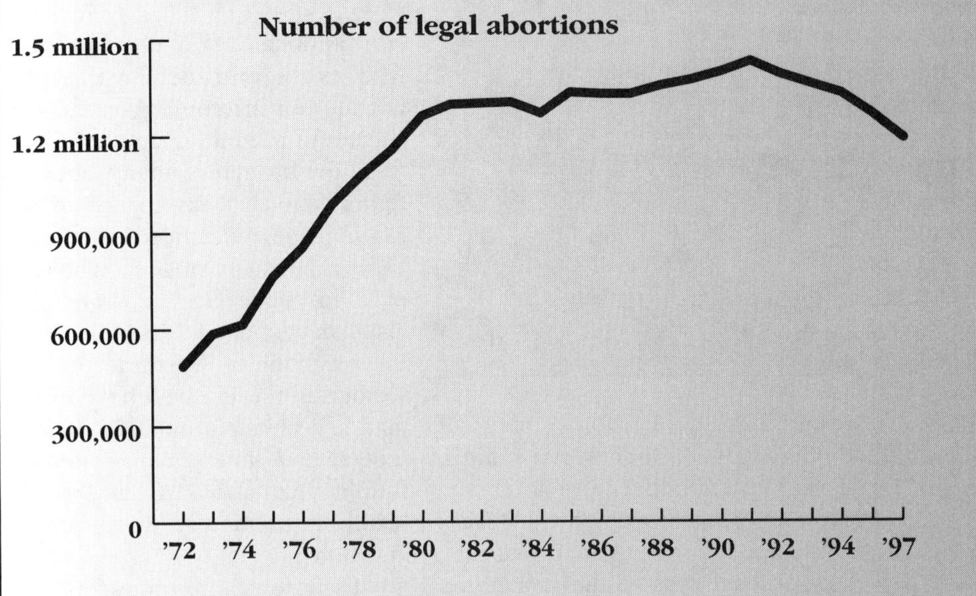

Source: U.S. Centers for Disease Control and Prevention, "Abortion Surveillance: United States, 1993 and 1994," Morbidity and Mortality Weekly Report, *Aug. 8, 1997*

• counseling stressing the disadvantages of abortions;

• requirements that minors notify their parents or receive their consent before obtaining an abortion;

• prohibitions on providing abortions to low-income women at public facilities; and

• restrictions on private or public-employee insurance coverage.

Michelman said the restrictions often force women to delay their abortions until later in pregnancy, increasing the potential health risks. Mississippi, for example, requires girls under 18 to obtain the written consent of both parents before obtaining an abortion.

"We're seeing an increase of second trimester procedures because young women are delaying telling their parents," said Hill, who opened a clinic in Jackson, Miss. seven years ago.

The number of hospitals, clinics and physicians' offices offering abortions decreased 14 percent between 1992 and 1996, according to AGI. One reason is a steep decline in ob-gyn residency programs that provide training in abortion, says the National Abortion Federation (NAF), which sponsors education programs for abortion providers.*

Another reason is harassment of abortion clinics and doctors, which represents an ongoing problem, abortion providers say. Since 1994, one doctor has been murdered and four others have been shot in the United States and Canada; a clinic escort and three clinic employees have been murdered, according to NARAL. "Many women have to travel out of state because abortion providers have declined in number due to intimidation and violence directed at them and their families," Michelman said.

Judging by the absence of arrests this year, blockades at clinics by anti-abortion activists and some other forms of harassment actually have decreased since anti-abortion demonstrations peaked in the early 1990s. There were no bombings and only two arsons last year, compared to one bombing and eight arsons in 1999. Eleanor Smeal, president of the Feminist Majority Foundation, attributed the decline partly to the passage and tough enforcement of the 1994 Freedom of Access to Clinic Entrances Act (FACE), which imposes federal fines and prison terms for intimidating patients and workers at abortion clinics.

But it also appears that other kinds of harassment and surreptitious attacks have mounted. The NAF reported 9,509 arrests last year for harassing calls, hate mail, bomb threats and illegal picketing, which equals almost three times the number of arrests in 1992.[3]

Wins and Losses for the Right to Life Movement

The Right to Life movement has made other political gains since *Roe*, in addition to state laws restricting

*In 1996, the agency accrediting ob-gyn residency programs, the Accreditation Council for Graduate Medical Education, required ob-gyn residency programs to provide abortion training, but according to NAF, it is too soon to tell what effect it has had.

abortion. In 11 states, majorities of the Senate and House as well as the governor are firmly anti-abortion, according to NARAL, and would most likely pass a ban on abortion if *Roe v. Wade* were overturned. The movement's most notable recent victory was the election of a strongly anti-abortion president, George W. Bush. However, the movement was also dealt some important political setbacks in 2000 and 2001.

On June 29, 2000, the Supreme Court ruled that the government may not prohibit doctors from performing a procedure abortion opponents dubbed "partial-birth" abortion because it may be the most medically appropriate way of terminating some pregnancies. Although not a medical term, "partial-birth" abortion was coined by anti-abortion activists seeking to outlaw the late-term procedure known medically as dilation and extraction (D&X).* In striking down a Nebraska law banning the procedure, the Court ruled that the law violated constitutional rights in *Roe v. Wade*, the landmark decision that guaranteed women's right to choose abortion 28 years ago. The anti-abortion movement had provided grisly descriptions of the procedure as a way of building public support for a ban. The 5–4 decision in *Stenberg v. Carhart* undermined that strategy. It rendered similar bans in 30 states unconstitutional and unenforceable. It also took the steam out of efforts by anti-abortion forces in Congress to pass a federal ban.[4]

On Sept. 28, 2000, the U.S. Food and Drug Administration (FDA) approved the use of the abortion bill mifepristone after more than ten years of political pressure by abortion opponents to block its use in the United States. During last year's election campaign, then-governor George W. Bush had called the FDA decision to approve the pill, known abroad as RU-486, "wrong," adding "I fear that making this abortion pill widespread will make abortions more and more common rather than more and more rare."[5] Bush's statement had given anti-abortion forces hope that he might reverse the FDA decision. However, those hopes were dashed in June when Secretary of Health and Human Services Tommy Thompson said the administration had no plans to review the drug's approval. "Nobody has written to me asking me to review it on any safety concerns," he said.[6] The administrations inaction also took momentum away from a legislative effort in Congress led by Sen. Tim Hutchinson, R-Ak, to limit the kinds of doctors who could prescribe the abortion pill.

Abortion-rights supporters in Boston protest violence at abortion clinics on the 22nd anniversary of Roe v. Wade *in January 1995.*

On Aug. 9, 2001, President Bush announced that he would permit federally funded research on stem cells from embryos that had already been destroyed. While the National Right to Life Committee, a leading anti-abortion organization, "commended" the decision for limiting the research to embryos already destroyed, other anti-abortion groups, including those representing America's Catholic Bishops, condemned it for undermining the concept that life begins at conception.[7] The implications of this decision for the abortion debate are primarily philosophical questions over when life begins, but some pro-choice activists fear it could spill over into legislation aimed at curbing abortion by inserting earlier definitions of when human life begins into current law. The decision could also have political implications for President Bush. Some political observers suggest that by moving slightly to the left on this issue and alienating some anti-abortion mem-

*The D&X procedure is one of several late-term abortion procedures. Others include a conventional dilation and evacuation (D&E) and induction, where labor is induced.

Experts Try to Explain Declining Abortion Rate

In 1990, for the first time since the Supreme Court's *Roe v. Wade* decision in 1973, the number of abortions began going down, according to government statistics.[1] By 1997—the most recent year for which statistics are available—the number of abortions in the United States declined to its lowest level since 1978.[2] And the percentage of pregnancies ending in abortion is also at its lowest point in 20 years.[3]

Experts point to a number of factors to explain the decline. As baby boomers age, they say, the age distribution of the female population is shifting toward the less fertile years.

It is also possible that Americans are getting better at using contraception, noted Lisa M. Koonin, an epidemiologist at the federal Centers for Disease Control and Prevention (CDC). In 1995 only 31 percent of all births were unintended, according to government surveys, compared with more than 40 percent in the 1980s.

As might be expected, abortions increased rapidly after the procedure became legal in 1973. Abortion rates were stable during the 1980s. Since 1990, both birth rates and abortion rates have declined, with abortion rates declining faster.

The concern that most abortions are employed in place of birth control appears to be unfounded, although an abortion often follows a contraceptive failure. A recent study by the Alan Guttmacher Institute in New York found that of women who had abortions in 1994 and 1995, 58 percent were using a contraceptive method in the month they became pregnant, compared with 51 percent in 1987.[4]

Among teenagers, abortions also have been declining since the beginning of the 1990s. However, this recent encouraging development follows a much longer period—between 1972 and 1990—when the teen pregnancy rate rose and a growing proportion of pregnancies occurred outside of marriage. The vast majority of teen pregnancies are unintended, and approximately one-third end in abortion, according to the National Campaign to Prevent Teen Pregnancy.[5]

Among African-American teens, the birth rate in 1996 plummeted 21 percent, compared with a 12 percent drop in the birth rate among teens overall. But the explanation does not seem to be that teenagers are getting more abortions. The percentage of live births ending in abortion for 15- to 19-year-olds was the lowest that the CDC had ever recorded for that age group, as reflected in 1995 data.[6]

The recent decreases in the teen birth rates reflect a leveling off of teen sexual activity and a growing number of teens using contraception effectively, according to the pregnancy prevention campaign and government surveys.[7]

Increased use of condoms in an age of heightened awareness about AIDS may be affecting the declining pregnancy and abortion rates, particularly among 18- to 19-year-olds, said Susan Tew, a spokesperson for the Alan Guttmacher Institute. "Introduction of new methods of birth control are very effective," she said, pointing to the injectables Norplant and DepoProvera. Approximately 15 percent of 15- to 17-year-olds were using DepoProvera in 1995, according to the institute.

Other factors that could be contributing to declining abortions are dwindling numbers of providers and a shift toward negative social attitudes about abortion, experts say.

Nonetheless, noted Tamara Kreinin, director of state and local affairs for the pregnancy prevention campaign, "U.S. rates of teen pregnancy are still twice as high as Great Britain and 10-15 times that of Japan and the Netherlands." As more unmarried teens give birth and keep their children, she added, "That's a strong cause for concern because it perpetuates the cycle of poverty."

---

[1] Lisa M. Koonin et al., "Abortion Surveillance—United States, 1997," *Morbidity and Mortality Weekly Report,* December 8, 2000, pp. 1–44.

[2] Centers for Disease Control, "Fact Sheet: Abortion Surveillance—United States, 1997." www.cdc.gov.

[3] Stanley K. Henshaw, "Abortion Incidence and Services in the United States, 1995-1996," *Family Planning Perspectives,* November–December, 1998, pp. 263–170 and 287.

[4] Stanley K. Henshaw and Kathryn Kost, "Abortion Patients in 1994–1995: Characteristics and Contraceptive Use," *Family Planning Perspectives,* July/August 1996, p. 140.

[5] National Campaign to Prevent Teen Pregnancy, *Whatever Happened to Childhood?*

[6] Sheryl Gay Stolberg, "U.S. Life Expectancy Hits New High," *The New York Times,* Sept. 12, 1997, p. A14; Koonin, op. cit.

[7] See Health and Human Services Department News Release, May 1, 1997. The percentage of teens who have had sexual intercourse declined for the first time after increasing steadily for more than two decades. The 1995 National Survey of Family Growth found that 50 percent of girls 15–19 had had intercourse, compared with 55 percent in 1990.

---

bers of his core constituency, Bush may feel pressure to stick more rigidly to the anti-abortion position on other related topics.

In 2001, the leadership of the Senate shifted from Republican to Democratic hands, making it extremely unlikely that the Senate leadership would schedule votes on bills pushed by conservative anti-abortion forces. This could mean the death knell, for example, to the House-passed Unborn Victims of Violence Act, which would establish criminal penalties for harming a human fetus during the commission of a federal offense against a woman. Supporters called the bill a way to ensure that a criminal who attacks a pregnant woman is charged with murder or manslaughter if the woman survives but her fetus perishes. Opponents called it a thinly disguised effort to undermine abortion rights by granting a new legal protection to a fetus.[8]

Political Implications

"The anti-abortion forces have been robbed of their most potent issues," Susan Cohen, deputy director for government affairs at the Alan Guttmacher Institute, said in a phone interview in August. She cited the recent Supreme Court decision on late-term abortions and the Bush administration's lack of interest in overturning approval of the abortion pill mifepristone.

At the same time, however, prochoice forces were sobered by the surprisingly slim majority for the Supreme Court decision in *Stenberg v. Carhart.* Until that decision, support for the underlying right to abortion had been counted as 6–3. The major surprise was the dissenting opinion of Justice Anthony M. Kennedy.

"Clearly the margin for any meaningful access to abortion is slim," said Cohen. "The retirement of one justice from the five-vote majority could have radical implications." A change in the composition of the Supreme Court could also mean a return to the legislative arena of the moribund but emotional issue of late-term abortion, she predicted. With a change of one vote, NARAL warns, Nebraska and the 30 other states that passed often vaguely worded bans on abortions could enact laws to eliminate second trimester abortions and could discourage doctors from offering services for fear of criminal prosecution. A shift in two votes "could allow state legislatures to end legal abortion" entirely, NARAL predicts.[9]

As the 25th anniversary of *Roe v. Wade* approaches, these are some of the issues being debated in state legislatures, Congress and the courts.

Will* Roe v. Wade *eventually be overturned?

Experts on both sides of the abortion issue agree that the right to abortion established by *Roe* is unlikely to be overturned in the foreseeable future. "I would agree *Roe v. Wade* will not be overturned in the near future, but we've seen a chipping away of reproductive rights that will leave nothing left to overturn," Monica Hobbs, federal legislative counsel for the Center for Reproductive Law and Policy in Washington, D.C., said in an August interview. The Center represented the Nebraska doctor who successfully challenged Nebraska's ban on late-term abortions in the landmark *Stenberg v. Carhart* case before the Supreme Court last year.

As examples of "chipping away" Hobbs cited laws in close to 30 states that prosecute criminals for hurting a fetus if they attack a pregnant woman. Some of these laws redefine a fetus as a human being. She also cited so-called "trap laws" in 16 states that impose regulations on the physical facilities of abortion providers "to make it more expensive for abortion providers to be in the business of providing abortions."

"Even with a change of personnel on the Supreme Court, it would be questionable whether the court would be willing to take [*Roe*] up again," said Douglas Kmiec, a conservative professor of constitutional law at the University of Notre Dame. "Dissenting members of the court are quite frustrated [with the current situation], but I don't think they will pursue reexamination of the right [to an abortion] any time soon." Kmiec added, "The court is uneasy with its abortion decisions" and "is going to stay silent and let the states work it out through the political process."

Emory Law School historian David J. Garrow, author of *A History of the* Roe *Decision*, was even more emphatic.[10]

"*Roe* will never be overturned," Garrow said. He pointed to the plurality opinion by Justices Sandra Day O'Connor, Anthony M. Kennedy and David H. Souter in the landmark 1992 case *Planned Parenthood v. Casey**. The court decided the case on a 5–4 vote, but the three moderately conservative justices surprised conventional wisdom by supporting the essential holding of *Roe v. Wade.* Their opinion reaffirmed "the right of a woman to choose to have an abortion" before a fetus can live outside the womb "and to obtain it without undue interference from the State."

Garrow said the opinion in *Casey* was less about abortion than about the stature of the Supreme Court in standing by its earlier, influential decision. "For the court to consider reversing *Roe* and *Casey* [in the future] would be the equivalent of reversing *Brown v. Board of Education* [outlawing school desegregation.] *Roe's* weight in history is such that it's impregnable," he said.

However, some prominent abortion-rights activists argue that the fundamental right of abortion in *Roe* has been severely undermined by subsequent court decisions, including *Casey*, and by mounting state legislative restrictions.

In *Casey*, the Supreme Court considered the constitutionality of several provisions of a Pennsylvania state statute that have since been widely adopted by other states. The provisions required include the following: "informed-consent" information prescribed by the state (such as information about the gestational age of the fetus and the risks of abortion) to be given the woman by the doctor; a mandatory 24-hour waiting period before undergoing an abortion; and, pregnant girls under 18 to obtain the permission of a court or the consent of one parent. Most controversial of all was a provision that a married woman could not obtain an abortion unless she first signed a statement

*A plurality opinion results when there is not a majority opinion.

Abortion Rights and Restrictions in the States

More than half the states impose at least one restriction on minors' abortions. Public funding for most abortions is restricted in 31 states.

States	Require parental involvement in minors' abortion decisions	Require mandatory delay following state-directed counseling	Require state-directed counseling without mandatory delay	Restrict private and/or public-employee insurance coverage	Restrict state funding for Medicaid recipients to life, rape or incest	Restrict abortion after viability or a specified point in pregnancy
Alabama	✓				✓	✓
Alaska			✓			
Arizona						✓
Arkansas	✓				✓	✓
California			✓			✓
Colorado				✓	✓	
Connecticut			✓			✓
Delaware	✓				✓	✓
Florida					✓	✓
Georgia	✓				✓	✓
Hawaii						
Idaho	✓	✓		✓		✓
Illinois				✓		✓
Indiana	✓	✓				✓
Iowa	✓				✓	✓
Kansas	✓	✓			✓	✓
Kentucky	✓	✓		✓	✓	✓
Louisiana	✓	✓			✓	✓
Maine			✓		✓	✓
Maryland	✓					✓
Massachusetts	✓			✓		✓
Michigan	✓	✓			✓	✓
Minnesota	✓		✓			✓
Mississippi	✓	✓			✓	
Missouri	✓			✓	✓	✓
Montana						✓
Nebraska	✓	✓		✓	✓	✓
Nevada			✓		✓	✓
New Hampshire					✓	
New Jersey						
New Mexico						
New York						✓
North Carolina	✓				✓	✓
North Dakota	✓	✓		✓	✓	✓
Ohio	✓	✓		✓	✓	✓
Oklahoma	✓				✓	✓
Oregon						
Pennsylvania	✓	✓		✓	✓	✓
Rhode Island	✓		✓	✓	✓	✓
South Carolina	✓	✓			✓	✓
South Dakota	✓	✓			✓	✓
Tennessee	✓				✓	✓
Texas	✓				✓	✓
Utah	✓	✓			✓	✓
Vermont						
Virginia	✓		✓	✓	✓	✓
Washington						✓
West Virginia	✓					
Wisconsin	✓	✓			✓	✓
Wyoming	✓				✓	✓

Source: Alan Guttmacher Institute.

attesting that she had notified her husband of her intended abortion. (The statute provided a narrow medical emergency exception to the restrictions.)

Unlike *Roe*, which barred states from interfering in virtually all abortions before the fetus was viable, *Casey* said the state could impose restrictions at that stage as long as they did not impose "an undue burden" on the woman seeking the abortion. In the view of Harvard University constitutional law expert Laurence H. Tribe, *Casey* is "a watered-down version of *Roe*" because of the new "undue burden" standard. *Casey* invalidated Pennsylvania's spousal-notification provision but upheld the other provisions.[11]

"They said you can burden women seeking abortion as long as it's not an 'undue burden' — and we're not sure to this day what that means," said Janet Benshoof, president of the Center for Reproductive Law and Policy. She views *Casey* as "part of a systematic political campaign to undermine *Roe v. Wade* that's been largely successful." She estimated there are now more than 100 state statutes restricting pregnant women and doctors that would not have been constitutional when *Roe* was decided in 1973.

"Over the last 25 years there has been a systematic assault on the right to abortion that weakened judicial resolve," Benshoof said. "The appointments on the Supreme Court for the 12 years of [the Reagan and Bush administrations] have served to weaken reproductive privacy." She pointed to decisions that said poor women were not entitled to government-funded abortions and that minors can be subject to restrictions on abortion (see *Background, p. 300*).

But Garrow, who has been studying how federal judges apply the undue burden test, said judges have used *Casey* to bolster abortion rights in some states. He noted in Indiana, for example, lower courts have applied the undue burden test and struck down the requirement that a woman make two in-person visits to an abortion clinic. At the same time, he added, "What a federal district judge in Indianapolis is willing to do is different from what a federal judge is willing to do in New Orleans."

Some leaders of the Right to Life movement said they're confident the Supreme Court will eventually overturn *Roe* because they believe its basis, a constitutional right to privacy, is weak. Helen Alvare, a spokeswoman for the National Conference of Catholic Bishops, estimated it would be at least a decade before the decision is overturned, however.

"[Regulation of abortion] will be handed back to the states," she predicted. "The social climate is very clearly sending the message that abortion has not been healthy for us. I never thought 20 years ago we would come to a time when people were incredibly worried about the rate of out-of-wedlock pregnancies, premartial sex, breakdown of the family. I don't think these problems will go away unless one of the fundamental problems is solved — the idea of a right that could allow abortion to be legal."

Kmiec of Notre Dame agreed with some abortion-rights lawyers that "*Roe* has been at least partially overturned by *Casey*" because it "reformulated the right to an abortion from a fundamental interest to one less than fundamental and capable of at least some litigated forms of regulation."

Even the toughest state laws, however, may not have deterred women from getting abortions. Some 23 states call for waiting periods or require doctors to give the pregnant woman prescribed information about abortions, including the risks.

"Most often," said Gloria Feldt, president of Planned Parenthood of America, such restrictions "make it more expensive, more pain- and shame-filled for women and result in abortions being performed at later dates in pregnancy."

A recent study found that Mississippi's 1992 law requiring abortion counseling followed by a 24-hour waiting period had led to a decline in abortions in the state. But in the year after the law went into effect, Mississippi women were more likely to get out-of-state abortions and to have them later in pregnancy, according to a recent study, especially as compared with women in neighboring states without the restriction. Total abortions in Mississippi declined by 16 percent during the year studied, but the researchers found no significant increase in the birth rate, according to the study published in the *Journal of the American Medical Association*.[12] Under the Mississippi law, the physician must describe the medical risks associated with abortion, inform the woman that medical assistance benefits may be available for prenatal care and that the father is liable for child support. In practice, because of the 24-hour waiting period, the law requires women in Mississippi to pay two visits to an abortion provider.

For poor women in some states, mandatory waiting periods often set up a no-win, "Catch-22" situation. Because they have trouble coming up with the money for an abortion, they often delay past the point where the clinic can legally do an abortion. By then the woman needs a later-term abortion, which costs still more.

"We've seen women sleeping in cars because there's not enough money to get a hotel room," said Hill, describing how some women from the Mississippi Delta coped with coming twice to her Jackson clinic. "It's just a general insult to them that the state thinks they need another 24 hours to think about it."

Will the expanded use of non-surgical abortion defuse the abortion controversy?

When the FDA last year approved the abortion pill known around the world as RU-486, pro-choice activists had high hopes that its availability would defuse the abortion controversy. Many of them had hoped it would permit women to take the pill in the privacy of a doctor's office rather than at abortion clinics, where women faced harassment and doctors faced threats from anti-abortion demonstrators.

The verdict is still out. A few months after the FDA announced its approval, many private doctors said they still had no plans to offer the pill to their patients, according to *The New York Times*. Many said they would advise their patents to choose a surgical abortion instead because they think surgery is a better method.[13]

In August, Richard Hausknecht, medical director for Danco Laboratories—the company that distributes the drug known as mifepristone under the trade name Mifeprex—could not give figures on how many women had taken the drug so far, nor how many physicians had prescribed it. (Hausknecht said sales information was proprietary. But he added it was difficult for Danco to tell how many women are taking the pill, since some doctors are prescribing less than the FDA's recommended dose, and may be dividing the standard pill package among more than one patient.)

Reuters/Vidal Medina

Anti-abortion protester confronts abortion supporters behind the White House on the 22nd anniversary of the Roe v. Wade *decision in January 1995.*

In international studies, women who chose the abortion pill said they preferred it over a medical abortion because it was more private, less invasive and more natural. Abortion with RU-486 has been described as similar to a miscarriage.[14]

Mifepristone, a synthetic steroid, works by blocking the hormone progesterone, which prepares the lining of the uterus for implantation of a fertilized egg. Without progesterone, the lining of the uterus breaks down during menstruation and a fertilized egg attached to the lining is dislodged from the side of the uterus and expelled.

A few days after taking mifepristone, a second drug, misoprostol, is taken in the form of a pill or suppository. It causes the uterus to contract and empty, completing the abortion.

One of the advantages of an abortion induced with a medication like mifepristone is that it can be performed as soon as a pregnancy is confirmed — but usually no later than about seven weeks. By contrast, women usually must wait until they are six or eight weeks pregnant to have a surgical abortion.

Debate Shifts to Side-effects, Limits on Prescribing Doctors

After 10 years of trying to block RU-486 from the U.S. market and failing, anti-abortion opponents have shifted their tactics to suggesting the pill has dangerous side-effects.

In Congress, Sen. Tim Hutchinson, R-Ak, and Rep. David Vitter, R-La., introduced the Patient Health and Safety Protection Act in February 2001 aimed at limiting physicians who can prescribe Mifeprex. Hutchinson said the purpose of the bill is "to ensure the health and safety of women who are prescribed RU-486." But abortion rights activists say the bill is designed to impede women's access to the pill.

Under the bill, physicians who prescribe Mifeprex would have to meet four conditions: they must be trained to perform surgical abortions, certified in ultrasound pregnancy dating and detection of ectopic (outside the uterus) pregnancy, trained to administer Mifeprex through a government-approved program and have admitting privileges at a hospital within one hour of their office.

The clinical trials uncovered no serious side effects of the drug, beyond heavy bleeding and nausea. But its supposedly deleterious health effects have become a rallying cry for opponents of medical abortion. Introducing the House version of the bill earlier this year, Rep. Vitter declared that approval of Mifeprex "will not only increase the number of abortions performed each year, it will create serious and potentially dangerous side effects for women using the drug. The least we can do is ensure that this drug does not endanger the life of the mother."[15]

In the same vein, the National Right to Life Committee maintains a statement on its web site stating that the pill poses dangers because one woman participating in the clinical trials nearly bled to death.

"There have been no serious complications," Danco's Hausknecht responded in an August interview, noting that any complications must be reported to both Danco and the FDA. He added that so far the only complications have been those reported in clinical trials, such as heavy bleeding, nausea and in some cases the need to do a surgical abortion if the pill does not succeed in completing the abortion. (Based on the clinical trial in this country, 92 percent of women experienced a complete abortion with the pill.)

According to an article published by the Alan Guttmacher Institute, the FDA reportedly considered the kinds of restrictions proposed by opponents Hutchinson and Vitter, but rejected them as medically unjustified. Instead, the agency required Danco to agree not to distribute Mifeprex to pharmacies but only to physicians who certify in advance that they have the necessary knowledge and skills to prescribe the drug appropriately and provide patients detailed information.[16]

Pro-choice supporters of the bill point out that the pill has been approved in 22 countries since 1988 and state that more than 650,000 women in Europe alone have taken it safely. As in other areas of standard medical practice, they argue, a doctor who prescribes the pill can always refer the patient to another doctor for surgical services if needed.

As for the argument that Mifeprex would lead to more abortions, the rate of abortion in England, France and Sweden actually declined during the 1990s when medical abortion was introduced in those countries, according to a report published by the Alan Guttmacher Institute's *Family Planning Perspectives* in 1999.[17]

Underlying Debate: is Abortion with a Pill Any Different?

The underlying debate over RU-486 has revolved around the question of whether a very early abortion by pill is any less objectionable than a surgical abortion later in pregnancy—both from the point of view of the woman involved and the American public. On the 25th anniversary of *Roe v. Wade*, 61 percent of respondents to a New York Times/CBS News poll in the United States said they thought abortion should be permitted during the first three months of pregnancy, but support dwindled for abortions performed later in pregnancy.[18]

In 1997, Smeal of the Feminist Majority said the ability to use a medication-induced abortion, also known as a medical abortion, very early in pregnancy is one of its major advantages — both for the women using it and for defusing the national debate.

"If the way most abortions are performed is you take a pill and have a heavier period, it changes the whole debate," Smeal said. At such an embryonic stage of pregnancy, Smeal argued, it would be harder for the anti-abortion movement to draw a parallel to "baby-killing" than with surgical abortions, in which a fetus is physically removed.

"It would encourage more early abortions," Smeal said. "It would make more women check [whether they are pregnant] right away. We think half of all abortions would be done this way."

Even before FDA approval of RU-486, however, anti-abortion demonstrators had not spared medical abortions from their ire. Planned Parenthood clinics participating in clinical trials of another medical abortion drug, methotrexate, had been specifically targeted by anti-abortion demonstrators, noted Feldt. Eric A. Schaff, an associate professor of daily medicine and pediatrics at the University of Rochester who has conducted clinical trials on both drugs, said his clinics had been picketed "pretty regularly" and that he had been harassed at home.

Smeal predicted that a large number of doctors would offer medical abortions once they could offer them in the privacy of their offices. Some surveys have suggested that more doctors would offer abortion if it were available via medication. "You will have so many more facilities that the opposition will no longer have just a few targets," Smeal said. Anti-abortion activists, she added, know "it will create more access and help defuse the debate."

But anti-abortion activist Alvare said Smeal's prediction of a defused debate is "a wish that will go unfulfilled." She noted that under the protocol prepared by the Population Council for Food and Drug Administration (FDA) review, an RU-486 abortion would require more visits to the doctor — at least three — than a surgical abortion. "I don't see how that will make it more private," Alvare said. "I don't see how leaving a dead unborn at the clinic makes it a happier situation for women. Women who've had a medical abortion will often say it's a more awful psychological experience."

Similarly, Alvare said, "the idea that you will persuade a bunch more doctors to involve themselves in abortion if you make it medical as opposed to surgical is a pipe dream." She contended the number of doctors performing abortions has been declining because they do not view the procedure as mainstream medicine.

Is Three Visits Too Many?

For several years, women's health activists have questioned why women must make multiple visits to a clinic for an abortion pill that was originally touted as a way to make the procedure a private one.

The FDA gave its final approval for mifepristone based on the three-visit regimen used in the clinical trials in this country. Under that regimen, women must make two separate visits to receive medication — one for mifepristone and a subsequent visit to take misoprostol. On the second visit the woman is to remain under observation at the clinic for four hours. The majority of women abort during this four-hour period. A third and usually final visit is to ensure the abortion is complete.

Schaff said the three-visit requirement was designed for "political reasons; it's not necessarily for medical reasons." Surveys in the United States and other countries indicate women would choose in-home self-administration of an abortion drug if given a choice, and that they can do so safely. In a 1999 study reported in *Contraception* of women who used vaginal misoprostol at home, no significant complications occurred.[19]

With these medical findings in mind, most medical abortion providers, including Planned Parenthood, have begun to provide women such choices as a lower dose of mifepristone or the option of taking misoprostol at home. Such modifications are allowed, since the FDA left administration to the discretion of individual physicians.[20]

Because of the long delay in getting mifepristone to market, much attention in the late 1990s focused on methotrexate, a medication that had already been approved by the FDA for treating some cancers. Any drug that has FDA approval for a particular use can be used to treat other conditions, so doctors can legally use methotrexate "off-label" for abortion in combination with misoprostol; however, it is not very widely administered for abortions, according to Schaff. The drug, given in the form of an injection, works by stopping development of the placenta or the embryo because it prevents cells from dividing and multiplying.

One of the advantages of methotrexate over mifepristone is that it is effective in aborting early ectopic pregnancies. However, with methotrexate an abortion can take significantly longer—up to a week for complete expulsion. In addition, because methotrexate is an anti-cancer agent and theoretically toxic to cells, it could cause multiple side effects, Schaff said. Nevertheless, in studies so far the side effects women complain of are similar to those with mifepristone, such as abdominal cramping and vaginal bleeding. According to Planned Parenthood, more than 3,000 women have used the drug for early abortion in clinical trials and doctors' offices, and there have been no reports of significant side effects or long-term risks.

"It's a good thing methotrexate is available now," Waldman said in 1997, "but when mifepristone gets on the market, there won't be real competition."

Would a ban on late-term abortions lead to bans on all abortions?

On June 29, 2000, the Supreme Court declared Nebraska's law banning "partial-birth" abortions unconstitutional, thus rendering all of the similar bans in 30 other states unenforceable.

However, because of the razor-thin majority of 5–4 in the decision known as *Stenberg v. Carhart*, both sides caution that the issue could be revived if the composition of the court were to change to an anti-abortion majority. In a Fox News Network interview January 18, newly-elected President Bush said he would not rule out having his Justice Department argue for a change in abortion law. The National Right to Life Committee posts this interview on its web site, commenting "Hopefully, any such re-examination would begin with review of last summer's disastrous 5–4 ruling [in *Stenberg v. Carhart*] that *Roe v. Wade* protects even the brutal practice of partial-birth abortion."[21]

At the height of the debate over late-term abortion, pro-choice forces argued that the state laws outlawing the method were so broadly worded that they could outlaw all abortions. But they also recognized that anti-abortion forces had found an issue that attracted broad public concern by describing a procedure that repelled even some of those who supported *Roe v. Wade.*

In 1997, Planned Parenthood president Gloria Feldt said, "The fact is that anti-choice extremists realize there is no public support for a constitutional amendment to ban abortion, so they don't even try that. Instead they have put forth this legislation that falsely maligns the health record of abortion and tries to make the debate around surgical techniques instead of debating the morality of making choice available to women."

"It's no secret that the Right to Life movement favors the restoration of the rights of unborn children," responded Johnson of the NRLC. But he added, "People who thought they agreed with *Roe* recoil in horror at

Chronology

19th Century

Doctors' campaign leads to laws banning abortion except to save the life of a woman.

1821
First U.S. abortion bill, passed in Connecticut, prohibits inducement of abortion with poison.

1859
American Medical Association (AMA) launches campaign to outlaw abortions, prompting more than 40 state anti-abortion laws.

— • —

1960s

Support grows for movement to liberalize abortion laws in states.

1967
AMA issues statement favoring liberalization of abortion laws.

— • —

1970s

Abortion is legalized; Supreme Court strikes down some state restrictions.

1970
Hawaii becomes the first state to repeal its criminal abortion law; New York state passes law legalizing abortion.

Jan. 22, 1973
Supreme Court hands down *Roe v. Wade* ruling, recognizing a woman's right to abortion as a "fundamental right," and striking down all state laws banning abortion.

1976
Supreme Court strikes down provisions of Missouri law giving veto power over abortion to husbands and parents in *Planned Parenthood v. Danforth.*

1977
In *Maher v. Roe,* the Supreme Court upholds Connecticut law permitting state Medicaid assistance only for "medically necessary" abortions.

— • —

1980s

President Ronald Reagan appoints three new conservative Supreme Court justices, which leads to rulings favorable to state restrictions on abortion.

1980
In *Harris v. McRae,* the Supreme Court upholds the congressional Hyde amendment, denying federal Medicaid funding even for medically necessary abortions.

1983
In *Akron v. Akron Center for Reproductive Choice,* the Supreme Court strikes down an Ohio law requiring a doctor to inform a woman seeking an abortion that a fetus is a human life from moment of conception.

1989
In *Webster v. Reproductive Health Services,* the Supreme Court upholds Missouri bans on the use of public facilities or public employees to perform abortions.

1990s

Supreme Court upholds* Roe *but gives states more leeway to restrict abortions. Anti-abortion forces win congressional victories in efforts to ban "partial-birth abortions," but the bill is vetoed twice by President Clinton.

1992
In *Planned Parenthood v. Casey,* the conservative-dominated court rules that states may restrict abortion as long as the regulations do not place an "undue burden" on the woman.

1994
In *Madsen v. Women's Center Inc.,* the Supreme Court says judges can create buffer zones to keep anti-abortion protesters away from abortion clinics.

Dec. 7, 1995
Senate passes its first ban on partial-birth abortions.

Sept. 26, 1996
Senate sustains President Clinton's veto of the partial-birth abortion ban.

Oct. 10, 1997
President Clinton vetoes second bill banning late-term abortions.

2000s

President George W. Bush, an outspoken opponent of abortion, is elected. Supreme Court strikes down ban on "partial-birth" abortion.

June 28, 2000
In *Stenberg v. Carhart,* Supreme Court strikes down Nebraska's "partial-birth" abortion ban, chilling state and Congressional efforts to ban abortion procedures.

Group Links Abortion Opponents in Debate

Can abortion rights and anti-abortion activists reach common ground on the divisive issue of abortion? Common Ground Network for Life and Choice, a national group based in Washington, D.C., thinks so. In a dozen cities around the nation, it has been gathering small groups of activists from opposite sides of the barricades to hold regular discussions about areas of possible agreement.

In a discussion in 1996, members of the local Washington, D.C., chapter generally agreed that anti-abortion demonstrations at clinics should be non-violent. Participants spoke surprisingly openly about aspects of their own activism that made them uncomfortable.[1]

John Cavanaugh-O'Keefe, a member of the anti-abortion group American Life Federation, described his participation in picketing the home of an abortion doctor. "I really feel mixed about it," he said. "One of the questions for us was, 'Can we pick a time when we know his kids won't be there?'"

Mary Haggerty said she had participated in an Operation Rescue demonstration outside an abortion clinic because "I saw what was going on outside the clinic to be a lesser form of violence than what was going on inside." But she said she became disenchanted with Operation Rescue's approach after demonstrators gave police a hard time.

Liz Joyce, an abortion-rights participant, questioned whether a woman about to enter an abortion clinic would perceive anti-abortion demonstrators who confronted her there as genuinely concerned about her and her ability to bring up a child.

Participants from both factions say one of the benefits of the D.C. discussion group, which meets every other month, is that it breaks down monolithic stereotypes each side has of the other.

Anti-abortion columnist Frederica Mathewes-Green says she joined Common Ground because she was frustrated by the distrust of abortion clinic staffers, whom she approached for information in the course of writing her 1997 book *Real Choices: Listening to Women, Looking for Alternatives to Abortion*.

She points out that anti-abortion members don't always agree on tactics. Of demonstrations outside doctors' homes, Mathewes-Green said, "I couldn't stand that. That sounds awful to me." There are also differences among abortion-rights members. "You see these distinctions and realize these are human beings thinking carefully, not just a faceless organization steam-rolling in one direction," she says.

One of the ground rules for group members, each of whom participates in a one-day mediation training session, is that individuals are not expected to change their minds on the fundamental issues, but are expected to change their stereotypes of people on the other side.

Jillaine Smith, a senior associate at a Washington, D.C., foundation, has marched for abortion rights, written letters, made phone calls and voted on behalf of the "pro-choice" cause. She said she thinks there are too many abortions but is opposed to legislating against them.

"I keep going [to the discussion group] because I really like the dialogue. I'm very moved by the sharing and listening that happens," Smith says. "While it hasn't changed any of my activism or my mind about my stance," Smith says, she's less apt to react angrily when she sees anti-abortion rallies on the news and more likely to be curious about the demonstrators' beliefs.

According to Mary Jacksteit, director of the national Common Ground organization, preventing teen pregnancy and encouraging adoption are two goals both sides tend to share. The organization has produced white papers on both topics.

But some abortion-rights activists fear that Common Ground's efforts will result inevitably in a victory for unyielding anti-abortion forces. Feminist Katha Pollitt charged last year that "when talking together becomes working together, the pro-choice people play a dangerous game, lending support to proposals that are both ineffectual and contrary to their own values." She cited the example of the Norfolk, Va., Common Ground chapter, where pro-choice participants supported a sex education program promoting sexual abstinence. Since abortion opponents also opposed birth control, she charged, the only common ground was an ineffective abstinence-only program, rather than comprehensive sex education. [2]

"We're not trying to arrive at a position or force people behind one another," Jacksteit responds. Pollitt, Jacksteit says, is "incorrect in saying people who see some value in talking about common ground on teen pregnancy will be pushed into abstinence-only." But there may be additional, less controversial approaches to teen pregnancy prevention that both sides can agree upon, Jacksteit suggests, even as each camp pursues different approaches to sex education.

In Buffalo, for example, the Common Ground group supports after-school activities to promote teens' self-esteem, such as supper clubs for Hispanic girls, according to Jacksteit.

While the national political scene remains divisive, Jacksteit says she senses interest among citizens at the local level in working peacefully to solve problems like teen pregnancy. "There's a weariness with the political people and that kind of debate," she says, "and a feeling they're not able to see the issue as anything but simplistic black and white."

---

[1] Common Ground Network for Life and Choice, "Finding Common Ground," videotape of meeting held Oct. 26, 1996. On September 1, 1999, the Network became a co-sponsored effort of Search for Common Ground and the National Association for Community Mediation. See www.nafcm.org or www.sfcg.org.

[2] Katha Pollitt, "A Dangerous Game on Abortion," *The New York Times*, June 18, 1996, p. A23.

partial-birth abortion....That's one value of this debate—it's educated some segment of the public as to how extreme the law on abortion is today. Most Americans had no idea abortion was legal after 20 weeks, had no idea it was done routinely." (Approximately 1 percent of the abortions performed annually are conducted after 20 weeks.)

Most of the state bans define late-term abortion as an abortion in which the person performing the abortion "partially vaginally delivers a living fetus before killing the fetus and completing delivery."

However, as advocates of the statutory bans readily admitted, "partial-birth" abortion is a political term created by the Right to Life movement, not a medical term that can be found in a medical textbook or journal. No solid information exists on how often the procedure targeted by the drafters of the statutes is used, but it appears to be performed by only a few doctors.[22]

The movement's interest in the issue originated in 1993 when the NRLC obtained a paper delivered at a 1992 National Abortion Federation meeting, according to Johnson. In that paper Martin Haskell, an Ohio doctor, described an abortion procedure for which he coined the term dilation and extraction, or D&X. (The procedure is also sometimes referred to as Intact D&X.) As Haskell described it, the procedure involved puncturing the skull of a fetus, suctioning out the contents and removing the fetus intact through the cervix. Haskell said he had performed the procedure more than 700 times, generally for patients 20–26 weeks pregnant.[23]

"If you look at the procedure from an obstetrical point of view, there may be advantages to the woman," said ob-gyn Diana Dell, past president of the American Medical Women's Association (AMWA). "The primary complication when the fetus is not intact is from lacerations to the cervix." The procedure's advantages include less bleeding and tearing, according to the NAF. "This sounds like one guy's way to avoid lacerating the cervix. I think a very small number are performed," Dell said. "For late-term abortions, it's probably a safer procedure."

Under a ban passed by Congress but vetoed by President Clinton in 1997, a physician who performed a late-term abortion would have been subject to two years in prison and fines. The only exception would have been if the procedure were necessary to save the mother's life. The bill permitted the father, if married to the woman seeking a late-term abortion, to file a civil suit if the abortion was conducted without his consent. Parents of a woman under 18 would have had the same right.

In May 1997, the American Medical Association (AMA) endorsed the late-term abortion ban after the Senate adopted several minor changes. President-elect Nancy Dickey said that the group decided to support the legislation because the changes made it clear "that the accepted abortion procedure known as dilation and evacuation is not covered by the bill."[24]

"If you look at the scientific literature, there's no support for doing this procedure," Dickey said. "Experts will tell you it's virtually never done and there are alternative procedures to it."

In the end, she said, the AMA decided to support the ban with changes because the public found the procedure repugnant, there was no good support for why it was needed and "the legislation appeared to be moving forward."

Abortion-rights lawyer Eve Gartner of Planned Parenthood Federation said, however, that even the revised bill language could cover a wide range of accepted abortion procedures. The ban is opposed by the American Medical Women's Association (AMWA) and the American College of Obstetricians and Gynecologists (ACOG). In a statement issued on Jan. 12, 1997, ACOG said, "An intact D&X may be the best or most appropriate procedure in a particular circumstance to save the life or preserve the health of a woman."

Advocates of the ban say the procedure is conducted anywhere from 20 weeks to full term. NRLC's Johnson argues that under numerous state laws, a baby expelled spontaneously at 20 weeks would be a live birth protected under the law. "This [procedure] is akin to infanticide," he said.

Vicki Saporta, executive director of the NAF, said the ban's advocates have distorted the issue by displaying pictures of perfectly formed, close to full-term infants. In the third trimester, she said the procedure is "most often used when women discover they have babies that can't survive outside the womb. Over a dozen of these women have come forward to tell their stories. These are very difficult decisions for people to make and decisions that can only be made by these women in consultations with their physicians.

"If you describe any medical procedure in detail to a lay person, they're usually uncomfortable. That doesn't mean the procedure isn't safe or shouldn't be used."

But the AMA's Dickey said that according to abortion doctors the procedure is done with more frequency and in less dire circumstances than groups like NAF suggest. "It is a procedure used for elective abortion in late second and third trimester without any fetal anomalies," she said.[25]

Much of the confusion over the

"partial-birth" abortion ban comes from its frequent description in the news media as a form of "late-term" abortion. In fact, the congressional legislation did not specify when in pregnancy the procedure is performed or is prohibited.

According to lawyers who challenged similar bans in state courts, this may be the legislation's greatest constitutional weakness. Under *Roe v. Wade*, the Supreme Court said the state may not interfere in a woman's decision to have an abortion in the first trimester. In the second trimester, the ruling recognizes a state interest in protecting the health of the woman. States can, for example, pass laws requiring that abortions be performed by a doctor or licensed professional.

After the fetus is viable, which *Roe* places approximately at the beginning of the third trimester, the ruling says states can ban abortions, except when they are necessary to protect the life or health of the woman.

A related ruling defined health broadly to include the woman's psychological health. The Supreme Court's 1992 *Casey* ruling said states could impose restrictions on abortions before the fetus is viable as long as they did not impose an "undue burden" on the woman's ability to get an abortion.

Opponents of bans on late-term abortions argued they would be unconstitutional because they

- describe the procedure in such vague terms that it could apply to all abortions;
- fail to include an exception for the health of the mother after the fetus is viable;
- ban abortions before viability; and,
- impose an undue burden on women before viability.

For the most part, the Supreme Court accepted those arguments in declaring Nebraska's ban on partial-birth abortion—and thus all bans—unconstitutional in its 2000 *Stenberg v. Carhart* ruling. Under Nebraksa's law a doctor who performed a late-term abortion not necessary to save the woman's life faced a sentence of up to 20 years in prison. Nebraksa's attorney general, Don Stenberg, argued that the Nebraska state legislature meant to ban one specific procedure, known as D&X. But the Supreme Court majority said the statutory definition also applied to the procedure known as dilation and evacuation, or D&E, which is used much more commonly for abortions after the first trimester of pregnancy.

Justice Breyer in his decision said the court had to review the statute as written. As a result, Justice Breyer said, all doctors who use the D&E method "must fear prosecution, conviction and imprisonment," making the law an "undue burden upon a woman's right to make an abortion decision." The majority of the court also insisted that a more precisely written law would still be unconstitutional because it lacked an exception to protect the woman's health. Nebraska and other state laws had only an exception to save the life of the mother.[26]

"None of the partial-birth abortion statutes in the states or the one passed in Congress has a viability line, and they don't recognize the different constitutional standard" before and after viability, Benshoof said in 1997. "They apply throughout pregnancy." According to Benshoof, the anti-abortion movement was focusing on late abortion "as a political campaign and meanwhile drafting statutes that encompass much more. They're trying to eviscerate the concepts of viability and health — both of which are preeminent in *Roe v. Wade.*"

Advocates of the ban contend that the legislation covers a category of person not specifically addressed by *Roe* — those "who are in the process of being born." In its report on the bill, the House Judiciary Committee noted that in *Roe*, the Supreme Court cited a Texas statute prohibiting killing a child during the birth process that had not been challenged.[27]

"This baby is four-fifths across the line of personhood," Johnson argued. "The theory is that partial-birth abortion is completely outside the scope of *Roe v. Wade.*"

But Planned Parenthood's Gartner found that argument weak. "In any abortion procedure, you'll have some part of the fetus out of the uterus before other parts are out, and the fetus will be living at the beginning of the procedure and the procedure itself kills the fetus," she says. "They're defining abortion as birth. I don't think there's any legal or medical support for it."

Michael W. McConnell, a University of Utah law professor opposed to abortion and Bush's nominee for the 10th Circuit Court of Appeals, argued in 1997 that it would not be unconstitutional to outlaw "partial-birth" abortions because alternative abortion procedures exist. (NARAL has gone on record opposing McConnell's nomination because McConnell opposes *Roe v. Wade*. The abortion rights group notes that abortion decisions from the circuit courts often find their way to the Supreme Court and that circuit judges are often tapped to fill Supreme Court vacancies.[28]) "In the vast majority of cases, it would not put an undue burden on the woman to have this one grisly procedure eliminated," he argued.

In the final analysis, the debate over late-term abortion has more significance as a surrogate for the larger abortion debate than as an individual issue.

"You can see it as a chink in the armor of the pro-abortion crowd," McConnell said. "For the first time the American public has become aware of the realities of abortion, and

At Issue:

Can abortion-rights and anti-abortion groups reach common ground?

yes

Naomi Wolf
***Author of* The Beauty Myth, Fire with Fire *and* Promiscuities: The Secret Struggle for Womanhood**

FROM *THE NEW YORK TIMES*, APRIL 3, 1997

From a pro-choice point of view, things look grim. Last month, came accusations that abortion-rights advocates had prevaricated about how frequently "partial birth" or "intact dilation and extraction" abortion is performed. Then the House of Representatives voted overwhelmingly to ban the procedure. The Senate may soon address the issue, but even if it fails to override President Clinton's promised veto, the pro-choice movement is staring at a great symbolic defeat.

This looks like a dark hour for those of us who are pro-choice. But, with a radical shift in language and philosophy, we can turn this moment into a victory for all Americans.

How? First, let us stop shying away from the facts. Pro-lifers have made the most of the "partial-birth" abortion debate to dramatize the gruesome details of late-term abortions. Then they move on to the equally unpleasant details of second-trimester abortions. Thus, pro-lifers have succeeded in making queasy many voters who once thought that they were comfortable with *Roe v. Wade*. . . .

What if we transformed our language to reflect the spiritual perceptions of most Americans? What if we called abortions what many believe it to be: a failure, whether that failure is of technology, social support, education or male and female responsibility? What if we called policies that sustain, tolerate and even guarantee the highest abortion rate of any industrialized nation what they should be called: crimes against women?

The moral of such awful scenes is that a full-fledged campaign for cheap and easily accessible contraception is the best antidote to our shamefully high abortion rate. Use of birth control lowers the likelihood of abortion by 85 percent, according to the Alan Guttmacher Institute. More than half of the unplanned pregnancies occur because no contraception was used. If we asked Americans to send checks to Planned Parenthood to help save hundreds of thousands of women a year from having to face abortions, our support would rise exponentially.

For whatever the millions of pro-lifers think about birth control, abortion surely must be worse. A challenge to pro-choicers to abandon a dogmatic approach must be met with a challenge to pro-lifers to separate from the demagogues in their ranks and join us in a drive to prevent unwanted pregnancies.

© 1997 The New York Times. Reprinted with permission.

no

Katha Pollitt
Author of Reasonable Creatures: Essays on Women and Feminism

FROM *THE NEW YORK TIMES*, JUNE 18, 1996

Can there be a truce in the abortion wars? A lot of people would like to think so. . . . The Common Ground Network for Life and Choice tries to get activists on both sides to lower the decibel level, so that they can work together to [reduce] unwanted pregnancies. . . .

Who can quarrel with civility? . . . But when talking together becomes working together, the pro-choice people play a dangerous game, lending support to proposals that are both ineffectual and contrary to their own values.

Adoption is a big item on the Common Ground agenda: It should be made easier, more respectable, less racially fraught, less expensive. Maybe so. But in its position paper on the subject, Common Ground goes so far as to suggest that states subsidize adoption with family planning funds — hardly a recipe for fewer unwanted pregnancies. Will pro-adoption campaigns result, as Hillary Rodham Clinton claimed in a letter to Common Ground, in "far fewer abortions?" Not likely.

Sex education is another area in which a well-intentioned search for common ground leads, in practice, to pro-life turf. In the chapter of Common Ground in Norfolk, Va., pro-choicers are working with pro-lifers to bring a program called "Better Beginnings" to the local schools. Aimed at 10-to-14-year-olds, it is essentially an advertising campaign to promote sexual abstinence. . . .

This is a laudable goal, but do such programs lower teen-age pregnancy rates? Not according to two respected research groups. . . . So why did pro-choicers, who support education about contraceptives, agree to support an abstinence-only education program? Opponents of abortion rights were also against birth control. Abstinence was common ground. . . . This may look like a coalition politics, but it isn't a coalition when one side simply adopts the other's agenda. Abstinence-based sex education isn't half of an abstinence- and contraception-based sex education. It's a wholly different program, one that denies young people life-saving information in the false belief that knowledge of birth control encourages sex.

Adoption? Abstinence? Abortion as a moral iniquity? Those who support a woman's right to choose have nothing to gain by taking on either the programs or the language of their opponents. It's the pro-lifers who stand to gain. They give up nothing, while looking ever so reasonable and flexible, and their marginal ideas become accepted as mainstream.

© 1997 The New York Times. Reprinted with permission.

they're horrified and willing to do something about it." But there's also a downside for the anti-abortion movement, he pointed out. "To distinguish between partial-birth abortions and other abortions is almost to concede the ideology of abortion rights," he said, because it ratifies the idea that abortion inside the womb "is not an act of grisly violence."

BACKGROUND

Road to *Roe v. Wade*

Until 1821, no state had enacted a statute outlawing abortion. Abortion was governed by English common law, which permitted the procedure until "quickening," or the first movement of the fetus.

The earliest abortion laws were aimed at protecting women's health. The first abortion statute, passed in Connecticut in 1821, prohibited the inducement of abortion through dangerous poisons. By 1840, only eight states had enacted statutory restrictions on abortion.

A 19th-century campaign by U.S. doctors to legitimize their profession and protect the health of women resulted in more than 40 anti-abortion statutes by about 1860. Typically, abortion would be permitted when necessary, in the opinion of a physician, to preserve the life of the woman. Versions of these laws remain on the books in more than 30 states today, Harvard Law Professor Laurence H. Tribe estimates.[29]

From the early 20th-century to the 1950s, a large number of abortions, particularly for middle-class women, were performed by physicians who interpreted the exception for therapeutic abortions broadly, Tribe notes.

Between 1967 and 1973, 19 states reformed their abortion laws. Professor Mary Ann Glendon, also of Harvard Law School, has argued that even if the Supreme Court had not ruled in *Roe v. Wade* in 1973, abortion would have become freely available at least during the first trimester of pregnancy under most state laws. But Tribe counters that history "undermines this claim." In 1970, New York's law legalizing abortion passed by a razor-thin margin, he notes, and measures to repeal abortion restrictions were defeated in several other states during this period.[30]

By 1973, only four states—New York, Alaska, Hawaii and Washington—guaranteed a woman the right to choose an abortion.

On Jan. 22, 1973, the Supreme Court handed down its *Roe v. Wade* decision. The case involved a Texas woman named Norma McCorvey, who used the pseudonym "Jane Roe" to protect her privacy. Abortion was illegal in Texas, and McCorvey lacked the money to get a legal abortion elsewhere.

The majority opinion written by Justice Harry A. Blackmun described "Roe's" right to decide whether to terminate her pregnancy as a "fundamental right"—part of the constitutional privacy right recognized in previous cases. The 7–2 ruling struck down all state laws banning abortion. Within a few years, abortion death rates were 10 times lower than they had been for illegal abortions.

The decision mobilized abortion opponents, who began trying to overturn the ruling by constitutional amendment or by enacting restrictive laws that limited its impact.

Over the next decade, the court struck down several restrictive, post-*Roe* laws that states had enacted. In 1976, in *Planned Parenthood of Central Missouri v. Danforth*, the court struck down provisions of a Missouri law that required a husband's consent for a first-trimester abortion; required parental consent for unmarried women under 18 to have an abortion; and prohibited use of the most common procedure for performing abortions.

Seven years later, in *Akron Center for Reproductive Choice v. City of Akron*, the court struck down an Ohio law that listed specific information a doctor must give a woman before an abortion, including a statement that a fetus is a human life from the moment of conception.

During the same era, the court upheld a legislative strategy adopted by abortion opponents: bans on use of taxpayers' funds to finance abortions for poor women. In 1977, in *Maher v. Roe*, the Supreme Court upheld a Connecticut law that permitted state Medicaid assistance only for "medically necessary" abortions. Three years later in *Harris v. McRae*, the court upheld a stricter federal provision — the Hyde amendment — that barred federal funding even for medically necessary abortions.

With the election of Ronald Reagan in 1980, the anti-abortion movement gained an important ally. Reagan appointed more than half the members of the federal bench and appointed three new Supreme Court justices considered hostile to *Roe*—O'Connor, Kennedy and Scalia—to replace three of *Roe's* 7 to 2 majority.

The effect of the Reagan appointments was seen in a 1989 decision, *Webster v. Reproductive Health Services*. The 5–4 ruling upheld major provisions of a Missouri abortion law that prohibited the use of public facilities or public employees to perform abortions. The law also required a test of the fetus for fetal viability in the case of a woman as much as 20 weeks pregnant.

With *Webster*, Tribe has written, the constitutional tide turned in favor of state regulation of abortion after years of Supreme Court rulings striking down state restrictions on abortion.[31]

In the term immediately after the *Webster* decision, the court upheld state laws requiring teenage girls to notify their parents before they got abortions.

Casey *Decision Upholds* Roe*, But Allows Restrictions*

As *Roe v. Wade* neared its 20th anniversary, abortion continued to be a major issue in American elections and in the courts. In 1992, the Bush administration filed a friend of the court brief asking the Supreme Court to overturn *Roe v. Wade* in the case of *Planned Parenthood v. Casey*. But the conservative-dominated court surprised experts by upholding *Roe*, ruling that states may not prohibit abortions performed before the fetus could be viable outside the womb.

But in *Casey* the court also adopted a new, more lenient standard for determining whether individual state restrictions infringe too far on the right to abortion. It abandoned the *Roe* standard, under which virtually all restrictions on abortion through the first two trimesters of a pregnancy were invalid. The plurality in *Casey* said the new standard should be whether the regulation puts an "undue burden" on a woman seeking an abortion.

Using that test, the court upheld all but one of the restrictions under a Pennsylvania law, striking down a provision that a woman must notify her husband before seeking an abortion.

"With the creation of the undue burden standard in *Casey*, the Supreme Court opened the door to states to limit reproductive rights as long as it didn't impose an 'undue burden,'" Monica Hobbs of the Center for Reproductive Law and Policy said in August interview, referring to state laws that, for example, impose mandatory delays before a woman can get an abortion. She added, "We still don't understand what an 'undue burden' is."

The Supreme Court's 5–4 ruling in *Stenberg v. Carhart* striking down Nebraska's ban on "partial-birth" abortions declared the law unconstitutional because it placed an "undue burden" on women by excluding them from the procedure and failing to make an exception where it was needed for the health of the woman. This ruling was hailed as a victory by abortion rights activists and as a defeat by abortion opponents. Nevertheless, Hobbs says, the ruling still didn't provide "a full explanation of what the 'undue burden' is."

The ruling chilled both state and congressional activity to ban late-term abortions. President Clinton twice vetoed congressionally passed bans in 1996 and 1997. In 2000, both houses passed bans that never reached the president. Even with the election in 2000 of a strongly anti-abortion president, George W. Bush, no action was expected on the legislation until or unless the Supreme Court's composition shifts to an anti-abortion majority.

The Supreme Court has also issued several rulings upholding attempts to control anti-abortion demonstrators at abortion clinics. In the early 1990s, the court heard several complaints against blockades of clinics by anti-abortion demonstrators. In the most important of the rulings, the court held 6–3 in 1994 in *Madsen v. Women's Center Inc.*, that judges can set up "buffer zones" requiring protesters to keep a minimum distance away from clinics. Last year, in *Hill v. Colorado,* the Supreme Court ruled that a Colorado law aimed at protecting abortion clinic patients and doctors from harassment by protesters did not violate the protesters' First Amendment rights. The law requires that within 100 feet of the entrance to a clinic, no one may make an unwanted approach to within 8 feet of another person, talk to the person or pass out a leaflet.[32]

CURRENT SITUATION

Legislative Initiatives

Abortion-rights groups have faced defeat on several fronts in both Congress and state legislatures. Since 1994, Congress has voted 134 times on reproductive rights issues, and pro-choice forces have lost all but 24 votes, according to NARAL.[33]

Among the congressional defeats cited by NARAL in 2000 were votes by Congress that:

• banned late-term abortions and subjected physicians who performed such abortions to jails, fines or civil lawsuits. Although the Partial Birth Abortion Act of 2000 passed both Houses, it was never sent to President Clinton, who was expected to veto it as he had on previous occasions (see chronology). With the Supreme Court decision in June 2000, declaring state bans on the procedure unconstitutional, the move in Congress has lost much of its momentum.

• extended the global "gag" rule prohibiting foreign family planning organizations that receive federal funds from using their own funds to provide abortions or advocate abortion policy. This gag rule was ultimately dropped in 2000. In January 2001, President Bush brought this policy back into force through executive order. Congress was poised for a fight over the rule in the fall of 2001 after two Senate committees approved language repealing the order.

- continued to bar low-income women's access to abortion services through the Medicaid and Medicare programs, except in cases of life endangerment, rape or incest (known as the Hyde amendment).
- continued to ban access to privately funded abortions at overseas military hospitals for servicewomen and military dependents.
- prohibited federal employees from choosing health insurance plans that cover abortions.
- denied access to abortion for women in federal prisons.

With the demise of the late-term abortion issue in the wake of the Supreme Court's ruling last year striking down state bans, the pro-life movement turned its attention to other bills, including the Unborn Victims of Violence Act. This bill, introduced by Rep. Lindsey Graham, R-SC, and passed by the House in April 2000, would establish criminal penalties for harming a human fetus during commission of a crime against a pregnant woman. The shift in the Senate leadership to Democratic control, however, makes it unlikely that the leadership will schedule this bill for a Senate floor vote, but supporters could attempt to attach it to another bill as an amendment.

Similarly, momentum seems to have slowed on legislation to limit physicians who can prescribe the abortion pill mifepristone on the grounds that women's health is endangered. Although President Bush originally stated he would sign the bill, his HHS secretary indicated later that no safety concerns had come to his attention, suggesting that the administration had little interest in reversing or curbing the FDA's approval of the drug.

State Legislation

At the state level, abortion-rights forces are still feeling beleaguered. A total of 23 states enacted bills restricting abortion or reproductive choice in 2000, according to NARAL.[34] More than half the states have at least one restriction limiting abortion, through such methods as mandatory delays, counseling or restrictions on minors' obtaining abortions.

For the future, pro-choice forces have their eye on state laws that claim to protect the fetus. About 30 states have laws that prosecute criminals for hurting the fetus as well as a pregnant woman in the commission of a criminal act, according to Hobbs of the Center for Reproductive Law and Policy. Abortion rights activists say such laws are aimed primarily at expanding the definition of a human life to include a fetus, not at protecting women. "Legislation these days is very undercover in how it attacks *Roe v. Wade*," Hobbs said in an August interview.

Abortion rights activists are also concerned about states' use of laws to prosecute pregnant women who use cocaine as another tactic for elevating the legal status of the fetus. The Center for Reproductive Law and Policy represented ten pregnant women in Charleston, S.C., who were subjected to urine searches for cocaine use. Nine of the ten were arrested for cocaine possession, distribution of cocaine to a minor or child abuse.

The Supreme Court struck down the scheme as unconstitutional March 21 in a 6–3 decision in the case known as *Ferguson v. City of Charleston*. The court found that the scheme, developed by local police and prosecutors in collaboration with doctors in a South Carolina hospital, was in direct violation of the Fourth Amendment, which provides protection from unreasonable searches.[35]

Proponents of such efforts say they are trying to promote fetal health and protect children. Critics say the supporters are hoping to gain legal states for "fetal rights," which would require women to subordinate their health, including decisions about reproduction, to the fetus. The Center lost on this issue in the lower courts in South Carolina, which is unusual in defining life as beginning at conception by state law, according to Hobbs. However, in 21 of the 22 states in which women have challenged such charges for hurting their unborn child, courts have rejected those charges or reversed penalties imposed on the women for their behavior during pregnancy.[36]

Some prominent abortion opponents have taken issue with the view of abortion rights activists that state laws have eroded a woman's constitutional right to abortion.

"I wish they were right, but it's utter and complete claptrap," said McConnell at the University of Utah College of Law. "I would say the abortion right is more firmly established today than it was a decade ago."

"I would call [state abortion laws] regulations," rather than restrictions, Alvare concurred. "There isn't much states can do," Alvare argued, because *Roe v. Wade* limited states' ability to ban abortions outright to the third trimester (after viability) and because the courts have defined the health exception to such bans so broadly that it encompasses a woman's psychological health.

OUTLOOK

FOR MORE INFORMATION

Alan Guttmacher Institute, 120 Wall St., 21st Floor, New York, N.Y. 10005; (212) 248-1111; www.agi-usa.org. This abortion-rights research group is a good source of statistics and research, much of which is published in its journal *Family Planning Perspectives.*

American Life League, P.O. Box 1350, Stafford, Va. 22554; (540) 659-4171; www.all.org; . This Christian group mounts legal challenges to abortion issues and runs a network of pregnancy crisis and child-care centers.

Center for Reproductive Law and Policy, 120 Wall St., New York, N.Y. 10005; (917) 637-3600; www.crlp.org. This organization has represented plaintiffs for the abortion-rights side in several landmark Supreme Court cases and has useful litigation information on its web site.

National Abortion Federation, 1755 Massachusetts Ave., N.W., Suite 600, Washington, D.C. 20036; (202) 667-5881; www.prochoice.org. This professional organization representing hospitals, clinics and other abortion providers produces fact sheets on the medical aspects of abortion, offers continuing education to abortion professionals and monitors clinic violence.

National Abortion and Reproductive Rights Action League, 1156 15th St., N.W., Suite 700, Washington, D.C. 20005; (202) 973-3000; www.naral.org. NARAL lobbies for abortion-rights legislation and puts out an annual report on state abortion legislation.

National Right to Life Committee, Suite 500, 419 7th St., N.W., Washington, D.C. 20004-2293; (202) 626-8800; www.nrlc.org. The NRLC is the nation's largest anti-abortion group, with 50 state affiliates.

Joining Forces

Increasingly, some segments of the abortion-rights movement stress that their underlying goal is to prevent unwanted pregnancy through better use of contraception and sex education so that fewer abortions are necessary. NARAL, for example, has lobbied for increased contraceptive research funding and for legislation requiring private health insurance carriers to cover contraception. Close to 20 states now mandate contraceptive coverage as part of private health insurance, according to Susan Cohen of the Alan Guttmacher Institute, and pro-choice advocates will be pushing for similar legislation at a national level in Congress this year. NARAL has also supported public education about the use of birth control pills as a morning-after contraceptive.

"I think the common ground where we can join forces is to make it possible for fewer women to have to face a decision on abortion by making abortion less necessary," said NARAL's Michelman. But the continuing battles over abortion legislation in the state legislatures and Congress make it tough for her organization to focus their efforts on pregnancy prevention, she said.

"The other side needs to have us re-fight over and over again the ground we win, because that war over abortion enables them to mask their real intent — which is to control reproductive decisions," she maintained.

But the anti-abortion movement's Alvare argued that the women's movement has made a mistake in thinking that a woman's control of her child-bearing is the key to her advancement in society.

"When you embrace abortion as a means to that end, you get yourself in trouble," Alvare said. "The women's movement did a disservice to women. Why? Abortion is an ugly, violent thing. People don't want to get cozy with a movement whose primary association is with abortion." Alvare argues that the movement's focus on abortion short-changed advancement for women. "Why have abortion on demand but not flextime, or leave on demand?" she asked.[37]

Utah law Professor McConnell saw no immediate prospect of serious challenge to *Roe v. Wade* in the near future when interviewed in 1997. But he said, "I'd be very surprised if [*Roe*] is not eliminated 50–100 years from now. It's so deeply inconsistent with the premises of our constitutional system. Our constitutional design protects the most vulnerable among us from violence and discrimination at the hands of the powerful. It is incongruous for the court to hold it unconstitutional for states to extend protection to the most vulnerable people [in the society]."

In a dozen cities around the country, a Washington, D.C., group called Common Ground Network for Life and Choice has been sponsoring discussions between abortion rights and anti-abortion activists in an effort to find areas of agreement. "Preventing teen pregnancy is a common concern for pro-choice and pro-life people," said Director Mary Jacksteit. The group has joined with the National Campaign to Prevent Teen Pregnancy to advance their common goals.

But activists in both camps are skeptical that a real middle ground can be reached without serious capitulations on both sides. Michelman pointed out that many abortion opponents are also opposed to contraception and want sex education to be limited to an abstinence message. Alvare retorted that rising rates of contraception use have had little impact on abortions, noting that 58 percent of abortion patients are contraceptive users. She attributes recent abortion declines to "an increased awareness of the social and personal consequence of getting pregnant where you and the man cannot commit to a child. I think people are talking about less sexual intercourse where they couldn't commit to a child together."

Despite some recent legislative victories by the Right to Life movement, abortion-rights activists are confident that women voters will not permit the basic right to an abortion to be abridged. But, the activists note, women have to be convinced that their rights are genuinely threatened.

Pro-choice forces say they once again face a precarious position with an anti-abortion president in power and a razor-thin majority for abortion on the Supreme Court. Whether the majority of Americans agree has yet to be seen.

"There's a latent giant of public opinion on our side," the Feminist Majority's Smeal said. "It doesn't get aroused often because most women don't think it's possible to lose. If the right to abortion were threatened, that giant would stir again."

Notes

[1] For background, see "Abortion Clinic Protests," *The CQ Researcher*, April 7, 1995, pp. 297–320 and "Teenagers and Abortion," *The CQ Researcher,* July 5, 1991, p. 441–464.

[2] "Summary Table 1: Major State Abortion Policies in Effect," Alan Guttmacher Institute, 2001 at www.agi-usa.org.

[3] Annual statistics on clinic violence were kept beginning in 1984.

[4] Linda Greenhouse, "The Supreme Court: The Nebraska Case: Court Rules that Governments Can't Outlaw Type of Abortion," *The New York Times*, June 29, 2000.

[5] Quoted in Heather Boonstra, "Voicing Concern for Women, Abortion Foes Seek Limits on Availability of Mifepristone," *The Guttmacher Report on Public Policy*, April 2001, p. 4.

[6] "On other Issues," *The Washington Post*, June 12, 2001, p. A8.

[7] See National Right to Life Committee Press Release, "President Bush's Statement," August 10, 2001, at www.nrlc.org and American Life League, "Analysis of Bush Stem Cell Decision," August 13, 2001, www.all.org.

[8] Alison Mitchell, "House Approves Bill Criminalizing Violence to Fetus," *The New York Times*, April 27, 2001, p. 1.

[9] NARAL Foundation, *Who Decides?* 2001.

[10] David J. Garrow, *Liberty and Sexuality: The Right to Privacy and the Making of* Roe vs. Wade (1994).

[11] The Associated Press, October 20, 1997.

[12] Theodore Joyce et al., "The Impact of Mississippi's Mandatory Delay Law on Abortions and Births," *Journal of the American Medical Association,* August 27, 1997, pp. 653–658.

[13] Gina Kolata, "Wary Doctors Spurn New Abortion Pill," *The New York Times*, November 14, 2000.

[14] See Beverly Winkoff, " Acceptability of Medical Abortion in Early Pregnancy," *Family Planning Perspectives,* July/August 1995, p. 142–185.

[15] Boonstra, op. cit.

[16] Ibid.

[17] Ibid.

[18] Boonstra, op. cit.

[19] Boonstra, op. cit.

[20] Ibid.

[21] "National Right to Life Statement Concerning President-Elect Bush and *Roe v. Wade*," Jan. 19, 2001, www.nrlc.org.

[22] See David Brown, "Late Term Abortions: Who Gets Them and Why," *The Washington Post Health Section,* Sept. 17, 1996, p. 12. Interviews with abortion doctors suggested that fewer than 20 perform the surgery, Brown reported.

[23] Martin Haskell, "Dilation and Extraction for Late Second Trimester Abortion," Presented at the National Abortion Federation, September 13, 1992.

[24] Mary Agnes Carey, "Foes of Controversial Procedure Boosted by Strong Vote," *CQ Weekly Report,* May 24, 1997, pp. 1196–1198.

[25] See Brown, op. cit., for interviews with doctors who said they use the procedure in this fashion.

[26] Linda Greenhouse, op. cit.

[27] House Judiciary Committee, "Partial Birth Abortion Ban Act of 1997, Report 105-23," March 14, 1997, pp. 15–16.

[28] "Memorandum: Michael McConnell Bush Nominee for 10th Circuit Court of Appeals," NARAL Online Newsroom, May 17, 2001, www.naral.org

[29] Laurence H. Tribe, *Abortion: The Clash of Absolutes* (1992), p. 30.

[30] Ibid., pp. 49–50.

[31] Tribe, Ibid., p. 24.

[32] Greenhouse, op. cit.

[33] NARAL Online Newsroom, "Congressional Record on Choice—106th Congress, 2nd Session," www.naral.org.

[34] NARAL Foundation, op. cit.

[35] See *Ferguson v. City of Charleston* at www.crlp.org.

[36] Center for Law and Reproductive Policy, "Punishing Women for their Behavior During Pregnancy," Sept. 11, 2000, at www.crlp.org.

[37] See "Feminism's Future," *The CQ Researcher,* February 28, 1997, pp. 181–204.

Bibliography

Selected Sources Used

Books

Bruno Leone, *Abortion: Opposing Viewpoints,* Greenhaven Press, 1997.
This collection of essays by authors with opposing viewpoints looks at such issues as whether abortion is immoral and whether abortion rights should be restricted.

Garrow, David J., *Liberty and Sexuality,* Macmillan, 1994.
Pulitzer Prize-winning historian Garrow provides a detailed chronicle of the personalities involved behind the scenes in the Supreme Court's landmark *Roe vs. Wade* decision and related decisions.

Tribe, Laurence H., *Abortion: The Clash of Absolutes,* W.W. Norton, 1992.
Harvard University constitutional lawyer Tribe, who favors abortion rights, provides a historical and legal overview of the abortion issue. He concludes that the Supreme Court's 1992 decision in *Planned Parenthood vs. Casey* watered down the *Roe* decision by permitting states new powers to restrict abortion but affirmed a woman's basic right to an abortion.

Articles

Brown, David, "Late Term Abortions: Who Gets Them and Why," *The Washington Post Health Section,* Sept. 17, 1996, p. 12.
Interviews with doctors who perform late-term abortions reveal that not all such abortions are done for medical reasons. The article quotes doctors who say they perform many late-term abortions for poor, young women who have waited until late in their pregnancy.

Greenhouse, Linda, "The Supreme Court: The Nebraska Case," *The New York Times*, June 29, 2000, p. 1.
This article describes the Supreme Court ruling that struck down state bans on "partial-birth abortion."

Seelye, Katharine Q., "Abortion Vote Signals a Shift in Political Momentum," *The New York Times,* March 23, 1997, p. A30.
Seelye discusses the partial-birth abortion ban in the context of the Right to Life movement's broader anti-abortion strategy.

Sontag, Deborah, "Doctors Say It's Just One Way," *The New York Times,* March 21, 1997.
In interviews, most doctors who perform abortions after 20 weeks say they prefer other methods to the "dilation and extraction" procedure targeted by the congressional ban.

Steinauer, Jody E., "Training Family Practice Residents in Abortion and Other Reproductive Health Care: A Nationwide Survey," *Family Planning Perspectives*, September/October 1997, pp. 222-227.
This 1995 survey found family physicians ill-prepared to provide abortions as only a minority of residency programs in the field provide abortion training. Sixty-five percent of family medicine residents said they "certainly would not provide abortion." The survey found family physicians ill-prepared to provide abortions.

Whitman, David and Stacey Schultz, "A Little Pill but a Big Dispute," *U.S. News and World Report,* Oct. 9, 2000, p. 18.
This summarizes the debate over the abortion pill RU-486 at the time of its approval for sale in this country.

Reports and Studies

Committee, Judiciary, U.S. House of Representatives, *Partial-Birth Abortion Ban Act of 1997, Committee Report 105-24,* March 14, 1997.
This report from the committee that wrote the ban on partial-birth abortions presents the arguments for banning the procedure along with dissenting views from 14 committee members opposed to the ban.

Action League Foundation, National Abortion and Reproductive Rights and, *Who Decides? A State-by-State Review of Abortion and Reproductive Rights,* (2001).
This report provides detailed descriptions of state legislation and regulations affecting abortion.